# Iceland

## the Bradt Travel Guide

**Andrew Evans**

www.bradtguides.com

Bradt Travel Guides Ltd, UK
The Globe Pequot Press Inc, USA

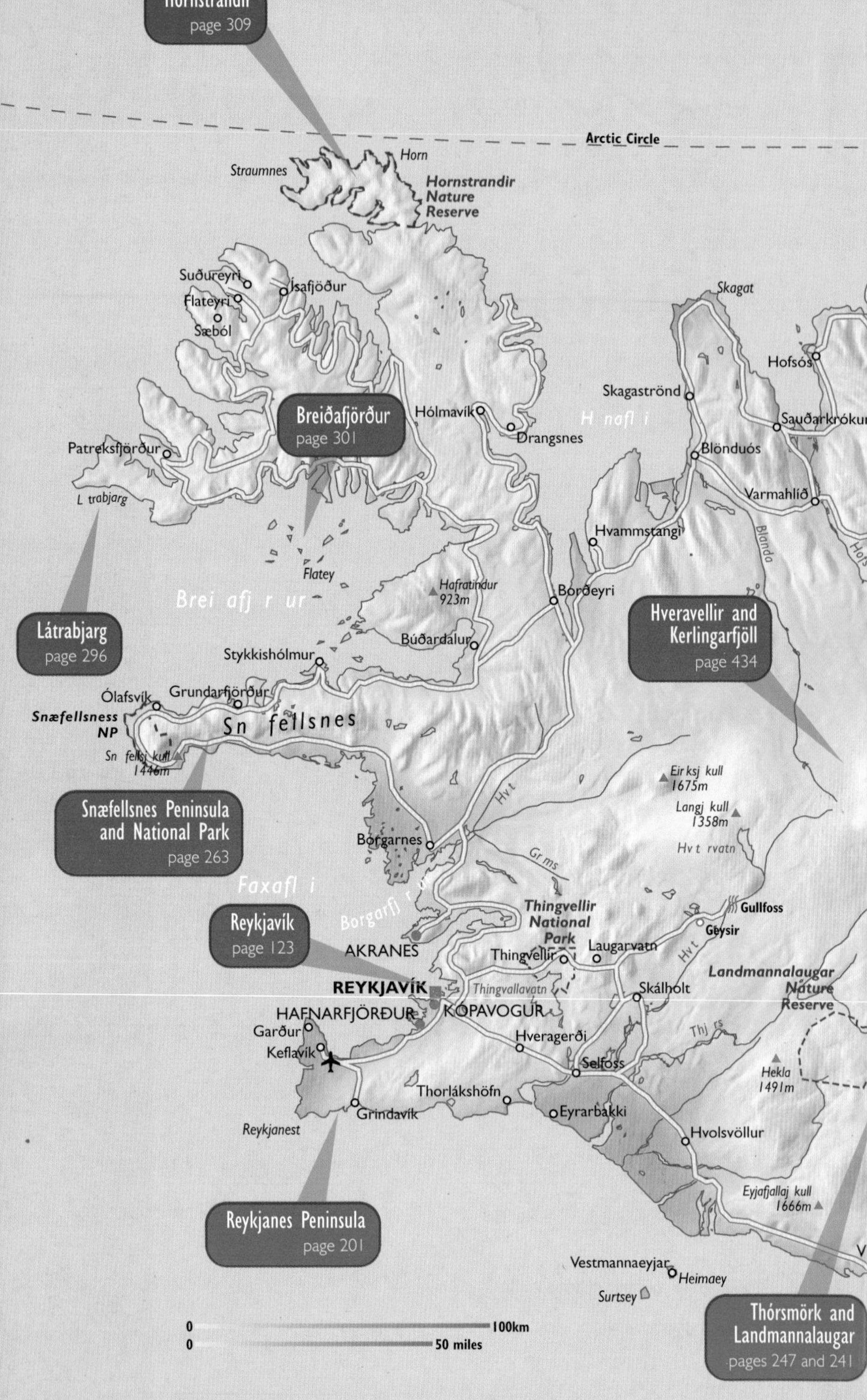

Hornstrandir
page 309
Arctic Circle
Horn
Straumnes
Hornstrandir Nature Reserve
Suðureyri
Ísafjöður
Flateyri
Sæból
Skagat
Hofsós
Skagaströnd
Breiðafjörður
page 301
Hólmavík
Drangsnes
Sauðarkrókur
Patreksfjörður
Blönduós
L trabjarg
Varmahlíð
Hvammstangi
Blanda
Flatey
Hafratindur 923m
Borðeyri
Brei afj r ur
Látrabjarg
page 296
Búðardalur
Hveravellir and Kerlingarfjöll
page 434
Stykkishólmur
Ólafsvík
Grundarfjörður
Snæfellsness NP
Sn fellsnes
Sn fellsj kull 1446m
Eir ksj kull 1675m
Snæfellsnes Peninsula and National Park
page 263
Langj kull 1358m
Borgarnes
Hv t rvatn
Faxafl i
Borgarfj r ur
Gullfoss
Reykjavík
page 123
Thingvellir National Park
Geysir
AKRANES
Thingvellir
Laugarvatn
Landmannalaugar Nature Reserve
REYKJAVÍK
Thingvallavatn
Skálholt
HAFNARFJÖRÐUR
KÓPAVOGUR
Garður
Hveragerði
Keflavík
Selfoss
Hekla 1491m
Thorlákshöfn
Grindavík
Eyrarbakki
Reykjanest
Hvolsvöllur
Reykjanes Peninsula
page 201
Eyjafjallaj kull 1666m
Vestmannaeyjar
Heimaey
Surtsey
0 100km
0 50 miles
Thórsmörk and Landmannalaugar
pages 247 and 241

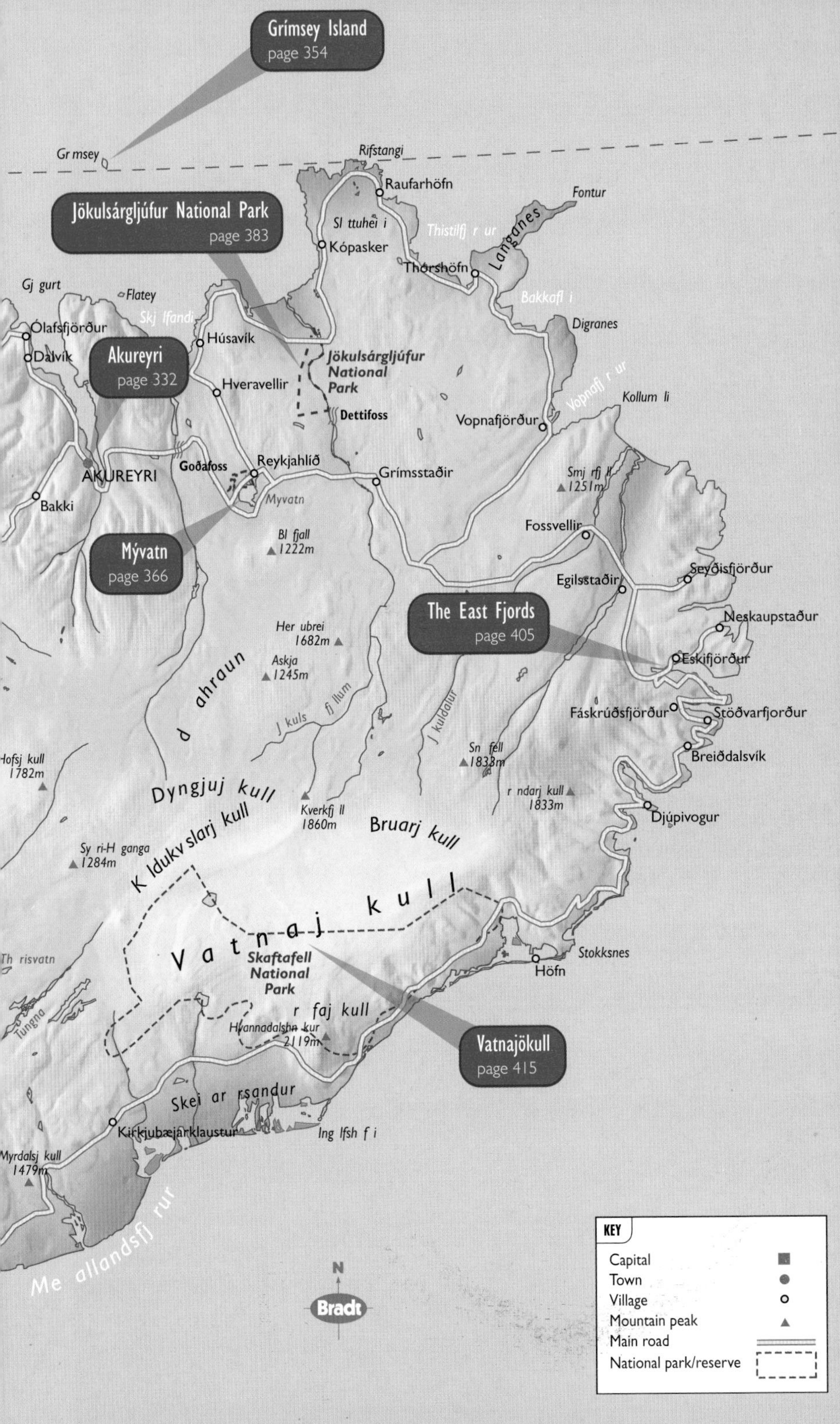

Grímsey Island
page 354
Gr msey
Rifstangi
Raufarhöfn
Fontur
Jökulsárgljúfur National Park
page 383
Sl ttuhei i
Thistilfj r ur
Langanes
Kópasker
Thórshöfn
Gj gurt
Flatey
Skj lfandi
Bakkafl i
Ólafsfjörður
Dalvík
Húsavík
Digranes
Akureyri
page 332
Jökulsárgljúfur National Park
Hveravellir
Vopnafj r ur
Kollum li
Dettifoss
Vopnafjörður
AKUREYRI
Goðafoss
Reykjahlíð
Grímsstaðir
Smj rfj ll
1251m
Bakki
Myvatn
Fossvellir
Mývatn
page 366
Bl fjall
1222m
Seyðisfjörður
Egilsstaðir
The East Fjords
page 405
Neskaupstaður
Her ubrei
1682m
Eskifjörður
Askja
1245m
ð ahraun
J kuls fj llum
J kuldalur
Fáskrúðsfjörður
Stöðvarfjorður
Sn fell
1833m
Breiðdalsvík
Hofsj kull
1782m
Dyngjuj kull
r ndarj kull
1833m
Kverkfj ll
1860m
Djúpivogur
Bruarj kull
Sy ri-H ganga
1284m
K ldukv slarj kull
Vatnaj kull
Stokksnes
Th risvatn
Skaftafell National Park
Höfn
Tungna
r faj kull
Hvannadalshn kur
2119m
Vatnajökull
page 415
Skei ar rsandur
Kirkjubæjarklaustur
Ing lfsh f i
Myrdalsj kull
1479m
Me allandsfj rur
N
Bradt
KEY
Capital
Town
Village
Mountain peak
Main road
National park/reserve

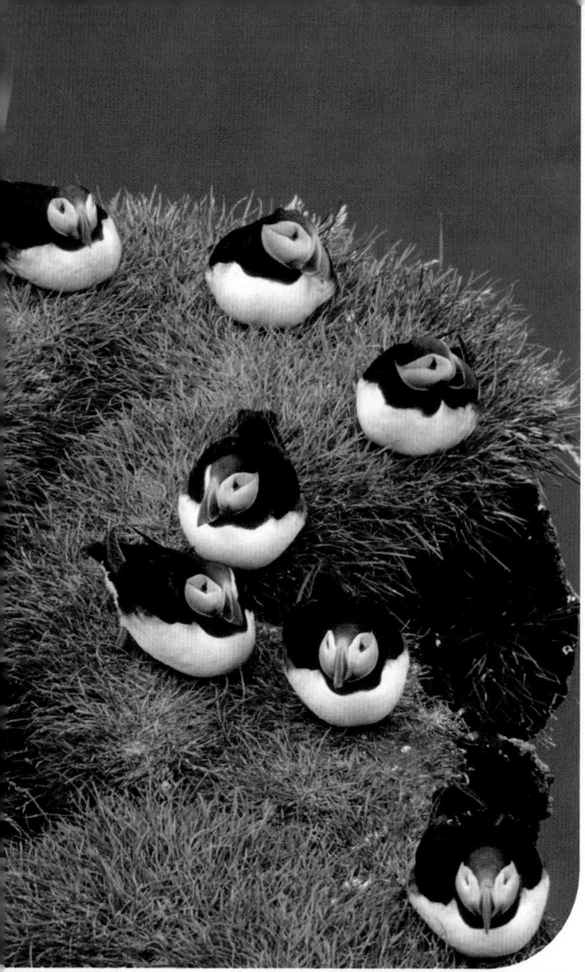

# Iceland Don't miss...

**Wildlife**

Puffins (*Fratercula arctica*), or *lundi*, are the iconic bird of Iceland

(FL/FLPA) page 56

**Islands**

Each of the Westmann Islands represents a different stage in a staggered chain of volcanic events

(HK/A) page 228

**Reykjavík**
Reykjavík's stainless-steel *Sólfar*, or 'Sun Voyager', sculpture is the work of local artist (and welder) Jón Gunnar Árnason
(R/A) page 172

**Spectacular landscapes**
The mountains of Landmannalaugar are pure rhyolite – a crystallised, slow-forming igneous rock
(C/D) page 241

**Hot pools**
Blue Lagoon is the most visited destination in Iceland
(CC) page 206

*above* At 245ft (74m) high, Hallgrímskirkja is Iceland's tallest building and Reykjavík's most prominent landmark (SS) page 174

*above left* Reykjavík's youth sports centre was built in 1908 and is one of several architectural gems on Fríkirkjuvegar (SS) page 168

*left* Reykjavík's Raðhús (City Hall) represents one of the city's greater architectural achievements (SS) page 170

*below* View over Reykjavík – Iceland's picturesque capital nestles against a spectacular backdrop (SS) page 123 *above left* Reykjavík street sculpture by Ásmundur Sveinsson (JS) page 192

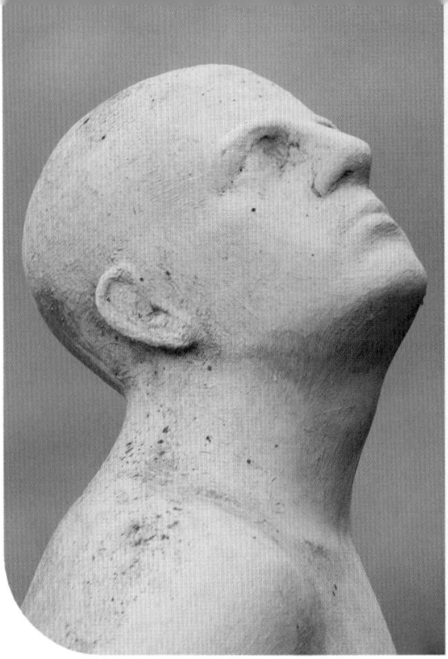

*above right* Stained glass detail from the interior of Hallgrímskirkja, Reykjavík (LM) page 174

*below* Sculptures outside the Perlan complex in Reykjavík, home to a revolving restaurant and the Saga Museum (SS) page 185

*above* Traditional Icelandic turf-covered house (S/D)

*left* Rock monument to Bárðar at Arnastapi; Bárðar is considered the 'man of the mountain' and guardian spirit to Snæfellsjökull (SS) page 267

*below left* Hafnarfjörður's International Viking Festival has become so popular you can now order one for your own country (SS) page 195

*below* Ingólfshöfði – before founding his farm in Reykjavík, Ingólfur Arnason first set foot on land here at 'Ingólfur's cape' (AE) page 427

## AUTHOR

Andrew Evans was born in Texas and educated in England. He made his first trip to Iceland in 1998, and has been back over a dozen times since. He is the author of a handful of books, including the Bradt guides to Ukraine and Kiev. He also writes for several travel publications – newspapers, magazines and online. In 2009, he won the Lowell Thomas Award (Silver) for the first edition of this book. Today, he is a contributing editor and columnist for *National Geographic Traveler* and spends a large amount of time on the road as their 'digital nomad'. He speaks Russian, French, Spanish, and some Icelandic. He lives in Washington, DC and may be contacted through his personal website (*www.walkedandwalked.com*).

### AUTHOR'S STORY

Before I fell in love with Iceland, I fell in love with a map of Iceland. As a boy, I used to spend hours with my atlas and I remember staring at Iceland's crazy coastline and trying to read all those impossible place names. I made my first trip right out of college – the fog never lifted once and yet I thought it the greatest country on earth. I went back six months later just to see the snow and have kept going back ever since.

When Bradt gave me a peek at potential new titles, I jumped on Iceland like a little kid ('me, me, pick me!'). While they were thinking on it, I jetted off to Iceland for a weekend of hiking and came home even more exuberant. I wanted to write a book that opened up the whole of Iceland, not just the easy places and not just in good weather. I have been fortunate to write for Bradt in the past and encouraged by their step away from the obvious. For this title especially, I was grateful for their support of personal exploration in lieu of mere fact-finding. What I learned was that Iceland is a huge place, much larger than I had ever imagined or experienced. All those fjords with long names have long histories to match and these are the stories I wanted to tell. Indeed, the most challenging aspect of this book was discovering that no place in Iceland is too small and that this country is changing constantly.

Over the past few years, a major financial crisis and some serious volcanic activity kept Iceland on the map and in the minds of people across the globe. Yet despite the agitated news stories and overwhelming public concern, I was never really alarmed. In writing this book I have learned that these events are mere hiccups among the real excitement and melodrama of Icelandic history. This new edition is the culmination of four years of collaborative research, comprising the updates of so many key friends and contributors in Iceland and at home. I am grateful to them all but most grateful of all that I still have the amazing opportunity to keep travelling to Iceland.

## PUBLISHER'S FOREWORD

*Hilary Bradt*

When I lived in the US in the 1960s, the cheapest way of getting to the UK was to fly via Reykjavík. One visit I broke my trip for a week to do some pony trekking. Forty years later it's a holiday I remember above many other more exotic ones because the country astonished me. I can still remember the crowds of people strolling the streets of the city at midnight, in sunshine, and the beauty of the green landscape, gushing geysers, chunky ponies, and the utterly charming – and extraordinarily well-read – Icelandic people. Andrew's *Ukraine* is one of our most highly praised books, and *Iceland* must surely gain the same following.

It has his hallmarks: meticulous research coupled with an infectious enthusiasm. I think it's time I made a return visit to this beguiling island.

**Second edition published September 2011**
First published 2008
Bradt Travel Guides Ltd
IDC House, The Vale, Chalfont St Peter, Bucks SL9 9RZ, England
www.bradtguides.com
Published in the USA by The Globe Pequot Press Inc,
PO Box 480, Guilford, Connecticut 06437-0480


Project Manager: Elspeth Beidas



ISBN: 978 1 84162 361 0

**British Library Cataloguing in Publication Data**
A catalogue record for this book is available from the British Library

**Photographs** Alamy: Ashley Cooper (AC/A), David J Slater (DJS/A), Hideo Kurihara (HK/A), imagebroker (i/A), Nisbetwylie photographs (NP/A), Realimage (R/A); Andrew Evans (AE); Chris Courteau (CC); Dreamstime: Bluedeep (B/D), Csld (C/D), Kaido Kärner (KK/D), Mirceax (M/D), Mogens Trolle (MT/D), Replayall (Re/D), Rzihlman (R/D), Solarseven (Sol/D), Sova004 (So/D), Svobodapavel (S/D); Frans Lanting/FLPA (FL/FLPA); Inger Helene Boasson/Photolibrary (IHB/P); Jon Smith (JS); Laurence Mitchell (LM); Superstock (SS)
*Front cover* Church, Flatey (IHB/P)
*Back cover* Jökulsárlón (Np/A), Icelandic horse (i/A)
*Title page* Statue of Leifur Eiríksson, Reykjavík (JS), Seljalandfoss (SS), Puffin (*Fratercula arctica*) (DJS/A)
**Maps** David McCutcheon (based on source material from ITMB)

Typeset from the author's disc by D & N Publishing, Baydon, Wiltshire
Production managed by Jellyfish Print Solutions; printed in India

# Contributors

**Nathan Evans** is a freelance writer from Katy, Texas, who first fell in love with Iceland back in July 2009 while hiking the Laugavegurinn (see page 244). When not running away to Iceland, he is pursuing his university degree in film. He continues to write for a number of online publications and teaches acting classes. For this update, Nathan travelled to nearly every corner of Iceland, which included a few snowy (and precarious) moments in the East Fjords.

**Nick Gilroy** is an experienced rider who likes to ride his motorcycle all over the world (New Zealand, Australia, southeast Asia, Africa, and all over Europe). When not travelling, he lives in York and Reigate, England. In July 2006, Nick completed a 1,500-mile tour of Iceland on his BMW R1200GS. He writes on travelling by motorcycle (see page 99).

**Dr Brian Gratwicke** is a conservation biologist from Zimbabwe. A talented wildlife photographer and avid birder, he writes about how to capture the best pictures of Iceland's seabirds (see page 116).

**Dr Guðni Thorlacius Jóhannesson** is a professor of history at the University of Iceland in Reykjavík. He is the author of the recent book *Óvinir Ríkisins* or *Enemies of the State*, which deals with the Cold War era in Iceland. He writes about the Cod Wars (see page 24) and sea-swimming in Iceland (see page 113).

**Eliza Reid** is a freelance writer who has lived in Reykjavík since 2003. She writes for the magazines *Iceland Review* and *Atlantica* and has contributed to various guidebooks on Iceland. Eliza writes about immigration (see page 76), Icelandic culture (see page 38), and *skyr* (see page 107). She can be contacted through her website (*www.elizareid.com*).

**Dr Dennis Riege** is a biologist and forester who lived in Iceland for three years. In collaboration with the Icelandic Forest Research Service, he initiated experiments at the Keflavík International Airport on how lupins can serve as a nurse plant to establish trees. He writes about forestry in Iceland (see page 48).

## FEEDBACK REQUEST

Like the weather in Iceland, everything changes so quickly in this country. Hotels open new floors, volcanoes explode and move mountains, restaurants hire new chefs, bus schedules vary, and the rivers might even change direction. No one person can keep track of it all, so any tips and new information from travellers is much appreciated. I also love to hear from readers, to hear your travel tales and to get your input on the guide and on Iceland in general.

If you have any comments, queries, grumbles, insights, news or other feedback, please contact Bradt on ☎ 01753 893444 or e info@bradtguides.com. Alternatively, you can add a review of the book to www.bradtguides.com or Amazon.

Periodically Bradt authors post travel updates and reader feedback on the website. Check www.bradtguides.com/guidebook-updates for any news.

# Acknowledgements

**ANDREW EVANS** Iceland has gone through so much in the past few years, it's been a challenge to keep up. Thankfully, I've had a lot of helping hands in Iceland and America and to them I am most grateful. I want to begin by expressing my sincere appreciation to Iceland Consul-General Hlynur Guðjónsson for all of his interest and support in my work. Thank you to Einar Gustavsson for his friendship and leadership of the Iceland Tourist Board (you will be sorely missed). A very big thank you to Icelandair and especially Michael Raucheisen and Arnar Mar Arnthorsson. *Takk.*

Thank you to the entire team at Bradt Travel Guides: to Hilary Bradt for first getting me into this, to Donald Greig, Adrian Phillips, Helen Anjomshoaa, Rachel Fielding, Anna Moores, Emma Thomson, Elspeth Beidas, Maisie Fitzpatrick, Janet Mears, Helen Calderon, Mary-Lou Nash, Debbie Hunter and Deborah Gerrard.

I made four separate journeys to Iceland during this update, but the truly detailed work I owe to my primary contributor, Nathan Evans, who so thoroughly researched the text and travelled to those places I couldn't get to. (Thank you Nate!)

And so I'll turn the space over to him:

**NATHAN EVANS** The people of Iceland are among the nicest and most generous in the world – it is necessary to thank almost all of them. I would like to thank the countless Icelanders (and Benny from Kosovo) for their patience and for giving me directions, the Icelandic Tourist Board for their invaluable support, especially Einar Gustavsson for making everything happen like magic, Hertz, for their good service to me, and in particular, Arnar Karl (*takk* for the snow tyres). To Eliza Reid, Dr Guðni Thorlacius Jóhannesson, and Duncan Tindur for providing a home away from home – congratulations on Donald! Also deserving of gratitude are simple everyday people across Iceland who assisted me in gathering information for this edition of the guide: Steinunn on her first day of work, Elin Thoroddsen at the Geysir Hotel, Ludo, Jimmy, and Solnúr at the Fosshótel in Fresynes, Hildur Helgadóttir for being a friend, Mary Frances Davidson of SEEDS for a familiar accent and a cheerful chat, Orlygur Hnefill, Inga and Sibba in Olafsfjörður for the quick tour and lots of information, Rósa Húnadottir, Erna Kaaber for two delicious meals 18 months apart, Svanhildur Pálsdóttir in Varmahlið, Glyfi Arnason of the Borganes Hostel, Shelagh Smith, and Mia for playing fetch with me.

Like any glittering firmament, a few stars always shine out. Special thanks to Olí and Dísa in Skjaldarvik for their hospitality, Dísa for her time, tour, and priceless networking, Olí for his kindness and for towing cables at 02.00. To Marie and Asgeir Valgarðsson who opened their minds, history, family, business and home to me; God bless you in Goðaland! To Jonsina Einarsdóttir and Jón Rafn Högnason for showing me the generosity and magic of Glymur, telling me stories and teaching me altruistic truths.

Finally, to the Lord who kept me safe on my trip, Michelle Kharas for keeping me company via the internet, and my brother Andrew for his guidance, encouragement, and faith in me, and in giving me this lifetime opportunity.

*Þakka þér fyrir* to you all.

# Contents

## NOTE ABOUT MAPS

Several maps use grid lines to allow easy location of sites. Map grid references are listed in square brackets after listings in the text, with page number followed by grid number, eg: [128 C3].

## LIST OF MAPS

# Introduction

The best part about writing a guidebook to a country is that it allows you to go back again and again. After so many years of continuous travel to Iceland, I am still amazed by this marvellous country – its incredibly raw nature, its ancient culture and its overwhelming beauty.

Travelling to Iceland is much less about sightseeing than it is feeling things you've never felt before – what it's like to be the only person on earth or how it feels to be outnumbered by a million-odd puffins. Iceland's gargantuan nature stirs the soul or it can shake you in your boots. That plume of mist on the horizon could be steam from a hot spring, the salty breath of a spouting whale, the early wisps of a week-long fog, or the conquering cloud of a massive volcano.

In some ways, the surprising eruption of Eyjafjallajökull volcano was symbolic of the country itself. Iceland might appear small and remote on world maps, but it has a funny way of affecting all of us. In turn, the great cataclysms of the rest of the world affect Iceland. Even today, the global financial crisis still marks Iceland's economic landscape and has returned Icelanders to their more frugal traditions of self-reliance.

And yet, in spite of exploding volcanoes and a dire economic crash, the numbers of tourists to Iceland continues to grow. They come for the rumbling waterfalls, to soak in heavenly hot springs and to witness the last great glaciers of Europe. They discover the strange shapes of the bright-green mountains, the colours of the daunting sky and the shimmering fjords, and the joy of sunbeams after a hard-hitting rain. This is a land where horses grow long hair on their backs and where the liquorice aisle is the longest one in the shops. It is a place where everyone calls each other by their first name, where all the churches have tiny gold stars painted on their ceilings, and where mailing addresses haven't changed in 1,000 years. What's not to love?

The first edition of this book found a loyal following all around the world, especially among readers and travellers who desire a deep historical and cultural background as they discover this great nation. In writing this second edition, I have tried to incorporate the drastic changes that have put Iceland on the map in recent years while staying true to the eternal spirit of the country itself. I hope that you enjoy Iceland as much as I do – may yours be a wonderful trip and may the sun shine brightly at least some of the time.

*Góða Ferð!*, Andrew Evans

## A NOTE ON SPELLINGS

The Icelandic alphabet uses a handful of letters not known in English (see page 439). The letter **Ð ð** represents the sound 'th' as in *their*, while **Þ þ** represents 'th' as in *thick*. For the ease of English readers, I have replaced the **Þ** with 'th' in labelling all place names. In this book, **Þ** is used only when referring to the official names of Icelandic organisations and for some cultural terms. Unlike many English texts of Icelandic origin, **Ð ð** has been retained to promote accurate pronunciation of place names. Hence *Thór* instead of *Þór*, but *fjörður* instead of *fjord*.

# Part One

## GENERAL INFORMATION

## ICELAND AT A GLANCE

**Location** Island in the north Atlantic, at 65°N and 18°W. Slightly east of Greenland and north of the United Kingdom.
**Size** 103,000 km²
**Geography** Active volcanic zone on the Mid-Atlantic Ridge with marked glacial features. Mountainous coast with deep fjords, high interior plateaux with permanent ice cover and deserts.
**Climate** Temperate with cool, wet summers and windy winters. Average temperature in January -1°C, in July 15°C.
**Status** Republic
**Population** 309,672
**Life expectancy** 80.3 years
**Capital** Reykjavík
**Other major cities** Hafnarfjörður, Kópavogur, Akureyri, Keflavík
**Administrative divisions** Eight regions; 23 counties
**People** Icelander 92%; other (predominantly European) 8%
**Language** Icelandic
**Currency** Icelandic króna (ISK)
**Exchange rates** US$1 = 115 ISK; £1 = 187 ISK; €1 = 165 ISK (June 2011)
**National airport/airline** Keflavík (KEF)/Icelandair
**International dialling code** +354
**Time** GMT year round (in summer one hour behind London; four hours ahead of New York City)
**Electrical voltage** AC is 220V; frequency 50Hz
**Flag** Red Nordic cross outlined in white set upon a blue background
**National anthem** *Ó Gúð Vors Lands* (Oh God of our Land)
**National flower** *Jöklasóley* or glacier buttercup
**Public holidays** 1 January (New Year's Day), April (third Thursday; first day of summer), 1 May (May Day), 17 June (Independence Day), August (first weekend; summer bank holiday), 25 December (Christmas Day)

1

# Background Information

## GEOGRAPHY

Iceland is situated in the north Atlantic, between Europe, North America, and the polar ice cap. The country's geographic centre is at 65°N, 18°W and the Arctic Circle barely grazes the northern island settlement of Grímsey. The country's northernmost point at Kolbeinsey 67° 08'N (see page 364) is disappearing fast, while its southernmost point of Surtsey 63°30'N (see page 238) is only just emerging from the waves. As an island nation, Iceland is surrounded by water. The Greenland Sea is due north, though Greenland itself lies only 287km (178 miles) to the west, across the Denmark Strait. The Scottish Hebrides lie 798km (496 miles) to the southeast, and Norway is 970km (603 miles) to the east, separated by the Norwegian Sea.

Iceland is the westernmost country in Europe, though technically speaking it could also be considered the easternmost country in the Americas: the Mid-Atlantic Ridge runs right through the middle, and in theory, splits Iceland into two continents. Reykjavík sits on the North American plate, but a one-hour drive to the east lands you right on the Eurasian plate. Continental drift is just one of many reasons why Iceland has such amazing landscapes. It's also why Iceland is considered a part of Scandinavia in only a cultural sense.

The area of Iceland is 103,000km$^2$ (37,769 square miles) and the state of Kentucky is an oft-quoted (yet unfortunate) size reference. Alternative comparisons might be Scotland and Wales combined, or England minus the Midlands, or Guatemala. Size matters very little in a country where travel times are determined by season, terrain, and weather – not distance. From Reykjavík to the east coast is about 400km, and the distance north to south is about 300km.

The shape of Iceland has been compared to everything from a human heart to a cow to a dragon. What makes it so unique are the stubborn peninsulas and the intricate coastlines cut with so many fjords and dotted with rocky islands. Iceland's terrain consists of a very high (and dry) inland plateau that breaks down near the coast in a series of cliffs, mountain ridges, and glacier-cut lowlands. The dramatic features of the landscape are shaped by 'fire and ice' – the continued effects of volcanic activity and glacier weathering upon the country's rather young geology. Millions of years ago, the rest of the world was formed by the same processes that are still going on in Iceland. That means lots of active volcanoes and fresh lava fields, while ice covers 11% (11,922km$^2$) of the country in the form of permanent glaciers. Because the centre of the country is a flat desert (complete with sand dunes), the melting ice flows into dozens of rushing rivers that pour over the coastal ledge in a series of powerful waterfalls. What is most amazing about the geography of Iceland is how all-encompassing and representative it is. The entire country is a textbook of geographic phenomena and even the most casual observer will suddenly remember all the stuff learned back in school.

**ICELAND RECORDS**

**Tallest mountain** Mt Hvannadalshnjúkur at 2,110m (6,925ft), though its peak is completely under ice. The tallest mountain that you can see is Mt Snæfell at 1,833m (6,013ft).
**Largest glacier** Vatnajökull (8,300km²) with a volume of ice equal to 3,300km³.
**Most active volcano** Mt Hekla (five eruptions over the last 70 years).
**Longest river** Thjórsá (230km) although the Jökulsá á Fjöllum (206km) is a close second.
**Highest waterfall** Glymur at 196m (643ft), though Dettifoss (see page 388) is the most powerful waterfall in Europe.
**Longest fjord** Eyjafjörður at 60km (37 miles). There are 80 named fjords in Iceland.

## CLIMATE

Iceland does not have the hellish climate that it's actually supposed to have. The country's name and Arctic latitude implies Siberia, Alaska, and Greenland, but the reality is far warmer thanks to the wonder of thermohaline circulation. In simpler terms, the warm waters of the Caribbean Sea move across the Atlantic (ie: the Gulf Stream), then north across Britain and all the way up around Iceland (known as the Irminger Current). The movement of this north Atlantic current explains why water temperatures in south Iceland are the same as those in southern England. The old adage that Iceland is green and Greenland is icy is very true: the Irminger Current ends just 50 miles west of Iceland and the temperature plunges about 10°C. Icelanders admit fatalistically that without the warm-water current, their country would be uninhabitable.

Fortunately, Iceland enjoys a temperate climate, which means it's not that bad but also not that great. In winter, things hover around freezing (average January temperature is -1°C), and in summer, life gets a good deal warmer (the average July temperature is 15°C). Spring and autumn are quite moderate – the temperature stays within such a limited range that even Icelanders get a little bored with it. There is more variation in the hinterland – the coldest place in Iceland is up in the highlands, on the northwest side of Vatnajökull glacier. The coastline tends to be far warmer.

When it comes to precipitation, Iceland is definitely in favour. Reykjavík is the most quoted statistic, but that's misleading given that the area is one of the wettest in the country. An average 800mm (32 inches) falls on the capital, with 215 'rainy' days per year (London receives an average 596mm over 196 rainy days). Despite its persistence, the dripping coastal rain contributes little to the water cycle. Most of Iceland's precipitation arrives in the form of snow on top of the glaciers, feeding the country's ice and rivers. Some parts of Vatnajökull receive more than 3,000mm (118 inches) of precipitation each year. Ironically, the driest place in Iceland is right next to the glacier, where all the water has been frozen and the mountain of ice creates a vast rain shadow.

**WEATHER** Climate and weather are two very different things – the first is a generalisation and the other is a guessing game. In Iceland, every day is partially cloudy with a strong chance of anything the skies might throw down at you. In less than an hour it can rain, shine, sleet, snow, hail, and gust – then go back through the cycle in reverse. That does not necessarily mean that Iceland has bad weather – Iceland simply has weather, and lots of it. Expect everything and you will never be disappointed.

The melodramatic conditions are due in large part to the island's position in the middle of the ocean. The confluence of warm water and cold Arctic currents (moving in opposite directions) promises exciting and unpredictable weather. New fronts and pressure systems get pushed across the country in a very short time, and with them comes all kinds of precipitation. Never underestimate the wind, which is a lot stronger than you are probably used to. Sustained, gale-force winds can blow through at any moment, along with extremely powerful gusts for which Iceland is famous. A sudden change in wind direction is also normal. The biggest storms come in winter – huge howling blizzards that are truly an amazing site to behold. Heavy snow accumulation is rare – any whiteouts are caused by a few inches of old, blowing snow. Fog is much more common – it can roll in at any time and roll out just as quickly, especially on the coast, out on the islands, or at the base of a fjord.

The country's varied terrain also plays a vital role in the day-to-day weather. The flat coastal areas (Reykjanes, Reykjavík, and the south) tend to be warmer but much more overcast and windy. The mountains are cooler, and some of the fjords are shielded from the country's worst weather. That's why the warmest and sunniest parts of Iceland are actually up in the north (Eyjafjörður, Vopnafjörður). Where you travel does have some bearing on what you encounter.

In Iceland, one checks the weather forecast like a smoker reaches for a cigarette: frequently and subconsciously. A sunshine on the TV weather map will cause Icelanders to drive to the other side of the country for a picnic. A bad forecast only means to sit tight because it might all blow over in an hour. Jokes like 'we get all four seasons in one day' or 'if you don't like the weather, just wait five minutes' become less funny as you learn to accept their truth. But does it get cold? Occasionally. And how do I plan my trip to coincide with good weather? You can't – there are T-shirt days and there are wool parka days and they're normally on the same day.

Indeed, the weather is one of Iceland's greatest attractions and should be enjoyed as such. In some countries the rain falls down; in Iceland, it rains sideways. In other countries, the wind is 'gentle'; in Iceland the wind is mighty. Some days you can't see your hand in front of you, but then the skies clear, giant sunbeams break through the clouds, and Iceland becomes the most glorious place on earth.

For more scientific data and daily forecasts, visit the Icelandic Meteorological Office (*Veðurstofa Íslands; www.vedur.is*).

**SUNSHINE** The amount of daylight in Iceland fluctuates a fair deal, due to the tilt of the earth in relation to the sun. Also, because of the earth's curvature and Iceland's place near the top, a 100km drive north or south shows a significant change in the length of daylight. For most of the country, spring and autumn see the same number of daylight hours experienced in the lower latitudes. The more extreme difference comes in summer (continuous daylight) and winter (continuous darkness).

Iceland's renowned 'midnight sun' is most evident in the very far north, where the sun never disappears from the horizon – by definition, you can only catch a glimpse of the midnight sun on or above the Arctic Circle. Most people are content to watch the pink sky at midnight followed by a slow dawn that arrives within the following hour. In Reykjavík, the weeks before and after the summer solstice see more than 22 hours of daylight. In winter, the capital gets less than four hours of daylight. The utter darkness can feel a little gloomy, just like the sunshine-filled nights can feel a little surreal. Visitors quickly pick up on what Icelanders learned long ago: when it's sunny, stay outside.

## POPULATION

Iceland has close to 310,000 inhabitants, which means that over the space of a year, Icelanders are outnumbered by tourists in their own country. More than two-thirds of the population live in the capital and its suburbs – by definition Iceland is an 'urban' society, although most Icelanders feel a strong connection to a specific rural area. On holidays and in summer, families still travel back to their districts. The largest towns outside Reykjavík include Akureyri, Keflavík, Selfoss, Höfn, Egilsstaðir, and Isafjörður. The rest of the population tends to live near the coast or on the smaller islands. Around 80% of the country is considered 'wild' and a good deal of the country's interior is uninhabitable, though it's not for a lack of trying. With only 2.8 people per square kilometre, Iceland is one of the least densely populated countries in the world.

About 92% of the population comprises ethnic Icelanders, making this one of the most homogenous nation-states in the world. Because of their size and homogeneity, Icelanders are still a prime target of study by geneticists who appreciate the controlled factors exhibited by such a concise group. It's not that every Icelander is blonde with blue eyes. Rather, they have all been related to one another for more than a millennium. A recent yet significant influx of immigrants and refugees is slowly changing that cultural make-up – much of the current population growth is foreign labour from the new EU member nations. Iceland also has the highest fertility rate in the European Community (almost two children per woman) and one of the lowest infant mortality rates in the world.

Icelanders are some of the healthiest people on earth, with a life expectancy of 83 years for women and 79.5 years for men (the highest statistic for men in the world). Longevity can be attributed to very low pollution, good healthcare and a strong social policy. Worldwide happiness surveys might seem dubious, but Iceland always scores among the top three happiest nations.

### PER CAPITA: ICELAND'S WINNING STATISTICS

As a wealthy and highly developed country with a very small population, Iceland always ranks highly on any given worldwide index. *Per capita* has become the common suffix to national achievement and the proud pedestal upon which the nation stands. Per capita, Icelanders:

- are the most literate nation on earth (99.9%)
- drink the most Coca-Cola; 115 litres (30 gallons) per year
- have the highest home internet access (84%)
- produce the most films (ten-times more than the USA)
- eat the most fish: 91kg (200lb)
- use the most electricity (28,787kWh per year)
- have the most Nobel laureates (1)

* Per capita, Iceland ranks in the top five worldwide for business efficiency, economic transparency, global competitiveness, GDP, car ownership, teacher to student ratio, and number of MRI units.

## ADMINISTRATION

The first Vikings to arrive in Iceland divided the country into quarters based on the cardinal directions (north, south, east, and west). This later grew into the eight traditional regions (*landsvæði*) that are used as chapter divisions in this book and are still in use by the post office and in the phone book. To cope with the shift in population towards the capital, Iceland is now divided into six constituencies (*kjördæmi*) that send a select number of representatives to the Althing (parliament). The rural districts include the northwest, northeast, and the south; the remaining three encompass Reykjavík and the surrounding urban areas.

Twenty-three counties (*sýsla*) were established back in the 13th century, and although the system is no longer officially recognised, the names and borders still hold strong cultural connotations. These traditional counties have since been replaced by 26 magistrates (*sýslumenn*), which are broken down into 79 municipalities (*sveitarfélög*).

## GOVERNMENT

Icelanders claim to have invented representative democracy, despite previous attempts in ancient Greece and Rome. The Althing was founded in AD930 (see page 215) and laid the foundation for Iceland's highly independent political culture of councils, debate, constitutional law, and fair judgement. The Icelandic Constitution was signed on 17 June 1944 and has been amended only four times since. The document declares an equal balance of powers, though the legislative branch tends to show a stronger arm. Today's Althing consists of 63 members elected every four years to serve within a unicameral legislature. Seats are decided as a proportional representation of party votes and that may be the most exciting aspect of Icelandic politics. The Althing assembly (*www.althingi.is*) is located in the centre of Reykjavík and visitors are welcome to sit in the gallery and observe the animated discussions. Parliament meets four days a week, from the first of October until the end of May.

The High Court of Iceland (*Hæstiréttur; www.haestirettur.is*) is made up of nine judges who are appointed for life by the President of Iceland. The judges hold court as a panel of three or five members and wear dark-blue robes with white collars. Iceland was the first country to simultaneously publish high court rulings on the internet while they were read aloud. Until quite recently, the high court was housed in Reykjavík's old Danish prison.

Iceland's president plays the role of national figurehead, much like the kings and queens of Europe's constitutional monarchies. He or she is elected to a four-year term in a nationwide vote with no limitations as to the number of terms served. The president's political powers are limited to diplomatic responsibilities, guardian of the high court, and a rare but restricted veto on parliamentary legislation. Even so, the president's picture is framed and hung in public buildings, shops, and offices. He or she is normally pictured wearing the Order of the Falcon, which is Iceland's highest decoration. The presidential office is based at the estate of Bessastaðir (*www.forseti.is*).

The real executive powers lie with the office of the prime minister, who is appointed by the president based on majority party representation after elections to the Althing. Typically, party coalitions will appoint cabinet ministers under the approval of the president. The prime minister has his offices at Government House in Reykjavík (*www.forsaetisraduneyti.is*) and Iceland's largest ministry (the Ministry of Fisheries) is just around the block.

## POLITICS

Iceland's government is best characterised as the Scandinavian model of liberal democracy, where a strong central government combines its aggressive economic policy with a tight social safety net. As a small and close-knit nation, the governing mentality tends to focus on policies that best suit families and individuals. Icelandic political culture favours welfare support to the less fortunate, equal opportunity, and minority rights. These traditions likely stem from a not-so-distant era when Icelanders were the minority subjects of the Danish monarchy and its strict trade monopolies.

Iceland is also fiercely democratic – Icelanders hate politics and politicians, but they tend to be quite vocal about politics. Close to 90% of the electorate cast votes in the last parliamentary elections and even the smallest villages are run by elected town councils who base their decisions on very vocal town meetings. Career politicians are far less common in Iceland. After working as a tour guide and managing the Reykjavík theatre, in August 1980 Vigdís Finnbogadóttir became the first elected woman president in Iceland (and the world).

President Ólafur Ragnar Grímsson comes from a leftist political background and was the former leader in the now defunct People's Alliance. The president is well-liked enough to have won re-election in 2004, though he caused quite a stir a few weeks prior when he was the first president ever to invoke Article 26 of the Icelandic Constitution, by vetoing a parliamentary bill that would have restricted privatisation of the media. Despite the political upheaval that followed the recent economic crisis, Grímsson was re-elected for a fourth term in 2008.

**PARTIES** Even though Iceland is an ancient country with a 1,000-year political history, much of its recent politics reflects a young and vigorous democracy. Nowhere is that more evident than in the consolidation and behaviour of Iceland's political parties. Since independence, more than a dozen political parties have come and gone. Also, allegiances and ideologies tend to shift wildly, though it seems to make sense to Icelanders.

Prior to the economic crash, the Independence Party (Sjálfstadisflokkurinn) functioned as the largest and most powerful political party in the country, favouring a strong base in Reykjavík. That changed at the end of January 2009, when, after months of angry protests in the capital, Geir Haarde resigned as prime minister and relinquished the Independence Party's political dominance. This led to the dissolution of a previous coalition with the Social Democratic Alliance (Samfylkingin) and the rise of the latter's new centre-left coalition.

The Social Democratic Alliance was created in 2000 out of several left-ish parties, namely the Social Democratic Party, the Women's Alliance and the People's Alliance. The coalition tends to represent standard-issue labour policy with a strong focus on social welfare – hence their current popularity and majority victory in 2009. The current prime minister, Jóhanna Sigurðardóttir, is head of the Alliance and represents a new progressive force working towards EU membership and honesty in dealing with the financial crisis.

Other parties include the Progressive Party (Framsóóknarflokkurinn), which represents a moderate brand of liberal democrats based on the rural interests of farmers and fishermen. They inherited Iceland's strong co-operative movement and were once known for their nationalistic sympathies. Traditionally the country's second-largest party, they have pandered to both sides of the political spectrum.

The much smaller Left-Green Party (Vinstrihreyfinging – Graent framboð) is a good jump further to the left, and is most focused on conserving Iceland's nature. They tend to the most radical of the current parties and are quite vocally opposed to EU membership. This poses an interesting problem as they supported the Social Democratic Alliance in the elections of 2009 yet differ on the larger party's EU policy.

**CURRENT ISSUES** The hottest political issue in Iceland today is achieving a full and total recovery from the economic crisis of 2008. Many blame the previous government for either turning a blind eye or actively participating in dodgy bank dealings that allowed the country's finances to descend into chaos. The public mood in Iceland is one of dissatisfaction with the government leaders and a desire for greater transparency in the financial sector.

Other political issues in Iceland today are not too dissimilar to those in other developed countries, namely the use of natural resources, conservation, tax and inflation, and immigration. As Iceland blossoms into a hefty worldwide financial power, Icelandic politics seems to be more focused on money: how it is made and how it is spent. The environmental controversy of the Kárahnjúkar Dam (see page 404) pinpoints past political struggles – to integrate Iceland with the global economy by capitalising on undeveloped resources (eg: clean energy) versus a conscious effort to preserve Iceland from the ills of global society (eg: pollution and economic disparity). In very simple terms, one brand of Icelander seeks 'progress' through economic development while another warily seeks to guard the best of Icelandic tradition. In Kárahnjúkaur, the choice was the elimination of a wilderness area for jobs and money. Future projects will be slowed by environmentalists who see the Icelandic wilderness as a unique resource that is not for sale.

Another real issue is the economic flight from the countryside to the big city – the only city. The question of coastal fishing quotas getting bought up by large corporations is of the same ilk. Some politicians seek to counter the abandoning of rural areas and a past way of life. Yet another raging debate centres on immigration: opponents fear the influx of non-Icelanders erodes Icelandic cultural values and burdens social security; proponents cite the high cost of Icelandic labour and the gap in Iceland's service industry. Immigrants from Poland, the Baltic States, and even Britain, are now filling the needs of construction, cooking, and cleaning. Whaling (see page 65) represents a twist in political logic, as it is the traditionalists who support the controversy and the internationalists who fear angering foreign trading partners. Up until 2006, the fundamental foreign policy issue for all of Iceland was NATO – in particular, should Iceland allow a foreign military base on its territory? Politicians fell into camps of for or against and the debate raged for decades.

Perhaps the largest question looming in the political sphere is Iceland's relationship to the European Union. While naysayers rejected membership because of a fear of foreign domination, the devastation and mistrust that stems from the banking crisis has made EU membership a fairly predictable outcome for Iceland. Politicians will continue to battle the pros and cons, but economic necessity of partnership will probably see Iceland join the EU in the very near future.

## INTERNATIONAL RELATIONS

Iceland is a truly transatlantic nation by means of both its position and function. The country continues to serve as a bridge between European and North American interests, as well as a small and neutral leader in the ranks of the world's highly developed countries.

For obvious historic and cultural connections, Iceland favours strong relations with Scandinavia and Denmark in particular (Danish is still a required subject in Icelandic schools). As part of the Nordic Council (*www.norden.org*), Iceland seeks greater political and economic co-operation with fellow northern European members, as well as Greenland, Iceland's closest neighbour. Greenland still relies heavily on Iceland's infrastructure, economic strength, and proximity. In much the same way, Iceland looks to Great Britain as a powerful neighbour and friend. This in spite of past skirmishes and, most recently, the tension and mistrust caused by the global financial crisis. These fraternal disagreements go back for centuries: the British have been fishing in Iceland for hundreds of years, their troops were the first to arrive in World War II, they helped build Iceland's roads and airports and London is still the nearest 'world capital'. Many Icelanders still receive their secondary educations in Britain and the business ties between the two countries are considerable (Britain is Iceland's largest trading partner). A strong cultural connection with France also dates back to early French fishermen – a number of Icelandic fishing villages still hold annual 'French' festivals and there exists a lively and idiosyncratic French–Icelandic yachting culture. Iceland is a member of the European Economic Area (EEA) which allows Icelanders open trade and travel within the European Union without having to join. The arrangement also facilitates immigration and temporary workers entering Iceland. Public opinion seems to be moving towards the idea of EU membership, though there is the fear that doing so would compromise Icelandic fish stocks.

Iceland joined NATO at its inception in 1949, though some claim the Icelanders did not have much of a choice since the American military was already there. During the Cold War, NATO forces used Iceland both as a major north Atlantic air base and as a communications centre to keep track of Soviet manoeuvres. Iceland is the only NATO member that does not have a military, though it did contribute finances and manpower to operations in Kosovo and Bosnia. Since World War II, Iceland's relationship with the United States has been important and American influence on modern Icelandic society is obvious and visible. Likewise, there is a definite closeness with Canada, who welcomed so many Icelandic immigrants in the 19th century (see page 22). Manitoba is home to the largest ethnic Icelandic community outside Iceland today.

Other countries fight for oil or land – Iceland fights for its fish. By far the largest of Iceland's international conflicts were the Cod Wars (see page 24), a series of conflicts with Great Britain over fishing rights between 1958 and 1976 (which Iceland won). Iceland has been very much in favour of the international law of the sea from the beginning although its exclusive economic zone (EEZ) of 200 nautical miles was only recognised in 1994. Iceland still rolls its eyes at the Faroe Islands, who claim their continental shelf extends beyond the 200 nautical mile limit, which would extend their fishing rights well into Icelandic waters.

Iceland's determination to hunt whales has been a cause for serious diplomatic concern and has soured relationships with some of Iceland's closest allies. Iceland left the International Whaling Commission (IWC) in 1992 but rejoined ten years later, although it continues to defy the worldwide ban on commercial whaling. It is a fundamental factor in Iceland's foreign relations today.

In total, Iceland manages 16 foreign diplomatic embassies plus six permanent missions to international organisations. Among the pomp and pageantry of international affairs, Iceland's Foreign Ministry takes pride in being small, personable and non-bureaucratic. It's one reason why Iceland plays such a unique diplomatic role in the world today. The most memorable case was the 1986

Reykjavík Summit when Reagan and Gorbachev met to negotiate disarmament and seek an end to the Cold War. Always rooting for the underdog, Iceland was the first country to recognise the independence of Latvia, Lithuania, and Estonia in 1991, and Montenegro in 2006. Iceland also has a strong record on international human rights, global economic development and aiding refugees.

**DEFENCE** As a sign of political neutrality, independent Iceland chose not to have an armed force. That desire was overridden in World War II, when tens of thousands of allied troops were stationed in Iceland. The **Iceland Defence Force (IDF)** was founded in 1951, and evolved into a 1,400-strong American military unit that was commissioned by NATO to defend Iceland. Hundreds of Icelanders were trained and employed by the IDF, most of whom were affiliated with the NATO base in Keflavík (see page 203). The IDF was officially disbanded in 2006.

Officially, Iceland still has no military. The **Icelandic Coast Guard** (Landhelgisgæsla Íslands) provides most of the necessary operations of protection and crisis management. It is world-renowned for performing daring rescues at sea, although its primary mission is to protect Iceland's Exclusive Economic Zone from illegal fishing activity. In order to capture foreign fish 'pirates', the force operates a few helicopters and four ships, all of which are named after Old Norse gods (like Odin). Instead of heavy artillery, the ships are armed with giant cutters, the same type once used to slice the nets of British trawlers during the Cod War. The coast guard still takes its motto seriously: *Föðurland vort hálft er hafið* ('the sea is half of our homeland').

The Icelandic **police force** (Lögreglan) consists of about 700 officers who maintain public order and manage law enforcement responsibilities. Because Iceland benefits from a low crime rate, the police do not carry guns and lack the sour demeanour typical of their position. Indeed, the Lögreglan are some of the kindest police in the world, but they are totally unforgiving when it comes to traffic violations.

The **Icelandic Crisis Response Unit** (Íslenska Friðargæslan) is a 100-person armed peacekeeping force that participates in foreign operations in honour of Iceland's international agreements and alliances. As part of the 'coalition of the willing', Iceland committed its support to the war in Iraq, although this came down to the deployment of only two soldiers who were withdrawn shortly thereafter.

## ECONOMY

Like Iceland's rugged landscape, the country's economy has had its ups and downs. Right now, Iceland is in recovery mode – it currently ranks 17th in the world for highest GDP per capita (nominal) – more than Belgium, but less than Denmark – and fifth highest for GDP per capita (purchasing power parity). Iceland also ranks 17th on the United Nations Human Development Index (HDI) after Finland.

Following the global economic crisis, the Icelandic government is dedicated to diversifying the economy away from fishing and into alternative energy and service industries, as well as tourism: it seems to be working. Iceland is a founding member of the Organisation for Economic Co-operation and Development (OECD), and joined the World Trade Organisation (WTO) in 1995. Lead trading partners are the United Kingdom, Germany, the Netherlands, Norway, Denmark, Sweden, the United States, China and Japan.

**BANKING CRISIS** In early 2008, the króna began to fall sharply against the euro, indicating serious issues within Iceland's powerful banking sector. By October 2008, three of Iceland's four major banks had failed: Glitnir, Landsbanki, and

Kaupthing – once perceived as cunning investment giants – all came under receivership and represented national losses worth over €50 billion. Iceland was essentially bankrupt.

In the months following the crisis, Iceland published some fairly grim statistics: unemployment tripled, significant pay reductions were made for a large part of the workforce, pension funds shrunk by a quarter, Iceland's GDP fell by at least 10% and inflation rose to nearly 75%. From a per-capita standpoint, Iceland's banking collapse was the largest suffered by any country.

The economic crisis that ensued was a serious wake-up call for the rest of the world as global markets battled with the wider financial crisis. Millions of foreigners who had invested either directly or indirectly in Icelandic banks suddenly found their assets frozen or evaporated. In November 2008, the IMF disbursed an emergency loan to Iceland of US$2.1 billion, and took a managing role in overseeing the recovery of the Icelandic economy.

Perhaps more difficult was the changed reality of everyday life in Iceland. Homeowners suddenly faced impossible repayments on their homes; retirees watched their life savings disappear. What was once a fairly wealthy, social-safe Scandinavian country was now cash poor. Imported goods became unaffordable, credit cards stopped working outside the country, and Icelanders were limited in the amount of money they could withdraw at one time.

Iceland's economic recession will likely continue and affect serious political changes. While the country has received a lot of attention for its economic woes, in

## SUSTAINABLE ICELAND

No country has achieved a truly sustainable society, though Iceland has come fairly close. Not only is Iceland one of the least polluted countries on earth, but 75% of its total energy consumption comes from hydro- and geothermal sources. With the growing concern over climate change, human impact on earth and the demand for clean energy, world leaders are now looking to Iceland's example of low-impact living and relative independence from fossil fuels. A good example is how Iceland's lamb, fish, and dairy industry are heavily regulated as they move towards total sustainability. The ability to feed one's own people (and produce surplus for export) without diminishing natural food sources is a policymaker's dream but a reality in Iceland. All Icelandic lamb is 'free-range', and 'organic' has been a way of life for the last thousand years.

Such a progressive state breeds two lines of thought – some Icelanders take pride in their nation's accomplishments and welcome outside interest, others feel a tad isolationist, wanting to protect themselves from the problems of more polluted nations. The abundance of low-cost, emissions-free energy has already attracted the aluminum industry to Iceland, who require huge amounts of electricity to refine bauxite ore into metal. This brings up the added controversy (page 404) of building new dams that cause environmental damage. Others see Iceland's capacity of clean energy as a revenue stream that can pick up the slack from the slowing fish industry. Sustainability has become one of Iceland's primary political concerns that sums up the wider concerns of immigration, tourism, the environment, and Iceland's future role in a global marketplace. As a visitor, you are part of the conversation.

many ways Iceland is only a microcosm of the broader global issues in international banking and finance.

**FISHING** Fish had always been Iceland's number-one money-maker until quite recently. The general decrease in worldwide fish stocks has seen new protections put in place and the government now controls the harvesting of certain species like cod. Fish once accounted for 90% of Iceland's exports, but that figure has dropped to 50%. In real terms, that's still well over 1,500,000 tons of fish per year worth close to US$1 billion. In the past, fishing quotas were issued to individuals and towns, but recent changes have seen larger fishing corporations buying up the fishing quotas and consolidating a nationwide fishing industry. As a result, many of Iceland's smaller fishing villages are in a state of economic stagnation as they seek to reinvent themselves. Today, only 8% of Iceland's population is directly employed by the fishing industry.

**TOURISM** Tourism accounts for the fastest-growing sector of the Icelandic economy and is now the second-highest earner in the country. There are now more foreign tourists to Iceland than there are Icelanders in Iceland, and their foreign currency-filled wallets pay about 15% of Iceland's total export earnings. The average tourist stays less than nine days and spends about US$1,100. The majority of visitors come from the Nordic countries, followed by North America, Great Britain, Germany, France, and Italy. The government continues to invest in developing tourism and it's hard not to miss the rush towards the tourist dollar – sometimes it seems that every small town is reinventing itself for tourists.

**ENERGY** Around 98% of Iceland's energy comes from ecologically clean hydro-electric and geothermal sources, which has the dual benefit of low pollution and low costs. Iceland is so pristine that according to the Kyoto Protocol, the country is allowed to increase its carbon emissions by 10% (Iceland has chosen to sell them instead). The pending limitations of Kyoto have seen several major industries looking to clean energy destinations like Iceland. Aluminium-smelting plants require huge amounts of electricity, and despite the high cost of labour and shipping raw goods, aluminium companies still come out on top by locating their smelters in Iceland and using inexpensive Icelandic power. Aluminium and metallurgical products are now a leading Icelandic export, and current plants would see output triple in the next decade. Despite the notable controversy around the ecological effects of the Kárahnjúkar Dam and the aluminium plant in Reyðarfjörður, this is just the beginning of a broader global trend. As the demand for clean energy increases worldwide, Iceland is likely to experience a great deal of foreign interest.

**AGRICULTURE** Less than 1% of Iceland's land is considered arable. The bright-green fields that you see in valleys and along coasts are filled with hay that grows naturally and is cut in late summer to feed the livestock during the dark and dreary winter months. Officially, Iceland produces no crops, even though Icelanders have been trying to grow vegetable gardens for well over 1,000 years. Icelandic greenhouses produce potatoes, cucumbers, and mushrooms primarily for the domestic market and these are heavily subsidised. Import tariffs on agricultural products are as high as 700% (!) which is why Icelanders tend not to eat salad. Sheep is Iceland's other white meat, though in general, sheep farming is in decline. About half is exported as mutton to both sides of the Atlantic; Icelandic wool is considered a speciality commodity and sells at a very high price. After sheep, dairy farms are the most common.

**COST OF LIVING** Despite the great humbling caused by the banking crisis, Iceland remains a very expensive country in the world and ranks number one on the global Big Mac index (the per-capita real cost of a McDonald's hamburger). Common explanations point to the small island population, astronomical import duties, high sales taxes, and your basic supply versus demand disparity. But even after you subtract all those factors, Iceland still comes out as very expensive. It's no secret that Icelanders find it much cheaper to fly to another country to do their shopping, especially for luxury items. To watch recently returned Icelanders entering the customs line at Keflavík Airport can be fairly entertaining as they unpack bicycles, television sets, and computers.

Iceland has 24.5% VAT, which is the third-highest tax in the world (after Norway and Denmark). Following the never-ending murmurs of Icelanders and foreign tourists, VAT on restaurants was reduced to 7%, although the bill at the end doesn't seem that much less. And yet in spite of the horrific prices, Icelanders enjoy one of the highest standards of living in the world. Home ownership is high, education levels are high, and there is an equal distribution of wealth. The one fundamental problem is high debt and easy lending: the word on the street is that the average adult Icelander owes somewhere in the vicinity of US$25,000 in credit-card debt.

**CURRENCY** The Icelandic króna (ISK) has a small circulation and its value is heavily controlled by Iceland's central bank. Prior to the financial crisis, the króna was not 'pegged' to any other nation's currency, but now follows the euro. Inflation is still a major frustration, and exchange rates fluctuate wildly. The need to reform monetary policy was a common criticism of Iceland's financial sector long before the current economic crisis. Most prices are now listed in euros, and there is much speculation that when EU membership does come, Iceland will quickly adopt the euro.

**LABOUR** Following the banking crisis, Iceland's rate of unemployment rose from one of the lowest in Europe (1.3%) to over 8.5% in 2010. At least 85% of the workforce belongs to a union and workers' rights are some of the best in the world. There is no standard minimum wage but only because Iceland's liberal labour laws prevent the need for one. The state is still the largest employer in Iceland.

# 2

# The Icelanders

## HISTORY

The early history of Iceland is such a well-told tale that it leaves very little room for embellishment. The sagas recall every event with great detail – pick any pretty spot in Iceland (an elegant fjord or mountain) and you will find a perfectly accurate description of that very same spot as it was written 1,000 years ago. Read on and you will find out exactly what happened there and how it happened. The name on the signpost is most likely the same name it was given by the Viking whose bones now lie beneath the turf.

To appreciate Iceland's history is to recognise that Iceland is timeless. That goes for the rocks and volcanoes, as well as its people who have changed very little in spite of the centuries. So much of what Iceland looks and feels like today is a culmination of things changing very little over a very long time.

**DISCOVERY** In 325BC, the Ancient Greek explorer Pytheas embarked on an epic journey of northern Europe which he detailed in his work *On the Ocean*. Among his many travels he described a land called Thule that was six days' sailing north of Britain and near a frozen sea. Some of his descriptions are fitting for Iceland (like the midnight sun), others less so (a land of milk and honey). Historians still argue over whether Iceland is Thule and not Ultima Thule – the name for the land beyond, which others believe to be Greenland. Regardless, Iceland is marked as 'Thule' on later medieval maps.

In 825, the Irish monk Dicuil penned his book on world geography and recounted the tales of fellow monks who had reached the land later known as Iceland. These early Christian Celts led a secluded life on the coastal islands, finding solace and a contemplative atmosphere in the midst of stark surroundings. The Norse settlers called these Irish monks *papar* and there are many place names in Iceland that still reference them, like the island of Papey (see page 415). The sagas recall how the *papar* became terrified and fled Iceland after the Norse arrived – not surprising given the earlier Viking raids on monasteries in Scotland (like Iona). Other than their mystical legacy, the *papar* left very little behind.

The first of the Norse to arrive in Iceland was Naddodur the Viking, who was sailing back to Norway from the Faroe Islands when a violent storm threw him off course and landed him in the East Fjords. He climbed the nearest mountain and found the land to be totally uninhabited. He left at summer's end when the snow began to fall and he called the new place *snæland* or 'snow-land'.

Not long after, the Swedish Viking Garðar Svavarosson sailed to Snowland after his clairvoyant mother had a vision and declared her son's fate in the new land. Garðar circumnavigated the country and confirmed it to be an island, after which he landed in the north and built a house at 'house bay' or Húsavík (see page 377).

He named the country after himself, Garðarshólmur or 'Garðar's isle', and made the puzzling remark about the land being covered in forest 'between fell and foreshore'. Garðar stayed for one winter and then accidentally left behind his servant Nattfari who became the de facto first settler in Iceland.

The Norseman Flóki Vilgerðarson was intrigued by the favourable reports and set off to find Garðarshólmur. For guidance he sailed with three black ravens that were especially blessed for navigation. He let the first one go after he had passed the Faroe Islands, but the bird just flew from the back of the ship up to the front. Further on he released the second raven who flew straight up into the air and then came back down to the ship's deck. It was only the third raven who flew straight ahead towards the west, prompting Flóki to follow the bird towards land. To this day, the 'great Viking' is remembered as Hrafna-Flóki or Flóki-Raven.

## ICELAND HISTORICAL OVERVIEW

| | |
|---|---|
| AD874 | Iceland is settled by Norse 'Vikings' |
| AD930 | Althing established at Thingvellir |
| 1000 | Iceland adopts Christianity |
| 1220--62 | Civil war: Icelanders made subjects to the King of Norway |
| 1397 | Kalmar Union: King of Denmark gains control of Iceland |
| 1402--04 | Black Plague: Iceland loses 50% of its population |
| 1550 | Reformation: Bishop Jón Arason beheaded for treason |
| 1584 | Bible printed in Icelandic |
| 1602 | Denmark establishes trade monopoly on Iceland |
| 1662 | Kópavogur meeting: Iceland accepts absolute rule by King of Denmark |
| 1707 | Smallpox epidemic: 18,000 die |
| 1783 | Famine of the mists: 10,000 die |
| 1786 | Reykjavík founded as a woollen goods company |
| 1814 | Treaty of Kiel (Denmark loses Norway but keeps Iceland) |
| 1845 | Althing re-established in Reykjavík |
| 1854 | Danish trade monopoly ends |
| 1870s | Icelanders emigrate to the New World: 25% of the population leaves |
| 1874 | Denmark grants Iceland autonomy and a constitution |
| 1904 | Denmark grants Iceland home rule |
| 1918 | Iceland enters equal union with Denmark |
| 1940 | Allied forces occupy Iceland |
| 1944 | Iceland becomes an independent republic |
| 1946 | Iceland joins the United Nations |
| 1949 | Iceland joins NATO |
| 1951 | US reopens NATO base at Keflavík |
| 1958 | First Cod War |
| 1972 | Second Cod War |
| 1976 | Third Cod War ends |
| 1986 | Reykjavík Summit between Ronald Reagan and Mikhail Gorbachev |
| 2006 | NATO base closes at Keflavík: American troops leave Iceland |
| 2008 | Financial crisis leads to failure of Iceland's top three banks |
| 2010 | Eyjafjallajökull erupts, disrupting European air travel |

Bad voyages tend to be more memorable than good ones, and such was the case with Flóki. First his daughter drowned *en route*, then he arrived and became trapped by the cold and bitter winter. Flóki found the fishing in Breiðafjörður to be so fantastic that he forgot to harvest hay for his livestock and they all died from starvation. Then his fishing boat broke loose with his closest friend inside and he watched them both drift away. Depressed and frustrated by the colder than average spring, Flóki climbed a mountain and looked across to the next fjord where he was met with a view of hundreds of floating icebergs. Crestfallen, he called the place *ísland* ('ice-land').

Flóki had landed at Barðarströnd in the West Fjords at a place now called Flókalundur (see page 299). The ice that he witnessed was most likely a common spring flow when the warmer temperatures cause winter ice to break away from the nearby Greenland coast and float south. These days, Iceland gets little to no drift ice, but the name has stuck ever since Flóki pronounced it. When he returned to Norway, the sagas recount how Flóki spoke ill of the place and that 'Iceland' was more of a slur. The new land might have been left alone if it wasn't for a younger member of Flóki's crew, Thorolf, who spun wild tales about this strange country where 'butter dropped from every blade of grass'. His exaggerations earned him the name Thorolf Smjör (butter) and started a chain of rumours throughout Norway about the rich paradise of Iceland.

**SETTLEMENT** Iceland's first permanent resident was Ingólfur Arnason (see page 124) who built a farm in Reykjavík around AD874 and declared the new land a suitable place to live. This was the last country in Europe to be settled – an event that is recounted in detail in the *Landnámabók*, or Settlement saga. The written record is made more fascinating by the physical evidence of the time when Vatnaöldur volcano (near Torfajökull) erupted and dropped a distinct layer of ash over the whole country. Iceland's oldest archaeological sites are all found just at or above this 'settlement layer', which carbon dating places at or around AD871.

Iceland's first settlers came from western Norway, which by this time had grown into a powerful Viking kingdom. Several powerful chieftains had fallen out of favour with King Harald the Fair-haired – formally known as 'the tangle-haired' because of the oath he had taken not to cut his hair until he was king of all Norway (a fate that took ten long years). Facing intimidation and demotion, many of the leaders who had opposed Harald chose to leave with their families and make a new life in Iceland. Others simply found that Norway had limited resources and was becoming overpopulated. New Viking settlements had already popped up in the Faroe, Shetland, and Orkney islands, and Iceland seemed the next step for any hard-working adventurer in search of new opportunities.

The newcomers sailed to Iceland in open boats with tools, supplies, and livestock. The journey from Norway took about three days, after which they laid claim to the new lands along all sides of Iceland's coast. These new settlers included the Norse, but also their servants – the majority of whom had been taken in Viking raids in Ireland and Scotland. The country's isolation and the eventual blend of Norse and Celtic peoples were key to the creation of a unique nation in Iceland. By the end of the 50-year era, an estimated 30,000 people had settled in Iceland.

**THE COMMONWEALTH** Iceland was settled quite haphazardly, with new arrivals claiming all the land they could see (and beyond) before giving away sections to family and friends. Within just a few decades, most of the coastline was accounted for, along with a good deal of the interior. The country was now a series of

## THE VIKINGS

We tend to think of helmets with horns, blood-stained battleaxes, and longboats with dragons' heads – but the typical Viking was the kind of neighbour you always wanted. They were intensely loyal but minded their own business – they valued personal freedom above all else. They also watched and raised one another's children as their own and threw great parties that could carry on for weeks.

The Vikings of Iceland were farmers first and foremost. They owned land, livestock and servants and lived by a code of mutual respect and occasional revenge. In search of adventure or riches – and sometimes as a right of passage – the Vikings would set off on long trading journeys. Boats were built, bought or borrowed, and commodities were traded from one port to the next. Trading voyages could last for a summer or for many years and the sagas tell of epic adventures spread across several different countries. If Vikings agreed to fight in a foreign war, it was only to seat an ally and improve trade relations in that country. The 'raping and pillaging' usually took place upon exposed enemy ports and could be entirely random – a year after some vicious raid, the Vikings might return looking for a trade.

The first recorded Viking 'attack' took place in AD787 when a group of Danish seamen landed in Dorset and stabbed an English bureaucrat through the heart (he was trying to get them to pay a customs tax). Historians believe the term *Viking* comes from the Norse word *vík* (bay) although alternative definitions are limited to their reputation for violence and not seamanship. The Vikings sailed in open wooden longboats called *knorr* and were the most skilled and able navigators of the time. They travelled as far as North America to Africa and Persia and their settlements stretched from Greenland to Kiev. Such an expansive trade route ultimately led to the Vikings 'settling down' and the eventual integration with other cultures; historians mark the end of the era with the Battle of Hastings in 1066.

Iceland was settled at the height of the Viking age, between the 9th and 10th centuries, and was the only independent Viking nation in the world. Most of what we know about the Vikings comes from the Icelandic sagas, which provide a sympathetic, behind-the-scenes look at some of Europe's most-feared villains. The real Vikings wore coned helmets (without horns) and had a soft spot for nature and pretty objects. They composed complex poetry filled with rhyme and double meanings and performed incredible feats of strength. 'Good' Vikings were just as prone to pragmatism as they were to outrage or fatalism. They enjoyed raising sheep as much as they enjoyed raising hell and valued strong family ties and lifelong friendships.

The more common image of Vikings as unkempt barbarians is the romantic invention of 19th-century Europeans who longed for wilder roots than their civilised histories permitted (if in doubt, just sit through an opera by Wagner). Today's Icelanders have no need for such imaginations – visitors will find that the best of Viking culture is alive and well in Iceland.

independent farms or steads (*staðir*) upon which stood a religious temple (*hof*). Every farm was ruled by a local chieftain called a *goði* (from the same Norse root that gives us the word 'god') and his jurisdiction was a *goðorð*. These *goðar* were self-appointed leaders of their household and their status was typically based on their prowess in building their own wealth through trade and marriage.

Having fled an unjust king in Norway, the *goðar* preferred a system of governance along the lines of 'live and let live' but eventually realised the benefits of a universal law for the whole of Iceland. In AD930, during the weeks of midsummer, the goðar gathered on the edge of a plain in southeast Iceland to establish a new legal system. Prior district councils were known as a *thing* and because this new nationwide parliament represented all of the *things*, it was simply called the *Althing*. The Althing was established upon the fields of parliament, or Thingvellir (see page 213), where the landscape seemed custom-made for large gathering assemblies and public speeches. Laws were read from the law rock (*lögberg*) to a legislature comprising the goðar known as the *lögrétta*. From this legislative body was elected the law-speaker (*lögsögumaður*) whose job it was to memorise the law and quote it whenever necessary. The law-speaker was elected for a three-year stint, and the very first man for the job was none other than the grandson of Iceland's first settler, Ingólfur Arnason: Thorkel máni ('moon') was remembered as a wise and righteous leader, 'for a heathen' (so disclaim the sagas).

The annual midsummer meeting of the Althing became the social event of the year – if it wasn't some big business deal or a wedding announcement, there was still a fair amount of gossip and political wheeling and dealing. The Althing became more sophisticated as it developed into a system of district and supreme courts where civic disputes could find resolution. This period of governance was known as the commonwealth (*Þjóðveldið*), and for it, Iceland is still remembered as one of the world's oldest functioning democracies. Others say that it resembled more of an anarchy, though whichever way you look at it, the commonwealth lasted for 300 years and the Althing is still around today.

**CHRISTIANITY** By AD1000, the Althing had split into two opposing groups: the Old-World pagans who were still loyal to the Norse gods versus the 'modern' Christians who believed that Iceland was better off as part of Christian Europe. Both groups arrived at the Althing that year, armed and ready for a brawl. The situation was tense and the debates became increasingly heated until the question was brought before the law-speaker, Thorgeir Thorkelsson Ljósvetningagoði. Thorgeir was himself a pagan, but as the elected speaker, both factions made a pact to abide by his decision. He retired to his tent and covered himself with a fur blanket, pondering on the question for a full day and night. He emerged the next morning and ascended the law rock to propose his compromise: Iceland must have one religion and one law, otherwise there would never be peace – Christianity would be that religion, but the pagans could still practise their rites in secret. As an example, Thorgeir was baptised there and then, after which he returned home and threw his pagan idols over a waterfall (see page 365). Other pagans were more reluctant, insisting on delaying their baptisms until they had reached a nearby hot spring.

The Icelanders fell into Christianity quite easily – the goðar temples were easily replaced with Christian churches, new monasteries were built, and a tithe was exacted. In 1056, a bishop was established at Skálholt (for southern Iceland) and another in 1106 at Hólar (for northern Iceland).

**THE GOLDEN AGE** Not only did Christianity bring peace to Iceland – it also brought the Latin language and the Roman alphabet. The tales that Icelanders once retold by heart or carved in runes were now put down with ink in Icelandic. The second half of the 12th century opened Iceland to a literary age with titles like *Íslendingabók*, or 'Book of the Icelanders', which gave a detailed account of the previous 300 years' history. By far the most celebrated author of the sagas is Snorri Sturluson (see page 261), a former law-speaker whose writings are so prolific that they still baffle the minds of Old Norse scholars. He wrote the *Edda*, the *Heimskringla* ('History of Kings'), and is the likely author of some of Iceland's most famous sagas. Saga writing continued from the 13th and well into the 14th century, and gave Iceland new status as a land of educated and entertaining storytellers. The sagas also forged a strong and separate Icelandic identity in which Icelanders viewed themselves as a separate nation from the rest of the Nordic lands.

**CIVIL WAR** The golden-age poet Snorri Sturluson played the poster boy to Iceland's not-so-golden age when the country's peace and prosperity disintegrated into a series of family feuds. Over time, a handful of goðar were able to consolidate their power by buying up the rights to neighbouring lands and winning over the people of one another's districts. By 1220, the whole of Iceland lay under the control of six wealthy families, the largest of which was the Sturlungs. Each family sought to broaden its power and the King of Norway (Hákon the Old) began to play them off against one another in an attempt to bring all of Iceland under his reign.

King Hákon first summoned the goðar of the Sturlung clan, Snorri Sturluson, who pledged to deliver Iceland but then never followed through. The jilted king made further attempts with Snorri's relatives and his rivals which led to a number of bloody battles as families fought for the king's favour. On King Hákon's order, Snorri was assassinated in 1241, and the man who did the deed – Gissur Thorvaldson – became the Earl of Iceland. The violence only came to a close with the 'old pact' (*gamli sáttmáli*) of 1262, an arrangement which in effect made all the Icelanders taxpaying subjects to King Hákon.

The 'Age of the Sturlungs' was a short but effective upheaval in which Iceland fell to a foreign monarch in just 40 years. The Althing survived as a governing body but was given a new code of laws (*Jónsbók*) that implemented a hierarchy of sheriffs and governors like those in Norway. A century later, Norway similarly fell to a foreign monarch. In the Kalmar Union of 1397, Denmark was granted rule over Sweden and Norway, as well as Iceland.

**THE 'ENGLISH CENTURY'** The Black Plague came to Iceland in 1402, 50 years after laying waste to western Europe. Oddly, rats arrived in Iceland 500 years later, but the plague still raged across the country and killed more than 50% of Iceland's population in just two years. A repeat plague hit the West Fjords in 1495 and decimated that region for a second time. The effect was devastating for all except the Church, which inherited the farms of the dead.

Iceland's 'English Century' was part of the broader trade war taking place among the seafaring nations of Europe. English ships had been fishing cod from the coast of Iceland since 1412 and soon began trading in saltfish – the English parliament even went so far as to claim a title to Icelandic fishing grounds. Meanwhile, the Hanseatic League (a powerful Germanic trading guild) set up its own trading posts in Iceland and attempted the same kind of fishing monopoly it had formed in the Baltic Sea. Competition with the English was fierce and sometimes violent – the first set of 'cod wars' was fought in Iceland and over Iceland, but not by Icelanders. By 1475, the Hanseatic League had shut off the supply of cod to the port of Bristol, which led to a search for alternatives and the British discovery of the Grand Banks (near Newfoundland). Still, the battle for trading rights continued, and in 1532 there was a last and final showdown in the streets of Iceland's primary saltfish port Grindavík (see page 207). An Englishman by the name of John the Broad was killed and the English were pushed out of Iceland. That same year, King Christian II of Denmark (who was apparently short on cash) offered to mortgage Iceland to England for the low price of 50,000 florins (about US$14 million today). Henry VIII turned him down, saying that he wasn't interested.

**REFORMATION** Denmark adopted Lutheranism in 1536 – the kingdom outlawed the Catholic Church, nationalised its property, and then ordered the same in Iceland. The Icelanders' vehement resistance was by and large politically motivated – the Catholic Church in Iceland was a powerful but independent counterweight to Danish power, and at the time, both bishops were Icelandic (a previous Danish bishop had been tied up in a sack and drowned in a river by his own diocese). The Bishop of Skálholt, Ögmundur Pálsson, was old and incapable of resisting Danish demands. He was arrested in 1541, and died in chains in Copenhagen. The south of Iceland quickly fell to a Lutheran bishop, while the Catholics rallied around the remaining Bishop of Hólar, Jón Arason (see page 225). Isolated from Rome and declared an outlaw by Danish king Christian III, Jón amassed his own army and tried to oust the new apostate leaders. In 1550, he marched on the Althing and conquered the Danish command, only to be arrested that autumn. The last Catholic bishop of Iceland was beheaded at the cathedral of Skálholt along with two of his sons (he had a number of children).

Iceland's status quickly changed from that of protectorate to a fully fledged colony of Denmark. The king now owned the Church's money, lands, and monasteries and Danish nobles were granted titles to whole regions of the country. Copenhagen became the administrative capital to which the Althing now answered. At the same time, religious life in Iceland flourished with the translation and printing of the Bible in the Icelandic vernacular in 1584. 'Guðbrandur's Bible' gave Lutheranism a popular edge and helped canonise the Icelandic language in spite of Denmark.

**TRADE MONOPOLY** In 1602, the Danish crown granted exclusive trading rights for Iceland, first to a single Danish company, and then a select few. The nation of Iceland soon became a lucrative contract on which competing merchants bid for a total monopoly on imports and exports. In 1660, King Frederik III of Denmark declared his absolute power over Iceland, and the Icelandic people (represented by one bishop and one lawyer) 'ratified' the decision at the infamous Kópavogur meeting of 1662. The monopoly was carried one step further: Iceland was divided into counties and districts and Icelanders were prohibited from buying and selling between these districts. Lawbreakers were sentenced to life imprisonment in Denmark. Icelanders could sell only to the monopoly at a price fixed by the monopoly. The result was the utter collapse of Iceland's already undeveloped economy. Farmers and fishermen were reduced to subsistence living, which was not enough to survive in Iceland. Widespread starvation was added to the list of ill fates suffered by the Icelandic people.

The effects of the monopoly were compounded by a rash of natural disasters and deadly disease. The 1707 smallpox epidemic killed 18,000, followed by five major volcanic eruptions which destroyed farms and their produce. The Lakagígar eruption of 1783 was by far the worst, covering the land with a poisonous sulphur haze that killed crops and livestock. The 'famine of the mist' (*moðuharðindi*) was a two-year stretch of poverty and starvation, followed by a devastating earthquake. At the end of 1784, Iceland's population had been reduced to 34,000. Apparently, the Danish government nearly threw in the towel – Copenhagen's response was to draw up a plan in which the entire population of Iceland would be resettled in the uninhabited parts of Norway or Denmark. Fortunately, someone decided a better response to the crisis was to loosen the trade monopoly (just a little). The city of Reykjavík was founded in 1786 after a trade charter was granted to Skuli Magnusson (see page 125), and the next year trade was opened up to all subjects of the Danish crown, including Icelanders. For the first time in almost 900 years, Iceland was permitted to build cities. Denmark further consolidated its power by dissolving the two bishops' seats in Hólar and Skálholt and placing the head of the Church in Reykjavík. In 1798, the Althing was also moved to Reykjavík, only to be abolished two years later and replaced by the Danish Supreme Court.

**NATIONALISM** The tumultuous events on the European continent added momentum to Iceland's rise towards self-determination: Denmark suffered a dressing-down in the Napoleonic Wars, revolutions raged in capitals like Paris and Vienna, and the German Romantic movement came into full swing. The 1814 Treaty of Kiel spelled out the Danish loss of Norway and Sweden – in the deliberations, the British also sought control of Iceland, Greenland, and the Faroes with the premise that the British navy had 'saved' (protected and fed) Iceland during the previous wars. Denmark prevailed, but grew more cautious regarding its distant colonies.

Iceland's nationalist movement found its legs both in Iceland and in Copenhagen. At home, the graduates of the Latin School (the only secondary school in the country) went on to make important contributions in Icelandic culture and thought. There was an increase of foreign interest, both in Iceland and in the Icelandic sagas. Iceland's national library and museum were established, as well as a free press. Meanwhile, back in the Danish capital, a group of young Icelandic intellectuals had founded an Icelandic-language journal *Ný félagsrit* ('The New Society Writing') that swiftly became the political platform for Icelandic autonomy. They were led by Jón Sigurðsson (see page 295), a student from the West Fjords who worked at the Copenhagen University Library and managed its huge collection of Icelandic manuscripts. Jón's demands (and the fear of a revolution in Denmark) led to a compromise in 1845, when the Althing was re-established in Reykjavík as a 'consultative' body.

Jón Sigurðsson won a seat in the new parliament and sought to increase Iceland's national freedoms through political means. He led a number of revolts with a few small victories, but the struggle was long. In 1854, Denmark finally ended the trade monopoly, and in 1871 the Danish king issued the Status Act, which nominally recognised Iceland's 'special national rights'. Iceland celebrated its millennium in 1874 – 1,000 years since the settlement of Reykjavík by Ingólfur Arnason. King Christian IX of Denmark travelled to Iceland (the first Danish monarch ever to visit) and granted the country its own constitution, expanding the Althing's powers to matters of taxation and law-making. Still, the king continued to practise his right to veto.

The new political freedoms did not help the general economic decline of the Icelandic people. The poverty of the 1870s led to 25% of the population emigrating, mostly to North America. Other Icelanders responded by banding together in co-operatives that granted individual farmers and fishermen part-ownership of a business and allowed the joint benefit of an economy of scale. Various forms of co-operatives had already existed for decades, but the wealth and power of Iceland's co-operative movement only took off at the end of the 19th century.

**INDEPENDENCE** Home rule was finally granted to Iceland in 1904 in the form of a 'Minister of Icelandic Affairs'. The new position was based in Reykjavík and worked directly with the Althing as a liaison to the Danish government. Hannes

Hafstein, an Icelander, was the first to fill the position – today he is remembered as the country's first prime minister. Bit by bit, dependence on Denmark was lessened. Iceland increased its economic capacity with the foundation of its own shipping company, the modernising of its fishing fleet, and the building of the harbour in Reykjavík. The University of Iceland was also founded, Icelandic women gained the right to vote, and the use of a separate flag for Iceland was approved in 1915.

Iceland fared well in World War I, as Denmark's neutrality allowed a raging export business to Europe's wartime shortages. Iceland gained boldness in trade and politics, while Denmark became bogged down in its troubles on the home front. In 1918, the Act of Union was passed, which stated that Iceland and Denmark were both free and sovereign states, with a joint king who happened to be Danish. The Icelanders got their own currency (the Icelandic króna), their own coat of arms, and a supreme court, but Denmark still controlled Iceland's foreign affairs. Iceland was independent in principle, but not in practice.

In 1930, Iceland celebrated the millennium of the Althing before falling into the same economic depression as much of the rest of the world. Icelanders fled the countryside for the cities in search of jobs that did not exist. An uppity labour movement finally blossomed with little results. Modern Europeans travelled to Iceland as tourists to an undeveloped nation – travel books of the time marvel at how quaint and primitive it all seemed.

Iceland found its real escape from poverty in World War II. The Althing had declared Iceland's neutrality in the Act of Union, but then Denmark was occupied by Nazi forces in less than two hours on 9 April 1940. That same day, the British allied command invited Iceland to join the war effort, but the Althing refused, again claiming neutrality. Instead, the Althing voted to control its own foreign policy and elected its own governor, Sveinn Björnsson. Winston Churchill continued to push for a base in Iceland on account of its strategic position in the north Atlantic and Iceland continued to refuse. A month later (in May) the British navy simply showed up and occupied the country. Iceland's then prime minister appealed to the Icelandic people to treat the troops as guests. The Icelanders decided instead to treat them as customers – unemployment disappeared overnight as the British military hired helping hands and the Icelanders supplied 25,000 troops with food and shelter. In 1941, the British were replaced by over 40,000 American forces and suddenly there was plenty of money and opportunity for everyone. Reykjavík boomed, along with Iceland's entire infrastructure – airports and roads were built in the name of the war effort and the standard of living increased. The only concern was the demographic imbalance: American troops outnumbered Iceland's adult male population, fostering a bitter competition for Icelandic women.

After years of success and development and with very little word from Denmark, Iceland held a referendum to dissolve the Act of Union. Voter turnout was almost 99%, of which 97% voted for total independence. Sveinn Björnsson was elected president and the Republic of Iceland was declared on 17 June 1944. It is the birthday of Jón Sigurðsson and is now celebrated as the national holiday of independent Iceland.

**INDUSTRIALISATION** In 1946, the American forces left Iceland but continued ownership of their base at Keflavík. Despite major opposition by Icelanders (eg: eggs thrown at the Althing), Iceland joined as a founding member of NATO in 1949 with the understanding that the country had no armed forces of its own and would never be asked to participate in offensive manoeuvres. Two years later, Iceland signed the Iceland Defence Agreement (IDA) with the United States –

the Americans took responsibility for defending Iceland, in exchange for the use of Keflavík as a NATO base. Some Icelanders regarded the entire affair as a replacement for the Act of Union with Denmark – Iceland had finally gained its sovereignty only to lose it to a new superpower. Resistance to the NATO base continued until its closing in 2006.

Independent, post-war Iceland was a prosperous place. Iceland exported fish *en masse* to war-torn Europe and imported luxury goods from both sides of the Altantic. Hoping to increase output and national revenue, the Althing chose to invest its new foreign-currency reserves into purchasing 33 high-tech fishing trawlers.

## COD WAR VERSUS COLD WAR

*Guðni Thorlacius Jóhannesson*

An award-winning television advertisement for non-alcoholic beer (alcohol ads are forbidden in Iceland) shows two animated Icelanders talking to a gullible British tourist at a bar in Reykjavík.

'No, no, no, not the *cold* war, the *cod* war,' says one.

'It was against England,' the other continues. 'We had these small fishing boats and you had these huge… these huge battleships, and they just kept on hitting them.'

'So what was the war like?' asks the Brit innocently, if not uninterestedly.

'That was the war!' exclaim the Icelanders in unison, clearly shocked that the visitor did not grasp the magnitude of the conflict.

The so-called Cod Wars between Britain and Iceland were by no means wars in the proper sense of the word. The origins of the conflict can be traced to the end of the 19th century, when British steam trawlers began to work the rich fishing grounds off Iceland. The locals, who still depended on small fishing boats, resented the competition, however the Icelandic authorities were powerless in driving out the newcomers. At the time, Britain was the master of the seas and Iceland was under Danish rule. In 1901, the governments in London and Copenhagen signed a treaty on three-mile territorial waters around Iceland, and for half a century the Icelanders had to content themselves with this state of affairs.

Only after independence could Iceland struggle for full control over its fishing grounds. In 1952, the Icelandic government extended the fishing limits to four miles from its shore. Back in Britain, the trawler owners retaliated by preventing Icelandic vessels from landing and selling their catches in the fishing ports of Hull, Grimsby, Fleetwood and Aberdeen.

The British boycott was a blow to Iceland, though the Soviet Union, sensing a means to increase its popularity in Iceland, offered to buy the bulk of Icelandic catches in return for oil and other commodities. This new deal upset the Americans, who looked to Iceland as a Cold War ally and worried about increased Soviet influence on the island. By 1956, the British government realised that the game was up and the trawler owners were forced to lift their ban on Icelandic landings. In early 1958, the United Nations convened its first Law of the Sea Conference. No agreement was reached, but many nations supported a territorial waters limit of 12 miles or more. Consequently, the left-wing government in Iceland at the time decided to extend the country's fishing limit to 12 miles. Britain was not ready to accept such 'encroachment on the high seas'. Royal Navy warships were now dispatched to protect British trawlers from harassment by the Icelandic Coast Guard in the disputed waters. British journalists quickly dubbed the dispute 'Cod War', a term which has been used ever since.

The modernisation of the fishing fleet marked the beginning of a delayed industrial revolution for Iceland. New technology earned Iceland more money than ever with which they could improve their own society. A nationwide telephone system was installed, and rural homes received their own phones; Iceland broadcast its first national television station and Icelandic families watched it on their own television sets (there was no television on Thursday however, as the channel's employees needed one day off). Rural communities felt less isolated and the Reykjavík suburbs exploded with growth. The somewhat bland, reinforced-concrete buildings you see throughout Iceland reflect an era – a building boom of housing, schools, and

In naval terms, Iceland's Lilliputian 'fleet' of seven to eight coast guard vessels (mostly converted fishing boats) was no match for the might of the British fleet. On the other hand, the strategic importance of Iceland in the midst of the Cold War increased the country's strength in the dispute. Obviously, Britain could not use its full force against a vital ally in NATO. In 1960, moreover, the United Nations convened its second Law of the Sea Conference where a proposal on a 12-mile fishing limit failed by merely one vote to reach the required two-thirds majority.

The tide was turning. In 1961, Britain accepted Iceland's 12-mile limit in return for a commitment by a new centre-right coalition in Reykjavík to refer any further disputes about fisheries jurisdiction to the International Court of Justice. For a decade, all was quiet on the Icelandic front. In 1971, however, a new left-wing government came to power in Iceland, determined to extend the fishing limits to 50 miles. The new limit took effect on 1 September 1972 and the rulers in Reykjavík ignored British (and West German) appeals to the International Court. Again, Royal Navy vessels were sent to the disputed waters but this time the Icelandic Coast Guard wielded a new 'secret weapon' – scissor-like cutters which could sever the trawler wires underwater and render naval protection useless. 'Ramming' became the new means of confrontation and a series of dangerous collisions occurred between Icelandic Coast Guard vessels and British warships. In late 1973, a two-year compromise on limited foreign fishing within the 50-mile zone was reached. As before, Iceland's strategic importance improved its bargaining position in the dispute.

By this time, the international community was moving towards an agreement on a 200-mile Exclusive Economic Zone (EEZ). In 1975, the new centre-right coalition in Iceland decided to extend the fishing limits to 200 miles, triggering the third and final Cod War. This was the nastiest of all the conflicts with repeated collisions at sea. Iceland broke off diplomatic relations with Britain and it was a miracle that lives and ships were not lost. In mid 1976, Britain had to give in. A general acceptance on the 200-mile zone was imminent and the Icelanders had threatened to leave NATO and expel US forces from the island.

Since the end of the last Cod War, Iceland has held sole jurisdiction over the 200-mile zone around the island. In the first years after the conflict, it was assumed that the Icelanders could now fish as much they wanted but the obvious danger of overfishing led to the imposition of the quota system and restriction of catches. In recent years, the determination to keep foreign vessels away from the fishing grounds has been the key factor in the more-or-less constant reluctance to consider membership of the European Union. The victory in the Cod Wars is also a source of immense pride for Icelanders. Foreign visitors – especially from Britain – should be prepared to hear tales like those in the television ad!

hospitals. The country's scant road system was also dramatically expanded and the ring road around Iceland was finally completed in 1974. Iceland had transitioned from a close-knit nation to a close-knit society.

What's wrong with this picture is that everything was built on fish: during the best years, more than 90% of Iceland's exports came from fishing. The fluctuations in fish catch from year to year caused horrific inflation of the Icelandic króna at an average rate of around 38% per year. Iceland received its biggest cash flow not from cod, but from the herring stocks that migrated to its shores. The 1950s and early 1960s were a heyday for herring production, which Iceland sold all over the world. Then, in 1967, the herring suddenly disappeared, turning a way of life into an empty coast of ghost towns. A small economic crisis ensued.

**DIVERSIFICATION** Overfishing had always been a problem for Iceland, although Icelanders never seemed to benefit from the catch. Until 1959, foreign ships accounted for about half the fish caught in Icelandic waters. Iceland only gained the exclusive right to its fishing grounds after a series of conflicts known as the Cod Wars. The dynamics surrounding the fray are important, namely Iceland's appeal to the international community, Britain's gradual respect of international law, and Iceland's strategic bargaining power.

Iceland was gaining the respect of powerful nations and regaining its own self-confidence in the process. The 1973 eruption of Heimaey in the Westmann Islands (see page 231) focused the world's attention on the unique struggle of the Icelanders and their unique homeland. There seemed to be a new interest at home in making the most of Iceland's own resources. For the first time, there was a singular, concentrated effort to control and maintain fishing as a sustainable natural resource. The country began tapping into its geothermal energy resources on a more advanced scale – the first aluminium-smelting plant opened in 1970 as the government sought additional sources of income. Iceland joined the European Free Trade Area (EFTA) and the European Community (EC) and began a steady process towards international integration.

**IN WHICH ICELAND BECOMES COOL** Iceland made its global debut in the 1980s, starting with the election of Vigdís Finnbogadóttir, the first woman ever to serve as elected president of a nation. In the following years, Iceland became synonymous with individuality, equal rights, and environmental awareness. In 1985, the Althing declared Iceland a nuclear-free zone, refusing to participate in the atmosphere of proliferation. The very next year Reykjavík celebrated its bicentennial and with just a few days' notice also hosted the 1986 Reagan–Gorbachev Summit, an event that eventually led to the end of the Cold War. In 1987, the country opened its first modern commercial airport terminal in Keflavík and was soon welcoming foreign tourists by the planeload. Just in time for the party, the Althing legalised beer in 1989.

Iceland continued to hone its image as a pristine, progressive-minded destination unlike anywhere else in the world. Areas once perceived as uninhabited wasteland were now the prized vistas for harried foreigners. In 1990, Iceland had about 150,000 tourists – that number has since tripled, thanks to creative marketing and Iceland's 'cool' factor. By the mid 1990s, the Icelandic singer Björk was selling millions of albums all around the world, followed by other stars. Overnight, it seemed, Iceland had become a global trend setter in fashion, art, and design. In 2000, the European Union confirmed what Iceland already knew by crowning Reykjavík as the European Capital of Culture. The city's nightlife became world famous and the rest is history.

**THE 21ST CENTURY** Iceland entered the new century with great optimism for a bright and independent future. What appeared to be savvy global investments were making Icelanders rich at home and abroad. In 2006, the NATO base in Keflavík was closed and for the first time in a very, very long time, Iceland was free from any foreign power. Opposition to EU membership continued to strengthen based on fears of neocolonialism, protection of fishing rights and economic and environmental self-determination. Already, the opening of Iceland's Kárahnjúkar Dam in 2007 caused huge controversies at home, while Iceland's open defiance of the international ban on commercial whaling (see page 65) attracted the ire of the same allies who fought to protect Iceland from overdevelopment.

The strong sense of self-determination was founded on the confidence that came out of the country's newfound financial capacity. After bank deregulation in 2001, Icelanders watched as a team of young and wily Icelandic investors took on the global marketplace with aplomb, earning billions of dollars in profits in a relatively short time. For several years, Iceland was very proud of its rogue financial cowboys and their ability to earn billions for their tiny country. That all came to a quick and dramatic end with the country's banking crisis in 2008, an event known locally as *Hrunið*, or *'the crash'*.

The Icelanders' general sense of optimism was suddenly crippled by the horrific realisation that their country had been completely overleveraged by a handful of investors. Three of Iceland's four main banks collapsed and the Icelandic króna went into freefall. Suddenly, Iceland was in the world news and not in a positive light. The crisis foundered a deep mistrust of the government among the Icelandic people – a generally peaceful population suddenly found themselves in the streets protesting for weeks and demanding someone take the blame for bankrupting the country.

The angry protests were successful in that they led to an ideological shift and significant power change in government. Today, more and more Icelanders accept the notion that integration with larger global institutions will be necessary in order to make a full recovery and find a sustainable economic future. Having once snubbed the European Union, Iceland now looks to the EU as its only hope for a quick recovery and establishing a stable currency once more.

After picking up the pieces of the financial crisis, Iceland came into the news again with the eruption of the Eyjafjallajökull volcano (see page 43), disrupting air traffic across Europe off and on over the course of a month. For more than a year, world headlines focused on Iceland as a source of chaos – both financial and physical.

And yet – despite all the sudden focus on Iceland's woes and misfortunes – the country continues to move forward. A review of Iceland's last 1,000 years puts financial crises and volcanoes well into perspective. The country has survived far worse ordeals and the Icelandic people are far more resilient than most people know.

## PEOPLE

Icelanders see themselves as quirky and distinct in a world that is fast becoming bland and similar. They know that their numbers may be few, but they are also confident in their personality as a nation. Traditions are not followed for the sake of tradition, but rather because Icelandic traditions are a lot of fun.

Icelanders are not mere 'Scandinavians' but represent a unique blend of Norse and Gaelic heritage. Historians still argue over percentages, but we do know that the first settlers to Iceland were Vikings and their servants – most of whom were captured in raids along the Scottish and Irish coasts. Irish women were considered prized booty and the sagas relay several tales of Norse and Irish couples who bore children. The two groups likely merged within the first century of Iceland's settlement.

The stereotypical Icelander has blinding blonde hair and piercing blue eyes, but their spectrum of physical appearance is much more diverse. Some Icelanders appear quite dark and Celtic genes contribute a higher-than-average number of redheads. What is distinct are the pronounced Nordic features, most noticeable in a person's eyes, nose, and cheekbones.

Because of its long-term isolation and homogeneity, Icelanders have been targeted by genetic researchers who delight in the de facto control group provided. In 1998, a 'biogenetic technology' company gained exclusive access to the country's genetic data to use in the research of diseases. The process of mapping the Icelandic genome was not without controversy, but it has successfully uncovered genetic links to common ailments.

The Icelandic population is very small and close-knit, so that people tend to know one other. It's uncanny how the random stranger you met on one side of the country is probably the cousin of the sister-in-law of a school friend of the bartender you're chatting with in Reykjavík. It's also funny how every time you happen to mention someone's name to an Icelander, they will stop and think about it before volunteering: 'No, I don't think I know him/her.' Iceland is not a good place for anonymity. The common belief is that all Icelanders are related by no more than four degrees of separation. As proof, there is a national website (*www.islendingabok.is*) where any two Icelanders can easily find out how they are connected by blood or marriage. The site is password-protected for Icelanders only, and goes back to the late 1700s (there is no need to go back any further).

**ICELANDIC NAMES** The most common names in Iceland tend to be those of early Christian saints – (for women) Anna, Sara, Katrín, Guðrun, and María – (for men) Sigurður, Guðmundur, Jón, Ólafur, Magnús, Einar, and Kristján. It's the less common names that seem the most poetic, either taken from Icelandic nature – Jökull (m 'glacier'), Sóley (f 'sun'), or Hlynur (f 'maple'), or from the sagas – Skarphédinn (m 'sharp coat'), Þórarinn (m 'Thór's fireplace'), and Ásgerður (f 'house of the gods').

Icelanders do not have surnames – a few of them do, but it's the exception to the rule and they tend to be of foreign origin (adopting surnames is now illegal). From the Vikings, Icelanders inherited a system of patronymics, where children are given their father's first name as their second name in the possessive form with the suffix *-son* or *-dóttir.* A girl named María whose father is Guðmundur would have the full name María Guðmundsdóttir and her brother Jóhannes would be called Jóhannes Guðmundsson. It is therefore possible for everyone in the same family to have a different 'last' name.

Icelanders are known by their first names – calling someone by their first name is a sign of respect, whereas calling someone by their full name sounds officious. Jaws may drop at the thought of the Icelandic phone book, which is only about two inches thick and where people are listed by their first names (under cities), followed by occupation and street address. However, the system is quite logical – much quicker than skimming through countless pages of 'Smiths'.

By law, anyone born in Iceland must be given at least one Icelandic name and until recently, immigrants seeking citizenship had to adopt an Icelandic name. There is also an official Icelandic naming committee (under the Ministry of Justice) that must approve a baby's name as 'Icelandic' before it is considered legal. Babies tend to receive their name at the time of christening, and foreign names can be the cause of small controversies. A while back, the entire naming committee resigned over the proposed name 'Eleonora'.

**FAMILY LIFE** Icelandic family reunions are like none other – 'relations' can be loosely interpreted and the 300 people who show up at your campsite may be celebrating a bond that outsiders just can't understand. To say that Icelandic families are close is both a generalisation and an understatement – in Iceland, family simply carries a lot of meaning. Because the country is small, Icelanders tend to visit one another often. Even in this global age when Icelanders live and work all over the world, they tend to make an effort to get home and spend time with family. It's not so different from most cultures, but then again, where else do you get treated like family because you once dated their aunt?

**BIRTH** Icelandic women bear more children than any other European nation, and begin having children at a much younger age. Unlike other developed societies, large families are desirable – Iceland scored the highest in a global survey for 'ideal number of children'. Cultural heritage and strong social support (nine months' paid leave to parents, shared between the father and mother) offer an incentive for having children in Iceland.

In Iceland, more children are born out of wedlock than in, another factoid with which Icelanders like to shock the rest of the world. By world standards, that might seem appalling, but inside Iceland it's the norm and carries no stigma whatsoever. Fathers and mothers stay very involved in a child's life – whether or not they remain involved with one another. Grandparents and uncles and aunts are also quite involved with a child's upbringing. Half-siblings also tend to be close.

**DEATH** There's an Icelandic saying that 'everyone wants to live long but nobody wants to be old'.

So true, though Icelanders seem to cope just fine: their men live longer than any other men in the world and the women come close to setting their own record. Bodies of the deceased tend not to be embalmed and the coffin (*kistu*) is usually white (a number of mountains in Iceland are ominously named *kistufell*). Within one or two days of death, a brief open-casket service (*kistulagning*) is held in a small chapel and is reserved for close family members only. The actual funeral is held one to two weeks after. Burial takes place in churchyards – looking at older Icelandic gravestones can be quite interesting. Most tend to bear a Lutheran cross, while non-Christians or those unaffiliated with the Church are marked with a radiant sun.

Rather than have a single, standard obituary, Icelandic newspapers first print a standard notice of death, followed later by a notice of the funeral, after which they will print any number of obituaries. Friends and family members can each send in their own obituary and condolences. Messages tend to be written letter-style in the first person and refer to the deceased in the second person (eg: 'Dear uncle, I miss you'). Numerous obituaries written to one individual can run for several days and in a national newspaper like *Morganblaðið*, obituaries may occupy four to five pages out of the entire 40-page paper.

## LANGUAGE

Icelandic is the official language of Iceland and is spoken by more than 300,000 people. It is classified a member of the West Scandinavian branch of the North Germanic languages in the Indo-European family. In the beginning, Old Norse was the lingua franca of the Vikings, who helped spread it all across Scandinavia and northern Europe. The bulk of settlers to Iceland in the 9th and 10th centuries came from three districts on the west coast of Norway, which meant their original dialect was already quite specific. Iceland's isolation kept Icelanders separate from the evolution and integration of other Scandinavian languages, and 1,000 years later, Icelandic is a wholly different tongue. Scandinavians often say that Icelandic sounds funny and old-fashioned, while Icelanders find Scandinavian sloppy and lacking in poetry. The closest living language to Icelandic today is Faroese, a language spoken by only 48,000 people – Faroese-speakers tend to understand Icelanders fine; Icelanders feign difficulty hearing through the 'thick accent'.

Icelandic is both a modern and ancient language, one of the oldest to survive unchanged for so long. A common idiom says that Icelanders can read the medieval sagas the same as they would read the newspaper. It takes a lot longer to get through a saga, but the point is that modern Icelandic varies little from 13th- and 14th-century syntax. Speakers of English, German or French would fail that test in their own languages.

Outsiders can find Icelandic daunting for its super-long compound words, the tongue-twisting sounds, and its impossible grammar. The rules of Icelandic are well organised, but complex to a dizzying degree. While younger languages have shed the burdens of things like complicated declensions (think Latin class), Icelandic has preserved a millennium of grammatical quirks that only a linguist could love.

Yet the sound of Icelandic is part of its appeal. Those acquainted with older forms of English or the King James version of the Bible will discover recognisable links with Icelandic. For example, the Icelandic *Þú ert hér* sounds a lot like 'thou art here'. Technically, only a few English words come from Icelandic (ie: 'geyser' from *geysir*, 'saga' from *saga*, 'eider' from *æðir*), but Old Norse has a huge influence on modern English. Over 1,000 years of words belong to Icelandic, which is why it is considered one of the 'largest' languages in the world. The rich vocabulary reveals something about the Vikings who first spoke it: there is no word for 'please' in Icelandic, but over 60 known words for 'devil'.

Speaking Icelandic is a badge of distinction for Icelanders. Historically, it is their language that has defined them as a nation, which is one reason why it survived centuries of foreign domination. The sagas played a vital role in keeping Icelandic alive – other Scandinavians who want to read their history must do so in Icelandic. This wealthy literary heritage – along with classics like Guðbrandur's Bible – offered Icelanders a sophisticated backbone against change. In spite of having relatively few speakers, Icelandic does not suffer the same threats as a 'minority' language. As the official language of an independent country, Icelandic is used in national newspapers, television broadcasts, on the internet, and in books and magazines. The Icelandic Language Institute (Íslensk malstöð) is the official government body responsible for language purity, similar to the Academie Française in France but a lot more reasonable. It maintains the country's vocabulary, passes judgement on 'loan words' and promotes the proper use of Icelandic and methods of Icelandic teaching.

Danish is taught as a second language to all Icelandic schoolchildren, and a fair number of Icelandic youth go to Denmark for their university education. All the tourist signs that say 'we speak Scandinavian' typically refer to compulsory knowledge of Danish. English is also required learning from a young age, but there is some concern that the prominence of English in multi-media is diluting the role of Icelandic in Iceland. Today, Icelandic children learn more English from video games than they do at school and English has replaced Danish as the lingua franca with other Nordic countries. Visitors may sigh in relief to find out that in

Iceland, 'everyone speaks English', but that expectation is callow and misses the point. Icelanders do their best to respond in English if English is spoken to them, but it is still their second language. Icelanders are well educated, yes, but younger generations manage better than older and there are some parts of Iceland where locals simply do not know English. Speaking Icelandic – even attempting to – will grant you a wholly different experience (see *Appendix 1*, *Language*, page 439).

## BELIEFS

**RELIGION** Icelanders are a deeply spiritual people. They may not go to church every Sunday (fewer than 10% do) but it's almost impossible to find any real atheists in their ranks. By creed, the country is overwhelmingly **Lutheran**. The National Church of Iceland (*Þjóðkirkjan*) or Church of Iceland is the **Evangelical Lutheran Church**, of which more than 80% of the population are members. This official State Church is led by the Bishop of Iceland (based in Reykjavík) and is the main heir to 1,000 years of Christian history. All the little red and white churches that you see are almost always linked to the State Church. About 5% of Icelanders belong to smaller 'free Lutheran' Churches which broke away from the State Church at a time when it represented the colonial government of Denmark. Lutheran worship follows the Christian Protestant norm: services last about an hour, there is a short sermon, the singing of several hymns by choir and congregation, and communion. Because so many of Iceland's churches are located in such rural areas, there tends to be a rotation schedule for a whole district where services are held in a different church each Sunday. Schedules are printed on single-sheet brochures and are distributed in tourist information centres or in local cafés and shops.

In Iceland, the Lutheran faith is equivalent to national identity – weekly attendance might be low but almost every Icelander will attend church at some point during the year *because* they are Icelandic. The church is the setting for cultural activities – concerts, plays, poems, and national celebrations – and the Icelandic flag is always present. All Icelanders are charged a Church Tax (regardless of their faith) which is paid to the official State Church. This dates back to the beginning of Christianity in Iceland, when tithes were enforced by the government. Non-Lutherans can choose to have their tax paid to a charity or the University of Iceland.

**Catholics** comprise the largest religious minority in Iceland (about 3%) with a few famous Icelanders among their ranks. About half of Iceland's Catholics are foreign immigrants. A dozen or so scant religious groups make up the remainder of Iceland's churchgoers.

In regards to faith, one can't help but notice a small paradox in Iceland. As liberal Scandinavians, Icelanders will speak disparagingly of organised religion and criticise the oppressive nature of 'The Church', remembering the injustices dealt to the Icelandic people. At the same time, Iceland is a blatantly Christian society in both word and deed. Christian ethics are universally accepted and expected (honesty, human rights, equality, humility) and there is a national aversion to hypocrisy. Icelanders generally take pride in their Church and the humanist achievements of their society.

**THE PAGAN PAST** The old religion was outlawed in AD1000, but with the caveat that pagans could still practise their faith in private. Few heathens take advantage of the loophole today, but the well of Icelandic belief seems shallow without some knowledge of the country's rich pagan heritage. A travel guide can do no justice to the elaborate world of Norse mythology – there is a reason why universities fund whole departments of Old Norse studies. It is all quite fascinating stuff.

## WHO'S THE BETTER PAGAN?

The early Icelanders took their conversion to Christianity seriously, ridding their weekdays of wicked heathen references. Not so in English, which still venerates the Old Norse gods.

| English | Old Norse root | Icelandic | Translation |
|---|---|---|---|
| Sunday | *Sun day* | *Sunnudagur* | Sun day |
| Monday | *Moon day* | *Mánadagur* | Moon day |
| Tuesday | *Týr's day* | *Þriðjudagur* | Third day |
| Wednesday | *Odin's day* | *Miðvikudagur* | Mid-week day |
| Thursday | *Thór's day* | *Fimmtudagur* | Fifth day |
| Friday | *Freyja's day* | *Föstudagur* | Fast day |
| Saturday | *Saturn's day* | *Laugardagur* | Wash day |

Practically everything we know about the Norse religion comes from the Icelandic sagas, namely the *Prose Edda* of Snorri Sturlurson (see page 261). The **Æsir** are the primary family of the gods who live in the highest world of the gods, **Ásgarð**. The chief god is **Oðin** (Odin) who embodies war, death, wisdom, and poetry. He has two whispering ravens (named 'thought' and 'memory'), and an eight-legged horse named Sleipnir. He sacrificed his left eye in exchange for eternal wisdom and the remaining eye shines like the sun. Oðin also hung himself upside down from the cosmic ash tree Yggdrasil for nine days, after which he died and was resurrected having attained the ultimate mystic knowledge – or enlightenment. Oðin was revered by the early Vikings and welcomed the victorious dead into Valhalla, a gilded fortress in Ásgarð.

**Thór** is the son of Oðin and the god of thunder. He travels in a chariot pulled by goats, and carries a magic hammer from which he tosses out thunderbolts. Thór was the preferred god of the Icelanders, evident in the names of people and places all around Iceland today. Likewise, Thór's hammer (*þórshammar*) was an important symbol throughout Iceland that was later incorporated into the Christian cross.

**Baldur** is Thór's younger brother and represents beauty, peace, and goodwill. He was doomed from the beginning, having foreseen his death in a dream. His mother **Frigg** made every thing on earth promise not to harm her son, with the exception of the mistletoe that eventually killed him. The Icelandic flower *baldursbrá* (see page 50) – literally 'Baldur's brow' – represents this god's fairness and beauty. Also, Baldur's son **Forseti** was the Norse god of justice – *forseti* is the modern Icelandic word for 'president'.

**Freyja** is the most powerful of the goddesses, a counterpart to Oðin in that she also gathered the dead of war but belonged to a separate family of gods, the Vanir. She represents fertility and love. In Iceland, Freyja was consulted most by farmers and those suffering from unrequited love.

The world of men is **Miðgarður** – literally 'middle-earth', surrounded by ocean. It is located beneath Ásgarð but above the underworld **Hel** ('hell'). The Icelanders believed that the fiery volcano **Hekla** (see page 239) was the entrance to Hel where the dead suffered endless cold.

**FOLKLORE** Icelandic nature tempts the most practical minds into considering the supernatural. The northern lights, the midnight sun, strange-shaped lava rocks, the wind, moss, and mist – all of it feeds the imagination. Icelanders have spent the last 1,000 years making sense of what all these sounds, shapes and spine-tinglings mean. Their explanations have more basis than first-time scepticism.

Foremost, there is a parallel spiritual realm that covers the whole of Iceland. The main occupants of this world are the ***huldufólk*** or 'hidden people'. The term is often translated as 'elves' – which delivers an awful and erroneous 'bells on toes' image to English-speaking minds. These are *not* the rank-and-file minions of Santa Claus. Instead, the hidden people are invisible to the human eye and have the same appearance as humans, though they are said to be tremendously beautiful. The Christian legend is that just prior to a surprise visit by God, Mother Eve (of Adam and Eve) hid away those of her children who were still unwashed. God called Eve on her deceit, but she feigned innocence. God then cursed the hidden people, telling Eve how 'that which you hid away from me shall be hidden from all'.

Iceland's hidden people live among the rocks – but not all rocks. Belief in the hidden people is usually revealed at construction sites, where altering the landscape – especially by moving a rock – can be an open offence to the hidden people. Plenty of tales exist where bulldozers and tractors are damaged in revenge. Whole roads are redirected in order to leave some rock in place. Even the untrained tourist eye will notice how in the middle of some cultivated field there might be a large pointed boulder that has been left untouched. There's a reason why.

Showing disregard to the hidden people has bad consequences. In times past, they would steal your milk or make you sick. Today, they can make your business fail and cause all kinds of setbacks. However, those who give help or show respect to the *huldufólk* are rewarded generously. The best way to endear the hidden people is to ask their permission before making changes to one's land or home, to leave food out for them, and to leave your door open. Thus, belief in the hidden people is made manifest in a general reverence of nature and the adherence to tradition. Some Icelanders claim the ability to commune with the hidden people, and in private, many will divulge personal stories of experiences they have had.

Because they are often referred to as elves, the *huldufólk* are easily confused with ***álfafólk*** which really *are* elves, but still different from what some might think. Other mystical creatures include the classic ***tröll*** or trolls, who tend to be giant, ugly, mean-spirited and stupid. Trolls turn to stone if the sun shines on them, and many of Iceland's more interesting lava forms are in fact the rocky remnants of surprised trolls.

Few fans know that J R R Tolkein wrote his senior thesis on the subject of Old Icelandic, and that the vivid folklore of Iceland had a very direct influence on the *Lord of the Rings* series of books. In addition to the aforementioned creatures, Iceland is also inhabited by frost and mountain giants, dwarves, monsters, and all kinds of spirits. The ***fylgjur*** are spiritual beings that often take the form of an animal or a woman. They are a reflection of a human's own character and tend to follow individuals – either to protect them or torment them (all of Iceland's supernatural beings tend to have ambiguous intentions). ***Draugar*** are bona fide ghosts – the restless spirits of the dead. You'll find that Icelandic homes suffer from a high number of hauntings – those lucky enough to hear a real ghost story will find that the Icelandic versions tend to be far spookier than the ones you hear back home.

Icelanders also place great importance on the spiritual mood of a particular location or landscape. Some places are happy, others are mysterious, sad, or lonely. Every place has its own emotions and energies, some of which are ***álagablettir*** (enchanted areas). Very good or very bad things can happen within an *álagablettir*, depending on its energy. Travelling through some of Iceland's more remote and spectacular regions, it's hard not to believe in such enchanted climes – in my opinion, the whole of Iceland is an *álagablettir*.

### RÚMFJALIR

One of the most curious forms of Icelandic craft is that of *rúmfjalir* from the words ***rúm*** (bed) and ***fjalir*** (board). In Old Icelandic homes, beds were built into the sides of the roof, with one open side to a centre aisle. Family members and farm workers often slept in the same communal room, so that one's bed was the whole of one's personal space. The bed board could be slipped into the side of the bed as a kind of guardrail or used to stuff the bed covers under the mattress when making the bed. The boards were also used as lap trays for eating meals and as makeshift desks. For poor farm workers, the *rúmfjalir* was a prized possession and the bed boards slowly evolved from a functional use to something more ornamental. Flowing designs were carved into the boards – either curved lines or floral patterns reminiscent of Celtic and Viking traditions. More elaborate motifs included images like birds' nests and suns, but the most intricate woodcarvers still left one side flat to keep it functional. A well-made *rúmfjalir* was meant to last a lifetime and several very old examples are on display in folk museums.

## CULTURE

**FLAG** Iceland's flag consists of a red Nordic cross outlined in white over a deep-blue background. If anything, the flag represents Iceland's prolonged fight for independence – after centuries under the Danish flag, the Icelandic Althing agreed in 1885 that a separate flag was needed. Blue and white have always been considered traditional colours of Iceland, and the first proposed designs included a blue background with a white cross. Such was the flag flown from a daring rowboat in Reykjavík harbour in 1913, upon which a Danish battleship quickly removed the offending item as contraband. An added red cross was proposed by Matthías Thórðarson, who was serving as the country's 'keeper of antiquities'. His design was approved in 1915, but lacked popular support in Iceland because the Danish king had approved the final decision. Icelandic nationalists often flew the blue and white flag in protest until the official adoption of Iceland's current flag in 1944.

The Nordic cross design originated with the *Dannebrog*, the national emblem of Denmark. Legend states that a red cloth with the white cross simply fell from the sky in the middle of the 13th-century Battle of Valdemar, after which the Danes were victorious. As a badge of divine right, Denmark flew its cross in the other Scandinavian countries it ruled and as each nation gained independence, they incorporated the Christian symbol. Today the Nordic cross is found on the national flags of Iceland, Sweden, Norway, Finland, and Denmark, as well as the flags of the Shetland, Orkney and Faroe islands. Some people tend to confuse the flag of Iceland with that of Norway, which sports an identical design but with inverse colours (though the shades are quite different).

Iceland's constitution is quite specific about the flag's colours, declaring them to be sky blue (*heiðblár*), fire red (*eldrauður*), and snow white (*mjallhvítur*). The flag is flown on all national and religious holidays. It is also considered improper for the Icelandic flag to be flown after midnight, even if it is still light.

**NATIONAL SYMBOLS** Iceland's national flower is the *jöklasóley* or **glacier buttercup** (*Ranunculus glacialis*), a light pink to whitish blossom that grows in the high fjords and snow-capped mountains, usually near the coast. The national bird

## ICELAND'S GUARDIAN SPIRITS (*LANDVÆTTIR*)

So many spirits inhabit Iceland that you cannot travel far without encountering a tale or two about them. One of the first stories recorded is in the *Heimskringla*, in which the ancient story of the kings recounts the evil designs of King Harald Bluetooth of Denmark who sought to invade Iceland in vengeance for its disrespect of his court. And so the king sent a spy – an evil wizard who changed himself into a whale and swam hurriedly to Iceland. He first tried landing in Vopnafjörður (see page 395) on Iceland's eastern shore, where he was attacked by a terrible, poison-breathing dragon (*dreki*). And so he headed north to Eyjafjörður (see page 331), where a giant eagle (*gammur*) swooped down and chased him away. The wizard then approached from the west at Breiðafjörður (see page 301), where a monstrous bullock (*griðungur*) waded out to him, bellowing mightily. The wizard fled and made a last attempt from the south at Vikarsskeiði where a tall mountain giant (*bergrisi*) charged down the hillside with an iron spear. The dismayed wizard finally gave up and left Iceland unharmed.

The message of the legend is clear, that Iceland is protected from evil intentions. The popular image of the Vikings is not complete without the menacing dragon prow on their warships, but Old Norse law demanded that all ships approaching Iceland remove these mastheads so as to not provoke the *landvættir*. Today, the *landvættir* comprise Iceland's coat of arms, with the dragon, eagle, bullock, and giant standing behind a flag of Icelandic shield upon a slab of lava rock. In Reykjavík, the *landvættir* are displayed on the front of the Althing (see page 166), and you can also see them on the back of Icelandic coins (the giant is on the 1 króna). Although it is rarely enforced, Icelandic law forbids any unofficial portrayal of the coat of arms and the *landvættir*.

is the **gyrfalcon** which is still represented on various insignia. For many centuries, the King of Denmark had absolute rights to capturing and hunting with falcons in Iceland – his falcon house is now a popular bar in Reykjavík. If Iceland had a national fish, it would be the **cod**, for its abundance and for the essential role it plays in the economy. Iceland's previous national insignia portrayed a headless, disembowelled cod, split down the centre, flattened and dried, beneath the Danish crown. If anything, the depiction of stockfish as a national crest is honest – dried, salted cod was Iceland's main export for a good 500 years.

**NATIONAL ANTHEM** Iceland's national anthem is *Ó Guð Vors Lands*, which means 'Oh God of our Land'. The words to the hymn were written by the Reverend Matthías Jochumsson and inspired by Psalm 90 (*Before the mountains were brought forth, or ever thou hadst formed the earth and the world… thou art God*). The music was written by Sveinbjörn Sveinbjörnsson, an Icelandic composer with whom Matthías was staying in Scotland at the time. The anthem was first performed to a royal audience (Danish King Christian IX) in Reykjavík's Dómkirkjan (see page 175) as part of Iceland's millennial celebrations in 1874.

**NATIONAL DRESS** Iceland's national dress is anything that keeps you warm and dry when you go outside. The national costume looks a little more provincial. The women's outfit is based around the *peysuföt*, a heavy grey or black woollen dress that

### THE LADY OF THE MOUNTAIN (*FJALLKONAN*)

In Iceland, all the mountains are referred to as women and should be respected as such. The *fjallkonan* is the mythical lady of the mountain whose bold, independent spirit represents Iceland as a nation. She is typically shown with long, wavy blonde hair and a crown of ice from which fiery flames are shooting. A raven sits on her shoulder and she carries a long sword in one hand and a rune stave in the other.

The *fjallkonan* has a steady role in Icelandic folk tales, but she made her first public appearance in the 19th-century poem *Eldgamla Ísafold* ('Ancient Iceland'), written by Althing member Bjarni Vigfusson Thorarensen. Now, on 17 June celebrations, a woman will dress up as the *fjallkonan* and recite the poem. *Eldgamla Ísafold* is still considered the unofficial anthem of Iceland, sung to the tune of *God Save the Queen*.

is gathered in the back and covers everything from wrist to neck to ankle. Fancier modern versions are made of velvet with extraordinary embroidery around the lower hems and sleeves. As a variation or accessory, women also wear the *upphlutur* which is a tight sleeveless bodice tied over a light blouse. The compromise arrangement is the *Skautbúningur*, which comprises a long skirt with a fitted jacket that is typically embroidered with shiny thread into floral designs (different flowers denote different regions). The *skotthúfa* is the small cap with a tassel worn to one side.

It should be noted that the idea of a national costume is a wee bit contrived. The artist and nationalist Sigurður Guðmundsson began drawing up fashion designs for women's costumes in the 1860s, convinced that a universal national costume was one step closer to self-determination. The *peysuföt* is quite traditional (a clear reference to the common dress long worn by Icelandic peasant women) but some of the elaborate headdresses are romantic imaginations. In 1994, a contest was held for a suitable 'male' costume, since there were too many variations floating around. The winning design consists of long black trousers (or knee breeches), with a dark-coloured double-breasted waistcoat and cravat. The Icelandic government manages a National Costume Board which conserves knowledge about national dress and promotes its proper wear. The very best time to see Icelanders in national dress is on Independence Day (17 June) and other summer festivals. Schoolchildren will also dress up for festivals.

**HOLIDAYS AND TRADITIONS** Icelanders make sure to have at least one holiday per month – it helps the long winter months go faster and the long summer days last longer. According to the Old Norse Calendar, Thorri is the fourth month of winter (from the end of January to early February). The weather can be ghastly at this time and so Icelanders huddle up inside and partake of some of the ghastly cuisine during the **feast of Thór** (*Þorrablót*). The feast is one of the most Icelandic of festivals, relishing Icelanders' strong pagan roots and celebrated with patriotic fervour. The menu is highly traditional and is vaguely referred to as 'food of Thór' – apparently the God Thór eats marinated shark, pickled whale blubber, ram testes, seal flippers, blood sausage, singed sheep's head, mutton tripe, and the list goes on (don't worry, there's usually mashed potatoes and bread on the side). The more sophisticated feast is **Árshátíð** – the annual festival, held in late winter/early spring. The lenten calendar is followed closely and the **Easter** (*Páskar*) holiday weekend is celebrated with church services and chocolate bunnies like much of the rest of the Christian world. The **first**

**day of summer** (*Sumardagurinn Fyrsti*) is 20 April although it might snow that day and still feel a lot like winter. The early Vikings did not embrace the concept of spring or autumn, and so when it was no longer technically winter outside (the spring equinox), they simply called it the first day of summer. Children normally get the day off school, there are big parades and homage is paid to the approaching warmer months. Iceland's **national day** (*Þjóðhátiðargurinn*) or independence holiday is on 17 June. Festivities normally include a big parade and picnics and a jubilant mood. People wear national dress and fly Icelandic flags – it's a great time to visit because these are the longest days of the year.

By law, Icelanders receive six weeks' paid holiday, the bulk of which they take in the summer. Icelanders tend to stay in Iceland in summer and travel to warmer climes in the depths of winter. The common practice is for families to own or rent a summerhouse in some rural district – the more remote the better. From July to August, the family enjoys the relaxed atmosphere of outdoor living; it's very civilised. The first weekend in August is **Labour Day** (*Verslunarmannahelgi*) when Icelanders like to camp and hold their gigantic family reunions. There's always a lot going on, but it's also one of the busiest times to travel. The **roundup** (*réttir*) takes place in the early autumn, between 1 and 30 September. After a summer of free grazing up in the highlands, the sheep are rounded up and chased back down to their respective farms. Icelanders show great skill on their horses, and it's a time of outdoor activities like camping and horseriding – those who can experience this annual event in person, should. **Christmas** (*Jól*) in Iceland is an extended and festive period, starting long before 25 December. Children place a shoe in the window 13 days before Christmas, hoping for daily visits from the 13 *jólasveinar*, a band of mischievous 'Christmas lads' who are actually descended from trolls and mothered by the evil ogress Grýla. A different lad comes to each home on the nights leading up to Christmas. Each has his own naughty trait (the 'pot-licker' and the 'door-slammer'). Good children get gifts in their shoes; naughty children get a potato. **St Thorlákur's Day** (*Þorláksmessa*) is on 23 December, to commemorate the patron (Catholic) saint of Iceland. Traditionally, fish is served, and it is the last day of Christmas shopping. The main Christmas festivities take place on Christmas Eve, including dinner and the giving of presents. Christmas Day and the day after (Boxing Day) are also holidays, typically spent at home with families. New Year's Eve (*Gamlárskvöld*) is the party to end all parties: Icelanders light giant bonfires and then blow up all kinds of fireworks – even winter-dark Reykjavík lights up like a rocket. Traditionally, New Year's Eve has also been a time of magic, when humans could trick the hidden people into giving them gold. Also, cows can talk and seals take human form (not unlike the selkies of Scotland). **New Year's Day** (*Nýársdagur*) is a day of recovery from all the madness, though the party goes on until 6 January which is celebrated as *Þrettándinn*, the **13th day of Christmas**. On this night, there tends to be another round of bonfires and another round of drinks. Then before you know it, it's already the feast of Thór.

**LITERATURE** Icelanders love to read and they love to write. Iceland is the most literate country in the world and one out of every ten Icelanders will write a book in their lifetime. One can easily argue that the entire Western literary paradigm is based on the **Icelandic sagas** (*Íslendingasögur*). The sagas are exactly like the word they gave us in English – long, meandering tales of history, family feuds, romance, wars, travels, and adventure. Despite handheld Western compilations, the sagas don't make for good in-flight reading. Some people spend their whole lives dedicated to studying just one saga, and there are close to 50 known Icelandic sagas out there. Most were written between the 12th and 14th centuries and recount the lives of the first three generations of Icelanders. The writings are based on oral tradition, which explains their loose structure but not their overwhelming length.

Tour operators may advertise 'sites from the sagas' or that a certain region is where the sagas 'happened'. In fact the whole of Iceland is a site from the sagas, down to every last river and rock. Some tales are more common or popular than others

### THE ANNUAL PARTY (*ÁRSHÁTÍÐ*)

*Eliza Reid*

The death throes of winter bring with them a modern Icelandic tradition – the *árshátíð*. Loosely translated as an 'annual celebration', an *árshátíð* is usually held sometime between February and April by almost all companies, as well as virtually every club or group of people which meets regularly (eg: if you play football with your mates on a Saturday morning, you'll hold an *árshátíð*). Most locals get invited to several each year.

The *árshátíð* is more than just another social evening with colleagues. It is a gilded, glossy, no-holds-barred affair where heavy drinking and sentimental recitals of ancient poetry go hand in hand.

Dress is formal. Many women buy a new gown for each *árshátíð* they attend and men sometimes appear in the double-breasted waistcoats of Icelandic national costume. In an effort to outdo their competition, many companies even hold their events in another country (city breaks in Copenhagen or London are the most popular), although the norm is to have the *árshátíð* at a restaurant, rented hall or hotel in the countryside.

Icelanders enjoy the ritual of tradition, and the *árshátíð* is no exception. The evening always begins with a free apéritif for the assembled guests. The meal itself is a three-course affair, usually with a seafood starter and a lamb, or possibly beef, main course (fish is not seen as upmarket enough for the entrée of a formal dinner). Vegetarians are few.

Once the free apéritifs and expensive wine begin to take effect, the biggest tradition of the *árshátíð* begins: *skemmtiatriði* (roughly 'fun activities'). Every attendee at the *árshátíð* (except partners) will be in a small group which pre-prepares one activity for the larger group on the evening. This might be a silly song, a poetry recital, a quiz show, or a game like charades. Like speeches at a wedding, good *skemmtiatriði* make the evening fantastic; boring poetry recitals make you wish you were at home reading the phone book.

In addition to the organised fun activities, anyone who wishes is able to give a speech, usually guided by the Master of Ceremonies (at larger *árshátíð*, a local celebrity is often invited to play this role). Many speeches feature quotes from the sagas, Icelandic limericks or in-jokes from the office which confuse people's partners. By midnight, the wine is really flowing. Once the speeches have finished, it's time to dance. Any *árshátíð* worth its salt will have hired a local celebrity entertainer to sing Icelandic songs that everyone will know the words to.

Visitors to Iceland are unlikely to get formally invited to an *árshátíð*. Like Christmas, this sacred occasion is reserved for members of the hosting organisation – be it company employees or members of the football team. But, like Christmas, if you find yourself in the right place at the right time (keep an eye open for speeches given in fancy dress), you may get invited to join in a round of *skemmtiatriði*. The modern Icelandic marriage of flashy materialism and fiercely proud traditions and friendships is never better epitomised.

– like Grettis or Egils saga – but the sagas themselves are far-reaching to the point of inexhaustibility. Everyone has their favourite stories and characters. The sagas do not include the ***Prose Edda***, and the ***Heimskringla***, both written by Icelander Snorri Sturluson (see page 261). The first is the bible of Norse mythology and the latter is a detailed history of the Norwegian kings. Both are an absorbing read.

The most widely read Icelandic writer in English is **Halldór Laxness** (see page 197), who won the Nobel Prize for Literature in 1951. His most well-known classic in translation is *Independent People*, which characterises the Icelandic nation in the story of one stubborn farmer who ekes out a humble living for himself and his disaffected children in a turf-covered home. The story is epic, if not slightly tragic. Other works by Laxness like *Iceland's Bell* and *Under the Glacier* take on some of Iceland's controversial historical and religious themes with humour and aplomb. He is considered the finest modern Icelandic novelist of all time and typically labelled as an 'expressionist'. His contemporary **Gunnar Gunnarsson** (see page 398) wrote primarily in Danish but later switched back to his native Icelandic. Gunnar also penned long epics of struggling farmers and their families, though he is best known in English for his murder story *Black Cliffs*. Much less known is author **Jón Thoroddson**, whose book *Boy and Girl* (1850) marked the birth of the modern Icelandic novel. A more recent international success is that of Hallgrímur Helgason's *101 Reykjavík* (1996) which grants a caustic view of contemporary Icelandic life. In case you haven't spotted a trend, Icelandic prose is not a particularly happy genre. For a more comprehensive list and background on contemporary Icelandic writers, visit www.bokmenntir.is (see also *Appendix 2, Further Information*, page 447).

**POETRY** The Icelandic poetic tradition is equal, if not greater than that of its prose. The ***eddas*** were the long poems of Norse history and mythology, whereas the ***skaldic*** poems of the Viking era were literary compositions composed by skilled court poets called *skalds*. Skaldic poetry is best known for its intricate use of metre, alliteration and metaphor, and talented poets were celebrated. In Egils saga, the condemned Viking Egil composes such an impressive skaldic poem – *Head Ransom* – that his life is spared. Another chiefly Icelandic tradition is that of ***rímur*** – poems that rhyme at the end of each line and that were sung to a rhythmic beat. Long ago, *rímur* were the primary form of entertainment in the long winter months and their effect on Icelandic music is obvious.

Poetry was at the heart of Iceland's nationalist movement, the best-known exponents being **Jónas Hallgrímsson** and **Bjarni Thorarenson**. For the Icelander, poetry is not some exclusive art form, but rather a god-given means of expression accessible to all. That's true of politician-poets like **Einar Benediktsson**, as well as farmer-poets. The hero of Laxness's *Independent People* composes thoughtful poems as he walks through the stark landscapes or works with his sheep. One of the best examples of the mental exercise of poetry is **Stephan Stephansson** who emigrated from Iceland to Canada in 1873. He lived the life of a hard-working farmer, but composed thousands of poems and wrote exclusively in Icelandic. Lastly, Iceland has inspired poets of all nations – W H Auden's *Letters from Iceland* relates his own three-month travels into perfect skaldic form.

**MUSIC** Icelanders have been making their own music ever since they arrived in Iceland. Sadly, very little pre-Christian music (*rímur*) has survived the ultra-religious period of the 16th and 17th centuries except for a few haunting relics. Older Icelandic music tends to be choral and religious. The renowned hymn writer **Hallgrímur Pétursson** set the standard for Iceland's ecclesiastical tradition with his Passion Hymns which are performed more than any other. Icelanders will form a choir at the drop of a hat but they still tend to be very good. Choirs are usually affiliated with schools or churches and organ recitals are common entertainment.

Just like every Icelander is a writer and a painter, sometimes it seems that every Icelander is in a band – a night out in Reykjavík is proof. What's more is that they tend to cover (well) every type of music that exists. Icelandic jazz is a whole little world unto itself and the band Quarashi rapped their way to the top of America's hip-hop scene. At the same time, the ghostly music of Sigur Rós attained cult following among alternative fans. The most famous Icelandic singer of all time is Björk, who has divided the world into psychotic fans and everyone else.

## BJÖRK GUÐMUNDSDÓTTIR (1965– )

Iceland's biggest icon happens to be a singer who is known the world over for singing and doing everything in very much her own way – that should make Icelanders proud. Björk Guðmundsdóttir was born in Reykjavík and schooled at the Barnamúsikskóli, where she studied piano, flute, and voice. She recorded her first album at age 12 – self-titled *Björk* – the songs are sweet and jaunty and reflect the time (late 1970s). An original copy is on permanent display at Iceland's National Museum. With the money she made from this first record, Björk bought herself a piano. She played in a number of groups as a teenager, diving into Iceland's fanatical punk scene and blazing a trail of scandal through Reykjavík. Her band Kukl (Sorcery) had some success, after which she helped found the Icelandic label Smeykklesa ('tasteless') and formed the new band Sykrumolarnir. 'The Sugarcubes' earned a devoted following in both Europe and America but eventually disbanded. Björk then moved to London where she sniffed out the electronic music scene. Her solo album *Debut* (1993) went platinum in the United States and raised her status from alternative star to world celebrity. She has since released a constant and steady flow of original music – always new and always different.

Björk's musical tastes are wonderfully unpredictable. She's sung Icelandic jazz (Gling-Gló), wrote the opening music for the 2004 Olympics, composed original film scores, recorded a 100% acoustic album, and conquered the pop world with chart-topping singles. Björk has also acted in a few Icelandic and foreign films – at the Cannes Film Festival she won best actress for *Dancer in the Dark* (2000).

It was Björk who put Iceland on the world map of contemporary culture and defined it as a place where creativity flourished. Journalists tend to attach Björk's music to things like Iceland's nature, her upbringing, and saga heroines (her very traditional name, pronounced *byurk*, means 'birch'). Really though, Björk is Björk – a highly creative individual who has made a living out of being herself. She is Iceland's first big international pop star, and a lot of Icelanders still don't know how to react to all the attention Iceland gets in her name. Being world famous and wildly different are not traditional Icelandic values, and although some Icelanders are big fans and feel just a little bit star-struck, others rebuke the hullabaloo. Today, Björk lives in a lot of places and travels a lot, though she does still own a home near the old harbour in Reykjavík: 'Björk spottings' are still common gossip fodder in the capital (PS my favourite song is *Unravel*).

# 3

# Natural History

Iceland is a very young country still in the midst of its own creation. It is the very attraction of this land and why the topography alone is so entertaining. Most of us come from gentle countryside tempered out of ancient geologies. Not so in Iceland, where the landscapes look positively prehistoric. The mountains in the distance or that lava field or waterfall did not happen 'hundreds of millions of years ago' – it's happening right now.

Iceland is a very large and high plateau formed from many layers of volcanic activity. One must travel up into the highlands to experience the flat and barren rock from which the rest of the country is cut, but the outer edges are more exciting. Here, the volcanic substrate is broken down by wind, water, and ice into valleys, sharp peaks, waterfalls, rivers and fjords. Travellers don't come to Iceland for the duty-free shopping or the cheap margaritas – they come to experience the most basic natural elements, namely earth, air, fire, and water.

## EARTH

As a volcanic island, Iceland is made from extrusive igneous rock, of which 90% is **basalt**, a black or dark-grey stone that is formed from rapid surface cooling of magma flows. Large-scale eruptions that coat huge areas are known as flood basalt, and these layers of black rock comprise the layered mountains so typical of Iceland. Each thick black layer reflects a solid volcanic period, divided from the next by a fine layer of organic growth and decay. These ancient soils accumulate over tens of thousands of years but get compressed into just a few inches' thickness. Their organic iron content turns this intermittent layer red and that colour tends to leak out onto the basalt. The black and red stripes of a mountain hillside are quite common. Columnar basalt is the vertical crystals formed at the time of eruption – the faster the cooling, the smaller the columns. The 'crystals' are hexagonal, but the columns can comprise anything from a four-sided square to a dodecahedron. You can see columnar basalt just about anywhere, but it tends to be more exposed on seacoasts and on the sides of waterfalls.

When lava cools so fast that no crystals form, the result is volcanic glass. The most vivid example is **obsidian**, which actually looks and feels like a shard of black or green glass. More common is **pumice**, which is filled with gas bubbles and very light. Pumice shoots out of a volcano as pyroclastic bombs – when it is heavy in basaltic mineral content, the stone is known as **scoria**. In Iceland, most of what is referred to as 'lava rock' is scoria – the rough, but almost weightless hunks of stone strewn across lava landscapes. It ranges in colour from black to red and is sometimes less dense than water (so it floats). Eldfell in the Westmann Islands is an example of a volcanic cone made out of scoria (see page 237).

Iceland's other building block is **rhyolite**, which differs from basalt in that it's heavy in silicates and formed from very slow-moving lava that has the time to crystallise. Rhyolite has the same chemical composition as granite, but with microscopic crystals. It also contains quartz and appears in much lighter colours than basalt – often white, grey, reddish-brown, and yellow. The angular mountains of Landmannalaugar form the most classic example of a rhyolite landscape. In general, Iceland has few mineral resources but for the record there is a reddish, iron-rich form of andesite officially known as **icelandite**. Also, **Iceland spar** is a clear and transparent calcite crystal (known for double refraction of light beams) used in making ocular prisms.

For its geological youth and a general lack of organic material, Iceland has very poor soil and very little of it. What is not rock is **sand**, or well on its way to becoming sand. The colossal black-sand beaches for which Iceland is famous are actually made from small grains of scoria, crushed by wind, ice and water. Indeed, the whole country is undergoing massive erosion to the extent that Iceland's landscapes are often referenced for their 'textbook' geology. School groups travel to Iceland for the abundance of classroom examples of everything from geomorphology to glaciology.

Iceland has two main types of **mountains**. The most classic are the steep layered slopes of basalt with either flat tops, or sharply eroded ridges, usually found near fjords. These have been carved out by ice or water erosion. The other form grows out of numerous volcanic eruptions (like Mt Hekla) and tend to be more rounded in shape.

**Earthquakes** are common to the point of being constant – with thousands of recorded tremors per year, there is at least one quake happening in Iceland at any given moment. The majority of these are very small shakes, rarely more than a three on the Richter scale. The country's earthquake zone is limited to the main fault line of the Mid-Atlantic Ridge (see box below) and most activity corresponds with that of the volcanoes. A government website reports all seismic activity that has occurred in the previous 48 hours; it can be viewed at http://hraun.vedur.is/ja/englishweb.

## THE MID-ATLANTIC RIDGE

Iceland is the largest land portion of the underwater mountain range that runs the length of the Atlantic Ocean. At over 14,000km (8,900 miles) long, the Mid-Atlantic Ridge marks a divergent boundary between the earth's plates. As the plates pull apart, the Atlantic Ocean grows at a rate of 2.5cm per year – as does Iceland, which is split between the North American and Eurasian plates. Iceland is the only place on land where you can witness the geological phenomenon of seafloor spreading; visitors can actually stand inside the rift of the Mid-Atlantic Ridge at Reykjanes (see page 209) or at Thingvellir (see page 219).

The divergent plates expose a number of undersea hotspots from which erupt volcanic islands all along the ridge. Examples include Jan Mayen, the Azores, and Tristan da Cunha, but owing to the size of this arctic hotspot, Iceland is the largest and most active of these mid-Atlantic islands. In a way, Iceland's mountains and trenches reflect an undersea topography, but that discovery is recent: the Mid-Atlantic Ridge was only recognised in the late 1950s after the ocean floor was mapped for the first time.

## EYJAFJALLAJÖKULL

Every few decades, Iceland reminds the rest of the world that their island country is in fact a highly active volcanic hotspot. In spring 2010, the volcano near Fimmvörðuháls (see page 248), erupted right across the famed Laugavegurinn hiking trail (see page 244) at the edge of the Eyjafjallajökull ice cap, above Thórsmörk.

The eruption soon spread to the middle of the Eyjafjallajökull glacier, which caused a rush of meltwater to push through the mountain rivers in south Iceland, a phenomenon known as *jökulhlaup* (see page 427). Eyjafjallajökull would most likely not have been more than a blip on the news screen if it hadn't been for that fact that the volcano caused a massive plume of volcanic ash that went high into the atmosphere. The mix of gas, dust, and mineral particles was quickly diffused across the north Atlantic and Europe – creating the infamous ash cloud that shut down air traffic in Europe and across the Atlantic for days. The disruption continued through April and into May 2010, reminding stranded travellers that Iceland was, in fact, a volcanic nation – and a part of Europe in more ways than one.

And in case you're still wondering, it's pronounced *Eh-ya-fyat-lah-yukutl.*

# AIR

The air in Iceland is so clean that just breathing tastes good. Chalk it up to low population, low pollution, and a strong wind that blows away any lingering poisons. The elation of foreign visitors just might be an oxygen high. The air in Iceland is so clean that the Kyoto Protocol has allowed Iceland a 10% increase in carbon emissions by 2012 (the Icelandic government has chosen to sell most of these emissions to dirtier countries). The main threat to air quality today is the Icelanders' general affinity for cars.

The **wind** (*vindur*) is a major force in Iceland and should be enjoyed as part of the landscape. It blows constantly, and everything – even the people – grow with it or against it. The Gulf Stream and cold arctic currents create some powerful air movement across the country, typically blowing towards the northeast, but on the ground the wind can hit you from anywhere. For fun, take five minutes and watch the windsock at any local airport as it flips around and changes direction.

This is the place where weather is made for the rest of Europe. Iceland does not experience tropical cyclones or hurricanes; it just gets all the leftover storms and in fast forward. Even on a pleasant sunny day, the wind speed will feel much stronger than you might be accustomed to – 20–30km/h is quite typical. That's why all precipitation happens sideways – be it rain, sleet, snow, or a sandstorm. Storm-force winds blow far stronger, especially in winter: that means 'hurricane force' on the Beaufort scale (upwards of 75mph) or 30–50m per second. The wind in Iceland is also very gusty. There is good reason behind the advice not to open your car door in heavy winds because a strong gust can easily rip the door off its hinges. And so Icelanders learn to park facing the wind. For the same reason, buildings are anchored on sturdy foundations and kept low to the ground. Ask any Icelander about the wind, and they can answer matter-of-factly with a story about something that was blown away 'a few years ago' (eg: a church, a bus, or a bridge).

With the ever-changing skies of Iceland, you can't help but notice the incredible **clouds** that pass overhead. Most likely, you will see colours and shapes that you've never seen before: pink, orange, blue and purple, white, slate grey and bright gold. There are days when it seems like the sky has been erased, and other days when only a few wispy white threads remind you that you're still on earth. Watching the constant transformation inspires vague recollections of forgotten school lessons. The range and shapes of Iceland's cloudscapes are quite complex, but here's a basic refresher:

Stratus are the low, layered clouds that tend to blank out the sky. They are normally eggshell white in colour and when these clouds drop a few hundred feet, they become **fog**. Iceland is probably the best country in the world to watch fog 'roll in'. In a matter of minutes, the whiteness can erase a fjord and the mountains behind it. For its general effect on mood, fog warrants two words in Icelandic: *thoka* is the heavy blanket that falls on a fishing village in an instant and goes away three days later, not to be confused with the less-daunting *mistur* that creeps up on high mountain roads and lingers in the harbour in the morning. Nimbostratus occur when several layers pile up to great heights and darken to grey. They appear thick and impenetrable and are the most common source of precipitation in Iceland. Cumulus clouds are the puffy round clouds of cartoons and children's paintings. They are low and small enough to see the sky behind them. Cumulus are the building blocks of more sinister cloud formations, though Iceland rarely gets the big thunderstorms of temperate climes. Instead, the cold fronts carry in dramatic pile-ups of cumulonimbus clouds – the ones that look like giant cauliflowers and promise wet and windy times. Cirrus clouds arrive on sunny days as gauzy wisps. These very high-altitude clouds are made of ice crystals and contribute to some amazing patterns in the Icelandic sky.

## AURORA BOREALIS (*NORÐURLJÓS*)

The Northern Lights (*norðurljós*) are just one of Iceland's many outstanding natural phenomena and reason enough to travel there in wintertime. The lights glow green, white, blue, red, violet or even pink, and it really is something everyone should see at least once in their lifetime. The luminosity of the aurora is a form of fluorescence: solar winds cause electronic particles to enter the magnetic fields of earth, typically in belts that form within 25° of the poles. The particles travel so quickly that they collide with molecules of atmospheric gasses, which expends the kinetic energy in an emission of light. All of this happens at least 100km above the surface of the earth and is visible to the human eye in the form of a dazzling swathe of coloured light across the sky.

The Latin name Aurora Borealis derives from the Greek goddess of the morning (Aurora) and the god of the north wind (Boreas). In Iceland, the northern lights are most visible from October to April. Every town in Iceland advertises itself as the best place from which to see the Northern Lights, though it's a hard sell seeing as the quality of any sighting is completely unpredictable. Other than the state of solar weather, what matters most is cloud cover and competing light. An optimal viewing will occur on a cold, clear night, and in total darkness. Thus, the farther north you travel and the closer to the winter solstice, the more impressive a display will greet you. Fortunately, in Reykjavík, there is one night a year when the entire city turns out its lights in order to see the aurora more clearly.

## VOLCANIC HIGHLIGHTS

Notable eruptions:

| | |
|---|---|
| AD934 | Eldgjá erupts: largest basaltic lava flow this millennium |
| 1104 | Hekla erupts: northern half of Iceland buried in ash |
| 1362 | Öræfajökull erupts: tephra makes the region uninhabitable for 100 years |
| 1510 | Hekla erupts: exploding rock kills a farmer in a field 40km away |
| 1660 | Katla erupts: falling ash sinks fishing boats in the Faroe Islands |
| 1693 | Hekla erupts for seven months: fluorine poisoning kills livestock |
| 1755 | Katla erupts beneath glacier: two men struck by volcanogenic lightning |
| 1783 | Lakagígar erupts: 10,000 die and world climate affected |
| 1967 | Undersea volcano erupts: creates the new island of Surtsey |
| 1973 | Eldfell erupts: 5,000 residents evacuated from the Westmann Islands |
| 1996 | Grimsvötn erupts: glacial flood destroys the ring road |
| 2004 | Grimsvötn erupts again: ash falls on continental Europe |
| 2010 | Eyjafjallajökull erupts: European air travel shut down for days |

## FIRE

In some ways, Iceland is a country that only a volcanologist could love. They are the only ones who can truly understand all the excitement taking place around them. The 'hotspot' beneath Iceland is actually a magma plume where a 'leak' in the earth's mantle allows molten rock to rise up to the top of the earth's crust. Magma reservoirs and bubbles form within the crust and account for some of the more active parts of Iceland today. For example, a bubbling pool of magma lies just two miles beneath the surface of Krafla (see page 375).

As part of the Mid-Atlantic Ridge, the majority of Iceland's volcanoes are fissures – long cracks in the earth's crust where the lava simply seeps out in fast-moving flows. These fissures form small cinder cones and crater rows, like the ones in Mývatn. Slow-moving lava forms shield volcanoes, a term that comes directly from the Icelandic volcano Skjaldbreiður (see page 217) or 'broad shield'. The standard-issue cone volcano is far less common in Iceland.

Lava flows and volcanic eruptions are part of everyday life in Iceland. There are 180 volcanoes listed, of which 18 are known to be active systems. A commonly known factoid is that Iceland accounts for one-third of the volume of lava extruded on the earth's surface, rivalling that of the Hawaiian islands. Most of that lava is mafic, which means it is very high in iron and very hot (more than 950ºC). Felsic lava is cooler (650°C), higher in silicates, and is more common among Iceland's most active volcanoes. Tephra is the term for anything that shoots out of a volcano that isn't lava (ie: ash, rock, gas) – the volcanic debris accounts for much of the desolate aftermath of an eruption.

While Iceland's volcanoes can be intensive and violent, most occur away from human habitations. Noted exceptions get all the media attention, like the eruption of Heimaey in the Westmann Islands (see page 231). Today, the Icelandic government keeps close track of the most active volcanoes: Hekla, Katla, and of course Eyjafjallajökull.

## WATER

The water in Iceland is some of the purest in the world. A lack of air pollution and the natural filters of volcanic rock make for a memorable drink out of any spring. In all its many forms, the water is part of the fun. **Ice** covers 11% of the country, mostly in the form of glaciers. The four largest are Vatnajökull, Hofsjökull, Langjökull, and Mýrdalsjökull, but there are dozens (if not hundreds) of smaller glaciers high up in the mountains and central highlands. Some of these remaining bits of ice date back to the last ice age of 10,000 years ago; others are younger, following periods of warming and cooling in the last millennium. From far away and up close, the ice of Iceland is beautiful and comes in many different shades of white, black and blue. Glaciers are constantly moving and either melting or freezing. **Crevasses** are the deep cracks in the ice that occur from the changing tension in the moving glacier, from just 1cm wide to several metres. One rarely sees to the bottom of a crevasse, but in Iceland they can open up to extreme depths. Narrow, slippery, hard to see, and impossible to get out of, crevasses are interesting but very dangerous. As the ice on the surface melts, it creates **ice streams** that flow across the top of the glacier and then forms deep wells that spin down to the bottom of the ice. Known as **moulins**, these natural mills carry water off the glacier and they are a common sight on all the glaciers in Iceland.

Glaciers cut deep channels through the layers of basalt and form the **U-shaped valleys** inside which most of Iceland's roads are built. If that valley is below sea level, the incoming water creates the characteristic **fjords** of the coastline. The receding glacier at the back of the fjord melts into a river, which deposits glacial sand and debris at the base of the fjord. The younger the fjord, the straighter the river and more open the channel. Old fjords are often closed off at the base with a sandy beach, a lagoon and a very curvy river. The sharp jagged mountains seen in the East Fjords and in the north are known as **arêtes**, where the ice has cut the rock into a pointed blade or a horn. **Cirques** are the bowl-shaped depressions carved out of the sides of the mountains, especially common in the West Fjords where they are perfectly round and precise. Here the glaciers have literally plucked the basalt rock from its base, and carried it along in the ice. Boulders can be dropped anywhere (another common form of 'troll'), but the rocks are most often ground down into pebbles and sand which are then flushed out and deposited as shiny black beaches, which are fairly wide and extremely long.

**Icebergs** are the broken remnants of glaciers that have broken off from the ice's edge and float out into a glacier lagoon or the sea. Jökulsárlón (see page 421) is the best and only example in Iceland today, because it is the only place in the country where a glacier meets the sea. **Drift ice** comes to Iceland from far colder places. Thirty years ago, the polar ice flow enclosed the north of Iceland from spring well into midsummer, but today that same flow sticks to the Greenland current. Rogue icebergs may still float over to the north of Iceland but it is considered rare. If you really want to see icebergs, go to Greenland.

Most of the water and ice in Iceland arrives in the form of snow, which can fall in any month of the year. Glaciers mark the areas of highest snowfall, and as this snow gets packed down, it turns into ice. In contrast, the lowlands and coastal areas rarely get the deep powdery alpine snows one might imagine for so far north. Even though the whole country looks white in the winter, it's mostly just recycled snow that gets blown around. Steep mountain areas are at more risk of heavy accumulations, and the subsequent threat of avalanche. The fjords in Iceland are particularly vulnerable to these violent cascades of snow, and two recent cases still haunt the West Fjords when dozens were killed. Protective dirt mounds have been built to direct future avalanche flows away from the villages at the base of these fjords, but even today, remote parts of Iceland can be cut off for weeks owing to snow.

Melting ice and snow feed the rivers of Iceland, which are relatively young and therefore much more dramatic than the calm, meandering variety you may know. For starters, all the rivers in Iceland 'rush' – they are short, quick, noisy and carry a huge volume of water from the glaciers to the sea. From the air, it is quite easy to see the radial pattern of Iceland's rivers flowing outwards (and downhill) from the centre of the country. The Thjórsá is the longest and most established river (230km) while some 'rivers' are only a few kilometres long. Many riverbeds are mere suggestions for the water to follow, and, historically, Iceland's rivers have changed direction frequently, branching into new rivers or jumping a few hundred metres. Perhaps to be expected, bridge-building has proven to be a difficult issue. The local term glacial river (*jökulsá*) typically refers to rivers whose flow is directly linked to the meltwater from prominent glaciers. The high content of glacial silt colours the water white or slushy grey. A far more violent event is the dreaded ***jökulhlaup*** – an Icelandic word that is now the internationally recognised term for a glacial outburst flood. Volcanic eruptions beneath the ice melt several cubic kilometres of water that are under the extreme pressure of the glacier. The heated water is finally forced out with such intensity that it can break through 1km of ice as it races to the sea. So many of Iceland's 'canyons' have been created by glacial floods.

Iceland's **waterfalls** are a testament to what a youthful country this is. The fall line around the coast is barely eroded so that most of the glacier melt takes a good drop getting down to sea level. For every big and famous waterfall (Dettifoss, Goðafoss, Gullfoss, and Skógarfoss), you'll encounter a dozen small ones, and hundreds of trickling rock faces that have yet to be named. As recent creations, Icelandic waterfalls tend to be broken into several angled layers – magnificent in height, but perhaps more tremendous in the volume of water that comes crashing through the narrow channels.

Indoors, water from the tap comes out in one of two ways: glacier cold or nuclear hot. Getting the shower temperature just right can be a little tricky. Approximately 99% of Iceland's energy is clean – either from **geothermal** or hydro-electric resources. Five major geothermal plants provide more than a quarter of the country's electricity, where cool, fresh water is piped down through the naturally hot crust and raised to temperatures well above 100°C. Steam exits through pipes into a plant that spins turbines to produce electricity. Leftover steam is cooled into condensation and the temperature reduced to the piping-hot water that comes out through the tap. Also, more than 90% of Icelandic homes are heated with hot water, with a system of pipes beneath the floors.

The abundant natural **hot springs** are beautiful to look at with the bright mineral-induced colours of ultramarine, pink, and ochre. These springs are usually on the verge of boiling and only 'swimmable' when mixed with nearby cold water. **Geysers** are hot springs that erupt periodically, ejecting boiling water and steam into the air. The term comes from Iceland's original *geysir* (see page 223) which is a name that derives from the Icelandic verb *gjósa* (to erupt or gush). The geysers in Iceland occur in areas of rhyolite, the rock which coats the hot springs and nearby area with silicate and allows for airtight subterranean channels. A geyser erupts from the gas explosion deep within its well when carbon dioxide bubbles (produced by the very hot water underground) escape upwards. As the amount of bubbles increases, they block the narrowness of the channel, so that the only way for the gas to escape is by pushing out all the water above it. Following an eruption, cooler water seeps back down into these underground channels where it is heated and the process repeated over and over. The cycle of hydrostatic equilibrium is what grants a degree of predictability to the geyser (ie: Strokkur erupts every ten minutes). Iceland is one of the five largest geyser fields in the world, along with Chile, New Zealand, Kamchatka, and Yellowstone. When only pressurised steam shoots from the earth, it is called a **fumarole**. Without the barrier of water, a constant emission of hydrogen sulphide gas creates a funnel of residue and adds to the sulphuric smell all around. The best places to see fumaroles are at Hveravellir (see page 434) and Namarskarð (see page 376). When these cracks and funnels of gas are blocked by shallow puddles of water and silicates, the result is a bubbling **mud pot**.

## FLORA

Iceland's plant ecosystem is common in its collection of sub-Arctic species, but unique in colour and diversity. Because of Iceland's poor soil, heavy water and high winds, plants put out dense root systems that create the turf (*torf*) once used to construct

### THE ONCE AND FUTURE TREES OF ICELAND

*Dennis A Riege*

When the Viking settlers disembarked on the shores of Iceland, they found woodlands. Granted, it was scrubby birch and not the tall conifers left behind in Scandinavia, but nonetheless, the resourceful homesteaders found the woods useful. The forests were devoured for firewood and charcoal production, reduced to isolated woodlots that were fought over in the civil wars of the 12th and 13th centuries. As the woods were removed, herds of sheep were loosed upon the land. These 'hoofed locusts' (quoting John Muir) ate up birch seedlings and anything green.

Sheep were vital to Icelanders' survival over the centuries, but disastrous to the forests. Overgrazing exposed the topsoil to the blasts of maritime wind. Today, you can still see erosion fronts where the winds have undercut the overhanging turf. You might not associate Iceland with desertification, but overgrazing and volcanic fallout have de-greened vast areas and prompting the Icelandic government to establish the world's first Soil Conservation Service in 1907 at Gunnarsholt in the desert south of Mt Hekla.

Through a century of patient trial and error, suitable plants were found for the re-vegetation of Iceland – primarily grasses and nootka lupin (*Lupinus nootkanensis*), a native of Alaska. Blue fields of flowering lupins now stand out in the landscape from May to September. The lupin is particularly proficient at reclaiming barren soil devoid of nitrogen, as bacteria living in its roots can convert the boundless store of atmospheric nitrogen into plant nutrients. Icelanders love debate and controversy, and the non-native lupin has many detractors. One concern is the fear that this persistent legume may spread into native cover, even into the few remaining pockets of native birch woods, such as Bæjarstaðarskógur ('farmstead forest') at Skaftafell National Park (see page 422). Still, natural recovery of denuded terrain is tortuously slow in a cold land that is short of pioneering plant species (especially nitrogen fixers). Given the choice of manmade lupin greenery or manmade grey barrens, most Icelanders favour the former.

The Iceland Forest Service (IFS) was also established in 1907 to combat desertification, but Icelanders, who had lived in a virtually treeless world for centuries, were sceptical that trees could grow. An aggressive programme of

homes, walls, and churches. A few hundred species of **moss** cover the hills and valleys with their densely packed leaves – it's always worth inspecting the differences up close. **Icelandic moss** (*Cetraria islandica*) or *fjallagrös* is the commonest type of brown-green lichen that grows everywhere and anywhere – truly the carpet of Iceland's hills and mountains (the Icelandic name means 'mountain grass'). Such thick growth acts like a sponge that holds a huge amount of water and allows hikers to bounce from rock to rock. Traditionally, Icelanders have made porridge with Irish moss in times of famine and it is still a coveted herb prized for its medicinal qualities. By the seaside you will notice another kind of orange flaky growth with the optimistic name maritime sunburst lichen (*Xanthoria parietina*) or *Veggjaglæða*. Beneath the water is a whole other world of unique **seaweed**. Dulse (*Chondrus crispus*) or *söl*, is the slimy, purplish-brown branches that wave back and forth with the tides. Rockweed (*Fucus distichus*) or *skúfathang* is green and with big bubbles of air that allow it to float. Inside the cool, clear lakes grow all kinds of strange and colourful Arctic algae.

Iceland bursts into bloom in spring and enjoys an intense two-month season of tiny blossoms everywhere. The flowers make for such a glorious experience (and

afforestation found success with varieties of northern conifer species, particularly Sitka spruce (*Picea sitchensis*) from Alaska and Siberian larch (*Larix siberica*). Sitka spruce does well in the maritime south and west. Spruce planting began in earnest after World War II and extensive forests can now be seen just east of Reykjavík at Heiðmörk, its municipal recreation area. Siberian larch is better adapted to the drier north and east. It is a major component of Iceland's largest and tallest forest, located near the IFS headquarters at Hallormsstaður (see page 403). Here, near the growing eastern hub of Egilsstaðir, trees cover the hillsides along the south shore of Lake Lagarfljót for over 20km.

The climate of Iceland fits that of the boreal forest, the circumpolar belt of spruce and fir that fills northern Canada and Eurasia. Why then, did the Vikings not find a boreal neighbourhood just like back home when they arrived in the 10th century? Because Iceland was never connected to the continents. Its volcanic rock began emerging from the sea about 125 million years ago, which limited the number of plant species that reached the island. Any species that did make the crossing were later obliterated in the ice age. Fossils show that boreal conifers grew in Iceland prior to the glaciations, but after the last retreat ten millennia ago, only downy birch (*Betula pubescens*) and few other low-growing woody species remained.

In the last two decades, afforestation has accelerated dramatically. Regional citizens' forestry associations subsidise farmers to plant seedlings. As you travel throughout Iceland, you will see young trees of various types in the fields – windbreaks of non-native willows and cottonwoods have become popular. Sheep numbers have declined in recent years, which also benefits seedling survival. In reaction to the preponderance of exotic trees, there is a surge of interest in promoting native downy birch. Hardy varieties were developed and are now planted extensively. The ambitious 'Hekluskógar' programme was launched in 2005 to convert the volcanic plains around Mt Hekla into a forest composed of native birch and willows. Don't worry about the panoramic vistas disappearing behind foliage though: Iceland's modest goal is to afforest a mere 5% of the lowland by 2040. The little dabs of green will enhance the already-picturesque farmsteads, but will never obscure the sweeping scope of stark geologic grandiosity that defines this beautiful island.

scent) that a midnight sun feels almost requisite. The national flower is the pale-pink glacier poppy (*Ranunculus glacialis*) or *jöklasóley*, which translates as 'glacier sun' and grows high in the mountains, close to glaciers. Down in the valleys and by the coast grows sea mayweed (*Matricaria maritima*) or *baldursbrá*, the daisy-like flowers worn on the forehead of the Norse God Baldur. More common are the purple stalks of alpine bartsia (*Bartsia alpine*) or *smjörgras* ('butter grass'). A favourite are the minuscule pink star flowers that grow in tight little bunches of moss campion (*Silene acaulis*) or *lambagras* (yes, 'lamb grass'). Good luck trying to keep all the pretty little yellow flowers apart because there are dozens. The meadow buttercup (*Ranunculus acris*) or *brennisóley* is perhaps most common, but looks a lot like the alpine cinquefoil (*Potentilla crantzii*) or *gullmura*. Both grow on hillsides, and at higher altitudes you'll find the larger yellow Arctic poppy (*Papver radicatum*) or *melasól*.

Iceland's blue flowers are a little more discernible thanks to their unique shapes. Wood cranesbill (*Geranium sylvaticum*) has five clover-shaped petals and grows near trees and on hillsides. It is actually more violet but known simply as 'blue grass' (*Blágresi*) in Icelandic. The oysterplant (*Mertensia maritima*) or *blálilja* (blue lily) is really blue and grows near the seaside in sprawling bunches. The tiniest (microscopic!) flowers grow on the end of these broad-leaved vines – if you press a few in a book, they appear as if watercoloured on the page. The fields of purple lupins (*Lupinus nootkanensis*) or *lúpína* are so beautiful and so controversial, given that they are considered an invasive weed from Alaska. And yet, they were introduced to stop erosion. Just as common but more traditional is the cotton flower, or *fífa*, which grow in great abundance in valleys and on islands.

What Icelanders call **blueberries** (*Bláberjalyng*) are actually bilberries (*Vaccinium uliginosum*). They grow in very small clumps or 'bushes' on the ground and are abundant on wet hillsides. The pink flower blossoms from May to June and blueberry picking commences in late July/early August. 'Blueberries' are a summer staple and eaten year-round. It really is the national fruit of Iceland and Icelanders will keep their special blueberry-picking spots a secret from both friends and strangers. For visiting hikers, blueberries provide welcome and abundant treats (they cannot be confused with anything else).

In Iceland, what doesn't grow is just as important as what does. Whether or not Iceland ever was a land of **trees** is somewhat controversial. The sagas provide early descriptions of wood 'from fell to foreshore' and some evidence that the Vikings deforested the entire country at the time of settlement. Iceland's harsh climate prevents quick recovery, and for the past millennium, nearly all timber has been imported. Frankly, Iceland wouldn't look like Iceland with a bunch of trees, but the fear of erosion inspires a national forestry department (see box on page 48). Birch (*björk*) is the most common tree and the most native. It grows in small bushes and covers protected hillsides – it's also difficult to walk in. Because of its small size, Iceland's proudest tree inspires two commonly told jokes – the first, a Japanese tourist in Iceland who is enraged to find the whole nation filled with 'natural' bonsai trees, and the second: What do you do if you get lost in the forest in Iceland? Just stand up.

## FAUNA

The creatures of Iceland are plentiful, especially the birds, and the fish. Some will be pleased to know that there are no reptiles or amphibians. There are however, lots of insects, but they are only active in the short summer period and none of them bites. On very rare occasions, a walrus or polar bear might float over to Iceland on a piece of drift ice, but they are not indigenous – just accidents. Trigger-happy Icelanders have prevented either from ever getting established.

**FISH** Fish is life in this country surrounded by water. Icelanders eat whatever they can catch in the sea and so the best way to know the local species is to pick up a restaurant menu. **Cod** (*Gadus morhua*) or *thorsku* is the heart and soul of Iceland's kitchen table, as well as its history and economy. At present, the Icelandic stock is considered the most prominent (and legal) codfish population in the world. The fish has a very distinct look, with three dorsal fins and two fins on the bottom. They are grey-green or brown in colour and can grow to very large sizes – the largest cod recorded in Iceland was almost 2m long and weighed over 90kg, though the fish unloaded in the harbour is generally only one-third that size. Cod live in large schools and prefer cold-water shallows and depths up to 200m. The fish are omnivorous, eating plants and marine life and each other. They are also threatened. The **haddock** (*Melanogrammus aegiefinus*) or *ýsa* is in the same family as the cod, but is smaller and silvery white, with a distinct black line along its side. The largest haddock-spawning ground in the world is off the Reykjanes coast. Iceland's **catfish** (*Anarhichas lupus*) or *steinbitur* is not the commonly known freshwater catfish with whisker-like antennae, but rather stands out as the most lugubrious-looking fish in the world. The Icelandic name 'stone biter' derives from the manner in which the long grey fish scours the rocks for molluscs. A row of giant front teeth help split open the shells. **Halibut** (*Hippoglossus hippoglossus*) or *heilagfiskur* is a giant deep-sea fish that provides ample white meat. The name 'holy fish' references suitable Catholic food on Fridays and during Lent. Vast schools of **herring** (*Clupea harengus*) or *síld* once migrated through Icelandic waters, but disappeared without a trace in the late 1960s. The fish are destined for a comeback, but most of Iceland's old herring boats have been re-outfitted for whale-watching tours. **Plaice** (*Pleuronectus platessa*) or *skarkoli* is a flat fish (like a flounder) that swims along the sandy bottoms around Iceland. It's a very popular food fish and a common ingredient in *plottfiskur,* and therefore at risk. **Monkfish** (*Lophius piscatorius*) or *skötuselur* are downright ugly looking and were once tossed aside as by-catch in the cod nets. Today, it's the darling of chi-chi restaurant menus, although only about a third of the fish is edible (the tail and liver). Monkfish live at the very bottom of the sea and have gigantic mouths that allow them to swallow prey half their size. Another odd-looking sea-bottom dweller is the **lumpfish** (*Cyclopterus lumpus*) or *hrognkelsi* with its lumps, dorsal spines, and underside suckers which allow it to stick to the seafloor. Lumpfish roe is prized food in Iceland.

**Skate** (*Raja radiata*) or *skata* swim all around Iceland's coastlines and can grow to huge sizes (more than 1m across). It is the traditional 'Christmas' dish for St Thórlakur's Day (see page 37). **Greenland shark** (*Somniosus microcephalus*) or *hákarl* is the northernmost species of shark. It is a reclusive animal, living at depths over 2,000m. Despite being close to the great white shark in size, it does not pose a threat to humans, feeding mainly on seals (although the stomach contents of one recently caught shark revealed the paws of a polar bear). Eating cured *hákarl* is a national tradition – because the flesh is toxic, the smelly meat undergoes a long treatment process (see page 106).

The rushing rivers of Iceland are perfect habitat for **salmon** (*Salmo salar*) or *lax.*This classic Atlantic fish is a staple of the environment and history of Iceland. Salmon fry are born in turbulent freshwater streams where they live for about two years. The young then swim out into the saltwater oceans to feed and mature. At around age five, the salmon return to the same river in which they were born. Starting in early April, the adult fish swim upstream to begin spawning in the

## LOOSE CHANGE – THE FISH IN YOUR POCKET

What's on the back of that coin?

| | |
|---|---|
| 1 króna | codfish |
| 5 krónur | dolphins |
| 10 krónur | capelin (or whitefish) |
| 50 krónur | crab |
| 100 krónur | lumpfish |

autumn. Icelanders refer often to 'salmon rivers', which is any river where salmon come to spawn (most of them). Salmon fishing is highly popular and heavily regulated in Iceland. Netting salmon out at sea is now illegal in Icelandic waters and fishing rights on the streams is a costly endeavour. Even so, it's hard to visit Iceland and not eat salmon. The **Arctic char** (*Salvelinus alpinus*) or *bleikja* is closely related to both the salmon and trout. It is the northernmost freshwater fish in the world and has a similar life cycle to that of the salmon. The flesh is pink (hence the Icelandic name 'pinky').

**BIRDS** Over 300 species of bird have been spotted in Iceland, but that oft-quoted figure says little about what Iceland means to birds. First and foremost, Iceland is home sweet home – the nostalgic birthplace for millions and millions of birds who live all over the world. Instinct brings them back year after year, often to their very childhood nest. The sub-Arctic island provides undisturbed summer breeding grounds and access to a good deal of food. When the brunt of tourists arrive in summer, the whole country is a bustling nursery of baby birds and expectant mothers. It's very exciting.

While seaside habitats have been destroyed on both sides of the Atlantic, most of Iceland remains untouched by humans. For migrating birds, Iceland also represents the final reach of the east Atlantic route from Africa and Europe, intersecting with North America's Atlantic flyway. Thus Iceland is home to both American and European species that overlap but do not occur beyond that point. For those that fly beyond, Iceland is a noted pit-stop and, given the ocean currents, it's no surprise that passing migrants outnumber summer breeders. The following is by no means an exhaustive list, but aims to help the traveller to know what to look for in different parts of the country.

**Seaside and islands** Iceland's long and intricate coastline is home to the majority of its birds. Habitats vary from steep fjords to low islands, rocky coasts, and black-sand beaches. A prime example is Breiðafjörður (see page 301), but on any coast there are certain key species to look out for. The commonest duck in Iceland is the **eider** (*Somateria mollissima*) or *æðir*. It is over one million strong, and Icelanders have relied on the prized down since the age of settlement. They are the only ducks to live almost exclusively by the sea, and most of them reside in Iceland year-round. The adult male is a sight to behold, with very elegant feathers of white and black. The female is brown and dappled but with a unique sloped head that sets her apart from the other species. The eider is one of the few duck species to live almost exclusively in the sea. They eat small marine life (shellfish and plants) and normally live in very large groups. While it is nesting (for one month) the female eats nothing, and leaves just once a day for a drink – like most birds in Iceland, eiders drink seawater and process the salt through nasal glands. They hatch three–six eggs and in July you will see the little black ducklings everywhere.

The Arctic tern (*Sterna paradisaea*) or *kría* is one of Iceland's most remarkable and gregarious birds. Slender and small, they migrate huge distances – more than any other bird in the world. They breed in Iceland for the Arctic summer and then

## KRÍA – ICELAND'S BLOODTHIRSTY BEAST

It seems like a scene from Alfred Hitchcock's *The Birds*: hundreds, if not thousands, of terns dive-bombing the innocent humans who are out strolling along the shore. Add to that a soundtrack of harrowing screams and birdwatching becomes a terrifying, extreme sport. Arctic terns have the physique of a sleek fighter jet and are equipped with a pointed, arrow-sharp red beak – when aimed and directed at high speeds it will puncture your scalp and draw blood (to this I can testify). What you have to remember (whilst rubbing your head) is that the Arctic terns don't hate you – they're just a little defensive.

Wherever nature is lacking, nature also tends to compensate. When it comes to building nests, Arctic terns lack skills – the birds lay a pair of eggs on open, gravel-strewn fields, typically inside a crude little indent of pebbles. The eggs are tiny, coloured greenish white with black and grey spots on them. Once they hatch, the babies are just teeny weeny balls of fluff with black speckles. The two-inch-tall birds tend to wander clumsily while their parents are out collecting fish to feed them with. It's no surprise that birdwatchers in heavy hiking boots can easily crush the eggs and babies and not even know it.

In response, the Arctic tern collective is a highly defensive bunch, with appointed lookouts that fly high and sound a piercing alarm call for incoming predators. Approaching threats are met with a regiment of tern forces that will actually line up and take turns dive-bombing the enemy until he or she runs away screaming. Arctic terns are also equal-opportunity defenders and will protect the nests and babies of all birds in the area. Even after their own fledglings have grown up, Arctic terns will keep an eye out for the young eider ducklings and the puffin chicks. In most seaside areas, it's a game of 'hot and cold': as you get closer to the baby birds, the terns get crazier.

The birds' message is clear: tread lightly! It's not hard to avoid the terns' territory, but there are times when you may have to cross. Watch where you step and keep your head low. The birds always aim for the highest point, so as long as you are shorter than others in your group, you're safe. As a deterrent, tourists are often handed plastic poles to carry over their heads, though something tells me that the terns are getting smarter and have learned the difference between plastic and flesh. Wearing a hat up high on your head might help.

Icelanders feel a great affinity towards the *kría*, the local name that matches the sound of the bird's banshee cries. They don't view the terns as violent, respecting instead the birds' solidarity and their passion for protecting all birds. You'll find the *kría* depicted on stamps, on the signs of restaurants and summerhouses and on the hulls of boats. It's not the lion or eagle crest of some nations, but quite fitting for Iceland – the bird is small, but if necessary, it's got a bite to match its bark.

fly to Antarctica for the austral summer – a good 32,000km (or 20,000 miles). They have black heads, grey backs and white undersides, with bright-red beaks and feet – although they will usually attack you before you recognise them.

**Gulls** add to Iceland's resident year-round bird population. They are not the most numerous, but they are often the most vocal and telling them apart can be a headache. The rest of the world refers to the Iceland gull (*Larus glaucoides*) in honour of its winter home, but *bjartmáfur* means 'bright gull' in Icelandic. They look a lot like the glaucous gull (*Larus hyperboreus*) which the Icelanders know as the *hvítmáfur* or 'white gull'. Much more prominent is the great black-backed gull (*Larus marinus*) or *svartbakur* and the very similar but smaller species of the lesser black-backed gull (*Larus fuscus*), which is *sílamáfur* or 'herring gull' – not to be confused with the herring gull (*Larus argentatus*) or *sílfurmáfur* ('silver gull'); *sigh!* Great blacks are the largest gulls in Iceland, with distinctive black wings and a red mark on the lower beak, and pinkish legs. The lesser black look the same, but are smaller, with thinner yellow legs. The herring gull has light grey wings with black tips; all three (great, lesser and herring) look almost identical as juveniles. The black-headed gull (*Larus ridibundus*) or *hettumáfur* has an easily identifiable black head and face, and like the Arctic tern, will defend its nest with its beak.

The **great skua** (*Catharacta skua*) or *skúmur* is the bully of the seabird schoolyard, chasing down other birds and forcing them to hand over their lunches – even making them vomit up the fish they just ate. They look like a large gull, but with the colouring of a brown hawk, and with a menacing glare. In Iceland, you can normally locate a great skua by the number of puffin carcasses strewn about. If skua babies are around, the parents will attack. Normally, they give a warning of a single overhead swoop before they come out with the claws. The great skua lives all along the southern coast, especially near Öræfi (see page 426).

Iceland's largest bird is the **white-tailed eagle** – also known as the sea eagle – (*Haliaeetus albicilla*) or *haförn*. With fewer than 200 birds in the country, they are highly endangered, though still much better off than they were in the 1960s when they numbered fewer than 20 pairs. The birds are true giants: adults typically weigh 5kg and have wingspans over 2m. They are mainly brown, with lighter colouring on their head (the American bald eagle is a close cousin). Their main prey is fish,

## EIDERDOWN

Like most ducks, eiders pluck the down from their breast to insulate their nests. What makes eiderdown so special is that it is incredibly light, soft, and warm – the most efficient down in the world. Medieval law still grants Icelandic landowners the right to collect the down from any nests on their property – hence the high demand for islands and coastal farms where the eider ducks breed.

Although never domesticated, there exists a respected ritual between man and duck in Iceland. Farmers sometimes build stone shelters to encourage nesting, and even feed the very hungry nesting females. Once the ducklings have hatched, the down is gathered up – one eider nest can provide about 30g of down. As a luxury item that comes from a wild source, the price of eiderdown fluctuates, but currently sells at around US$1,500 per kilo. That's about the minimum amount needed to fill a duvet or comforter, which can easily sell for US$10,000 back home. Iceland remains the largest exporter of eiderdown in the world.

which they catch with their very sharp talons right out of the water, but they are also known to eat eider, fulmar and ptarmigan. Adult eagles build their nests of twigs on small islands, perhaps in a fjord, or at the tops of high mountains. It's difficult to say where one might see an eagle – they are most prominent in the West Fjords, but they are heavily protected and known nests are kept a secret.

The **gannet** (*Morus bassanus*) or *súla* is a beautiful and graceful bird – large, tall and white, with a pale yellow-orange shading on the head and long black wing feathers. One of the world's largest gannet colonies is on Eldey Island (see page 210), in Reykjanes. Other known colonies include the remote outcrops of Skrúður Island (in the east) and Langanes (see page 393). Unless you can get out to these rocks, you are most likely to see a gannet from a boat out at sea.

**Oystercatcher** (*Haematopus ostralegus*) or *tjaldur* live all along the coast, but mostly in the west. Other well-known species of seabirds inhabit very specific areas of Iceland. **Shags** (*Phalacrocorax aristotelis*) or *toppskarfur* and **cormorants** (*Phalacrocorax carbo*) or *dílaskarfur* are concentrated in Breiðafjörður, while the Westmann Islands represent the crossover of the European **storm petrel** (*Hydrobates pelagicus*) or *stormsvala* and the western hemisphere's **Leach's petrel** (*Oceanadrama leucorrhea*) or *sjósvala.* On these same islands you can find a few overachieving **Manx shearwater** (*Puffinus puffinus*) or *skrova* who overshot their summer migration from Britain.

***Bird cliffs*** Any seaside rock face that's covered with birds for some of the year is called a bird cliff, and in Iceland that constitutes most of the mountainous coastline and the offshore islands. In columns or in layers, the basalt cliffs offer the perfect nesting spot for so many birds. Cliffs range from 10m to 400m high – in summer, the magnificent number and concentration of birds is astounding. On a cliff like Látrabjarg (see page 296), more than one million birds will cling to a sheer and vertical surface, protected from harm and with easy access to the sea. In the summer breeding season, different bird species divide up the cliffs like an apartment building – floor by floor (see page 297). Somehow they all co-exist. Nests are small and narrow and the eggs of cliff-dwellers are conical in shape so that they spin back on the heavy end as opposed to wobbling and falling off the edge. Most cliff birds are pelagic – they spend the majority of their life out at sea in very deep waters. They are also terrific divers who plunge from a great height into the sea and swim down to even greater depths to catch fish. Watching them push down through the clear water is often more fascinating than watching them fly.

**Razorbills** (*Alca torda*) or *álka* have a telltale thin white stripe that streaks upwards from the lower beak all the way to the eye. They have black backs and heads with white bellies with a distinctive sharp, parrot-like bill. The largest razorbill colony in the world is in Iceland, at Látrabjarg. Three types of **guillemots** live in Iceland: the common guillemot (*Uria aalge*) or *langvía* is the most abundant, with over one million breeding pairs. It looks a bit like the razorbill (white belly, black back, head and wings), but is slimmer, with a smaller head and a pointed beak. Sometimes they also have a very unusual and pretty white doe-eyed outline around their eye. Common guillemots are very sociable and can make a real racket. The Icelandic name for Brünnich's guillemot (*Uria lomvia*) or *stuttnefja* means 'short nose', which is the best way to tell them apart from the more common variety, since they look and behave almost identically. Their shorter beak also has a small white streak on the side. Nearly all of Iceland's *stuttnefja* live on the cliffs in the West Fjords. The less common black guillemot (*Cepphus grille*) or *teista* is black all over, except for small white patches on the wings. They also have bright-red feet and mouths. The species lives close to the water – either at the bottom of the cliff or on islands; most of the local population lives in Iceland year-round.

Although the **fulmar** (*Fulmarus glacialis*) *or fýll* looks like a gull, it is actually a large petrel, sporting a sizeable white body with tinted dark-grey wings. Unlike gulls, fulmars glide and dive and rarely squawk. They also have the unique habit of vomiting on you if annoyed or alarmed. Primarily a cliff-dweller in Iceland, they can also be found a good distance inland. They love to follow fishing boats and are a common sight around village harbours and fish factories. With over 1.5 million breeding pairs distributed all around the coast, the fulmar is one of the most commonly seen birds in Iceland. The **kittiwake** (*Rissa tridactyla*) or *rita* is a gull that is often found alongside the fulmar and likes to follow the fish. Kittiwake are smaller and more streamlined, with unique colouring: the adults are white with grey wings, black wingtips, and sharp yellowish beaks – younger birds have distinctive black stripes along the front of their wings. Kittiwakes nest right in the middle of the cliffs and hatch the fluffiest, all-white babies of any bird in Iceland.

**Puffins** (*Fratercula arctica*) or *lundi* are the iconic bird of Iceland, and quite an entertaining species. They are irresistibly cute, intelligent and highly expressive – for centuries their character has been compared to that of whimsical parrots or clowns. Their Latin binomial 'little brother of the north' pinpoints their monkish appearance and reveals a long-standing affection for the bird, and with good reason. You can watch puffins for hours and never get bored.

The puffin's appearance is unmistakable: black wings, necks and hood, with a podgy white tummy and white cheeks. Their eyes look like triangles, and their parrot-shaped beaks show bright red, yellow and blue in summer (winter sees the colours fade to grey). They waddle on bright-orange webbed feet but with such small and stubby wings, puffins are not nimble flyers – to stay airborne they must flap their wings at around 100 beats per minute. Puffins are, however, incredible divers and swimmers. They can easily outdo some of the other birds, diving to depths of 15m and staying underwater for up to one minute. They also have a jagged palate that allows them to hold fish against the roof of their mouths while they fish for more. It is common to see a puffin flying around with as many as ten fish in its mouth (the photographed record is 62!).

Puffins live long and interesting lives. They spend the winters in the deep waters of the Atlantic, feeding mainly on eels, capelin, and herring. The first three years of life are spent exclusively at sea, after which they fly back to the very cliff on which they were born. By age five, the sexually mature males will have finished digging a burrow at the very top of a sea cliff. Puffins typically mate for life, laying a single egg in the same burrow year after year. A puffin burrow is between 1m and 2m long with a fork at the back – one side is where the egg is incubated and the chick is fed, with the other side used to collect waste. From an early age, the chick is trained to relieve itself in this other chamber and keep itself clean, dry and – most importantly – waterproof. The newborn chick is an awkward greyish bundle that bit by bit transforms into the black-and-white patterns of its parents. In Iceland, puffin parents spend their days zipping back and forth between clifftop and sea. They are feeding a demanding chick who (by the end of the summer) weighs twice as much as its parents. In the long days of summer, the adults only return to the cliffs to rest late at night – typically after 22.00. That's why the best time to watch puffins up close is around midnight.

Iceland is home to the world's largest population of puffins, with an estimated six million birds arriving every summer. You can find puffins along most high coasts and islands, but the largest colonies are found in the Westmann Islands (see page 228), Látrabjarg (see page 296), the islands of Breiðafjörður (see page 301), and on Grímsey (see page 355). Puffins arrive in Iceland by May and disappear by mid-August. Their departure is instantaneous – nobody knows exactly when it will occur, but when the time comes, it is quick and exact. The adults group together in 'rafts' out at sea and within 48 hours they're gone. The fledglings stumble out of their holes and flop around, eventually making it out to sea and repeating the cycle.

**Rivers, lakes and fjords** Few places in the world see the concentration of **swans** (*Cygnus cygnus*) that Iceland does. The *álft* (f) or *svanur* (m) occupies a vital place in the landscape and folklore, and although not numerous, the elegant white bird is quite visible. Many of the wintering swans of Britain and Ireland breed and summer in the fjords and ponds of Iceland. Back at home, swans are often seen alone or in small families, but the migration of swans in Iceland is a tremendous sight. Around mid-September, hundreds – if not thousands – of swans gather together and began preparing for their journey south.

Lots of other waterbird species come to breed in Iceland – the real jackpot is at Lake Mývatn (see page 366). It's the best place to see **divers** and ducks. The red-throated diver (*Gavia stellata*) and the great northern diver (*Gavia immer*) are relatively few in number, but are well protected and a real treat when you spot them. The horned grebe (*Podiceps auritus*) is the only **grebe** to breed in Iceland. About two-dozen species of **duck** are seen regularly in Iceland, including Barrow's goldeneye (*Bucephalus islandica*), the long-tailed duck (*Clangula hyemalis*), scaup (*Aythya marila*), tufted duck (*Aythya fuligula*), teal (*Anas crecca*), and wigeon (*Anas penelope*). The area around Mývatn is also the only breeding area in Europe for the harlequin duck (*Histrionicus histrionicus*). Iceland's two prominent species of **goose** have divided the country up nicely. The low-lying fjords and rivers are the domain of the greylag goose (*Anser anser*) or *grágæs*, while the highland ponds and glacial riverbanks are home to the curious-looking pink-footed goose (*Anser brachyrhynchus*) or *heiðagæs*. The two are easy enough to tell apart. As part of the Arctic migration route, huge numbers of barnacle goose (*Branta leucopsis*) and white-fronted goose (*Answer albifrons*) pass through the southwest corner of the country in the spring and autumn.

**Marshes** The 'waders' of Iceland are many and show up everywhere: seaside deltas, inland marshes, and the drier heath that's further inland. Making a recent comeback is the **black-tailed godwit** (*Limosa limosa*). The bird is very tall, with a very long neck and a long pointed beak. Its tail is indeed black, but much of the body is reddish-brown. The godwit's call ('*weeta*') is unmistakable; you can be assured of a summer sighting on Viðey Island (see page 186). The commonest wader is the **snipe** (*Gallinago gallinago*) which has acquired a habit for gathering near hot springs in Iceland. Other waders include the larger **whimbrel** (*Numenius phaeopus*), the smaller **dunlin** (*Calidris alpine*) and the podgy, round **purple sandpiper** (*Calidris maritima*). Spring and autumn see fair migrations of **knot** (*Calidris canutus*) and **sanderling** (*Calidris alba*).

**Inland and highlands** The **ptarmigan** (*Lagopus mutus*) or *rjúpa* is the ubiquitous Arctic bird of the grassy heath. Their plumage changes with the season – mottled grey and brown in summer and all-white in winter with distinctive red marks above the eyes. Not great flyers, they are the easy prey of foxes and raptors. Their number-one predator is the **gyrfalcon** (*Falco rusticolus*) or *fálki* – although few in number, it is the national symbol of Iceland and quite a noble-looking creature with a white

## HRAFN – CORVUS CORVAX

The raven is the largest member of the corvid family (crows, rooks, jackdaws) and lives in Iceland year round. Ravens are thought to be territorial and many farms in Iceland have their 'own' pair of ravens. They mate in mid-April, and chicks hatch in May–June. Despite their magnificent size, fledgling ravens spend a month or so flopping about and cawing ungraciously. At full-size, the raven's wingspan reaches up to 2ft (60cm). The raven is considered a mischievous and cunning bird with high intellect and is a common figure in Old Norse mythology. It's a raven that brought Flóki to Iceland (see page 16) and there are tales in Iceland of ravens warning people of avalanches.

and dark-grey pattern on its chest. The falcons nest in the rocks of mountaintops and are most numerous in the northeast of the country. The more commonly seen raptor is the **merlin** (*Falco columbarius*) or *smyrill.*

The less habited inland areas are also home to the **Arctic skua** (*Stercorarius parasiticus*) or *skúmur* which is smaller and sleeker than its greater cousin, but just as much of a bully, making a living from stealing other birds' food. Instead of the robin, Icelanders declare the arrival of spring based on the first spotting of the **golden plover** (*Pluvialis apricaria*) – the *heiðlóa* or 'heath plover' lives on the expansive heath and dry highlands where you can locate them by their very distinct call ('*derr-eee*').

Also be on the lookout for the very cute **snow bunting** (*Plectrophenax nivalis*), or *snjótittlingur*, which changes its coat with the snow; the Icelandic *snjótittingur* means 'snow sparrow'. They are quite common in the highlands and you will hear them chirping a song before you see them. Iceland's tiniest bird is the **wren** (*Troglodytes troglodytes*), or *músarrindill*, best identified by its pretty song and its affinity for the few tree limbs that grow in Iceland.

**Birdwatching** Iceland has become one of the prime birdwatching sites in the world thanks to its undisturbed habitats and easy access for humans. In actuality, the diversity of Icelandic bird species is relatively low – only about 70 species are regular breeders, with 75% rare or passing migrants. It's just one reason why the casual observer can recognise and enjoy a handful of common species, while the serious birder should come prepared for surprises and with a good bird guide in hand.

Like their claims on good weather, every village in Iceland advertises the best birdwatching of all. The fact is that you really can't go wrong in Iceland – even Reykjavík has some great wildlife flying about. As a rule, every town in Iceland has its own pond (*tjörn*) set aside solely for ducks and waders. It's always worth taking a look at what's there when you are visiting. Birdwatching tours focus on the high-impact destinations like Mývatn and Breiðafjörður, which are indeed spectacular – but travellers should be encouraged to head out to the islands, like Grímsey, Papey, and the Westmann Islands. Also, never assume that an area which looks barren is really barren. Even Iceland's interior has its surprises.

Be sensitive to the fact that most of the birds you see in the summer are either newborns or new parents. If you get too close to them, birds will treat you as a predator. Mother ducks and others are known to fake a broken wing and try to lead you away. Others (like the terns, gulls, and skuas) simply aim straight for your head (see box on page 53).

**MAMMALS** The only known indigenous mammal in Iceland is the **Arctic fox** (*Algopex lagopus*), which is quite a special creature. They have adapted to the extreme conditions of the north in so many ways – the fox has tiny triangular ears, high body fat, fur on the bottom of its paws (like slippers with treads) and the warmest coat of any mammal in the world – even more efficient than a polar bear's fur. They are omnivorous, eating everything from bird eggs to shellfish to little lambs, although their main prey in Iceland is the ubiquitous ptarmigan. Visitors most often spot a fox when it is chasing birds in a field.

In Iceland, the foxes have blue-black fur in the summer and go totally white in the winter – the in-between moments see a staggered colouration of tan, grey, and red. Come spring, the foxes give birth to litters of seven to 14 pups. Today, there are fewer than 5,000 foxes left in Iceland, most of which live in the unpopulated corners of the country. Their highest numbers are in the remote reserve of Hornstrandir (see page 309) in the West Fjords and in Skaftafell (see page 422), where they are protected. Count yourself very lucky if you see one.

Mice were the first non-native land mammals to arrive in Iceland, stowing away with the settlers. Today, the **wood mouse** (*Apodermus sylvaticus*) and **house mouse** (*Mus musculus*) have adapted comfortably to the farms and homes of Icelanders and can be seen in the bushes of Reykjavík gardens as well as in the foundations of country churches. Rats arrived much later – some think that the **brown rat** (*Rattus norvegicus*) only became widespread in Iceland during the early 20th century, having arrived earlier from Denmark (not Norway). The smaller **black rat** (*Rattus rattus*) showed up around the time of industrialisation and continues to be a pest. Iceland's offshore islands are proud to be free of rats and mice, because the rodents are bad swimmers.

By far the most annoying species in Iceland is the **American mink** (*Mustela vison*) – the result of a Depression-era fur-farming scheme gone awry. By the 1960s, escaped mink covered the whole country, living near streambeds and eating everything from duck eggs to birds and bumble bees. The pest led to a few species of waterbirds simply disappearing from Iceland – as a result, hunting mink is now a government-sponsored sport. For every mink you shoot, the local police will pay you a bounty in króna that's just enough to pay for a nice dinner out.

Iceland's **reindeer** (*Rangifer tarandus*) or *hreindýr* were introduced from Norway in the late 1700s in the hope that the hardy Nordic animals could populate the uninhabited parts of Iceland with game. Reindeer are the same animal as caribou, but have been semi-domesticated in Scandinavia for many centuries and are slightly smaller in stature. Their coats are brown-grey in summer and become white in winter with antlers on both sexes. The males lose their antlers in winter, the females drop theirs in the spring, when they give birth to a single calf. In Iceland, the animals went feral from the word go and have suffered a number of ups and downs related to disease, harsh climate, and periodic lack of food. Around 3,000 animals remain in the country today and that population is heavily regulated. All of Iceland's reindeer herds live in the eastern highlands, with the largest concentration just north of Vatnajökull glacier.

**Domestic animals** You don't see that many fences in Iceland – a testament to the fuzzy line between what is wild and what is not. Icelanders take great pride in the animals that helped settled their nation, and recognise their livestock as special and highly resilient breeds that bear only a vague resemblance to the more common lookalikes in the rest of the world. These animals were carried over in open-air Viking ships and were then left to fend for themselves in a very harsh climate. From

## HOW DO YOU SAY 'SHEEP' IN ICELANDIC? THAT DEPENDS . . .

| | |
|---|---|
| *Sauðfé* | the animal known as sheep |
| *Rólla* | a sheep |
| *Kindur* | many sheep in a flock |
| *Hrútur* | ram |
| *Gimbur* | ewe |
| *Lamb* | a baby lamb |
| *Gemlíngur* | one-year-old lamb |
| *Gemsí** | farmer slang for *gemlíngur* |

* Because it sounds similar to 'GSM', *gemsí* is now the common Icelandic slang for mobile phone. Thanks to Agnar and Smári Kristjánsson for their help with research.

the beginning, the hardest factor in keeping animals in Iceland has been feeding them. Come winter, there is almost nothing for grazing animals to eat – hence Icelandic farmers grow hay wherever they can. The grass is left to grow during a very short season: cutting begins in late July and early August, after which the bundles are wrapped in plastic and used for feed from October to May. A few extra weeks of winter can spell disaster for an Icelandic farmer – if the food is all gone or there's none yet on the ground, the animals must be rounded up again.

About 750,000 **sheep** live in Iceland today, making it the most common mammal in the country. Icelandics are considered the oldest and purest breed of sheep in the world, as there has been no cross-breeding for over 1,100 years. The animals usually have horns and their tails are naturally short and skinny. Their coats come in all different colours and patterns, and they actually have two separate layers of wool – a short and soft layer undercoat, and then longer, coarser strands on the surface. Sheep are typically shorn at the beginning and end of winter, and Icelandic wool is considered rare and exported as a speciality product for hand-knitting. Traditional knitting patterns feature the natural colours of the sheep.

Mating takes place in late November–December, and the lambs are born in May. The Icelandic breed is associated with a high percentage of multiple births – up to six – and the country's sheep population doubles in lambing season. Come June, the animals are turned out into the wild and it's amazing how you can run into sheep in the oddest places. The ***réttir*** (roundup) takes about a week in September, when Icelanders mount their horses and go riding off into the wilderness in search of their sheep. It is very hard work but a lot of fun as one gets to explore the most uninhabited corners of the country. There's a fair number of legends regarding sheep that have missed the roundup and been located the next summer with new lambs in tow.

The roundup is just one of the jobs done by the Icelandic **sheepdog**, or *fjárhundur*. On the farm, they herd and protect sheep, horses, and cows. They are especially adept at finding sheep buried in the snow and are often used in rescue operations – in the old days, no Icelander travelled anywhere without a dog. The original breed is a small version of a spitz dog (like the Siberian husky) with a big fluffy coat that is normally tan or yellow, with some variation. Icelandic sheepdogs are considered a rare breed – by 1935, disease had reduced their number to just 35 and there are fewer than 5,000 in the world today.

The **horse** is essential to the Icelandic landscape – watching a few dozen animals thunder across a stormy horizon is a heart-swelling and familiar scene. More than

80,000 horses live in Iceland today, all of them descended from a controlled group first carried over by the settlers. In AD982, the Althing passed a law forbidding the future import of any foreign horses, and so for more than 1,000 years, Icelandic horses have evolved and were bred expressly for the land and climate of Iceland. That means today's Icelandic horses can swim a glacial river and cross a highland desert. The breed is so specialised and pure that once a horse leaves Iceland, it is never allowed back in. A constant debate rages as to whether or not Icelandic horses born and raised in Europe and North America can still qualify as the original breed.

Icelandic horses are incredibly durable animals – they are custom-built for carrying heavy loads (like Vikings and well-fed tourists) over very rough terrain, and remain completely unfazed by high winds and snowstorms. In fact, they seem more beautiful in bad weather. They have big, dense bones, stocky bodies, strong necks and thick hair. Come winter, their coat grows long and shaggy, so that they look bearded and full. Colouring is totally variable – from dappled to all-white to brown with blonde hair to grey to reddish, but often the hair colour will be different from that of the coat. Icelandics also live to be very old – over 40 years.

While most horses only have four gaits (walk, trot, canter, gallop), Icelandic horses have a fifth. *Tölt* is unique to the Icelandic breed and occurs between the trot and canter. Riding at a *tölt* is remarkably smooth because there is no 'moment of suspension' – the horse always has one foot on the ground and changes at an equal beat. Only some Icelandic horses can do the much faster *skeið* (pace) in which two legs on the same side touch the ground at the same time. The result feels like flying – the horse is airborne between each pace and can reach speeds in excess of 50km/h (30mph).

Icelandic horses are known for their kindly comportment and affability. You haven't been to Iceland unless you've communed with a friendly horse and looked into its amazing eyes. They are not skittish and do not spook easily – instead they are very stable and centred, bold and persevering, with a mind and will very much their own. Also, the naming of Icelandic horses is a poetry unto itself (eg: *Farfús* – 'likes to travel'). Never ride a horse whose name you do not know or understand.

Like Iceland's sheep and horses, Icelandic **cattle** are 1,000-year-old purebreds direct from the Viking-era gene pool. This means they are quite hardy, smaller than most breeds and represent a true rainbow of colours. They do not have any horns (usually) and produce a lot of milk. The buttery, mild flavour of Icelandic cheese comes straight from cows that eat only clean, unadulterated food. Fewer than 30,000 cows live in the country today, and they are kept indoors for eight months of the year.



## NOT A PONY

Better to insult an Icelander's mother than to call the animal they are riding a 'pony'. By definition, ponies are smaller (under 14.2 hands), stockier and have shorter legs than horses. They also have a thicker coat, mane and tail. Though all of these characteristics of a pony apply to the Icelandic breed, it is still very much a horse. Some argue that its ancient genetic make-up is more horse than pony, others say it's all about semantics. Despite the 'neigh'-sayers of the international equestrian world, Icelanders remain the qualifying authority and they say horse. After 1,000 years without a word for 'pony', Icelandic invented one – *smáhestur* or 'small-horse' – but for the record, there are no *smáhestur* in Iceland, only *hestur.*

**Seals** It's hard not to see a seal in Iceland, as long as you know where to look. When not diving for fish and crustaceans, seals like to hang out on the rock skerries and low-lying islands around the coast, as well as the barren stretches of sand along some of Iceland's remote peninsulas. Seals can be equally curious and wary of humans and will slip underwater if you move too close. Better to sit and wait patiently in a spot known for seals – they will appear, either playfully swimming or sunning themselves on their sides.

The most common species in Iceland is the **harbour seal** (*Phoca vitulina*) or *landselur.* They can be any colour – brown, tan, grey, or white – with lighter under bellies and mottled backs (every seal has its own unique pattern of spots – like a thumbprint). They can weigh up to 100kg and are about 1.5m long. About 10,000 harbour seals remain in Iceland – one-third of the population of 30 years ago. Harbour seals are most abundant on the west and north coasts of Iceland, and Hvammstangi (see page 315) has established itself as a seal-watching centre. Less commonly seen is the **grey seal** (*Halichoerus grypus*) or *útselur* which is darker grey (with silvery spots) and a lot bigger (up to 200kg and 2.5m long) than the harbour seal. About 6,000 grey seals live in Iceland today, usually near unpopulated islands.

The easiest way to distinguish the two seals is by their Icelandic names. Although both species migrate for feeding and breeding, the *landselur* (harbour seal) sticks close to land, while the *útselur* (grey seal) spends more time out at sea. Also, look at their heads – harbour seals have the mug of a friendly dog, while grey seals have a longer snout with an upturned nose (their Latin name means 'hook-nose sea pig').

A number of rarer seal species are sometimes spotted in Icelandic waters in spring and summer. The **harp seal** (*Phoca groenlandica*) or *vöðuselur* is the easiest to identify, of medium size and often marbled white and black. The **ringed seal** (*Phoca hispida hispida*) or *hringanóri* is quite small with distinctive rings on its back (like leopard spots) and is most commonly spotted in Eyjafjörður. **Bearded** and **hooded seals** have been known to wander all the way to Iceland but are still considered exceptions.

Harbour and grey seals have inverse mating seasons – harbours give birth to a single pup in spring and greys do the same in the autumn. During pregnancy, the seals feed and fatten up a good deal, then quickly lose all the weight – a nursing cow burns up to 29,000 calories a day (!). The baby seals are absolutely adorable and start fending for themselves after just one month.

**Whales** In Iceland, you have a good chance of seeing a whale any time that you are on or near the water. Most whales arrive in May and leave by September or October. In summer, keep an eye on the fjords in the morning or evening and near islands, and watch for where the birds are feeding on fish stock. Down below there is likely to be a whale. Fourteen different species of whale have been spotted in the waters around Iceland, although only half of these are seen commonly. While the **narwhal** (*Monodon monoceros*) and **beluga whale** (*Delphinaptesrus leucas*) are still both listed for Iceland, they are extremely rare.

***Toothed whales*** Whales with teeth eat fish and larger sea animals. Unlike baleen whales, which tend to be either loners or travel in pairs, toothed whales tend to be much more communal, moving about and hunting in large pods. Iceland's dolphins and porpoises are the easiest animals to see leaping in the air, the most common of which is the **white-beaked dolphin** (*Lagenorhynchus albirostris*) or *hnyðingur.* Because they do not migrate and tend to stick close to shore, the white-beaked is a sure-fire sighting for whale-watching boats. The dolphins weigh around 300kg, measure about 3m, and tend to travel in pods of six–12 animals. The white-beaked is often confused with its close relative the **white-sided dolphin** (*Lagenorhynchus acutus*) or *leifturhnýðir*, although the latter is smaller (200kg; 2m) and the distinctive side marking of white and yellow stripes is unmistakable. White-sided dolphins outnumber the white-beaked by three to one, but both species are seen arching through the water along the southern and western shores of Iceland. The **harbour porpoise** (*Phocoena phocoena*) or *hnísa* is shy and elusive, and is the smallest of Iceland's whales (60kg; 1.5m). They are most easily identified by their small size, their dark-grey colouring, and the manner in which they swim just beneath the surface, barely exposing their dorsal fin and rarely leaping or arching like dolphins do. As their name suggests, they are frequent visitors to harbours, bays, and fjords.

Larger members of the dolphin family include the **longfin pilot whale** (*Globicephala melas*) or *grindhvalur*, which can grow up to 8m and weigh five tons. Unlike large whales, however, the pilot has its dorsal fin closer to the front, a very tiny fluke and long, slender front flippers. They also have an abrupt, rounded head. About 30,000 are meant to still swim along Iceland's southern coast, but this is the northernmost limit of their range. The **northern bottlenose whale** (*Hyperodon ampullatus*) or *norðsnjáldri* is about the same length (7–8m) as the pilot but weighs more – up to eight tons. They are a light grey or brown colour with a tiny dorsal fin and tiny front flippers. The distinctive 'bottlenose' resembles the beak of a dolphin, compounded by the exaggerated round bulge on its head. Bottlenose whales prefer very deep water and are therefore not frequently spotted.

The much larger **orca** (*Orcinus orca*) or *háhyrningur* – also known as the **killer whale** – is a prominent species in Iceland, with an estimated population of 5,000 but easily spotted as they travel and hunt for fish; typically herring. Tradition has marked the East Fjords (see page 405) as the most likely place to see orca, although in the summer months they have been spotted feeding on every coast in Iceland. Their appearance is unmistakable: sleek black bodies with distinctive white markings behind the eye and underbelly and a black, sharply angled dorsal fin that stands straight up (just under 2m high). They also bare their sharp, angled teeth. Orcas are the fastest whales in the world, swimming up to 50km/h. They are also highly communal animals. The **sperm whale** (*Physeter macrocephalus*) or *búrhvalur* is the largest of the toothed whales, at 18m long and weighing 50 tons. Sperm whales are fascinating on so many levels: they have the largest brain of any animal ever to have existed (over 7kg) and are the largest toothed predator on earth (humans need both hands just to hold one of their cone-shaped teeth). They are also the deepest-diving mammal, recorded to reach depths of 2,200m (over 7,000ft). Although many believe their name comes from their unmistakable shape (a big head and tiny tail), 'sperm' whale derives from the name given to the white, waxy substance extracted from the whale's head (*spermaceti*), once used to make pharmaceuticals and ointments. Although the world population of sperm whales is high, sightings in Iceland are considered fairly rare. Only about 1,200 sperm whales are known to swim here in the summer, and they spend a lot of time deep beneath the surface.

***Baleen whales*** Instead of teeth, baleen whales have long bony plates covered with fine hairs (baleen) that catch huge amounts of plankton, krill and other small marine life. When baleen whales feed, they often turn on their side, open their mouths and allow the food to gush in. The **minke whale** (*Balaenoptera acutorostrata*) or *hrefna* is one of the most common 'big' whales seen around

Iceland, either from a boat or the shore on every coast. The whales are curious and friendly and are known to prefer shallow waters, even to swim into fjords and along the sides of boats. They are easily identified by the white strips across their flippers, their greyish underbellies and the manner in which they arch their dorsal fin before diving. The small glimpse that most people catch represents only the lowest third of their backs. The Minke grows up to 11m in length, weighs up to ten tons and can live for up to 50 years. Their current population is estimated at 50,000. The **humpback whale** (*Megaptera novaeangliae*) *or hnúfubakur* is easy to identify because they do have a have a hump on their backs, along with a bony spine and very large paddle-shaped front flippers. Their skin is often covered with barnacles, which can attach themselves to the whales at birth. They grow up to 15m in length and weigh 35 tons so that when they breach (which is often), it makes quite a splash. Humpbacks are known to be extremely intelligent, with very large brains. Although their numbers in Iceland are quite small (fewer than 1,500), they are more commonly seen by whale-watching boats due to their inquisitive nature, and their affinity for swimming up fjords. They live for up to 90 years.

The **blue whale** (*Balaenoptera musculus*) or *steypireyður* is the largest animal to have ever lived on earth (considered larger than any of the dinosaurs). The largest specimen ever recorded was 33m in length and weighed nearly 200 tons, though most are considered to weigh around 170 tons (equal to 30 elephants). Blue whales also have a massive lung capacity of 5,000 litres which enables them to blow a water spout 9m high and makes them easily recognisable from afar. Another distinctive trait is that when they breathe, blues show much more of their body above the surface than do other species. Blue whales are bluish-grey and dappled with darker spots across their sides and backs. Their triangular-shaped heads have a distinct bony ridge from lip to blowhole, and their flippers are white underneath. Any blue whales seen in Iceland make up the larger of two north Atlantic groups, with an estimated population of 600. This group is believed to swim along the Mid-Atlantic Ridge to Iceland, where they feed during July and August. Nobody ever knows where they might pop up, but they have been known to feed for long periods in Breiðafjörður (see page 301). Because of their endangered status and small numbers, you should feel very fortunate if you happen to spot a blue.

The **fin whale** (*Balaenoptera physalus*) or *langreyður* is one of the fastest swimmers among whales, known to travel at speeds of up to 35km/h. Fins are also the only species of whale to show asymmetric colour patterns (dark on the left side and white on the right). They are also the second-largest species of whale after the blue. They grow up to 25m in length, weigh up to 80 tons and live to 100 years. A fairly optimistic estimate claims that around 10,000 fin whales still pass through Icelandic waters in summer, though the world population is classified as endangered.

**Sei whales** (*Balaenoptera borealis*) or *sandreyður* are quite elusive, preferring deep, open waters. They are also harder to identify, since they closely resemble the minke whale. Sei are darker and a lot bigger – up to 20m in length and weighing up to 30 tons. *Sei* is the Norwegian word for 'pollock', a fish that would arrive in Norway in the same season as the whale, even though the sei eats plankton and krill and not fish. Fewer than 8,000 sei are known to summer off the coast of Iceland, about one-fifth of the world's remaining population. They are most commonly seen in the west beyond Snæfellsness and the West Fjords. The sei is still a targeted species for modern-day whalers and classified as endangered. Their natural life expectancy is 80 years.

***Whaling versus whale-watching*** Ever since settlement, Icelanders have used whales for food, light, and making tools. A 13th-century instruction manual depicts the harpooning and butchering of a whale. Still, for centuries the history of 'whaling' in Iceland was limited to taking advantage of beached or stranded whales. The meat, fat, oil and bones were perceived as a great fortune – in Icelandic, the modern word for 'jackpot' is *hvalreki*, or 'beached whale'. Thus, whale meat was eaten rarely and on special occasions. Large-scale commercial whaling only came about in the late 19th century and Icelanders benefited little. Tens of thousands of whales were taken during this 'Moby Dick' era, but mainly by Norwegian whaling crews under a royal Danish mandate. In 1915, the Althing banned whaling off the coast of Iceland. During the 1930s–1980s, a single Icelandic whaling operation killed an average of 400 whales per year, both for home consumption and for export to Norway and Japan. In 1986, the International Whaling Commission (IWC) banned commercial whaling in the same year that environmental activists sabotaged and sank two Icelandic whaling ships in Reykjavík harbour. Iceland finally agreed to stop whaling in 1990, but Iceland left the IWC two years later, only to return a decade later stating its intent to resume whaling for 'scientific purposes'. This research began in 2003, under the guise of trying to determine how much of Iceland's fish stock was being consumed by whales. Then, in 2006, licences were issued for commercial whaling, much to the chagrin of the international community. *Démarches* and protests aside, an Icelandic whaling ship killed a fin whale in October 2006. In 2007, licences were issued to kill another 40 whales.

### FREE WILLY

In 1979, when he was just two years old, a young orca (or killer whale) was captured in Iceland and sold to a small aquarium near Hafnarfjörður. The Save the Whales movement had sparked a public fascination for the 'playful' black-and-white creatures – the Icelandic whale was bought by a marina in Niagara Falls where he lived cooped up in a warehouse for two years. He was later resold to a theme park in Mexico City and christened with the Japanese name Keiko, or 'lucky one'. Art reflects life, and in 1993 the orca was typecast as the star in *Free Willy*, an American blockbuster film about a whale trapped in a cruel marina whose only hope is the young boy who eventually frees him.

The anthropomorphic killer whale gained such a following among children (and parents) that two more sequels and a TV series followed before public opinion wondered aloud: why not 'free willy'? Bake sales were baked, money was raised, and Keiko was purchased and brought to Oregon (by UPS) to recover from his long ordeal in Mexico. Two years later, Keiko was flown in a hefty US air force C-17 transport plane to the Keflavík NATO base and ferried to his new home in a fjord of the Westmann Islands (see page 228).

In 2002, after four years of training to survive in the wild, Keiko was released. In less than a week, he swam 870 miles (1,400km) to the west coast of Norway where he began seeking out humans and playing with them in the water. The whale was too acclimatised to humans and attempts were made to isolate him from the public. Sadly, Keiko died suddenly of pneumonia in 2003. He was buried in the middle of the night on a rocky beach in Norway, but Icelanders still claim him as their own.

While a few Icelandic traditionalists hold out for the right to kill whales, a number of entrepreneurs have started up successful whale-watching ventures. Today, large-scale tours run out of Olafsvík (see page 270) in Breiðafjörður, Húsavík in Skjálfandi (see page 377), Reykjavík, and off the Reykjanes coast at Reykjanesbær (see page 203). These companies are severely disappointed in the recent return to commercial whaling and are active in Icelandic politics to bring it to an end. The battle is not likely to end any time soon. Most Icelanders are upset about the public relations disaster created by whaling, but in their own homes, they are not above serving whale meat now and again. Tourists do play an important role however, and should be discouraged from consuming whale products.

# 4

# Practical Information

## WHEN TO VISIT

You can visit Iceland at any time of year and have a wonderful time, but what kind of experience you have depends a lot on when you go. A trip to Iceland in July versus a trip to Iceland in December feels like two different countries. Summertime allows you the freedom to go almost anywhere in the country, to hike outdoors, to stay up all night, and to experience Iceland's tourist industry in its prime. Best of all is summer, when all the animals (especially birds) are out in full force, as well as all the flowers. The landscapes glow bright green and Iceland feels like an undiscovered Eden.

Come winter, everything in Iceland turns white, diverting your eyes to the bright wooden houses and the subtle changes in the sky. The weather may or may not be treacherous, but where you go and what you can do is more limited. You can, however, ride horses in the snow, ski and snowmobile, see the Northern Lights at their best, soak in hot springs whilst thumbing your nose at the cold, and experience Iceland at its iciest.

For travellers, the main difficulty is the way in which Iceland has developed into a seasonal destination. Hotels, restaurants, museums, airlines, and tour operators try to cram all their profits into a six-week summertime blitz. That's why the summer is always booked solid and why everything costs twice as much. Don't buy into that mindset and you'll feel liberated. Rather, plan your trip based on what it is you want to do. If you want to hike glaciers, go early (April/May) or late (October) when the ice is firm and less prone to crevasses. If you want to see puffins *en masse*, then go in July; if you want to see their puffin chicks, then go in August. If you want to ride in the sheep roundup, go in mid-September. If you want to witness the Northern Lights, go in November; if you want to test the theory that limited

### SUNRISE, SUNSET

Take daylight into consideration when planning a trip in Iceland. Around the time of the winter and summer solstices, a few hundred kilometres north or south make a significant difference. The following hours of daylight are for Reykjavík:

| Season | Sunrise | Sunset |
|---|---|---|
| 1 January | 11.20 | 15.45 |
| 1 April | 06.45 | 20.20 |
| 1 July | 03.05 | midnight |
| 1 October | 07.30 | 19.00 |

daylight affects mood, then try late December, and if you want to conserve your cash, go in February. The wind blows all year round.

Of course, if you are plotting an epic journey all around Iceland, it is best to travel in summer just because you will see so much more. In winter, a lot of rural roads are closed and most of the tourist industry shuts down (though ferries, planes, and buses still run). On the flip side, don't try planning your trip for 'when it's warm and sunny'. Rarely is Iceland both of these things at once. In fact, Iceland never gets warm – only 'pleasant'. Sunny days happen often enough, but no Icelander has ever won any money betting on it.

Nothing beats the glory of Iceland in July, but besides the obvious, my favourite time to visit is early October. All the tourists are gone, the temperature is still not that cold (around 5°C), you still get a full day of sunlight, hiking is still viable and some tourist amenities are still open. Luckily, even in the high season of July–August, there are only a few spots where the crowds are almost unbearable (namely the Golden Circle, Reykjavík, and the Blue Lagoon). In relative terms, the hustle is nothing compared with back home, but you probably didn't come to Iceland to feel jostled. Step away from the obvious and all that disappears.

## HIGHLIGHTS

**NATIONAL PARKS AND NATURE RESERVES** Iceland has four official national parks: **Thingvellir** (see page 213) is the most historic and nothing at all like the frozen volcano of **Snæfellsjökull** (see page 265), the dramatic gorges of **Jökulsárgljúfur** (see page 383) and the great glaciers of **Skaftafell** (see page 422). Of Iceland's many nature reserves, **Mývatn** (see page 366) offers pure serenity and **Askja** (see page 436) the volcanic wilderness, **Ingólfshöfði** (see page 427) is steeped in historical meaning and a gorgeous bit of seashore, **Hornstrandir** (see page 309) is Iceland at its most extreme, and the lakes and rivers of **Vatnsfjörður** (see page 299) are stunning.

**ISLANDS** Every one of Iceland's offshore islands is a unique gem. To strand yourself on some poetic isle, consider the volcanic **Westmann Islands** (see page 228), the windswept cliffs of **Grímsey** (see page 355), or the history of tiny **Flatey** (see page 302). For romantic day trips, visit the homestead on **Vigur** (see page 286), the grassy hills of **Papey** (see page 415), easy-access **Hrísey** (see page 330) or hard-to-get-to **Drangey** (see page 321).

**FJORDS** Picking fjords is like picking perfume – it's very personal. A few favourites include the now-forgotten **Hvalfjörður** (see page 254), the secluded channel of **Arnarfjörður** (see page 291), and Iceland's longest fjord, **Eyjafjörður** (see page 331).

**GEOTHERMAL SPOTS** Besides the well-known **Geysir** (see page 223), visit the scorched-earth landscape of **Námaskarð** (see page 376), the hot pools and natural steam jets of **Hveravellir** (see page 434), 'smoky' **Reykjanes** (see page 201), and the largest springs in Iceland at **Deildartunguhver** (see page 262).

**TOWNS** Obviously **Reykjavík** (see page 123) is the must-see capital and the most vibrant urban space in Iceland. The other 'big city' of **Akureyri** (see page 332) is artistic and quirky, and isolated **Ísafjörður** (see page 281) is an architectural treasure chest. For obscure Icelandic fishing villages with that something special, visit **Grundarfjörður** (see page 271), **Siglufjörður** (see page 325), **Eskifjörður** (see page 410), **Djúpivogur** (see page 413), or **Suðureyri** (see page 288).

**HIKING** The most touted trails for their volcanic/glacial terrain include **Landmannalaugar** (see page 241) and **Thórsmörk** (see page 247), and both deserve the fame. All the national parks offer prime trekking, especially **Skaftafell** (see page 422) and **Snæfellsjökull** (see page 265). **Tröllaskagi** (see page 324) in the north is fantastic climbing country. For wanderings with less mountain and more mystique, walk the under-appreciated lava fields of **Reykjanes** (see page 201), or the landscapes around Mývatn (see page 366). To really step off the beaten track, venture into **Í Fjörðum** (see page 354), **Borgarfjörður eystri** (see page 405), and **Lönsöræfi** (see page 420). Though it's not easy, the hiking in **Hornstrandir** (see page 309) is in a league of its own.

**WILDLIFE** For seals, visit **Hvammstangi** (see page 315), for whales, visit **Húsavík** (see page 377) or **Ólafsvík** (see page 270), for reindeer, visit **Snæfell** (see page 404), and for Arctic fox, try **Hornstrandir** (see page 309) or **Skaftafell** (see page 422). The birds are everywhere (see *Chapter 3, Birds,* page 52), but for mind-blowing birdwatching, you must visit the cliffs at **Látrabjarg** (see page 296).

**COMMON MISTAKES** On a map of the world, Iceland looks so small. When you finally get there and stand at the edge of a lava field, or a glacier, or a fjord, the country feels endless. There are a lot of beautiful, empty spaces and infinite journeys to be had, so take your time. Iceland is not a good country for rushing. In a way, Iceland has become a victim of its own marketing – so many Europeans and Americans now view the country as a stopover to the other side of the Atlantic. Iceland is a great country in that you can be there for just 24 hours and have an amazing time, but that's really just an appetiser.

The most common blasphemy occurs when misguided travellers attempt to 'do' Iceland by taking five or six days to drive around the ring road. Sure it can be done (you can drive it in two days if you want), but it's an exercise in self-torture. Every day you'll be trying to get to the next place, instead of stopping to see the glacier up close, or getting out for a better look at the puffins, or enjoying some fishing village or taking a walk on the sand. Everything gets sacrificed in the name of 'getting there' and it feels like watching your favourite movie in fast-forward. If your time is limited, just pick one or two regions and focus on those environs, otherwise you'll spend all your precious time driving. To complete the ring road in seven–ten days, plan on at least three to four hours of driving per day. Also note that flying to one destination and renting a car from there makes sense, costs the same, and saves you a lot of time.

In that same vein is the manner in which most tour operators treat every destination as a day trip out of Reykjavík. That makes life easier for them, but you'll end up wasting your time travelling back and forth to Reykjavík every day. A rule of thumb is that if it's more than two hours outside the capital, it deserves an overnight stay.

## SUGGESTED ITINERARIES

Iceland is a great place for either independent or pre-planned itineraries, but it's not wise to have a really tight schedule or be fixated on a single plan. Unexpected fog can erase the view that you hoped to see on Day 3 and a sudden storm might force you indoors. As long as you're flexible, everything will be fine. The suggested itineraries are simply guidelines that might help you think about what you want to see and do.

## Three days

### *From Reykjavík*

**Generic** Reykjavík–Golden Circle (Thingvellir, Gullfoss, Geysir)–Blue Lagoon
**Lava rocks** Keflavík–Reykjanes Peninsula
**Hot springs** Hveragerdí–Laugarvatn–Reykjavík pools–Blue Lagoon
**Nature fix** Snæfellsnes (2 nights)

### *From Akureyri*

**City break** Akureyri (2 nights)
**Whirlwind** Akureyri–Mývatn–Húsavík
**Nature fix** Jökulsárgljúfur (2 nights)
**Arctic break** Grímsey (2 nights)

## One week

**Town and country** Westmann Islands (2 nights)–Thjórsárdalur (2 nights)–Reykjavík (2 nights)
**The west** Reykjavík–Borg–Reykholt/Húsafell–Stykkishólmur–Grundarfjörður–Snæfellsnes

### *Nature*

**Classic trekking** Laugavegurinn (Landmannalaugar–Thórsmörk) (5 nights + 1 night recovery in Reykjavík)
**Mountain climber** Mt Esja (Reykjavík)–Mt Hekla–Mt Hvannadalshnjúkur–Mt Herðubreið (via East Fjords)

### *Fly/drive*

**The north** Fly to Akureyri–Mývatn–Jökulsárgljúfur–Húsavík
**West Fjords** Fly to Ísafjörður–Hornstrandir (boat)–Látrabjarg–Flókalundur
**East Fjords** Fly to Egilsstaðir–East Fjords (4 nights)–Höfn (1 night)–Reykjavík
**Interior** Fly to Akureyri–drive the Kjölur route via Hveravellir and Gullfoss to Reykjavík
**Ice** Fly to Höfn–Vatnajökull, Jökulsárlón, Skaftafell–drive to Skógar (Mýrdalsjökull)–Reykjavík

## Ten days

**Classic ring road** Reykjavík–Borgarnes–Skagafjörður–Akureyri–Mývatn–Egilsstaðir–Höfn (Vatnajökull)–Skógar–Golden Circle–Reykjavík
**Far from the madding crowd** Keflavík–Hveravellir (Kjölur route)–Siglufjörður–Öxarfjörður–Langanes–Eskifjörður–Lönsöræfi–Hvolsvöllur–Krýsuvík

## Two weeks

### *National parks of Iceland (by bus or car, camping or guesthouses)*

Reykjavík (1 night), Snæfellsjökull (2 nights), Akureyri (travel) (1 night), Mývatn (2 nights), Jökulsárgljúfur (2 nights), East Fjords (travel) (1 night), Skaftafell (2 nights), Thingvellir (1 night), Reykjavík (1 night)

***From the ferry (a fair amount of driving in parts)*** Möðrudalur (1 night) via Seyðisfjörður and Egilsstaðir, Mývatn (2 nights) (via Dettifoss), Akureyri (1 night), Varmahlíð (1 night), Stykkishólmur (1 night), Snæfellsjökull (1 night), Reykjavík (2 nights), south coast (Vík, Skógar, or Kirkjubæjarklaustur) (1 night), Skaftafell (1 night), Djúpivogur (1 night), Seyðisfjörður (1 night)

***Go west*** Reykjavík (1 night), Borg (1 night), Snæfellsjökull (2 nights), Stykkishólmur (take Breiðafjörður ferry) (1 night), Flatey (1 night), Flókalundur (1 night), Látrabjarg (1 night), Thingeyri (1 night), Ísafjörður (2 nights), Hólmavík (1 night), Brú (1 night), return via Reykjavík

### Three weeks

**Week 1** Reykjavík–Golden Circle–south–Skaftafell–East Fjords
**Week 2** Mývatn/Jökulsárgljúfur–Akureyri–Grímsey–Hólar/Sauðárkrókur
**Week 3** Hvamsstangi–west Iceland–Reykjavík

### *4x4 tour – interior*

**Week 1** Reykjavík–Thórsmörk–Landmannalaugar
**Week 2** Sprengisandur–Vatnajökull–Askja–Goðafoss
**Week 3** Varmahlíð–Kjölur route–Reykjavík

***The ultimate bird tour (three weeks' minimum, best in July)*** Reykjanes–Viðey Island (Reykjavík)–Breiðafjörður–Látrabjarg–Hornstrandir–Grímsey–Mývatn–Langanes–Papey–Ingólfshöfði–Westmann Islands

### One month

### *Grand tour*

**Week 1** Reykjavík–Borgarnes–Snæfellsnes Peninsula–Breiðafjörður–West Fjords
**Week 2** Látrabjarg–Ísafjörður–Hólmavík–Skagafjörður–Siglufjörður–Akureyri
**Week 3** Húsavík–Mývatn–Jökulsárgljúfur–Melrakkaslétta–Vopnafjörður
**Week 4** East Fjords–Vatnajökull–Westmann Islands–Golden Circle–Reykjavík

**24 hours** Pick up a car at Keflavík but go the opposite way to everyone else (Route 44), stopping to see everything along the southwest coast of Reykjanes, going past the lighthouse and then on to Grindavík. Have a morning soak at the Blue Lagoon, then head to Reykjavík (Route 41), have a bite to eat and take about two hours to see the sights. Then drive to Mosfellsbær, climb Mt Esja, drive all the way around Hvalfjörður but take the tunnel back. Spend the evening in Reykjavík, but spend the night in a guesthouse outside the city (perhaps in Reykjanes), drop off your car at the airport and check in to your flight. From experience, I can say that it's possible to drive the five hours' round trip from Keflavík to climb Mt Hekla and go swimming and make your next flight, but I wouldn't recommend it.

## TOURIST INFORMATION

### UK

**Iceland Tourist Information Bureau** Embassy of Iceland, 2a Hans St, London SW1X 0JE; ☎ +44 (0)20 7259 3999, 020 8391 4888; e icemb.london@utn.stjr.is; www.visiticeland.com

### DENMARK

**Islands Turistråd** Strandgade 89, Opgang C, 2nd Floor, Copenhagen; ☎ +45 32 833 741; e scandinavia@icetourist.is; www.visiticeland.com

### GERMANY

**Isländishces Fremdenverkehsamt** Frankfurterstrasse 181, D-63263 Neu-Isenburg; ☎ +49 6102 254 388; e info@icetourist.de; www.visiticeland.com

## ICELAND

**Ferðalag Íslands** Lækjargata 3; Reykjavík; ☎ +354 535 5500; e info@icetourist.is; www.visiticeland.com

## USA

**Icelandic Tourist Board** 655 3rd Av, New York, NY 10017; ☎ +1 212 885 9700; e usa@icetourist.is; www.goiceland.com

# TOUR OPERATORS

## UK

**Discover the World** Arctic Hse, 8 Bolters Lane, Banstead, Surrey SM7 2AR; ☎ 01737 218 800; e travel@discover-the-world.co.uk; www.discover-the-world.co.uk/iceland. The world's leading Iceland specialist tour operator offering both independent & escorted holidays & a full tailor-made service. They also run www.icelandadventuretours.co.uk, a definitive collection of active day tours & multi-day adventures available in Iceland, from white-water rafting to glacier hiking, snowmobile safaris to snorkelling adventures.
**Exodus Travel** Grange Mills, Weir Rd, London SW12 ONE; ☎ 020 8675 5550; e info@exodus.co.uk; www.exodus.co.uk. A variety of select tours to Iceland.
**Explore Travel** Nelson Hse, 55 Victoria Rd, Farnborough, Hampshire GU14 7PA; ☎ 0870 333 4001; e res@explore.co.uk; www.explore.co.uk. Package family tours.
**Original Travel** Crombie Mews, 11A Abercrombie St, London SW11 2JB; ☎ 020 7978 7333; e ask@originaltravel.co.uk; www.originaltravel.co.uk. Truly original tours, mostly to west Iceland.
**Regent Holidays** Regent Hse, 31A High St, Shanklin, Isle of Wight PO37 6JW; ☎ 0845 277 3301/2; e icelanddept@regent-holidays.co.uk; www.regent-holidays.co.uk. Iceland specialist, with over 30 years of experience.
**Voyages Jules Verne** 21 Dorset Sq, London NW1 6QG; ☎ 0845 166 7003; e sales@vjv.co.uk; www.vjv.co.uk. Journeys all around Iceland.
**Yes Travel** 1 High St, March, Cambridgeshire PE15 9JA; ☎ 01778 424499; e vip@yes-travel.com; www.yes-travel.com. Iceland specialist.

## NORTH AMERICA

**Adventure Women, Inc** 300 Running Horse Trail; Bozeman, MT 59715, USA; toll free ☎ +1 800 804 8686; e advwomwn@aol.com; www.adventurewomen.com. Women-only tours around Iceland.
**Borton Overseas** 5412 Lyndale Av South, Minneapolis, MN 55419, USA; ☎ +1 800 843 0602; e ino@bortonoverseas.com; www.bortonoverseas.com. A plethora of upmarket package tours, plus other parts of Scandinavia.
**Brekke Tours** 802 North 43rd St, Grand Forks, ND 58203, USA; ☎ +1 701 772 8999; e tours@brekketours.com; www.brekketours.com. Short stopover tours in Iceland to & from Scandinavia.
**Discover British Isles & Europe Travel** 7447 Egan Drive, Suite 300, Savage, MN 55378, USA; ☎ +1 952 226 9132; e info@discoverbritishtravel.com; www.discoverbritishtravel.com. 1–2-week group & self-drive package tours.
**Icelandair Holidays** 5950 Symphony Woods Rd, Suite 410, Columbia, MD 21044, USA; toll free ☎ +1 800 779 2899; e holidays@icelandair.is; www.icelandair.is. All-inclusive land tours with flights.
**Iceland Experience Travel** 333, Chicago, IL 60601, USA; ☎ +1 312 263 0333; The Great Canadian Travel Company 158 Fort St, Winnipeg, MB R3C 1C9, Canada; ☎ +1 204 949 0199; toll free ☎ +1 800 661 3830; e info@icelandexperience.com; www.greatcanadiantravel.com/tours/iceland. Big travel company specialising in arranging a diverse number of package or independent tours.
**Iceland Saga Travel** 3 Freedom Sq, Nantucket, MA 02554, USA; ☎ +1 508 825 9292; e icelandst@aol.com; www.icelandsagatravel.com. Diverse, 1–2-week escorted tours all year round.
**Nordic Saga Travel** 320 Dayton St, Suite 240, Edmonds, WA 98020, USA; ☎ +1 425 673 4800; e NSTours@nordicsaga.com; www.nordicsaga.com. Escorted & independent tours in Iceland as well as some cruises.

**IN ICELAND** Activity and region-specific tour operators are listed under the appropriate headings or chapters. The following are nationwide tour operators based in Iceland.

**Arctic Rafting** Reykjavík, Laugavegur 11; ☎ 562 7000; e info@arcticrafting.is; www.arcticrafting.is. Adventure ecotourism in Iceland.
**Eco-logy** Reykjavík, Torfufell 23; ☎ 587 7335; e info@www.eco-logy.com; www.eco-logy.com/customized-botanical-tours.html Short, botanical tours of Iceland.
**Guðmundur Jónasson Travel** Reykjavík, Borgartún 34; ☎ 511 1515; e gjtravel@gjtravel.is; www.gjtravel.is. Unique overland tours with a long-standing reputation.
**HL Adventure** Reykjavík, Lækjargata 2; ☎ 568 3030; e info@hl.is; www.hl.is. Adventure travel of all sorts in the highlands.
**Iceland Excursions** Reykjavík, Höfðatún 12; ☎ 540 1313; e iea@iea.is; www.icelandexcrsions.is. Day tours from the capital in buses & jeeps.
**Iceland Express** Reykjavík, Síðumúla; ☎ 570 2700; e sales@icelandexpresstours.com; www.icelandexpresstours.com. Quick tours (3–7 days) of nature & history sites.
**Iceland on Track** Kópavogur, Grófarsmári 18; m 899 5438; e icelandontrack@icelandontrack.is; www.icelandontrack.is. Short & long 4x4 tours of Iceland.
**Iceland Travel** Reykjavík, Skútuvogur 13A; ☎ 585 4300; e info@icelandtotal.com; www.icelandtotal.com. Self-drive packages, coach tours, & activity organisers.
**Ísafold Travel** Garðabær, Suðurhraun 2B; ☎ 544 8866; e info@isafoldtravel.is; www.isafoldtravel.is. Intimate travel to less well-known places with small groups – a winning combination.
**Luxury Adventures** Kópavogur; ☎ 577 1155; e info@lux.is; www.lux.is. High-end, personal tours all around Iceland.
**Mountain Taxi** Hafnarfjörður, Trönuhraun 7; ☎ 544 5252; e info@mountaintaxi.is; www.mountaintaxi.is. Adventure tours in the remote highlands & custom-built expeditions in super jeeps.
**Nature Explorer** Reykjavík, Skalagerði 17; ☎ 691 3900; e info@NatureExplorer.is; www.NatureExplorer.is. Iceland's natural wonders by 4x4 or mountain bike.
**Nonni Travel** Akureyri, Brekkugata 5; ☎ 461 1841; e nonni@nonnitravel.is; www.nonnitravel.is. Conservation-focused tours in Iceland, Greenland & the Faroe Islands. Great for off-season travel.
**Nordic Visitor** Reykjavík, Austurstræti 17; ☎ 511 2442; e Iceland@nordicvisitor.com; www.nordicvisitor.com. Comprehensive incoming tour operator offering just about everything.
**Tour Iceland** Reykjavík, Frostaskjol; ☎ 517 8290; e tour@tour.is; www.tour.is. A wide range of spa, adventure, & nature tours along with sensible self-drive packages.
**Vikingaslóðir** Reykjavík, Fannafold 165; ☎ 567 2288; e vikingaslodir@islandia.is; www.vikingaslodir.is. 'Viking trails': invigorating, 1–2-week tours of the whole country.

## SPECIALIST ACTIVITIES

### Biking

**Freewheeling Adventures** 2070 Hwy 329, RR #1, Hubbards, Nova Scotia B0J 1T0, Canada; ☎ +1 902 857 3600; toll free ☎ +1 800 672 0775; e bicycle@freewheeling.ca; www.freewheeling.ca
**Pack & Pedal Europe, Inc** RR 1 Box 35A, Springville, PA 18844-9578, USA; ☎ +1 570 965 2064; e hennie@tripsite.com; www.tripsite.com

### Cruises

**P&O Cruises** Richmond Hse, Terminus Terrace, Southampton SO14 3PN, UK; ☎ 0845 678 0014; e reservations@pocruises.com; www.pocruises.com. Cruises to Iceland from Britain, Ireland, & Norway.
**Polar Star Expeditions** PO Box 9510 A, Halifax, Nova Scotia B3K 5S3, Canada; ☎ +1 902 423 7389; e info@polarstarexpeditions.com; www.polarstarexpeditions.com. Round-the-world cruise with annual ports in Iceland.

**Voyages of Discovery** Lynnem Hse, 1 Victoria Way, Burgess Hill, West Sussex RH15 9NF, UK; ☎ 01444 462150; e info@voyagesofdiscovery.com; www.voyagesofdiscovery.com. Luxury Arctic cruises to Iceland.

## RED TAPE

Icelanders hate bureaucracy as much as the rest of us. Plus, there aren't enough people in Iceland to man that many desks or warrant that much paper. Even so, they do make a noble attempt at keeping up appearances in the officiousness department. Be honest, straightforward and law-abiding and you won't get into trouble.

**VISAS AND PASSPORTS** All travellers must have a valid passport that expires three months after the intended date of departure. Visitors from the UK, Ireland, the USA, Canada, Australia and New Zealand who are travelling on holiday or business for 90 days or less do not require a visa. For longer periods, you must apply for a visa with the Icelandic Directorate of Immigration (*www.utl.is*). Visas are issued to individuals as tourists, for family visits, official business, commercial business and as students.

Iceland is part of the Schengen Agreement, which means visitors from Schengen countries do not require a passport, and those visitors requiring a visa must apply for a Schengen visa. In countries without an Icelandic embassy or consulate, visa applications are typically accepted at the embassies of Denmark or Norway. For the latest information and for any questions, check out the website for Iceland's Ministry of Foreign Affairs (*www.mfa.is*).

**CUSTOMS** Clearing Icelandic customs is a breeze compared with most countries, unless you're an Icelander who goes shopping overseas. The main contraband concern of Iceland is people evading the hefty VAT by bringing in consumer goods from abroad. You can bring as much currency in and out of Iceland as you like, but anything that's worth a lot of money is a no-no. Because Iceland is so expensive, many people arrive with a large amount of food from home. The official new rule is 3kg of 'consumable food' per person not to exceed 13,000ISK (about US$200) in value. The rule tends to be more enforced with travellers arriving by ferry than by air. All meat, unpasteurised dairy, and raw-egg products will be confiscated. Naturally, all birds and bird products are prohibited, but the old rocks you pick up on the beach are legal souvenirs (just not stalagmites!). Note that Iceland has a zero-tolerance policy on drugs, and customs officers use drug-sniffing dogs at all entry points. Travellers bringing cars into the country are exempt from paying duty unless you fail to take the car back out of the country, if you choose to stay beyond three months, or if you get caught selling the car. For additional information, contact the Directorate of Customs (*Tollstjórinn; Reykjavík, Tryggvagata 19;* ☎ *560 0300;* e *info@tollur.is; www.tollur.is*).

## EMBASSIES AND CONSULATES

**Australia** (see China)
**Austria** Botschaft von Island Naglergasse 2/3/8 1010 Vienna; ☎ +43 1 533 2771; e emb.vienna@mfa.is; www.iceland.org/at
**Belgium** Ambassade van Ijsland, Schumanplein 11; 1040 Brussels; ☎ +32 02 238 5000; e emb.brussels@mfa.is; www.iceland.org/be
**Canada** Embassy of Iceland, 360 Albert St, Suite 710, Ottawa, ON K1R 7X7; ☎ +1 613 482 1944; e emb.ottawa@mfa.is; www.iceland.

org/ca; Consulate General of Iceland, Winnipeg, One Wellington Crescent, Suite 100, Winnipeg, Manitoba R3M 3Z2; ☎ +1 204 284 1535; e icecon.winnipeg@utn.stjr.is; www.iceland.org/ca/win

**China** Embassy of Iceland, Landmark Tower 1, #802, No 8 Dongsanhuan Bei Lu, 100004 Beijing; ☎ +86 10 6590 7795; e emb.beijing@mfa.is; www.iceland.org/cn

**Denmark** Islands Ambassade, Strandgade 89, DK-1401 Copenhagen; ☎ +45 3318 1050; e icemb.coph@utn.stjr.is; www.iceland.org/dk

**Faroe Islands** Icelandic Consul, Svabasgøta 31, Tórshavn; ☎ +298 301 100; e info@faroeyard.fo; www.iceland.org/fo

**Finland** Islannin suurlähetystö, Pohjoisesplanadi 27 C, FI-00100 Helsinki; ☎ +358 9 612 2460; e emb.helsinki@mfa.is; www.iceland.org/fi

**France** Ambassade d'Islande, 8 Av Kléber, 75116 Paris; ☎ +33 1 44 17 32 85; e emb.paris@mfa.is; www.iceland.org/fr

**Germany** Botschaft der Republik Island; Rauchstrasse 1, 10787 Berlin; ☎ +49 0 30 5050 4000; e emb.berlin@mfa.is; www.iceland.org/de

**Italy** Permanent Mission of Iceland in Rome, Via di San Saba, No 12, 7th Floor, 00153 Rome; ☎ +39 06 5725 0509; e emb.rome@mfa.is; www.iceland.org/it

**Japan** Embassy of Iceland, 4-18-26 Takanawa, Minato-ku, Tokyo 108-0074; ☎ +81 03 3447 1944; e emb.tokyo@mfa.is; www.iceland.org/jp Norway Islands Ambassade, Stortingsgata 30, NO-0244 Oslo; ☎ +47 2323 7530; e emb.oslo@mfa.is; www.iceland.org/no

**Poland** (see Germany)

**South Africa** Embassy of Iceland, Parioli Office Park, Phase II, Block A2, Pretoria; ☎ +27 0 12 342 5885; e emb.pretoria@mfa.is; www.iceland.org/mo

**Spain** (see France)

**Sweden** Islands Ambassad, Kommendörsgatan 35, SE-114 58 Stockholm; ☎ +46 0 8 442 8300; e emb.stockholm@mfa.is; www.iceland.org/se

**UK** Embassy of Iceland, 2A Hans St, London SW1X 0JE; ☎ +44 20 7259 3999; e icemb.london@utn.stjr.is; www.iceland.org/uk

**USA** Embassy of Iceland, 1156 15th St, NW, Suite 1200, Washington, DC 20005-1704; ☎ +1 202 265 6653; e emb.washington@mfa.is; www.iceland.org/us; Consulate General of Iceland, 800 Third Av, 36th Floor, New York, NY 10022; ☎ +1 212 593 2700; e icecon.ny@utn.stjr.is; www.iceland.org/us/nyc

## GETTING THERE AND AWAY

**BY AIR** Flying to Iceland is the simplest and cheapest part of the journey. Few travellers realise that **Icelandair** (*www.icelandair.com*) is the longest-running transatlantic airline still in operation today (since 1937). With Keflavík as its hub, Icelandair services 24 destinations in North America (Boston, Halifax, Minneapolis, New York, Orlando, San Francisco, Seattle and Washington, DC) and Europe (London Heathrow, Glasgow, Manchester, Paris, Barcelona, Madrid, Milan, Munich, Frankfurt, Berlin, Copenhagen, Oslo, Bergen, Gothenburg, Stockholm and Helsinki). Flights from North America typically arrive in the early morning, while flights from Europe tend to arrive in the mid afternoon, though increased trips in high season may not follow that pattern. From Europe, the flight is about two–three hours; from the east coast of North America the flight lasts four–five hours.

Iceland's position in the middle of transatlantic routes started a trend of stopping over en route between Europe and North America. The airline typically offered bargain tickets to passengers crossing the entire ocean, while flights to and from Iceland were much more costly. Thankfully, that logic is changing now as more travellers focus solely on Iceland as their destination. One-way tickets are now available and prices are becoming even more competitive. For many, the seasonal change in prices is a deciding factor when they travel to Iceland. In winter and off season, it is possible to fly from either side of the Atlantic for as little as US$400 return. In summer, prices can jump up to well over US$1,000.

## THE LONG HAUL: RELOCATING TO ICELAND

*Eliza Reid*

Only 6% of Icelandic residents are foreign citizens. Compared with most countries, the figure is minuscule but as recently as 1996, the statistic was 1.9%. While many new arrivals land for seasonal work, there is a growing community of foreigners who come to the north Atlantic with longer-term goals. The bureaucracy for moving to Iceland has expanded in recent years and regulations on paperwork are changing. For the latest information, your first port of call should be the Icelandic Directorate of Immigration, (*510 5400; www.utl.is*).

**RESIDENCE AND WORK PERMITS** For a long-term stay, you'll need to start the process before landing at Keflavík Airport. Citizens of the other Nordic countries (Denmark, Norway, Sweden and Finland) can move to Iceland without a residence permit and find work as any Icelander would. Citizens of the EU/EEA can apply for a residence permit after they arrive in Iceland, but for everyone else, the process is more complicated. Non-EU/EEA citizens intending to move to Iceland must apply for a residence permit before entering the country. If you are coming to study or have a job offer, your institution/employer should help you with this. The residence permit allows you to apply for a work permit, which is linked to a particular employer for the first three years. After three years of residency in Iceland, you can apply for a green card that lets you seek employment in Iceland without restrictions. Immigrants are normally eligible for Icelandic citizenship if they have resided in the country for seven years and have met certain language requirements. Spouses of Icelandic citizens are eligible earlier.

**NOW WHAT?** After the various permits are stuck in your passport, the last vital ingredient to your status as a resident is the *kennitala*, or national ID number. This number is your key to everything from pension benefits to renting DVDs. To sign up, contact the National Registry (*Þjóðskra; 569 2950; e thjodskra@thjodskra.is; www.thjodskra.is*). You should also pay a visit to the Intercultural Centre (*AHUS; Hverfisgata 18; 530 9300; e ahus@ahus.is; www.ahus.is*) in Reykjavík. AHUS helps new arrivals in the country with legal advice, information on people's rights, translation services, and Icelandic classes. It runs a very informative website.

**TALAR ÞÚ ÍSLENSKU?** Virtually everyone in Iceland speaks passable English and it is quite possible to eke out a happy existence in the country without ever learning the difference between *pils* and *pylsa* (one's a skirt and one's a hot dog). Those who arrive on limited-term contracts are often not inclined to study the language, both for its complex grammar and its extremely limited use elsewhere in the world. However, those who make an effort find it pays off in terms of wider employment opportunities and integration into Icelandic society. Even if you mix up genders and decline verbs incorrectly, just giving it a shot will win you a lot of points with locals. To pick up the basics, buy a CD-Rom of the language or try a free online course (*www.icelandic.hi.is*). Once in Iceland, enrol on a course at the School of Continuing Education at the University of Iceland, or if you've got the

**Iceland Express** (*www.icelandexpress.com*) is Iceland's budget airline, offering daily low-cost flights between Keflavík and London Stansted (STN), along with a dozen more continental European destinations, typically to smaller, secondary

time, the university offers a three-year Bachelor of Arts degree in Icelandic for Foreigners (*Háskóli Íslands;* e *hi@hi.is; www.hi.is*). The other main school for Icelandic classes is Mímir (*www.mimir.is*), which offers several levels of instruction at various times throughout the year. Employees' unions or employers often pay the cost of language lessons.

**HOME SWEET HOME** Home ownership in Iceland is high and Icelanders usually try to get on the property ladder as soon as they can. The main challenge for finding a flat to let is the limited selection available. The best way to find out about places to let is through word of mouth or by looking in the newspapers. You can also pay a monthly fee to be sent the *Leigulistinn* list of rental properties (*www.leigulistinn.is*). For information on student housing with the University of Iceland, visit its website (*www.studentgardar.is*). The Intercultural Centre (AHUS) can provide basic information on how to apply for loans to buy a home.

**NINE TO FIVE** Iceland has a very low unemployment rate and it is usually fairly simple to find a job, although the high cost of living means many people hold two positions in order to pay the bills. Clearly those who can't speak Icelandic are more limited in their options, but employers who require a high degree of skill in some area like computer programming will not mind any linguistic limitations. Areas which have lower salaries or many vacancies, such as working at day cares or homes for the elderly, are often primarily staffed by foreigners. EEA citizens can visit the European Employment Portal (*www.eures.is*), for a list of jobs in Iceland which don't require Icelandic language skills. Unions are very influential in Iceland and have collective bargaining agreements, including minimum wages, with employers. The unions are also helpful resources for everything from filling out tax returns to access to summer cottages.

**SETTLING IN** Adapting to life in a new country is both challenging and thrilling. It goes without saying that the more effort you put into integrating and learning about the new culture, the more quickly you will feel at home. The key to successfully settling in the country is not comparing everything with 'back home'. Of course it's different – that's part of the point.

It's fairly easy to meet other foreigners in Iceland, often through Icelandic classes or clubs representing various countries. Developing social connections with Icelanders takes a little longer – this is a close-knit society where bonds are formed and maintained from a very early age. Still, locals are generally welcoming and hospitable. Aside from work, meet people by getting involved in other activities: join a gym, play a team sport, sing in a choir (there are many!) or volunteer. Staying busy also helps keep the winter blues away; one of the hardest things for any foreigner in Iceland is adjusting to the winter darkness and the island's general isolation. There are plenty of resources available to help you adjust happily and quickly to Icelandic life. Whatever your reason for moving to this northern island, and however long you stay, the cliché applies: the more you put into it the more you'll get out of it.

airports. Prices are cheap – about £100 each way (with taxes), and in summer, there are direct flights from Copenhagen (CPH) to other cities, like Akureyri. **British Airways** (*www.ba.com*) flies direct from London Gatwick (LGW) to Keflavík, and

**SAS** (*www.sas.com*) flies direct from Oslo (OSL) to Keflavík. Travellers can also fly to Iceland from the Faroe Islands or Greenland. **Air Iceland** (*www.airiceland.is*) offers a regular service to Tórshavn in the Faroe Islands, and to Kulusuk, Narsarsuaq, and Nuuk in Greenland.

**BY SEA** Nothing compares to catching your first glimpse of Iceland from the sea. The first Viking to spot Iceland sailed in to the East Fjords, and today the tradition continues. **Smyril Line** (*Broncksgata 37; Tórshavn, Faroe Islands; ☎ +298 345 900; e office@smyril-line.fo; www.smyril-line.fo*) is the Faroese shipping company that operates the ferry *Norröna* with a service to Iceland. Most travellers go by boat in order to bring their own caravan, car, 4x4, motorcycle, or bicycle. Taking your own vehicle to Iceland can save you a pile of money. Paying for passage and cabin space on a ferry, even with the option of an extra stay in the Faroe Islands, is still cheaper than renting something in Iceland. More importantly, travelling by ship is far more fun and exciting than flying. The gigantic *Norröna* feels more like a pleasure cruise than a ferry, and it's a great place to meet fellow travellers.

The *Norröna* bounces about the North Sea in an odd weekly circuit including the ports of Hanstholm (Denmark), Tórshavn (Faroe Islands), Bergen (Norway), Lerwick (Shetland Islands) and Seyðisfjörður (Iceland). It's a bit of a mind-juggle trying to figure it all out, but it suffices to say that a journey from Denmark to Iceland forces you to spend three days in the Faroe Islands (that's a good thing)..

From Britain, travelling to Iceland by ship can be cheaper than flying. At the time of writing, Smyril Lines was operating a direct summertime link from Scrabster (north Scotland) to Seyðisfjörður. If you plan it right, you can sail from Britain to Iceland in about 32 hours. Otherwise, getting to Iceland from Britain entails taking two different ferries, with stops in the Shetland and Faroe Islands. **North Link Ferries** (*Kiln Corner, Ayre Rd, Kirkwall KW15 1QX, Orkney; ☎ 0845 600 0449; e info@northlinkferries.co.uk; www.northlinkferries.co.uk*) sails once a day between Aberdeen, Scotland and Lerwick (about 12 hours) in the Shetland Islands. This is typically an overnight ferry with a midnight stop in Kirkwall, Orkney Islands. From Lerwick, passengers catch the *Norröna* from Lerwick to Tórshavn and then on to Seyðisfjörður. Outside the high summer season (especially for those in the south of Britain or western Europe), it's just as easy to drive to Denmark (via the Chunnel) and catch the ferry from Hanstholm. Plus, the winter fares are incredibly cheap.

**Cost** Like most ferries, prices are meant to add up. The Smyril Line has three separate pricing periods, the highest being in midsummer (late June to mid-August), when a return fare (car + two persons) from Denmark to Iceland runs to around US$1,350. A single individual with a motorcycle or bicycle is about half that, and if you're a traveller on foot, it's about US$550. From Scotland (Scrabster) to Iceland, high-season return fares run in the range of US$750 (car + two persons), US$400 for a motorcycle or bike, and US$325 for a foot passenger. Note that these prices are for couchettes in the very bottom of the ship, and any upgrades to a berth will tack on another US$200+ per person. Smyril Line also offers affordable package tours that include ferry transportation plus car passage and accommodation in Iceland. In the off season, prices are halved, but even in high season, four adults travelling by car and paying for berths will cost less than if they flew.

**The small print** The ferry is a lot of fun, but bear in mind that you are still 'at sea'. In times of inclement weather (this is the North Sea), those prone to seasickness will feel it, and although the *Norröna*'s a big enough ship to soften the waves, you might want to bring something along to quell the queasiness. Also, bring your own food (there's a big grocery store at the port in Hanstholm, with smaller shops in Scrabster). On the ship, your only choices are the super-fancy, all-you-can-eat buffet, an overpriced cafeteria, or duty-free chocolates and whisky. To amuse guests, there's a pool and sauna, but being out on deck is amusing too. The ship passes several islands and oil platforms, and there's a good chance to see whales and birds. Budget travellers often accept the cheapest couchettes without thinking, but think about it. The couchettes are basically in steerage (at the bottom of the ship) where U-boat-style bunks are stacked three people high and bathrooms are shared. This is not a good idea if you are claustrophobic. Pay the extra cash and get a berth above the waterline.

Seyðisfjörður (see page 406) is a small fjord and a small port. Many travellers are shocked that their grand arrival in Iceland doesn't feel so grand (the ferry is the largest 'building' in east Iceland except for the aluminium plant (see page 409). The ferry schedule works in such a way that travellers must often spend a night in Seyðisfjörður or close by.

**Cruises** Cruise lines are now so popular in Iceland that in summer, the main ports of call (Reykjavík, Akureyri, and Ísafjörður) have a new ship almost every day. Rarely is Iceland offered as a cruise destination in its own right, combined instead with Norway, Greenland, or the Arctic in general. Some cruises do allow for a pickup or drop-off in the country to further your journey on your own, so it is quite possible to travel to and from Iceland via cruise ship.

**Yachts** Sailing on your own to Iceland is a special adventure and I truly admire all the salty sailors who steer their own boats northward. There's a worldwide secret society of dedicated arctic sailing enthusiasts (fetishists?) and I won't even try to pretend to know what they know. If you are considering a trip north, make sure you've got the right kind of boat that can handle what you might encounter, and make sure you have an experienced crew. The one sure thing is that you always have wind. For more information, contact the **Icelandic Sailing Association** (*www.silsport.is*), or the major ports of call: Akureyri (*www.port.is*), Reykjavík (*www.faxafloahafnir.is*), Ísafjörður (*www.isafjordur.is*), Grundarfjörður (*www.grundarfjörður.is*), and the Westmann Islands (*www.vestmannaeyjar.is*).

**Cargo ship** It is not well advertised, but it is quite possible to travel to and from Iceland by freighter on the national shipping line **Eimskip** (*Reykjavík, Korngörðum 2; ☎ 525 7000; e info@eimskip.com; www.eimskip.com*). Travellers are only granted passage in summer (April–October) and can embark from the ports of Rotterdam or Hamburg. It takes more than a week to get to Iceland as you service several ports of call in Denmark and the Faroe Islands. The trip from Reykjavík to Rotterdam is more direct and takes about three days. Charges are calculated based on the number of days spent on the ship. Book passage through the travel agent **Iceland Travel** (*Skútuvogur 13A; ☎ 585 4270; e info@icelandtotal.com; www.icelandtotal.com*).

## HEALTH

**PREVENTION** Happily, you do not need any immunisations to travel in Iceland (although it is advisable to be up to date with all UK recommended vaccines, including MMR and DTP). Even better, because of the climate, there are very few bacteria in the air. Also, the water in Iceland is some of the cleanest in the world. Drink as much as you like, but only out of clean sources. 'But it all looks clean!' – it does, but if you drink from a valley with lots of cows defecating nearby, you risk getting an upset stomach. The higher up you are, the safer it is. Mountain waterfalls, glaciers, streams, and cold springs are optimal. Otherwise, health concerns for travellers in Iceland are minimal. When hiking, avoid blisters by wearing boots that fit and bring plasters to cushion sore spots. Also use caution on rough paths and in dangerous places (like high cliffs). Bring lip balm for wind-burn and lotion for dry hands. Avoid mass-produced seafood at all-you-can-eat tourist buffets, and in misty mountainous areas, beware of large trolls.

**FIRST AID** Smart travellers always carry a basic first-aid kit, which should include:

- Plasters/band-aids
- Blister plasters for hiking
- Antiseptic wipes and cream
- Aspirin or paracetamol
- Wound dressing (gauze and tape)
- Anti-diarrhoea pills

**COLD WEATHER** Weather only becomes a concern when people are exposed. Dress properly (warm and waterproof) and wear a woolly hat. Iceland never gets the deep, harsh freezes like in Russia or Canada, but the weather can whip up the perfect recipe for a sniffly cold. The shift in climate alone can be enough to unbalance your stamina. If you get drenched in cold drizzle, drink plenty of hot liquids (coffee, tea, or soup). Even in the midst of the Icelandic summer, travellers can get caught in the wet and cold. Travel in high altitudes can also be a lot colder than you might expect. Long-term exposure can cause hypothermia, when your body's core temperature drops below what it needs to function properly. Shivering and numb hands are some of the first symptoms of hypothermia. Treat by removing wet clothing immediately and warming up the victim indirectly (external heat source) or directly (body-to-body contact).

**SEXUALLY TRANSMITTED DISEASES** Among developed (OECD) nations, Icelanders are the youngest to become sexually active, a cultural phenomenon that may give rise to false impressions and expectations. Like much of Scandinavia, the age of consent is 14. Always be wise in your encounters. Statistically, Icelanders have the lowest rate of HIV infection in the world, but as a foreigner you are not included in that statistic. Condoms (*smokkur*) are available in pharmacies and in every counter of every *sjoppa* or petrol station in Iceland.

**HEALTH CARE** Health care in Iceland is of superb quality, so there is nothing to fear. Large towns have hospitals and smaller villages have health clinics. In any emergency situation, dial ☎ 112 and you will get immediate help. Most medical professionals speak very good English and most foreigners find that they receive better care in Iceland than they would back home. Iceland and Britain have a reciprocal health agreement, so all UK citizens should travel with their European Health Insurance Card (EHIC), which is valid for care in Iceland. Non-EU/EEA citizens must pay at the time a service is rendered. Obviously, if your health insurance does not cover you outside your own country, then travellers' insurance is a good idea.

**PHARMACIES** The Icelandic Apótek is easily spotted for the green cross, typically open 09.00–17.00 and later in Reykjavík. A breadth of pharmaceutical needs is covered, and most shops carry everything a traveller needs: contact-lens solution, first-aid materials, sunscreens, moisturisers, etc.

**TRAVEL CLINICS** A full list of current travel clinic websites worldwide is available on www.istm.org. For other journey preparation information, consult www.tripprep.com. Information about various medications may be found on www.emedicine.com/wild/topiclist.htm.

## SAFETY

Iceland is the safest country on earth – it is highly unlikely that you will get pickpocketed, kidnapped, caught up in a coup, attacked or contract malaria. However, Iceland is also one of the most dangerous places on earth, with a possible threat of volcanic eruption, earthquakes, avalanche, glacier outbursts, tidal waves, blizzards, and other treacherous weather conditions. Expect nothing, but be prepared for anything.

The number-one concern for foreign travellers is road safety. All too often, foreigners assume (wrongly) that driving in Iceland is the same as anywhere else. Drive very carefully (see *Driving in Iceland*, page 94) and take extra precautions. Never speed, and always remain alert, obey signs and carry plenty of fuel.

Weather is another root cause of safety concerns. Icelandic weather is unpredictable and can be highly problematic. Icelanders cope by going with the flow and never testing the limits. The first rule is to check the weather (*www.vedur.is*) and the second is to never take the wind for granted. Hurricane-force gusts are serious business that can blow cars off the road and make travel impossible. Add a random bout of rain, sleet, or snow and it's not a pretty picture. If anyone warns you not to go out, then don't.

The same thing that makes Iceland beautiful (isolated, uninhabited landscapes) can also be hazardous. The 'middle of nowhere' is a good description of much of Iceland – one step off the main road is a step away from civilisation and carries the same potential risks as a hike across the Sahara Desert or a trek in the Himalayas. Specific safety tips on hiking, glaciers, and geothermal landscapes are covered in depth later in this chapter (see *Hiking*, pages 114–15). Iceland's universal emergency number is ☎ 112, emergency huts (see page 105) are available in remote areas, and the **Icelandic Search and Rescue** (*www.icesar.com*) can be a vital resource. Still, common sense and emergency preparedness always make for the safest travel.

**CRIME** Crime in Iceland is so petty, it's almost pitiful. Cases of vandalism and public intoxication outnumber theft. The rare violent crime that does take place almost always involves late-night drinking and carousing. Avoid drunk people. Because Iceland is packed full of tourists in summer, thieves may target unassuming foreigners who have let down their guard in a perceivably 'safe' situation. If you are a victim of a crime, dial 112 and report it to the police (*www.police.is*) or **Lögreglan**. They are always helpful and most speak excellent English.

**WOMEN TRAVELLERS** Iceland is a very progressive country that is light years ahead of most when it comes to women's rights. Icelanders will be the first to remind you how they elected the first woman president in the world and insist that Icelandic women face little discrimination in their society. For women travellers, Iceland is a place to wander freely and experience nature fully without apprehension or taking special precautions. Even so, the savvy woman traveller should always travel with a good set of 'street smarts'. Potential threats (injury, theft, intimidation) are just as likely (if not more so) to come from fellow foreign travellers. Take special care in campsites and remote mountain huts where potential lack of protection and sheer isolation might place you in a vulnerable position. Most hostels or guesthouses with sleeping-bag spaces will offer women-only rooms. Likewise, women should not hitchhike on their own. Potential confusion might also arise within Iceland's particular club culture, where women often play a dominant role that may lead some men to expect more than you are willing to give. Bar-hopping in the middle of the night (even when it's light outside) poses the exact same risks. There is safety in numbers, while pairing off with strangers is always a huge risk. For more information, contact the **Icelandic Feminist Association** (*www.feministinn.is*) – the largest women's advocacy organisation in the country. A rape crisis centre inside the national hospital (see page 165) and **Stígamót** (*www.stigamot.is*) is the Icelandic non-profit organisation dedicated to survivors of sexual violence.

**RACIAL MINORITIES** Not all Icelanders are blonde with blue eyes, but almost all of them are really, really white. For that reason, a variation in skin tone is enough to make you stand out. In general, Icelanders are open minded, well educated, hospitable, thoughtful and discard the notion of prejudice. Like most Scandinavians, Icelanders are all about cosmopolitanism and equality, which means that racism gets expressed in more subtle tones. Nobody will shout ethnic slurs at you, but you may get the sense that some people are just a little bit unnerved by your presence. That's not so much the case in Reykjavík, which is now very much a global city, but the remote hinterland may respond differently. A new wave of African refugees, Filipino workers, and other non-European residents has established a foothold in the country, so a tiny twinge of anti-immigrant fervour just might get projected your way. The issue is less about race per se and more about the potential for a less-Icelandic Iceland. You might get stared at a lot, and some kids might even run up to rub your skin, but most people will treat you fairly. To break any tension, say something in Icelandic.

**DISABLED TRAVELLERS** Travellers with disabilities will find Iceland to be a place that cares about giving all people the right to experience the country fully. There is a very real and sincere push to make the entire travel industry wheelchair-friendly, and in principle, Icelandic law grants disabled travellers equal-opportunity access to most public activities (swimming pools, museums, etc). This includes the latest technology to assist those with visual and hearing impairments. For more information on services available to deaf travellers, contact the **Icelandic Association of the Deaf** (*Félag Heyrnarlausra;* ☎ *561 3560;* e *deaf@deaf.is; www.deaf.is*). Icelandic sign language is interesting in that it derives from Danish and is therefore quite different from spoken Icelandic – interpretation services are available at the association. Likewise, the **Icelandic Association of the Blind** (*Blindrafélagið;* ☎ *525 0000;* e *blind@blind.is; www.blind.is*) can help arrange for an appropriate guide for visually impaired travellers. While a majority of hotels and farms claim to offer wheelchair-accessible rooms, I have made special note in the reviewed accommodation of those that actually do. These include hotels with at least one ground-floor unit, ramps, and equipped bathrooms. A great online resource is the Icelandic equal rights organisation **Sjálfsbjörg** (*www.sjalfsbjorg.is*), which provides updated coverage on travel topics for less-mobile people and also offers accessible rooms in Reykjavík. For more in-depth consideration, please refer to Gordon Rattray's helpful tips (see pages 84–5).

**GLBT TRAVELLERS** By law, all gay, lesbian, bisexual, and trans-gendered persons are equal and protected from discrimination. For more than a decade, same-sex couples have been allowed to marry and adopt children. Icelanders are very accepting of GLBT persons as a minority group, but the numbers of GLBT individuals in Iceland are so few (per capita) that there is no prominent gay subculture. For example, Reykjavík's gay pride festivities (*www.gaypride.is*) attract a predominantly heterosexual crowd that just like a good party. The political issue is such a non-issue that there is no need to sequester anyone for the sake of solidarity. Similarly, there is no gay 'scene' in Iceland. Reykjavík boasts a single official gay bar (see *Truno*, page 161) and a few other noted clubs – though their status of 'gayness' is in constant flux. The best resource for tapping into Iceland's gay community is the gay rights organisation Samtökin 78 (*www.samtokin78.is*), which hosts a weekly gathering in its upstairs lounge/library. In general, GLBT travellers should face no ill will or difficulty. Booking a room as a same-sex couple is hardly an issue, and there is no need to hide the fact that you are a couple. Iceland being Scandinavia, public displays of affection are frowned upon, regardless of gender and orientation. For more information, check www.gayice.is.

**TRAVELLING WITH CHILDREN** Children rule supreme in this Scandinavian welfare state, which leaves you little reason to leave the kids back home. Despite Iceland's high prices, nearly every service (transport, museums, shows, tours, accommodation, etc) offers at least a 50% discount to children under the age of 16 and, more often than not, young kids get in free. The potential cost should be secondary to the experience that awaits. Iceland offers amazing adventures and incredible learning opportunities – it is very hard to be bored.

In general, Iceland is a very safe place for children – one could argue that young Icelanders enjoy more freedoms than do their counterparts in other European countries. Come summer, children are allowed to stay out way past their bedtime to play in the midnight sun. They also get fed a good deal of ice cream and sweets. Other times you may witness the very Scandinavian practice of mothers and fathers parking baby carriages (with baby) outside a shop. Instead of fearing the bogeyman, caution is necessary when dealing with Iceland's challenging terrain and unpredictable weather. So much of the volcanic landscape is fun (and safe) to climb on, but let common sense guide you. In remote areas, do not let children wander unattended. Take extra precautions around high cliffs, areas of geothermal and volcanic activity, and around bodies of water. On boats, all children should always wear life jackets, even if they are strong swimmers. Certain coastal towns enforce the rule that young children must wear life jackets on land when they are near the harbour or shore (signs will be posted).

Iceland's universal health care is of the highest quality, perhaps better than what your children get back home. That said, travellers of any age should be covered by sound medical insurance. In Iceland, your kids won't catch malaria, but they can catch a nasty cold in the middle of July. The key to keeping kids happy is keeping them warm and dry. Along with a waterproof jacket or poncho, pack a few extra pairs of dry socks, a sweater, some mittens and a woolly hat – even in the summer. Packing a general children's antihistamine is another good idea, especially if your child is susceptible to allergies. Some parents also like to take along motion-sickness tablets or patches to prevent nausea in small planes, boat rides, or long trips in a car or bus. Extra plasters take care of scraped hands and knees in a jiffy.

Most restaurants will offer a children's menu or at least one children's dish, although these tend to be 'junk' food (hamburgers, hot dogs, pizza, fried chicken,

## NOTES FOR TRAVELLERS WITH LIMITED MOBILITY

Older buildings may be difficult to enter, with steps and narrow doorways, but a growing number of shops and restaurants are accessible and proprietors are always willing to help if need be. New developments are now designed with less-mobile people in mind and many features like pavement drop-offs (curb cuts) in Reykjavík are already in place. With tour companies becoming more aware and attractions more accessible, everybody, irrespective of physical ability, can enjoy Iceland's frosty and fiery features.

**ACCOMMODATION** Many of Iceland's larger hotels have accessible rooms, with Reykjavík's Loftleiðer (see page 139) and Grand Reykjavík (see page 139) even providing shower chairs. The situation is less comfortable if you are looking for accommodation in small guesthouses or bed and breakfasts, but most can be contacted via email in advance and your needs discussed. Recently, the Icelandic Tourism Board (see page 72) has made great strides forward on this issue and its website now indicates accessibility of hotels. If you wish to explore rural Iceland, Icelandic Farm Holidays (see page 104) has evaluated the suitability of all its farms to visits for people with disabilities and is continually updating this information.

**TRANSPORT**

**By air** Keflavík Airport has aisle chairs to help people to and from their seats on the plane, and there are airline-owned wheelchairs to assist people within the terminal. Personnel will assist as needed and there are wheelchair-accessible toilets. By law, all domestic airlines must accommodate travellers in wheelchairs.

**By sea** The larger ferries in Iceland (to Breiðafjörður, Grímsey, and the Westmann Islands) all accommodate wheelchair travellers.

**Taxis and car hire** Minibuses with lifts and ramps can be hired from Iceland Excursions (*+354 540 1312; mob: +354 660 1312; e iceland@grayline.is; www.icelandexcursions.is*), although they are usually working for local schools so may only be available during weekends and holidays in the off season. If you use other taxi companies, you will need to be able to transfer into standard cars. If necessary, drivers are normally happy to help, although it's worth remembering that they are not trained in this skill. Avis (*www.avis.is*) offers rental vehicles with hand controls.

**By bus** A large percentage of Reykjavík's city buses, at least on the more common routes, have large doors, space allocated for wheelchairs and a 'kneeling' facility to allow easy boarding. Mindy Desens (see opposite) says that the drivers are

etc). If a child cannot be persuaded to eat 'icky' fish, then hotel breakfasts can sometimes come to the rescue. Carrot sticks are also easy to buy or make and may counter the ill effects of a holiday diet. Baby formula, baby food, and nappies are all readily available in any supermarket and sometimes even at petrol stations.

## WHAT TO TAKE

'Pack light' is the traveller's mantra but it doesn't always hold true in Iceland, where a variety of situations demands a variety of stuff. Still, you can buy everything

normally prepared to help if need be, but warns that she did not see any sort of tie-downs on these vehicles. Reykjavík Excursions (see page 137) now runs a large lift-equipped bus as one of its regular Fly Buses. This vehicle can be used for airport transfers or day trips and can accommodate many wheelchairs, but has to be pre-booked.

**ACTIVITIES** Reykjavík's Laugardalur Swimming Pool (see page 179) and the Blue Lagoon geothermal spa (see page 206) both have accessible toilets and facilities for changing and showering. The former has a hydraulic lift chair into one of the pools and the latter has a wheelchair available for use on site (as the highly mineralised water can be corrosive). Several other pools in Reykjavík indicate from their descriptions that they are wheelchair-accessible. One older indoor pool, Sundhollin, states that it's accessible in some brochures, but apparently it is not. Various waterfalls and geyser sites have hard, flat paths to them, and the popular 'Golden Circle' tour (see page 221) is possible using the lift-bus (if booked through Reykjavík Excursions). Although wheelchair users are not able to get very close to the waterfall, they can still get a good view of it, and, with minimal assistance, can easily reach the viewing area for the geyser.

**WHALE-WATCHING** Most boat crews will do their best to provide whatever help you need, but there are none with comprehensive facilities. The most accessible vessel is the *Hafsulan* (see page 171) on which the main viewing area is reached with good ramps; however, the indoor area is below deck via steep stairs, as is a small whale museum. The Whale Museum in Húsavík (see page 380) claims to be suitable for people with limited mobility, with bathroom facilities and several places for people to sit down and either rest, read or watch one of the presentations.

**HEALTH** Doctors will know about 'everyday' illnesses, but as with anywhere, you must understand and be able to explain your own particular medical requirements. If possible, take all necessary medication and equipment with you, and it is advisable to pack this in your hand luggage during flights in case your main luggage gets lost.

**SPECIALIST TOUR COMPANIES AND FURTHER INFORMATION** A US-based operator that visits Iceland frequently is **Lucky Mindy Adventures** (☎ *+1 877 291 1053;* e *luckymin@hutchtel.net; www.luckymindy.com*). Mindy Desens, who runs the company, is a fount of knowledge on access in Iceland. For details of other tour operators, see page 72.

you need for Iceland in Iceland – it just costs a lot more. A few items to consider: sunglasses, a small sewing kit, some cold medicine and extra batteries. In summer, bring earplugs to block out the noise of other travellers and eye shades to block out the midnight sun.

**LUGGAGE** Because Iceland is perceived as a luxury destination by most, the entire travel industry caters to travellers with a lot of luggage. Interior highland buses, tour operators, and big coaches will pull whole trailers filled with people's large suitcases. If you are in a group tour, you'll find that a great deal of time and ritual is spent shifting luggage around. Having something that's discernible (coloured) and smaller gives you a competitive advantage in the fray. Travelling by rental car is convenient as you can simply roll your luggage from the airport into the back of your car. If you're travelling around the country by bus or plane, then smaller is better (internal flights have strict limitations). Smart backpackers will bring medium-sized, waterproof packs. Avoid the cumbersome, super-size packs used by novices. Such packs work like a sail in Iceland and the wind will blow you right over. If you're planning on hitchhiking, then take an absolute minimum.

**SHOES** A pair of sturdy, but light, comfortable walking shoes is best for urban and roadside travel. The rest of Iceland requires a good strong pair of hiking boots. It's imperative that your boots are waterproof, warm, and insulated. If not, you'll be miserable. Iceland is not a good place to break in a new pair of hiking boots. The walking is glorious, but expect sharp rocks, steep climbs, ice, snow, thick mud, deep puddles, sinking sand, and turf landscapes that are custom-made for twisted ankles. If you want to treat yourself to a new pair for your trip, buy them several months prior and go on a few really good blistery hikes before you head to Iceland. Buying at home is nearly always cheaper – a pair of half-decent hiking boots in Iceland costs at least US$250.

**SOCKS** *Sokkur* are essential so bring a few more pairs than you would normally anticipate. It's also not a bad idea to put a few clean, dry pairs in a waterproof bag to save for the day after a rainy day. Thick, heavy-duty hiking socks are recommended for any outdoor activities. Icelanders knit their own woollen socks, and these bristly homemade lovelies are sold on farms, in petrol stations, and just about everywhere else. They can feel a little scratchy and uncomfortable if you're not used to them, but they're great insulators.

**CLOTHING** A holiday to Iceland does not warrant the wardrobe of an Arctic explorer, yet watching tourists file out of a tour bus sometimes looks like Robert Peary's 1909 North Pole expedition. If wearing a fur-ringed parka makes you feel the part, then by all means do it, though you'll get by with a lot less. Wearing layers is key and will allow you to keep up with the weather throughout the day. In that regard, packing for winter or summer is pretty much the same. If you plan on spending time outdoors (which is the whole point of Iceland), then bring long underwear and long-sleeve T-shirts to wear underneath comfortable, casual outfits. Jeans and cotton trousers are fine for low-impact travel (tour buses, driving, museums, shopping, etc), and you should also take at least one good, thick sweater (preferably wool). The most important consideration is how to waterproof yourself. Nobody should come to Iceland without a raincoat or a serious waterproof jacket (with a hood). If you are doing any hiking, climbing, or serious birdwatching, you'll also need a pair of waterproof trousers. Serious long-term hikers typically wear a pair of thermal tights or leggings underneath wind-resistant, waterproof trousers. Gaiters protect you from ice, snow, and mud and are the next best thing to a pair of waterproof trousers. For your upper body, wear breathable, synthetic underclothing (not cotton) that allows you to sweat without getting wet. Synthetic jackets and windbreakers are optimal in summer. Icelanders dress up for work, for church, for funerals, and to go clubbing. If you plan on doing any of these things, then bring at least one formal outfit. Remember to pack a bathing suit for the many pools and hot springs. Also, don't bring a pair of shorts just in case it gets warm. It won't.

**OUTER WEAR** No matter what time of year, bring a wool hat and insulated, waterproof gloves. Summer demands a light coat, and in winter something heavier. A waterproof is imperative. 66° North (*www.66north.com*) is an Icelandic company that specialises in outdoor clothing made especially for Iceland. It's what everyone in Iceland wears and it's very good clothing, but it also costs a small fortune.

**CAMPING GEAR** When travelling in Iceland you should bring along lightweight woollens, a sweater or cardigan, a rainproof (weatherproof) coat and sturdy walking shoes. Travellers who are camping or heading into the interior will need warm underwear and socks, rubber boots and a warm sleeping bag. It's pretty amazing to see the kinds of things people bring to Iceland, some of these souped-up from Germany.

**TENTS** If you plan on camping in a tent, then plan on bringing the best of the best. That means a waterproof, four-season tent that can stand up in 75mph winds (the expensive kind). Most likely, the sturdy tent you take camping back home doesn't stand a chance in Iceland. I've seen plenty of rugged-looking tents get ripped to shreds, even in midsummer. Though some may disagree, I advise using an alpine tent – the kind used by professional mountaineers at high altitudes. Although ventilation is poor, they are warm, compact, and very adept at withstanding high winds. In Iceland, the high price of a good tent pays for itself in four–five nights, but if you're only camping for one–two nights or don't want the added expense, then consider a few factors. Make sure you bring a tent that can stand on its own, preferably with a flexible interior frame as driving tent pegs into the Icelandic earth is sometimes impossible. Also, extra tarpaulins and flysheets are important. Even if your tent says waterproof on the label, it pays to waterproof it again for good measure (use the spray-on stuff sold in outdoor shops). It is possible to rent tents at campsites in Iceland, but if you plan on doing so for more than a few nights, it will cost less to bring your own.

**SLEEPING BAGS** Taking a sleeping bag or *svefnpok* is a great way to save money in Iceland. If you're only using it in hostels and guesthouses, any bag will do. If

### POETIC ADVICE

In 1936, the great English poet W H Auden made a summer voyage all around Iceland, the subject of his wonderful travel book *Letters from Iceland*. Here are some of his suggestions on what tourists should bring:

- Stout gumboots (with at least two pairs of socks worn inside)
- Oilskin trousers, coat, and sou'wester
- A pair of warm, flexible gloves
- Tinted glasses
- A roll of toilet paper ('invaluable')

Auden also understood the value of wearing layers. He confesses to wearing his pyjamas, two shirts, a golf jacket, and a coat underneath his oilskins.

*Taken from* Letters from Iceland, *Faber 1965 edition by W H Auden and Louis MacNeice.*

you're going to be camping or sleeping in mountain huts, bring a very good quality sack that keeps you warm and dry. Regular down-filled sacks are good for severe cold, but not ideal for Iceland because they are useless if they get wet. Instead, go for something synthetic and light. In summer, a sleeping bag should insulate to a threshold of at least -9°C (15°F) in case of wind chill. In winter, you will need a serious sub-zero bag (-18°C/0°F) which means special waterproof, goose-down, or a high-tech synthetic bag.

**COOKING** Open fires are prohibited in all official campsites, and although some offer cooking facilities, almost everyone depends on small camp stoves. Purchase gas cylinders for stoves after you get to Iceland, sold in any food shop or petrol station. Bring stainless-steel pots, pans, and utensils which are easily compacted and plastic dishware that is easily cleaned. Don't pack huge bags of flour or dried milk or bread. Those are the few things you can buy in Iceland cheaply. Instead, use up your food allowance (3kg) on luxuries like energy bars, sauces, and processed foods.

**ELECTRICITY** Current is standard European (220V/50Hz), using the same plugs as you find in continental Europe. Buying an adaptor or converter before you go will save you a good deal of cash. Otherwise, you can purchase either at the airport, at the mall in Reykjavík, or in any of the tourist shops and some tourist information offices. In case you're wondering, Iceland belongs to DVD region number 2.

**MAPS** In Iceland, you can buy maps at most major bookshops, tourist information centres, and petrol stations. Having a quality and current map is essential and will help you enjoy your trip a lot more. A lot of tourists rely on the free maps given out at the airport or tourist information office. These are alright for context and planning, but not optimal for travelling. If driving, make sure that you have a detailed map with correct road markings showing both paved and unpaved sections. Also, beware of any map that seems too cartoon-like. You want something that's accurate and informative. **ITMB** (☎ *+1 604 879 3621;* e *itmb@itmb.com; www.itmb.com*) publishes a great double-sided, waterproof and tear-free travel map of Iceland, which is perfect for backpackers, tourists and anyone driving around the country. In Iceland, the official mapmaker is the **National Land Survey of Iceland** (*Landmælingar Íslands;* ☎ *430 9000;* e *lmi@lmi.is; www.lmi.is*). They print some of the highest-quality maps that are also fairly pricey (about US$20 apiece). Their general travel map of Iceland (Ferðakort Ísland 1: 500,000) is recommended for anyone driving the ring road, and their regional maps (1: 100,000) are optimal for in-depth travelling. Their land survey and hiking maps are the best on the market for serious trekking. In national parks and nature reserves, the information offices will often sell small booklets or pamphlets with hiking maps, and these are also quite useful. For certain areas, I have included specific map recommendations in the relevant sections of this book.

## MONEY

**PRICES** After the financial crisis, Iceland went from being one of the world's most expensive destinations to one of its cheapest. The economic crisis and falling króna allowed foreigners to come and enjoy Iceland at hugely reduced rates. Alas, prices have since adjusted themselves – so don't expect a budget holiday simply because Iceland is pulling itself out of a small depression. As a whole, real prices are lower than they were, but Iceland is still very expensive. Certain imported items, such as food, have actually gone up in price owing to the country's trade deficits. Due to continued inflation and the general instability of the króna, many hotels are listing their prices in foreign currency (US dollars or euros).

Iceland stopped being a budget-travel destination back in 1940, when Icelanders discovered they could make a lot of money by selling foreigners the most basic items for exorbitant prices. With nowhere else to buy the stuff, visitors can only grumble and pay up. And so shopping in Iceland feels like getting mugged at gunpoint. Things like plasters and shoe polish cost five times as much as they do at home, and that's just the tip of the iceberg.

No matter what your wealth, the high cost of travel in Iceland will affect your plans in one way or another (you know it's bad when the Swiss are complaining). What irks most travellers is that one cannot simply avoid high prices by shunning luxury items. In Iceland, all consumables are luxuries: clothing, food, petrol, transportation and accommodation (even postcards and stamps). The price of books is simply outrageous. So why is Iceland so expensive? First, it's an island nation with a small population. Second, most import businesses are sheltered monopolies that can do whatever they like. Third, consumerism isn't a driving force in Iceland, and fourth (like icing on the cake) is Iceland's record-breaking VAT of 24.5%. Now that tourism is a mainstay for foreign investment, you as a tourist are expected to invest heavily. Be ready to spend.

**CURRENCY** The first step to enjoying Iceland is to stop doing currency exchanges in your head. If every time you pay for dinner you think 'that burger, fries and Coke just cost me €60!', then your trip will be nothing but one panic attack after another. Start thinking in króna, with 1,000ISK as a baseline (like a US$10 bill or £10 note), and adjust your own personal consumer price index from there.

The Icelandic króna (ISK) or 'crown' is the official currency of Iceland, with a long-standing reputation for volatility and very high inflation. Following the economic crisis, prices are still very much in flux – foreign currency (cash) has since become much more desirable. Currency exchange is available at all banks, airports, many hotels and major tourist information offices. At Keflavík Airport, ATMs distribute króna and sometimes US dollars and euros. (Note that many banks will have certain restrictions for Icelanders regarding the amount of foreign cash they can exchange at any one time.) Icelanders joke that foreigners are the only ones who ever use the 2,000ISK notes because they are typically only drawn from banks. With a few very remote exceptions, credit cards and debit cards are the preferred method of payment (even on city buses). Icelanders themselves use plastic to pay for everything and anything, even if it's just a chocolate bar or a plastic comb. It is quite possible to come to Iceland and never perform a cash transaction. Travellers' cheques were once easy to use around Iceland, but since the economic crisis, it is difficult to find a place that will cash them.

**BANKING** All banks in Iceland are open from 09.15 to 16.00 (because bankers deserve that extra 15-minute morning break). Banks give the best rates for changing currency. ATMs are widespread, but even in very remote places, banks can draw cash from a debit card. Although the banking crisis is now past, some ATMs might still limit cash withdrawals from foreign debit cards. Credit cards continue to be safe and give the best exchange rate; however, you might want to consider bringing a little extra foreign cash (US dollars, euros, or pounds sterling), and only changing as much as you need for one or two days.

## ON THE MONEY

In case you wondered whose face you're spending ...

| | |
|---|---|
| 500ISK | Jón Sigurðsson, Icelandic nationalist (see page 295) |
| 1,000ISK | Brynjólfur Sveinsson, 17th-century Bishop of Skálholt |
| 2,000ISK | Jóhannes Kjarval, Icelandic painter (see page 183) |
| 5,000ISK | Ragnheiður Jónsdóttir, expert embroiderer who married two bishops |

## BUDGETING

Travelling in Iceland is very, very expensive. Starting with accommodation, summer-season prices range from campsites, huts and youth hostels (US$20–40 per night per person) to farms (US$50–70 per room) to guesthouses (US$80–100 per room) and average hotels (US$140–200) to 'nice' hotels (US$250–500). That might seem typical, but cost is little indication of quality – a US$200 hotel room in Iceland might resemble a US$50 bed and breakfast back home. Next comes food, which is outrageously expensive. Eating out at tourist-class restaurants will set you back at least US$40 per person per meal (lunch and dinner); nicer restaurants cost upwards of US$75. If you are driving, budget around US$100 per day for the rental car, plus US$90 per tank of fuel; inter-city flights are about US$100 each way and ferries too. Then there are admission prices to museums and historical sites (US$10–20), swimming pools, guides and extra activities... and start tacking on imaginary digits to your bottom line. If you really want to come to Iceland, plan on spending more money than you would on any other trip, then actually come and spend twice that amount.

**CUTTING COSTS** And yet despite the horrific cost, hundreds of thousands of travellers visit every year without going bankrupt. The secret to cutting costs in Iceland is to lower expectations. Delusional travellers will attempt to maintain a standard of travel equal to the average experience in continental Europe or North America and shell out close to US$400–500 a day. If you accept Iceland as it is, a couple driving a rental car can get by on a budget of US$250–300 per day. To cut costs further take your own bedding (sleeping bag), stay only in accommodation with shared bathrooms (like hostels), prepare your own meals from food purchased at grocery stores, pre-book your accommodation online (often discounted), bring your own car, and enjoy Iceland's free nature as opposed to its 'consumables'. Travelling in groups can help, too. Package tours are sometimes cheaper (not always) and individual travellers who band together can save a lot of cash. Some of the best deals include getting four or more travelling together who can share suites and apartments, car-rental costs, and cook together. A common sight is two couples travelling together. Likewise, families can also make their money stretch out farther, per capita. Children get huge discounts and family-style accommodation is often available for a lower cost. Your tourist dollar also goes a lot further in spring and autumn than it does in July – travelling off season cuts accommodation costs by half. Another cheaper option is to travel like Icelanders do by renting a summer home and staying in one place.

Hikers, cyclists and campers can travel for much less: if you're walking or biking, sleeping in campsites or huts, and cooking your own food, you can budget under US$50 per person per day. If that still isn't low enough, there is a way to get around Iceland on a shoestring: 1) hitchhike, 2) camp rough, 3) bring your own dry food or eat at grocery stores. It's a recipe for adventure and being miserable and wet.

**TAX REFUNDS** With such an astronomically high tax, it seems unfair to punish the foreigners who don't live here and reap the benefits of a Scandinavian tax structure. Thus, visiting non-Icelanders are entitled to a refund of up to 15% on consumer goods purchased in Iceland. The small print is that this does not include payments for food or accommodation – only retail items that you take outside the country. Each individual sale must exceed 4,000ISK. Departure from Iceland must be within 30 days of the purchase.

It's a bureaucratic process that enriches someone else, but if you've done a lot of shopping and want to get some of your money back, why not? Slightly confusing is how there are two different tax reimbursement systems in place. Different shops are linked to a specific system and can only issue receipts for one or the other. Allegiance to one tax-free plan is not necessary, but it does make your life easier in the end, so pay attention to the strikingly similar logos. **Global Refund** (*www.global-blue.com*) is the 'TAX FREE Shopping' inside a blue and grey box; **Euro Refund** (*www.eurorefund.com*) is the 'TAX FREE' arrow inside a red and blue circle.

Here's how you do it: whenever you make a tax-free purchase, ask the cashier for your 'tax-free cheque'. Keep all of these, and then get them validated (export stamped) at one of the tax-free offices in Reykjavík or at the 'tax-free' stand at the airport in Keflavík. There is more paperwork to be filled out to get your totals, after which you can submit all of it at the cash-refund office at Keflavík Airport. This is the only place where you will be issued an immediate cash refund. Otherwise, you will get the refund by way of a credit to your credit card.

**TIPPING** Tipping is not something you do in Iceland. Prices are high enough as it is, and powerful labour unions ensure that even part-time restaurant waiters are getting paid enough to not depend on tips as income. If it makes you feel uncomfortable, just pretend your VAT is a giant cover-all tip.

## GETTING AROUND

**BY AIR** Flying is the very best way to see Iceland's marvellous landscapes. With so few roads and such massive wilderness, a flight can show you what you cannot see on your own (so always request a window seat). Planes are also quick and convenient, allowing you to drop down into the remotest places and saving you days of driving. The downside to air travel is that flight schedules are susceptible to Icelandic weather. Fog, wind, rain, or storm can delay or cancel a flight with little notice. If you're patient and make flexible plans, then there's no problem, but flight mishaps can wreak havoc on tightly packed itineraries. Flying around Iceland is also relatively inexpensive, with most flights costing US$90–120 each way. Backpackers are surprised to find out that flying across Iceland by air can be cheaper than taking the bus. Check current schedules as they change from winter to summer, and always book tickets in advance (purchase them online or by phone).

Reykjavík City Airport (see page 130) is the national hub for all domestic flights.

**Air Iceland** (☎ *570 3030*; e *websales@flugfelag.is*; *www.airiceland.is*) is the country's main airline, with regular flights between Reykjavík and Ísafjörður,

Egilsstaðir, the Westmann Islands, and Akureyri, and from Akureyri to Grímsey, Thórshöfn, and Vopnafjörður. Air Iceland also flies to Greenland and the Faroe Islands, as well as operating a number of 'action-packed day tours' from Reykjavík. These are short, intense excursions which normally entail a one–two-hour flight to a distant corner of Iceland and a day of activities such as kayaking, bird- and whale-watching, or touring natural reserves. If your time is limited, these are a great experience. They are pricey though (around US$500–600), and if your time is not limited, then you should simply buy the flight and take your time enjoying the unhurried destination. By the way, the logo on the tail of Air Iceland's planes is not Pegasus, but Sleipnir (see page 32), Oðin's eight-legged flying steed. **Eagle Air** (*562 4200; ernir@ernir.is; www.eagleair.is*) is another Icelandic airline that also flies out of Reykjavík City Airport. Because it services a number of Iceland's secondary towns and remotest climes (like Höfn, Sauðárkrókur, and Bíldudalur and Gjögur in the West Fjords), it has a strong reputation among outdoorsmen and trekkers. It also offers fantastic sightseeing flights right out of Reykjavík into the wildest parts of Iceland. One minute you can be sitting in a taxi and 20 minutes later you'll be flying over the valley of Thórsmörk, the glacier of Snæfellsjökull, or the vast uninhabited interior. Eagle Air also features flights to the Faroe Islands and Greenland, and manages its own charter air service which allows you to plan your own adventure. There are almost 100 paved airports in Iceland, and a seemingly limitless number of airstrips. If you have a small group, want to save time, or go somewhere far away from anyone else, this is the way to do it. Several smaller charter airlines offer sightseeing flights in different areas of the country, like Mýflug in Mývatn (see page 370) and Atlantsflug in Skaftafell (see page 426). Obviously, charter airlines can be expensive but are definitely worth the cost. There really is no better way to experience the landscapes of Iceland, and if you've come all this way to see a glacier, why not really see it?

**BY CAR** Driving in Iceland offers total freedom and is one of the most extensive means of travel in the country. Iceland has a car culture, so travellers who aren't driving often feel stranded or limited. So much of what there is to see and do in Iceland is only accessible on wheels, and without a car, travellers must resort to scanty 'public transport' and overpriced tour operators. Having a car is just easier, and in the long run, less expensive. For example, for what it costs two people to take a fixed coach excursion of the Golden Circle (see page 221), those same two travellers could rent a car in Reykjavík with a full tank of fuel, visit the exact

### WHERE'S MY PLANE?

Figuring out when a plane might leave is a common pastime in Iceland. Larger airports will list flights in English, but some smaller airports do not. This is how to read the board of Arrivals (*Komur*) and Departures (*Brottfarir*):

| | |
|---|---|
| *Á Áætlun* | On time |
| *Brottför* | Departure time |
| *Staðfest* | Confirmed |
| *Innritun* | Checking-in |
| *Athugun* | Delayed |
| *Farin* | Departed |
| *Lent* | Arrived |

## STUDENT DRIVER

The basics of driving in Iceland are:

- Drive with headlights on at all times (day and night, rain, sun, or snow)
- Always wear your seat belt
- Never drive off-road
- Do not speed
- Slow down for bridges, hills, tunnels, and animals
- Do not drink and drive
- Be careful in high winds

same route and see a lot more in the process. All too often, people who think they cannot afford to hire a car will end up spending a lot more money on day trips from Reykjavík than the price of having a car for the same time period.

Driving in Iceland (see next) is totally different from driving in most countries, so prepare yourself and always be super careful. Route 1 is the omniscient circuit that goes all the way around the country and is commonly referred to as the ring road or *hringvegur.* The route was only completed in 1974, is 1,339km in length and is thereby Iceland's largest and longest 'highway'. Driving the ring road is a wonderful way to enjoy the diversity of Iceland's landscapes, but it is not the only way. Having a car in Iceland does not require a race around the ring road, nor does a complete circumnavigation qualify as 'seeing all of Iceland'. The country has many roads to explore and many places to explore without any roads. Where you go and what you see depends largely on what it is that you are driving. Regular cars are fine for the ring road, but about half of Iceland's roads require a meaty 4x4. Taking your own car from Europe can save money; if you are taking your own vehicle into Iceland, be sure to have a copy of your registration documents with you. Drivers of their own vehicles from EU/EEA countries do not require proof of third-party **insurance** (ie: green card), but everyone else does. If you do not have such proof upon arrival, you will be required to purchase an insurance policy in Iceland.

In case you need a reminder, gas or petrol is offensively expensive in Iceland. The main **fuel** providers are **Esso** (*www.esso.is*) and **Shell** (*www.shell.is*), and they both have stations dotted around the ring road. Icelandic petrol stations are often the heart of small communities (see page 110) and stay open late, usually from 07.00 to 23.30. More remote areas follow their own schedules. If you stick to the ring road, fuel options are of no concern; however, travel in remote areas (like the West Fjords) demands some careful fuel planning. On some roads, petrol stations might be located more than 100km apart. As a rule, top up your tank before heading off into an empty space on your map. If you are travelling in very remote areas (ie: parts of the interior), you should carry extra fuel with you as a precaution. Icelandic law dictates that any extra fuel tanks must be attached to the exterior of the vehicle. Most petrol stations will have a designated area for car cleaning with several jet-powered water hoses and brushes. This is a gratis service and a necessary practice as the Icelandic elements are merciless to cars. At any time of year, mud, gravel, sand, ice, and snow (or an ugly combination of all those things) will build up on the body and wheels. Periodic cleanings make driving safer and protect your car from permanent damage – be sure to clean underneath.

## ICELANDIC ROAD SIGNS

Icelandic road signs use fairly depictive graphics to aid the less intuitive among us. If a picture of a car zooming over the edge of a cliff says nothing to you, then study these phrases closely:

| | |
|---|---|
| ***BLINDHÆÐ*** | Blind hill |
| ***LOKAÐ*** | Road closed |
| ***MALBIK ENDAR*** | Paved section ends |
| ***EINBREIÐ BRÚ*** | One-lane bridge |
| ***ÓBRÚAÐAR ÁR*** | River crossing |
| ***ILLFÆR VEGUR*** | 4x4 vehicles only |

**Driving in Iceland** This section should have exclamation points all over it because it's so important. There's a reason why special driving instructions are printed in English on everything from travel brochures and maps to restaurant menus in Iceland. Foreign tourists wreck a lot of cars, and in the process, many of them wreck themselves. It's not that Iceland's roads are so terribly dangerous, they are just different from what most people know and expect. The number-one cause of fatal car accidents in Iceland is foreign drivers who speed on a paved road that suddenly meets an unpaved section. Wheels spin, the driver loses control, and the car flies off the road. Sometimes that road is in the middle of some innocent lava field, but it could also be at the edge of a 200m-high cliff. Don't speed. Officially, the maximum speed limit for the whole country is only 90km/h (55mph). In most areas it's much less, and in towns it's 50km/h. A 60km/h speed limit does not mean 100km/h when nobody else is around. Speed cameras are placed all along the ring road in both directions. Speed even a little and you will get caught and severely fined. Do not plan driving times between destinations based on your own understanding of road quality and speed limit. Neither is comparable to what you already know.

Route 1 may be the country's main highway but it's really just a narrow two-lane road. Be very careful when attempting to pass the car in front of you. Blind hills and curves are very common, and if you can't see a good distance ahead, you're begging for a head-on collision. The same goes for single-lane roads, many of which are unpaved. Most tunnels are only one lane wide, with periodic sections to allow for travellers in the opposite direction to pull over. In tunnels, slow down, keep your lights bright and be ready to pull over quickly. Also slow down on all dirt and gravel roads (less than 80km/h) and pay attention to areas where paved and unpaved sections meet. Roads labelled 'F' represent mountain passes – typically one-lane, unpaved, gravelly dirt roads that are often blocked by snow and ice in winter. Likewise, the roads across the interior are only opened up during the summer months, dates that fluctuate from year to year based on conditions (like river levels). To check road conditions in English, contact the **Public Roads Administration** (☎ *1777 (toll free), 563 1500;* e *info@vegagerdin.is; www.vegagerdin.is/English*). **Driving off road in Iceland is illegal** and is punished severely (as in arrested). To avoid the police, there are a few more dos and don'ts. Always drive with your headlights on (day or night). Never drink and drive – Iceland has a zero-tolerance policy for drink-driving. Always wear your seat belt, and again, don't speed. You don't want to get a ticket in Iceland.

Smaller roads often cross glacier rivers and streams and the letter 'V' represents a ford (*vað*). Don't assume that because a road crosses at one spot that it's the safest ford. Water levels fluctuates by the hour, so take a good look before you cross, checking where other cars have been crossing most recently. Typically, the most shallow places are where the water is roughest or loudest (because of rocks), but not always. Always drive into a river diagonally against the current and in first gear. If you stall – don't panic. Starting a car in the middle of a river is not impossible, though it's also a good way to flood the engine.

A few more words of caution: animals (namely sheep) roam freely in Iceland and have no respect for your space. Be alert and ready to slow down or stop, although it's always better to hit an animal than to swerve off the road. If you do hit an animal, you are financially liable to the owner – try to locate the closest farmer. Other things to watch out for are falling rocks and large rocks that have already fallen. Also use caution in severe winds. Bear into the wind with your steering wheel, but not too much as a gust might suddenly subside and leave you swerving into the opposite lane. Park your car facing the wind and open the door against the force. Opening a car door to the wind can cause it to simply bend, snap off or blow away (no kidding). If you have an accident, call the emergency number 112. As flat tyres are quite common, make sure that someone in your car knows how to fix a flat and make sure you have a spare. Be aware that in remote areas, mechanics and car-repair shops are few and opening hours limited.

## WINTER DRIVING

*Nathan Evans*

Driving through Iceland in winter can be an incredible experience but it can also be very dangerous. If you lose focus for just a few seconds, it can kill you. As stated at the beginning of this guide, driving time in Iceland is determined less by distance and more by season, weather conditions and visibility. If you intend to do lots of driving in Iceland, get a 4x4, or at least get a solid vehicle with special winter tyres, and pack plenty of supplies.

On either side of the road are markers called 'priests'. The markers on the left side of the road have two reflective stripes on them; those on the right have one. The purpose of this is that when there is a horrible snowstorm, travellers can tell where the road is. Taller priests will have double markings on them. You can guess how bad the weather can get in your area by how much of the priests remain visible.

When setting out on a drive, always carry some food and more water than you think you will need. Iceland's weather changes so drastically that often all you will need to do is pull over for a while and wait until driving conditions are better. At other times, however, it can be dangerous to pull over: snowploughs may not see you, or the storm may not stop, leaving you stranded. Perhaps the biggest problem of all is that Icelandic roads do not have hard shoulders, therefore if you are stopping along the road for any reason, you'll need to find a lookout point or tourist rest stop. Simply pulling towards the edge and flipping on your blinking emergency lights only offers minimal protection. Check the Icelandic weather website compulsively (*www.vedur.is*). Always do so before you get in the car, and if you have internet access with you, check along the way.

**Do not** take mountain roads in winter. Many small, one-lane roads traverse parts of the interior and offer short-cuts to destinations; however, in winter these roads are impassable to most cars. Yours will not be an exception, so don't try it.

## Tickets

***Speeding and parking*** Getting a parking ticket can ruin your trip, or at least put a dent in your travel budget. Akureyri has a particular reputation for issuing tickets to foreigners (see page 345), so watch where you park. Speed cameras photograph plenty of tourists zipping around Iceland at unsafe speeds. When issued with a ticket, the first thought that crosses many foreign minds is 'hey, if I'm never coming back to Iceland, why pay my overpriced ticket?'. Over 1,000 years ago, Iceland was settled by Vikings who had similar thoughts about escaping the law in Norway. A lot of them got away, but a few faced some pretty grim consequences. Plus, if you're driving a rental car, it is the rental company who will be charged, and they will gladly forward the charge to your credit card along with their own hefty fine. Better to search out the closest police station and confess to your crimes.

**Car hire** Iceland boasts the most expensive car rental in the world, the result of a simple mathematical equation: start with a country that's already pricey, add a responsible socialist government that holds companies liable and makes insurance mandatory, then multiply the enormous risk of renting to non-native drivers in a land renowned for extreme weather and catastrophic events. In principle, renting a car in Iceland is easy and convenient and highly recommended, but there are a few things you should know.

A wise lawyer once said, 'The big print giveth, the small print taketh away.' As demanded by Icelandic law, car-rental companies in Iceland offer 'full insurance' with each rental, which is only the mandatory third-party insurance. Drivers are even offered extra insurance (Collision Damage Waiver (CDW), etc) for that extra sense of security, but it's practically worthless. In Iceland, the small print states that insurance does not cover damage caused by ice, snow, water, falling rocks, wind, lava, earthquake… and the list goes on and on, striking out just about everything that damages cars in Iceland (trolls?). The point is that you are liable for everything except the car as a whole. If you get a flat tyre, you pay for all of it; if a pebble dents your car door, you'll get tagged with a hefty bill; if saltwater sprays the car whilst being transported on a ferry and corrodes the bumper, you pay. According to this logic, it's better for you to shove your slightly damaged car over the edge of a cliff than to turn it in with a scratch (except that it's fraud). On a similar note, a graveyard of totalled vehicles lies behind every car-rental office in Reykjavík. It's a testament to the downside of their own risk (renting in Iceland) and your need to be a cautious driver.

Now that you know the downside of car rental (cost, liability, headache, etc), here's why you should still do it. Because other than renting a private plane to take you around the country, driving is the fullest way to experience the beauty of these landscapes. As long as you're careful and keep your fingers crossed against any volcanic eruptions, you'll be fine. As proof, there are literally hundreds of car-rental agencies in Iceland. Flying to a more remote corner of the country and then renting from that spot is a smart way to explore Iceland. Know that car-rental prices change frequently and skyrocket during the summer season. In my experience, you get what you pay for. The most expensive car rentals (like Hertz) are also the least hassle, the exception being a few mom-and-pop-car-rental operations in Reykjavík (see page 136) and other regions that offer good cars for low(ish) cost. The following companies are all located at Keflavík International Airport (see page 128):

**ALP** ☎ 562 6060; e alp@alp.is; www.alp.is
**Avis** ☎ 591 4000; e avis@avis.is; www.avis.is
**Budget** ☎ 567 8300; e budget@budget.is; www.budget.is

**Hertz** ☎ 522 4400; e hertz@hertz.is; www.hertz.is

**National** ☎ 568 6915; e holdur@holdur.is; www.holdur.is

***Choosing the right car*** Currently, the cheapest car rented throughout Iceland is a super-small Toyota that gets great fuel mileage. This makes good sense, and despite size limitations, the car is fine for getting around the ring road and any other major paved roads, and even some well-trodden unpaved routes. The minute you start wanting to venture off onto rough roads and mountain climes, then you should consider getting a 4x4. These range from compact Suzukis to giant Land Rovers. Bear in mind that most car-rental companies do not cover regular vehicles for the interior or any mountain (F) roads, including the Kjölur route and Landmannalaugar. If you plan on going anywhere that's seriously unpaved, you must have a 4x4. Many rental companies now offer mobile homes and caravans as well.

**BY BUS** In principle, an extensive bus network covers the whole of Iceland. **BSÍ** (*www.bsi.is*) is the national bus station in Reykjavík (see page 131) and the starting point for most journeys. There is no national bus line per se, but rather a loose configuration of private bus companies that appear to align their schedules (not unlike the British rail system). That means co-ordinating long-distance trips and complex, multi-day itineraries can be a small headache. To make it easier, travellers are offered a series of convenient bus 'passports' that allow for unlimited transport over a specific period of time (one–four weeks) over a particular region or the whole country. You can also purchase discounted passes like the full circle passport, which allows unlimited summer travel (June–September) on the ring road as long as you keep moving in the same direction (no backtracking). Add-ons include the Kjölur route and the West Fjords. You can also get away without a pass or pre-booked tickets. Hikers and bikers are always flagging down buses for a lift, and the driver will simply charge you for the portion of the trip (they even take credit cards).

Riding the bus is a great way to meet fellow travellers and to tour the country. It's also a reliable way for hikers to get to and from places like Landmannalaugar, Thórsmörk, and to visit the interior without worrying about a car. If you're a backpacker with a lot of spare time who wants to roam, then a bus pass can be a good investment. However, before you decide to travel by bus, crunch the numbers and make sure that it's worth it. Time is money and Icelandic buses are very expensive and not always the most convenient option. For one, you might spend a lot of your time waiting for a bus. If you pair up with fellow travellers, it can often be cheaper to rent a car, and without exaggeration, it is often cheaper to fly between two cities than it is to take the bus. For the latest information on buses, check with the operator **Reykjavík Excursions** (*www.re.is*) and the smaller companies such as **SBA-Norðurleið** (*www.sba.is*) and **Trex** (*www.trex.is*).

**BY BOAT** One could argue that Icelanders fare better in boats than they do cars. Quoting the Icelandic Coast Guard ('half our homeland is the sea'), going by boat lets you see the other half of the country. Main ferries include the Westmann Islands (see page 232), Grímsey (see page 359), and Breiðafjörður (see page 301), as well as the boat to Hornstrandir (see page 310). Smaller boat tours (whale-watching, island excursions) are also widespread.

**BY MOTORCYCLE** Rough riders love riding in Iceland, and it's at the top of the list for extreme motorcycle destinations. It's definitely a different experience for which you need to be prepared. Group cycle tours are available from the operator **Northenduro** (☎ *562 6469;* ✉ *northenduro@northenduro.is; www.northenduro.is*).

**BY BICYCLE** Pedalling around Iceland is a totally thrilling endeavour, which is precisely why thousands of cyclists rush to Iceland every year. The challenge of impossible weather, pain and suffering, and the vast rugged distance – well, if you're into that sort of thing, Iceland is the place to be. Exposing oneself to the harshest side of Iceland and using your own steam to get through it can be exhilarating. Plus, cyclists can get away with seeing a lot of the country for very little money and this is one of the few places where you're almost guaranteed NOT to have your bike stolen. Still, Iceland's not for every cyclist, even the hardest of the hardcore.

Nobody should attempt a bike tour around Iceland without some serious pre-planning. There's a whole community of serious cyclists who know all the quirks of riding in Iceland and it behoves you to learn from them. Start with the **Iceland Mountain Biking Club** (*Íslenski Fjallahjólaklúbburinn; www.mmedia.is/~ifhk/touring.htm*). Know that this is less of a ride and more of an expedition. Roads are rough and the weather worse.

Checking a bike onto your flight is easy and it seems there's always at least one cyclist putting a bike together in the Keflavík arrivals hall. Be it domestic or international, normal airline regulations apply: bikes should be in a bike bag or box, with tyres deflated, pedals removed, and handlebars parallel to the frame. The maximum size of the package permitted is 221cm long by 102cm wide by 56cm deep. A flat charge typically applies (less than US$100). Also, if you don't want to worry about the bike box, know that you can pick up a new one at any of the bike shops in Reykjavík for your way back. Carrying bikes on the ferry is no problem.

Most first-timers want to ride the ring road, a challenging course in and of itself. Allow for at least two–four weeks to complete the ride and be flexible about your daily goals. Traffic is only a problem in busy tourist areas and close to towns, especially Route 41 between the airport and the capital. Otherwise, bikers are treated with a lot of respect and room. You'll often find drivers cheering you on and checking up to make sure you're alright. Besides the cold and wet, the most common biker's ailments are windburn and chapped hands. Wear gloves and bring Vaseline (petroleum jelly) or hand cream and lip balm.

A good-quality road bike (with a lot of gears) is fine for the ring road, but for other parts of Iceland, you'll need a strong mountain bike with wide-gripped tyres (and good shocks). Riding across the Kjölur route or the hills in Landmannalaugar offers some of the best mountain biking in the country. The road from Dettifoss to Askja is another challenging, desolate but beautiful route and if you've got something to prove, try biking around the West Fjords. For something shorter that's relatively light but with great scenery, bike around the Snæfellsnes Peninsula. Riding off-road is illegal in Iceland, but that's not a problem given the number of designated mountain paths. Use extreme caution when crossing glacier rivers and if it looks too deep, wait for a mountain bus or a passing truck to take you and your bike across.

If you choose to bike in Iceland, bear in mind that you will never really feel dry. The best campsites and hostels have drying rooms that cyclists tend to dominate, but the next morning you'll be soaked in five minutes. Wear waterproof and windproof clothing, preferably Gore-Tex, Lycra, or Neoprene cycle-wear that is comfortable, form-fitting and warm, but gives you enough freedom. Have good gloves (bring an extra pair) and a warm, waterproof hat. Goggles can be a good idea too. Other things to have with you: a big roll of duct tape, an extra water bottle, a bike-repair kit with extra inner tubes, a really good road map or atlas, extra grease for bearings,

## ICELAND BY MOTORCYCLE

*Nick Gilroy*

For the experienced and adventurous motorcyclist, Iceland is fast becoming an exciting destination. A trip from the UK can be challenging, though less time-consuming with the opening of the ferry link at Scrabster. Ferry companies are well equipped; however a cautionary note: while Northlink deck crews are particularly attentive to bikers' needs concerning marshalling on board and securing machines, Smyril Line is certainly not. Once onboard and pointed to the deck area to park, it is very much a situation of looking out for your own bike.

Any good biker will have researched what type of roads to expect on arrival in a new country, and in Iceland the road infrastructure is dominated by the mainly asphalt ring road. Thereafter, the road network varies from single-track hard surface to an abundance of gravel and sub-graded roads. The latter is ideal for the biker with an off-road-style bike, but know that actually riding off-road (any type of road) in Iceland is prohibited. The ring road itself can be challenging and provides an excellent 1,400km circuit of the country. Few coastal areas have safety barriers and sheer 'fall-aways' to the ocean are common, which can be challenging when it is windy.

Iceland is well served with fuel stations along main routes, but fuel planning is still vital. Riders taking on the gravel roads of the interior must plan their bike range and fuel stops carefully, as facilities are less common. The weather needs to be respected and is certainly not what you get in mainland Europe. The main weather hazard all year is the wind, which can make riding extremely dangerous. One day, I experienced such strong and gusty windy conditions that I aborted my ride and laid up for the day. Additionally, mountain wave action (the wind's wavelike effect, characterised by updrafts and downdrafts that occur above and behind a mountain range, especially in the southeast), can take the rider by surprise. In such areas such as Vatnajökull, it can be common to be riding in still conditions and suddenly be confronted with uncomfortable, multi-directional turbulence pounding down from the glacial highlands to the coastal plain.

Undoubtedly a destination not to be overlooked, Iceland is, however, not for the inexperienced rider. Respect the weather and plan your route in order to make it back for your ferry departure at Seyðisfjörður. Administratively, ensure your bike insurance is valid in Iceland and, most important, check you have satisfactory breakdown cover.



patience and resilience. Take whatever bike luggage works best for you, but make sure you've got plenty of straps to secure everything with. The wind will try to rip everything open.

Between destinations and to give your soul a rest, you can strap your bike onto a bus for a very minimal fee (under US$15). If you don't want to take your own bike, most of the tour operators listed (see page 72) offer bike tours, from short, half-day trips, to week-long riding safaris. Bike rentals are also available through some hotels and youth hostels. The bike-repair shop and rental that everyone knows and loves is **Borgarhjól** in Reykjavík (*www.borgarhjol.net*) (see page 133).

Most cyclists have a love/hate relationship with Iceland. There will be days when you want to quit; for instance, when you have snow piling up on your hands or when the wind keeps knocking you over. There will be other moments when you

## VEÐUR: WEATHER IN ICELAND

The weather in Iceland changes suddenly and frequently (see page 4), especially near the coast, in the highlands, and near any mountain slope (so, most of the country). Being sufficiently prepared for anything can help you have a safe trip. When outdoors, always have warm, waterproof clothes on hand. Know that in Iceland, it can snow anywhere at any time of the year. A smart outdoorsman knows that the air temperature drops 1°F (0.6°C) for every 100m elevation that you ascend. In Iceland, you face the added treachery of the wind which can bring temperatures down below freezing in a matter of minutes. Always check the weather before you go anywhere. For current weather information in English, contact the Icelandic Weather Bureau (*Veðurstofa Íslands;* ☎ *902 0600;* e *office@vedur.is; www.vedur.is/English*).

feel like the luckiest person alive, with wind pushing you from behind and the most incredible landscape unfolding before you. For those who are up for the challenge, I definitely recommend it.

**BY HORSE** Icelanders have been exploring their country by horse for the last 1,100 years. Despite modern technology (speedboats, snowmobiles, 4x4s, and planes), nothing compares to getting out in the wilds of Iceland on the back of the resolute Icelandic horse (see page 60). The animal is such a part of the landscape that some would say that horseback is the only way to go. The fact is that horses can go where no-one else can. That's why horseriding tours across the interior are ideal.

Riding is such serious business in Iceland that travellers have a wide number of choices. Hundreds of tour operators and farms offer horseriding tours and horse rentals. You do not need to be a pro-rider to go on a tour. Short tours are fine for first-timers, however some of the longer tours (one week or more) are best for those with some riding experience. Probably the most popular and invigorating tour is the cross-country trek along the old Kjölur route. Tour groups normally provide all the gear you need (similar to English riding) – just dress warmly and pack light. Get to know your horses, as most treks bring a whole team of horses, allotting two or three per rider and working them in shifts. Usually, these are all-inclusive deals, with night stays in old schools, mountain huts, or campsites. An all-inclusive week of riding costs around US$1,800 and a short ride can be less than US$50. The following are recommended tour operators; for details of other tour operators see page 72.

**Eldhestar** Hvergaerði; ☎ 483 4884; e info@eldhestar.is; www.eldhestar.is. A major Icelandic tour operator, Eldhestar ('fire horse') offers package tours across Kjölur & Sprengisandur, along with shorter horse treks through the natural reserves. Its tour between the deserts is one of a kind & goes to an area that is off limits to most.

**Hestasport Activity Tours** Varmahlíð, Vegamót; ☎ 453 8383; e info@riding.is; www.riding.is. An experienced tour operator, offering fun trips (both short & long riding tours) all across Iceland.

**Íshestar** Hafnarfjörður, Sörlaskeið 26; ☎ 555 7000; e info@ishestar.is; www.ishestar.is. One of the largest tour groups in Iceland, Íshestar ('ice horse') offers a myriad of experiences on horseback, from country tours to Mývatn, to Kjölur & Sprengisandur in the interior. These are also the people to contact for the Sep roundup.

**Lýtingsstaðir** Varmahlíð; ☎ 453 8064; e info@lythorse.com; www.lythorse.com. This family-friendly horse farm in Skagafjörður has wonderful horses & is great at custom-building a tour or ride that fits your desires.

**HITCHING** Iceland is one of the easiest countries for travellers to catch a free lift, especially in summer when thousands of tourists are circling the ring road in both directions. Hitching is legal and almost a tradition in the more remote stretches of Iceland. Local youths often avoid the high cost of transportation by hitching, and some backpackers find they can tour the entire country by thumb. This is definitely the case if you stick to the main ring road (Route 1) and other well-travelled routes such as Snæfellsnes and Reykjanes. Otherwise, know that off the beaten path means far fewer lifts. There are roads in Iceland where a whole day can pass without a car going by.

Although the practice is generally safe in Iceland, follow the same precautions you would in other countries. Don't get into a car with a driver who gives you the creeps and agree on the destination beforehand. To improve your chances of getting picked up, pack light and maintain a clean and well-kempt appearance. Also, be courteous. There's nothing worse than picking someone up who makes a mess of the car or who starts making demands. Do not abuse the kindness of strangers. Offer to contribute some money for fuel and express gratitude.

**TAXIS** Like much of the rest of the world, a yellow-lit sign indicates the taxi is available. If you are on the street searching, the Icelandic for taxi is *leigubíll.* Regular taxis fit one–four passengers, larger vans fit five–eight. With such high fares, drivers' unions, and so forth, tipping is not common. Reykjavík's taxi companies go above and beyond the drive across town, offering taxi tours to destinations like the Blue Lagoon and Snæfellsnes. Taxi tours range from Reykjavík's noted sights (including Oskjuhlidð and Esja) to the Golden Circle or exotic personal day trips. The price can be staggering (US$1,000 for four people on a single day trip), but the benefit is that someone else is driving, allowing you the freedom to just watch. Almost every taxi company in Iceland offers some kind of tour. To find out more, contact **Iceland Taxi** (m *892 0501;* e *info@icelandtaxi.com; www.icelandtaxi.com*).

## ACCOMMODATION

It's heartbreaking to watch what Iceland does to people: luxury travellers suddenly turn into penny-pinching backpackers who sneak complimentary breakfast buns back to their 20,000ISK room. Actual backpackers resort to camping out indoors or just plain camping, and among all tourists there exists a strange sense of solidarity in which all of us are just trying to get by in the midst of surreally high hotel bills. Indeed, accommodation is the number-one expense for travel in Iceland: where you lay your head determines just how expensive your trip will be. The good news is that Iceland has a lot of variety in accommodation (hotels, guesthouses, hostels, and homestays); the not-so-good news is that standards are not at all standard. Iceland follows its own sense of service, backed by a Scandinavian austerity that makes you feel lucky to even get a bed.

The reason behind all of this is that Iceland's accommodation is still a sellers' market. The supply of rooms coincides with the supply of tourists, who until recently have been very seasonal. That explains why the six-week period from July until mid-August is booked solid, and why they can charge you so much for a room that feels average compared with back home. Don't judge too harshly. Standards are improving and you can help the process by being choosy about where you stay. For now though, adjust your sights to fit the reality. If your travel budget normally gets you hand-fluffed pillows with a goodnight chocolate, Iceland might feel like a school trip. If you're used to paying for middle-rate chain hotels, then Iceland might seem like an institutional summer camp. To avoid lowering your standards, one must spend upwards of US$500 a night, after which one is taken care of quite splendidly.

The bright side of Icelandic accommodation is how impeccably clean it all is – not a lick of dust or smudge of dirt anywhere. The Icelandic sense of home is to make a haven from the harsh outdoors and this they do well. Rooms tend to be light and cosy, with fluffy beds that are covered in big duvets and the heat cranked up high. That is the definition of luxury in Iceland, so enjoy it. Visitors are often aghast when confronted with a US$200-per-night room bill in which they must share a bathroom down the hall with strangers (welcome to Iceland!). While most hotels have private bathrooms for each room, many guesthouses do not. As a discerning feature, bathrooms have become a defining factor in hotel reviews. In choosing a place to stay, also recognise that a fair number of guesthouses, farms, and hostels are open only in the summer months (as listed).

**CUTTING COSTS** Accommodation prices quoted in this book are based on double-occupancy rooms with private bathroom during the high season. Before you give up and decide that Iceland is unaffordable, realise that there's a lot you can do to lower the price. Travelling in the off season (spring, autumn, and winter) sees hotel rooms discounted by nearly 50%. Not having a private bathroom will also drop the price significantly and if you are going to be travelling in summer, then book ahead. Discounted specials are always available to guests who book through the hotel's website, and even high-priced luxury hotels have great deals. Likewise, following an allegiance plan (booking with one chain or with a tour operator) will normally get you very good hotel rates. Because labour is the real expense of Iceland's hotels, cheaper accommodation is often available to those guests who are willing to lighten the laundry load by not using any bedding. Getting a 'sleeping-bag space' (*svefnpokplass*) costs US$15–40 a night, and in the long run will more than halve the cost of your trip. Sleeping-bag spaces are usually offered in middle-range hotels, farms, and guesthouses. The cost will differ based on the amount of privacy, the cheapest situation being about 45 strangers all snoring in unison in a school classroom (but hey, you just saved 5,000 króna!).

**HOTELS** Iceland's most formal accommodation ranges from the passably decent to sleek design hotels to woody country lodges and a few stalwart classics like the Hótel Borg (see page 138). To make the most of the seasonal shift, a lot of Iceland's schools and colleges are outfitted as tourist hotels in summer and this is the prime habitat for most large groups – if your room feels like a dormitory, that's because it is. To help outsiders know what they're getting, the tourist association has its own five-star classification system that grades tourist accommodation annually. For now, it is only relative internally: the only hotels to advertise their status have three or more stars, and at present, there are no five-star hotels in Iceland. A four-star hotel is the international standard for a 'nice' hotel and this is exactly what most people expect in Iceland, but don't get. On the upside is an emerging class of creative boutique hotels that now dot Iceland's towns and countryside. These are original, unique, and truly pleasant.

Iceland does not have any big international chain hotels (hopefully it will stay that way), but there are a number of local chains that are sure to cover every corner of the country. Icelandair hotels (*www.icehotels.is*) tend to be more upmarket, with modern design and very good restaurants. Fosshótels (*www.fosshotel.is*) are

## ACCOMMODATION PRICE CODES

Based on a single room in summer high season.

| | |
|---|---|
| Luxury **$$$$$** | 37,500ISK+ |
| Upmarket **$$$$** | 28,000–37,499ISK |
| Mid range **$$$** | 17,000–27,999ISK |
| Budget **$$** | 6,000–16,999ISK |
| Cheap **$** | up to 6,000ISK |

probably the most similar to what foreigners expect of a nice, normal hotel (big beds, big rooms and good service). Hótel Edda (*www.hoteledda.is*) advertises its own set of tourist-class hotels, which is not intended to make you feel bad about being a tourist. Most of these are re-outfitted schools, but to a comfortable degree. A new wave of Edda Plus hotels offers a higher standard of year-round accommodation.

Although you can get better discounts sticking to one hotel chain, it can feel a bit formulaic – diversity is a good thing. Also, don't assume that all hotels are outside your budget. Since prices are listed per room, if you're travelling as a couple, a decent hotel can still work out to be less than a guesthouse.

**GUESTHOUSES** The Icelandic *gistiheimilið* combines traditional Icelandic hospitality with the demand for something more personal and local. Some guesthouses look and act more like boutique hotels and others like grandmotherly bed and breakfasts. Obviously, prices are higher than the concept of a guesthouse might imply, but there are also some real gems out there that are definitely worth every penny. The best part about staying in a guesthouse is that you get to meet local Icelanders and really connect with the area you're in. It's worth doing the research to find a good guesthouse and book in advance.

**HOSTELS** Once you've been to Iceland, you'll be too spoiled to stay in a hostel anywhere else. Icelandic youth hostels are top quality – clean, efficient, user-friendly, and affordable. Because the cost of hotels is so prohibitive, the clientele at hostels tend to be more mature and even family-oriented. In general, that means quiet times are respected, people are more courteous, and everything is always kept very clean. Because the demand for clean, quality, and affordable accommodation is so exasperatingly high in summer, you absolutely must book ahead. **Hostelling International Iceland** (*Sundlaugarvegur 34;* ☎ *553 8110;* e *info@hostel.is; www.hostel.is*) oversees 25 privately owned hostels, all of which are better quality than you'd find in mainland Europe. If you are planning on staying in several hostels, it is definitely worth becoming a member of **YHA** (*Hostelling International, Gate Hse, Fretherne Rd, Welwyn Garden City, Herts AL8 6RD, UK;* ☎ *01707 324170;* e *yhf@hihostels.com; www.hihostels.com*). Members receive a significant discount that pays for the membership in just a few stays.

**FARMS** Ever since people lived here, travellers crossing Iceland have found refuge from the wilderness by staying in remote farms all around the country. It was the Viking code of hospitality to welcome all strangers, feed them, keep them warm, and give them a good bed for the night. This practice continued on for centuries, and in the national museum (see page 180) there's a 19th-century travel map of Iceland that pinpoints 'farms in which you can stay'. As Iceland turned into a cash economy, the farmers had to start charging for the night (given the constant flow of tourists) and there now exists a federation of farms that welcomes travellers. Some of these are legitimate farms with hundreds of sheep and lots of horses. Others are simple homesteads in the middle of nowhere that allow you to stop in the middle of Iceland and breathe it all in.

Farmstays are still the most authentic way to see Iceland, and in certain parts of the country, you won't have any choice but to stay on a farm. Amenities are what they are – some might offer private cottages with hot tubs, others might be a re-converted barn with a single bathroom for 20 people. This guide recommends as many farms as possible, but there are hundreds and hundreds to choose from. For more information, contact **Icelandic Farm Holidays** (*Ferðaþjónusta bænda; Reykjavík, Síðumúla 2; ☎ 570 2700; e ifh@farmholidays.is; www.farmholidays.is*). Also note that some farms offer space for tents and caravans to spread out, including access to amenities.

**CAMPING** Camping in Iceland is for masochists – not only for the wetness, cold, and wind (which are admittedly bad) – but also for the crowds and general chaos that surround the practice. In Iceland, every town, village, national park and nature preserve has a designated campsite in order to keep travellers from ruining the countryside. Some campsites are very plush (hot showers, kitchens, drying rooms, clean toilets, etc); others are pretty basic (toilets and cold water only). The Icelandic government should be applauded for its efforts to provide a safe and comfortable place for campers, and kudos to the locals who go to great lengths to keep these sites clean. Alas, the main threat to campsites is the campers themselves, who, as a whole, can be downright obnoxious and untidy. Summer crowds in campsites become so concentrated that their populations outnumber many of Iceland's small villages. That means tent-to-tent apartment blocks and the most unbelievable noise. Despite quiet times (total silence from 23.00 to 07.00), summer campsites are anything but, with people coming and going all through the night-time sunshine. If you happen to be camping next to an Icelandic family reunion, then you might as well just give up on getting any sleep and join in the festivities. With so many people washing, cooking, playing, and grooming, things get messy fast. The worst example of this is the campsite in Reykjavík (see page 146).

Of course, camping is seen as the cheapest way to travel across Iceland and you may land in a campsite that's clean and empty and gorgeous. If you do, don't let anyone else know about it. A common location for campsites is right next to the town swimming pool, which is very convenient for grimy campers who need a good hot shower (and you will). Others are next to farms, guesthouses (even some hotels), and mountain huts, and usually your fees as a camper grant you access to the amenities indoors. Each campsite will let you know where you must pay for the night and a typical charge is US$10–15 a night either per person or per tent (always check). Upon payment, you will be issued with a dated sticker to be attached to your tent or caravan to let them know you're paid up.

The Icelandic word for camping is *tjaldsvæði* and the sign is a blue tent. Free directories of the country's campsites are handed out all over Iceland, or you can do your research online. The English site (*www.camping.is*) is less informative than the Icelandic equivalent (*www.tjaldsvaedi.is*). It is possible to book a space at campsites but not all. A good number of campsites are reviewed/recommended/not recommended in this guide.

If money is your main impetus for camping, then consider carefully. Two to four people sharing a tent will be charged individually. You can then also face additional charges for access to the pool's showers. When all the little costs add up, staying at a youth hostel is of comparative cost to camping out (but a heckuva lot more comfortable). If you still insist on camping, bring earplugs to keep out the noise, flip-flops for the showers, and a lot of goodwill towards strangers.

You may hear that rough or wild camping is against the law. That is not the case – you may camp at will. The practice is not widespread simply because wild camping is not pleasant. Campsites offer wind barriers and facilities with plumbing – a lava field in the middle of nowhere does not. Also, Icelanders take property rights very seriously and chances are that you are camping on someone else's land. If you do camp wild, always seek permission from the farmer who owns the property. Building a fire is illegal and littering will get you a terrible fine.

Caravans and motorhomes are a whole different world and in Iceland's campsites they trump the whole tent scene. Most urban campsites offer limited hook-ups, and in summer, you might want to book ahead to ensure that you can turn on your lights and flush the toilet. Recognise also that while certain campsites might be flooded with caravans (ie: Egilsstaðir, Reykjavík, Akureyri, Húsavík, and Höfn), there's always another one nearby that is far less crowded.

**MOUNTAIN HUTS** The Icelandic Touring Association manages nearly 40 mountain huts (*skálar*) located throughout the remotest parts of Iceland. Most of them are cute little cottages with wooden or tin-siding, ample bunk space, gas stoves, and access to fresh water nearby. This is not luxury accommodation by any means, but a place for hikers to unroll a sleeping bag and get out of the weather. Guests are expected to contribute to the upkeep of these cabins by paying a fee (typically 1,000–2,000ISK per night), paid into a lockbox in the cabin. While some huts are left virtually unused, others (like Landmannalaugar and Thórsmörk) get booked out solid. If you're planning a mountain hike, then guarantee a space by booking in advance (*Ferðafélag Íslands; Reykjavík, Mörkin 6;* ☎ *568 2535;* e *fi@fi.is; www.fi.is*).

**EMERGENCY HUTS** You know things are bad if you're staying in one of these. Iceland's emergency huts are painted bright fluorescent orange and are situated in the most isolated and dangerous parts of the country: think barren coastlines, high mountains, empty deserts, and the tops of glaciers. Almost every decent map of Iceland will show all the locations of emergency huts (normally a red house symbol). Inside the huts you'll find emergency rations of food, bedding, and a radio to contact emergency help. If you are caught up in terrible weather, then the huts are there to help you survive. They are not there to camp out in and non-emergency use is illegal.

## EATING AND DRINKING

**TRADITIONAL FOOD** Icelandic cuisine relies on anything that could be harvested from the barren landscape. It is simple in that its ingredients are what can be pulled from the ocean or what can live off the earth. That means fish, sheep, and the few things that do grow in Iceland – potatoes, blueberries, rhubarb, and caraway seeds. Once upon a time, Icelanders ate a greenish porridge made from boiled moss. Lifestyles have since improved, but there is still a blend of what nature provides and whatever can be shipped from Scandinavia.

Learn your Icelandic **fish** and you'll know something about what's on your plate (see *Chapter 3*, *Fauna*, page 51). Cod (*thorsku*) is a mainstay and on every menu, cooked in so many different ways. Tourists are served gratins and cod cheeks, but historically it was salted cod (*saltfiskur*) that got Icelanders through lean times. Traditional throughout Scandinavia is *fiskbollur* – fried balls of fish and herbs –

## SHARK!

*Hákarl* means shark in Icelandic, but in Iceland it means so much more – almost an edible national medal of honour. The shark in reference is the Greenland shark (*Somniosus microcephalus*), the northernmost shark species in the world. The fish is toxic to eat because its flesh is laced with heavy doses of trimethylamine oxide and urea, a cocktail that works like antifreeze in the shark's body, allowing it to swim in Arctic waters as cold as -2°C. To render it edible, Icelandic tradition advises burying the shark for at least two months to let it decompose. This releases the urea and the flesh begins to break down, after which the meat is hung up to cure for another four months. The half-year process makes the shark safe to eat, though safe does not mean good. Eating *hákarl* tastes like a lump of chewy, pungent blue cheese chased with a shot of ammonia.

though the quintessential Icelandic dish is *plokkfiskur*: flaked white fish (typically plaice) cooked in white sauce with onions and mashed potatoes. *Plokkfiskur* is Iceland's most comforting comfort food, a recipe that only an Icelandic mother can make just right. Try it at least once, and appreciate how it offsets a nasty, dark day outside. Halibut and monkfish were once the poor man's fish that have now entered the realm of gourmet cooking. Both fish are typically poached, baked, or grilled and covered in sauce. Traditional Icelandic fish sauce is pretty bland (butter is all that matters), but that's changing with Iceland's penchant for fusion cuisine. Icelandic salmon (*lax*) is some of the best in the world. In restaurants it's almost always incredibly fresh and cooked to perfection. A more casual snack is *hardfiskur* – white dried fish (traditionally wind-dried) that's chewed much like beef jerky and sold in all the petrol stations as driving food.

With so many sheep around, **lamb** is the red meat option most preferred by Icelanders. Lamb fillets and roasts are what you see on menus, but the pinkish *hangikjöt* (literally 'hanging meat') is the most traditional. Normally served as slices alone or on open-faced sandwiches, the lamb is smoked in sheep dung, which gives it that unique carboniferous flavour. Icelanders also eat every other part of the sheep, including *svið* (singed head), the intestines, stomach, and on holidays *hrútspungar*, or pressed ram's testicles. Icelanders use their cows for dairy, so beef is not traditional (though steak is now listed on every menu). The same goes for horse meat, which was once taboo, but is now a common tourist dish. Whale is unfortunately not taboo, and is still more common than people think. Both the meat and the blubber are eaten, often heavily salted or pickled.

Vegetables and fruit were never Iceland's forte, but potatoes did catch on in the 19th century. Icelanders avoided getting scurvy by eating scurvy grass (see page 364) and blueberries. *Bláber* are actually bilberries and they grow so ubiquitously that you can get filled up just by picking them as you walk. The berries are sweet, juicy, and tart (and blue) and are best from August and into September. The other Icelandic plant is *rabarbari* (rhubarb) that everyone grows in their garden and cooks into tarts, soups, stews, and jams.

Compared with the rest of Europe, Icelanders devour an alarming amount of **dairy** products. Icelandic butter, milk, yoghurt and ice cream are some of the best you'll ever taste, and the truly unique *skyr* (see opposite) is downright addictive. Traditional Icelandic cheese is little known outside the country, but ranges from very soft brie-like cheese to harder Edam-style cheeses.

Iceland does pretty well in the **pastry** department and most towns have at least one daily bakery that warrants a good taste-testing. Icelandic baked goods are dreamt up from the simplest ingredients but are diverse enough to differ from region to region. *Brauð* (bread) comes in many different shapes, and ranges from white, to seeded, to the traditional slightly sweetened brown bread that is sometimes steamed in hot springs.

Icelandic pastries are also never too sweet – the perfect accompaniment to coffee or tea. *Kleinur* are the lovely twisted doughnuts that look like diamond-shaped knots. Once upon a time they were fried in melted sheep fat, but now you can find the very common lighter version sold everywhere from museum cafés to petrol stations. Iceland's other doughnut is the *ástarpungar* or 'love balls', which are round and dotted with sweet raisins. *Flatkakka* is the traditional 'flat cake' on which butter and meat (lamb or salmon) is served, and the *hveitikakka*, or 'flour cake', is a very basic flat bread only found in the West Fjords. Gingerbread-like spice cake is very traditional, and for weddings and happy occasions, one eats *hjónabandsæla* or 'happy marriage cake': a layered jam and pastry tart.

## *SKYR*: ICELAND'S DAIRY DELICACY

*Eliza Reid*

Iceland's marketing gurus may enjoy painting the nation's traditional cuisine as replete with pickled ram's testicles, sheep's heads, putrefied shark, and spiced innards, but there is food originating from this little island that is delicious, flavour-packed, and cheap. And I don't just mean hot dogs. *Skyr* is the quintessential Icelandic dairy product. Some describe it as thick yoghurt, others as sour curds. It is high in protein and calcium and very low in fat (though some add a lot of sugar).

*Skyr* has been mentioned from as early as the 11th century. The saga of Grettir the Strong (see page 321) recounts a fight that Grettir has with Auðunn, who throws a bag of *skyr* at Grettir. The strong man 'thought this a greater insult than if Auðunn had given him a bad wound'. One of the biggest fans of *skyr* in Iceland is known for his addiction. His name, Skyrgámur, means '*skyr* gobbler', and he is the eighth of 13 Icelandic yule lads to visit children in the days leading up to Christmas (see page 37). Skyrgámur will eat any *skyr* that is in the house and, with the super-powers befitting a Santa, can even open any locked container of *skyr*.

*Skyr* has found its uses into the 20th century. The last death sentence ever handed down by the Icelandic courts was in 1914 to a woman who was convicted of killing her brother by feeding him poisoned *skyr*.

*Skyr* is available in all local shops, in either individual portions complete with plastic spoon, or larger shareable tubs. The best way to enjoy this treat is the traditional way: plain *skyr* with sugar and milk added on top to taste and possibly spiced up with some fresh fruit or jam. Restaurants often offer *skyr* desserts either served plain with berries or used as the slightly tart base to delicious *skyrkökur* (*skyr* cakes).

There's an old Icelandic proverb '*Þeir sletta skyrinu sem eiga það*' (literally 'they throw around the *skyr* who own it'), which means that those who can afford to waste usually do so. *Skyr* has been a valuable commodity over the centuries; we residents need to make the most of living in the country that invented it. And for visitors – dig in! Those who can afford to buy *skyr* should do so.

**TOURIST FOOD** Iceland has embraced fast food with a worrisome vengeance. In some places, restaurants serving pizza, hamburgers, hot dogs, fried chicken, and fish and chips outnumber traditional eateries. At the other extreme is the trend of serving culinary curiosities to tourists. This includes traditional game (puffin, guillemot, and whale) along with oddities for the sake of oddities (eg: horse and dolphin). Certain game (like puffin and reindeer) are said to be harvested sustainably; others are not. Eating any type of wild game should be discouraged because it contributes to a tourist market for wild animals. At the forefront of this issue is whale meat, which continues to be a heated political debate in Iceland. Tourists wrongly assume that because whale is on the menu, 'it must be OK'. It's not – restaurants rarely know the origins of the whale they are serving and Icelandic whaling ships continue to hunt endangered species. Another controversy surrounds puffins – though Icelanders reassure visitors that there are millions and millions of puffins (which is true), Iceland is the last major breeding ground left for these birds in the world. Know that the great numbers of puffins have disappeared from the United States and parts of Britain because tourists were eating them. As tourism in Iceland grows, it is vital that the market does not decide the future of Icelandic wildlife.

**SWEETS** Icelanders consume a staggering amount of sugar. A walk through any food store or petrol station reveals a national penchant for sweets that rivals the sweet tooth of America and Great Britain. *Lakkrís* (liquorice) is a Scandinavian staple, though you'll find it here in every way, shape and taste (allsorts, black and salty, soft, hard, chewy, brittle, and chocolate-covered). Icelandic Síríus chocolate is unique with its honey-like flavour and their kilo-size boxes of dark chocolate-covered raisins are perfect driving food. Some may find that soft-serve ice cream laced with gummi bears is a bit much.

**DRINK** The first thing that anyone should drink in Iceland is the water, which is incredibly pure and tastes so good that upon returning home, you'll feel disappointed by your tap. In most places, it is quite safe to simply dip into the clear rocky streams, waterfalls, and lakes and drink the cool water. Almost all the cold water you encounter is glacial run-off and free from the sulphur smell that comes with naturally heated groundwater. When searching for a spot to drink from, look for clear water flowing over rocks. If you are somewhere remote and there's nothing animal or human upriver, the water is safe. Otherwise, use caution if drinking water near farms, cities and dams. Mineral springs dot the countryside, some of which are naturally carbonated (see page 264) and bottled Icelandic water is sold everywhere.

### *PYLSUR*: ICELAND'S FAMOUS HOT DOGS

The Japanese have their tea ceremony and Icelanders have their hot dogs. Both are beloved traditions, though Iceland's adoration for *pylsur* only goes back to World War II when American troops introduced the sausage. Sold mainly in petrol stations and fast-food diners, ordering *einn með öllu* ('one with everything') is a must, even if you would never dream of touching a hot dog back home. Everything means ketchup, raw chopped onions, crispy fried onions, regular mustard, spicy sweet mustard and remoulade (a kind of pickled mayonnaise). It's sloppy but delicious.

Even with all that clean water, Icelanders imbibe more Coca-Cola per capita than any other nation on earth (115 litres (30 gallons) per year). Icelandic shops even carry one-litre cans of Coke sold for individual consumption! Malt extract is a traditional Icelandic non-alcoholic beverage that tastes like sweetened Guinness.

Alcohol is sold at the Vínbúðin, the government-approved off-licence. Wine is prohibitively expensive and French and Spanish are the most common. Iceland's national liquor is *Brennivin* which derives from the Icelandic verb 'to burn'. Known as *svarti dauði* ('black death'), the liquor is distilled from potatoes and caraway seeds, and is utterly repulsive. Lately, a number of designer vodkas have emerged in Iceland, though none of these is traditional. Icelanders have been brewing ale since the age of the sagas, but **beer** or *bjór* was officially banned in 1915. The country's prohibition lasted for decades, during which time breweries sold non-alcoholic beer to the disgruntled populace. The ban was only lifted in 1989 after a pair of Icelandic students (recently returned from Germany) opened a bar selling non-alcoholic beer with a hidden shot of vodka. The bar quickly outdid all others in Reykjavík and it is still a popular drinking spot (see *Gaukur á Stöng*, page 161). Beer is still not a preferred beverage in Iceland today, but two breweries have made their mark on the nation. **Egils** (*www.egils.is*) is named after the saga hero Egil Skallagrímsson (see page 258) and makes a variety of pilsners, malts, and lagers. **Vífilfell** (*www.vifilfell.is*) is named after Ingólfur's good servant Vífil (see page 190) and is the creator of Víking lager. Because of its expense, beer is often sold in half-pints, while club-goers will carry pint-size cans inside their bags and purses when going out. In the last ten years, Iceland's beer consumption has more than doubled.

The Icelandic national religion that is coffee has been in force ever since the Danes first brought it here. No matter where you go, you will be offered a cup of coffee, typically with lots of sugar and lots of milk. Even when people speak of 'tea' they usually mean coffee.

**RESTAURANTS** Most restaurants open right before lunch (around 11.30) and stay open until late, though the kitchen always closes by 22.00. Almost every menu in Iceland is printed in English and reading between the lines is a good way to learn the language. Hotel restaurants are open for breakfast from about 07.00 onwards and tend to serve a formulaic breakfast: coffee with a smorgasbord of a few Icelandic delights (eg: pickled herring, smoked lamb, etc) next to continental staples like muesli, yoghurt, sausage, cold-cut ham and cheese, along with bread, butter and jam.

Icelanders get a little sensitive to criticism about their cuisine – as they should, considering that most of the past critics were eating in bad restaurants. The core of Iceland's tourist restaurants fall under a category that I refer to (affectionately) as 'fish-and-lamb'. This being Iceland everyone serves fish and lamb, yes, but 'fish-and-lamb' denotes the tourist standard in which 'a taste of Iceland' is so monotone that it begs an aftertaste of somewhere else. The early days of mass tourism have now passed and Iceland's dining culture has matured a great deal. Today it's the Icelanders who are the discerning critics and they have zero patience for an uncreative chef.

If you find yourself eating at a 'fish-and-lamb', all is not lost. The identical menus always have at least one good fish dish (salmon or something white), a slew of pasta dishes, chicken (always), and a choice of hearty desserts. That said, try to avoid doing it too often because there are a lot more exciting places where you could be spending your money.

Most visitors are appalled by restaurant food prices (gasp!), some of which are comically high. To lure foreigners to the table, VAT was reduced to 7% in restaurants, but this has had little effect. The fact is that food is expensive in Iceland, and good

## RESTAURANT PRICE CODES

Based on the average price of a single main dish.

| | |
|---|---|
| Expensive $$$$$ | 3,200ISK+ |
| Above average $$$$ | 2,500–3,199ISK |
| Reasonable $$$ | 1,800–2,499ISK |
| Good deal $$ | 1,200–1,799ISK |
| Cheap $ | under 1,200ISK |

food is very expensive. For that reason, it's hard to categorise restaurants merely by the price of an entrée – appetisers and light meals might cost around 1,500ISK, a fish dish will cost slightly more, but the full-bodied red meat options will be double that. Furthermore, there's not always a correlation between price and quality.

On the top of the spectrum are Iceland's glitzy gourmets that mix over-the-top flamboyance with artistic experimentation. Some of these restaurants are spectacular, others not so much. Their main flaw is that Iceland is a small country and its chefs like to chase trends as a collective. If one guy starts doing Icelandic pan-Asian fusion, suddenly every 'nice' restaurant is doing the same thing to a sickening degree. Fortunately, the trends are moving back towards fresh, organic, and traditional Icelandic food with just a little flair.

**CUTTING COSTS** If you're trying to keep food costs down but you're sick of eating carrot sticks, it is possible to dine out and not break the bank. To start, go to fancy restaurants and just order the house's fish soup. *Fiskisúpa* is a fail-safe Icelandic staple, served in a generous bowl with fresh bread and butter on the side. It's warm and filling and only costs around 1,000ISK. Likewise, just ask the chef to grill you a fillet from the day's catch. Normally that gets you a piping-hot plate of fresh fish minus all the frilly accoutrements and at a much lower price. Also, do not assume that ordering salads will save you cash – all lettuce is imported and therefore very expensive. Conserve your money by breaking tourist protocol. Don't waste money on paid breakfasts at hotels and restaurants. Instead, eat your morning meal at a bakery or on your own, and put that money towards lunch. Eat your restaurant meals at lunch and your home-cooked meals in the evening – two can eat for the price of one at dinner. Lastly, go and splurge once. Better to eat hot dogs all week and save your money for some fabulous restaurant, than to eat at fish-and-lambs the whole time.

**SHOPS** No matter how small a place it is, every Icelandic crossroads or village has its own ***sjoppa*** (pronounced 'shyoppa') where you can buy just about everything you might need in Iceland. Normally these are part of the petrol station, and in the smallest towns, the *sjoppa* is the beacon of civilisation amid a lifeless landscape. Diverse groceries are packed onto the shelves (milk, bread, canned food, etc) along with new tyres, antifreeze, windshield scrapers, maps, hiking boots and so much more. There's always at least one pay phone, the public toilets, and the town's hot-dog and ice-cream stand. The *sjoppa* is open longer than any other store, from around 08.00 until midnight, or sometimes for 24 hours.

**SELF-CATERING** You can save a lot of money in Iceland by skipping the pricey restaurants and buying your food right off the shelf. **Bonus** (*www.bonus.is*) is the largest supermarket chain with the lowest prices in the country (the one with the pink piggy bank). The chain of **10/11** or **11/11** stores is meant to be open during those times, but isn't always. Dried soup packets mixed up with boiling water is standard travellers' fare, as is whole-wheat bread, Icelandic butter and cheese, smoked salmon and sausage. The only vegetables grown in Iceland (in greenhouses) are tomatoes, cucumbers, mushrooms, and carrots. It's amazing how much you can do with those few ingredients. Everything else that's green is imported and that's why a chocolate bar is cheaper than an apple.

**VEGETARIANS** Icelanders are pretty tolerant people but vegetarians do befuddle them (this is, after all, a country that eats seal flippers). Reykjavík has a number of top-quality vegetarian restaurants (see page 153), and other large towns like Akureyri cater to diverse dietary restrictions. Plus, anywhere that has an Asian restaurant normally has a few veggie dishes. More remote areas are plainly carnivorous and green salads are rare the whole country over. About half the restaurants that serve fish soup also carry vegetable soup, and if you tell the waiter that you are vegetarian, they're likely to point out the pasta menu. Chefs in the nicer restaurants pride themselves in coming up with some really adventurous vegetarian dishes, and most vegetarians are surprised to find that they fare quite well in Iceland. Vegans will have a tough time since dairy is such a staple in Iceland.

## PUBLIC HOLIDAYS

| | |
|---|---|
| **1 January** | New Year's Day |
| **Maundy Thursday** | |
| **Good Friday** | |
| **Easter Sunday** | |
| **Easter Monday** | |
| **6 April** | First day of summer |
| **1 May** | Labour Day |
| **1 June** | Fisherman's Day |
| **17 June** | Independence Day |
| **First weekend in August** | Bank holiday |
| **25 December** | Christmas Day |
| **31 December** | New Year's Eve |

You'll find that few people work on or around midsummer's day (21 June), that the *réttir* (roundup) in September is a time of diversion, and no matter what time of year, Sunday morning is totally dead – nobody moves before noon. Big parades take place both on 6 April (the first day of summer) and on Iceland's Independence Day, when children march in the streets wearing traditional Icelandic dress.

## SHOPPING

The most abundant shopping to be done is in Reykjavík (see page 162), but if you're looking for Viking helmets with plastic horns, then tourist shops will oblige you all the way round the ring road. The most traditional souvenir is hand-knitting, in particular, the Icelandic wool sweater. Traditional designs are snowflake-like patterns that radiate from the neckline in white, grey, and black, and the real thing will cost you plenty. Handmade socks, mittens, and hats are just as wonderful. Duty-free stores will also sell pre-packaged salmon, which is usually legal to take back into your own country.

## ACTIVITIES

Iceland is fast becoming an adventure destination, where adrenalin junkies can throw themselves into rushing rivers or snowmobile off the edge of a glacier. Other activities to consider in Iceland are kayaking, and diving (see page 219), which is something quite unique. Adventure tour companies are listed in the regional chapters, though here's a few in the capital:

**Activity Group** Reykjavík, Tunugháls 8; ☎ 580 9900; e activity@activity.is; www.activity.is. Offering glacier, snowmobile, jeep, all-terrain vehicle (ATV) & dog-sledding tours.
**Explore** (or Arctic Rafting) Reykjavík, Laugavegur 11; ☎ 562 7000; e info@arcticrafting.is; www.arcticrafting.is. Offering white-water rafting, jumping into canyons, caving, & ice-climbing. One of the most diverse activity companies.
**Iceland Rovers** Reykjavík, Bíldshöfði 14; ☎ 567 1720; e icelandrovers@icelandrovers.is; www.icelandrovers.is. Offering Jeep & glacier tours in the southwest.

For details of other tour operators, see page 72.

**FISHING** Fishing in the sea is what Icelanders do for a living. The politics of who has the right to catch fish where goes way back to the beginning (see *Chapter 2*, page 21). By law, anyone can fish from the dock in the harbour, but all coastal fishing rights belong to the 'farmer' or landowner of the property. With the recent buying up of fishing rights by larger fishing corporations, it's not so simple anymore. The point is, if you want to go fishing, it's best to do so with another party. Guests who stay on a farm that has fishing rights will often be issued a day pass for a minimal fee. Tour operators (mainly the whale-watching and ferry companies) offer deep-sea fishing excursions. These are half-day to full-day affairs that cost upwards of US$250. Of course, the best option is to hitch a ride on a real Icelandic fishing boat.

**ANGLING** The first Vikings who arrived in Iceland defended their rivers to the death. The same protective spirit surrounds this precious resource today and angling rights coincide with land rights for individual rivers. When an Icelander refers to a stream as a 'salmon river', they mean that a certain river has been designated solely for catching salmon. The same goes for trout. The salmon season for rod-fishing lasts from June until August, but every river's own particular 'season' stops and starts at different dates. Because this is some of the best fly-fishing in the world, foreign anglers are charged about US$1,000 per day for the rights to fish on a premier salmon river. For trout rivers, the price is about US$400 per day. Salmon fishing other than on designated rivers is illegal. Also, all fishing gear and tackle brought into the country must be disinfected at customs. For the authority on the subject, and to plan an angling outing, contact the **Federation of Icelandic River Owners** (*Landssamband Veiðifélaga; Reykjavík, Hagatorgi;* ☎ *533 1510;* e *info@angling.is; www.angling.is*).

**SWIMMING** If God made Iceland to be cold and miserable, His consolation prize was a land of naturally hot water. Today, you could easily fit the entire population of the country into the 120+ public swimming pools that benefit even the remotest villages. Swimming indoors and outdoors is a great thing to do in Iceland, especially when the weather stinks. Some pools are conducive to swimming laps with designated exercise lanes. Others are perfect for children, with waterslides, and playful wading areas. But the real pastime of 'going to the pool' involves sitting in the hot pots and chatting with friends and strangers. This guide lists as many pools as possible, but is by no means complete.

Proud of their clean and natural hot water, Icelandic swimming pools have little to no chlorine in them. Therefore, hygiene demands that all bathers shower before and after their swim WITHOUT a bathing suit. That means completely naked, and although Icelanders have learnt to be sensitive to the qualms of bashful foreigners, they will still make you do it. In some areas, locker-room attendants are paid to stand guard and watch to assure that you use soap in all the right places. In case you need guidance, the graphic signs on the wall show you exactly what body parts need special attention. Do as the natives do and dry off completely in the shower area. Dripping water all over the place will earn you a brisk finger-wagging.

**HOT POTS** Despite what tourist brochures might tell you, there are no hot tubs in Iceland, only 'hot pots'. In Icelandic ***heittur pottur*** (which sounds too much like 'Harry Potter' to go unmentioned) are typically kept at human body temperature (a cool 38°C). At public swimming pools, there's a few hotter pools. Once you start venturing into 40–45°C pools, then beware and don't overdo it. Bright-red skin and a light head means you've been in there too long. Few natural hot springs in Iceland are cool enough for bathing, so only visit 'natural hot pots' that use diverted rivers to cool it down. My favourite is at Hveravellir (see page 434), but if you come upon one with fewer patrons, test the water with your hand held slightly above the steam. Nature's thermostat is fickle and changes at will. Also, it's a good idea to remove any silver jewellery before stepping into a natural hot pool (like the Blue Lagoon).

## SEA SWIMMING

*Gúdni Thorlacius Jóhannesson*

The sea temperature around Iceland ranges from just above 0°C in wintertime to around 10–15°C in summer. Consequently, swimming in the sea is not a common affair. Still, a few sea-swimming clubs exist and in summertime this type of physical exercise is invigorating and risk-free, though you should never venture far from shore. In Reykjavík, Nauthólsvík Bay is a popular place to jump in for a quick swim, especially because surplus water from the Reykjavík heating system increases the water temperature there. Those who prefer 'normal' sea temperatures often go to Bakkatjörn in Seltjarnanes. Only experienced swimmers should attempt to go for a dip in wintertime, and make it quick!

The boldest sea swimmers in Iceland traverse fjords or repeat the feat of Grettir the Strong who, according to the saga of Grettir, swam from Drangey in Skagafjörður to the mainland, a distance of 7.5km (see page 321). The sagas contain other tales of epic feats of this kind and similarly great achievements have taken place in more recent times. In March 1984, a fishing boat sank around 6km east of the Westmann Islands. Four men drowned but the fifth one, Guðlaugur Friðthórsson, managed to swim ashore and then struggle to safety across treacherous lava fields (see page 237). Those who have attempted to swim for a minute or two in the seas around Iceland in winter will easily comprehend the magnitude of this effort.

For more information on local sea-swimming clubs, visit www.sjosundfelagislands.com (the official group) or www.skitkalt.com (a local group in Reykjavík).

The water won't ruin anything beyond repair, but the sulphur will turn your rings a strange sort of black that takes a while to polish off.

**HIKING** Hiking can mean scuffling around a pile of lava rock behind your hotel and it can also mean trudging for weeks across the inland desert. Take a good pair of hiking boots and do your research. Have a good hiking map that shows contours and river crossings. In Iceland, the land survey maps (1:100,000) are the best and you can pick these up at any bookshop in Reykjavík, or check them out online (*www.lmi.is*). Some hikers swear by a GPS and most hiking maps today do give GPS co-ordinates. This can be very important in Iceland, when weather distorts the look of places. Speaking of weather, watch out for wind, especially near cliff tops and on mountain slopes. A single, unexpected gust can blow you over. When planning a trip, you might consider linking up with the **Icelandic Touring Association** (*Ferðafélag Íslands; Reykjavík, Mörkin 6;* ☎ *568 2535;* e *fi@fi.is; www.fi.is*). They manage all the hikers' mountain huts, and also plan some wonderful treks, both short ones and very long ones – sometimes truly epic journeys. There is no better way to get to experience those parts of Iceland that seem inaccessible than to join this ruddy group of Icelandic hikers. Their all-inclusive package tours are good value and their guides do all the hard work for you.

Hiking on ice is a whole different story and it's best to do this with a professional company like the **Iceland Mountain Guides** (*Reykjavík, Vagnhöfði 7B;* ☎ *587 9999;* e *info@mountainguides.is; www.mountainguides.is*). They offer training and excursions for ice-climbing, glacier walking, etc. They also do trips onto all the southern glaciers and this really is the most intimate way of connecting with Iceland's ice. If you are planning a serious trek to somewhere remote on your own, you should register with **ICE-SAR** (*Icelandic Association for Search and Rescue; Reykjavík, Skógarhlíð;* ☎ *570 5900;* e *slysavarnafelagid@landsbjorg.is; www.landsbjorg.is*). This is a volunteer organisation with some serious equipment – they will be the ones looking for you should you get lost, so it's worth helping them out by letting them know the general area where you might be.

## BEYOND ICELAND

Iceland's closest neighbour is so close that you just might feel Greenland beckoning you from the east. Iceland is still the main gateway to Greenland and getting to the world's largest island is an easy hop from Reykjavík City Airport. Either of Iceland's domestic airlines (see pages 91–2) fly the two-hour+ flight to Kulusuk, Ilulisat, Narsarsuaq, and the capital Nuuk. Day tours are also increasingly popular, allowing you all the comforts of big-city Reykjavík, but dropping you down in the real land of ice for just a spell. These packages are very expensive (about US$1,000) and pure punishment since it feels like snatching an ice cream from a young child who's just taken his first lick. For more information on Greenland, visit www.greenland.com.

To the west lie the misty Faroe Islands, a most vivid destination in the middle of the North Sea. On the Smyril Line ferry (see page 78), it's just a day away from the port in Seyðisfjörður, and by air it's less than two hours. Air Iceland (*www.airiceland.is*) and the Faroese carrier Atlantic Airways (*www.atlantic.fo*) both fly from Reykjavík City Airport to Tórshavn. If you do venture to the isles, do be sure to read the wonderful guidebook by James Proctor *Faroe Islands: the Bradt Travel Guide*. For more information, visit www.faroeislands.com.

**Glacier safety** People get hurt badly on glaciers – a few from bad luck and misfortune, many others from sheer stupidity. Ice is a totally different element with which most of us have little experience: it's very slippery and it breaks and melts and refreezes in all kinds of interesting ways. Glaciers are very beautiful and worth exploring, but do it properly and assume nothing.

Don't go scrambling up a glacier as if you're climbing a mountain. If you have no previous experience of ice-climbing/walking, then go with an organised tour led by a professional guide. They can introduce you to the equipment and teach you what to look for on the ice.

Glacier tongues tend to be bumpy and slippery, which means the easiest ice to access can also be the most treacherous. Use crampons and ice-axes, and be especially alert near the sound of trickling water – *moulins* are extremely interesting but deadly. Also with ice, what is above you is just as important as what is beneath you. Use great caution entering ice caves and avoid standing next to giant walls of ice. At any moment, a house-sized chunk might fall on you – this happens more frequently than you might think.

Flat, snow-covered ice caps require a different approach: on glaciers covered with snow, always use ropes (tied between two people). Beware of snow bridges, where snow has drifted over a crevasse, and beware of crevasses themselves. This is best done by going with a guide who knows the glacier or knows how to avoid crevasses. It is very tricky to pull someone out of a crevasse – those who do not die from the fall tend to perish from shock or hypothermia. Snowmobile tours on glaciers are quite common and a great way to explore vast distances of ice. Never stray from the guide, who will navigate a way around the crevasses.

A few key reminders:

- Never walk alone on the ice
- Have and use proper gear: crampons, ropes, and ice-axes
- If you've never received proper ice training, go with a professional guide
- Avoid steep ledges, ice walls and caves, flowing water, and crevasses

**Geothermal areas** In areas of high geothermal activity, always stick to the path. If there is no path then be smart about where you step (not between two boiling mud pots or hot springs). Don't trust appearances as what's happening on the ground looks very different from what's happening beneath it. Foolhardy hikers who step out of bounds have broken through the crust and scalded their legs. Even in old volcanic areas, the rocks can get so hot that it will melt shoes and burn feet. I really shouldn't have to say this, but don't stick your hand into a hot spring to check 'if it's really hot'. A majority of these pools have a water temperature close to boiling (100°C), and yet there's always someone who tries to put their hand in it.

## ARTS AND ENTERTAINMENT

Every Icelander is an artist, or an actor, or a musician, or a filmmaker. Thus the 'arts' are rarely held in a separate realm but are part of everyday life. You might be sitting in a restaurant when suddenly the owner picks up a violin and starts playing to his diners, or you may comment on the painting in your hotel room only to find the manager painted it herself. Such is the delightfulness of Iceland.

The 'high arts' of theatre, opera and ballet are all available in the city (see *Reykjavík*, pages 161–2). However, the cost can be prohibitive and, honestly, it rarely

## GOING ON THE *RUNTUR*

Notwithstanding the false perceptions of British tourists, a *runtur* is not a mad alcohol binge or 'pub crawl'. Rather, the *runtur* is a solid Icelandic tradition of going out on the town in your car. The phenomenon is best exhibited on Saturday night in smaller Icelandic towns, when cars swarm bumper to bumper and inch along a well-designated route in the city centre. Out of nowhere, the empty streets turn into a midnight traffic jam and the cars go around and around the same few blocks. In Reykjavík, there may be an equivalent mass of people moving about the streets, but in smaller towns, and even in a city like Akureyri, the *runtur* is made up of cars only and it is the event of the week. People dress up to 'go out', knowing they will spend most of their time in the back seat of a car.

Above all, the *runtur* is a social event. When the streets are frigid, the party just moves into the comforts of a car heater and stereo. All you have to do is cram a car full of good friends and join in the parade. Everyone is in search of the scene and one another – passengers might change vehicles to chat with friends and find out who's out and who's not. A stop for snacks or fast food is almost requisite, and there may be venturing into bars, but it's the driving that makes the *runtur*.

has anything to do with Icelandic culture. If you want to see opera, go to Vienna. An exception might be the stage (there are many wonderful Icelandic playwrights), and even if you don't understand the language, the drama itself is top quality.

Live music is where Iceland really shines, be it a symphony orchestra or an outdoor rock concert. Icelandic choirs are an art form in themselves, and you can catch a concert at local churches almost any time of the year, though autumn to spring is the more obvious time of year. This is not necessarily religious music, but churches are regular concert venues in smaller towns, and a lot of traditional Icelandic polyphonic music is religious. In Reykjavík, check the *Grapevine* (*www.grapevine.is*); it posts extensive music listings for the upcoming week, which can include anything – folk, jazz, rock, electronic. In smaller towns and fishing villages, go to the main restaurant or pub and look at their sign board. There will always be at least one Icelandic singer passing through, and even the smallest places have a local band that will pick up their instruments once the beer starts to flow.

Going to the cinema is an Icelandic tradition and the common remedy for bad weather or severe darkness. Though the experience can be costly (US$15–20 per seat), the theatres are some of the most comfortable in the world. Besides the usual American and British blockbusters, Scandinavian films are popular, as are international films in general. Iceland has a small but passionate film industry with devotees around the world. Foreign films are always subtitled into Icelandic, while Icelandic films are often subtitled into English. For something uniquely Icelandic, check out the national film archives in Hafnarfjörður (see page 194).

Icelanders hold the visual arts in such high esteem that the capital has a disproportionate number of art museums and galleries (see pages 182–4) in relation to its petite population, as does Akureyri (see page 351). Buying art in Iceland is fairly straightforward and the Icelandic post is good about shipping large works of art in a protected and secure manner.

## MEDIA AND COMMUNICATIONS

**PRINT MEDIA** Iceland's national morning newspaper is ***Morgunblaðið*** (*www.mbl.is*); ***Fréttablaðið*** is the free daily paper that is comparable to the *Daily Mail* or *New York Post*. Reykjavík's main English-language newspaper is the ***Grapevine*** (*www.grapevine.is*) and although it started as an edgy alternative weekly, it's grown into the official unofficial resource on travel, music, and all cultural goings on in the country. To find out what's going on while you're in Iceland, check it out. The ***Iceland Review*** (*www.icelandreview.com*) is an artfully presented glossy magazine known for its stunning photography and thoughtful articles (in English) dealing with Iceland's most current issues. Similarly, ***Icelandic Geographic*** (*www.icelandicgeographic.com*) shows off gorgeous photographic spreads of Icelandic nature backed up with serious articles on conservation and wildlife. ***Atlantica*** is the in-flight magazine for Icelandair, and although it covers airline business matters and foreign travel destinations, there is always at least one piece on Iceland.

**POST** The ***postur*** (☎ *580 1000*; e *postur@postur.is; www.postur.is*) is open 09.00–16.30 Monday–Friday. Every medium-sized town has its own office, visible for the red and yellow colour scheme. You can also buy postage stamps at any petrol station, bookshop, or *sjoppa*. It is possible for travellers to receive letters and parcels at a particular office.

### PHOTOGRAPHING BIRDS IN ICELAND

*Brian Gratwicke*

In summertime, Iceland's breeding-bird cliffs, offshore islands and insect-rich lakes are a paradise for bird paparazzi. When visiting seaside habitats, it pays to be out between 11.00 and 03.00 when the light is most dramatic and when seabirds like puffins and razorbills visit the cliffs in the highest numbers. In some places you can get so close to puffins that a wide-angle lens offers a rare chance to capture them in a landscape setting. The sheer drops and uncertain footing of the Swiss-cheese-like turf could quickly deliver you to the rocky shore below, so it's best for you and the birds if you stick to paths and stony outcrops. Be sure to head out to the puffins if the wind picks up. Puffins are normally such poor fliers that they will glide for minutes as they try to figure out how to land. Rarely do puffins pose in mid air, just a few feet away and with sand eels in their beaks!

At some stage, summer bird photographers will get attacked by Arctic terns or *krías*. This clearly means that you are in their nesting space, so keep to the paths and watch where you tread – terns often lay their eggs on roadsides, while their flightless chicks scuttle rapidly between the grassy tussocks. If you want to get a classic tern 'dive-bombing' shot, try using a wide-angle lens set on manual focus, and sit down in one place on the road edge waiting for the bird to fill your frame. The terns are quite obliging and will not stop harassing you until you have your shot. Staying in one place minimises the chance of you stepping on a chick or an egg while your eye is focused elsewhere.

Look out for other opportunities too, such as fishing boats coming into the harbour, followed by fulmars and kittiwakes brawling over the fish scraps. Having a few slices of bread in your pocket is always a useful bribe for black-headed gulls, which can be coaxed to pose nicely in front of a backdrop like the Icelandic flag. Don't overdo it though as too much unregulated contact between photographers and birds is irresponsible.

**TELEVISION AND RADIO** Until very recently, Icelandic television only broadcast a single station that would turn off after nine at night (Thursdays played snow because it was the channel's day off). The information age has blessed Icelanders with more TV channels than they could ever watch but you probably didn't come to Iceland to watch subtitled soap operas. **RÚV** (*www.ruv.is*) is Iceland's national broadcasting service and its most entertaining show is the morning weather report in English at 07.30.

**TELEPHONE** Iceland's country code is +354 (omitted from listings in this book). There are no separate city codes in Iceland. Once in the country, just dial the seven-digit number. To call outside Iceland, dial 00 followed by the country code and phone number and to make an international collect call, dial 800 8050. Pay phones are still around at transportation stations and public places, but chucking 100ISK coins into the box becomes dull. Purchase phonecards at any *sjoppa* or the post office. International phonecards are also available and can be used from any phone.

Iceland sports more mobile phones than it has people. Foreigners can rent phones (though this ends up costing a lot) or bring their own phone and buy a chip from one of two operators: Síminn (*www.siminn.is*) or Vodafone (*www.vodafone.is*). The tourist information office in Reykjavík (see page 136) has a starter package for tourists with their own phone that includes an Icelandic chip and talk time. Additional pay-as-you-go cards can be bought at the stores of the mobile provider (whose hours always seem inconvenient). Mobile coverage is great on the ring road and in towns but gets spotty near ice or a recent lava field (due to the magnetic disruption). Iceland's emergency number is ☎ 112; for directory assistance (in English), dial ☎ 118. In case you wondered, the Icelandic word for telephone – *sími* – means 'thread'. In the olden days (not so long ago), a long line of farms would all be attached to a single party line along which messages would get passed.

**INTERNET** Iceland is one of the most wired countries on earth and getting on the net is never a problem. Service can cost, though – tourist information offices will charge US$5–10 for 30 minutes, and nicer hotels will offer high-speed connections at outlandish prices. Wi-Fi is now available in all of the upmarket, corporate-style hotels in Reykjavík and in a surprisingly high number of medium-priced hotels elsewhere in the country. Smaller hotels and youth hostels will make one or two computers available to guests for a small fee. There are very few expressly defined internet cafés in Iceland, simply because so many of them already have Wi-Fi and public hotspots now cover much of the city centre.

## BUSINESS

Business hours are from 09.00 to 17.00, though weekends fluctuate and Sunday morning is never a good time. Icelanders work hard and rest hard – one reason why the country has been so successful on the international market. The best way to learn how to do business in Iceland is to read the sagas, many of which are business histories of family enterprises. The Icelandic Vikings had figured out shares, percentages, and shared profits centuries before any of our currencies came into existence. Likewise, Iceland's longstanding co-operative movement has played an important role in the development of business and industry. Iceland's modern business culture is still just as straightforward – there is no enigma waiting to be cracked by some outside hotshot consultant. Icelanders are out buying, developing, and selling like everyone else in the world. What is unique in Iceland is how small a place it is – everyone knows everyone else and word travels quickly. You might be surprised at how many people know of your presence and mission when you arrive. Other side effects of a small country and the concise economy include a very limited banking structure, which basically means that all the money flows from a single source. Also, there are a number of de facto monopolies that are in place, where all major enterprises are owned by a very limited number of people. Furthermore, Icelandic companies do not have the extensive hierarchies known in the rest of Europe and North America. You might sit down for a meeting with a marketing director only to have the CEO walk in for a direct chat.

Icelanders conduct business freely in English, but don't assume they're catching all the jargon and buzzwords that you're importing from back home. Speak clearly and use plain terminology. Above all else, Icelanders appreciate directness. Business meetings tend to be concise and to the point, starting with an exchange of business cards and then the matter at hand. The pleasantries and personal exchanges normally take place afterwards. Meeting over coffee, a drink, or dinner is quite typical. If you are on a business trip in Iceland, you are likely to be invited to participate in some recreational activity: to see the wilderness, to go hiking or boating or horseriding, or visit some cultural or historical monument. A genuine interest in Iceland and Icelandic culture is appreciated.

## CULTURAL ETIQUETTE

The most incorrect assumption outsiders make is that because Icelanders are (in principle) Scandinavians, they behave like Scandinavians. That is simply not the case and you'll find it quite impossible to place Icelanders into any box. Your typical Icelander embodies the rugged individualism of Americans, the can-do attitude of Canadians, an English sense of propriety, a cultural solidarity not unlike that of the Japanese, the stoicism of the Danes, the hardiness of the Scots, the musicality of the Welsh, the devastating romanticism of the French and an almost Hindu sense of fate.

For the most part, cultural etiquette consists of the same basic 'good manners' your grandmother taught you. Here are a few other pointers:

Icelanders do not appreciate the art of spin or flattery. Back up your words with actions, or better yet, only say what you mean. Icelanders will do the same back, so be prepared for open and honest words that might sound a little jarring until you get used to it.

An Icelander's home is a clean and quiet refuge against the vicious outdoor elements. A common sight is a frosty windowpane, behind which sits a row of potted cacti, soaking in whatever sunshine might linger overhead. Because Iceland can be a muddy place, or at least a wet and snowy place, always, always, always take your shoes off when entering someone's home. Typically, you will leave your shoes right inside the doorway. Your host may fuss and say that you really shouldn't, but they are simply being polite. If you leave your shoes on and track mud all over the place, you'll be seen as uncultured and uncouth.

In principle, punctuality is respected and expected. In practice, Icelanders have far too many excuses to be on time, starting with the weather.

Icelanders shake hands and look each other in the eye when they are doing it. Be prepared for a firm grip and a single shake.

It is polite to address someone by their first name only. In formal or business situations, you may use the first name and patronymic (see page 28). Expect total strangers to call after you by your first name.

As a guest, you will always be offered coffee as a refreshment. Coffee is served at all times of the day and night, and most Icelanders take it pretty sweet.

When entering a shop or crossing paths, people in Iceland will greet each other with a firmly enunciated *Goðan daginn* or *Goðan dag*, or a nod of acknowledgement.

Icelanders appreciate casual dress for any outdoor activities and even in some professional situations. For parties and going out on the town, everyone dresses up in their very best.

## VELKOMIN!

The Icelandic word for foreigner is *útlendur* (literally 'out-lander') – a strange person from the outside world who typically does not belong in Iceland. Ever since the age of the sagas, *útlendurs* have been treated with a mutual feeling of admiration and caution. New visitors had a couple of chances to prove their mettle but repeat offenders were normally dealt a swift blow by the first short-tempered Viking they crossed. The battleaxe has since fallen out of fashion, but impressions still matter. You are not the first *útlendur* to show up on these shores, so get to know your stereotype: most of us foreigners show up for a short, intense season, wear the wrong clothes, drop copious amounts of cash, gawk at the prices, complain about the food, make no attempt to learn even a phrase in Icelandic, have preventable car accidents, then get lost in the wilderness and have to be rescued. Two days later, we leave with a vague sense of accomplishment that we have 'done' Iceland.

The best way to break the mould is to stay curious about Iceland every minute that you're there. Get to know what place names mean, ask why it's called that, learn to order your dinner in Icelandic (and then how to compliment the chef), make efforts to meet new people and ask them questions about their country, learn the flowers in summer and the different fish in winter, don't rush through museums (even if they're bad), and always take the chance to sit still and watch. Most of all, don't readily swallow the tourist paradigm that's presented to you. Instead, observe how Icelanders travel in their own country and take your cues from them. Iceland is such an empty and open land that its own people are in a constant state of exploration. You should feel the same way.

### TRAVELLING POSITIVELY

Iceland has so much to offer that travellers can forget what they might have to offer in return. Remember that the best kind of travel is a two-way street and that Iceland's transition to a sustainable tourist economy depends as much on you as it does them. As you experience Iceland in full, consider how your presence affects the country and how you might give something back. This can range from the choices you make, eg: what you choose to eat or not eat (see page 108), to a direct contribution of your time and resources. This guide aims to promote local business and community-based initiatives and describes a few opportunities to help out directly; for example, identifying and counting whales (see page 380), aiding baby puffins on their way to the sea (see page 239), and patronising rural museums. Further opportunities to get involved are listed under the websites in *Appendix 2, Further Information*, page 450. Also, do not be afraid to simply ask. Icelanders are very active volunteers and always have some project at hand. If you have any future suggestions on how travellers can give something back (or experiences to share), please do not hesitate to contact me directly.

# Part Two

## THE GUIDE

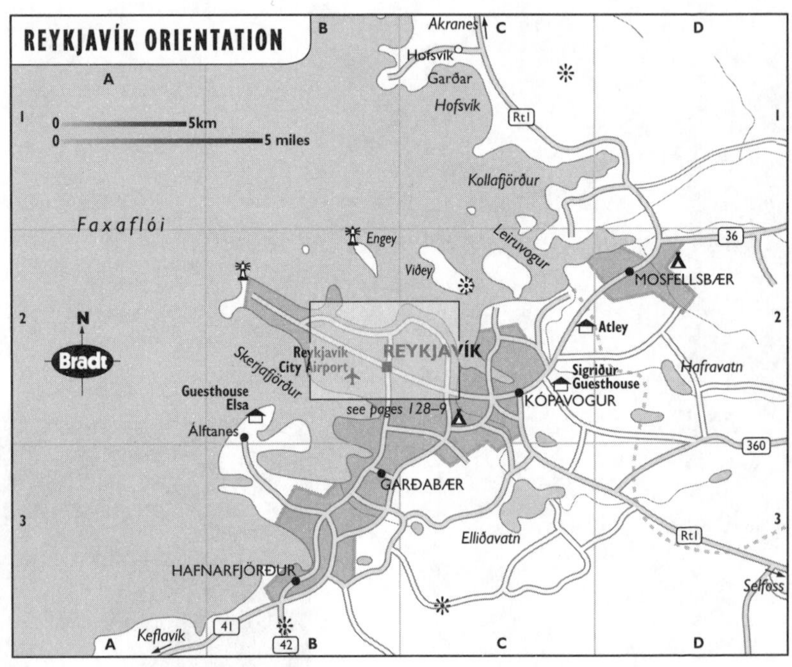
REYKJAVÍK ORIENTATION
0 5km
0 5 miles
Faxaflói
Akranes
Hofsvík
Garðar
Hofsvík
Rt1
Kollafjörður
Engey
Viðey
Leiruvogur
36
MOSFELLSBÆR
Atley
REYKJAVÍK
Reykjavík City Airport
Skerjafjörður
Guesthouse Elsa
Álftanes
Sigríður Guesthouse
KÓPAVOGUR
Hafravatn
see pages 128–9
360
GARÐABÆR
Elliðavatn
HAFNARFJÖRÐUR
Rt1
Selfoss
41
42
Keflavík
N
Bradt

5

# Reykjavík

A stunning backdrop pronounces Iceland's picturesque capital: on one side of town stand rows of prim coloured rooftops outlined by a silvery, swan-filled lake. On the other, city streets slope down to the wind-capped bay of Faxaflói and a pair of quiet, bright-green islands. The mighty ridge of Mt Esja rises in the distance, perhaps the most treasured landmark in Reykjavík. The city proper spreads out across Seltjarnanes, a peninsula whose optimal position affords (on a clear day) a tremendous panorama that extends from the tip of the Reykjanes Peninsula (near Keflavík Airport) all the way up to the icy dome of Snæfellsnes glacier, a good 100km away. This incredible view – and the remarkable sky that frames it – seems an open invitation to explore.

What sets the capital apart from the rest of the country is the presence of people, cars, and trees – all rare species elsewhere in Iceland. Indeed, appreciating Iceland's largest town raises the question, is Reykjavík a village that acts like a city or a city that feels like a village? On the metropolitan side of things sit the Icelandic stock exchange, a massive harbour filled with massive ships, a national parliament building, and an art, music, and restaurant scene that rivals anything in either London or Manhattan. Village-wise, the air is unbelievably clean, whales are jumping in the harbour, the tallest building is a church, and by the second day you'll start recognising the faces you pass in the street. It's comforting to find such big-city delights in such a small and unusual package.

Aside from the spectacular view, Reykjavík is known best for its highly individual style, having the strange effect of making one feel rather cosy through its unstuck version of minimalism. The city displays some true architectural gems, including the massive housing projects built for the population influx following World War II. Other highlights can be spotted in the perfect little Art Deco hotels, painted Scandinavian timber houses, fervent steeples upon tiny cathedrals, and a few functional classics from the Danish era. The honest ensemble is part of the attraction and begs a walk down unknown streets in all of their two- and three-storey glory.

Reykjavík also boasts the title of the world's northernmost capital (at 64° 08′N), which should by no means be interpreted as the coldest. Rather, this balmy harbour town features the kind of hazy undecided weather felt in San Francisco or Cardiff, which makes those blue-sky days all the more splendid. Winter's few hours of reluctant daylight – followed by a slight chance of horizontal sleet – can deter the more superficial visitor, but even indoors, this city is unique.

Visitors often wonder how many Icelanders live in Reykjavík and the answer is that most do. The official tally for the city proper is 115,000. If you include all of the neighbouring towns that have now merged into the 'city', the capital area has a total population of around 200,000, which comprises nearly 60% of Iceland's total population of 300,000 people. Still, the summer months see much of the city pick up and venture out to more rural climes, exchanging the pressures of 'city life' for the joys of the wilderness.

It's nearly impossible to make any generalisations about the people of Reykjavík in terms of attitude, dialect, culture, or lifestyle. Instead, consider this town as the urban expression of Iceland as a whole, which is pretty diverse. One face of the city is dedicated solely to tourists, which is welcoming and sincere, if not slightly seasonal. Within that same grid lies the busy heart of Reykjavík where Iceland's intellectual, financial, and cultural elite put in their serious hours. Weekends witness the outrageous nightlife for which the city is famed, but by Sunday morning, the streets are as silent as the sleepy suburbs nearby. In fact, just five minutes from the city centre you'll find wide pavements, clipped grass and open gardens, single-family houses with two-car garages, and giant shopping malls connected by four-lane highways (not the party town you might have expected).

Owing to its infrastructure, Reykjavík receives the lion's share of tourists to Iceland. To be sure, the city surely deserves a more intimate acquaintance than the one to three days often allotted by harried visitors, but if that's all the time you've got, then only feel a little bit dismayed. Reykjavík's the one kind of town where it's not too difficult to make every minute count, as long as you've got the energy. One unfortunate result of the developing tourist industry is the trend to market nearly every destination in the country as a day trip from Reykjavík, squeezing the city's delights in at night or in between glacier tours and horseriding. Avoid falling into that trap, or else entertaining the faulty notion of 'doing' the capital, and you're bound to have a great time.

## HISTORY

Thanks to the sagas, the story of Reykjavík can be traced back over 12 centuries. The *Landnámabók* recalls the colourful tale of the city's first resident, Ingólfur Arnason. The Norwegian farmer sought new opportunities after a typical Viking feud left him persona non grata in Norway (he'd also lost his estate to the family of a man he had killed). He consulted the earlier reports of Flóki (see page 16) on the possibilities in Iceland and made a preliminary voyage to the East Fjords to check things out for himself. Finding conditions agreeable enough, Ingólfur sailed back to Norway and consulted an oracle, which confirmed that his destiny did in fact lie in Iceland.

And so in AD874, Ingólfur set off with his family and that of his brother-in-law Hjorleif (Leif of the Sword), notorious for his merciless ransacking of Ireland. When Ingólfur caught sight of Iceland, he threw his two 'high-seat pillars' (chair backs) into the sea, making an oath to the Norse gods that he would settle wherever they came to rest. Then he landed his own ship at a cape in southeast Iceland – still known as Ingólfshöfði (see page 427) and commanded his two trusty slaves Vifill and Karli to walk westward along the coast of Iceland until they located the omen. Three years later, the exhausted hikers found the two carved pillars washed ashore inside a small bay.

Ingólfur named the area Reykjavík or 'smoky bay' for the plumes of steam that floated up out of the ground. He most likely accepted the geothermal activity as a plus, attributing the gods' foresight and direction, though one of his slaves disagreed. After three years of trekking through some of Iceland's more breathtaking landscapes, Karli wondered aloud as to why they should end up in such a forsaken spot as this. He ran away with an Irish slave woman and settled near Ölfusá River in the southwest. Ingólfur let it go, then granted Vifill his freedom to do the same.

Thus began Reykjavík. The city's official seal (as seen on street signs and the sides of public service vehicles) shows two white pillars floating upon the waves of the blue sea, and a statue of Ingólfur Arnason stands on top of Arnarhóll (see page 169), right next to Ingolfsstræti ('Ingólfur's street'). The city's Viking founder was both ambitious and prophetic in surveying his own farm, claiming a territory wider than the commuting zone of today's greater Reykjavík area. His first *toft* – or farmhouse – was most likely located near the main city square of Austurvöllur. As a close confirmation, the city's earliest archaeological find lies beneath Aðalstræti, in what is now the Settlement Exhibition (see page 180). These ruins are presented as the original Reykjavík farmstead, although no direct link has been made to Ingólfur Arnason himself.

For the next 800 years, Reykjavík was no more than a family farm on the bay. Other Viking settlements like Borg (see page 261) were larger and more prominent, but it was Ingólfur's descendants in Reykjavík who took the lead in establishing a government for Iceland with the founding of the Althing in AD930. Reykjavík's first pagan temple became a Christian church around AD1000, and in 1225, the chieftain Thorvaldur Gissurarson built a Catholic monastery on Viðey Island, in the bay of Reykjavík. As a recipient of tithes from over 100 neighbouring farms, the monastery flourished until 1539, when Danish troops razed Viðey in the name of the Reformation.

Reykjavík's first paved street (Aðalstræti) only appeared in 1752 as part of the larger development undertaken by the Inréttingar Wool Company. Prior to this, most wool was exported as unprocessed bulk from Iceland to the rest of Scandinavia. To encourage industrialisation the King of Denmark granted the domain of Reykjavík to Skúli Magnusson, a trustworthy capitalist and the first Icelandic treasurer of Iceland. Skúli put up some of the very first buildings in Reykjavík in the form of warehouses, wool-processing and textile factories, shops, and accommodation for labourers, as well as his own impressive stone residence on Viðey Island. Several of these early buildings remain today and Skúli Magnusson is revered as the 'Father of Reykjavík' (see page 186).

Such swift economic growth established the city as a centre of power and influence. In 1785, the bishopric of Iceland's national Lutheran Church was centralised and relocated to Reykjavík. The following year, the King of Denmark granted the town free market status, issuing an official town charter to the 200 residents. From henceforth, the city celebrates 1786 as the year in which it was founded. The trade monopoly was abolished soon after, and industry continued to expand into new fields. By 1796, the Dómkirkjan was completed on Austurvöllur, adding a flourish to the emerging town centre.

From this time and well into the mid 19th century, the odd group of travellers and traders who made it to Reykjavík always commented on the sheer beauty that encompassed the area. They also expressed surprise at how small a place it was – no more than a village with a few roads. Turf houses predominated, seeing as timber buildings still had to be imported. Compared with the mighty cities of Europe, Reykjavík was still quite lowly and isolated.

Reykjavík only gained the title of Iceland's capital after a series of events: in 1845, the Althing was re-established in Reykjavík, albeit nominally, though the gesture recognised the city's prominent role. In 1874 – a millennium since Ingólfur Arnason's first settlement – Iceland was granted its own constitution, followed by the construction of the stone parliament building on Austurvöllur Square as a permanent home for the Althing in 1881. In 1904, Iceland was granted 'home rule' in the form of its own Minister of Icelandic Affairs who would be based in Reykjavík. Then, in 1911, the University of Iceland was founded, marking Iceland's intellectual independence from Copenhagen, followed by the creation of the Kingdom of Iceland in 1918 under the ambiguously titled 'Personal Union' with Denmark.

Of equal significance was the construction of Reykjavík's old stone harbour, which began in 1913 and was completed in 1917, allowing for much larger ships to dock and thereby improving Iceland's access to the rest of the world. The only railway ever to exist in Iceland was built in 1914 to carry the giant volcanic stones from the nearby mountains to the port.

The 1920s and early 1930s saw Reykjavík emerge as a thriving centre for Icelandic culture, politics, and art – a brief era of enlightenment prior to the turmoil of the Great Depression. Poverty, hunger, and unemployment led to a wave of migration from the countryside into Reykjavík, nearly doubling the size of the city. In the capital, the sudden evidence of disparity and class struggle sparked an uprising of a magnitude hitherto unknown in Iceland. The capital was now dealing with the politics and social concerns of urban society.

Reykjavík eventually found release from its economic woes in the form of World War II. Fearing the Nazi invasion of Denmark would carry into Iceland, the Allies occupied the country in the form of the British navy sailing into Reykjavík in 1940. At one stage there were nearly 25,000 British troops stationed in Reykjavík, followed by an even greater number of Americans. The fact that foreign troops outnumbered the citizens of Reykjavík was cause for a few controversies, although Icelanders did welcome the sudden cash flow of wartime military expenditure. The British military constructed Reykjavík's city airport in 1940, and in 1943, Reykjavík's high-tech central heating system was completed, bringing geothermal energy into city homes. The very next year, Reykjavík was declared the official capital of a wholly independent Iceland, justifying the pomp and circumstance to which it was already accustomed.

The late 1940s and 1950s witnessed a boom in population followed by mass construction. Iceland's talent for making reinforced concrete look artfully pleasant is most evident in the vaguely Bauhaus apartment blocks seen all around the city – an answer to quick and convenient housing for a growing city. The essence of Reykjavík's unique style dates back to this period when some of the city's most interesting buildings were built or designed. Nor can one look past the telltale American influence of the 1960s and 1970s, when grassy suburbs sprawled out from the compact centre and the joys of car culture made way for a city without limits.

Enter Reykjavík's small but furious music scene, which evolved in the late 1970s into the punk phenomenon of the early 1980s. Dozens of semi-famous bands joined in the cultural experimentation and the rest of the world began to see Iceland's capital in a new light. Reykjavík was not some fishing backwater or isolated military outpost, but a place where things were happening in poetry, art, music, and fashion. The Reykjavík Summit of 1986 between the Soviet Union's Mikhail Gorbachev and the US president Ronald Reagan marked the city's bicentennial and brought significant international attention to this under-appreciated Nordic capital. Throughout the 1990s, the city's derelict harbour area underwent a speedy gentrification and Reykjavík became a tourist destination in its own right. In 2000, the city was named one of nine 'European Cities of Culture' – a title that helped secure its reputation as the cool place that it is.

During the 'bubble' years of fast economic growth, Reykjavík emerged as a kind of Nordic party town, with an elite and expensive club scene, high-priced luxury real estate and the glamour that comes with fast money. Alas, the glitz was short-lived, because after the September 2008 crash, Reykjavík suffered the most. Enterprises shut down overnight, the high street of bank offices became a kind of silent ghost town and ambitious building projects were left unfinished.

Post-crisis Reykjavík is a little more tempered and modest than the city of the last decade – but the party hasn't stopped. Friday and Saturday nights still comprise the city tradition for sleeplessness and big noise.

Today, Reykjavík continues to grow at the expense of other cities in Iceland. The issue is of some concern to Icelanders, who see their country's broad appeal giving way to the capital's commercial dominance. Also, Reykjavík's recent financial prowess has transformed the city from a uniquely Icelandic place to a fairly cosmopolitan mix of nationalities and languages (for Iceland). This is not the city it was 15 years ago, let alone 1,100 years ago, though that means little when you're looking ahead. There's a definite attraction to the city's current pace and the notion that almost anything can – and will – happen here.

## GETTING THERE AND AWAY

**BY AIR** Reykjavík is amazingly accessible by plane. Direct flights connect the capital to most every regional airport, including the Westmann Islands. *Chapter 4* (see page 91) details these particular internal routes, the majority of which fly in and out of Reykjavík City Airport. From the much larger but much farther Keflavík Airport, there are daily connections serving dozens of convenient international destinations, with more details in *Chapter 4* (see page 75).

### Airline offices in Reykjavík

**Air Iceland** 101 Reykjavík, Reykjavíkurflugvöllur; ☎ 570 3030; e websales@flugfelag.is; www.flugfelag.is
**British Airways** Airport; ☎ 421 7374; e info@ba.com; www.britishairways.com
**Icelandair** 101 Reykjavík, Reykjavíkurflugvöllur; ☎ 505 0100; e sales@icelandair.is; www.icelandair.is
**Iceland Express** 108 Reykjavík, Grímsbæ-Efstaland 26; ☎ 550 0600; e (info@icelandexpress.is; www.icelandexpress.is
**SAS** 113 Reykjavík, Kristnibraut 12; ☎ 577 6420; www.flysas.is

#### POSTAL CODES IN REYKJAVÍK

London SW1, Beverly Hills 90210… so where's posh in Iceland? Out of the 1,000 postal codes doled out by *Íslandspóstur*, Reykjavík occupies the numbers 100 to 172. Of these, the only address that will get you any respect is 101 Reykjavík – the heart of the city and the part that most tourists visit anyway. How disappointingly logical? Perhaps, but not so long ago, 101 was anything but cool or residential. Instead, this particular strip of the city seemed a mass of boring offices and old warehouses from which commuters fled in the evening. The re-blossoming of the city centre in the 1990s saw an influx of new restaurants and shops, followed by trendy apartments and renovated homes. Today, 101 Reykjavík represents urban renewal and a stake in the city's future. The idiom gained even wider notoriety following Hallgrímur Helgason's best-selling novel-turned-film *101 Reykjavík* – a story that could very well be a metaphor for Reykjavík itself.

Getting technical, 101 Reykjavík spans the middle section of the Seltjarnanes Peninsula, from the old harbour in the north to the city airport in the south, westwards to Hringbraut and east to Snorrabraut. As long as you stay inside that area, you're cool.

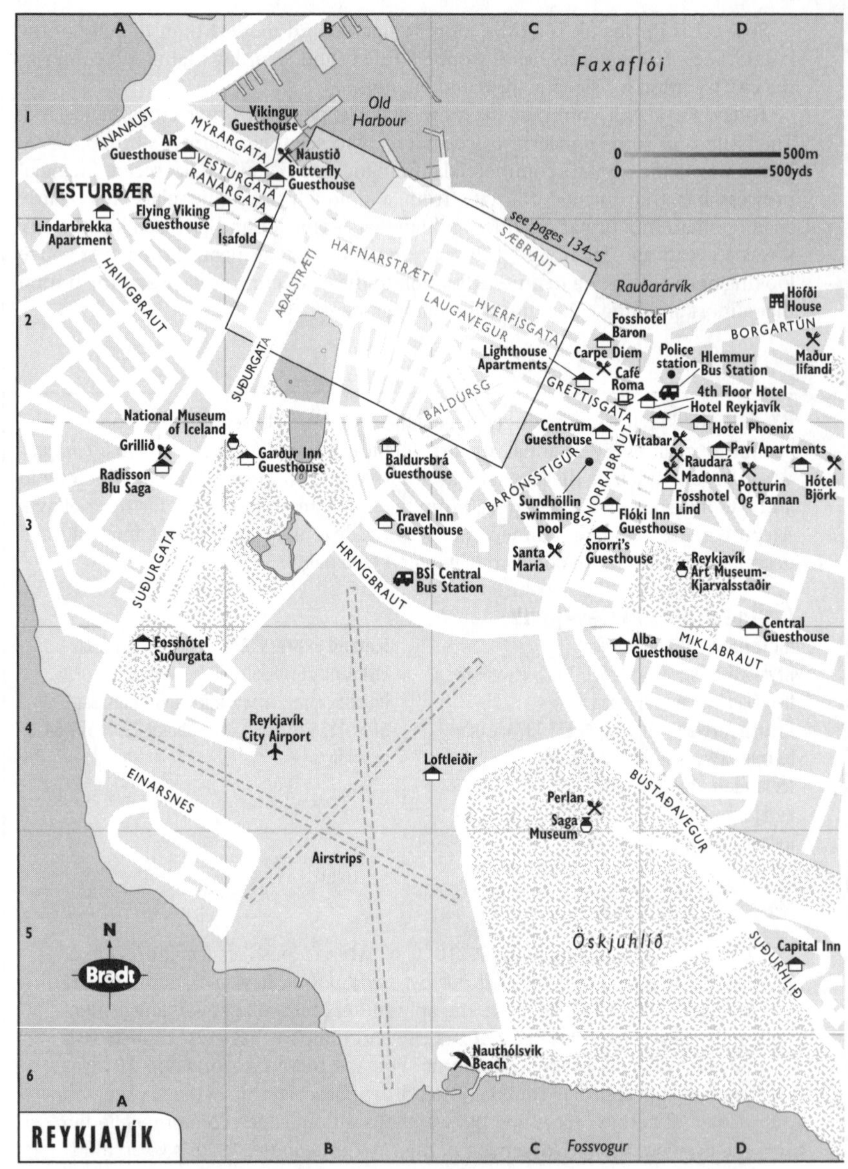


**KEF Keflavík International Airport/Flugstöð Leifs Eiríkssonar** Keflavík's Leifur Eiríksson International Airport (*235 Keflavík Airport;* ☏ *425 0680;* e *airport@fle.airport.is; www.flugstod.is*) serves as Reykjavík's international airport and the largest entry point into Iceland (see page 202). The terminal is located not far from the town of Keflavík, but a good 50km from Reykjavík. Travel time into the capital varies depending on time of day and traffic (typically under an hour), but transportation is regular and efficient. Enjoy the ride, as this is the newest, widest, and best-paved road in the country.

The primary means of getting from the airport into Reykjavík is the **Flybus**

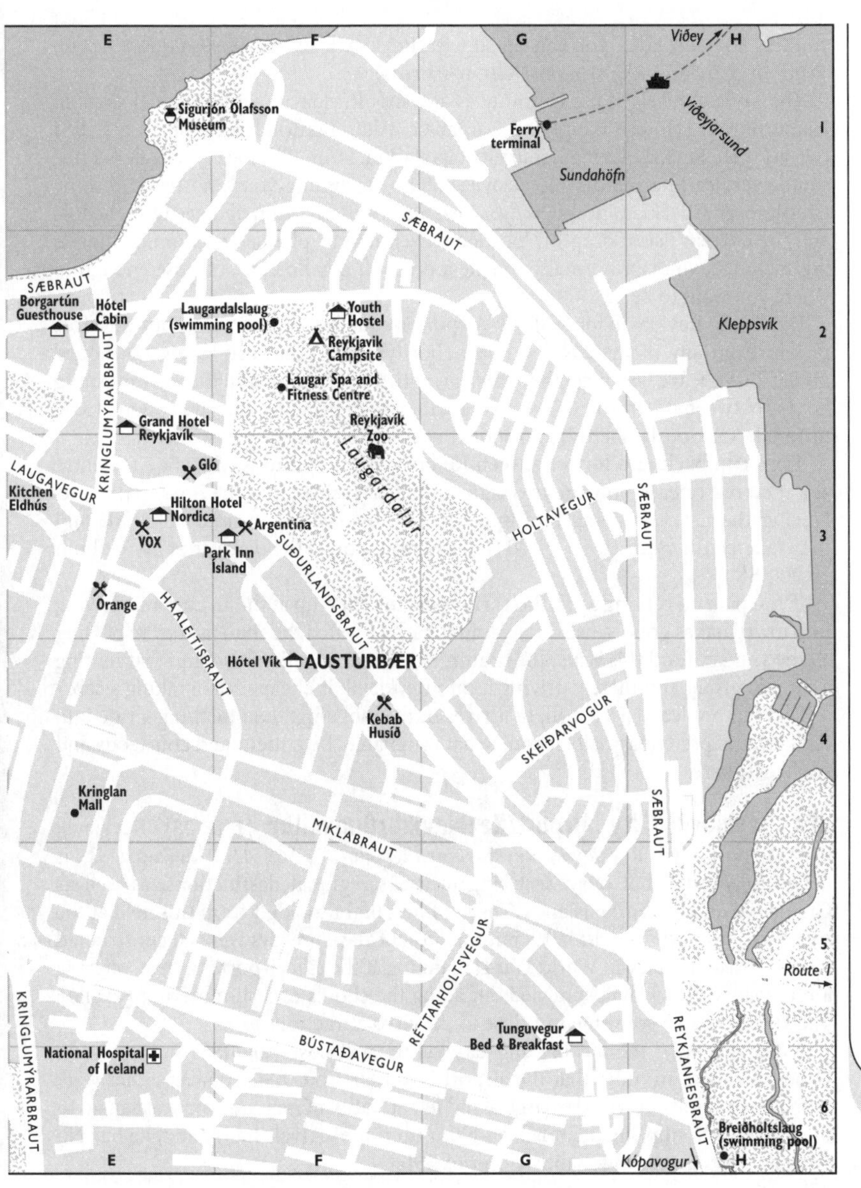




(*www.flybus.is*), your typical boxy tourist motor coach with all of the luggage shoved underneath. The bus advertises as departing the airport 40 minutes after each international flight arrival. After you've picked up your luggage and cleared customs, exit into the arrivals lobby (the one with all the tourist brochures and car-rental offices). Go to the Flybus booth and purchase a ticket. Off the bus you can pay with plastic, on the bus is cash only. A single one-way fare costs 1,200ISK; and a round trip is 2,000ISK (50% off for children aged 12–15; free for children under 11; NB: return tickets do have a limited time of validity, so check to make sure you're OK to come back). It is not necessary to purchase a ticket in advance, but if it makes you less stressed, than you can do so with Reykjavík Excursions (*200 Kopavogur, Veturvör 6;* ☎ *580 5400;* ✉ *main@re.is; www.re.is*).

The Flybus travels along Highway 41 towards Reykjavík, with optional stops in Hafnarfjörður (Hótel Viking) and Garðabær (Aktu-Taktu). The terminus is at **BSÍ** (*www.bsi.is*), Reykjavík's main intercity bus station. From BSÍ, the Flybus offers a free shuttle service to around 30 Reykjavík hotels – including youth hostels and some guesthouses. Check online (*www.flybus.is/schedule.html*) for an updated bus schedule and the current list of drop-off locations. Even if your planned accommodation is not included, you can normally wangle a drop-off at a hotel that's close enough to where you want to be.

Departing Reykjavík for Keflavík Airport is equally simple. You can arrange free pickup from any of the covered hotels, but typically you need to give 24 hours' notice. Buses leave BSÍ throughout the day, with a large number in the early morning hours (between 04.45 and 06.00) and another rush period in the afternoon (13.00 to 16.00). Obviously, there are far more buses in summer than in winter.

Taxis run back and forth between Keflavík Airport into Reykjavík city centre at a metered rate. Follow the taxi signs in the arrivals hall to the line-up outside. During the day, the going rate into central Reykjavík is around 8,000ISK and they take credit cards. After 17.00 (in either direction) the price goes up to about 10,000ISK.

If you plan on renting a car, then arranging to pick it up at the airport and driving into town makes good sense. Many find it hard to watch the road as they're passing all the scenery (and this is just the beginning). Some travellers also find that renting a car as a group and merely driving it into Reykjavík is cheaper than taking a cab.

Last but not least, if your flight arrives in the morning, then hitching a ride into Reykjavík is pretty easy, albeit somewhat unreliable. Be patient and courteous and you'll get there.

**REK Reykjavík City Airport/Reykjavíkurflugvöllur** [128 28] Reykjavík City Airport (*101 Reykjavík, Reykjavíkurflugvöllur;* ☎ *569 4100; www.caa.is*) is delightfully small but busy, servicing Iceland's regional destinations, as well as Greenland and the Faroe Islands. The very first flight took off from this field at the southern end of the city in 1919, but the present-day runways were all constructed by the British military in World War II. Landing at the city airport is a treat, offering a rare view of Reykjavík sprawled out along the shores of a shimmering Faxaflói. The airport is also conveniently close to the city's attractions.

A taxi between the airport and city centre will cost 1,000ISK and upwards. Otherwise, bear in mind that the airport is not far from BSÍ. You can either walk to the bus station (down Njarðargata and left at Vatnsmýrarvegur) or you can go to the airport bus stop Innanlandsflug (400m from the arrivals hall) and take bus No 15 to the stop that's only slightly closer to BSÍ.

**Transfer between airports** Many travellers are shocked to find there is no official transportation service between Keflavík International Airport and Reykjavík City Airport. The airlines will suggest you take a direct taxi, which is fairly quick but will set you back about 7,000–8,000ISK. Otherwise, you can take the Flybus, since BSÍ is right next door to the city airport – sort of (this should really be easier than it is). Whether you fly into the city airport with the intention of taking the Flybus to Keflavík, or else you arrive at BSÍ with the intention of connecting to an internal flight, there will be plenty of taxi drivers waiting to pick up unassuming tourists and drive them around the block for US$15. Most choose this option, because if you have luggage, it's really your only option. Otherwise you can walk or take the No 15 bus – the walk is less than 1km (0.6 miles).

**BY CAR** All roads lead to Reykjavík, or rather – *the road* leads to Reykjavík. No matter where you are in the country, you're bound to find some sign that tells you how many hundreds of kilometres you are from the capital, or from Route 1 if you're not already on it. The driving distance to Reykjavík from Keflavík is 50km (30 miles) on Route 41; from Akureyri it's 389km (233 miles) on Route 1; from the ferry port at Seyðisfjörður in the East Fjords it's 680km (408 miles).

**BY BUS** All major public and private bus lines service Iceland's capital regularly, although prior planning is imperative for making connections to and from more remote places (ie: the West Fjords or the east of the country). Departure times and frequency change with the seasons, so check the latest schedules online (*www.bsi.is*) or those printed and distributed by the individual bus companies. The service between Reykjavík and Keflavík is frequent year-round and takes about one hour. Other daily routes include Selfoss (via Hveragerðí) (1 hour); Hellisandur (via Grundarfjörður) (3 hours); Akureyri (on Route 1) (6 hours); and Höfn (via Vík and Kirkjubæjarklaustur) (9 hours). *Chapter 4* (see page 97) details bus routes throughout the country.

**BSÍ Central Bus Station** [128 B3] (*101 Reykjavík, Vatnsmýrarvegur 10; ☎ 562 1011; e bsi@bsi.is; www.bsi.is; ⏲ 1 May–31 Oct 24hrs; 1 Nov–30 Apr 05.00–22.00*) Reykjavík's terminus for intercity buses is located at BSÍ (Umferðamiðstöðin). It is also the connecting point for the Flybus and the departure point for most day tours. BSÍ is really the only place in the country that emits the kind of gritty excitement of travel often felt in European train stations. Big-wheeled buses come and go and exhausted travellers rub shoulders with cheery newcomers just off the plane. Besides offering a cash machine (ATM), internet access, and toilets, BSÍ is one of the few public places where you can check and store luggage. The luggage office is located inside the station (*☎ 591 1000; ⏲ 07.30–19.00*). The cost is about 500ISK per 24 hours.

The in-house café is called **Fljótt og Gott** (Fast and Good) (*Vatnsmýrarvegur 10; ☎ 552 1288; e fljottoggott@fljottoggott.is; www.fljottoggott.is*). Think hamburgers, pizza, fried chicken and fish, sweets, and soup – then think bus station. Even so, the food and atmosphere are warm.

Alas, despite the tempting moulded plastic seats, you cannot spend the night in the bus station. Even when it is open all night in summer, they kick everyone out at midnight and open the doors again at 04.30.

## GETTING AROUND

Moving about Reykjavík can be fairly easy given its good pavements, extensive bus service, numerous taxi ranks and relatively small size. In spite of this, Reykjavík still tends to disappoint those with strong preconceptions about Scandinavia and user-friendly transportation. Indeed, there are times when getting from A to B feels a lot less like Nordic Europe and a lot more like North America. When venturing beyond the compact city centre, it helps to plan a little. Patience and a fondness for walking are also of great benefit. In addition to the listed modes of transportation, a lot of upmarket hotels will have shuttles to transfer guests to various attractions and the city centre.

**BY TAXI** Rarely does one hail a cab in Reykjavík. Instead, you call, get someone else to call, or you walk to a recognised cab queue. In addition to BSÍ and Reykjavík City Airport, you are likely to find cabs at the other city bus stations (eg: Lækjartorg, Hlemmur), the Reykjavík Information Centre on Aðalstræti, and sitting outside any of the city's main hotels.

Normally cabs arrive in five to ten minutes from the time you call. All fares are fixed and you will pay exactly what is on the meter, though expect that fare to be around a US$10 minimum, no matter how short the journey. Remember that fares increase by about 25% after 17.00 until the following morning and that tipping is not expected.

The most prominent taxi companies servicing the capital include:

**Borgarbílastöðin** ☎ 552 2440
**BSH Taxis** ☎ 555 0888; e taxi@bsh.is; www.bsh.is
**BSR Taxis** ☎ 561 0000; e info@bsr.is; www.bsr.is
**Hreyfill-Bæjarleiðir** ☎ 588 5522, 553 3500; e tour@hreyfill.is; www.hreyfill.is

**BY BUS** Reykjavík's bus system is called Strætó (from 'street'), recognised by the yellow 'S' inside a red circle (☎ *540 2700;* e *info@bus.is; www.bus.is*). The extensive network of nearly 30 bus routes includes the city centre and beyond, reaching from Hafnarfjörður all the way to Akranes. Individual routes are numbered and coloured (although four lines share varied shades of red) and practically every tourist pamphlet that you're handed will have a free bus map inside. Plan your route, find the nearest bus station and wait. Then wait some more.

On weekdays, buses run every 20 minutes between 07.00 and 18.00 and every 30 minutes from 18.00 to midnight. In winter (20 August–1 June), the main routes (S1–S6) run every ten minutes during the morning (07.00–8.30) and evening (15.30–18.00) rush hours. On weekends, buses run every 30 minutes from 07.00 to midnight on Saturday and from 10.00 to 23.00 on Sunday.

Taking the bus may be the cheapest way to go, but that's all relative seeing as a single fare costs 250ISK (about US$4). Also take note that buses do not give change, so you'll need to keep a heavy pocketful of 50 and 100ISK coins. If you're planning on doing any swimming or museum visits, it's definitely worth purchasing a Reykjavík Welcome Card (see below) for the bus fare alone. Otherwise, you can buy individual tickets or long-term passes at any of the major bus stations: Lækjartorg [134 D2] (☎ *510 9805*); Hlemmur [128 D2] (☎ *540 2701*); and Mjódd (☎ *567 0588*).

## REYKJAVÍK WELCOME CARD

The Reykjavík Welcome Card (Gestakort Reykjavíkur) is probably the best deal you can find in this city. The card allows free access to the city's seven thermal swimming pools, free entrance to nearly all city museums, and unlimited travel on Strætó city buses. Plus, you get a bit of free internet and significant discounts on certain tours and in some shops. Cards are sold for 24-, 48-, and 72-hour periods (about US$15, US$23, and US$30 respectively), starting from the moment you begin using it.

You can purchase the card at the Visit Reykjavík office at Aðalstræti 2, as well as the city hall, BSÍ, Strætó bus stations, the art museums, the Laugardalslaug swimming pool, the youth hostel and campsite, and at any of the offices of Reykjavík Excursions.

For more frequent bus travel, consider the option of buying ten discounted single tickets for 2,000ISK, a yellow card (unlimited travel for two weeks) for 3,000ISK, or a green card (unlimited travel for a month) for 5,000ISK. If you plan to switch buses (or not, but just in case) be sure to ask the bus driver for a transfer (*skiptimiðinn*). You'll have 45 minutes to use it.

Overall, getting around on Stræto can seem a little complex, though the website (*www.bus.is*) is very helpful and can spell out an individualised itinerary based on your starting point and destination. On the plus side are Reykjavík's bus drivers, who tend to be very friendly, helpful, courteous, English-speaking, and patient, even when they have to spend a significant time dealing with confused tourists. The buses are shiny new and fairly comfortable – when the weather's really acting up, you'll be glad that you're riding.

**BY FOOT** Yes, by all means, do walk. Everyone else does, and you'll see lots of wonderful things. Parts of the city centre are designated pedestrian-only, and the outlying areas offer some interesting nature trails by the sea, to local geysers and into the mountains. For a few suggested city walks, see page 185. Also, beware of falling into the tourist trap of walking up and down Laugavegur 20 times and thinking you've checked the box for Reykjavík. If you're really going to explore on foot, then explore. Step away from the quaintness of Aðalstræti and discover some of the other colourful residential streets. You'll be safe – there's no such thing as a 'bad area' of the city where you shouldn't walk.

But can one get by just on foot? Maybe. Much of Reykjavík is made for walking, some of it is not. For those coming right off the Flybus from the airport at BSÍ, it's not so bad walking into the city centre – less than a mile (1.6km) away. If you're staying outside the city centre (eg: the campsite), then coming and going becomes quite a hike. A sudden stab of wind and rain can also discourage even the staunchest pedestrian. Plus, getting to certain attractions (like Viðey Island or Esja) fall well outside comfortable walking distance.

**BY BICYCLE** Weather is the only thing keeping Reykjavík from being a biker's dream. The elements aside, you've got well-marked bike lanes, bike-only paths, cool terrain, conscientious drivers, and it's totally legal to ride on the pavements. Specified bike paths criss-cross the city and link up with more extensive paths along the seashore, harbour, and into the surrounding hills. Plus, there's plenty of bike racks and bike theft/damage is practically a non-issue.

Even if pedalling is not on your agenda, you should definitely consider it on the off chance you catch a bit of good sky. Cycling makes a lot of sense in terms of the way the city is laid out and you'll also discover that Reykjavík has more hills than you once imagined. You can rent bikes from some hotels, as well as the youth hostel and campsite at Laugardalur. In the city centre, try **Borgarhjól Bike Rental** (*Hverfisgata 50; ☎ 551 5653; e borgarhjol@simnet.is; www.borgarhjol.net; ⏲ 08.00–18.00 Mon–Fri, 10.00–14.00 Sat*). Prices range from 2,000ISK to 2,500ISK per 24 hours, with discounts for longer rentals.

If you don't trust your sense of direction, then guided bike tours offer a pleasant mode of exploring the capital and its stunning natural surroundings. Most advertised tours are not too physically demanding and last around four hours. They tend to originate in the city centre and work up to Oskjuhlöíð for a panoramic view, then follow the coastline around Seltjarnanes and back to the harbour and city centre. For more information, contact **Explore Adventures** (*☎ 562 7000; e info@explore.is; www.explore.is*).

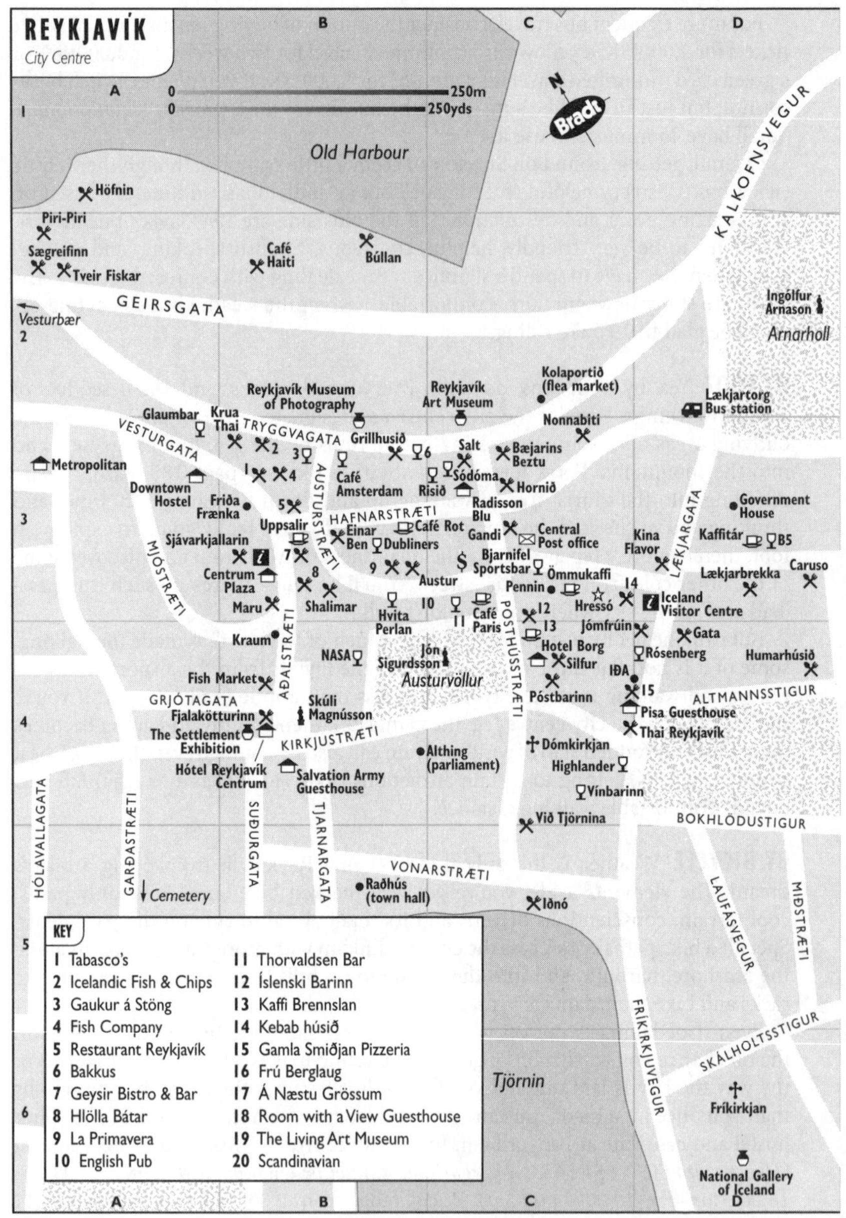


**BY CAR** Driving your own vehicle in Reykjavík is really quite nice, although not necessary. Benefits include not having to take a bus or taxi, staying warm and dry, not feeling restricted to a certain area of the city, and having total freedom to travel whenever and wherever you want. The downside is that there's a whole lot to do in Reykjavík without a car, during which time it will just occupy a parking space.

Despite its size (or maybe because of its size) Reykjavík has some splendid traffic jams that are brief but intense. Rush hour starts at about 07.30 and ends by

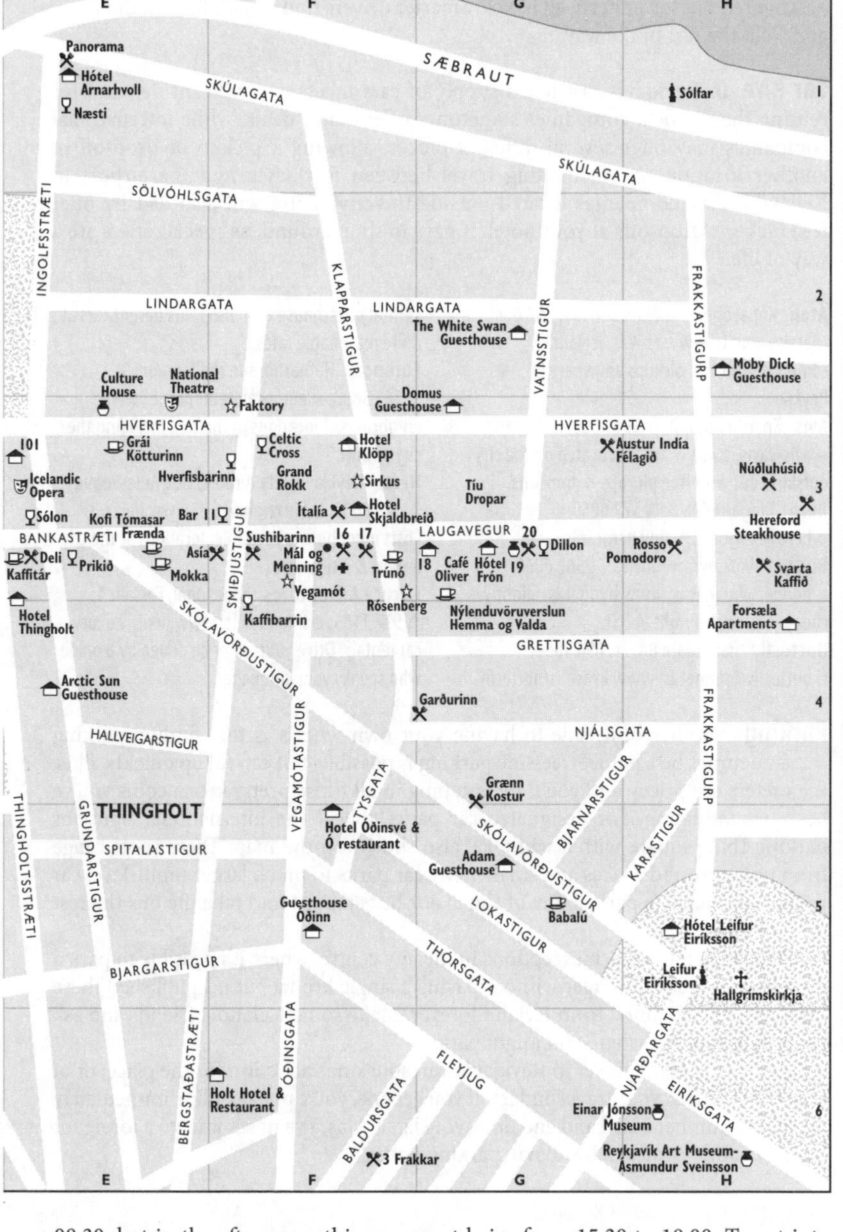




08.30, but in the afternoon, things can get hairy from 15.30 to 18.00. To get into the city centre, take Reykjanesbraut (akin to the ring road) up to the big cloverleaf intersection – turn onto Miklabraut (left if facing north) and follow until it turns into Hringbraut.

Reykjavík's city centre is rife with one-way streets, dead ends, and a few impossibly narrow lanes that are easily cut off by a refuse truck or light construction. It's enough to make you feel like a rat in a maze, but once you've circled a few times and figured out the pattern, all is well. Smarter drivers find a place to park their cars and walk the rest of the way.

**Car hire** In Reykjavík, a trusted supply of cars meets a significant demand for renting them. Local companies sometimes offer better deals, while international companies may offer several different offices, allowing a pickup or drop-off in another location (eg: facilitating travel between Reykjavík and the airport in Keflavík). Any companies located outside the city centre will also usually offer free pickups/drop-offs at your hotel. It pays to shop around, as special offers are a way of life.

**Átak** Kópavogur, Smiðjuvegur 1; ☎ 554 6040; e atak@atak.is; www.atak.is. Icelandic company with free pickups anywhere in Reykjavík.
**Avis** Knarrarvogur 2; ☎ 591 4000; e avis@avis.is; www.avis.is. Located on the city outskirts but with free pickups & drop-offs.
**Berg** Tangarhöfða 8; ☎ 577 6050; e berg@bergcar.is; www.bergcar.is
**Budget** Vatsmýrarvegur 10; ☎ 562 6060; e budget@budget.is; www.budget.is. Slightly cheaper & located right at BSÍ.
**Butterfly** Ranargata 8A; m 894 1864; e butterfly@simnet.is; www.kvasir.is/butterfly. Central guesthouse that also rents decent cars at quite reasonable rates.
**Europcar** Hafnarfjörður, Hjallahrauni 9; ☎ 565 3800; e europcar@europcar.is; www.europcar.is. 2 locations in the city, including the city airport.
**Hertz** Reykjavík City Airport, Flugvallarvegur; ☎ 505 0600; e hertz@hertz.is; www.hertz.is. Costs more but very reliable; locations at the city airport & city centre.
**Luxury Adventures** Kópavogur, Forsalir 1; ☎ 577 1155; e info@lux.is; www.lux.is. Luxury car rentals. Drive yourself or be driven by a guide who speaks your language.

**Parking** Another downside to having your own wheels is that finding parking can sometimes be a pain. Streetside parking is possible, but can fill up quickly. Plus, the meters are pricey and you'll be pumping in all those pretty króna coins you've been accumulating. For designated car parks, follow the international signs for parking (blue square with a white P), also shown on the map. These spots range from underground spaces and smaller city car parks to much larger multi-level car parks. You can also park at any of the major bus stations and take the bus the rest of the way.

There are a few known exceptions in the city centre, where it's possible to park a car for up to a day or longer without paying a single króna, but if I published these locations I'd be banned from Iceland forever. Make some Icelandic friends and ask them (wink, wink) where you might park.

Getting a parking ticket in Reykjavík can sour one's affection for the place, or at least put a dent in your travel budget. If you get one, you can pay online immediately or call the number listed and end up paying later. Alas, I've never known a foreigner to successfully contest a Reykjavík parking ticket.

## TOURIST INFORMATION

**REYKJAVÍK TOURIST INFORMATION CENTRE** [134 B3] (*Aðalstræti 2; ☎ 590 1550; e info@visitreykjavik.is; www.visitreykjavik.is; ⏲ Jun–Aug 08.30–19.00 daily; Sep–May 09.00–18.00 Mon–Fri, 09.00–14.00 Sat/Sun*) The Visit Reykjavík office is the capital's official tourist information centre and functions as the hub for all travel-related queries regarding Iceland in general. A full-time, helpful staff can answer any question you have, make any bookings that you want, and provide free literature on practically everything. They also carry a huge collection of maps, books for sale, and tickets for just about anything. Plus, they have an in-house internet café, phone booths and phonecards, a currency exchange and tax refund office, as well as two of the city's finest restaurants. Definitely worth a stop.

Following a rise in tourism, several private companies have opened their own information centres that target foreign tourists. While labelled 'Tourist Information Centres', none of these is as comprehensive as the Visit Reykjavík office. They are also privately funded, meaning they are far more commercial and paid to direct tourists to their own clients.

**KLEIF ICELANDIC TRAVEL MARKET** (*Bankastræti 2; ☎ 510 5700; e kleif@kleif.is; www.kleif.is; ⏲ Jun–Aug 08.00–19.00 daily; Sep–May 08.00–12.00 & 15.00–19.00 daily*) A bustling place at the end of Laugavegur and extremely touristy. Includes a restaurant, internet café, car hire and hotel bookings, forex currency exchange and tax refund office.

**IDA ICELAND VISITOR CENTRE** [134 D3] (*Lækjargata 2; ☎ 511 2442; e info@icelandvisitor.com; www.icelandvisitor.com; ⏲ Jun–Aug 09.00–22.00; Sep–May 10.00–18.00 Mon–Sat*) A smaller and quieter centre with a lot more for the active adventure tourist.

## TOUR OPERATORS

Almost every major tour operator for Iceland features some kind of representation in Reykjavík. Some of them offer comprehensive sightseeing trips for the capital itself.

**Arctic Rafting** Laugavegur 11; ☎ 562 7000; e info@arcticrafting.is; www.arcticrafting.is. The king of adventure travel in Iceland, offering plenty of creative ways to explore the city & beyond. Their main office is nicely located in the middle of Reykjavík.
**Iceland Excursions** Höfðatún 12; ☎ 540 1313; e iceland@grayline.is; www.icelandexcursions.is. As a bus line turned tour company, IE offers a wide range of interesting trips & a comfortable way to accomplish them. Their extensive city tour takes in a few of the less-visited locales.
**Reykjavík Excursions** Kynnisferðir, BSÍ, Vatnsmýrarvegur 10; ☎ 562 1011; e main@re.is; www.re.is. One of the leading tour operators for day trips in & out of Reykjavík, as well as a 2½hr 'grand tour' of the city. The company manages 6 different offices around the city, including one at BSÍ, & others at hotels Loftleiðir & Nordica.

For details of other tour operators, see *Chapter 4*, page 72.

## WHERE TO STAY

Reykjavík probably has more hotel rooms per capita than anywhere else in the world. There's a wide range of shelter in terms of location, style and comfort, but less so in terms of price. Recently, Reykjavík has seen a burst of fabulous upmarket hotels – some have wonderful style, others are all money and no personality. Being just a little picky can pay off. For the budget-minded, there are a few guesthouses and other less expensive options to choose from, but you may have to suck it up and pay luxury prices for so-so accommodation. Reykjavík's unwritten rule seems to be nearing a US$100 minimum per person for anywhere that's close to the centre. Also, keep in mind that this is a small town by world standards, and it is not uncommon for every one of these rooms to get fully booked on any given weekend, especially during special events that get flooded by tourists (summertime, musical festivals, New Year, etc).

## LUXURY

**101 Hotel** [135 E3] (38 rooms) Hverfisgata 10; ☎ 580 0101; e 101hotel@101hotel.is; www.101hotel.is. It may be that all of Iceland's boutique hotels secretly aspire to the sophistication & art of Reykjavík's '101', a member of the world-famous Design Hotels group & a full-blown fashion experience in its own right. Wooden floors, a fireplace & a few thoughtful furnishings all soften the otherwise stark black-&-white minimalism, while the entire space is used to showcase the work of Iceland's latest & greatest artists. The serenely private bedrooms come totally decked out with every amenity you could want, the bar & restaurant are renowned, & a petite health spa (with jacuzzi) is tucked away in the basement. All this is just 1 quiet block away from Laugavegur & the city's crazy nights. Overall, this is one of the most personable hotels in Reykjavík, although it's also one of the priciest, with no request too big or small, as long as you're willing to pay. If you can't afford to sleep here, it's still worth stopping by for a drink & to take in the latest of Icelandic design. **$$$$$**

**Hilton Hotel Nordica** [129 E3] (252 rooms) Suðurlandsbraut 2; ☎ 444 5000; e nordica@icehotels.is; www.icehotels.is. The Nordica's reputation for incomparable taste & service is well deserved. Preferred by choosy business travellers & official international delegations, this quintessentially Scandinavian hotel favours the kind of grandiose comfort you might expect in other Nordic capitals. Rooms are graciously large & the beds pretty much flawless. In addition to the celebrated Nordica spa, occupants of business & executive suites are granted access to the top-floor Panorama Lounge & its longing view of Faxaflói Bay & Mt Esja (the stunning view pictured in almost every brochure you pick up in Reykjavík). The in-house VOX Restaurant offers constant discussion material among serious Icelandic foodies. There's ample parking & a constant shuttle that connects to the city centre; you're also not far from the diversions of Laugadalur. **$$$$$**

**Hótel Borg** [134 C4] (56 rooms) Posthússtræti 11; ☎ 551 1440; e hotelborg@hotelborg.is; www.hotelborg.is. A city icon & a legend for the rest of Iceland, the Borg's reputation rests on its name rather than its chic. The 6-storey classic faces the tidy green of Austurvöllur Sq, making this a prime location for those who want to be in the middle of everything but still enjoy the quiet refuge of their own castle. The hotel's rooms were completely renovated in 2006 & feature an elegant black-&-white décor that's fresh & inviting. The showers are the best in the city & the tower suites are as regal as Reykjavík gets. Despite jaw-dropping prices, don't assume that the Borg is out of your league (insert Trekkie joke). It's a good place to wrangle for a deal, especially off-season. Summer **$$$$$**; winter **$$$**

## UPMARKET

**4th Floor Hotel** [128 D2] (23 rooms) Corner of Laugavegur & Snorrabraut; ☎ 511 3030; e info@4thfloorhotel.is; www.4thfloorhotel.is. The newest location to try & break into the posh hotel scene. Priced accordingly, you get sleek, urban black-&-white rooms with wooden floors, lots of black leather & zebra-print duvets. The bathrooms are small, but perfect. The in-house lounge Studio 29 presents delectable food. **$$$$**

**Holt** [135 F6] (40 rooms) Bergstaðastæti 37; ☎ 552 5700; e holt@holt.is; www.holt.is. Swanky to the core, the Holt holds its own against many of the other upmarket hotels in Reykjavík on account of its commitment to style & art (they purport that theirs is the largest private collection in the country). Pieces are displayed throughout the halls & in all the rooms, which are furnished in a modern, business-friendly style. It's no coincidence that you're only a few steps from the National Gallery. The Holt was also home to the entire US delegation when President Ronald Reagan attended the Reykjavík Summit in 1986. The immaculate in-house French restaurant may just push things over the top. Free parking, free Wi-Fi. **$$$$**

**Grand Hotel Reykjavík** [129 E2] (313 rooms) Sigtún 38; ☎ 514 8000; e reservations@grand.is; www.grand.is. Iceland's only high-rise hotel is also the country's largest, with hundreds of sleek, modern rooms entombed in a shiny glass tower. Room sizes are bigger than average (the junior suites can be a decent deal) & the bathrooms state of the art. Add extensive conference facilities, a lush spa & fitness centre & a fairly generic gourmet restaurant & you have the Grand – Reykjavík's ultimate in corporate chic. Ironically, the 'tower' is located outside 101 & the main business district, though a regular shuttle bus ferries you into the city centre. **$$$$**

**Hótel Óðinsvé** [135 F5] (43 rooms) Óðinstorg (corner of Óðinsgata & Thórsgata); ☎ 511 6200; e mottaka@hotelodinsve.is; www.hotelodinsve.is. A progressive little hotel in the middle of the shopping district (on the descent from Hallgrímskirkja), the Óðinsvé's rooms have wooden floors & are non-smoking while the décor is highly individualistic – sensible, stylish & with lots of light. Bathrooms feature showers only; a naturally splendid b/fast buffet is included. **$$$$**

**Hótel Reykjavík** [128 D2] (79 rooms) Raudarárstígur 37; ☎ 514 7000; e reservations@hotelreykjavik.is; www.hotelreykjavik.is. A standard upmarket hotel, the Reykjavík is modern, private, & comfortable, with a penchant for sound service & accommodating groups that might have slightly higher standards. The hotel is located just outside the main core of the city, but within walking distance of Laugavegur. All rooms have private bath/shower & a glossy veneer was added during renovations in 2007. Still, that doesn't change the fact that this will always be a nice place. The 2-storey suites are also worth mentioning (despite their outlandish price) as is the eager-to-please steakhouse restaurant. B/fast inc. **$$$$**

**Hótel Reykjavík Centrum** [134 B4] (89 rooms) Aðalstræti 16; ☎ 514 6000; e reservations@hotelcentrum.is; www.hotelcentrum.is.Opened in 2005, the Centrum is quite new, although the façade incorporates 3 of the oldest wooden structures in Reykjavík. In fact, it was the construction of the Centrum that led to the discovery of the oldest archaeological site in the city (now the Settlement Museum), which overlooks a quiet square that was once a Viking cemetery. The hotel's appeal lies in its delicate blend of old & new, merging Classical 19th-century Scandinavian elements with light-filled atriums & serene interiors. The rooms tend to optimise limited space, featuring wooden floors, framed botanic prints, & well-fitted bathrooms (rooms with bathtubs are available). Also, the entire hotel is non-smoking, with the exception of the adjoining bar. The in-house restaurant (see *Fjalakötturinn*, page 149) is excellent. **$$$$**

**Hótel Skjaldbreið** [135 F3] (33 rooms) Laugavegur 16; ☎ 595 8510; e skjaldbreid@centerhotels.is; www.centerhotels.com. One of the 4 hotels owned & operated by CenterHotels, the Skjaldbreið is the most traditional, occupying a trademark corner house that overlooks the non-stop parade on Laugavegur. Some might find the bedrooms a little old-fashioned, but that (& the high ceilings) contribute to the generally comfy & relaxed mood of the place. The all-glass breakfast room serves a complimentary morning buffet with a view. The inner-city garage parking is another nice perk. Summer **$$$$**; winter **$$**

**Loftleiðir** [128 C4] (220 rooms) Hlídarfótur; ☎ 444 4500; e loftleidir@icehotels.is; www.icehotels.is. Owned & operated by Icelandair since the very beginning, the Loftleiðir was built as a one-stop shop for tourists fresh off the plane. That explains the location (next to the city airport), the convenient tourist amenities (excursion, bike & car rentals, shuttle buses, & foot massage) & the rates, which can be significantly discounted when booked with your flight. Still, the all-inclusive set-up tends to irritate the independent-minded. The building itself is the epitome of 1960s style with smallish narrow rooms & ordinary interiors, with the exception of the romantic 'poetry rooms', furnished as a tribute to some of the greatest Icelandic bards. An indoor swimming pool & conference facility complete the ensemble. **$$$$**

**Radisson Blu** [134 C3] (88 rooms) Posthússtræti 2; ☎ 599 1000; e reservations@radissonblu.com; www.reykjavik.radissonblu.com. Such is the reincarnation of the central offices of Iceland's first shipping line (Eimskip), built in 1919. Fortunately, this posh hotel preserves all the charm of its past life, including the polished grand staircase, high moulded ceilings, giant windows, & a nod to old Reykjavík. Still, the general attitude is all things new & minimal. Ample-sized rooms feature long desks, soothing beds, & sleek bathrooms (with showers). The location is within the heart of hearts of the city, such that you really can't get any closer. Guests also have access to a smallish fitness centre, the luxurious restaurant, & a surprisingly lavish b/fast buffet. **$$$$**

## MID RANGE

**Centrum Plaza Hotel** [134 B3] (180 rooms) Aðalstræti 4; 595 8500; e info@centerhotels.is; www.centerhotels.is. Spanning 3 buildings, the Plaza is a pretty sweet deal. Located at the foot of Hverfisgata & Laugavegur, every room has a stunning view of the city, & the location is exceptional, although the price for this is having front-row seats to the rowdy weekends in the square below; despite the windows being triple-glazed for sound, there are half-a-dozen clubs & the concert venue NASA within shouting distance. That said, the Plaza is a cosy & charming hotel, modern with a twist of functionality, boasting a new $150m^2$ conference room. Prices are set by availability, so book early for better deals. The Plaza is fantastically priced for where & what it is. Summer **$$$**; winter **$$**

**Fosshótel Suðurgata** [128 A4] (42 rooms) Suðurgata 121; 562 4018; e info@fosshotel.is; www.fosshotel.is; summer only (Jun–Aug). The Suðurgata is a set of student dormitories open to travellers & favouring groups. Near the University of Iceland, you are only a short distance from the rest of the city.
The 'studio' apartments contain mini kitchenettes & bathrooms with showers. The practical design underscores simplicity, but for this much money, you could probably find something that feels a little less like a student dormitory. B/fast inc. **$$$**

**Hótel Arnarhvoll** [135 E1] (104 rooms) Ingólfsstræti 1; 595 8540; e arnarhvoll@centerhotels.is; www.centerhotels.is. The latest addition to the CenterHotels portfolio embraces the renewal of Reykjavík's harbour area with this mini modern high-rise right at the water's edge. That means visitors get exclusive access to the city centre & a one-of-a-kind bay view from the all-glass top-floor restaurant/conference centre. Rooms are square, bold, & forthright. B/fast inc. **$$$**

**Hótel Björk** [128 D3] (55 rooms) Bratarholt 22–24; 511 3777; e bjork@keahotels.is; www.keahotels.is. The 'Birch' falls outside the heart of the city centre, but is still within walking distance of Laugavegur & a few other Reykjavík attractions. The reinforced concrete construction is pretty utilitarian, while the interior is that of a fairly average yet comfortable hotel. All rooms have a private bathroom, & the conscientious staff are helpful. B/fast buffet inc. **$$$**

**Hótel Cabin** [129 E2] (152 rooms) Borgartún 32; 511 6030; e booking@hotelcabin.is; www.hotelcabin.is. As a totally functionalist but colourful hotel, the 'cabin' affords a tremendous view over the harbour towards Mt Esja. Rooms are narrow & tight, as are the teeny bathrooms. Popular with large groups in tour buses but also good for travellers who want a decent location, total cleanliness & no frills. Buffet b/fast inc. **$$$**

**Hótel Frón** [135 G3] (91 rooms) Laugavegur 22A; 511 4666; e info@hotelfron.is; www.hotelfron.is. The Frón is an eclectic little boutique hotel that's right on Reykjavík's main drag. Refined rooms & a laid-back atmosphere make a nice combination, & for what you get, these are some of the most reasonably priced beds in town. Of note are the very well-equipped apartments that make perfect sense for groups of 5 or less. **$$$**

**Hótel Leifur Eiríksson** [135 H5] (47 rooms) Skólavörðustígur 45; 562 0800; e info@hotelleifur.is; www.hotelleifur.is. Directly facing the mighty Hallgrímskirkja & a statue of their namesake, this old-style Danish mansion occupies an enviable position at the top of Reykjavík's most central descent. Rooms are smallish & without too many frills – this is what you might expect from a mid-market chain hotel back home. Still, the atmosphere is pleasant & private. B/fast inc. Summer **$$$**; winter **$$**

**Hótel Phoenix** [128 D3] (9 rooms) Laugavegur 140; 511 5002; e hotel@phoenix.is; www.phoenix.is. Proud of being the country's first entirely non-smoking hotel, the Phoenix could also win the title of most Rococo hotel in Iceland. Expect lots of chandeliers & curlicues, except for the bathrooms, which are quite modern & sensible. Despite the posh Laugavegur address, it's still a fair walk to civilisation (past the Hlemmur bus station). B/fast inc. **$$$**

**Hótel Thingholt** [135 E4] (50 rooms) Thingholtsstræti 3; 595 8530; e thingholt@centerhotels.is; www.centerhotels.is. As a very hospitable boutique hotel (right off Laugavegur), the Thingholt has it all: perfect location, impeccable taste, & a cool staff who appreciate the hotel as much as the guests. The unique interior finds inspiration in Iceland's untamed nature – complete with a trickling waterfall in the entryway. Although just renovated, the building dates back to 1877, when this was one of Reykjavík's primary printing shops. Rooms feature all-glass 'rain showers' & fluffy, queen-sized beds. A lounge bar on the ground floor is quite popular. **$$$**

**Hótel Vík** [129 F4] (24 rooms) Síðumúla 19–21; 588 5588; e lobby@hotelvik.is; www.hotelvik.is. Private & inviting, the rooms are good-sized, with an excellent view. Each comes with a private sink, refrigerator, & microwave. If you feel like splurging, upgrade to the superior rooms. Summer **$$$**; winter **$$**

**Metropolitan Hotel** [134 A3] (31 rooms) Ránargata 4A; 511 1155; e bookings@metropolitan.is; www.metropolitan.is. The Metropolitan delivers the basics of a hotel stay without any fuss except for a touch of floral fabric here & there. Surely the selling point is location, inside a quaint residential neighbourhood just 2 blocks from the city centre. Otherwise, some of the smaller rooms feel a bit cramped, as do the closet-like shower-only bathrooms. Still, the staff are quite congenial & eager to assist in any arrangements you might need. B/fast inc. Summer **$$$**; winter **$**

**Park Inn Ísland** [129 F3] (119 rooms) Ármúli 9; 595 7000; e info.reykjavik@rezidorparkinn.com; www.reykjavik.rezidorparkinn.com. A sensible traveller's base on the edge of Laugadalur, the charm of the Park Inn is that it's nice, clean, & comfortable – minus any of the pretensions found in some of the city's more extravagant hotels. The rooms are cheerful & airy, with good beds & spotless bathrooms. The hotel also goes to great lengths to be wheelchair-friendly, including custom-fit rooms. The in-house restaurant is only open in summer. **$$$**

**Radisson Blu Saga Hotel** [128 A3] (209 rooms) Hagatorg; 525 9900; e reservations.saga.reykjavik@radissonsas.com; www.radissonblu.com. The Saga Hotel has been welcoming travellers to Iceland for almost 5 decades, though a smart renovation has transformed the formerly nondescript building into something a little more futuristic. Rooms are colourful, classy, & modern, with everything a weary traveller might need. The beds are nice & wide & guests can choose between a bath and a shower. The Saga is situated a fairly good walk from the city centre, which isn't so terrible, seeing as the rooms are more spacious than average & you're also right next to the national museum. There's also free internet, a vibrant health care centre & 2 restaurants (1 that favours carnivores & another that's kinder to vegetarians). Summer **$$$**; winter **$$**

## BUDGET

**Fosshótel Baron** [128 C2] (121 rooms) Baronsstígur 2–4; 562 3204; e sales@fosshotel.is; www.fosshotel.is. Massive, central, & relatively new, the 'Baron' is the best of the Fosshotel chain in the Reykjavík area. Rooms are clean & comfy, the staff attentive, & there's a nice range of accommodation. The majority of double rooms have been recently renovated with new furniture & new décor. Some (not all) rooms also offer free Wi-Fi. Some 30 apartments are available for larger groups or longer stays; each has a small kitchen & a bathroom with shower. The 'Baron' is located right between the main drag Laugavegur & the seaside. The view is spectacular for one half of the hotel's guests, & the location fairly decent for both business travellers & tourists. The first floor features a very original Korean barbecue restaurant, Galbi. B/fast inc. **$$**

**Fosshótel Lind** [128 D3] (56 rooms) Rauðarárstígur 18; 562 3350; e sales@fosshotel.is; www.fosshotel.is. This 4-storey concrete block of a hotel is outside the main city centre but within reasonable walking distance of some attractions. As part of Iceland's Fosshotel chain, the Lind stays true to the needs of mid-market tourists, offering standard unadorned rooms (with showers) & the bed as the main attraction. Indeed, some of the economy double rooms make a very tight fit. They are most proud of their restaurant 'Carpe Diem' that serves very picturesque food. B/fast inc. **$$**

**Hótel Klöpp** [135 F3] (46 rooms) Klapparstígur 26; ☎ 595 8520; e klopp@centerhotels.is; www.centerhotels.is. This cool 1930s Art Deco classic has had a facelift, leaving rooms clean & newly furnished (all functional/all wood). Staying at the Klöpp makes you feel a bit like you live in Reykjavík, as it occupies the corner of a hidden side street but is just steps away from anything you could want. Some rooms are quite smaller than others (ask for a corner room if you can). The staff are very warm. B/fast inc. **$$**

**GUESTHOUSES** Reykjavík's many bed-and-breakfast-style guesthouses provide a logical refuge for the budget-minded traveller. They also make a nice alternative to more impersonal hotels as most are just typical Reykjavík homes. These fill up fast in summer, so always book ahead.

## Mid range

**Adam** [135 G5] (12 rooms) Skólavörðustígur 42; m 896 0242; e adam@adam.is; www.adam.is. Guesthouse Adam occupies a modern shopfront-style house that faces the descent from Hallgrímskirkja into the heart of the city. The location & a laissez-faire staff make this a very popular residence for serious clubbers & those who want the city at their doorstep. For that reason, prices go up 45% on weekends. Also, because space is so limited in the centre, rooms tend to be very small & the shower-only bathrooms even smaller (read tiny). Still, the rooms are decent & clean, & come equipped with kitchen sink & microwave. Think of it as basecamp for nights out. Summer **$$$**; winter **$$**

**Alba** [128 C4] (10 rooms) Eskilhlíð 3; ☎ 552 9800; e stay@alba.is; www.alba.is. One of the more tranquil guesthouses in the city, set in the residential neighbourhood between BSÍ, Perlan & Hallgrímskirkja. Rooms are modern, clean & smoke-free & the staff very accommodating. Free Wi-Fi. B/fast inc. **$$$**

**Arctic Sun** [135 E4] (7 rooms) Ingolfsstræti 12; ☎ 587 2292; e arcticsun@arcticsunguesthouse.com; www.Arcticsunguesthouse.com. A kindly establishment with an advantageous location, the Arctic Sun delivers clean & comfortable accommodation to the discerning traveller. Smaller rooms come with a shared bathroom, while the apartment (sleeps 8) & the 'penthouse' with a view have their own bathrooms with bath. Solid furniture & comfy beds are a tribute to the IKEA empire. Free internet & free parking. B/fast inc. **$$$**

**Baldursbrá** [128 B3] (8 rooms) Laufásvegur 41; ☎ 552 6646; e baldursbra@centrum.is; http://notendur.centrum.is/~heijfis. Situated on a shady city street in one of the residential sections of Reykjavík, the Baldursbrá offers a quiet but central alternative to some of the larger urban hotels. Owned & operated by a very hospitable Icelandic/French couple, guests are made to feel very welcome & at home. Bedrooms are large, carpeted, & cosy – bathrooms are shared. There's a closed-in garden with jacuzzi hot tub in the back. B/fast inc. **$$$**

**Butterfly** [128 B1] (12 rooms) Ránargata 8A; m 894 1864; e butterfly@simnet.is; www.kvasir.is/butterfly; ⏲ 31 May–31 Aug. This lively little house is one of the most popular in the city, & with reason. The place is always filled with very interesting guests & there's a wonderful ambiance among visitors & management. The colourful, old-fashioned façade looks onto a charming little street connecting the centre with the harbour – a coveted location that explains the slightly higher prices. All rooms have wooden floors with lots of light pouring in through the windows. You have the choice between shared or private bathroom, & there's 1 'apartment' that's very roomy & convenient. Internet, both hardline & Wi-Fi, is available, as are affordable car rentals. **$$$**

**Centrum** [128 C3] (12 rooms) Njálsgata 74; ☎ 562 0100; e mail@guesthouse-centrum.com; www.guesthouse-centrum.com. Not to be confused with the Central Guesthouse (see

Budget section), the Centrum is a delightfully prim yellow guesthouse that is actually close to the centre of Reykjavík – between Hlemmur bus station & Laugavegur. The rooms (sleeping 1–4) are quite simple, but do show a bit of affection. Very clean bathrooms are shared by guests (1 on each floor) & the very low prices almost qualify the Centrum as budget accommodation. B/fast inc in summer. **$$$**

**Domus Guesthouse** [135 G3] (12 rooms) Hverfisgata 45; 561 1200; e domus@simnet.is; www.domusguesthouse.is. Once upon a time, this squat white house was the Norwegian embassy, & before that, it was a famous music school for precocious Icelandic children. Recently renovated, Domus houses 6–12 people per room in hostel-style bunkbeds. Bring your own sleeping bag, or rent linen for a nominal fee. Bathrooms are shared. A kitchen is available for use & breakfast is offered, but will cost you. **$$$**

**Flóki Inn** [128 C3] (30 rooms) Flókagata 1; 552 1155; e info@inns.is; www.inns.is. Don't judge this inner-city guesthouse by its grey exterior. Inside, the rooms are spacious, clean, & fairly modern. All in all, the Flóki is rather conducive to visitors who want comfort & proximity without spending an arm & a leg. Rooms sleep 1–4 guests. Each room has a sink, while individual bathrooms cost more. For the price, the location is not half bad, right behind Hallgrímskirkja & next to Reykjavík's historic swimming pool. B/fast inc. **$$$**

**Garður Inn** [128 B3] (43 rooms) Corner of Hringbraut & Sæmundargata; 562 4000 (winter), 511 5900 (summer); e info@inns.is; www.inns.is. A hotel in summer only, the Garður is used as a university dormitory in the off-season, which explains its location on the University of Iceland campus. It also explains the interior, which is fairly basic, with sinks in rooms & shared bathrooms at either end of the hallways. The regular rooms are priced at much the same rate as a boutique guesthouse – what you're paying for is location, not the beds. The Garður is right next to the National Musuem of Iceland & a very pretty 1km walk (along the Tjörnin) into the city centre. Sleeping-bag accommodation is also available at a budget rate. **$$$**

**Moby Dick** [135 H2] (6 rooms) Lindargata 50; 561 4093; e mobydick@internet.is; www.internet.is/mobydick. Irresistibly cute & friendly, this metal-sided cottage adds a lot of personality to your stay in Reykjavík. Simple & well managed, the rooms are tidy & efficient. This is a non-smoking house. Some share bathrooms, with the option of a private bathroom upon request. There's also a grocery store nearby & open kitchen facilities. B/fast inc. **$$$**

**Pisa Guesthouse** [134 C4] (8 rooms) Lækjargata 6b; 578 7200; e pisa@pisa.is; www.pisa.is. Formerly the Ugly Duckling Guesthouse, following a tasteful renovation the Pisa has transformed into the Mediteranean beauty that it is. The single rooms vary in square footage from Harry Potter's understair room to the size of the private bathrooms in the bigger rooms, which are some of the nicer ones in the city, with wood floors & Viking-esque beds. While it may seem a bit pretentious, the Pisa's prime location makes it a good choice. **$$$**

**Sigriður** [122 C2] (12 rooms) Viðarhöfði 2A; 699 7885; e gistiheimli@gistiheimli.is; www.gistiheimli.is. Most ideal for car drivers, as it's located on the far eastern outskirts of the city. Pristine, all-white interiors, but small, shared bathrooms & teeny weeny-showers. A backyard wooden deck with jacuzzi is an added attraction. **$$$**

**Snorri's Guesthouse** [128 C3] (15 rooms) Snorrabraut 61; 552 0598; e guesthousereykjavik@guesthousereykjavik.com; www.guesthousereykjavik.com. A standard Reykjavík residence-turned-guesthouse, Snorri's is clean & relatively well priced, given its prime location near BSÍ & the city airport. The winding stone staircase gives it a castle-like feel, & the nicely furnished rooms accommodate 1–4 people & are available with or without individual bathrooms (with bathtubs). Use of the kitchen is encouraged. B/fast inc. Sleeping-bag accommodation is sometimes available in double rooms for less than half the cost (around 4,500ISK). **$$$**

**Sunna Guesthouse** (50 rooms) Thórsgata 26; 511 5570; e sunna@sunna.is; www.sunna.is. Light, upmarket, modern guesthouse that is very centrally located – at the top of the hill near Hallgrímskirkja. Everything inside is beige with light wooden floors & big windows, with very high standards of cleanliness. Sunna also caters to families with children, with discounts &

special services available. They offer open access to a kitchen for your own cooking & there is the option to take rooms with shared bathrooms for significantly lower costs. They also have a separate studio apartment that sleeps 4 & serve a very good breakfast buffet which costs extra. **$$$**

**The White Swan** [135 G2] (16 rooms) Vatnsstígur 11; 533 4101; e info@whitesvanur.com; www.reykjavikguesthouse.is. Fairly new & very progressive, here's a guesthouse that feels like a boutique hotel. A converted factory, the larger-than-average rooms benefit from smart design, lots of light, & a fresh perspective. 2 price categories of rooms (sleeping 1–5 people) allow for some range in price. The location near the top of Laugavegur is not bad at all; about a 10min walk into the city centre. B/fast inc. **$$$**

**Travel Inn** [128 B3] (12 rooms) Sóleyjargata 31; 561 3553; e dalfoss@dalfoss.is; www.dalfoss.is. Informal & IKEA-furnished, this guesthouse caters to small families, with 2 'family' rooms that sleep 4 & feature full cooking facilities & en-suite bathrooms. Other rooms have sinks & shared bathroom facilities. The small backyard garden adds a degree of ambiance, & the atmosphere is helpful. Bike & car rentals are available. B/fast inc. **$$$**

**Tunguvegur Bed & Breakfast** [129 G5] (9 rooms) Tunguvegur 23; 561 3553; e dalfoss@dalfoss.is; www.dalfoss.is. A homey residence in the midst of Reykjavík's suburban sprawl, the Tunguvegur reflects the everyday lifestyle of the city's local population & evokes the feeling that you are staying with distant relatives. The split-level house features craft-laden rooms of varied shapes & sizes – & 3 bathrooms, to be shared by guests. Getting there & away is not bad if you have a car; otherwise it's a 15min bus ride. B/fast inc. **$$$**

**Vikingur** [128 B1] (10 rooms) Ránargata 12; 562 1290; e ghviking@simnet.is; www.travelnet.is/vikingur. This old-style Reykjavík home is just 1 block from the city centre & its many tourist attractions. Rooms are petite & weathered & tiny bathrooms are shared (sinks in the rooms). The real charm is being situated on such a cute side street in such a cute red house & being able to walk everywhere. The triple rooms are a good deal. B/fast inc. **$$$**

## Budget

**AR Guesthouse** [128 A1] (10 rooms) Bræðraborgarstígur 3; m 857 2007; e info@arguesthouse.is; www.arguesthouse.is. AR is filled with an air of unpretentiousness & an aim to please, and the bathrooms have been recently renovated, but you have to share them with the rest of the floor. Rooms are available for 1–4 people, & as far as single rooms go, these are some of the nicer ones in the city. **$$**

**Central Guesthouse** [128 D4] (8 rooms) Bólstaðarhlíð 8; 552 2822; e cgh@visir.is; www.central-guesthouse.com. A very basic but decent guesthouse that's not so central despite the tricky name. You're a good 1km walk from where the city begins to get interesting. Still, not bad if you're in a car or if you don't care & want to save money. Rooms are tight but secure & cosy, with shared bathrooms. Kitchen facilities are available. *Sleeping-bag accommodation is available in shared rooms for 2,500ISK pp.* **$$**

**Flying Viking Guesthouse** [128 A1] (4 beds, 10+ people) Ránargata 10; m 896 6335; e info@flyingviking.is; www.flyingviking.is. Nice, quiet & quaint. Double rooms are small, but the studio apartment is pretty classy for a guesthouse. Check the website for log cabin rentals 10mins from the city centre. Perfect for people who need a place to leave their stuff while exploring. Plus, it's really close to the best parking in the city. **$$**

**Guesthouse Óðinn** [135 F5] Óðinsgata 9; 561 3400; e info@odinnreykjavik.com; www.odinnreykjavik.com. Well situated in the 101, this guesthouse feels like visiting relatives for the holidays. It's very clean, & very friendly, & very relaxing. A kitchen is available for guests. Rooms can accommodate 1–4 people, with a 6-person apartment also available. B/fast inc. **$$**

**Salvation Army** [134 B4] (41 rooms) Kirkjustræti 2; 561 3203; e guesthouse@guesthouse.is; www.guesthouse.is. Owned & operated by the Salvation Army since 1898, this guesthouse is not a hostel, even though it looks, feels, & acts like one. The main difference is that it's kept quite clean & is also very well managed. The whole Salvation Army presence has a rather interesting history in Iceland, & the attached church is one of the oldest in Reykjavík (the free coffee hour leaves a religious aftertaste). Take note that this is ground zero for the mature backpacker in Iceland & that with such a killer location & relatively low prices, competition for rooms is cut-throat – for a bed in summer, you should book months in advance. Individual rooms feature basic slatted beds with clean, warm linen & shared bathrooms on each floor. The more people sharing a room (2, 3, or 4) the cheaper the room. A kitchen is available for general use, with breakfast for a price. Internet available. *Limited sleeping-bag accommodation available (around 2,000ISK; mattresses available for rent). Monthly rent 35,000ISK.* **$$**

## ECONOMY

**Reykjavík Bed & Breakfast** (6 rooms) Grensávegur 14; 588 0000; e info@rbb.is; www.rbb.is. Whether you're travelling solo or in a group (up to 5), this B&B has a spot for you. Deceptively small on the outside, the rooms are big enough to make yourself at home. **$$$**

**Atley** [122 C2] (18 rooms) Fossaleyni 1; 594 9600; e info@atley.is; www.atley.is. This guesthouse is pretty much a glorified youth hostel housed inside a sleek new sports complex. Located well outside the city, the main appeal is the price & the Atley's connection to the Egilshöllin sports centre. Rooms sleep 2–6 people in made-up bunk beds with the option of paying more for a private room. There are significant discounts available for groups & long-term stays (more than 7 nights). A cafeteria/grill is open day & night. *Sleeping-bag accommodation is available for 2,500ISK.* **$$**

**Borgartún Guesthouse** [129 E2] (22 rooms) Borgartún 34; 511 1500; e gjtravel@gjtravel.is; www.gjtravel.is. Conveniently located just above the Guðmundur Jónasson Travel Agency, this guesthouse is about a half-hour walk from the city centre. However, it's very close to Árbæjarlaug, Reykjavík's main swimming pool. The rooms are bigger than usual, & TV & internet are available. **$$**

**Capital Inn** [128 D5] (23 rooms) Sudurhlíd 35d; 588 2100; e info@capitalinn.is; www.capitalinn.is. The private rooms give you space to stretch, & there's laundry facilities as well. Dorms for the weary hiker, doubles for the getaway. The inn also rents bicycles & scooters. **$$**

**Downtown Hostel** [134 A3] (15 rooms) Vesturgata 17; 553 8120; e reykjavikdowntown@hostel.is; www.hostel.is. While it's pricier than the Reykjavík City Hostel, the location is closer to the ground zero of Reykjavík life, & has earned the Nordic eco-label 'The Swan' for being environmentally friendly. Beds are available in dorms of 4 or 10 people, with a shared bathroom. There are also double rooms available, but you could find a hotel room for cheaper. New & squeaky clean, the hostel comes with a full load of facilities like laundry, Wi-Fi, a tiny café, & lots of camaraderie. Recommended. **$$**

**Guesthouse Elsa** [122 B2] (3 rooms) Fálkastígur 4, Álftanes; 565 0966; e guesthouseelsa@internet.is; www.internet.is/guesthouseelsa. Situated across the fjord from the city centre, you're trading proximity for solitude. That said, Elsa is as close to Reykjavík as you can get & yet enjoy the jaw-dropping beauty & peacefulness that the rest of the country is full of. The rooms are elegant, but breakfast is extra. It's a small guesthouse, so you won't be crowded out by other guests. Enjoy the surrounding scenery. **$$**

**Ísafold** [128 B2] (12 rooms) Bárugata 11; 561 2294; e isafold@itn.is; www.itn.is/~isafold. This traditional Scandinavian house is full of character & set inside one of Reykjavík's more historic neighbourhoods (right near the city centre). Rooms are generally inexpensive, although some of the beds might be categorised as flimsy. A few rooms have private bathrooms (not en suite), while others offer shared facilities. Breakfast served up in the attic. **$$**

**Youth Hostel** [129 F2] (40 rooms) Sundlaugavegur 34; 553 8110; e reykjavik@hostel.is; www.hostel.is. If only all hostels were like this: big, sleek, clean, friendly & eventful. The very metallic Reykjavík City Hostel is one of the best in the country with high-quality rooms, kitchens & bathrooms, free Wi-Fi & a lot of planned social events. As a notable destination, it's never a problem getting affordable transportation to the city centre, airport, or BSÍ. The hostel is next to the campsite & on the grounds of the Laugadalur recreation complex & its huge outdoor geothermal swimming pool. Private rooms can be booked for 1–6 people, however only the 2- & 4-person rooms offer private bathrooms. If you're looking for a really cheap place to sleep in the city, this is it. You can get a single bed in a shared room for under 2,000ISK but always, always book ahead. This place is impossibly full year-round. **$$**

## APARTMENTS

**Forsæla Apartments** [135 H4] Grettisgata 33B/35B; 551 6046; e info@apartmenthouse.is; www.apartmenthouse.is. Just 1 block away from Laugavegur, this series of apartments sleep 2–4 & offer both independence & proximity. You can also choose B&B-style accommodation, with shared bathrooms & a luxurious buffet b/fast. Finally, there's also a wonderfully unique option of renting out an entire cottage (8 sleep comfortably). Inside & out, the house stays true to older Icelandic traditions – an attraction in its own right. All units are smoke-free. **$$$**

**Lighthouse Apartments** [128 C2] (6 apts) Vitastígur 11; 551 6580; e lighthouse@lighthouse.is; www.lighthouse.is. Just off of the top of Laugavegur & inside a super-quaint red house, these apartments have character & class. The apartments (1–2 bedrooms) have comfy beds & en-suite toilet & shower, but the kitchenette is a little spartan. They also offer 2 rooms with a shared bathroom at a discounted price. **$$$**

**Lindarbrekka Apartment** [128 A1] (1 apt) Vesturvallagata 6; m 897 8699; e lindarbrekka@rekatravel.com; www.rekatravel.com/lindarbrekka. The house is 100 years old, but the 2-bedroom apartment offers evey convenience available. Equipped kitchen, comfy beds, & just a hop skip & a jump from downtown. **$$$**

**Paví Apartments** [128 D3] Brautarholt 4; 561 3553; e dalfoss@dalfoss.is; www.dalfoss.is. Owned & managed by Travel Inns, the Paví apartments occupy a blank glass & panel building right next to the Hlemmur city bus station. Inside, the 'luxury' apartments include a bedroom, sitting room, kitchen & bathroom (with shower) & offer a bit more space than that of a hotel, although 'luxury' might be pushing it just a bit. Still, for 2 or more travellers, the apartments are one of the best deals for price per person (they also have sofa beds, which helps cut costs further). Paví also offers nice & simple double rooms with kitchenettes, as well as far cheaper 'backpacker accommodation' with shared bathroom facilities. **$$$**

**Room with a View** [135 G3] (40 rooms) Laugavegur 18; 552 7262; e info@roomwithaview.is; www.roomwithaview.is. As far as apartments go, it's hard to find a better location than these upper rooms in the heart of the shopping district. It's also hard to find such a good deal: from nice-sized studios up to 4-bedroom apartments with hotel-like amenities (furnished, linens, towels, pickup services, etc) & fully functioning kitchens. The view can be seen from your room or from the 2 hot tubs on the balcony. If you're in a group of 3 or 4, this is the biggest bang for your buck. **$$$**

**CAMPING** The **Reykjavík Campsite** [129 F2] (*Tjáldvæðið; 568 6944; e info@reykjavikcampsite.is; www.reykjavikcampsite.is; 15 May–15 Sep;* **$**) is Reykjavík's main campsite and located at Laugadalur, the green quarter that's also home to the youth hostel and the recreation complex - about two miles (3.2km) from the city centre. There's no resemblance to actual camping, other than you might sleep in a tent. Instead, think sub-Arctic refugee camp. On a given summer night, there are around 700 campers trudging back and forth through a muddy field, dodging a road rage of rental cars and caravans each racing for their own piece of wet ground. Add the crowded, greasy kitchens, the disgusting bathrooms, the frazzled camp staff and an all-night cacophony of shouting in every officially recognised EU language. It's not pleasant, even when you compare it with Woodstock or Glastonbury. This may be the least desirable place to stay (and the least Icelandic), but it is also your cheapest option within the Reykjavík city limits. That said, it's the priciest campsite in the country, and for about US$10 more you could stay at the hostel next door, stay clean and dry and get some sleep.

If you're still bent on camping, try to stake out a spot on the south side, away from the chaos. Pitch your tent in line with all the others to avoid getting run over. Use the facilities in odd hours and you'll miss the crazy lines to the bathroom at peak times. If you crave hygiene, you can perform your ablutions in the showers of the Laugadalur swimming pool next door.

The campsite takes no reservations and sells pitches on a first-come, first-served basis. The exception is if you are arriving in a group of two or more caravans, in which case you should give prior notice. For caravans, there are over 40 electrical hook-ups available. Also, a pair of small cabins is available for rent for under 5,000ISK a night. Each contains a bunk bed that sleeps two.

Check-in takes place at the reception, on the north side of the campsite, right next to the main car park. Pay your fee, get a ticket and find a place. Needful things are sold at the front desk (stamps, gas, lighters, snacks, batteries, etc – but no earplugs). From the Laugadalur campsite, it's a fairly clear-cut bus ride (take No 14) into the city centre, or else a longish hike. The Flybus also makes a regular stop here.

## WHERE TO EAT

Reykjavík's reputation as the destination for avant-garde cuisine is based upon a sound advertising campaign and the creative competition that carries on among local chefs. For us that means a huge amount of choice for such a small place and elaborate food trends that sweep the city's menus every few months. Globalisation has brought every flavour and cuisine to Iceland's capital, along with a new appreciation for the few ingredients that Icelanders claim as their own. The resulting mix can often be artistic, bold, colourful, fresh, and delicious (or else completely over the top). Current fashion favours austere settings and bite-sized gourmet installations that are almost too pretty to eat. Beneath the upper crust lies a core of tried and tested fish-and-lamb restaurants beloved by tourist and native alike, while the day-to-day goes in for the capital's long-standing fast-food tradition. Needless to say, dining out costs a lot more than it does back home – a half-decent, sit-down meal at any upmarket restaurant can easily set you back US$100 per person (add drinks and your credit card's the limit). If you'd rather spend your travel budget on something besides gratins and reduction sauce, you can easily find and prepare your own meals for a lot less (see page 158), but going out is still a huge part of what makes Reykjavík the cool town that it is.

### VERY REYKJAVÍK

**Grillið** [128 A3] Hagatorg; 525 9960; grillid@grillid.is; www.grillid.is; 18.00–22.00 daily. The fact that Grillið has outlived a good 5 decades of Icelandic culinary whims says a great deal about this 8th-floor restaurant above the Radisson Blu Hotel, overlooking the city & surrounding fjords. Fortunately, its long-standing reputation as Reykjavík's premier dining experience hasn't affected the meals, which are good in that flawless sort of way. Grillið features an extensive wine list from virtually every cultural sphere of the world. An array of grilled meat & seafood dishes predominate (eg: venison tenderloin, rack of lamb, lemon sole, etc) but there's always an impressive vegetarian option. Save room for one of their delicate desserts. *Mains from 4,500ISK.* $$$$$

**Sjávarkjallarin** [134 B3] Aðalstræti 2 (next to the Reykjavík Tourist Information Centre); 511 1212; info@sjavarkjallarinn.is; www.sjavarkjallarinn.is; 11.30–22.00 daily. The 'seafood cellar' boldly defines Iceland's culinary new wave, setting the standard for all the other 'chi-chi' restaurants in town that now seek to imitate its unbelievable flavours & blissful mood. Designer lighting, handmade tables, & the rough stone walls of this – the oldest cellar in town – all add to the dining experiences, as does the long bar that's really an aquarium of tropical fish. The menu evolves weekly, but the concept is stable: classic Icelandic seafood (plaice, salmon, halibut, or smoked eel) dressed up in the chosen ingredients of Asia, Africa, & Australia – be it wasabi, lotus root, liquorice, curry, or kangaroo. The results are divinely unpredictable, & any traveller looking to splurge on 'one nice meal' should seriously consider an evening here. *Mains start at around 3,000ISK, or you can leave yourself to the creative hands of the chef, who concocts a worthy tasting menu for the table at 7,000ISK pp (3,500ISK for lunch).* $$$$$

**Potturinn Og Pannan** [128 D3] Pósthússtræti 17; also Brautarholti 22; 511 1690; slokabru@potturinn.is; www.potturinn.is; 12.00–22.00 Mon–Fri, 17.00–22.00 Sat/Sun. Priding themselves on being family friendly & catering to individual tastes, the 'Pot & Pan' wins the award for creativity. Their 'Adventure Menu' fills your tummy with Icelandic fare & gives you a history lesson at the same time. *Mains from 2,590ISK.* $$$$

**Geysir Bistro & Bar** [134 B3] Vesturgata 2; 517 4300; www.geysirbistrobar.is; 11.30–21.00 daily. Geysir offers a gamut of dishes; from soups & salads to nachos, hamburgers, seafood quesadillas & chicken-filled pancakes. The real highlight of Geysir is its prime location, looking out onto the main square in town, & the 'downtown lodge' interior design. *Mains from 1,995ISK.* $$$

**Jómfrúin** [134 D4] Lækjargata; 551 0100; jomfruin@jomfruin.is; www.jomfruin.is; summer 11.00–22.00 daily; winter 11.00–18.00 daily. Unapologetic Icelanders re-purposed the Danish *smørrebrød* long ago – today these open-face sandwiches are a proud Reykjavík tradition for lunch, dinner, or anytime in between. Jómfrúin offers a staggering variety of sandwiches to choose from, some quite authentic, others more experimental – everyone in this town has a favourite. Live jazz makes it even more popular. *Mains from 1,200ISK.* $$

**Búllan** [134 B2] Geirsgata 1; 511 888; 11.00–21.00 daily. This tiny dome of an Art Deco diner sits right on the edge of Reykjavík's old harbour & embodies all the goodness & grit of the neighbourhood – there's not a pretence (or foreigner) to be found for at least another 4 blocks. The quick service really does come with a smile, the general mood is laid-back, & the hamburgers are so outrageously delicious you'll gain a new respect for Iceland. Also, Búllan's got the best ice-cream milkshakes in the city. Attracts all ages, shapes, & creeds. *Mains from 700ISK.* $

**Icelandic Fish & Chips** [134 B3] Tryggvagata 8; 551 1118; erna@fishandchips.is; www.fishandchips.is; 11.30–21.00 Mon–Fri, 12.00–21.00 Sat/Sun. A must on a visit to Reykjavík. All-organic ingredients & their famous 'skyronnaise' make for a world-class meal that leaves you feeling good on all levels. Pick your fish, pick your sauce, pick your side, & be amazed. The unassuming exterior belies the homey inside & the culinary wonderland that's waiting to be explored to the sound of Billie Holliday & Louis Armstrong. *Mains from 990ISK.* $

## ESPECIALLY FOR TOURISTS

**Lækjarbrekka** [134 D3] Bankastræti 2; 551 4430; info@laekjarbrekka.is; www.laekjarbrekka.is; 11.30–23.00 daily. Tea time at Aunt Lulu's. Because tourists crave fancy food like reindeer carpaccio & trout roe, *n'est-ce pas*? What matters most here is presentation, from the pretty piles on your plate to the house itself (built in 1834 & the city's first bakery way back when). A few of the gourmet concoctions are truly splendid (like the signature lobster & lamb), but the hectic travel mart atmosphere eats away at the attempted grandeur. Stiff atmosphere, steep prices, & you'd better sit, not slouch. *Mains 3,220ISK.* $$$$$

**Perlan** [128 C4] Öskjuhlíð; 562 0200; perlan@perlan.is; www.perlan.is; 18.30–22.30 daily. An address all by itself, 'the Pearl' was Reykjavík's very first tourist trap: a revolving classy restaurant inside a crystal glass dome that sits atop 6 hot-water tanks, 1 of which is now home to a wax museum (see page 181). True, this is some of the finest fine dining around, with immaculate silver, table linens, a breathtaking 360° view & Secret Service-esque waiters. The Perlan is an exquisite dining experience. Recommended. *Mains 4,000ISK.* $$$$$

**Restaurant Reykjavík** [134 B3] Vesturgata 2; 552 3030; kaffireykjavik@kaffireykjavik.is; www.kaffireykjavik.is; 11.00–22.00 Sun–Thu, 11.00–03.00 Fri/Sat; fish buffet begins at 18.00. You can't miss this brightly painted (historic!) yellow restaurant, which is precisely the point.

Every evening sees a new roundup of tour bus groups who go in for the suspicious all-you-can eat seafood buffet. In all fairness, it does allow you a taste of the whole gamut, from fish balls to smoked trout, but you can do far better in this town. Perhaps most disappointing is their Ice Bar, which is nothing more than tourist misconceptions turned to profit: dress up like an Eskimo, walk into a refrigerated, blue-lit bar decorated with ice blocks, then drink hideously overpriced liquor. Surely a legend in the making. *Mains 2,800–3,400ISK.* $$$$

**Tabasco's** [134 B3] Hafnarstræti 1–3; 511 1980; e info@tabascos.is; www.tabascos.is; 11.00–23.00 Sun–Thu, 11.00–midnight Fri/Sat. Slap-bang in the middle of tourist country, Tabasco's is traditional Icelandic-meets-Tex-Mex, with entrées like fish enchiladas, lamb burritos & the like. Lots of bright flashy colours & fake sombreros. *Mains from 2,300ISK.* $$$

**Frú Berglaug** [135 F3] Laugavegur 17; 551 5979; e info@fruberglaug.is; www.fruberglaug.is; 10.00–23.00 daily. Traditional Icelandic soup (read very filling) & the 'Icelandic Trio' – lamb, fish & whale. Berglaug is famous for its lobster sandwich, & the hearty, artsy salad gets kudos too. Splurge & finish your meal with one of the homemade cakes. $$

## ICELANDIC

**101 Restaurant** [135 E3] Hverfisgata 10; e 101hotel@101hotel.is; www.101hotel.is; 07.00–23.00 daily. Never judge a restaurant by its cover: it may be the most polished boutique hotel in the country, but the in-house restaurant endorses an unaffected menu that's just plain refreshing (giant cheeseburgers, poppadoms with chutney, or lobster canapés). While some high-class dishes remain, the majority of the current menu caters to American tastes. *Mains from 3,900ISK.* $$$$$

**Einar Ben** [134 B3] Veltusundi 1 (Ingólfstorg); 511 5090; e einarben@einarben.is; www.einarben.is; 18.00–22.00 daily. In honour of the colourful nationalist poet Einar Benediktsson (see page 39), this namesake restaurant serves florid Icelandic dishes with a twist, in his former home, a comfy & bourgeois setting near the city centre. Expect refined, better-than-average fish, or chicken & lamb served in the style of Sunday dinner. Afterwards, don't hesitate to try the skyr tart. *Mains from 3,620ISK.* $$$$$

**Fjalakötturinn** [134 B4] Aðalstræti 16; 514 6060; e reservations@hotelcentrum.is; www.fjalakotturinn.is; 18.00–22.00 Sun–Thu, 18.00–23.00 Fri/Sat. The 'mousetrap' is an intimate, upmarket restaurant on the ground floor of the cheery red building that makes up a historic wing of the Hótel Centrum. The creative menu evolves weekly & relies heavily on Icelandic ingredients with a few deliberate bits of exotica tossed into the mix. Examples include the crispy duck salad, salted cod with pistachio crust, seasonal puffin & the superb reindeer in cowberry jelly. The wine list is one of the more extraordinary in this town & the lunch buffet makes a very gourmet afternoon treat. *Mains from 3,200ISK.* $$$$$

**Iðnó** [134 C5] Vonarstræti 3; 562 9700; e idno@xnet.is; www.idno.is. What started as a town hall has become a historical restaurant, remaining just as it looked in 1897. The food is classic Icelandic, with classic Icelandic prices, but you can get away with wearing striped suspenders & a top hat. The theatre hall seats 120, & a further 300 can be seated in the banquet room. *Mains from 4,745ISK.* $$$$$

**Naustið** [128 B1] Vesturgata 6–8; 554 0500; e naustid@naustid.is; www.naustid.is; 18.00–22.00 Sun–Thu, 18.00–23.00 Fri/Sat. A Reykjavík classic, the 'boatshed' has been serving hearty Icelandic meals since the end of the war, in this converted boatshed. Authentic & cosy, the food is the stuff of grandmotherly recipes: roasted chicken, braised lamb, & baked fish. Somehow it's avoided becoming too touristy. *Mains from 3,000ISK.* $$$$

**Carpe Diem** [128 C2] Rauðarárstigur 18; 552 4555; e carpediem@carpediem.is; www.carpediem.is; 11.30–14.00 Mon–Fri, 18.00–22.00 daily. One of the few places in town where smoked puffin & guillemot are on the permanent menu. Otherwise, it's fish & lamb but with special attention to Icelandic tradition. Also, a very nice variety of vegetarian choices. *Mains from 2,000ISK.* $$$

**Póstbarinn** [134 C4] Pósthússtræti 13; 562 7830; e postbarinn@postbarinn.is; www.postbarinn.is; 11.30–01.00 Sun–Thu,

11.30–03.00 Fri/Sat. A popular bar that's also not a bad restaurant, serving candid Icelandic meals like salt fish & potatoes. Live music makes this a popular place to eat, drink, & talk. *Mains from 2,200ISK.* $$$

**Scandinavian** [135 G3] Laugavegur 24; 578 4888; info@.scandinavian.is; www.scandinavian.is; 12.00–22.00 Sun–Thu, 11.30–23.00 Fri/Sat. A salute to all things Scandinavian in design, pictures, & food. It specialises in open sandwiches, and the walls are covered with menus in every Scandinavian tongue: Danish, Greenlandic, Finnish, Icelandic, & Norwegian. Soups, salads, burgers, & pastas round off the deal. *Sandwiches from 1,790ISK.* $$$

**Íslenski Barinn** [134 C3] Pósthússtræti 9; 578 2020; info@islenskibarinn.is; www.islenskibarinn.is; 11.00–15.00 Sun–Thu, 11.30–03.00 Fri/Sat. An old-time, split-level pub that attracts the indie crowd. This place offers your basic burger while flashing its Icelandic roots with whale, reindeer, puffin & lamb. There's a free-for-all piano & altruistic quotes painted on the tables. *The 1,000ISK lunch menu is a great deal.* $$

## ASIAN

**Austur Indía Félagið** [135 G3] Hverfisgata 56; 552 1630; www.austurindia.is; 11.00–22.00 daily. The 'East India Company' specialises in upmarket, authentic Indian cuisine with a focus on detail & flavour. The kebabs, curries, & rice dishes are all splendid, the various naan breads very much the real thing, & the vegetarian options tasty & filling. Recommended. *Mains from 2,700ISK.* $$$$

**Gandhi** [134 C3] Pósthússtræti 17 (downstairs); 511 1691; Gandhi@potturinn.is; http://gandhi.pano3d.eu/; 18.00–22.00 Mon–Fri, 18.00–23.00 Sat/Sun. Chic trip to India with stylish mains & lots of vegetarian-friendly entrées. The interior is authentically ethnic, as is the music (until you realise it's American rap *à la* sitar). *Mains from 2,590ISK.* $$$$

**Indian Mango** Corner of Frakkastígur & Grettisgata; 551 7722; info@indianmango.is; www.indianmango.is; 11.00–22.00 daily. Gourmet Indian cuisine cooked in a precise & colourful manner. The chef (who hails from Goa) has presented Iceland with its spiciest dining option yet. *Mains from 1,800ISK.* $$$

**Kitchen Eldhús** [128 D3] Laugavegur 60a; 517 7795; www.kitchen-eldhus.is; 12.00–14.30 & 17.30–22.00 Mon–Sat, 17.30–22.00 Sun. Iceland's first Nepalese restaurant, with all the best spicy entrées like tikka & pasanda Khyber & a healthy list of vegetarian dishes. *Mains from 2,290ISK.* $$$

**Shalimar** [134 B3] Austurstræti 4; 551 0292; shalimar@shalimar.is; www.shalimar.is; 11.30–22.00 Mon–Thu, 11.30–23.00 Fri, 16.00–23.00 Sat, 16.00–22.00 Sun. Right in the city centre, Shalimar dishes out the kind of Indian/Pakistani food that makes Brits feel right at home: tikka masala, vindaloo, tandoori & korma galore. Lots of healthy Indian vegetarian options too. *Mains from 1,290ISK.* $$

**Maru** [134 B3] Aðalstræti 12; 511 4440; maru@maru.is; www.maru.is; 10.00–23.00 daily. From the owners of Apótek comes this Asian take-away. Sushi & Thai curries & lots of grilled meat & fish. Tasty, quick, & affordable. *Mains from 1,700ISK.* $$$

**Asía** [135 F3] Laugavegur 10; 562 6210; 10.00–midnight Sun–Thu, 11.00–02.00 Fri/Sat. The trusty Chinese take-away that you know from back home. Beef, chicken or shrimp? *Mains from 1,550ISK.* $$

**Kina Flavor** [134 D3] Lækurgata 10 (downstairs); 527 0800; www.facebook.com/kina-flavor; 17.00–22.00. Another stop on the Oriental food circuit. Imagine a bright-orange restaurant with a fairly standard menu. $$

**Krua Thai** [134 B3] Tryggvagata 14; 561 0039; kruathai@restaurantkruathai.net; www.kruathai.is; 11.30–21.30 Mon–Fri, 12.00–21.30 Sat, 17.00–00.30 Sun. You never know when you'll start craving pad thai. Krua offers all the Thai classics you know & love: red & green curries, beef salad, yummy noodle soups & fried rice. Probably the most authentic Thai in town. *Mains from 1,300ISK.* $$

**Sushibarinn** [135 F3] Laugavegur 2; 552 4444; 16.30–22.00 Mon–Wed, 11.30–22.00 Fri/Sat, 17.30–22.00 Sun. Right above Kofi Tómasar Frænda, Sushibarinn serves yummy sushi to both venues. $$

**Thai Reykjavík** [134 C4] Lækurgata 8;

571 2222; 11.00–22.00 daily. Legit Thai food with an occasional Icelandic twist. *Mains from 1,390ISK.* $$

**Núðluhúsið** [135 H3] Laugavegur 59 (above Bónus); 552 2400; 11.30–21.00 Mon–Fri, 17.00–21.00 Sat/Sun. Lots of yummy meat dishes with surprises & rice. They don't skimp on portions or imagination. *Mains from 1,100ISK.* $

## MEDITERRANEAN

**La Primavera** [134 B3] Austurstræti 9; 561 8555; e laprima@laprimavera.is; www.laprimavera.is; 12.00–14.00 & 18.00–22.30 Sun–Thu, 12.00–14.00 & 18.00–23.30 Fri, 18.00–23.30 Sat. Very precise, northern Italian cuisine & one of the best-known restaurants in the city. Each dish is fresh & delicate, with updates to the menu every season & the service is supreme. It's the kind of place where you can either enjoy a 5-course meal or else simply sit down for a quiet bowl of risotto & glass of white wine. Either way you're content. Non-smoking. *Mains from 3,090ISK.* $$$$

**Madonna** [128 D3] Raudarástígur 27; 562 1060; e madonna@madonna.is; www.madonna.is; 11.00–23.00 Sun–Thu, 11.00–midnight Fri/Sat. Pasta & pizza predominate in this retro Italian eatery by candlelight. Dishes are traditional, but with an occasional twist (eg: blue-cheese lasagne). A cosy wine list completes an unpretentious dining experience. Mains from 2,600ISK; *pizza & pasta from 1,600ISK.* $$$$

**Rosso Pomodoro** [135 H3] Laugavegur 40A; 561 0500; e info@rossopomodoro.is; www.rossopomodoro.is; 13.30–22.00 Mon–Sat, 17.00–22.00 Sun. It's a global Italian chain, yes, but it's the only one in Iceland & the food is good enough to mention here. They're proud of their few core meat & fish dishes (mainly stuffed fillets) but for something less expensive, try the pasta (lasagne, cannelloni, linguini), pizza, or any of the hearty green salads. *Pizza from 1,950ISK; meat dishes from 3,600ISK.* $$$$

**Tapas** Vesturgata 3b; 551 2344; e tapas@tapas.is; www.tapas.is; 17.00–23.30 daily. Not even Iceland can resist the beloved tradition of Spain, & they've added a few of their own. Tapas dishes range from classics like Spanish omelette, calamari, & manchego, to things like Icelandic foal, smoked puffin or salt cod. The food & tavern décor are reminiscent of Spain, while the prices are blatantly Icelandic. The restaurant offers a few prix fixe menus for just under 4,000ISK; the average price is 1,150ISK – otherwise, your curiosity can kill your wallet. Dessert is worth sticking around for. *Tapas from 600ISK.* $$$$

**Caruso** [134 D3] Thingholtsstræti 1; 562 7335; e caruso@caruso.is; www.caruso.is; 10.30–22.30 Mon–Fri, 11.30–23.30 Sat/Sun. French & Italian cuisine that's just the right amount of fancy. Besides their homemade pasta dishes (ravioli, lasagne, spaghetti, etc) & lovely thin-crust pizzas, they've got some terrific bistro classics like pepper steak, veal, & mussels provençales. *Mains from 2,100ISK.* $$$

**Ítalía** [135 F3] Laugavegur 11; 552 4630; e italia@italia.is; www.italia.is; 11.30–23.30 daily. A classic Italian restaurant owned & operated by real live Italians with a penchant for frills. The rich entrées cover the 4 Italian staples: meat, seafood, pizza, & pasta – many cooked with fresh herbs & decadent sauces. Also, dessert never disappoints & there's a huge & ultra-refined collection of Italian wine. *Mains 2,400ISK.* $$$

**Trocadero** Suðurlandsbraut 12; 535 1400; 11.00–22.00 daily. Neighbourhood Italian diner for sit-down or take away. The lunch buffet is popular among businessmen, busy parents & time-constrained tourists. *Mains from 1,500ISK.* $$$

**Gata** [134 D4] Laugavegur 3; 527 0077; e info@gata.is; www.gata.is; 10.30–23.30 Sun–Thu, 10.00–midnight Fri/Sat. On Reykjavík's main shopping street, Gata offers a good variety of Italian-inspired pizza & pastas & Icelandic fish & meat dishes. The brunch served daily is the restaurant's selling point, but it's also a calm, refined escape from from hubbub of Laugavegur. *Mains from 1,650ISK.* $$$

**Gamla Smiðjan Pizzeria** [134 C4] Lækjargata 8; 578 8555; e info@gamlasmidjan.is; www.gamlasmidjan.is/; 11.30–22.00 Mon–Thu, 11.00–06.00 Fri, 12.00–06.00 Sat, 12.00–22.00 Sun. This spot gets mentioned, not for its refined dining but for being a popular pizza joint that serves a bajillion different types of pizza. The blues & jazz music overhead, chill atmosphere, & cosy interior make for a pretty ritzy café, but in the end, it's the local, albeit awesome, pizza place. *Pizzas from 1,400ISK.* $$

**Hornið** [134 C3] Hafnartsræti 15; 551 3340; hornid@hornid.is; www.hornid.is; 11.00–23.30 daily. Bohemian pizzeria on a quiet corner in the city centre, hence its name 'the corner' where the warm, open atmosphere & lots of green potted plants offer a welcome escape into what feels like a garden in a lighthouse. All day long you've got hot pizzas popping out of the brick oven with an aroma that gently lulls you from the dark, wet streets. Simple but tasty dishes & the best pizza in the city make this a local favourite. *Mains from 1,500ISK.* $$

## RED MEAT

**Argentina** [129 F3] Barónsstígur 11A; 551 9555; salur@argentina.is; www.argentina.is; 18.00–midnight Sun–Thu, 17.30–01.00 Fri/Sat. Big hunks of Icelandic beef, grilled South American-style. T-bone, ribeye, tenderloin, peppersteak – every cut is prepared to maximise its strengths & served with gusto. The same care goes into the long list of wine (including Chilean & Argentine) & the notorious cigar collection. Non-steak alternatives include fish, chicken, reindeer & other grilled meats, but you still won't escape the heavy testosterone of the place. *Mains from 4,500ISK.* $$$$$

**Austur** [134 B3] Austurstræti 7; 568 1907; info@austursteikkus.is; www.austursteikkus.is; 18.00–midnight Sun–Thu, 18.00–04.00 Fri/Sat. Austur prides itself on serving only Icelandic meat (minus the kangaroo) cooked on a charcoal grill & claims to be the only venue that combines fine dining & partying. By night it's a ritzy red-velvet restaurant; by later night it's a cool, raucous club. *Mains from 2,890ISK.* $$$$

**Hereford Steakhouse** [135 H3] Laugavegur 53B; 511 3350; hereford@hereford.is; www.hereford.is; 17.00–22.00 Sun–Thu, 17.00–23.00 Fri/Sat. Upmarket dining for the meat & potatoes set. The well-set tables look out from the all-glass walls onto Laugavegur & the scent of sizzling Herefordshire beef is mouthwatering. The restaurant specialises in New York-style steaks (strip, porterhouse, etc) as well as everyday European cuts (prime rib, entrecote, etc), & also offers seasonal puffin & whale. Also choose from delectable grilled salmon & lamb & the huge list of red wines. *Mains from 3,900ISK.* $$$$

**Rauðará** [128 D3] Rauðarástigur 37; 562 6766; raudara@raudara.is; www.raudara.is; 11.30–23.00 daily. The 'red river' steakhouse is housed in one of Iceland's oldest & largest breweries – a unique building that adds a truly local ambiance to a great meal. The steaks are everything a steak-lover could want (served with baked potatoes & stir-fried veggies) but it's their richly flavoured lamb fillets that set this restaurant apart from the rest. For the very, very hungry, there's a fixed menu for 5,000ISK that covers all the bases. *Mains from 2,700ISK.* $$$$

## SEAFOOD

**Fish Company** [134 B3] Vesturgata 2a; 552 5300; info@fiskfelagid.is; www.fiskfelagid.is; 11.30–14.00 & 17.30–22.30 daily. The wall blanketed with nice notes from customers speaks for this restaurant. The menu is stocked with premier seafood dishes, served in a way you'd never have imagined, along with a totally inique preparation & presentation, like cod & mussels with vanilla bean, sweet potato & tomato jelly. *Mains from 3,400ISK.* $$$$$

**Fish Market** [134 B4] Aðlstræti 12; 578 8877; info@fiskmarkadurinn.is; www.fiskmarkadurinn.is; for lunch Mon–Fri, for dinner 18.00–23.30 daily. While it might sound like a soggy, fishy side-street affair, the Fish Market is actually a very reputable & dress-up-for restaurant, with the only robata grill in the entire country. King crab claws, monkfish, salmon steaks, quail & cumquat make for an enjoyable evening in a quiet, exotic setting. *Mains from 3,700ISK.* $$$$$

**Humarhúsið** [134 D4] Amtmannsstígur 1; 561 3303; humarhusid@humarhusid.is; www.humarhusid.is; 11.30–22.30 daily. The 'lobster house' is all about lobster – cream of lobster soup, grilled lobster tails, even lobster burgers. If lobster's not your thing, then choose a variety of seafood or 'surf & turf' options that leave you full. The presentation is gorgeous, as are the flavours. *Mains from 4,500ISK.* $$$$$

**3 Frakkar** [135 F6] Baldursgata 14; 552 3939; 11.30–14.30 & 18.00–22.00 Mon–Fri, 11.00–06.00 Fri, 18.00–23.00 Sat/Sun. The '3 overcoats' is a friendly, family-run outfit serving lots of local fresh fish, but namely sole, cod, halibut, & catfish. The many different soups make a deliciously affordable lunch, & if nothing else, the 'fried-fish chins' are unique. *Mains from 2,750ISK.* $$$$

**Við Tjörnina** [134 C5] Templarasund 3; 551 8666; e vidtjornina@simnet.is; www.vidtjornina.is; 10.30–22.30 daily. 'By the lake' is just 1 block away from the lake – the central Tjörnin where people gather to feed the ducks. A homey refuge inside the city, the restaurant aims to please with sensibly prepared Icelandic seafood like bacalao, pickled herring, & whatever's being caught that day (the creamy fish soup is divine). Non-fish options include roasted guillemot or lamb fillet. Whatever bits of the delicious homemade bread you haven't finished off get bundled up so that you can join in & feed the ducks too. *Mains from 3,780ISK.* $$$$

**Tveir Fiskar** [134 A2] Geirsgata 9; 511 3474; e restaurant@restaurant.is; www.restaurant.is; for lunch 11.00–14.00, for dinner 17.00 onwards, daily. This gourmet fish restaurant covers seafood recipes from the entire globe while pronouncing the very best of Reykjavík's own tradition. If you keep longing for 'something local' then this is a good bet – the fish comes in from the harbour & the rhubarb for the rhubarb tart was grown in the chef's nearby garden. Non-smoking. *Mains from 3,100ISK.* $$$$

**Sægreifinn** [134 A2] Verbúð 8; 553 1500; e saegreifinn@saegreifinn.is; www.saegreifinn.is; 08.00–21.00 daily. Down by the harbour, this fish shop serves up the local catch of the day, whatever it may be. This includes rare Icelandic delicacies like Greenland shark, whale & hardfiskur. Eat in, or take it home & cook it yourself. *Mains from 1,000ISK.* $$$

## VEGETARIAN

**Gló** [129 E3] Engjateigi 19; 553 1111; e glo@glo.is; www.glo.is; 07.30–18.00 Sun–Fri, 10.00–14.00 Sat. All-organic hipster joint serving lots of fresh & creative plates for health-conscious clients. Enjoy fresh soups, great vegetable plates, & a daily vegetarian special. *Mains from 2,500ISK.* $$$

**Á Næstu Grössum** [135 F3] Corner of Laugavegur 20B & Suðurlandsbraut 52; 552 8410; e ang@anaestugrosum.is; www.anaestugrosum.is; 11.30–22.00 Mon–Sat, 17.00–22.00 Sun. The Icelandic version of 'the grass is always greener' is definitely greener than anything else you'll find in the country. As a fresh & feel-good upstairs restaurant above Laugavegur, it's not to be missed by vegans, vegetarians, & anyone else who likes organic, & tasty, healthy food. Along with your regular lentils, veggie lasagne, & tofu dishes, there's a fair amount of filling & creative surprises. Meals are served cafeteria-style as a mixed plate – point & choose. On weekends, the busy kitchen highlights a dazzling array of Indian cuisine, along with several vegan & gluten-free options. *Mains from 1,100ISK.* $$

**Garðurinn** [135 G4] Klapparstígur 37; 561 2345; e info@gardurinn.is; www.gardurinn.is; 11.00–20.00 Mon–Fri, 12.00–17.00 Sun. This hideaway café of a place is where local vegetarians/vegans sip hearty soups & chow down healthy meals before heading back out into the elements. It's also a great place for coffee & cakes. *Mains from 850ISK.* $$

**Grænn Kostur** [135 G4] Skólavörðustígur 8B; 552 2028; e info@graennkostur.is; www.graennkostur.is; 11.30–21.00 Mon–Sat, 13.00–21.00 Sun. The 'green choice' is 100% free of alcohol, smoke, & animal products. Couscous, veggie burgers, spinach lasagne, & bright salads are made with the kind of raw & organic produce for which Iceland is not generally known. *Mains 1,000ISK.* $$

**Maður lifandi** [128 D2] Borgartúni 24; 585 8700; e madurlifandi@madurlifandi.is; www.madurlifandi.is; 10.00–20.00 Mon–Fri, 10.00–17.00 Sat. This organic food store was so popular they opened an upstairs café – 'Man Alive' – which serves yummy meals made from the same products they sell. There's not one bit of processed/refined anything here. Meat (mainly poultry) is served, but at a safe enough distance to make vegetarians still feel welcome. *Mains 1,200ISK; salads from 650ISK.* $$

## FINE DINING

**Hótel Holt** [135 F6] Bergstaðastræti 37; 552 5700; holt@holt.is; www.holt.is; 12.00–14.30 & 18.00–22.00 daily. Old-school gourmet is what makes the 'gallery' such a focal point among Iceland's finer restaurants. There's always a hint of creativity on the menu, but nothing that sways too far from the steady French influence upon which its reputation was built (think duck à l'orange, escargots, foie gras). Some of the food is truly exquisite, but there's no guarantee. Non-fish lovers may want to be slightly more adventurous here, as their preparation of Icelandic seafood is quite unique to anywhere else – wine connoisseurs will also find contentment with the on-staff sommeliers & a cellar of over 4,000 bottles. If you want to experience all the finery but at half the cost, try one of their 3-course lunches. *Mains from 4,200ISK.* $$$$$

**Silfur** [134 C4] Hótel Borg, Pósthússtræti 11 (Austurvöllur); 551 1440; silfur@silfur.is; www.silfur.is; 12.00–14.00 & 18.00–23.00 Sun–Thu, 12.00–14.00 & 18.00–01.30 Fri/Sat. 'Silver' is all about nouvelle cuisine: model-sized portions of dressed-up food in brightly dribbled sauces served with a slightly upturned nose. If you like this sort of thing, you've probably seen it all before & with better results. One suspects one is chasing trends, but the menu does aim to cover every possible combination in the Icelandic/French set (eg: vanilla-salted cod, veal à la crème, reindeer with chanterelle mushrooms, etc). Much hype surrounds the 'flavours menu', which at US$100 per plate makes you want to be impressed. The restaurant's lofty décor makes up for what it lacks in personality. Best left to high-powered business dinners. *Mains from 4,200ISK.* $$$$$

**Höfnin** [134 A1] Geirsgata 7c; 511 2300; marina@hofnin.is; www.hofnin.is; 11.30–22.00 daily. Classy Icelandic specialities served, like salted cod, lobster, & reindeer meatballs with some bizarre dishes thrown in; mussels & French fries, caviar for lunch. Rather random, rather expensive. *Mains from 2,570 ISK.* $$$$

**Orange** [129 E3] Geirsgata 9; 561 1111; orange@orange.is; www.orange.is; 12.00–22.00 Sun–Thu, 12.00–23.00 Fri/Sat. Experimental molecular gastronomy finally makes it to Iceland – the latest craze in Reykjavík is the 5-course 'Let's go Crazy' taster menu that mixes food & chemistry. Reindeer & horse are just some of the bizarre meats in the dishes. Expect funky cocktails as well. *Mains from 3,800ISK.* $$$$

**Ó Restaurant** [135 F5] Thórsgata 1; 511 6677; o@orestaurant.is; www.orestaurant.is; 12.00–23.00 daily. Located in the Hótel Óðinsvé, Ó serves a blend of local Icelandic gourmet & seafood with a bold new European twist (eg: cod cheeks in dill sauce). Bright-purple walls & clean white linen offer an elegant setting for a fine meal in the city centre. *Mains from 3,400ISK.* $$$$

**Pisa** [134 C4] Lækjargata 6b; 578 7200; pisa@pisa.is; www.pisa.is; for dinner, 18.00–22.00 daily. Below the guesthouse by the same name is an upmarket restaurant, specialising in Italian with the Icelandic troika: lamb, fish, & vegetables. *Mains from 2,630ISK.* $$$$

**Panorama** [135 E1] Ingólfsstræti 1; 595 8540; panorama@panorama.is; www.panoramarestaurant.is; Open perched atop the Hótel Arnarhvoll, the eponymous Panorama offers just that with views overlooking the bay & faraway Mt Esja. Refined Scandinavian cuisine employs gourmet French techniques to produce subtle, luscious dishes that are light, artistic, & filled with wonderful flavours. A favourite of Reykjavík's posh set. *Mains from 4,000ISK.* $$$$

**Salt** [134 C3] Pósthússtræti 2; 599 1020; salt@saltrestaurant.is; www.saltrestaurant.is; 12.00–14.00 & 18.00–22.00 Sun–Thu, 12.00–14.00 & 16.00–23.00 Fri/Sat. One of the headliners in Reykjavík's sleek new parade of chi-chi dining options. Expect odd-shaped plates, a rainbow of flavours, lots of colour & texture & fair reason for pretension. The menu frequently shifts but always reveals a dedication to Icelandic staples (smoked eel, cod, & lamb) with plenty of continental accoutrements. *Mains from 3,000ISK.* $$$$

**VOX** Restaurant & Bistro [129 E3] Suðurlandsbraut 2; 444 5050; info@vox.is; www.vox.is; b/fast 07.30–10.00, lunch 12.00–14.00, dinner 18.00–midnight daily. As the dining room of the ritzy Hótel Nordica – & as one of Reykjavík's younger restaurants – VOX is still earning its wings, but not without significant notice at both home & abroad. Instead of seeking out the foreign & mysterious, their forte seems to be their supply of very fresh fish & a general faith in local ingredients & produce. The accompanying bistro offers equally thoughtful meals: the 'nordic tapas' (shrimp, caviar, smoked salmon, & herring with rye) is a fun example of their overall approach to high-minded Scandinavian cuisine. Hotel guests receive an automatic 10% discount. *Mains from 2,200ISK.* $$$

**CHEAP EATS IN REYKJAVÍK** Is it all just hamburgers, hot dogs, and fried chicken? For the most part, yes, but here's a few worthy exceptions.

✕ **Deli** [135 E3] Bankastræti 14; ☎ 551 6000; e deli@deli.is; www.deli.is; 🕒 10.00–19.00 Mon–Fri. Central deli with plenty of fresh options: stuffed baguettes, salads, pizza by the slice, lasagne, & grilled panini. *Mains from 600ISK.* $$

✕ **Grillhusið** [134 B3] Tryggvagata 20; ☎ 562 3456; e grillhusid@grillhusid.is; www.grillhusid.is; 🕒 11.30–22.00 Sun–Thu, 11.30–23.00 Fri/Sat. 1950s America all over again. From the décor to the menu, which offers a total smorgasbord of burritos, fish & chips, burgers & lamb. Try the 'West Side Story burger'. *Mains from 1,490ISK.* $$

✕ **Heitt og Kalt** Grensásvegur 10; ☎ 533 3060; e eldhus@heittogkalt.is; www.heittogkalt.is; 🕒 11.00–15.00 Mon–Fri, 11.00–14.00 Sat. 'Hot 'n' cold' serves one of the healthiest low-cost lunches in the city. A big soup & salad bar, lots of fresh veggies, & a strict no-smoking policy. *Mains from 900ISK.* $$

✕ **Mmmmm** Laugavegur 42; ☎ 445 7000; e info@mmmmm.is; www.mmmmm.is; 🕒 12.00–14.00 & 18.00–22.00 Sun–Thu, 12.00–14.00 & 16.00–23.00 Fri/Sat. Yes, that's 5 m's. Stepping in to Mmmmm is like stepping into a whitewashed spring day. Soups & salads are served up in a healthy, bright way, along with nouvelle vogue tortilla wraps & daily dishes of chicken, fish, & vegetables. *Mains from 950ISK.* $$

✕ **Piri-Piri** [134 A2] Geirsgata 9; ☎ 515 1500; e piripiri@piripiri.is; www.piripiri.is; 🕒 11.00–21.00 Sun–Thu, 11.00–22.00 Fri/Sat; lunch specials daily. Chicken everything & hearty servings, done the Portuguese way. Take-away is the thing to do, but there are snazzy booths inside as well. *Mains 1,480ISK.* $$

✕ **Santa Maria** [128 C3] Laugavegur 22a; ☎ 552 7775; e info@santa-maria.is; www.santa-maria.is; 🕒 06.00–23.00 Sun. Reykjavík's one & only stop for legit Tex-Mex. The music, decorations, flavour & feel are right off the border. There are a few Italian & gringo courses too. Strongly recommended. *Everything is 1,490ISK.* $$

✕ **Svarta Kaffið** [135 H3] Laugavegur 54; ☎ 551 2999, 🕒 11.30–midnight Mon–Thu, 11.30–01.00 Fri/Sat, 12.00–23.00 Sun. Breadbowls & soup, meats & veggies. Svarta Kaffi means a full belly. (Actually, it means 'black coffee'), but you'll be well fed with a good view of Laugavegur. *Mains 1,390ISK.* $$

✕ **Vitabar** [128 D3] Bergþórugata 21; ☎ 551 7200; 🕒 10.30–23.00 Sun–Thu, 11.00–04.00 Fri/Sat. The city's ultimate hamburger bar & grill.



**CAPITAL HOT DOGS**

A hot dog is a hot dog is a hot dog, or is it? Iceland's hot-dog stands are ubiquitous, but only one has a national reputation as the very best. **Bæjarins bestu** (*The Town's Best; 🕒 10.00–00.30 Sun–Thu, 10.00–04.00 Fri/Sat; mains 280ISK;* $) is no more than a wooden hut by the harbour, but there's always a line that stretches all the way around the corner. Indeed, these do taste better than your average frankfurter, and everyone in Reykjavík holds a theory as to why (cooked in beer/fresh-baked buns/homemade sauce). Whatever they do, Bæjarins bestu attracts a faithful clientele representing Reykjavík's bustling centre: businessmen out for lunch, famished clubbers, and mums pushing prams. Reputation allows them to charge just a bit more than the going rate for hot dogs.

Almost anyone you ask will tell you that this is their favourite, & with good reason. The blue-cheese burger has a countrywide reputation. *Mains from 600ISK.* $$

**Hlölla Bátar** [134 B3] Ingólfstorg; 511 3500; hlolli@hlollabatar.is; www.hlollabatar.is; 10.00–22.00 Sun–Thu, 10.00–midnight Fri/Sat. Hot & cold sandwiches galore in the city centre. Would you like French fries with that? *Mains from 1,100ISK.* $

**Kebab húsið** [134 C3] Grensásvegur 3; 561 3070; 11.00–midnight Sun–Wed, 11.00–02.00 Thu, 11.00–07.00 Fri/Sat. The city's beloved kebab house answering to late-night cravings for skewered meat, & your basic falafel needs, fish & chips, or just plain chips. *Mains 500ISK.* $

**Kornið** Lækjargata 4 07.00–17.30 Sun–Thu, 08.00–17.00 Fri/Sat. The great little bakery we all want to go to for breakfast. Icelandic pastries & bread, prepared with lots of love & friendliness. Makes for a good start to the day. *Cinnamon rolls from 200ISK.* $

**Nonnabiti** [134 C3] Hafnarstræti 11; 551 2313; 08.30–02.00 Sun–Thu, 10.00–05.30 Fri/Sat. Reykjavík's most beloved sandwich & hamburger shop. Super-fresh fixings. *Mains 500ISK.* $

**CAFÉS** Scandinavians and coffee go together like cream and sugar. It's part of what makes café culture so vibrant in Reykjavík and why it's so easy to while away the hours in some cosy corner waiting for the sky to clear. There's no right time to have coffee, but the ritual tends to centre on the social.

**Café Oliver** [135 G3] Laugavegur 20a; 552 2300; cafeoliver@cafeoliver.is; www.cafeoliver.is; 11.45–01.00 Sun–Thu, 11.45–05.30 Fri/Sat. Hipster café/bar/club that prides itself on its taste in fine dining, fine décor, fine music & fine clientele. The menu is almost entirely Indian, but caters to Westerners too. Their motto 'Eat like a man, party like an animal' sums up the metamorphosis the café goes through. While Oliver is a ritzy restaurant by day, at night it becomes one of Reykjavík's premier party sites. Lots of blue & red lights & raving 20-somethings. *Mains from 1,350ISK* $$$

**Café Paris** [134 C3] Austurstræti 14; 551 1020; cafeparis@cafeparis.is; www.cafeparis.is; 09.00–01.00 daily. Modern, artsy café in the city centre with comfy chairs & just the right amount of chic. The menu includes soups, salads, crêpes, healthy shakes & sugary pastries; the bar is famous for its wild array of cocktails. *Mains 1,390ISK.* $$$

**Babalú** [135 G5] Skólavörðustígur 22A; 552 2278; 09.00–22.00 Mon–Thu, 09.00–midnight Fri/Sat. A laid-back Cuban-themed coffeeshop in downtown Reykjavík? Yeah, it works. Decadent desserts, comfy chairs, & an up-&-coming venue for live music. Definitely a cool place to hangout. *Mains 800ISK.* $$

**Café Róma** [128 C2] Laugavegur 118; 562 0020; 08.30–18.00 Mon–Fri, 10.00–17.00 Sat/Sun. A bit beyond the known centre, but worth mentioning for its healthy lunches (sandwiches, pasta, salads, etc) & its laid-back, friendly feel. *Mains 800ISK.* $$

**Grái Kötturinn** [135 E3] Hverfisgata 16A; 551 1544; 08.15–15.00 daily. The 'grey kitten' is the local favourite of bibliophiles & brainiacs, with lots of books on the shelf & hot drinks that help fuel deep conversations. It's refreshingly uncontrived, which is exactly why it's been around for so long. Plus, it's one of the only places in Reykjavík you can get pancakes. Well-intentioned service, even if it's not the best. *Mains from 1,390ISK.* $$

**Kaffi Brennslan** [134 C4] Posthússtræti 9; 561 3600; brensslan@brensslan.is; www.brennslan.is; 09.00–01.00 Mon–Thu, 09.00–03.00 Sat, 12.00–01.00 Sun. A favourite among the city's young & effortlessly hip. By day you'll find a wonderful & brooding coffee shop; by night it's Reykjavík's chattiest beer hall. Foodwise, sandwiches reign supreme on the menu, although you have the option for juicy steaks & there's a complete children's menu. Also, Brennslan may be the only place in Iceland where you can get a slice of pecan pie. *Mains 800ISK.* $$

**Kaffitár** [134 D3] Bankastræti 8; 511 4540; kaffitar@kaffita.is; www.kaffitar.is; 07.30–18.00 Mon–Sat, 10.00–17.00 Sun.

This chain location only gets mentioned for its popularity & status in the city centre. Otherwise, it's pretty much the Starbucks of Iceland, with locations at the National Gallery, the airport & anywhere else you might happen to go. You'll find fresh-roasted coffee & all that goes with, plus they sponsor the annual Icelandic barista championship (a contest in coffee excellence). *Mains from 300ISK.* $$

**Mokka** [135 E3] Skólavörðustígur 3A; ☎ 552 1174; e mokka@mokka.is; www.mokka.is; ⏲ 09.00–23.30 Mon–Sat, 12.00–23.30 Sun. Reykjavík circa 1958; the only thing that's changed inside this café/diner is the staff. Otherwise, the menu, décor, & even music (sometimes) reflect an era heavily influenced by the American military presence in Iceland. Famous for its all-day breakfasts. *Mains from 500ISK.* $$

**Nýlenduvöruverslun Hemma og Valda** [135 G3] Laugavegur 21; ☎ 551 6464; e www.verzlun.com; ⏲ 10.00–01.00 Sun–Thu, 10.00–03.00 Fri, 11.00–03.00 Sat. Between the worn wooden walls & the amiable beer, Hemma og Valda feels a bit like you've stepped onto an Icelandic fishing trawler. With a distinct 'captain's cabin' feel, you can't help but feel at home. Weekends see local bands squeeze into the corner & music you can hear down the street. *Mains from 1,200 ISK* $$$

**Ömmukaffi** [134 C3] Austurstræti 20; ☎ 552 9680; ⏲ 08.30–21.00 Sun–Thu, 09.00–02.00 Fri/Sat. 'Grandmother's café' plays the blues & serves fresh-baked Icelandic pastries that go quite nicely with your steaming mug of coffee. Right across from the post office, it's a very warm & cosy refuge. Semi-healthy light lunches make you linger longer & it's non-smoking. *Mains from 750ISK.* $$

**Uppsalir** [134 B3] Aðalstræti 16; ☎ 514 6000; e dining@hotelcentrum.is; www.hotelcentrum.is; ⏲ 11.00–23.00 Mon–Thu, 11.30–01.00 Fri/Sat. A quiet & very central coffee bar taking up the first floor of the historic Hótel Centrum. Slow jazz, potent drinks, & a lax atmosphere. While there's a menu of 'healthy choices' like veggie lasagne & wholewheat wraps, the restaurant's interpretation of food is a little skewed: from the 'light courses' list you can order the British burger with sausage, bacon, fried onion, cheese, fried eggs, with a side of salad & fries. *Mains 1,580ISK.* $$

**Tíu Dropar** [135 G3] Laugavegur 27; ☎ 551 9380; ⏲ 09.00–18.00 Sun–Thu, 10.00–18.00 Fri/Sat. Personality is what really makes a coffee house worth your time, & 'ten drops' has plenty of it. Down underground – beneath the commercial fray of Laugavegur – all ages & types squeeze into the tiny space for coffee, smokes, & yummy cakes. Traditional to the core. *Mains from 600ISK.* $

**Café Haiti** [134 B2] Geirsgata 7b; ☎ 588 8484; e info@cafehaiti.is; www.cafe-haiti.is; ⏲ 08.00–23.00 Mon–Sat, 09.00–23.00 Sun. Half coffee house, half cultural bastion. Run by a sweet Haitian lady, Café Haiti's the place to unwind with a banana brownie. The open mic guarantees entertainment, local artists' work on the walls guarantees enlightment, & the patrons offer camaraderie. *Mains from 200ISK.* $

**Café Rót** [134 B3] Hafnarstræti 17; ☎ 662 1114; e info@ywamiceland.org; www.ywamiceland.org; ⏲ 15.00–23.30 Tue–Fri, 13.00–23.30 Sat. A standard non-alcoholic cafe, it's not the soup or sandwiches which set Rót apart, it's the story behind it. Rót is run by Youth With A Mission, an international, interdenominational Christian organisation which also runs a rather vague 'all-ages school' in the basement. *Mains from 700ISK.* $

**Kofi Tómasar Frænda** [135 E3] Laugavegur 2; ☎ 551 1855; http://en-gb.facebook.com/people/Kofi-Tómasar-Frænda; ⏲ 10.0–01.00 Mon–Thu, 10.00–05.30 Fri/Sat, 11.00–midnight Sun. Like much of Reykjavík, 'Uncle Tom's Cabin' is a coffee house during the week, serving trademark breadbowls & soup, & a party bar at weekends, whipping up alcoholic milkshakes. Think basement bohéme, troubadour songs, & eclectic, funky décor. *Mains from 1,300 ISK.* $$

**Trúnó** [135 F3] Laugavegur 22; ☎ 578 7800; e info@truno.is; www.truno.is; ⏲ 11.00–01.00 Sun–Thu, 11.00–02.00 Fri/Sat. While Truno is advertised as a gay bar, it's really just another friendly spot for coffee & a chat dressed up in fabulous decorations & pastel design to a groovy soundtrack. Truno's popular with the after-school crowd. Read the mini character bios on each table. *Mains from 1,600ISK.* $$$

**SELF-CATERING** If you're tired of nifty restaurants, prefer your own food or just want to conserve cash, then it's a breeze to go out and buy groceries yourself. In the city centre you've got the trusty **10/11** at Austurstræti 17 (*552 1011*) and a little farther out at Barónsstígur 2–4 (*511 5311*). Reykjavík also features somewhere around ten **Bónus** stores – just look for the pink pig. The two locations closest to the city centre are Skútuvogi 13 (*588 8699*) and at the Kringlan mall (*Kringlunni 4; 568 0140*). For something less predictable, check out some of Reykjavík's speciality food shops.

**Bakarí Sandholt** Laugavegur 36; 551 3524; www.sandholt.is; 07.30–18.15 Mon–Fri, 07.30–17.30 Sat, 08.30–17.00 Sun. More carbs that smell & taste nice.

**Bernhoftsbakari** Bergstaðastræti 13; 551 3083; 08.00–17.00 Mon–Fri, 08.00–16.00 Sat/Sun. One of Reykjavík's most famous establishments, baking bread & incredible pastries since 1834.

**Ferskt og Fljótt** bakery 08.00–18.00 daily, market 08.00–23.00 daily. Always 'fresh & ready', one half is a café working miracles with hot drinks & delicious baked goods; the other half is a grocery store with all the necessities.

**Ostabúðin** Skólavörðustíg 8; 562-2772; 11.00–18.00 Mon–Fri, 11.00–15.00 Sat. A dainty delicatessen with cheese & cold-cut meat, along with lots of yummy take-away hot & cold dishes.

## ENTERTAINMENT AND NIGHTLIFE

Reykjavík's reputation for insane all-night carousing is one part truth and one part sound marketing. People don't fly to the Arctic for cheap beer – it's the scene that counts. On a given weekend you have around 50 bars, nightclubs, and cafés open all night long in the city centre. The simple fact that partygoers can stumble from one hip spot to the next in just a few steps already sets tiny Reykavík apart from more glamorous global capitals. What's more is that every club competes for the coolness factor, constantly reinventing itself with new décor, new themes, new drinks, new menus, and new music. The novelty of endless dusk heightens the mood in summer, when it seems the party will never end and it will never get too late. And it never does. A lot of clubs live as restaurants by day but stop serving food at 22.00 when tables are cleared and the disco balls lowered. Anticipatory eleven o'clock pre-drinks are a Reykjavík institution and locals only start 'going out' around midnight. Things pick up two to three hours later and by 05.00 or 06.00 everyone slithers home to bed.

What makes going out in Reykjavík such fun is the sheer energy that erupts onto the streets – or street, seeing as it all happens along the Laugavegur/Bankastræti/Austurstræti thoroughfare. There's really no such thing as a 'dead' spot or a dull moment with the crowds swarming from club to club. Unruly street behaviour is a given but usually limited to sodden teenagers shoving each other in jest. The key to a good time is to stay loose and do a bit of everything (dance, drink something you can't pronounce, catch some live music, etc). It also helps to keep moving. Doing the rounds might include going back to a place you left an hour ago or waiting until everyone else shows up – it all depends on what's happening. To plan your clubbing strategy, check out the latest lay of the land at the *Grapevine* (*www.grapevine.is*).

For a little more handholding, check out **Nightlife Friend** (m *822 6600;* e *jonkari@nightlifefriend.is; www.nightlifefriend.is*). They publish a bi-weekly nightlife guide that highlights the weekend calendar and describes what's happening, who's playing, etc. All people timid and shy can hire a nightlife friend as a personal guide – locals who wilfully play the role of the hipster friend you never had. As a bona fide escort who knows the scene, your guide will take you from club to club and keep you at the centre of the buzz, and even introduce you to the pretty people at the bar. Prices start at US$500 per night (for a group of five or fewer), which buys you about six hours of friendship and insider cool. Perhaps the best part is that your guide knows all the bouncers who let you jump the lines.

**BARS AND CLUBS** Over half the city's nightspots exist as quiet cafés or fancy restaurants by day. The list below is by no means comprehensive, but includes those establishments that have made their name well after midnight. You can pretty much dance, drink, lounge, or listen to live music anywhere – the following categories are simply based on primary focus and reputation.

## Dancing

☆ **Faktory** [135 F3] Smiðjustig 6; ☎ 551 4499; e factory@faktory.is; ⌚ 17.00–01.00 Sun–Thu, 17.00–05.30 Fri/Sat. One of the places to be. Chessboard tables & pastel signs belie the rockin' disco inside. Weekends see this joint become a wall-to-wall mass of bodies, & the upstairs stage is on the 'Need to Perform Here' list for bands. In short, Faktory is one cool place.

☆ **Hressingarskálinn** [134 C3] Austurstræti 22; ☎ 561 2240; e hresso@hresso.is; www.hresso.is; ⌚ 09.00–01.00 Sun–Thu, 10.00–17.00 Fri/Sat. Pretty much a Reykjavík institution, 'Hressó' (kresso) is an eatery that's seedy in a harmless kind of way but offers free internet, live music, & plenty of seating. It serves soups, salads, & paninis, & like the rest of downtown, becomes really popular at the weekends.

☆ **Sirkus** [135 F3] Klapparstígur 31; ⌚ when it's open. Reykjavík's little anti-establishment temple has a very 1980s feel to it. The outer walls are an ever-changing mural by local artists & the inner walls are something to experience. The fun is getting packed into the raucous show that goes on inside. Live music & very lively dancing. *Paid cover.*

☆ **Vegamót** [135 F3] Vegamótastígur 4; ☎ 511 3040; e vegamot@vegamot.is; www.vegamot.is; ⌚ 11.00–01.00 Sun–Thu, 11.00–06.00 Fri/Sat. Honestly, it's impossible to classify Vegamót since everyone in Reykjavík loves it for a different reason. Depending on what time you show up, it's a café, restaurant, disco, or bar. The only constant is the party that seems to never stop. So much that you really can't avoid this place even if you try. At mealtimes the menu is seafood/pasta/Tex-Mex, & in between you've got coffee, tea, & bagels. Once the kitchen closes (at 22.00, 23.30 on weekends), there's a whole lot of drinking & gabbing, & then the dancing takes off. Still popular after so many years, with a popular brunch on weekend mornings. *Mains from 1,590ISK.* $$

## Drinking

🍸 **Bar Gallery 46** Ingólfsstræti 3; ☎ 561 0700; ⌚ 11.00–01.00 Sun–Thu, 11.00–03.00 Fri/Sat. Part bar, part art gallery, the 46 is a classy, quiet place, with music, cool art pieces, & friendly chat with the old timers.

🍸 **Bjarnifel Sportsbar** [134 C3] Austurstræti 20; ☎ 561 2240; e bjarnifelsportsbar@gmail.com; ⌚ 10.00–22.00, cocktails from 15.00; daily. Reminiscent of an Irish tavern, Bjarnifel is a mix of whitewashed walls, mismatched bricks, & sleek plasma TVs. 'All sports for all people', & all day long.

🍸 **Celtic Cross** [135 F3] Hverfisgata 26; ☎ 511 3240; ⌚ 11.00–01.00 Sun–Thu, 11.00–05.00 Fri/Sat. Reykjavík's ultimate Irish pub experience, complete with Guinness on tap.

🍸 **Dubliners** [134 B3] Hafnarstræti 4; ☎ 527 3232; e dubliner@dubliner.is; www.dubliner.is; ⌚ 15.00–01.00 Sun–Thu, 15.00–05.30 Fri/Sat. Guinness is the reigning favourite in this time-machine of a pub. Straight out of Old Ireland, it's low ceilings & wine-bottle candles, wooden floors & flowing beer.

🍸 **English Pub** [134 C3] Austurstræti 12b; ☎ 578 0400; e enskibarinn@enskibarrin.is; www.enskibarinn.is; ⌚ 12.00–01.00 Sun–Thu, 12.00–05.30 Fri/Sat. Just what it sounds like. The English Pub has spent 6 years as a scrappy upstart & has become one of the livelier joints in the Reykjavík party scene. It's a popular spot any night of the week, with continuous music, a huge whisky selection, cheap beer in Oct, football, & is home to the famous 1,500ISK spin-the-wheel game. Recommended.

**Grand Rokk** [135 F3] Smiðjustígur 6; 551 5522; grandrokk@grandrokk.is; www.grandrokk.is; 11.00–01.00 Sun–Thu, 11.00–03.00 Fri/Sat. Undergound chess bar with a pint on the side. Also famous for its malt whisky & as an intimate venue for small unknown bands.
**Highlander (House of Guinness)** [134 C4] Lækurgata 10 (upstairs); 578 0440; 17.00–01.00 Sun–Thu, 17.00–03.00 Fri/Sat. Straight-up ethnic Irish. Live music every Thu night. This venue is a little more upmarket than your standard Irish pub.
**Kaffibarinn** [135 F4] Bergstaðastræti 1; 551 1588; 16.30–01.00 Sun–Thu, 15.00–03.00 Fri/Sat. Where Icelanders go to run into someone famous then say they did. Partly famous because it used to be part-owned by British band Blur & partly because it's so hard to get into, although the back room makes it bigger than it looks from the front. Tiny space, tiny drinks, long lines, but nonetheless interesting. The Fidel Castro is the drink of choice.
**Næsti Bar** [135 E1] Ingólfsstræti 1a; 551 7776; 15.00–01.00 Mon–Thu, 15.00–05.00 Fri/Sat. A good-sized bar, with lots of smoke to boot.
**Prikið** [135 E3] Bankastræti 12; 551 2866; 08.00–01.00 Mon–Thu, 08.00–05.30 Fri, 12.00–05.30 Sat, 12.00–01.00 Sun. Weird drinks & the young, carefree drinkers who drink them. By day, it's a toned-down café/bistro with coffee, pastries, sandwiches & small meals. *Mains from 1,200ISK.* $$
**Sólon** [135 E3] Bankastræti 7A; 562 3232; solon@solon.is; www.solon.is; 11.00–01.00 Mon–Thu, 11.00–05.00 Fri, 11.00–05.30 Sat, 12.00–18.00 Sun. Ritzy food & drinks for those who like to dress smart & wear lots of makeup & jewellery. The service leaves a lot to be desired. *Mains from 2,500ISK.* $$$
**Thorvaldsen Bar** [134 C3] Austurstræti 8–10; 511 1413; thorvaldsen@thorvaldsen.is; www.thorvaldsen.is; 11.00–22.00 Wed, 11.00–01.00 Thu, 11.00–05.00 Fri/Sat. Distinguished, modern bar that attracts pretty people who come for the light atmosphere, cool décor & friendly bartenders. By day, one dines off the delicate menu (Asian fusion), & weather permitting, you can grab a seat on the patio overlooking Austurvöllur. By night, the music gets going (rhythmic techno jazz) & the drinks flow. Try the famous killer mojitos. *Mains from 1,790ISK.* $$$
**Vínbarinn** [134 C4] Kirkjutorg 4; 552 4120; 16.00–01.00 Mon–Sat. It makes sense that the 'wine bar' has one of the most diverse wine collections in the country. For those who like wine, elegance, & people their age.

## Lounge

**101 Lounge** [135 E3] Hverfisgata 10; 580 0101; 101hotel@101hotel.is; www.101hotel.is; 11.00–midnight Sun–Thu, 11.00–01.00 Fri/Sat. Already listed as a restaurant & hotel, the very small bar & entrance lounge still has its own late-night scene, what with the roaring fireplace, elegant cocktails & a completely separate mood.
**B5** [134 D3] Bankastræti 5; 552 9600; b5@b5.is; www.b5.is; 11.00–22.00 Sun/Mon, 11.00–01.00 Thu, 11.00–05.00 Fri/Sat. The first thing your eye catches is the neon-lit back wall that's stocked with exotic bottles of alcohol, which serves as a metaphor for B5. It's partly a café, with books & internet, part private club with barred-off rooms, but through all of that it's a yuppie bar with chill music & cool lights. *Mains from 1,500ISK & up.* $$$
**Bakkus** [134 B3] Tryggvagata 22; 578 3200; 20.00–01.00 Sun–Thu, 20.00–05.30 Fri/Sat. When the revolution starts, it will be at Bakkus. The ghosts of nightclubs past meet here for the young bohemian atmosphere, varieties of vodka, cheap beer, & fooseball. Recommended.
**Glaumbar** [134 A3] Tryggvagata 20; 552 6868; glaumbar@glaumbar.is; www.glaumbar.is; 11.00–01.00 Sun–Thu, 11.00–03.00 Fri/Sat. Sports bar with football on the big screen, lots of beer & lots of camaraderie. The best place to catch the big international matches.
**Hverfisbarinn** [135 F3] Hverfisgata 20; 772 6635; www.hverfisbarinn.is; 20.00–01.00 Wed, 20.00–01.00 Thu, 20.00–05.30 Fri/Sat. As close to heaven & hell as the Reyk club scene gets; the top of this split-level club is well lit with wood floors & hip booths; downstairs has black furniture, coloured shadows & buckets of empties.
**Posthusið** Posthússtræti 13; 551 1800; 11.30–01.00 Sun–Thu, 11.30–03.00 Fri/Sat. Small, chic after-work place for the mid 30s

crowd. The happy hour is worth checking out. *Mains from 1,490ISK.* $$

**Truno** [135 F3] Laugavegur 22; ☎ 578 7800; ⌚ 11.00–01.00 Sun–Thu, 11.00–02.00 Fri/Sat; Club Barbara ⌚ 21.00–01.00 Thu, 22.00–05.00 Fri, 22.00–05.00 Sat. Iceland's flagship gay bar. While it's previously listed as a coffee shop, it deserves mention as a nightlife hotspot as well, especially since the very gay Club Barbara is right upstairs.

## Live Music

**Bar 11** [135 F3] Corner of Laugavegur & Smiðjustígur (Hverfisgata 18); m 821 6921; ⌚ 11.00–01.00 Sun–Thu, 11.00–03.00 Fri/Sat. Rock & roll à la Icelandic, led by the slogan 'Lead us into Temptation'. Coffins on the bars, & skulls everywhere, but the dark stuff is all show; on Fri night, everybody just wants to have fun.

**Café Amsterdam** [134 B3] Hafnarstræti 5; ☎ 551 3800; ⌚ 11.00–01.00 Sun–Thu, 11.00–03.00 Fri/Sat. Live, guitar-smashing music every weekend.

**Dillon** [135 G3] Laugavegur 30; ☎ 511 2400; ⌚ 14.00–01.00 Sun–Thu, 14.00–03.00 Fri/Sat. This tiny (& very old) Reykjavík home is known for its live mixing by a run of new DJs & live music. Beer is the preferred beverage.

**Gaukur á Stöng** [134 B3] Tryggvagata 22; ☎ 551 1556; e gaukurinn@guakurinn.is; www.gaukurinn.is; ⌚ 11.30–01.00 Sun–Thu, 11.30–04.00 Fri/Sat. Live music every night with everything from folk to electronica. Noted as the first restaurant to break Iceland's long-standing ban on beer by mixing vodka with non-alcoholic brew. Now they serve real beer, & their well-known grill sticks to hamburgers & fries. Always fun. *Mains from 900ISK.* $$

**Hvíta Perlan** [134 B3] Austurstræti 12a; ⌚ 11.00–01.00 Sun–Thu, 11.00–06.00 Fri/Sat. 3 storeys of live music, poker, dancing, intricate drinks, & a killer nacho menu. $

**NASA** [134 B4] Austurvöllur; ☎ 511 1313; e nasa@nasa.is; www.nasa.is; ⌚ for events. World famous at this point – all the biggest, hottest bands play here as it's the largest indoor venue in the city. Things get fairly exciting on the huge dance floor. *Paid cover.*

**Risið** [134 C3] Tryggvagata 20; ☎ 552 6868; www.risid.is; ⌚ 'flexible hours'. 'The Rising' features football during the day & lots of live music at night. A cosy, hip, friendly place with an empowering view of the square outside.

**Rósenberg** [134 D4] Lækjargata 2; ☎ 551 8008; ⌚ 11.00–01.00 Sun–Thu, 11.00–03.00 Fri/Sat. Noted jazz venue & very cool, relaxed café with good sandwiches & motherly meals. *Mains from 1,200ISK.* $$

**Sódóma** [134 C4] Tryggvagata 22; m 821 6921; e sodomarvk@gmail.com; ⌚ 22.00–05.00 Sun–Thu. While it houses a reputable bar with snare-drum taps, Sódóma is primarily a concert venue, hosting a variety of musical talent. It's always dark, always loud, & always exciting. Recommended.

**MUSIC** The Reykjavík scene is sensational, huge, and diverse. For classical performance, try to catch the **Reykjavík Symphony Orchestra** (*Sinfóníuhljómsveit Íslands; ☎ 545 2500; e sinfonia@sinfonia.is; www.sinfonia.is*). They perform the classical greats and tend to collaborate with many internationally acclaimed soloists and groups, holding regular concerts at the university auditorium *(Háskólabíð; Hagatorg)*. Also, the **Reykjavík College of Music** (*Skipholti 33; ☎ 553 0625; e tono@tono.is; www.tono.is*) often showcases talented students and faculty in regular recitals during the school year.

Reykjavík's jazz scene goes way back to the very beginning and is known for its very eclectic expression and enthusiastic local following. You can find something almost any night of the week, but weekends are obviously best. Check local listings and noted jazz venues (eg: Rosenberg), which also tend to be the smokiest bars. The city's annual jazz festival normally takes place in the autumn (*www.jazz.is*).

Reykjavík's real musical reputation is grounded in the incredibly loud and raucous, although anything and everything is possible. It is yet another reason why weekends are so exciting in this city. Walk into a bar at 01.00 and you'll catch a young female devouring the microphone or a waif-ish teenager battling an electric guitar with gusto. Sometimes they're good, often they're really good, and other times it's so bad you realise that it's just a big joke. For big names or big shows, NASA is most famous, although the largest concerts are held in the local indoor stadium. A word of warning: Icelandic crowds can get pushy and out of control, especially under the influence of music. That's especially applicable to DJ spots at any of the clubs.

The city's streets and cafés will be littered with announcements of upcoming shows, and the websites of individual venues normally list who's playing in the weeks ahead. Check the *Grapevine* (*www.grapevine.is*) for current listings in English or ask your friends or strangers who is playing and who's cool right now. **Iceland Airwaves** (*www.icelandairwaves.com*) is the mega-huge, much-talked-about music festival that rocks Reykjavík every October. The hype is well deserved and if you happen to be around, you'll hear well-known international headliners play alongside Reykjavík's many bands, both crazy and sane.

**DRAMA** Perhaps not the city's forte, but there is a somewhat active and stimulating scene nonetheless.

**Broadway** Hotel Ísland; Ármúla 9; 533 1100; broadway@broadway.is; www.broadway.is. Reykjavík's cheesy dinner cabaret serving 3-course meals with a lively side of singing & dancing. Think tribute bands.

**Iðnó** [134 C5] Vonarstræti 3; 562 9700; idno@xnet.is; www.idno.is. What started as a late 19th-century cultural hall for a skilled labour union evolved into Iceland's main stage for over 100 years. Today, the lakeside hall is the ultimate in dinner theatre, serving a fancy Icelandic smorgasbord banquet-style in the midst of entertaining shows aimed at an international audience.

**Reykjavík City Theatre (Borgarleikhúsið)** Listabraut 3; 568 5500; borgarleikhusid@borgarleikhusid.is; www.borgarleikhusid.is. Home to the city's dramatic troupe & the Icelandic Dance Company. The repertoire tends to showcase the latest work of Icelandic playwrights.

**The Icelandic Opera (Íslenska Óperan)** [135 E3] Ingólfsstræti 2A; 511 4200; opera@opera.is; www.opera.is. Classical opera & music inside a neoclassical theatre. Quality, government-sponsored music for the masses.

**The National Theatre of Iceland (Þjóðleikhúsið)** [135 E3] Hverfisgata 19; 551 1200; leikhusid@leikhusid.is; www.leikhusid.is. As the title suggests. Established in 1950 to promote Icelandic/Scandinavian dramatic arts, although international & classical theatre are strongly represented. The plays are renowned for their exceptional visual effects. The guild acts on 3 different stages in 3 different locations, but the box office is at the main Hverfisgata location.

## SHOPPING

Reykjavík offers lots of fabulous ways to spend money quickly. If retail is what you crave most, you'll find plenty of free pamphlets and shopping guides telling you how, when and where to consume. As a rule, never judge a shop by outward appearance alone. Sophisticated window displays may give way to super-tacky inventory, whilst grungy basement boutiques hold one-of-a-kind treasures. Nowadays you have more and more international chains showing their faces and watering down all that used to make shopping in Reykjavík so unique. This doesn't change the fact that Icelanders are incorrigible collectors and some of that talent still makes its way onto shop shelves. Be prepared to spend.

Fortunately, the bulk of commerce lies within a concentrated area. **Laugavegur** is synonymous with shopping, and most tourists spend hours tramping up and down the hill, in and out of the few hundred shops that line either side of the city's main drag. Laugavegur has it all, but the area favours upmarket clothing and fashion boutiques, many of which sell the work of local designers. Some of these shops make you feel cool just by stepping inside them. **Skólavörðustígur** also features a number of art galleries, boutiques, and souvenir shops filled with various knick-knacks.

Current and comprehensive shop listings can be picked up in the form of free guidebooks distributed at any of the tourist information centres. Here are a few favourite places for buying stuff, special to Reykjavík:

**Friða Frænka** [134 B3] Vesturgata 3; ☎ 551 4730; ⌚ 10.00–18.00 Tue–Fri, 11.00–18.00 Sat/Sun. The city's most endearing antique shop, right in the city centre. Old prints, statuary, furniture, china, costume jewellery, traditional toys & century-old postcards. Gathered under a careful eye from the attics of Iceland. Everything in here has a story, so take your time.

**Kisan** Laugavegur 7; ☎ 561 6262; e info@kisan.is; www.kisan.is; ⌚ 11.00–18.00 Mon–Sat. Eye-catching inventory from around the world in a shamelessly post-modern display. Every little *objet d'art* is pretty & useful – it's not likely you'll find any of this elsewhere. Fun for browsing & touching.

**Kolaportið** [134 C2] Tryggvagata 19; ☎ 562 5030; e kolaportid@kolaportid.is; www.kolaportid.is; ⌚ 11.00–17.00 Sat/Sun. Reykjavík's anything-goes flea market down by the harbour. A living, breathing museum of all that locals tend to hoard: old music, strange Icelandic curios, secondhand clothing & long-lost objects.

**Kraum** [134 B4] Aðalstræti 10; ☎ 517 7797; www.kraum.is; ⌚ 09.00–18.00 Mon–Fri, 12.00–17.00 Sat/Sun. Icelandic design began in this building in 1762, when a cashier of the Danish king wanted to diversify Iceland's resources. He began experimenting with making clothes from Icelandic wool & now over 200 designers have their wares exhibited in this part museum/part store landmark. It's a humble building, filled with great gifts for the folks back home & something that will let you blend in and stay warm.

**Naked Ape** Bankastræti 14; ☎ 551 1415; e shop@dontbenaked.com; www.dontbenaked.com; ⌚ at random, but usually open. A creative design workshop where clothing is invented, created, decorated & sold on the premises. The in-house hair salon is the perfect place to get blue highlights.

**Nornabúðin** Vesturgata 12; ☎ 552 3540; e nornabudin@nornabudin.is; www.nornabudin.is; ⌚ 14.00–18.00 Mon–Sat. The witch's shop: herbal remedies, spells, candles, trinkets, good fortunes, jewellery, along with your everyday aromatherapy & New Age stuff. Stop in for a quasi-traditional rune reading or tarot cards.

**SHOPPING MALLS** Located in Kópavogur, **Smáralind** [122 C2](*Hagasmári 1; ☎ 528 8000; e smaralind@smaralind.is; www.smaralind.is; ⌚ 11.00–19.00 Mon–Thu, 11.00–21.00 Fri, 11.00–18.00 Sat, 13.00–18.00 Sun*) is now considered 'the mall' for the whole of Iceland and its name translates ironically as the 'tiny well'. Only 30 seconds inside will destroy all those hard-earned feelings that you had about travelling somewhere obscure. Smáralind is the best place for the exact same stuff you can get back home but for double or triple the price. Reasons you might make the trip include picking up no-brainer souvenirs, stocking up on travel necessities (there's an extensive food store and lots of shops that sell socks), and getting hooked up with an Icelandic mobile phone.

**Kringlan** (*Kringlunni 4–12; ☎ 568 9200; e kringlan@kringlan.is; www.kringlan.is; ⌚ 10.00–18.30 Mon–Wed, 10.00–21.00 Thu, 10.00–19.00 Fri, 10.00–18.00 Sat, 13.00–17.00 Sun*) is the city's older shopping centre that's a tad closer to the city centre and still feels a little like the 1980s. As the city's main commercial hub, you may get directed here if you need to visit a bank, buy a book, catch a movie at the cineplex, go grocery shopping, or eat in a food court.

**SOUVENIRS** You should be able to sniff these out on your own, as most people selling them will be sniffing you out. Woollen goods dominate the merchandise found on the racks.

**Handprjónasamband Íslands** Skólavörðustígur 19; ☎ 552 1890; e handknit@handknit.is; www.handknit.is; ⌚ 09.00–18.00 Mon–Fri, 09.00–16.00 Sat, 11.00–16.00 Sun. The Handknitting Association of Iceland is made up of 200 very active knitters who turn out beautiful, traditional Icelandic sweaters & sell them as a woman's co-operative. This is the real deal – nothing made in China.

**Handverk og Hönnun** Aðalstræti 12; ☎ 551 7595; e handverk@handverkoghonnun.is; www.handverkoghonnun.is; ⌚ 09.00–16.00 Mon–Fri. Unique gifts featuring contemporary craft & design. Everything here is quite original & Icelandic: jewellery, ceramics, textiles, & chachkas.

**The Viking** Hafnarstræti 3; ☎ 551 1250; e theviking@simnet.is; ⌚ 09.00–19.00 Mon–Fri, 09.00–18.00 Sat/Sun. Reykjavík's biggest & cheesiest souvenir shop carrying all the things that people expect you to bring back from Iceland: wool products, plastic Viking helmets, pretty pictures, & knick-knacks galore.

**BOOKSHOPS** Reykjavík is a literary town in every possible way with its writers living and dead, passionate readers, and books galore. You're never far from something good to read.

**Eymundsson** Austurstræti 18. The main branch of this national book chain.

**IÐA** [134 C4] Lækjargata 2A; ☎ 511 5001; e ida@ida.is; www.ida.is; ⌚ 10.00–20.00 daily. Books about everything & a huge choice of good souvenirs: T-shirts, coffee-table books, breathtaking postcards, stamps on Iceland, etc. A huge English-language collection.

**Mál og Menning** [135 F3] Laugavegur 18; ☎ 515 2500; e malogmenning@edda.is; www.malogmenning.is; ⌚ 09.00–17.00 daily. A shop named 'Language & Culture' sells just that. Owned & managed by Iceland's leading publisher who still prints the sagas, & the classics of Icelandic literature (ie: Halldór Laxness), along with the Icelandic edition of Stephen King's latest.

**Pennin** [134 C3] Austurstræti 18; ☎ 540 2130; e austurstraeit@pennin.is; www.pennin.is; ⌚ 08.00–17.00 daily. Thorough collection of English-language magazines & books. Stationery, fancy pens, computer & phone technology. They also have locations in both of the malls.

## OTHER PRACTICALITIES

**BANKS AND CHANGING MONEY** You can change money (cash) at the tourist information office [134 B3] (*Aðalstræti 2*), at any other travel market (see page 137) or at any number of banks. ATMs are ubiquitous, but remember, paying for everything in plastic is *de rigeur*. If in doubt, head to Bankastræti.

$ **Landsbankinn** Branch at Austurstræti 11; ☎ 410 4000; e landsbankinn.is; www.landsbankinn.is; ⌚ 10.00–17.00 Mon–Fri. Branch at Smáralind, Hagasmára 1; ⌚ 11.00–19.00 Mon–Fri, 11.00–16.00 Sat, 13.00–16.00 Sun.

**DOCTORS** If you simply need a doctor (*læknir*), then dial ☎ 525 1000. You can also always find the right specialist at the clinic of the Kringlan mall (*Kringlunni 4–12; ☎ 568 6811*). Out of hours or at holidays, you can also contact a doctor or make an appointment at the city's main medical clininc in Kópavogur (*Læknavaktin; Smáratorg 1; ☎ 1770; ⌚ (fully staffed) 17.00–23.30 Mon–Fri, 09.00–23.30 Sat/Sun & holidays*).

For a **dentist**, call ☎ 575 0505.

**HOSPITALS** For medical emergencies dial ☎ 112. Dial the emergency room (☎ *543 2000*) or go directly to Reykjavík's University Hospital in Fossvogur.

✚ **National Hospital of Iceland (Sjúkraþjálfun Íslands)** [129 E6] Suðurlandsbraut 34; ☎ 520 0120; e sjukratjalfun@sjukratjalfun.is; www.sjukratjalfun.is

✚ **National University Hospital (Landspítali)** Fossvogur; ☎ 543 2050; e landspitali@landspitali.is; www.landspitali.is

**NEWSPAPERS AND MAGAZINES** The long-running 'morning paper' for Reykjavík and all of Iceland is ***Morgunblaðið*** (*www.mbl.is*), whereas ***Fréttablaðið*** (*www.sunnlenska.is*) is the city's left-leaning 'news-paper' that loves to antagonise Morgunblaðið. Both are printed in Icelandic only. The ***Grapevine*** (*www.grapevine.is*) is the city's longest-running English-language newspaper distributed free (bi-weekly in summer and monthly in winter). Copies will find their way into your hand via shops, cafés, hotels, etc. Besides local news and listings, this is your best guide to the ins and outs of Reykjavík's music scene (besides word of mouth). ***Iceland Review*** (*www.icelandreview.*is) is the high-quality, English-language glossy magazine that covers the whole country, but with due attention to the capital.

**PHARMACY (*APÓTEK*)** Look for the little green cross.

✚ **Lyfja Apótek** e lyfja@lyfja.is; www.lyfja.is. City centre; Laugavegur 16; ☎ 552 4045; ⏲ 09.00–19.00 Mon–Fri, 10.00–16.00 Sat. Laugadarlur; Lágmúli 5; ☎ 533 2300; ⏲ 09.00–midnight daily

✚ **Lyf og Heilsa** www.lyfogheilsa.is. City centre; Egilsgata 3; ☎ 563 1020; ⏲ 09.00–19.00 Mon–Fri. Austurver; Háaleitisbraut 68; ☎ 581 2101; ⏲ 24hrs

**POLICE** For emergencies, dial ☎ 112. Reykjavík's main police station is located at Hverfisgata 113–15 (☎ *444 1000*). The police also tend to maintain a healthy presence on Laugavegur/Austurstræti at weekends.

**POST** Reykjavík's **Central Post Office (Pósturinn)** [134 C3] (*Pósthússtræti 3–5;* ☎ *580 1000;* e *postur@postur.is; www.postur.is;* ⏲ *09.00–18.30 Mon–Fri, 11.00–14.00 Sat (summer only)*) is located on the corner of Pósthússtræti and Austurstræti, where all your shipping and mailing needs will be met. Though honestly, very few places in Reykjavík don't carry stamps. Ask at hotels, petrol stations, bookshops, and anywhere they sell postcards.

**TELEPHONE** The tourist information office [134 B3] (*Aðalstræti 2*) sells starter packs for your own European mobile (tri-band) that include a chip, an Icelandic phone number and a limited amount of talk time. They also sell local and international phonecards to use from both land lines and mobiles. You can purchase top-up time for your mobile phone almost anywhere – if a shop sells cigarettes, they're likely to sell phonecards (ie: food and magazine shops, petrol stations, etc).

**Síminn** (Iceland Telecom) (☎ *550 6000;* e *8007000@siminn.is; www.siminn.is;* ⏲ *09.00–17.00 or during mall hours*) has three locations in Reykjavík where you can purchase mobile phones, chips, accessories and phone time. The shop at Ármúla 27 is the one that is closest to the city centre, though by public transportation, you'll have more luck getting to **Kringlan** mall [129 E4] (*Kringlunni 4–12*) or **Smáralind**.

## WHAT TO DO IN REYKJAVÍK

A few humble suggestions:

**WHEN THE WEATHER'S NICE...**

- Take in the view from the top of Hallgrímskirkja
- Eat a hot dog with everything on it
- Watch skateboarders crashing on the square by Aðalstræti
- Walk around the harbour and see all the old ships
- Feed the ducks on the Tjörnin
- Walk/bike/skate out to Seltjarnanes
- Skip town and climb Mt Esja

**WHEN THE WEATHER'S NOT SO NICE...**

- Absorb an art museum or two or three
- Plot your journey on the giant topographic model of Iceland in the Raðhús
- Go swimming outdoors
- Slurp fish soup in one café then wander to a different café and get coffee
- Go to one of the bookshops or the fantastic city library and read
- Find a different painted house for every colour of the rainbow, then do roofs
- Find out who's playing and enjoy the live music

## WHAT TO SEE AND DO

Reykjavík is a small town with big diversions: with a credit card and a power nap you can do pretty much anything. Take those away and you've still got a wonderfully strange city at your feet begging to be explored. Just be sure to step away from Laugavegur, take some unexpected turns, and go swimming.

**CITY CENTRE** A nice focal point is **Austurvöllur** (the 'east field'), which plays the part of the city's main square and most central park. Over a millennium ago, this was a cultivated field of Iceland's very first settlement – sheep have continued to graze on the green ever since. On sunny days, the field is packed with young and old lying on the grass and chatting, mums and dads pushing baby carriages, and businessmen doing business with their sleeves rolled up and a beer in one fist. At other times Austurvöllur reflects the utter tranquillity and small size of Iceland's capital city. A number of nice restaurants surround the square, as well as the famous Hótel Borg, but it's the presence of **Dómkirkjan** [134 C4] (see page 175) and Iceland's parliament building that reverence the square today. The field's criss-crossed paths meet at the statue of Icelandic national hero Jón Sigurdsson (see page 295), sculpted by Einar Jónsson in 1931 following the millennial celebrations of the Icelandic parliament. The statue proudly faces the front of the **Alþingishúsið**, or **parliament house** [134 B4], the modern seat of Iceland's government. As impressive as it may appear, the two-storey stone building seems a faint counterpart to the law rock at Thingvellir (see page 213) and the Althing's 1,000-year-old legacy. The present building was designed by Danish architect Ferdinand Meldahl and constructed of grey-black dolerite, a hard local stone that gives a unique colour and texture to the outside. The building was completed in 1881 as indicated on the façade – also note the crowned C9 emblem covered in verdigris that represents King Christian IX of Denmark, the sitting monarch at the time of construction. The figures above the four arches on the front of the building represent the *landvættir* (see page 35), Iceland's guardian spirits who showed themselves as a dragon, eagle, giant, and bull in order to defend the country from a different Danish king. As one of the more stately and solid buildings in Reykjavík, Alþingishúsið has been used as temporary homes for the country's national archives, the national library, and the University of Iceland (classes were taught on the main floor for nearly 30 years). Today, this is where Iceland's 63 members of parliament meet to govern the country. The attached modern glass building was added in 1999 to provide additional office space.

Designed and planted in 1893, **Alþingisgarðurinn** was the country's first public garden and is probably the only place in the world where you can walk into parliament unannounced and not have a gun pointed at your face. Go to the back of the left side (when facing the front of the building) and enter at the swinging gate that opens on to the circular path. The tiny garden is planted with flowers, bushes and trees and forms one of the most peaceful spots in the city, not the kind of solitude you might expect behind the house of national government. A back gate leads out onto Vonarstræti.

A walk down **Aðalstræti** takes in the city's oldest street and also happens to be the location of the very helpful and progressive tourist information centre (see page 136). The oldest house in Reykijavík proper is at Aðalstræti 10, built in 1762 as part of Skúli Magnusson's woolworks (the city's first stone house is on Viðey Island). The other historic homes and former warehouses have now been integrated into hotels and restaurants. Continuing to the end of the street brings you to Reykjavík's other town square, the **Fógetagarður**, or 'magistrate's garden', named after town magistrate Halldór Daníelsson who bought the square in 1893 and designated the area as a public garden. It took a good while for locals to be convinced, as this was the town cemetery for nearly 800 years and burials only ceased in 1838. The area was eventually paved over and planted with trees in a vague attempt to reduce the stigma of a Viking graveyard, but the snooping tourist can still spot a few stone markers beneath the bushes. The corner of Aðalstræti and Kirkjustræti pinpoint the city's original settlement, as detailed in the Settlement Exhibition (see page 180) and the square was also the site of Reykjavík's first Christian church. The ugly concrete tower was one of Iceland's first 'skyscrapers' and currently houses the offices of *Morgunblaðið*, Iceland's national newspaper.

**LÆKJARTORG** Lækjartorg Square is the first open area outside the small cluster of the city centre, at the intersection of Lækjargata and Bankastræti. Today it's a central vantage point for shopping, touring, dining, and clubbing and the city's main transportation throughway. Stand near the square and you'll spot whatever it is that

### BRONZED: REYKJAVÍK'S MEMORIAL STATUES

**INGÓLFUR ARNASON** [134 D2] First settler and founder of Reykjavík (see page 124). On top of Arnarhóll. By Einar Jónsson, 1907.
**JÓN SIGURDSSON** [134 C4] Leader of the Icelandic independence movement (see page 295). In the centre of Austurvöllur facing the Althing. By Einar Jónsson, 1931.
**LEIFUR EIRÍKSSON** [135 H5] Icelandic Viking believed to have discovered North America (see page 276). In front of Hallgrímskirkja.
**SKÚLI MAGNÚSSON** [134 B4] Broad-shouldered 'Father of Reykjavík' (see page 186). On the corner of Aðalstræti and Kirkjustræti.

you need (the main bus station is on the corner). Sightseeing-wise, the white, slate-roofed **Government House (Stjórnarráðshúsið)** [134 D3] sits in the grassy centre of the actual square. The sturdy stone building was erected in 1770 as a prison but now serves as the offices for Iceland's prime minister. Perhaps a poignant commentary on the evolution of Icelandic independence, the building's location also pinpoints the city's outer limits at the time of Reykjavík's founding. Visitors are free to enter, but there is little to see as it is no more than a working office. Two statues grace the front lawn: on the right, the first native 'prime minister' of Iceland Hannes Hafstein (see page 22), and on the left, King Christian IX of Denmark holding forth the Icelandic constitution which he brought to Iceland in 1874.

## REYKJAVÍK STREETWISE

Each and every street name in Reykjavík's city centre tells a story of its own. Here's some context to go with your wandering:

**AÐALSTRÆTI** (Main Street) The name says it all, except that this is the oldest street in the city with the oldest house (No 10), first built in 1762.

**AUSTURSTRÆTI** (East Street) Leads eastward past Austurvöllur (East Field) from Aðalstræti. The hollow square where the two streets intersect is popular with teenage skateboarders because in Iceland, skateboarding is not a crime. The next-door ice-cream shop is also one of the city's most popular.

**BANKASTRÆTI** (Bank Street) Iceland's national bank (Landsbanki) took up its offices here in 1886 and re-purposed the entire street. An atmosphere of money continues with a number of banks and ATMs, and a variety of high-end clubs, pubs, and restaurants.

**FRÍKIRKJUVEGUR** (Free Church Way) The construction of Iceland's Free Church in 1902 finally gave a name to the path along the west side of the Tjörnin. See the National Gallery of Iceland, Fríkirkjan, and the youth sports centre (built in1908) decorated with Adonis statues and the 'pavilion park' Hljómskalagardurinn.

**HAFNARSTRÆTI** (Harbour Street) Back in the 18th century, this path marked the city's waterfront. The street took shape with the long row of shipping warehouses that went up along one side and piers that extended from the dock on the other. The dock area was eventually filled in to the breakwater, which became Tryggvagata (Secure Street).

**HRINGBRAUT** (Ring Road) Reykjavík's ring road alters the original concept, but it still allows you the most direct access in and out of the city when driving a car. Hringbraut becomes Miklabraut (Great Road).

**HVERFISGATA** (Neighbourhood Street) Leads to one of Reykjavík's original residential quarters (*hverfi* is the Old Norse root for the English 'quarter'). Look for some truly fantastic old Reykjavík houses from the city's Modernist era: colourfully painted concrete, great rounded windows, interesting rooftops, etc.

**INGÓLFSSTRÆTI** (Ingólfur's Street) Named after Ingólfur Arnason, the man who picked the spot on which Reykjavík was built about 1,000 years before the street was here. See his fierce statue atop Arnarhóll.

The broad hill just north of the square is known as **Arnarhóll** [134 D2], recognised by the statue of Reykjavík's first settler Ingólfur Arnason. From the base of the statue you can get an active view of the bustling city and harbour – definitely worth the short uphill climb.

The huge building right behind the statue is the Ministry of Fisheries, one of the most important branches of government for most of Iceland's history (perhaps the reason why it's a lot bigger than both parliament and Government House). The smaller, more architecturally astute building that faces Hverfisgata is **Culture House** [135 E3] (see page 181).

**LAUGAVEGUR** (Bath Way) The road still leads from the old city centre all the way to Laugardalur (Bath Valley), where the natural thermal pools are still put to good use. As Reykjavík's main drag, visitors can't help wandering up and down this street more than any other because of the prime window shopping, restaurants, clubs and bars. It's the place to see and be seen.

**LÆKJARGATA** (Brook Street) The small brook that trickled down from the Tjörnin into the harbour was the de facto sewage outlet for the city centre until the early 20th century. For sanitary reasons, the stream was completely covered, which explains the great width of Lækjargata today.

**KIRKJUSTRÆTI** (Church Street) A public Christian church has stood on this spot since AD1200. Before that, there was a church closer to the original settlement at the intersection with Aðalstræti. The most recent version is Iceland's national cathedral, Dómkirkjan, across from the Althing.

**PÓSTHÚSSTRÆTI** (Post House Street) Iceland's first national post office was built here back in the 18th century (but is now a bar). The national post office still sits on the corner, but the rest of Pósthússtræti is a narrow alley of posh addresses and several high-end hotels.

**SKÓLAVÖRÐUSTIGUR** (School Cairn Path) Reykjavík's straightest street ascends the hill where, in 1790, boys from the Hólavallaskóli school built a tall pile of stones to mark the road into Reykjavík. The cairn was twice rebuilt (1834 and 1868) but was finally removed in 1930 to allow for the Leifur Eiríksson statue.

**TJARNARGATA** (Pond Street) Forms the west side of the Tjörnin waterfront and one of the prettiest walkways in the city. Home to some of the city's older and more traditional homes, several of which are ambassadorial residences; you can also get a glimpse of the water through tallish trees (a rare site in Iceland).

**VESTURGATA** (West Street) Leads west from the city centre into Vesturbær (West Town), one of the city's oldest neighbourhoods and longest streets.

**VONARSTRÆTI** (Hope Street) Like much of Reykjavík's waterfront, the northern edge of the Tjörnin is built from landfill. Although construction began in 1899, it took seven years to complete due to the sinking mud that caused periodic collapse. By the time the little street finally opened in 1906, the area had become synonymous with wishful thinking.

**TJÖRNIN** The Tjörnin, or 'pond', separates the city centre from the east and west neighbourhoods and provides a scenic cross-section of the city, as portrayed in countless postcards and vacation photographs. It's bigger than it looks, and a walk all the way around (take the bridge) is just under a mile in length (1.6 km). In winter, the pond freezes solid, and up until World War II, the Tjörnin was the main source of ice used for the city's refrigeration purposes. Geothermal runoff now empties in at the head of the pond, which prevents a small area from freezing and keeps all the waterbirds quite happy, of which there are many. Bird-wise, anything is possible, so don't head off into the wild until you've had a look here. The range of species obviously shifts through the year, but you are always guaranteed to see some big swans and ducks (mainly scaup, eider, and black ducks). Feeding the ducks is imperative. The basalt steps leading down to the water facilitates bread-throwing.

By the way, there are no fish in the pond whatsoever. Legend blames an old Viking curse, but it might also have something to do with the fact that the water's neither fresh nor salty and that 200 years of raw sewage is still settling. Nevertheless, it's one of the most picturesque spots in the city, with lots of quaint skyline and pretty reflections of pretty buildings. Some of these include **Iðno** [134 C5] (see page 162), the **Fríkirkjan** [134 D6] (see page 178) and the **National Gallery** [134 D6] (see page 182). The contemporary concrete-and-glass building wedged into the corner of the Tjörnin is the **Raðhús** [134 B5], or City Hall. Built in 1987, the play of water, pillars, and glassed-in office space represents one of the city's greater architectural achievements. Still controversial, it's hard not be curious about how it all fits together. Public visitors enter on Vonarstræti – past the shallow, round duck pond and sometimes-functioning fountain. Other than Reykjavík's city council, the most fascinating thing here is the **Íslandslíkan** – a painstaking topographic model of Iceland that grants visitors a vivid understanding of the country's living geology. A team of four individuals spent five years building the model using 1mm-thick cardstock, tiny knives and a whole lot of glue. The map's horizontal scale is 1:50,000, while the vertical scale is doubled for effect. It's especially fun to take a good look after you've completed a journey around Iceland and can recognise the landscapes you've passed along the way. Anyone who's driven through the East Fjords or crossed the interior gains a new appreciation for the feat after a good, long look at these deep fjords and high plateaux. The 75m² map is on wheels, which allows for it to be moved during official events, but for the most part it's open at the same time as the city's private information centre (✆ *411 1000;* 🕒 *08.30–17.30 Mon–Fri, 12.00–16.00 Sat/Sun*).

South of the Tjörnin lies the **National Museum of Iceland** [128 B3] (see page 180) and the **University of Iceland (Háskoli Íslands)**. Founded in 1911, the university opened with 45 students who gathered for lectures in the Althing. Today, the university boasts a roll of 10,000 students. Its main building is the most visible – built in 1940. The statue out front depicts the Icelandic legend of *Sæmundur and the Seal*, sculpted by Ásmunder Sveinsson. Sæmundur was a dark magician who tricked the devil into carrying him to Iceland in exchange for his soul. The deal was only good if Sæmundur's coat remained dry until he reached the shore, so the devil transformed himself into a seal and carried Sæmundur on his back. When Sæmundur saw land, he hit the seal on its head with a Bible, jumped into the water and swam to shore, having arrived in Iceland, but getting wet and thereby cancelling the devil's due. Quite the school mascot.

West of the Tjörnin (off Suðurgata) lies the **Reykjavík Kirkjugarður**, or the 'new' cemetery, dating from the 1840s. Part of its beauty is that the graves lie beneath a small wood forest and this is one of the greenest gardens in the city. The individual markers are also very unique and expressive.

**HARBOUR AND WATERFRONT** Reykjavík's less-dressed quarter is also one of its most exciting for the simple fact that it's still in flux. As a candid slice of urban history, the maze-like harbour is filled with all kinds of boats and grungy warehouses and fish smells that all confirm your travels. As a once-depressed industrial quarter, there's plenty of artful graffiti and cool urban decay, though now in mid gentrification, all that's changing into trendy homes, lofts, restaurants, boutiques and guesthouses. One fears an onslaught of shopping centres and pony rides, but for now things are still very subtle. A brief walk down Geirsgata allows a fair taste of the neighbourhood, but if you are more curious, head out to the piers.

Locals call this the '**old harbour**' [128 B1] because several larger and more industrial harbours exist to the west (Örfirisey) and farther from the city centre. The old harbour was built in 1913–15. Rough-hewn basalt was quarried out of the city's two main hills, Skólavörðustígur (where Hallgrímskirkja stands) and Oskjuhlið (where Perlan stands) and carried down to the water's edge on the only railway ever to exist in Iceland. Most cruise ships anchor in or near the old harbour, but tend to shuffle all their passengers into the city centre via taxi. Several whale- and birdwatching tours also originate in the harbour, leaving from the main pier, Ægisgarður.

You're never far from the sea in Reykjavík, but the 'waterfront' usually refers

## WHALE- AND BIRDWATCHING TOURS

Reykjavík harbour pales in comparison with what you can see in northeast Iceland (see page 381) and west Iceland (see page 275), but it does open onto Faxaflói, a prime whale habitat. A growing number of whale-watching tours now leave from the capital, although these are often no more than glorified boat tours. Trips tend to last under three hours and most visitors get away with only seeing dolphins and harbour porpoise. If you're lucky, you just might spot a minke or humpback whale or perhaps something truly rare, but this is the country's busiest waterway and bigger whales can be shy. The boat trip does afford an interesting vantage point from which to view the city and a closer look at the local birds, but you can see the same just by finding a quiet spot near the water and waiting patiently.

Most tours also take a turn past 'Puffin Island', which is a generic tourist name for any of the puffin colonies on the harbour islands. The largest of these colonies are on Lundey and Akurey. If you're dying for a puffin photo and you've got a big lens, this will do the job, but if you're eager to experience puffins in their full glory, then nothing beats the West Fjords (see page 277) or the Westmann Islands (see page 228).

**Elding Whale Watching** Elding I & II; Ægisgarður (main pier, Reykjavík habour); ☎ 555 3565; e info@elding.is; www.elding.is; ⏲ 1 Apr–31 Oct. 2 smaller boats that go out regularly – they report a high success rate & keep an online diary (in English) telling of the day's finds. Proper attire is provided & hotel pickups are available for a fee. They also offer popular sea-angling tours that are expensive but fun. Whale-watching US$55 per adult (US$25 for children).

**Whale Watching Centre** Hafsúlan; Ægisgarður (main pier, Reykjavík harbour); ☎ 533 2660; e hafsulan@hafsulan.is; www.hafsulan.is; ⏲ 1 Apr–31 Oct. A little larger & more commercial, Hafsúlan claims a 98% success rate in whale sightings & offers the guarantee of another trip if you don't see your whale. Hotel pickups are available for a fee. Whale-watching US$55 per adult (US$25 for children).

to the area east of the harbour. It's one of the most peaceful areas in town (by the shore) next to one of the busiest roads (Sæbraut). Of note is the iconic stainless-steel sculpture ***Sólfar***, or 'Sun Voyager' by Reykjavík artist (and welder) Jón Gunnar Árnason. Sólfar has become the Eiffel Tower picture of the Reykjavík tourist portfolio and with good reason. Somehow it's the perfect spot to take in the changing colours of sky, mountain and sea. Plus, the skeleton structure and its shiny frame do wonderful things in the light – a factor that has granted the Viking ship a worldwide following among photographers. The path that continues onward is extremely popular among cyclists, skaters, runners, and anyone who likes a nice walk by the sea. A lot of tall modern buildings are popping up, but there's still a nice view of the back of **Höfði House**.

**HÖFÐI HOUSE** [128 D2] Reykjavík's most famous residence also happens to be its most haunted, or at least one of its better documented cases. *Höfði* means 'cape' or 'promontory', and the little white Höfði House appropriately sits right on Reykjavík's open waterfront (just off Borgartún). Constructed in 1909, the squat structure expresses the influence of *Jugendstil*, a Nordic version of Art Nouveau that made its way to Iceland by boat. Like so many wooden buildings of the time, the house was completely prefabricated in Norway and shipped in pieces to Reykjavík for the customer, one Monsieur Brillouin – the French consul. This was at a time when French fishing interests granted significant weight to diplomatic relations with Iceland, though the consul spoiled his welcome by raising his official residence before the city planning department had approved its location. Monsieur's nonchalance ruffled bureaucratic feathers and the Versailles-like quality of the house (the largest private estate in the city limits at the time) led to his being generally envied, admired, and despised by Reykjavík society. He also found his new home uncomfortable and complained that the house was haunted. Brillouin stayed in Iceland for less than four years, selling the unlucky address to the lawyer and poet Einar Benediktsson. Einar already felt haunted by the ghost of a young woman (Sólbórg Jónsdóttir) who had poisoned herself following his judgement in a notorious court case. Accusations of incest led to her child being taken away and although the suicide occurred in the faraway north, Einar felt that Sólbórg's ghost followed him when he moved to the capital. At Höfði House, the woman's ghost would appear to him in the night so that he began to sleep with the lights on. In exasperation, Einar sold the house.

Ten different owners followed, none of whom occupied the building for more than three or four years. In the course of sales and resales, Höfði became the British embassy and was visited by Winston Churchill in 1941 and later by Queen Elizabeth II. The last man to ever live in Höfði was British ambassador John Greenway, who arrived in 1950 with great ambitions. A confirmed bachelor, Ambassador Greenway realised quickly that he did not like to be left alone in the house. The dark spooked him and the ghosts caused such a racket that he couldn't sleep. He was most terrified by the 'white lady' who wandered in and out of his bedroom and office day and night. Nerve-wracked and sleepless, he sent London's foreign office a rush of eccentric and harried dispatches recounting the phantasms and demanding that a new residence be found immediately. The embassy did eventually move to Laufásvegur, but not in time for Ambassador Greenway, who returned to Britain and was promptly suffixed with CMG (Commander of The Most Distinguished Order of St Michael and St George). Greenway went on to become a scholar in Nordic mythology; meanwhile Höfði House was sold, subsequently abandoned, and eventually condemned as unfit and unsightly. Reykjavík's mayor gave orders to tear it down, but the city's planning department covertly restored the building to its current state. Höfði became the property of the city government and was only opened for official receptions. Even so, things continued to go bump in the night (and in the day). Kitchen staff reported dishes crashing to the floor, paintings flying off the walls, and the lights turning on and off by themselves.

Fast forward to 1986 – Reykjavík's bicentennial and a dramatic turn in the Cold War. Following failed talks in Geneva that summer, Soviet leader Mikhail Gorbachev sent a letter to US president Ronald Reagan suggesting 'a one-on-one meeting, let us say in Iceland or in London, maybe just for one day', to enable negotiations regarding nuclear disarmament. The Icelandic government was given about one week's notice and Höfði House was designated as the chosen site. At such a sensitive moment in world history, the little house symbolised Iceland's strategic geography and its diplomatic significance. While the two world leaders chatted privately on the first floor, the delegations were sequestered upstairs. The Americans were given a bathroom and two bedrooms on the left side, while the Soviets were allotted the same on the right side. A central sitting room was accessible by both parties (seen from the rear), where coffee was served and informal, open discussion encouraged. After Reagan and Gorbachev retired from Höfði, the Soviet and American arms specialists stayed up all night talking – from 20.00 until 06.00 – hammering out the many details of the Strategic Arms Reduction Treaty (START). Alas, no final agreement was reached at the time, but Höfði is remembered as the beginning of the end of the Cold War. Apparently, a visiting Japanese businessman found Höfði so inspiring (such a cute house and the exit ramp from global annihilation), he built a same-scale copy in Japan.

Despite its history, or perhaps because of it, Höfði is closed to the public. Inquisitive visitors should still feel encouraged to walk around the exterior, take in the grand view, feel the ghosts, and just maybe take a peek in the windows. The bizarre copper sculpture out front was constructed in 1971, which makes it a little more forgivable. *Öndvegissúlur* is the work of Sigurjón Ólafson (see page 183) and represents the two throne pillars thrown overboard by Ingólfur Arnason that washed ashore at Reykjavík (see page 124). To get to Höfði, say 'Höfði' (*huv-thee*) to a taxi driver, take bus No 16, or just walk east along the waterfront (from the *Seafarers* sculpture).

**NEIGHBOURHOODS** Reykjavík doesn't like labels – different parts of the city mean different things at different times, and all that changes from year to year. Still, a few of the central residential areas make for an interesting stroll. **Thingholt** is the triangle-shaped quarter between Thingholtsstræti (west of the Tjörnin) and Skólavörðustígur, the streets of which bear the names of Norse gods (ie: Thórsgata, Oðinsgata and Baldursgata). Thingholt sprung up as a shanty town of sorts – after Iceland's industrial advance in World War I, rural immigrants rushed to Reykjavík for jobs. They built their ramshackle cottages here, and now it's become quite a trendy neighbourhood of quaint streets and colourful homes. **Vesturbær** forms the city's western quarter – the part that normally gets chopped out of tourist maps or covered with advertisements. The part closest to the city centre (Vesturgata, Bárugata, Öldugata and Ránargata) is also the oldest. Here you'll find straight streets, orderly rows of houses, and optimistic flowerboxes. The further west you go, the newer the houses – in recent years there's been an influx of young families. If you want to see 'how they live' in Reykjavík, this is the real thing. **Austurbær** centres at the crossroads of Snorrabrut and Laugavegur (where the shops end). The eastern side of town has a penchant for concrete but is not without its own personality. The park benches near Hlemmur bus station make for good people-watching. The rest of Reykjavík is rather suburban and can feel a little repetitive at times.

## A WALK THROUGH REYKJAVÍK

This city is all about doing your own thing and going your own way (*blessed are the curious and wandering, for they shall see more*). If you enjoy seeing sights for the sake of the sights themselves, then it's quite feasible to work in a good deal of them into a nice calorie-burning stroll. Here's one way to get started:

- Begin at **Austurvöllur** [134 C4] (see page 166) and check your bearings: face the Hótel Borg, with the **Domkirkjan** [134 C4] (see opposite) and **Althing** [134 B4] (see page 166) on your right.
- Turn left on Pósthússtræti and then take a right on Austurstræti; head to **Lækjartorg Square** and cross over to **Government House** [134 D3] (see page 168).
- Head up Arnarhóll to the statue of **Ingólfur Arnason** [134 D2].
- Continue uphill on Hverfisgata, past **Culture House** [135 E3] (see page 181) and the **National Theatre** [135 E3] (see page 162).
- From Hverfisgata, take a right on Klapparstígur, cross Laugavegur and go another block to Skólavörðustígur. Trudge your way uphill to **Hallgrímskirkja** [135 H5] (see below).
- Take a left on Frakkastígur and walk back to Laugavegur. Either A) take a left on Laugavegur and head down the main drag back to the city centre, or B) stay on Frakkastígur to the waterfront to see the **'Sun Voyager'** (see page 172).
- A) Pass by all the shops and restaurants on Bankastræti, cross Lækjargata and continue down Austurstræti to Aðalstræti. B) Take a left on the waterfront, walk along the path with the ocean on one side and busy traffic on the other. Go all the way to the harbour, turn left on Pósthússtræti then right on Hafnarstræti and continue to Aðalstræti.
- Take a left and walk down Aðalstræti; continue to the **Raðhús** [134 B5] (see page 170).
- If you want to add an extra mile, then walk all the way around the **Tjörnin** (take the bridge on Skothúsvegur) which has lots of pretty views. If you want something shorter, then simply walk along Vonarstræti and take a right on Fríkirkjuvegur, dipping into the **National Gallery** [134 D6] (see page 182).
- Now head back into the city centre via Lækjargata. You should recognise the area by now.

## CHURCHES

**Hallsgrímkirkja** [135 H5] (*Skólavörðuholt;* ☎ *510 1000;* e *hallgrimskirkja@hallgrimskirkja.is; www.hallgrimskirkja.is;* 🕒 *09.00–17.00 daily, 11.00 Sun, mass 08.00 Wed, 12.00 Fri free organ recital; church tower entrance 350ISK*) The grey tower of Hallgrímskirkja defines the Reykjavík skyline in a most impressive way. At 245ft (74m) high, this is Iceland's tallest building and the city's most prominent landmark – you can see the church from a good 25km away. Such totally unique architecture outweighs its very unique height. Indeed the church's design has become a symbol of Reykjavík in its own right: an ancient theme that honours a past hero by invoking nature with modernism.

The bold structure honours Hallgrímur Petursson (see page 39), the country's famous post-Reformation reverend and a man who authored so many classical Icelandic hymns. It is the most well-known work of Guðjon Samúelsson, Iceland's state architect who designed so many buildings in what is now a telltale Reykjavík style. What is different is the tower's almost parabolic shape, built to mimic the crystallised columns of basalt formed by cooling lava – a feature seen throughout Iceland. Tall Gothic windows and a fairly Classical nave add a traditional twist. The distinct design was finalised in 1937, but construction only began after World War II in 1945. Made of reinforced concrete, the church's tower was finished in 1974, and the entire structure only dedicated as part of the city's bicentennial celebration in 1986. Like anything new and different, Hallgrímskirkja ruffled some feathers among the city's conservative element, but nowadays, the church seems to serves as a universal source of pride and accomplishment for all of Reykjavík.

The church seats 1,200 people – a number set by the Althing in 1929 when they first commissioned the project for a large, modern national church. Besides general Lutheran services, the main hall is used for all sorts of events (state funerals, national concerts, poetry readings, theatre, etc). It's definitely worth trying to catch a concert if you can (check the church's website or the events calendar at www.visitreykjavik.is). Weekly recitals are your best bet, played on Hallgrímskirkja's stunning organ. This is the country's largest instrument (5,275 pipes), built by the German craftsmen of Orgelbau Klais and only finished in 1992.

The inside of Hallgrímskirkja may not wow the visitor in the same way the exterior does. For the most part, it is quiet and unadorned. Noted exceptions include the transcendent statue depicting the baptism of Christ and the statue of Hallgrímur Petursson by the sculptor Einar Jónsson (see page 183). Also, an original Guðbrandur Bible – printed in 1584 (see page 325) is on display. Upon entering, note the carved doors by contemporary Icelandic artist Leifur Breiðfjörð, who also designed the crystal baptistry.

Hallgrímskirkja stands atop one of the highest points in the city, pronouncing the ascent up Skólavörðustígur and offering an unbeatable view from its open tower. On a clear day, you should drop everything and go to the top for the panorama. You can climb the stairs (or take the lift) and take in the entire city, along with the Seltjarnanes Peninsula on which it is built, Mt Esja and Faxaflói Bay, the Reykjanes Peninsula (by the airport) – and if the weather is really kind – a hazy glimpse of Snæfellsnes.

In front of the church stands a copper statue of Viking explorer Leifur Eiríksson (see page 276), who is thought to be the first European to have set foot in North America. The statue was presented as a gift from the United States government in 1930, in recognition of the millennial anniversary of Iceland's Althing.

**Dómkirkjan** [134 C4] (*Lækjargata 14A; ☎ 520 9700; e domkirkjan@domkirkjan.is; www.domkirkjan.is; ⏲ 10.00–17.00 Mon–Fri, Sat/Sun according to service schedule (check website)*) Known locally as 'the cathedral', Dómkirkjan is considered Iceland's national church despite its humble size. Petite and precise, the beige church stands on the southeast corner of Austurvöllur as an essential prop to Reykjavík's village-like centre. Like many churches in Iceland, the site has been a place of worship since the settlement era (9th century) and a Christian church has stood here since the 13th century. The building's symbolic legacy of national struggle and the location right next to the Althing make this the Westminster Abbey of Iceland. The parliament opens its annual session with a service at Dómkirkjan and this is the place for awards ceremonies, government-sponsored concerts, and high-profile weddings.

After Iceland's bishop was moved to Reykjavík in 1785, King Christian VII of Denmark granted the city its charter and ordered an ecclesiastical centre for the newly

## GUÐJÓN SAMÚELSSON (1887–1950)

Rarely does a city bear the imprint of a single individual, though Reykjavík's compact size and isolated history provide a charming exception. Guðjón Samúelsson was born in Iceland's capital just as the real building of the city was taking off. His father was Samuel Jónsson, an architect who designed many of the rambling, turn-of-the-century. Victorian homes you see around the city today. Gúðjón followed his father's profession, receiving his education in Denmark just as Art Nouveau was fading into Art Deco. At age 25, Guðjón published a series of essays pronouncing his thoughts on urban planning in Reykjavík – he believed physical structures influenced the disposition of local residents and called for tall, distinctive buildings and green open spaces throughout the city centre. His very first designs reflected a student-like precision to the era, but each new building brought more confidence to Guðjón's work and a more individualised aesthetic.

All this at a time when Iceland was becoming its own modern nation (politically) and Reykjavík its capital. The demand for buildings of national prominence led to Guðjón's appointment as Iceland's state architect in 1924 (the first and last person ever to hold such a title). With his position he sought to find a style that was uniquely Icelandic: along the lines of Modernist and nationalist philosophy but particular to Iceland. His search is evident in the buildings you see in Reykjavík today. Critics peg his work with an array of labels: late Art Deco, neoclassicalism, Functionalism, and national Romanticism. Square forms and parallel lines predominate and castle-like towers are an important feature (in a country that never had castles). Guðjón also seemed very focused on height – his earliest buildings were always designed a bit taller than the one previous and his ultimate vision for Reykjavík saw a shining acropolis of buildings on top of Skólavörðuholt Hill.

For 25 years (until his death in 1950), nearly every notable building in Reykjavík was either designed or overseen by Guðjón Samúelsson. His prolific work not only defines the Reykjavík skyline and its streetscapes, but also continues to influence its style, most notably in the blend of natural and abstract forms. The well-known Icelandic painter Jóhannes Kjarval called him the 'artist's artist', and the architect's designs are still consulted as a reference. The casual observer will bump into most of Guðjón's buildings just by walking around the city centre, but knowing their chronology helps appreciate the architect's own progress:

**National Hospital of Iceland (Landsspítallin)** (1915) Hringbraut: blatantly neoclassical with an upright centre and two side wings.

unified Lutheran diocese of Iceland. Danish court architect Andreas Kirkerup was commissioned in 1787 to design a diminutive version of the neoclassical cathedrals of Copenhagen – large enough to house the 200 citizens of Reykjavík, but small enough to feasibly complete the task in such a faraway place. Construction began in 1788 with a boatload of Danish contractors who were sent to Iceland for the express purpose of maximising the short summer work period. Cold and uninspired, the builders drank their time away, all but halting the construction. After four years, the shoddy foundation and stonework passed muster but the rotting roof had to be torn down and completely rebuilt. The church was only finished in 1796, with little resemblance to the Scandinavian precision seen today.

Needless to say, Dómkirkjan has suffered a troubled existence ever since. Within

**National Gallery (Listasafn Íslands)** (1916) Fríkirkjuvegur 7: one of Guðjón's very first buildings, still reliant on neoclassical structure but with a Modernist touch.
**Reykjavíkurapótek** (1917) Austurstræti 16: The tallest building in the city when it was built. Over the decades it's been used as temporary office space for everyone and everything, but most notably as the city pharmacy.
**Eimskipafélagshúsið** (1919) Pósthússtræti 2: the first building in Iceland to be equipped with a lift (elevator), designed for Iceland's main shipping company. Today, it's the Radisson 1919 Hotel. Sneak in and take a look at the impressive staircase.
**Landsbanki** (1924) Austurstræti 11: Iceland's 'new' national bank to replace the original which burned down in the Reykjavík fire of 1915.
**Kristkirkja** (1929) Hávallagata 16: Reykjavík's Catholic cathedral follows neogothic principles, but with a very square tower and Art Deco corners.
**Hótel Borg** (1930) Pósthússtræti 11: considered a toned-down version of the neobaroque style with its arched ground-floor windows, square upper windows, and its mansard-like roof. Guðjón felt self-conscious that this was Reykjavík's tallest building at the time.
**Swimming hall (Sundhöllin)** (1937) Barónstígur: at first glance, quite Functionalist, but up close and inside, a truly unique structure and a must-see (behind Hallgrímskirkja).
**University of Iceland (Háskóla Íslands)** (1940) Suðurgata 1: a stern Art Deco design that's still just a little controversial.
**National Theatre (Þjóðleikhúsið)** (1950) Hverfisgata 19: Iceland's National Theatre. One of the most explicit examples of Art Deco in the city. Designed by the architect in 1928, construction commenced in 1930, was stopped by the Althing in 1932, restarted in 1944, and only completed after the architect's death in 1950.
**Hallgrímskirkja** (1986) Slólavörðuholt: considered to be the architect's masterpiece, and at present the tallest building in Iceland. The church was commissioned in 1937 and its iconic tower completed in 1974, mimicking the crystallised columns of basalt seen throughout Iceland's landscape. Hallgrímskirkja was the only part of Guðjón's 'acropolis' that was ever realised.

You can see Gúðjón's other works throughout the rest of Iceland. A few more examples include the cathedral in Akureyri (see page 346), the school in Laugarvatn (see page 225), Culture House in Ísafjörður (see page 285) and the red-and-white lighthouse at Dýrhólaey (see page 249).



20 years of opening its doors, the building was condemned and closed for major repairs. Upon reopening, creaky roof joints gave rise to hideous ghost stories that led to the church's haunted status today (a severe deterrent to high church attendance). By 1848, a total reconstruction was ordered, led by Danish architect Laurits Albert Winstrup. His overhaul was so extensive (doubling the size of the church) that he is given credit as Dómkirkjan's designer. In its new form, the church made a suitable centrepiece for the millennial celebrations of Iceland's settlement in 1874. King Christian IX of Denmark attended the ceremony where he heard *Ó guð vors lands* sung for the very first time – the hymn that later became Iceland's national anthem. Just a few years later (1879) the church's weathered internal woodwork had to be completely rebuilt. The most recent restoration (in 1999) involved more than your

average facelift, adding the fresh exterior and interior on display at present. Most of Dómkirkjan's problems can be traced to Iceland's long dependency on imported wood, but some Icelanders find room for a metaphor. That one of Reykjavík's very first stone buildings should be plagued with such drama bears political meaning – namely that Icelanders know their country better than outsiders do and that Denmark never really got it right.

Visiting Dómkirkjan becomes a priority not only for its status as a national sanctuary, but also for the mere fact that it is so different from the more typical red-roofed churches seen everywhere else in Iceland. The prim exterior embodies the simplicity of Protestantism, while a more decorative interior highlights the pomp associated with a national church. Note the encircled 'CVIII' emblem of King Christian VIII of Denmark (1786–1848) on the front of the building, as well as the bell tower, which chimes on the hour. Inside, one gets a much better sense of the Danish influence, especially in the gilding and decorative artwork. The wooden benches date from the 1879 refitting, and the balconies allow for the church to accommodate over 700 people today. Also note the ornate baptismal font carved by renowned sculptor Bertel Thorvaldsen (see page 347). There are no official tours offered, but many tour groups and city tours include Dómkirkjan, and it is generally open to visitors.

**Fríkirkjan** [134 D6] (*Laufásvegur 13;* ☎ *552 7270;* e *frikirkjan@frikirkjan.is; www.frikirkjan.is*) The 'Free Church' implies that this picturesque waterfront chapel is completely separate from Iceland's national Lutheran Church. In fact, the Fríkirkjan was built as an independent church that was free from the jurisdiction of the greater Lutheran (read Danish) Church. Established in 1899, the Fríkirkjan had its roots in an Icelandic organisation comprising labourers, tradesmen and seamen and their families. This church building was built in 1902 and later played a significant role in both the Icelandic independence movement and the wider labour movements of the 1920s. There was a time when over half of the population of Reykjavík belonged to the Free Church.

Today, the church is still a church as well as an overlooked attraction next door to the National Gallery of Iceland (see page 182). For many, a long glance at the reflection in the Tjörnin suffices, or else a brief walk around the white, tin-sided walls and a recognition of its distinctive steeple. The inside reflects some of the same

### THE BEACH

Rarely do Icelanders tamper with nature – they merely take advantage. Reykjavík's hot-water beach at Nauthólsvik [128 C6] (*Nauthólsvík;* ☎ *551 6630;* ⏲ *15 May–15 Sep 10.00–20.00; entrance 250ISK*) is a borderline example. Here, the capital's geothermal runoff is pumped into an artificially enclosed harbour, raising water temperatures to 20°C (around 70°F). Noble efforts have been made to create the kind of beach that exists in warmer climes, complete with volleyball, ice-cream stands and imported yellow sand. Even so, the experience can be slightly surreal, especially when air temperatures are severely cool and people still splash about in bathing suits. The spot has become quite popular among families with children as it allows them to frolic in the outdoors in spite of grey skies. Probably not why you came to Reykjavík, but it's there for the curious. The beach lies just beneath the Perlan on Öskjuhlíð; to get there, drive, take a taxi, or take bus No 16 to Nauthóll.

character as Dómkirkjan, with plain arched windows and a wraparound balcony on the second floor. The apse also features a dark-blue ceiling with tiny gold stars and the mantelpiece is quite extravagant. Fríkirkjan is only open for church services and specified events, of which there are still plenty. The church continues to be very 'free' and has become a popular venue for concerts of all persuasions, be it rock, punk, folk, jazz, or traditional music.

**SWIMMING** If you don't go swimming, you haven't been to Reykjavík. Really. The city's geothermal pools are simply marvellous and it's an integral part of the Reykjavík lifestyle. There's a variety of geothermal swimming pools open year-round, each with its own personality and special features. Locals tend to patronise different pools depending on location, time of day, and their general mood. Visit one or visit them all. Admission typically costs around US$5, unless you have a Reykjavík Welcome Card.

## Reykjavík thermal pools General (☎ *530 3000*).

**Árbæjarlaug** Fylkisvegur 9; ☎ 411 5200; ⏲ 06.30–22.30 Mon–Fri, 08.00–22.00 Sat/Sun. Located on the banks of the Elliðará River, this 25m pool benefits from the very natural surroundings & offers a unique view of the city. The children's waterslide is a big hit, as is the indoor children's pool.
**Breiðholtslaug** [129 H6] Austurberg 3; ☎ 557 5547; ⏲ 06.30–22.00 Mon–Fri, 08.00–22.00 Sat/Sun. A leisure pool on the far southeast edge of the city, Breiðholt feels more like the public pools you may know back home. There's a 25m outdoor pool & smaller indoor pool, popular with children.
**Grafarvoglsaug** Dalhús 2; ☎ 510 4600; ⏲ 06.30–22.00 Mon–Fri, 08.30–20.30 Sat/Sun. In the far northeast suburbs, this very sporty pool is part of a state-of-the-art sports complex & a hangout for local athletes. 3 hot pots & the hydro-massage are an added attraction.
**Laugardalslaug** [129 F2] Sundlaugavegur 30; ☎ 411 5100; ⏲ 06.30–22.30 Mon–Fri, 08.00–20.30 Sat/Sun. The city's largest pool complex & the one that foreign visitors are most likely to frequent as it is right next to the hostel & campsites & easily accessible. The very wide 50m pool is perfect for serious exercise, & the varied-temperature hot pots are super-relaxing. There's also a sauna & steam bath, a shallow warm pool for sunbathing in the cold, a children's pool & a giant waterslide.
**Seltjarnaness** Suðurströnd 8; ☎ 561 1551; ⏲ 07.00–21.00 Mon–Fri, 08.00–20.00 Sat/Sun. On the far tip of the peninsula for which it's named, the proximity to the sea allows this pool to be filled with salt water – a fairly unique experience. The isolated location & quiet neighbourhood offer a tranquil swim.
**Sundhöllin** [128 C3] Barónstígur; ☎ 551 4059; ⏲ 06.30–21.30 Mon–Fri, 08.00–19.00 Sat/Sun. Reykjavík's only indoor pool is also one of the oldest, built in 1940 by state architect Guðjón Samúelsson, not far from the city centre. The Art Deco building for the 'swim hall' is an admirable attraction in its own right, including the rows of long, square windows & a labyrinth of tiled changing rooms. The 25m pool was recently refurbished to top quality. There's also an outdoor sundeck with a view of Hallgrímskirkja, 2 large hot pots, & a steam room.
**Vesturbæjarlaug** Hofsvallagata 104; ☎ 566 6879; ⏲ 06.30–22.00 Mon–Fri, 08.00–22.00 Sat/Sun. Located in the city's quiet, older, west-side neighbourhood, this pool offers a pretty authentic Reykjavík experience with local families the primary patrons. Aside from the 25m pool, there are 4 hot pots & a nice steam room & dry sauna.

**SPAS** Reykjavík likes to sell itself as a spa town, although by their definition, so is the rest of the country. For a pleasant half-day getaway, you can always head out to the Blue Lagoon (see page 206) although you can experience near the same effects in any of Reykjavík's pools. Otherwise, here's two options, with a few more likely to arrive.

**Laugar Spa & Fitness Centre** [129 F2] Sundlaugavegur 30A; ☎ 553 000; e laugar@laugarspa.is; www.laugarspa.is; ⏲ 06.00–23.30 Mon–Fri, 08.00–22.00 Sat, 08.00–20.00 Sun. Fairly new, the city's largest private spa is situated in the Laugardalur complex (camping, swimming pool, & hostel). Besides the adrenalin-fuelled mega-gym, there are a number of hot pots, whirlpools, steam baths & saunas to enjoy, as well as a sporty indoor Olympic-sized pool. The spa itself is gaining in reputation, offering an extensive number of wraps, massage, manicures & pedicures, waxing, facials & their tempting 'pamper day' packages. Most individual treatments last about an hour & start at a US$100 base rate. Entrance to the gym & pools costs around US$25 pp for the day.

**Nordica Spa** [129 E3] Hilton Hotel Nordica; Suðurlandsbruat 2; ☎ 444 5090; e nordicaspa@nordicaspa.is; www.nordicaspa.is; ⏲ 06.00–21.00 Mon–Thu, 06.00–20.00 Fri, 09.00–18.00 Sat, 10.00–16.00 Sun. The city's 'posh' spa is exactly what you'd expect from an intimate hotel setting, with a pronounced mood of peace & luxury. A few hot tubs, Turkish baths & saunas serve for relaxation, while treatments focus on technique, & healthy indulgence. All services depend chiefly on Icelandic beauty products like volcanic scrub & locally produced salt scrubs. The gym is smallish but user-friendly, with a free, post-workout shoulder massage included. A little pricey (1hr massage for around US$150).

**MUSEUMS** Remember that the Reykjavík Welcome Card (see page 132) allows you free entrance to many of the museums listed.

## The National Museum of Iceland [128 B3] (*Þjóðminjasafn Íslands; Suðurgata 41; ☎ 530 2200; e natmus@natmus.is; www.natmus.is; ⏲ summer 1 May 1–15 Sep 15 10.00–17.00 daily, winter 16 Sep–30 Apr 11.00–17.00 Tue–Sun; entrance: adults 600ISK, senior 300ISK, free on Wed & for under 18*)

State-of-the-art interactive technology explains the vast collection of objects and images found at this museum, weaving the complex story of 1,200 years of human history in Iceland. Prize moments include a 1,000-year-old silver stature of Thor, Viking weapons, an original copy of Guðbrandur's Bible from 1584 (see page 325), Icelandic national costumes, a recreated *baðstofa* (farmhouse living room), a model fishing schooner, and an impressive collection of 20th-century memorabilia. The English and Icelandic narrative is highly informative; however, the protective mood lighting can cause severe eye strain. Another fair warning: this is not the kind of museum you want to rush through – visitors tend to spend far more time than anticipated due to the comforting amount of detail and the amazing story that unfolds. Overall, the national museum caters to history buffs, antique lovers and the genuinely curious, with a few hands-on exhibits for young children. The in-house café is overpriced and busy, but this is definitely one of the city's better gift shops for books, postcards, and more sophisticated souvenirs.

## The Settlement Exhibition [134 B4] (*Landnámssýningin; Aðalstræti 16; ☎ 411 6370; e info@reykjavik871.is; www.reykjavik871.is; ⏲ 10.00–17.00 daily; entrance: adults 600ISK, senior/child 300ISK*)

In 2001, the construction of the Hótel Centrum led to the discovery of a 10th-century Viking hall beneath its foundation, as well as a wall which experts say dates back to AD871 plus or minus one–two years. This is the oldest manmade structure in Reykjavík (and in Iceland) and therefore deserves a museum of its own, featuring the ultimate in high-tech interactive multi-media displays. The underground exhibit is built around the remains of the Viking home, which was most likely inhabited from AD930–1000. Animated computer reconstructions and virtual-reality technology portray the rows of dirt mounds in a far more fascinating light and provide a detailed understanding of Reykjavík's earliest origins.

**Reykjavík City Outdoor Museum** (*Árbæjarsafn; Kistuhyl; ☎ 411 6300; e minjasafn@Reykjavik.is; www.minjasafnreykjavikur.is; ⌚ summer 1 Jun–31 Aug 10.00–17.00 daily, winter 1 Sep–31 May guided tours are offered Mon/Wed/Fri at 13.00; entrance 500ISK*) Located on the far eastern edge of the city, the outdoor museum comprises dozens of old dwellings that have been transplanted, renovated and arranged in a village setting to push your imagination back to Reykjavík in its earlier years. Period costumes, barnyard animals, and a passionate, good-humoured staff make this a great destination for children, while the informative exhibit on the history of Reykjavík prevents the experience from becoming too Disney. One can lunch at the local coffee shop or bring a picnic – the village is nicer when the weather is co-operating.

**The Saga Museum** [128 C4] (*Sögusafnið; Perlan; ☎ 511 1517; e agusta@backman.is; www.sagamuseum.is; ⌚ summer 1 Apr–30 Sep 10.00–18.00 daily, winter 1 Oct–31 Mar 12.00–17.00 daily; entrance: adults 1,000ISK, senior/students 800ISK, children 500ISK*) Housed inside one of the giant water tanks that sits beneath the Perlan dome, visitors walk through 20-odd 'scenes' that depict key moments of the sagas. In the spirit of Madame Tussaud's, but with sound effects, the life-size and very life-like silicon figures leave little to the imagination in their graphic representation of the more dramatic and treacherous events of Iceland's early history. Individual audio guides (in English or German) accompany the 45-minute tour. It's fun, fairly comprehensive and educational.

**Culture House** [135 E3] (*Þjóðmenningarhúsið; Hverfisgata 15; ☎ 545 1400; e thjodmenning@thjodmenning.is; www.thjodmenning.is; ⌚ 11.00–17.00 Mon–Fri; entrance: students 300ISK, 200ISK seniors*) Culture House is the public showcase of the Árni Magnússon Institute, the world's foremost collection of Icelandic letters and manuscripts. The beautiful white building was completed in 1908 as Iceland's very first national archives and library, although the Danish architect Johannes Nielsen never once visited Iceland. Note the names of prominent Icelanders above the windows (eg: Snorri Sturluson, Guðbrandur Thorláksson and Hallgrímur Petursson) along with the impressive granite doorway decorated with the Danish crown over the falcon shield – Iceland's crest of Iceland under late Danish rule. The museum's permanent exhibition focuses on the medieval manuscripts of Iceland's sagas (histories) and *eddas* (poems) – these fragile vellum documents constitute Iceland's 'crown jewels' and are displayed with similar reverence and care. These include the *Codex Regius* (10th-century poems), fragments of Egils saga (see page 258), numerous illuminated Christian texts and the 14th-century copy of the *Flateyarbók* (see page 305) handwritten on a series of 113 calfskins. Visitors can also see the *Sagas of the Icelanders* – a manuscript that (for Icelanders) holds the symbolic weight of the US Constitution or the Magna Carta in Britain. The museum's many temporary exhibits typically pay tribute to historic moments, and past and present cultural issues of Iceland. The renowned reading room is worth a peek, if not a long read.

**Reykjavík Zoo** [129 F3] (*Húsdýragarðurinn; Laugardalur; ☎ 575 7800; e postur@husdyragardur.is; www.mu.is; ⌚ summer 15 May–21 Aug 10.00–18.00 daily, winter 22 Aug–14 May 10.00–17.00 daily; entrance: adults 500ISK, children 400ISK*) Not lions and tigers and bears – not even an elephant. Instead, the overall atmosphere resembles that of a petting zoo, featuring Icelandic farm animals (sheep, goats, pigs, cattle, etc), as well as Iceland's major land mammals, including the Arctic fox, reindeer, mink, and seal. Also, as a holding place for wounded birds, you might be lucky and see some of Iceland's rare species up close. A smallish aquarium introduces visitors to the major species of Iceland's coastal waters and the Science World museum caters to children's self-discovery. The 'family park' section contains several children's rides of the mechanical and pony variety.

**Nordic House** (*Norræna Húsið; Sturlugata 5;* ☎ *551 7030;* e *nh@nordice.is; www.nordice.is;* 🕒 *12.00–17.00 daily; entrance 300ISK*) Nordic House is the local 'embassy' and cultural centre for the Nordic Council, an international organisation representing the combined interests of Denmark, Finland, Iceland, Norway, and Sweden. Iceland's chapter was built in 1968 by Finnish architect Alvar Aalto. Despite frequent exhibits, the building is less of a museum and more of an active space in promoting the latest in Nordic art and culture – check their website for the latest events listings. Their library of Scandinavian literature is also quite large and interesting to some.

**ART MUSEUMS** It is doubtful that a city of equivalent size can boast such a vibrant and compelling art scene as the one in Reykjavík. Local art museums offer far more than the casual visitor can handle and the city's many galleries hold stunning exhibits of their own (complete with stunning price tags). In case you didn't notice, visual expression is in the air.

**National Gallery of Iceland** [134 D6] (*Listasafn Íslands; Fríkirkjuvergur 7;* ☎ *515 9600;* e *list@listasafn.is; www.listasafn.is;* 🕒 *11.00–17.00 Tue—Sun; entrance free*) Iceland's national art museum is a converted freezer warehouse designed by the prolific Guðjón Samúelsson (ice cut from the nearby pond was kept here year-round). The unique building is a work of art in and of itself and showcases the largest and most prominent public collection of Icelandic art in the world. Exhibitions include the nation's classic greats (Jóhannes Kjarval, Ásgrímur Jónsson, etc) and some of the more contemporary contributions by Iceland's living artists. Expect depictions of the sagas (eg: *Grettir and the Ghost)* and impressive Icelandic landscapes, some of which you may recognise from your travels. Temporary exhibits also tend to be Iceland-focused and very thought-provoking. If you've only got time for one art museum, I recommend this one. When you're done pondering it all, there's a wonderful artsy café up on the top floor serving coffee, cakes and sandwiches, and the downstairs gift shop sells delightfully unusual souvenirs.

**Reykjavík Art Museum** [134 C3] (*Hafnarhús; Tryggvagata 17;* ☎ *590 1200;* e *listasafn@reykjavik.is; www.listasafnreykjavikur.is;* 🕒 *10.00-17.00 daily; entrance: adults 600ISK, senior/child 300ISK*) The all-white 'harbour house' was constructed in 1939 as a major shipping warehouse and the offices for Reykjavík harbour. The very cool cement-and-steel building reflects the utmost austerity of Icelandic design – so fitting for the artwork it holds.

The city's contemporary collection is bold and eclectic, unveiled in stark flashes as you wander among the cement staircases, corridors and balconies. The in-your-face exhibit of Icelandic pop artist Erró is permanent, while other oversized rooms house gigantic installations or the winners of recent art competitions. There's a colourful shop that sells prints on the ground floor, the restaurant offers a unique view of the harbour and just entering the library space makes you feel like an artist. It's the perfect place if flipping through heavy art books on a rainy afternoon sounds like fun.

**Reykjavík Art Museum – Kjarvalsstaðir** [128 D3] (*Kjarvalsstaðir; Flókagata; ☏ 517 1290; e listasafn@Reykjavik.is; www.listasafnreykjavikur.is; ⏲ 10.00–17.00 daily; entrance: adults 600ISK, senior/child 300ISK*) One of the three branches of the Reykjavík Art Museum, Kjarvalsstaðir is dedicated to the works of Icelandic painter Jóhannes Kjarval (see page 406) who is best known for his rough and emotive Icelandic landscapes. The bulk of his personal collection was left to the city of Reykjavík, who in turn built this sizeable museum in order to house the work of such a prolific artist. Even a short visit provides strong insight into Iceland's cultural heritage and the legacy of the country's most beloved artist, not to mention a pictorial tribute to Iceland's iconic natural monuments. Recommended.

**Reykjavík Art Museum – Ásmundur Sveinsson** [135 H6] (*Ásmundarsafn; Sigtún; ☏ 553 2155; e listasafn@Reykjavik.is; www.listasafnreykjavikur.is; ⏲ May–Sep 10.00–16.00 daily, Oct–Apr 13.00–16.00 daily; entrance: adults 600ISK, senior/ students 300ISK, under 18 free*) Completes the trio that makes up the Reykjavík Art Museum, housing the massive sculptures and working sketches of Ásmundur Sveinsson (see page 184). The artist designed the geometric building himself, which is surrounded by a garden featuring a few dozen of his own sculptures. Guided tours in English available upon request. There's also a museum shop and cafeteria.

**Note:** Purchasing a ticket to any one of the three Reykjavík Art Museums grants you free admission to the other two (Hafnarhús, Kjarvalsstaðir and Ásmundarsafn).

**Einar Jónsson Museum** [135 H6] (*Eiríksgata 1; ☏ 551 3797; e skulptur@skulptur.is; www.skulptur.is; ⏲ summer 1 Jun–15 Sep 14.00–17.00 daily, winter 16 Sep–31 May 14.00–17.00 Sat/Sun, Dec/Jan closed; entrance: adults 400ISK, seniors 200ISK, students free*) Einar Jónsson was one of the country's greatest sculptors, whose symbolist representation of Icelandic folklore and religious heritage marks the modern departure of individual Icelandic artistic expression. A few of his more prominent works adorn Reykjavík's public places, including the statue of city founder Ingólfur Arnason. The abrupt square building represents the country's very first art museum and the artist actually lived in the upstairs penthouse apartment until his death in 1954. His home is part of the permanent exhibit, along with casts of his more famous sculptures and several paintings.

**Sigurjón Ólafsson Museum** [139 E1] (*Listasafn Sigurjóns Ólafssonar; Laugarnestangi; ☏ 553 2906; e lso@lso.is; www.lso.is; ⏲ summer 1 Jun–30 Sep 14.00–17.00 Tue–Sun, winter 1 Oct–30 Nov & 1 Feb–31 May 14.00–17.00 Sat/Sun, Dec/Jan closed; entrance 500ISK*) Experimental sculptor Sigurjón Ólafsson was a founding father among Icelandic contemporary art, known for his gigantic abstract monuments. His modern studio sits on the city's northeast shore overlooking the bay, and is now a private museum that features the artist's work as well as that of several more contemporary artists. This is one of Reykjavík's least-visited art museums, perhaps due to the fact that during much of the year the museum is only open for six hours on weekends. Worth a visit if you adore non-representational art or miss the 1960s. Summer concerts are also popular.

**Reykjavík Museum of Photography** [134 B3] (*Ljósmyndasafn Reykjavíkur; Tryggvagata 15; ☏ 563 1790; e photomuseum@reykjavik.is; www.photomuseum.is; ⏲ 12.00–19.00 Mon–Fri, 13.00–17.00 Sat/Sun; entrance free*) Since the invention of the camera, Iceland's people and landscapes have inspired photographers and most of their pictures are archived in this lovely little city museum. New exhibits come and go regularly, demonstrating both the classic images artfully chosen from their vast photo library, as well as new and unusual – sometimes foreign – photography displays. The museum is contained and deliberate, so that a good 30 minutes does the trick. Their cool gift shop is also noteworthy: the only place to find high-quality, postcard-size reproductions of old-time, black-and-white shots detailing Reykjavík's vibrant past. Take the lift up to the sixth floor (top floor) of Grófarhús (above the city library).

**ASÍ Art Museum** (*Listasafn ASÍ; Freyjugata 41;* ☎ *511 5353;* e *listasi@centrum.is; www.asi.is;* 🕒 *13.00–17.00 Tue–Sun; entrance 300ISK*) A small, contemporary art museum managed by Iceland's Labour Federation and housed in the former studio of sculptor Ásmundur Sveinsson (not to be confused with the eponymous sculpture museum listed above). Exhibits change monthly and focus on lesser-known Icelandic artists who favour the avant-garde and the proletariat.

**The Living Art Museum** [135 G3] (*Nýlistasafnið; Laugavegur 26;* ☎ *551 4350;* e *nylo@nylo.is; www.nylo.is;* 🕒 *13.00–17.00 Wed–Sun, 13.00–22.00 Thu; entrance fee varies*) The Living Art Museum is exactly that – a building that houses ever-changing art exhibitions, art experimentations, and a place where lively discussions take place among artists and those who appreciate art. As a non-profit gallery and artists' collective, there's always something interesting afoot. Wander in, or check ahead to see what might be going on when you're around.

## GALLERIES

**101 Gallery** (*Hverfisgata 18A;* ☎ *511 6999;* e *101gallery@101gallery.is; www.101gallery.is;* 🕒 *14.00–17.00 Thu–Sat*) The latest and greatest of the Reykjavík art scene and a hotspot for serious collectors. Around the corner from the 101 Hotel [135 E3].

**Anima** (*Ingólfstræti 8;* ☎ *698 7807;* e *list@animagalleri.is; www.animagalleri.is;* 🕒 *for individual shows*) Intimate and independent-minded: regular shows of photography, contemporary visual art, sculpture.

**Gallerí Fold** (*Rauðarástígur 14–16;* ☎ *551 0400;* e *info@myndlist.is; www.myndlist.is;* 🕒 *10.00–18.00 Mon–Fri, 11.00–14.00 Sat, 14.00–16.00 Sun*) One of the city's largest galleries and the one most frequented by foreign tourists, featuring big names.

**i8** (*Klappastígur 33;* ☎ *551 3666;* e *info@i8.is; www.i8.is;* 🕒 *11.00–17.00 Tue–Fri, 13.00–17.00 Sat*) Frequent shows by up-and-coming Icelandic and international contemporary artists.

**Kling & Bang** (*Laugavegur 23;* ☎ *696 2209;* e *kob@this.is; www.this.is/klingogbang;* 🕒 *for events*) Cool artists' co-operative where anything goes. Think installations, live shows, found art, and gratuitous experimentation.

**Safn** (*Laugavegur 37;* ☎ *561 8777;* e *safn@safn.is; www.safn.is;* 🕒 *14.00–18.00 Wed–Fri, 14.00–17.00 Sat/Sun*) Icelandic artists tend to 'make it' once they get a show at Safn. The gallery favours the austere and contemporary side of Scandinavian style.

## NATURAL REYKJAVÍK

Iceland's capital is unique when compared with most European cities in that it's completely surrounded by real wilderness. On land or on sea, you're never far from getting away from it all. **Birding** enthusiasts should be eager to leave the capital for the country's nether regions, but the city's active bird population is only part of the attraction. A lot of the common species spotted throughout Iceland can and do pass through Reykjavík. Expect to see swans, several species of ducks, gannets, and gulls – namely (in winter) the glaucous gull (*Larus hyperboreus*) and the Iceland gull (*Larus glaucoides*). For the best birdwatching on offer, either visit the Tjörnin (see page 170) or take to the coast and islands. One of the most remote spots that you can access on foot is the tip of the **Seltjarnanes Peninsula**. Walking and cycling paths connect to the city, and the magnificent seascape makes this a popular outing for locals. Here, Reykjavík's outer suburbs thin into a causeway that connects to Grótta 'island', a low, diamond-shaped point on which stands **Grótta lighthouse**, built in 1947. A beacon has stood on this spot for well over 200 years, directing ships safely into Reykjavík harbour. Grótta is a beautiful and windy place that still captures the wistful nature of Iceland's far-flung locales. There's always plenty of seabirds, and in summer, eider ducks and varied species of geese. **Bakkatjörn** is a pond on the lower end of Seltjarnanes and another fantastic spot for birds. Know that both Bakkatjörn and Grótta are protected nesting spots with restricted access, so tread lightly. During nesting season (July), certain areas are completely off-limits to visitors. For more information, check online at www.seltjarnanes.is. Overlooking the pond is the historic black-and-white **Nesstofa**, built in 1763 as the home of Iceland's first surgeon-general Bjarni Pálsson. The building was Iceland's very first apothecary and now houses the **Medical Museum** (*Nesstofa; ☎ 561 1016; e nesstofa@natmus.is; www.natmus.is; ⏲ 15 May–31 Aug 13.00–17.00 Mon–Fri, 13.00–17.00 Sat/Sun; entrance 350ISK*). Old-time medical gear and antique pill bottles dominate the exhibit – one should visit for the sake of the house itself as it is one of the oldest in the county. To get out to Seltjaranes, drive, walk, cycle, or take bus No 11 to the end, then continue on foot either to the island or the pond.

The longest 'official' marked **walking path** in Reykjavík starts at Seltjarnanes and follows the southern coastline (up around Bakkavík and then below Suðurströnd). Stay on the coast all the way around the airport, past Nauthólsvík thermal beach, along the rocky shores of Fossvogur and then finally beneath the rushing highway that is Kringlumýrarbraut. Continue in the lowest point of the valley (Fossvogsdalur) with the Reykjavík suburbs to the north and those of Kópavogur to the south. Pass underneath Reykjanesbraut and follow the path along the **Elliðaár River** (still a source of fresh water and salmon). From this point it's fairly easy to reach the outdoor museum (Árbærsafn; see page 181), the swimming pool, or the lakeshore of Elliðavatn. Or do it all in reverse (starting in Elliðavatn, follow the river to Fossvogdalur and back out to Seltjarnanes).

**Öskjuhlíð** is also touted as a local 'nature' area, albeit a disappointing one. The rounded hill is an important Reykjavík landmark, formed in the last ice age and now home to the **Perlan** complex of hot-water tanks, a revolving restaurant and the Saga Museum (see page 181). The panoramic view is what stands out here. Otherwise, all the waist-high trees are transplants and the 'geysir' is a fake, piped in conveniently close to the tour-bus parking area. (When the real thing's so close, why bother?)

Indeed, just to the southeast is the city's main 'conservation area' **Heiðmörk**. The stark lava landscape is what remains of the last eruption of Mt Búrfell, while the green area with trails and picnic tables is the result of a vigorous tree-planting campaign in the 1950s. This is a very popular recreation area and organised tours often leave from Hafnarfjörður (see page 192).

Equally impressive are the five **islands** just outside Reykjavík harbour: Akurey, Engey, Lundey, Therney and Viðey. Each is unique in landscape and ecology and these are by far the city's most exciting bird colonies. Large puffin populations nest on Lundey and Akurey in summer, and fulmars, Arctic terns and guillemots are everywhere. Boat tours (see page 171) will often make short tours near all the islands, but Viðey is the only island with a regular ferry service.

**VIÐEY** Viðey is the largest and most accessible of the five bay islands and a definite natural highlight. At its closest point, the island is just 600m (650 yards) from the bustling mainland, and yet Viðey offers a completely separate experience from that of the city: low grassy hills, utterly quiet shores, basalt rock formations, clear water pools and abundant birdlife. Oddly, this very serene spot is where the city began.

Like so many of the coastal islands around Iceland, Viðey was inhabited from the 10th century, most likely by Irish monks. In 1225, an **Augustinian monastery** was founded in the centre of the island. Despite the community's vow of poverty, the monastery controlled over 100 farms and became extraordinarily rich by collecting a tax on cheese. That all came to an end in 1539, when royal Danish forces 'enforced the Reformation' by killing all the monks and burning the church and monastery to the ground – archaeologists have recently uncovered the foundations of the monastery, still visible behind the main house. The cairn on top of the closest hill (Danadys) commemorates the Danes who were killed when the monks fought back, while a modern statue of the Virgin Mary remembers the Catholics who lived and died on Viðey.

During the 16th and 17th centuries, Viðey functioned as a beggar's refuge under the royal Bessastaðir estate (see page 191). In 1751, Skúli Magnusson – the treasurer of Iceland – chose to make his home and office on Viðey. The Danish architect Nicolai Eigtved (of Copenhagen's Christiansborg Castle fame) designed **Viðeyjarstofa,** which is why it resembles the old estates of Denmark. Completed in 1755, it is the first stone building ever constructed in Iceland and looks far more sturdy than the 'Rococo' label implies. Skúli lived and worked in Viðey House until his death and today the home serves as a museum in his honour. Visitors can walk through his 18th-century office where he used to collect rents, then wander upstairs to the well-preserved attic floor. The heavy wooden beams and central fireplace make this a popular banquet hall that's still used for traditional parties.

Next door is **Viðeyjarkirkja,** built in 1774 as the private church of the treasury and the oldest church in Iceland (that's still standing in its original form). The stout stone church is remarkable for its unique shape and colour scheme, but also because practically everything inside is original (pews, doors, woodwork, etc). Skúli Magnusson is buried beneath the front altar, and today Viðey church is becoming a trendy place to get married. In 1794, the property went to Iceland's governor Ólafur Stephensen, whose son purchased the entire island from the crown, along with a printing press. From 1819, he printed books (including the Icelandic Bible) – Viðey Bibles are now considered a rare and treasured antique. The island went through several short business ventures, including a dairy farm and fish-processing plant – the 'Million' company, so named for its capital investment of one million krónur. The factory, docks, and surrounding village are now the ruins at Sundbakki, on the southern end of the island.

Following Reykjavík's bicentennial, the city sought to renew the island's purpose and appeal. Viðey House and church were restored in 1988, followed by recreational

## SKÚLI MAGNUSSON (1711–94): THE FATHER OF REYKJAVÍK

Skúli was born on the farm of Keldunes, situated on a remote plain of northeast Iceland (see page 382). He grew up in a country that was no more than a vassal state to Denmark, where raw goods (namely wool and fish) were produced and then shipped away by the Danish government. Only when he attended university in Copenhagen did Skúli witness the wealth produced by trade. Winning high marks in the national examination, he became the sheriff of the Skaftafell district in south Iceland at age 24 and was later promoted to Sheriff of Skagafjörður in the north. These first two jobs earned him a reputation for sound management and he was appointed Treasurer of Iceland in 1747, the first ethnic Icelander ever to hold such a high position within Denmark's colonial government. His position allowed him certain luxuries, including a personal challenge to the centuries-old Danish trade monopoly. In 1751, he finally received a licence to open the Innréttingar woolworks, Iceland's very first 'company'. He chose Reykjavík as his corporate headquarters for its mild weather, good harbour, freshwater river, hot springs and easy access to both sheep and market. As the first shops and warehouses went up on Aðalstræti, Skúli made his home on the island of Viðey, from where he managed his own company as well as the economy of Iceland.

Rarely does a tax collector gain the status of national hero, but Skúli's business success saw Reykjavík grow into Iceland's largest (and only) city, later to become the capital. He is also attributed with introducing the Enlightenment to Iceland and represents the 'try anything' optimism still endorsed by Icelanders – he knew both success (ending a trade monopoly) and failure (growing tobacco on Viðey). Perhaps the Viking Ingólfur Arnason deserves credit for finding the spot, but if it wasn't for Skúli, this would all still be a farm. After a good life and almost 50 years as treasurer, Skúli died on Viðey Island. He is buried beneath the altar of the church that he helped build.

sites (ie: barbecue pits) and a couple of pieces of large-scale conceptual art. The first of these installations is ***Áfangar*** ('stages') by American environmental sculptor Richard Serra (quote: 'My work is very hard to hurt'). Nine pairs of columnar basalt pillars stand in a circle on the north end of the island. Each provides a frame through which the observer can appreciate the amazing views, and a trail connects each of the stages. ***Blind Pavilion*** (*blindi skálinn*) by Ólafur Elíasson arrived in 2005 as 200 panes of black and clear glass. Enjoy stepping inside and finding the blind spot. Most recently, Yoko Ono added her peace column of light to the centre of Viðey, visible from the city. What makes a visit to Viðey so magnificent is the opportunity to experience Iceland's nature up close and personal in just a five-minute boat ride from the city. A leisurely trek from end to end (and back) takes about 1½ hours – a nice afternoon escape from the city. It's important to pay attention to the simple things, starting with the grass and flowers. Look for caraway (introduced by Skúli Magnusson), and the fields of wild daisies (*baldursbrá*) and buttercups (*sóley*). The island is the faint remnant of a caldera, the rim of a local volcano that was covered in the ice age, then submerged shortly after, only to resurface about 9,000 years ago. The eastern shore exhibits some interesting rock formations, including Kattarnef (cat's nose) Thórsnes (Thor's nose) and Virkishöfdi (fortress cape). Probably the best 'columns' are in the cliff face of Eiðisbjarg (isthmus cliff) on the west shore.

The island's highest point is on top of Skúlahóll (Skúli's hill) at 32m, marked with a compass point.

Birds own the whole island, with large numbers of common shorebirds: eider ducks, fulmars, greylag geese, purple sandpipers, oystercatchers, and snipes. Perhaps the most interesting summer inhabitant is the somewhat threatened **black-tailed godwit** (*Limosa limosa islandica*) that nests on the south end of the island. This is a different subspecies from the one more commonly seen on British shores (slightly larger) and you will hear its very particular cry followed by its repeated call (*weeta, weeta*). The best spots for birdwatching include the southern fields and beaches, and the ponds at the isthmus – Kríusander (Arctic tern beach) is exactly that. Note that in summer, a large section of the south is closed off for nesting birds, so always stick to the trail. Another factoid: there are absolutely no mice on Viðey – a local mystery and the common defence against building a bridge to the city.

Two ferries travel to Viðey from Reykjavík. In summer (6 May–10 September), a small boat connects to and from Sundahöfn (the new harbour; take bus No 16); fare 750ISK; children 350ISK; return departures every hour on the hour from 13.00 to 17.00 with a final run at 19.00. Another ferry comes and goes from Reykjavík's old harbour in the city, leaving from the Ægisgarð pier (25 May–10 September) at 12.00 and returning from Viðey at 15.15. In winter months, private parties and individuals can gain access through the ferry company; **Viðey Ferry** (m *892 0099;* e *ferja@ferja.is; www.ferja.is*).

Visitors may camp on Viðey free of charge within the designated campsite but should first check in at Viðeyjarstofa and inform the island staff of your intentions. Hot and cold water are available. The staff 'office' doubles as the café at Viðey House; **Mulakaffi** (*553 7737;* e *mulakaffi@mulakaffi.is; www.mulakaffi.is;* *whenever the ferry's running*). The menu sticks to the basics (fish soup, sandwiches, coffee, tea, and beer) while the upstairs restaurant serves very traditional Icelandic fare, but only for private dinners. For general information on Viðey: e videy@reykjavik.is; www.videyjarstofa.is.

**MT ESJA** Reykjavík's most permanent scenery just begs you to get out there and climb the thing. It's that constant pull towards Mt Esja that makes it the favourite mountain of anyone who lives in Reykjavík and the reason why you can't help staring – the majestic ridge is the first thing you notice when you arrive, and it's the visual you keep long after you've left. No wonder Mt Esja harbours such spiritual meaning for those who live in its shadow. You will likely hear professions of loyalty and how the mountain watches over the city. You will also notice the perpetual gaze of others towards the mountain – from office windows, while crossing the street or waiting out a traffic jam.

Scholars still argue about what Esja really means and how the mountain got its name. In Old Norse, '*esja*' means 'clay', which makes a lot of sense when you take off your boots after hiking near the bottom. The *Kjalnesingasaga* also tells the story of the nearby farm Esjuberg and the people who lived there, including an Irish bondswoman by the name of Esja. Regardless, it's a pretty name and probably the only mountain in Iceland that foreigners can pronounce without spitting.

Mt Esja is actually a span of peaks in a long range that stretches from the fjord above Reykjavík all the way out towards Thingvellir. The highest point of that range is 914m (3,000ft) above sea level, but for most, reaching the top means getting to **Thverfellshorn** (780m), which feels a lot more like a mountain peak. The whole range of Mt Esja is a classic Icelandic volcano, meaning layers of hard, grey-black basalt (lava flow) interspersed with lighter grey rhyolite tuff (look for the sparkly bits

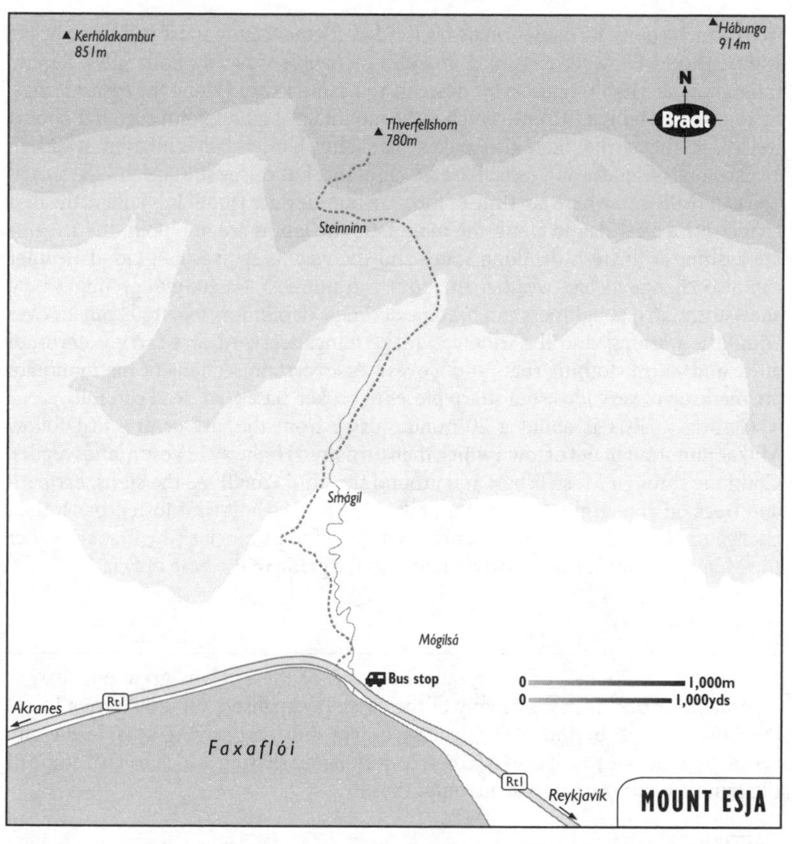


of quartz). The base of the mountain has a number of birch bushes and small pine trees, while further up you get whole valleys of flowers and then the incredible range of Icelandic moss. For those who plan on doing some serious walking/climbing in Iceland, Esja makes a nice starter mountain, while for those who normally shun uphill treks, it is remarkably novice-friendly. The trails are well maintained and marked with cairns (piles of stones), with several routes of varied climbing ability. This is the mountain that grandfathers climb with their young grandchildren and the one that teenagers stumble up after a crazy night of clubbing. It takes about two hours to go up and another hour to come back down.

The simplest and most well-travelled path starts at the main car park and heads up the left side of the valley. Wooden footbridges allow you to cross the Mógilsa stream and lead you up to the steeper ledge, aptly named *steinnin* (stones). Like a lot of mountains in Iceland, the climb starts off very easy and becomes steeper the higher up you go. The last 25m or so is climbing sheer rock faces (with the help of convenient stone steps and chain handrails). 'Thverfellshorn' means 'stubborn mountain peak', which requires no further explanation. Needless to say, the view from the top is incomparable: tiny Reykjavík hangs on the edge of a vast empty landscape and given clear skies, you can see for ever – at least 60km. Add your name to the guestbook and look for mine.

If you want to keep climbing, Esja provides ample space for rambling. **Kerhólakambur** (851m) is the next plateau over with a very subtle, arched ascent from which comes its name 'whale back ridge'. It's the feature most people associate with Esja and the walk westward provides incredible views on both sides. Several trails allow alternative options for descent. You can also head along the eastern ridge, up towards **Hábunga** (914m), which is the mountain's highest point even if it doesn't feel like it. The narrow ridge also makes this slightly harder than it might first appear.

Esja looks friendly and feels like easy climbing, but this is still Iceland: be smart! You can really come here anytime of the year, but summer (June–July) offers the best chance for a clear day to climb the mountain: the lupins are in bloom, the streams are rushing with fresh drinking water and the view is spectacular. Good weather can also change to bad weather in about two minutes – a sunny day might be a snowstorm up top, lightness can become darkness or blinding fog, trails can ice over with little warning, and the wind can make things scary. Always carry waterproof attire and warm clothing (hats and gloves). Also, certain sections of the mountain are made up of very loose but sharp pieces of broken basalt, so tread carefully.

Getting to Esja is about a 20-minute drive from the city centre: just follow Milkabraut straight out of town which then turns into Highway 1 (Vesturlandsvegur). Continue through Mosfellsbær and around the fjord. You'll see the signs, car park and trees on your right. For the bus, take No 15 to Háholt (in Mosfellsbær), then change to No 27 (headed to Akranes), but get off at Esjumelar (the first stop after the Mógilsa station). Let the driver know you're going to the base of Esja.

## GREATER REYKJAVÍK

Maybe it all looks like urban sprawl, but each of these towns grew out of very separate histories. Today, so many of the capital's expansive suburbs have a life of their own, not to be too easily dismissed. Not only can staying outside the city centre be a lot cheaper, it also makes a convenient base from which to visit some of the remote natural areas that surround the city.

**GARÐABÆR** If you're on the highway and going the speed limit, you'll pass Garðabær in about 90 seconds. It's the kind of suburb that's great for parking big cars and raising small children. The school system is superb and there are a lot of parallel streets, safe pavements, and single-family houses with big back gardens. The very young population just hit 10,000, which makes it Reykjavík's smallest satellite and one of Iceland's largest municipalities.

Garðabær's first settler was the man Vífill, one of Ingólfur Arnason's slaves who spent three years searching for his master's wooden pillars (see page 124). After his first disgruntled slave ran away, Ingólfur gave Vífill his freedom and this land as a farm, hence its name (Vífilstaðir) and that of the lake (Vífilsstaðavatn). One farm became many farms, and the resulting number of turf walls (*garða*) between fields gave the area its name. Halfway between Reykjavík and Hafnarfjörður, it stayed farmland for a fairly uneventful millennium until the 1950s, when it was cut up into cul-de-sacs with names like 'Pine Street'. Today, the good life is the town's main attraction, along with some very important historic sites in the close vicinity – like the presidential estate Bessastaðir.

### Where to stay

**Fell Guesthouse** Smiðsbúð 3A; 565 8800; e bjarki3@torg.is; www.islandia.is/fell; 10 Jun–31 Aug. This converted multiplex home features 'apartments' that sleep 1–4 people & includes kitchenettes & individual bathrooms with showers. Price-wise, a good deal for families. **$$$**

**Where to eat** Fast-food and grocery stores cater to the local demographic. The 11/11 shop is at Gilsbúð 1 (*585 7520*). For something more substantial, head to the adjoining suburbs.

**What to see and do** The nation's contribution to Scandinavian design (both austere and funky) is on display at the **Icelandic Museum of Design and Applied Art** (*Hönnunarsafn Íslands; Garðatorg 7; 544 2434; design@medusa.org; www.mudesa.org; 14.00–18.00 Tue–Sun; entrance free*). The temporary exhibits vary widely but the permanent collection reviews the past 100 years in furniture and product design. Expect to see everything from futuristic bowls and cutlery to 1950s chairs and groovy textiles. Looking to the past, visitors can walk freely through the archaeological site of **Hofsstaðir** (*Kirkjulundur; 525 8500; gardabaer@gardabaer.is; www.garðabær.is; 24hrs; entrance free*). The turf foundations of a 10th-century farmhouse outline how Iceland's earliest settlers once lived, while high-tech multi-media helps fill in the gaps. Then there's the local **swimming pool** (*Sundlaug Garðabæjar; Ásgarður; 565 8066; 07.00–21.00 Mon–Fri, 08.00–19.00 Sat/Sun*).

**BESSASTAÐIR** Iceland's official presidential 'palace' reflects perfectly the country's attitude towards pomp and politics. As a peaceful little farm with white walls and red roofs, the president's home is stately but not the least bit ostentatious. What makes it so lovely is how quiet and simple a place it is in the midst of the surrounding scenery – the city, the water, the faraway mountains, and the wind. Most visitors catch an unknowing glimpse of Bessastaðir when driving into Reykjavík from the airport – in the midst of concrete suburbs it may be the first traditional-looking thing you see.

Some sort of farm and church have stood on the spot for at least 1,000 years, though the actual buildings have evolved with the status of highly envied real estate. In addition to his Reykholt property (see page 262), the medieval hero and saga author Snorri Sturluson purchased the farm at Bessastaðir, most likely while he was speaker of the Althing. After Snorri's failed coup against the Norwegian crown, King Hákon got the title deed to Bessastaðir by having Snorri assassinated with a battleaxe in 1241 (see page 261). From the 13th century, the estate was used as the visiting residence for royal emissaries from Norway and Denmark. From the moment Reykjavík became a city, Bessastaðir became the permanent residence of the Governor of Iceland, the highest office in the country at the time. The main house (in which the president now lives) was completed in 1766 and could not look any more Danish. Note how the neoclassical façade contrasts the Rococo style of Viðeyjarstofa (see page 186), built just a decade before – a significant change in taste by the absolutist King Frederick V of Denmark.

Bessastaðir **church** was constructed from locally quarried lava stone and opened in 1796, though the square steeple took another 26 years to complete. The real beauty of the church lies in its very basic shape and colours. On the inside, eight fabulous stained-glass windows recount the history of Christianity in Iceland (installed in 1956). Along the left side, individual windows depict the first Irish monks arriving in Iceland by boat, Guðbrandur (see page 325) who printed the Bible in Icelandic, the hymn-writer Hallgrímur Petursson (see page 39), and Christ preaching the Sermon on the Mount. Windows on the right side depict the Vikings accepting Christianity at the Althing, Iceland's last Catholic bishop Jón Arason (see page 21), the renowned Lutheran bishop Jón Vidalin, and the Virgin Mary.

The very first secondary school in the whole of Iceland opened at Bessastaðir in 1805. For 40 years, the Latin or 'learned' school (*lærði skólinn*) tutored the country's best and brightest youth in classical texts, including the poet Jónas Hallgrímsson (see page 39). After the government moved to Reykjavík, Bessastaðir went back to private ownership to be finally purchased in 1941 by a local businessman. He gave the estate to the Icelandic government on the condition that it be used as the presidential residence, and in 1944 Iceland's very first president (Sveinn Björnsson) moved in. Since then, Bessastaðir has been the venue of Iceland's officialdom, including visits by Scandinavian royalty and heads of state such as Georges Pompidou and Richard Nixon. That doesn't make it off-limits – it's unbelievably easy to visit the property and the church is open to the public during the day.

Bessastaðir is located on the Álftanes Peninsula with a fairly wild shoreline that's home to many, many birds. There's also a very beautiful lake to explore (Bessastaðatjörn) and the cutesy next-door village of Álftanes. To get there, drive to Garðabær and turn on Álftanesvegur or take bus No 23 to the end.

**HAFNARFJÖRÐUR** Hafnarfjörður is exactly how one imagines an Icelandic fishing town: lots of busy boats, a stripey lighthouse, and a volcanic past. Indeed, 'harbour fjord' owes its ideal harbour to the last eruption of the Búrfell crater over 7,000 years ago. After the lava swirled into the sea and cooled, there was no safer shore on which to dock a boat in Iceland. So says the *Landmánabók* and until the last century, Hafnarfjörður did more business than Reykjavík. The Danish trading post became a town thanks to entrepreneur Bjarni Sívertsen, who founded a commercial fishing enterprise in 1793 that later grew into the biggest operation in the country. If you've ever bought 'Icelandic fish' in your own country, chances are it came from Hafnarfjörður.

Today, 25,000 people live here, and while some of them commute the 5km to Reykjavík, most enjoy a very separate existence from that of the capital. About half of Iceland's immigrant population live here, mostly because they can get jobs. While fishing towns are drying up all over Iceland, Hafnarfjörður survives on account of its great harbour and equally successful shipping business, not to mention one of the largest aluminium smelters in Europe. The town has also made a somewhat vigorous turn to tourism, focusing its efforts on cashing in on Icelandic folklore. There's always a lot going on here, including a number of annual festivals and gaudy tourist attractions.

Yet the real attraction is the town itself, which seems to summarise all the quirks of modern Iceland. Fishing is corporate, the townspeople re-enact Viking battles, their houses are wedged between rugged cliffs and lumps of lava rock (where 'elves' abound), and the radio sometimes broadcasts in Polish. Thus marks the end of Iceland's civilised 'capital area' and the beginning of the wild lava fields that stretch out to Reykjanes (see page 201). That happy Hafnarfjörður should be surrounded by such inhospitable landscapes is part of the fun. Head out into the nothingness but be back in time for hot water and dinner.

**Tourist information** Smack bang in the city centre you'll find the tourist information service centre (Hafnarfjörður Town Hall) (*Strandgata 6; ☎ 585 5555; e info@hafnarfjordur.is; www.hafnarfjordur.is; ⌚ 08.00–17.00 Mon–Fri (summer also 10.00–15.00 Sat/Sun)*). It's the starting point for local tours, buying tickets, transportation, and getting answers to any questions that you may have about exploring the area.

## Where to stay

**Hótel Viking** (42 rooms) Strandgata 55; ☎ 565 1213; e booking@vikingvillage.is; www.vikingvillage.is. Part of the Viking Village experience, with cosy rooms done up in Viking style (& as a tribute to the Faroe Islands & Greenland). All rooms have a separate bathroom with shower, & a regular shuttle bus connects you to Reykjavík city centre. Free internet, free parking, & a big hot tub outside. B/fast inc. **$$$$**

**Arahús Guesthouse** (8 rooms) Strandgata 21; ☎ 555 1770; e arahus@arahus.is; www.arahus.is. Steps away from the tourist information office, the museum & other main attractions, this very sensible but homely guesthouse is popular for a reason. Bathrooms are shared on each floor & kitchen & laundry facilities are available for use. B/fast inc. **$$$**

**Helguhús** (3 rooms) Lækjarkinn 8; ☎ 555 2842; e helguhus@helguhus.is; www.helguhus.is. Friendly guesthouse close to the town centre with tiny but motherly rooms, shared bathrooms & kitchen facilities. The separate 3-bedroom apartment sleeps up to 6 people at a very good rate. **$$$**

**Hótel Hafnarfjörður Apartments Hotel** Reykjavíkurvegur 72; ☎ 540 9700; e info@hhotel.is; www.hhotel.is. Newly expanded corporate hotel with spacious individual apartments – from studios to family suites that can sleep 6. The latest furnishings & modern bathrooms are a plus, as is the very professional service. Probably the 'fanciest' hotel in town. Located just off the main highway to Reykjavík, & within walking distance of everything. Summer **$$$**; winter **$$**

**Hafnarfjörður Guesthouse** (12 rooms) Hjallabraut 51; ☎ 565 0900; e info@hafnarfjordurguesthouse.is; www.hafnarfjordurguesthouse.is; ⌚ 15 May–15 Sep only. Huge & uncompromising, this is a hostel that has it all: good prices, family rooms, a nearby grocery store, giant kitchens, & generally clean bathrooms. However, regulating dingy crowds of backpackers day after day just might have made management a little nit-picky (you're charged an extra US$1 for the privilege of having a sink in the room). It's also 100% smoke- & alcohol-free. The guesthouse is located in the midst of Hafnarfjöðjur's lush green area & sculpture garden, Viðistaðatún. **Camping** is also available in the back for about US$10. To get there, take bus No 41. **$$**

**Við Lækinn** (4 rooms) Lækjarkinn 2; ☎ 565 5132; e olgunn@simnet.is. Cheery B&B with shared bathrooms & a sweet matron running the place. B/fast inc. **$$**

## Where to eat

There's a diversity of options, be it fast food or gourmet, but in limited amounts. For groceries, visit the busiest Bónus in the country (*Helluhrauni 18; ☎ 565 0101*).

**A Hansen** Vesturgata 4; ☎ 565 1130; e ahansen@ahansen.is; www.ahansen.is; ⌚ 18.00–midnight daily. Fine dining that's so pretentious they rent out white stretch limos to pick you up. This is the place to come for escargots by candlelight, but the food's actually not that adventurous (steak & more steak). *Mains from 3,700ISK.* **$$$$$**

**Fjörukráin** Viking Village; Strandagata 55; ☎ 565 1891; e vikings@fjorukrain.is; www.fjorukrain.is; ⌚ 18.00–23.30 Sun–Wed, 12.00–15.00 Thu–Sat. The very best of Icelandic theme dining with Viking waiters & bawdy waitresses, much carousing, & greasy fingers. Meals are traditional old Icelandic dishes toned down just a speck: fish soup, braised lamb shank, & skyr. A sit-down 3-course meal with drinks (& show) costs around US$90 pp. The restaurant Fjaran is the upmarket, upstairs alternative serving a little more sophisticated à la carte. *Mains from 2,100ISK.* **$$$**

**Jósalir** Sörlaskeið 26; ☎ 564 6100; e josalir@isl.is; ⌚ 11.00–18.00 daily. The in-house restaurant for the Íshestar Horse Riding Centre, so if you take a tour, you'll most likely lunch here, banquet-style. The menu is that of most cafés (hamburgers, chicken, pasta, salads, etc), but done with a little more care. *Mains from 1,500ISK.* **$$$**

**Tilveran** Linnetstígur 1; ☎ 565 5250; e tilveran@centrum.is; ⌚ 12.00–22.00 Mon–Fri, 17.00–23.00 Sat/Sun. Hafnarfjörður's 'affordable' Italian & seafood restaurant. *Mains from 1,600ISK.* **$$$**

**Kænan** Óseyrarbraut 2; 565 1550; kaenan@simnet.is; 07.00–18.00 Mon–Fri, 09.00–14.00 Sat. Laid-back diner near the harbour. Where local fishermen eat with their families. Grilled food (hamburgers, fish, etc). *Mains from 850ISK.* $$

**Súfistinn** Strandgata 9; 565 3740; 08.00–23.30 Mon–Thu, 08.00–midnight Fri, 10.00–midnight Sat, 13.00–midnight Sun. Cool local café with vegetarian food & global coffees. *Mains from 800ISK.* $$

**What to see and do** Catching the fish auction (the largest in Iceland), is about as real a thing as you can do here. Or just head down to the harbour and watch the fish being unloaded from the boats. If it's snowing that day, then step into the **Hafnarfjörður Museum** (*Byggðasafn Hafnarfjarðar; Vesturgata 8; museum@hafnarfjordur.is; www.hafnarfjordur.is; Jun–Aug 13.00–17.00, Sep–May 13.00–17.00 Sat/Sun only; entrance 600ISK*). Inside an old fishing warehouse, the permanent exhibit includes the history of Hafnarfjörður, photography and a very large collection of old-time Icelandic toys which will find more of an audience with antique-lovers than with children. Next door is the restored **Sívertsen house** (*Vesturgata 6*), the oldest building in Hafnarfjörður, built in 1805 by the city's founder Bjarni Sívertsen (open at the same time as the museum). If you want to see how his latter employees lived, then check out **Sigga House** (*Kirkjuvegur 10*), built in the early 1900s for a 'working class' family and depicted as such. The local **art museum** is known as Hafnarborg (*Strandgata 34; 555 0800; hafnarborg@hafnarfjordur.is; www.hafnaborg.is; 11.00–17.00 daily except Mon; entrance 500ISK*). The centre offers up austere modern art and frequent musical concerts, though the town's real cultural gem is Iceland's **National Film Archive** (*Kvikmyndasafn; Hvaleyrarbraut 13; 565 5993; kvikmyndasafn@kvikmyndasafn.is; www.kvikmyndasafn.is*). The archive presents two films a week at **Bæjarbíói**, a restored on-site 1940s movie house.

Hafnarfjörður's **Viking Village** is the Disneyland of Iceland, to be enjoyed as such (*Strandgata 55; 565 1213; booking@vikingvillage.is; www.vikingvillage.is*). Either stay at the hotel, eat at the restaurant, hit the gift shop or catch the festival. The outrageous Viking theme is offset by attention to historical accuracy and artistic detail. It's becoming a popular 'last night in Iceland' activity before heading to the airport the next morning.

Local **swimming** options include **Sundhöll Hafnarfjörður** – an indoor pool with outdoor hot pots and a nice sauna (*Herjólfsgata 10; 555 0088; 06.30–21.00 Mon–Fri, 08.00–12.00 Sat/Sun; entrance 250ISK*), and **Suðurbæjarlaug** – an outdoor pool that's good for swimming laps with a waterslide, steam bath and several hot pots (*Hringbruat 77; 565 3080; 06.30–21.30 Mon–Fri, 08.00–17.30 Sat/Sun; entrance 250ISK*).

**Hiking** in, around, and outside town is worthwhile as several trails head out over the stark but beautiful lava fields. Detailed hiking maps can be picked up at the tourist office, but the most popular trail ascends **Mt Helgafell** (339m). The remaining lava cone makes an interesting climb and is fairly easy and close. Bear in mind that this is just one of many *helgafells* ('holy mountains') in Iceland.

**Tours** Hafnarfjörður is headquarters to several tour specialists, some of which offer local excursions. One of Iceland's leading **horseriding** operators is just outside town at the **Íshestar Riding Centre** (*Sörlaskeið 26; 555 7000; info@ishestar.is; www.ishestar.is*). In addition to their incredible cross-country trips, Íshestar offers several fun half-day and whole-day trips, most of which take in the nearby lava landscapes. Easy enough for inexperienced riders, a three-hour tour costs around

US$65. If you prefer wheels, then try **Blue Biking** (*Stekkjarkhvammur 60;* ☎ *565 2089;* e *bluebiking@simnet.is; www.simnet.is/bluebiking*). They do easy-going bike tours in and around Reykjavík, and slightly more invigorating off-road tours on the rough terrain that surrounds Hafnarfjörður. By far the most interesting is the trip through Heiðmörk and up to the volcanic crater Búrfell, from which the harbour was born.

Although it sounds like a bad tourist stunt, Hafnarfjörður claims to be the capital of Iceland's hidden people (see page 33), along with a whole zoo of folk creatures (elves, dwarves, and gnomes), though it is unclear why they choose to inhabit a post-industrial fishing village. The intrigued can find out more on a guided tour with **Hidden World Walks** (☎ *694 2785;* e *sibbak@simnet.is; www.alfar.is; cost 2,800ISK*); ask at the tourist information office. The 90-minute walk meanders through some of the town's natural lava features and cliffs while a local clairvoyant recounts the presence and history of those you can't see. It's not nearly as hokey as it might sound and gives a deep insight into Icelandic folklore. The main elfin concentration is around Hamarinn, the park and cliff southeast from the city centre.

**Festivals** Hafnarfjörður's **International Viking Festival** has become so popular you can now order one for your own country (*www.vikingvillage.is*). Typically held in mid-June, the festival focuses around an outdoor market, swordfights, music, dancing, and your usual Renaissance fair fare but with a Viking twist. This is not to be confused with the town's **Bright Days Festival**, held around midsummer's eve when the sun is up all night. The two-week-long arts fair features outdoor performance, food stands, balloons and face-painting, etc. The **Christmas village** picks up at the end of November and is open every weekend (🕒 *12.00–18.00 Sat/Sun*) until Christmas Day. It's all about shopping and Santa Claus (and elves!), but with enough Icelandic flavour to make it credible.

**KÓPAVOGUR** 'Seal pup bay' takes its name from the small cove beneath the Kársnes Peninsula, most likely named by Iceland's first settler Ingólfur Arnason who claimed the land as part of his very first farm. Just minutes away from the city centre, Kópavogur gets treated like just another one of Reykjavík's neighbourhoods. Still, the border between the two is quite clear (Fossvogur) and with a population nearing 30,000, Kópavogur is officially Iceland's second-largest 'city'.

In addition to competing with the capital, Kópavogur also gets tagged with the negative connotations of *Kópavogsfundinum*, or the Kópavogur Meeting of 1662 (see page 21). That's when Icelandic bishop Brynjólfur Sveinsson and lawyer Árni Oddsson signed the country over to the King of Denmark, proclaiming absolute monarchy over Iceland. It's not that anybody blames the townspeople for setting a legal precedent backing an exploitative colonial regime that lasted for 300 years, but schoolkids still learn it that way.

There was no town here until the late 1930s, and it was only in the post-war years that an influx of job-seekers settled here and began forming a separate existence from the capital. Kópavogur really got its wings in the 1980s, when urban decay saw jobs moving out to the suburbs. Before long, this was the land of housing developments and industrial parks and the epicentre of Iceland's high-tech industry. Kópavogur is also 'the mall' where the entire country comes to shop at the largest stores in the country. People travel to Kópavogur on business, to visit friends who live there, and to get slightly less expensive accommodation. Otherwise, you will pass through Kópavogur on your way to and from Reykjavík.

## Where to stay

**Hótel Smári** (48 rooms) Hlíðarsmári; 558 1900 e hotelsmari@hotelsmari.is; www.hotelsmari.is. New-ish, pre-fab travellers' hotel right next to the gigantic mall. The interior is much more appealing, with big sturdy beds, nice carpets & a cosy professional atmosphere. Location is convenient to public transportation but best if you come with your own car. The in-house Chinese restaurant is not bad at all. **$$$**

**Kriunes Guesthouse** (10 rooms) Við Vatnsenda; 567 2245; e kriunes@simnet.is; www.kriunes.is. On the shores of Lake Elliðavatn, this quiet hotel allows you to experience great natural scenery while just 15km from the city centre. Furnishings are new & comfortable, & they offer a lot of outdoor activities. The suites make a lavish but homely experience. B/fast inc. **$$$**

**BB44 Guesthouse** (8 rooms) Borgarholtsbraut 44/Nýbýlavegur 16; 554 4228; e info@bb44.is; www.bb44.is. Sensible & affordable, this little guesthouse is a total gem with 2 locations – both houses converted to suit the traveller's needs. Family-friendly on all counts, with rooms that sleep 1–3 people, family studios & sleeping-bag space for under US$25. Convenient transportation (the Flybus stops here) & hot tubs out back. **$$**

**Where to eat** Most people will direct you to the mall at Smáralind (see page 163) where you have a sizeable food court, a few decent restaurants and several giant food stores. Otherwise, the fast-food signs will beckon from all directions. For groceries, there's the 11/11 (*Thverbrekku 8; 585 7565*) and the other Bónus (*Smiðjuvegur 2; 567 0800*).

**Café Catalina** Hamraborg 11; 554 2166; 08.00–20.00 Sun–Thu, 08.00–midnight Fri/Sat. Everyday Icelandic dishes & a local favourite (lots of fish & starch) not far from the main bus station. *Mains from 1,000ISK.* **$$**

**Kínahofíð** Nýbýlavegur 20; 554 5022; 10.00–22.00 daily. Chinese food as you know it. *Mains from 1,200ISK.* **$$**

**What to see and do** Kópavogur boasts two very praiseworthy museums (listed) and a famous music hall (*www.salurinn.is*) for evening concerts. And don't forget the **swimming pool** (*Borgarholtsbruat 17; 570 0470; 06.30–22.00 Mon–Fri, 08.00–19.00 Sat/Sun*). Among Icelanders, Kópavogur is the most-referenced example of *húldufolk* or hidden people (see page 33). The straight and narrow Álfshólsvegur (elf hill road) was meant to be the town's main street, but when workmen attempted to remove a giant boulder in order to add a few lanes, they were highly unsuccessful. Eventually, it was decided to leave the 'elves' alone and divert the road – you can still see the unmoved boulder.

For further information on activities that are available in Kópavogur, see www.kopavogur.is.

***Natural History Museum*** (*Náttúrúfræðistofa; Hamraborg 6A; 570 0430; e natkop@natkop.is; www.natkop.is; 10.00–20.00 Mon–Thu, 11.00–17.00 Fri, 13.00–17.00 Sat/Sun; entrance free*) The best of its kind and a great place to get acquainted with the building blocks that make Iceland: a huge collection of rocks and minerals and informative displays on the country's animals and plants (their mollusc collection is a source of pride).

***Kópavogur Art Museum*** (*Listasafn Kópavogs, Gerðarsafn; Hambraborg 4; 570 0440; e gerdarsafn@kopavogur.is; www.gerdarsafn.is; 11.00–17.00 Tue–Sun; entrance: adults 500ISK, children 200ISK*) A striking building holding a substantial collection of contemporary art, including the major works of the Icelandic sculptor Gerður Helgadottir, and the impressive lifelong collection of a local businessman.

**MOSFELLSBÆR** Travellers hit Mosfellsbær as they go north from Reykjavík. From the main road it seems like a bunch of houses and hay farms, but the peaceful countryside and a rich history make this town one of the special corners of Iceland that too often gets passed by in order to 'get somewhere'.

The ancient farm of Mosfell figures prominently in the sagas, settled first by Thórður Skeggi, who was given land here by Reykjavík's Ingólfur Arnason at the end of the 9th century. The farm and church were a noted stopping point for travellers in the Viking age – the spot was especially appealing for its many rivers, hot springs, and the valley that opens a passage to the Althing. The rushing waterfalls of the Varmá River would later power the Álafoss woollen mills (built in 1896 and still operating) and the hot springs were tapped for their energy. Even today, much of Reykjavík's hot water is piped in from Mosfellsbær. And yet the area never 'developed'. In World War II, the British military stationed over 15,000 men here, only to abandon the site a few years later. The road to Reykjavík was only paved in the 1970s and Mosfellsbær only became a *bær* (town) in 1987. Before that, this was simply a rural district of sheep farmers. It's the memory of local farm life that inspired **Halldór Laxness** – Nobel Laureate and the Icelandic novelist most renowned outside Iceland. Although born in Reykjavík, Halldór grew up on the nearby farm of Laxnes (from which he took his pen name). Nearly all of his books reference Mosfell somehow and after he achieved early fame, he returned and built his home in the very same valley. His estate was only recently opened as a museum and is attracting literary pilgrims from around the globe.

Today about 8,000 people live in Mosfellsbær and although it's a recognised Reykjavík suburb, it's also the smallest, farthest, and least suburban of them all.

## EGIL'S SILVER

The memorable Viking hero Egil Skallagrímsson (see page 258) spent his retirement at Mosfell, depressed by his ageing self (he was going blind and deaf) and loss of respect in the community. Egil's pension included two giant chests of silver paid out to him by King Athelstan of England (AD895–939) as compensation for Egil's brother Thorolf, who was speared to death defending the king. Rich and miserable, Egil concocted a plan to bring his treasure to the Althing and throw the money into the crowd, hoping to incite a riot and destabilise the annual government meeting. He was prevented by his step-daughter Thordis, who kept him from getting a ride to the Althing. Instead, Egil snuck out one night on the pretext of wanting to take a bath in a hot spring. He brought with him two slaves who carried the chests on horseback. The blind Egil was only found the next morning, wandering in circles with his horse. The treasure was never found and neither were the two slaves. Egil's silver is probably the best-known Viking treasure in Iceland and it's somewhere near Mosfellsbær. Archaeologists and treasure hunters have been searching ever since.

After Egil died, he was buried Viking-style in a mound. Later his son-in-law (who had just converted to Christianity) dug up the bones and placed them under the altar of the church at Mosfell. When a new church was built, the local priest (Skafti Thorarinsson) picked up the heavy, over-sized skull and tried to break it with an axe. He struck it as hard as he could but only left a small white mark. The impossibly thick skull convinced him that this was indeed the head of Egil.

Travel-wise, the town has pleasantly little tourist amenities but a grand collection of hills, valleys, and rivers – here you are truly on the verge of innocent hiking. Mosfellsbær also allows an alternative (and more scenic) route to Thingvellir (see page 213) which is coming into wider use.

**Getting there and away** Mosfellsbær is the junction of Highway 1 to the west and Route 36 to Thingvellir, a 15-minute drive from the city. You can also take bus No 15 from Reykjavík, which comes to Háholt. From there, bus No 27 stops at the sights outside the town.

**Tourist information** The town's tourist information centre is located inside the local library, which is inside the shopping centre (*Thverholt 2; ☎ 566 6822; e bokasafn@mos.is; www.mosfellsbaer.is; ⏲ 09.00–17.00 daily*).

## Where to stay

**Fitjar Guesthouse** (6 rooms) 270 Mosfellsbær; ☎ 565 6474; e fitjar@internet.is; www.fitjarguesthouse.com. A great little family-run inn occupying a Modernist house that borders a stunning view & babbling brook. Some rooms have a small private shower, others share a bathroom. You do have free rein over the kitchen & breakfast can be provided for a fee. The Fitjar is most ideal for drivers as there's not much of anything nearby. **$$$**

The **campsite** is next to the Varmá sports centre, at the end of Háholt (*☎ 566 6754; e mos@mos.is*). Hot and cold water are available and your payment includes free admission to the swimming pool.

## Where to eat

Fast food abounds (the kind you recognise from back home).

**Draumakaffi** Háholt 14; ☎ 586 8040; e draumar@binet.is; ⏲ 08.00–19.00 daily. Small coffee shop that serves sandwiches too. *Mains from 650ISK.* $$

**Mosfellsbakarí Urðarholt** Háholti 13–15; e mosbak@mosbak.is; www.mosbak.is; ⏲ 07.00–18.00 Mon–Fri, 08.00–17.00 Sat/Sun. A wonderful little local bakery in the town centre. Delicious cakes, pastry, bread, sandwiches & light meals. *Mains from 400ISK.* $

**What to see and do** To see the original site of **Mosfell**, head out 8km on Route 36. The modern angular church that you see was built in the 1960s but replaces a long line of churches going back to before the 13th century. The bones of Egil Skallagrímsson are buried somewhere around here, as is his treasure, and archaeological digs continue to this day. Several paved **hiking and biking paths** connect the town of Mosfellsbær to the valley of Mosfelldalur and the many surrounding hills, and along the rivers and various waterfalls. Note that the mouth of the Varmá River is a conservation area owing to the very rare saltwater rush (*Juncus gerardi*) which grows along the edge of the fjord. You're also not too far away from **Mt Esja** (see page 188). To enjoy some of the natural hot water, go to the **swimming pool** at Varmárlaug, near the riverbank (*☎ 566 6254; ⏲ 16.00–21.00 Mon–Fri, (summer 06.30–20.00), 09.00–18.00 Sat/Sun*).

***Gljúfrasteinn*** (*270 Mosfellsbær; ☎ 568 8066; e gljufrasteinn@gljufrasteinn.is; www.gljufrasteinn.is; ⏲ 1 Jun–31 Aug 09.00–17.00, 1 Sep–31 May 10.00–17.00; entrance 500ISK*) 'The stone in the glen' was the home of Icelandic novelist and Nobel Laureate **Halldór Laxness** from 1945 until his death in 1998. He grew up in this spot (Laxnes), and visitors are encouraged to walk around his gardens bordering the Kaldakvísl (cold branch) River. A film details the author's life and the tour (available in English) shows you the house, unchanged from when he lived there. The gift shop sells many of his books in translation.

***Álafoss wool factory shop*** *(270 Mosfellsbær, Álafossvegur 23; ☎ 566 6303; e alafoss@islandia.is; www.alafoss.is; ⏲ 09.00–18.00 Mon–Fri, 09.00–16.00 Sat/Sun)* The town's main industry is still going strong at this old-time wool factory. Renovated to preserve memories, the oldest building is now an outlet shop selling fine woollen products, including decorative blankets and bulk Icelandic wool yarn for knitters. You'll see plenty of old wool factories turned into souvenir shops all over Iceland, but honestly this is one of the better ones – if not for their focus on the historical aspect, then for the quality of what they make today.

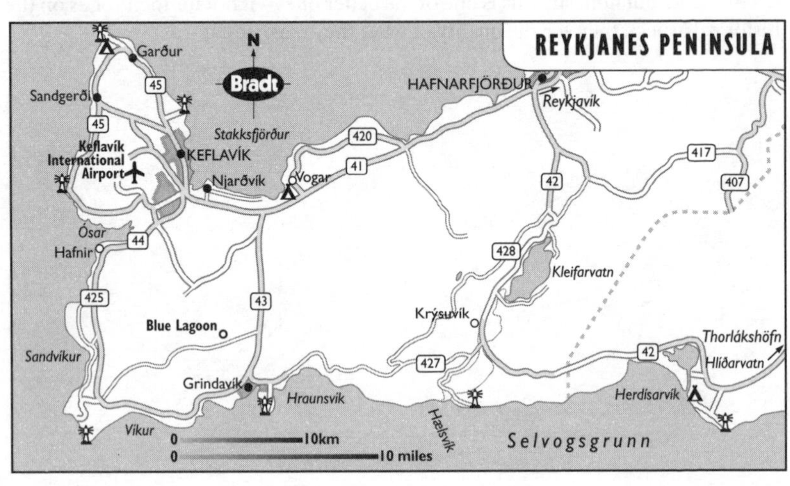
REYKJANES PENINSULA
N
Bradt
Garður
45
Sandgerði
45
Keflavík International Airport
KEFLAVÍK
Njarðvík
Stakksfjörður
420
41
Vogar
HAFNARFJÖRÐUR
Reykjavík
42
417
407
Ósar
Hafnir
44
425
43
Blue Lagoon
428
Kleifarvatn
Krýsuvík
Sandvíkur
427
42
Thorlákshöfn
Hlíðarvatn
Grindavík
Hraunsvík
Herdísarvík
Víkur
0
10km
0
10 miles
Hælsvík
Selvogsgrunn

# 6

# Reykjanes

There's a lot more to Reykjanes than simply the airport and the Blue Lagoon. If you're flying to Iceland, you'll pass through the former and you'll feel a lot better having passed through the latter, but that's only just the beginning. The southwest peninsula of Reykjanes, or 'smoky point', is an utterly strange region of surreal landscapes and desolate volcanic fallout. There are only crumbled lava rocks carpeted in thick, grey-green moss as far as the eye can see. There is no soil – only shifting, metallic black sand. The low mountains on the horizon are sleeping volcanoes, their forms the crusted spouts from whence flowed all this lava. As an active geothermal hotspot, the broken ground exhales the wispy puffs of steam that gave the peninsula its name. The wind blows without cease and the frontal gusts of the Gulf Stream shoot out from across the ocean. The land is forever streaked with drizzle or sleet.

Most travellers are motivated by a faulty notion that getting away from the airport gets them closer to Iceland's boundless wilderness. What they don't realise is that here they already are. Stark and almost uninhabitable, the Reykjanes Peninsula was overlooked as a fruitless wilderness until the American military thought it was the perfect place for a top-secret naval base. Perhaps the constant comparison of Reykjanes to the moon reaches back to bored military housewives who saw lunar living as a metaphor for life on the base. Most likely, their kitchen window granted enough of a view of pseudo-craters and pyroclastic flow for it to be convincing. Reykjanes doesn't feel like planet earth, but then neither does much of Iceland.

Whether you're on a quick stopover, exploring Iceland in depth, or if you've got a spare day at the end of your trip, Reykjanes is a surface worth scratching beneath. Nowhere else captures the same curious beauty and bleak mood of this peninsula's empty places. There is great hiking to be done, a magnificent coastline to explore, and pure heat bubbling up from the depths. Reykjanes is also ideal for winter travel – it's close, convenient, and compact. It's also warmer than the rest of Iceland and there's rarely any snow because it all gets blown away.



## GETTING AROUND

Reykjanes is home to Iceland's very best and very worst road. Route 41 connects Keflavík to Reykjavík with a smooth, newly paved wide surface that gives newcomers a false sense of confidence about driving in Iceland. With the exception of the paved roads to Grindavík and Hafnir, the rest of Reykjanes is fundamentally road-less. A harrowing rock path skirts the entire southern coast, a drive that tests one's mettle and one's axles.

Tiny Reykjanes also has more buses than any other region in Iceland, so it's never too hard to get from A to B, when A is the airport and B the Blue

Lagoon. The ubiquitous **Flybus** (☎ *562 1011*; e *main@re.is; www.flybus.is*) travels about 20 times each day to and from Keflavík Airport and Reykjavík's BSÍ bus terminal (1 hour). **SBK** (*Keflavík; Grófin 2–4;* ☎ *420 6000;* e *sbk@sbk.is; www.sbk.is*) travels between Reykjanesbær (Keflavík) to Reykjavík city centre (1 hour 15 minutes), and runs another bus from Keflavík to Sandgerði and Garður. The **Blue Line** bus does a continuous run between Reykjanesbær to the airport (10 minutes) to the Blue Lagoon (20 minutes) to Grindavík (30 minutes) and back again. Another 'Blue Lagoon Express' travels between BSÍ and the Blue Lagoon and the airport (*www.bluelagoonbus.is*).

To visit the rest of the peninsula, it truly helps to have a car. Hitching is unreliable given the sporadic traffic and surprise jolts of weather. Riding a bike is painful and comedic. Hiking is more fitting and will take you into lava landscapes that nobody else can see.

## KEFLAVÍK INTERNATIONAL AIRPORT (KEF)

Known simply as Keflavík or 'the airport', KEF seems a kind of national hospital where foreigners are born into Iceland. About 50km west of Reykjavík, this is the country's only international airport and thereby carries the same weight of importance as the capital, if not more. The constant energy of travel keeps the terminal busy and exciting, and it is the only place in Iceland where you will see an actual crowd or a queue.

Iceland's earliest airports were merely short, grassy strips for landing small planes. When the British arrived in Iceland in 1940, the Royal Air Force began immediate construction on an airport in Reykjavík for their fighter planes. When the Americans arrived the following year, they found the city airstrip was not long enough to accommodate their B-17 bombers (the largest military plane at the time). So they began construction of a new base in 1942. Keflavík was chosen because it was the flattest piece of ground near the capital. Removing a straight path of lava rocks was a gruelling task, but despite the great difficulty, Keflavík's first runway was operational in less than two months.

After the war, military – then civil – aircraft continued to stop at the American base in Keflavík for refuelling. So many tourists hopping about a NATO base made the people in uniform uneasy, so in 1987, a separate civilian section was opened and dubbed the Leif Eiríksson Air Terminal (*Flugstöð Leifs Eiríksonnar;* ☎ *425 0680;* e *airport@airport.is; www.airport.is/english*). As travel to and through Iceland increased, the airport expanded by several more terminals – first in 2001 and again in 2007. Today, over two million passengers fly through Keflavík Airport each year – seven times the population of Iceland. That's why it feels like a small city with its own workforce, so many shops, and more infrastructure than your average Icelandic town.

Getting to and from the airport is simple (see page 128). For most vistitors, the airport is where they get their first glimpse of Iceland, so make sure to pay attention when you land. In addition to the lumpy pumice landscape and the milky Blue Lagoon, look out for the lupins (see page 50) in summer, and the distant white mountains in winter. Exiting the airport takes you past the colourful stained-glass sculpture *Regnbogi* ('rainbow') by Icelandic artist Rúri, and the Surrealist *Þotuhreiður* (the 'jet nest') by Mangús Tómasson, in which a baby jet wing breaks out of a stainless-steel egg. This was all done in the late 1980s and is therefore entirely forgivable.

## REYKJANESBÆR

Reykjanesbær is Iceland's mini megalopolis that combines the towns of Keflavík, Hafnir, and Njarðvík into one dynamic community of 12,000 souls. That makes it the third-largest city in Iceland after the capital (not counting the suburbs) and Akureyri. As the heart of it all is Keflavík, a very functional town with row after row of perfect square blocks lined with two-storey concrete homes painted gaily in contrast to the lifeless lava mounds beyond. The harbour still serves as an active shipping and fishing port and continues to grow along the seashore.

Like so many ports in Iceland, Keflavík was founded as a fishing station by the Hanseatic League (see page 20). It went through the same ups and downs of a Danish trading post, except in 1799 when the next town over (Básendur) was demolished in a tidal wave. Business in Keflavík doubled and from the consequent boom comes the remaining historic homes in the town centre. Otherwise, Keflavík went relatively unnoticed until World War II when the Allies needed a very flat piece of ground for an airport. After the war, the Americans handed the base over to the newly independent Icelandic government, but then quickly took it back. The Cold War demanded a close watch over the 'trans-Atlantic tier', and for the next 50 years Keflavík was home to NASKEF (Naval Air Station Keflavík). And so Keflavík grew into its own modern military town, unlike any other in Iceland. This was an important era for Iceland and Reykjanes, and for better or worse, the NATO base waged a huge influence on Keflavík. No visitor can deny the American footprint that infiltrates Keflavík today: city planning, fast-food restaurants, and suburban gardens. Likewise, thousands upon thousands of Americans came and lived here, learning to love or hate Iceland based on the years they spent in the drizzle of Hafnargata. The base finally closed in 2006 and despite the decades of protests against foreign military presence by Icelanders, it seemed as though everyone was a little sad to admit the end of an era, especially the businesses in Keflavík.

Now home to the country's airport and a major shipping centre, Keflavík is the gateway into Iceland. The town is home to a thriving immigrant community and one of the youngest populations in the country. It's also the first impression most travellers get. Take it all in with a grain of salt. Keflavík is Iceland at its very tamest.

**Note:** The following listings are all located in Keflavík unless otherwise noted.

### TOURIST INFORMATION

**Tourist information** Hafnargata 57; ☎ 421 6777; e reykjanes@reykjanesbaer.is; www.reykjanes.is; 🕒 summer 10.00–22.00, winter 10.00–16.00 daily. Located inside the 'mall' as an office in the Reykjanesbær library.

### WHERE TO STAY

**Flughótel** (60 rooms) Hafnargata 57; ☎ 421 5222; e icehotels@icehotels.is; www.icehotels.is. Icelandair's posh airport hotel is just minutes from the terminal but conveniently located in the centre of town. The rooms are plush & shiny with modern bathrooms & stylish beds. Things get more elegant the higher up you go (try for the top floor). An in-house spa (sauna, jacuzzi, massage, etc) make this the perfect pre- or post-flight hangout. B/fast inc. **$$$$**

**Alex Guesthouse** (15 rooms) Aðalgata 60; ☎ 421 2800; e alex@alex.is; www.alex.is. The Alex is probably the closest & cheapest night's stay, located next to the airport. Choose between the pleasant guesthouse or the self-contained 'motel huts' with private bathrooms & b/fast, the very clean & comfortable hostel with shared bathroom & b/fast, or the full-service summer campsite (with kitchens & jacuzzi). Regular transport to & from the airport. High demand requires booking ahead. Motel huts **$$$**; hostel **$$**

**Guesthouse Keflavík** (6 rooms) Vatnsvegur 9; 420 7000; e stay@kef.is; www.kef.is. The humble stepsister of the hotel of the same name across the street. As a reconverted house, there's a bit more personality to the place. Bathrooms are shared & guests have access to the hotel's amenities. B/fast inc. **$$$**

**Hótel Keilir** (20 rooms) Hafnargata 37; 420 9800; e info@hotelkeilir.is; www.hotelkeilir.is. Keflavík's luxurious hotel, located in the town centre. A sleek tribute to the all-white room, the modish minimalism seeks to compensate for the tight rooms & tighter en-suite bathrooms with vertical shower – the deluxe rooms are slightly bigger, & the sizeable family suite sleeps 5 comfortably. **$$$**

**Hótel Keflavík** (68 rooms) Vatnsvegur 12; 420 7000; e stay@hotelkeflavik.is; www.hotelkeflavik.is. Despite the outward appearance of some lowbrow resort in Las Vegas or Blackpool, this huge travellers' hotel is surprisingly classy. Its fancy rooms (all with private bathroom), are a bit tight, but have everything you'd need & some stunning views to boot. The in-house restaurant is a bit pricey, & meant to give tourists their first Icelandic meal. Although the interpretation of luxury is a bit grandiose & outdated, the staff do go the extra mile. Overall, a nice hotel. **$$**

**Keflavík Youth Hostel** (100 beds) Fitjabraut 6A; 421 8889; e fithostel@fithostel.is; www.fithostel.is. The youth hostel is in Njarðvík, just off the main road (Route 41) – most of the buses will make a stop if you ask the driver. Besides Reykjavík, this is the busiest hostel in Iceland, with hordes of travellers coming & going from the airport. It also feels totally deadbeat & is the only hostel in Iceland to correctly mimic the grimy hostels of mainland Europe. Alas, it's really cheap. Rooms sleep 2–6 people & bathrooms, kitchens, & laundry facilities are shared. Tourists tend to occupy 1 building, the other houses long-term residents, mainly migrant workers. B/fast is available. **$$**

**B&B Guesthouse** (10 rooms) Hringbraut 92; 421 8989; e book@bbguesthouse.is; www.bbguesthouse.is. Right in the centre of Keflavík & within walking distance of everything, this laid-back (& affordable) B&B is extremely popular. The 10 comfortably furnished rooms share 3 bathrooms. Free airport pickup & drop-off. B/fast inc. **$**

## WHERE TO EAT

**Raín** Hafnargata 19A; 421 4601; e rain@mi.is; 11.00–15.00 & 18.00–22.00 daily. A distinguished supper club, Raín defines the ambiance of Keflavík with its potted trees, a roaring fake fireplace & banquet-style seating arrangements. The food is frilly: veggie hors d'oeuvres, baked cod, smoked salmon, lamb tenderloin, or lobster, followed by US$10 desserts. *Mains from 2,500ISK.* $$$$

**Langbest** Hafnargata 62; 421 4777; e langbest@langbest.is; www.langbest.is; 11.30–21.30 daily. Pizza & steak house in the heart of town. *Mains from 1,350ISK.* $$

**Létt & Ljúff** Hafnargata 57; 421 5222; 05.00–18.00 daily. Small café inside the mall specialising in meal-specific buffets (breakfast & dinner), with lots of fresh fruits & veggies. This is the de facto restaurant for the Flughótel. *Mains from 1,200ISK.* $$

**Panda** Hafnargata 30; 421 8060; 11.00–22.00 Mon–Fri, 16.00–22.00 Sat/Sun. Keflavík's resident Chinese take-away. Everything you've been craving. *Mains from 890ISK.* $

**Thai Restaurant** Hafnargata 39; 421 8666; www.thaikeflavik.is; 11.30–22.00 Mon–Fri; 12.00–22.00 Sat; 16.00–22.00 Sun. The younger sister of the Reykjavík location, this one's bigger & more elegant, with lots of Thai decorations & a nice bar. *Mains from 2,000 ISK.* $$$

**Self-catering** In town, there's the very convenient grocery store **10-11** (*Hafnargata 55; 421 8300; 24hrs*). More extensive food shopping can be done at the Reykjanesbær **Bónus** (*Fitjum; 421 4655; 12.00–18.30 Mon–Thu, 10.00–19.30 Fri, 10.00–18.00 Sat, 12.00–18.00 Sun*). The shop is located in Njarðvík (on the south side of town), within (a long) walking distance of the youth hostel. For baked goods, I would recommend trying **Nýja Bakaríið** (*Hafnargata 31; 421 1695; 08.00–18.00 daily*).

## ENTERTAINMENT AND NIGHTLIFE

☆ **Blues Lounge** Hafnargata 30; ⌚ 19.00–23.00 Sun–Thu, 19.00–04.30 Fri/Sat. The town bar meets chic lounge. It looks humble, but the Moby Dick of all bars means it can light up quickly.

☆ **Paddy's** Hafnargata 38; ☎ 421 8900; ⌚ 17.00–01.00 Mon–Thu, 17.00–05.30 Fri–Sun. Icelanders love Irish pubs as much as the rest of the world & this award-winning bar is Keflavík's salute to Celtic culture. It's the (only) place for live music, & gives off a friendly, clean vibe.

**WHAT TO SEE AND DO** Everyone gets directed to the **Reykjanes Folk Museum** (*Bugðasafn Suðurnesja; ☎ 421 6700; e www.reykjanes.is; ⌚ 11.00–18.00 daily; entrance 500ISK*). The old red fishing warehouse, known as Duus hús, was built in 1877. Today it is home to 59 models of fishing boats – all different, all in glass cases, and all the workmanship of Keflavík local Grímur Karlsson. If you don't think model ships are cool, then you might not want to attempt this on your own. Another stab at history is the **Viking ship** the *Icelander* (*Íslendingur; Stapagata; m 894 2874; ⌚ 13.00–16.00 Mon–Wed, Sat & Sun*), docked in Njarðvík. In 2000, the recreated Viking longboat was built and sailed from Iceland to Greenland to New York City in celebration of Leifur Eiríksson's journey to North America. There are a lot of young kids in Keflavík, which means there's a great **swimming pool** (*Sunnubraut; ☎ 421 1500; ⌚ 07.00–21.00 Mon–Fri, 08.00–16.00 Sat/Sun*), and in summer there's a very successful **whale-watching tour** out of the harbour (*Moby Dick Whale Watching; ☎ 421 7777; e moby.dick@dolphin.is; www.dolphin.is; ⌚ Apr–Sep*).

# VOGAR

Halfway between Reykjanesbær and Reykjavík lies the nondescript bayside village of Vogar. Because it's so close to the fork in the road between the Blue Lagoon (10 minutes) and Keflavík Airport (15 minutes), it's becoming a service centre of sorts. When arriving or departing Iceland, travellers in cars like to stay at the **Motel Best** (*38 rooms; m 866 4664; e motelbest@visir.is; www.motelbest.is;* **$$$**). This big, new and ultra-clean motel caters to the real needs of travellers, especially those of families, couples, and those in wheelchairs. Most rooms are furnished with huge beds, and most have private bathrooms. The complimentary breakfast buffet is better than average, and overall, this is good value for money. Nearly every bus will make a stop at Vogar upon request. The **swimming pool** is close by (*Hafnargata; ☎ 424 6545; ⌚ 10.00–19.00*).

# GARÐUR

The northwest tip of Reykjanes is pretty typical seashore with lots of screeching gulls and fishing boats. The main highlight of Garður is the pair of **lighthouses**, the old traditional one (built 1847) and the new square one built in 1944. Garðskagi is the northernmost point in Reykjanes, and given the right weather, you can capture Reykjavík in all its glory and see right across to the other side of Faxaflói. Heading down the coast brings you to the village of **Sandgerði**. If your idea of fun is barren isolation by the sea, there are cosy little summerhouses for rent (*Þóroddsstaðir; ☎ 423 7748; e putti@simnet.is*). Descending further down the west coast (on Route 45) takes you past the colourful little church of Hvalsnes, built in 1887. **Hvalsneskirkja** is unusual because of its stone structure, green-painted roof and the jovial red and yellow steeple. The site is best remembered for Hallgrímur Pétursson (see page 39) the Icelandic psalmist who served as pastor of this parish from 1644 to 1651. His daughter is buried at this church. Keep going to the 'end' and you'll be at the lighthouse at **Nýlenda** on Stafnes. The vague rock ruins below are those of **Básendar**, once the largest city in Reykjanes until a tidal wave cleaned it out in 1799.

## BLUE LAGOON

Blue Lagoon or Bláa Lónið (*Grindavík;* ☎ *420 8800;* e *bluelagoon@bluelagoon.com; www.bluelagoon.com*), is the most visited destination in Iceland, the proverbial 'T-shirt' proving you've been to the country. In the midst of the spooky black lavascape that is Reykjanes, the ethereal blue waters of this enormous manmade hot spring seem absolutely weird and strangely inviting. The minute you see a picture, you have to go, and once you've been, you have to go back. With every billboard, brochure, and tour guide pointing this way, it's hard to avoid it.

**HISTORY** It's not every day that industrial effluent becomes a wildly popular international attraction. The fact is, the Blue Lagoon phenomenon was just a lucky accident. In 1976, the Suðurnes Regional Heating Co-operation was assigned the task of finding a new energy source – mainly to feed power to the NATO base at Keflavík. The search for a reliable geothermal source brought them to Svartsengi, an area of black crater mounds and an active fissure swarm that keeps things underground very hot. Drilling deep wells allowed access to the heat and the constant flow of steam.

In short, the new power plant had planned for the factory runoff to simply flow back into the ground and disappear. What they didn't count on was the high silica content of the flow, which creates a slippery white coating that seals the rocks into a giant reservoir. By the early 1980s, people were sneaking into the area to go swimming and enjoy all that lovely hot water. Rumours of healing qualities and cured skin ailments led to a cult following and the power plant finally built the bathers a place to change their clothes. Only in 1999 did the 'Blue Lagoon' open as a spa for the masses.

**THE ENERGY PLANT** Svartsengi is still one of the largest geothermal energy plants in the world and is quite amazing in its design. Because the groundwater is so heavy in minerals and salt and is also extremely hot (150°C), the plant pipes in cold fresh water through this steam to heat it up. This secondary steam powers turbines that generate electricity (that feeds the lights on the runway at Keflavík), while the hot water is pumped directly into homes all around Reykjanes. Meanwhile, the natural underground steam condenses around the cooler pipes and gets dumped into the reservoir that is the Blue Lagoon.

**THE WATER** The water in the lagoon is actually re-condensed geothermal mineral steam from about a mile (1.6km) beneath the ground. This is exactly the same kind of water you see in the natural hot springs of Mývatn and Geysir, but has been cooled significantly. The Blue Lagoon tries to keep the water close to body temperature (39°C/98.6°F) though it gets a lot hotter towards the back wall. The bright-blue glow of the water comes from a type of blue-green algae unique to hot springs. The milky-white appearance comes from the silica in the water. Lucky for you, blue-green algae and silica are really good for your skin, improving skin tone and making you feel all soft and smooth. No chlorine is added to the water because it's in there naturally.

**BATHING** Without a doubt, the Blue Lagoon is a gigantic tourist trap but my, what a lovely tourist trap to be trapped in. The lagoon is open year-round (*Sep–May 10.00–20.00 daily, Jun–Aug 07.30–21.00 daily*) and the swimming is fine at any time. Entry is around US$30 with available discounts for senior citizens (30%) and teenagers (50%); children under 11 are free. With a few thousand guests every day, the process is a lot more high-tech than your typical public pool. Entrants are fitted with a wristband that controls your entrance and grants you electronic access to your locker, located in one of the enormous locker rooms. Be sure to bring your own towel, though you can rent towels and swimsuits at the main desk.

The lagoon is not deep (less than 5ft/180cm), but fluctuates based on the irregular shape. The bottom is covered with white silica mud, the result of a natural process of re-condensation. The silica does wonders for your skin, which is why everyone's fighting over the little boxes and buckets to get a fistful of their own. Obviously, avoid your eyes when spreading it on your face. There's also a dry sauna and two steam baths and a massage area, but none of that compares to a languorous soak.

The Blue Lagoon is almost always busy, but if you want to be all alone, go at about 10.00 in February (this is the only pool in the world where the lifeguards wear snowsuits). Swimming in the middle of a snowstorm, or under the Northern Lights, or in the daylight of summer nights – each offers its own heightened experience, so don't be afraid to be unconventional.

Everyone in Iceland is plotting to get you to spend time at the Blue Lagoon, and there isn't a tour out there that doesn't drop you down here at some point. Most independent travellers expressly plan for a day or half day to 'do the Blue Lagoon'. However, since the Blue Lagoon is right next to the airport, it makes sense to catch it on your way in or out (if you're flying), rather than make a special round trip from elsewhere.

## WHERE TO STAY AND EAT

**Blue Lagoon Clinic** (15 rooms) 420 8806; e reservations@bluelagoon.com; www.bluelagoon.com/Clinic. The Blue Lagoon has been proven to lessen the effects of psoriasis & eczema & there is now an on-site clinic with the sole aim of treating skin ailments. To be accepted at the clinic, foreign guests must have a referral form completed by their dermatologist. Patients are given access to a private pool & undergo a series of medical treatments using Blue Lagoon products. **$$$**

**Northern Light Inn** (21 rooms) Svartsengi; 426 8650; e welcome@northernlightinn.is; www.northernlightinn.is. Right across the road from the Blue Lagoon, this country lodge is committed to comfort & making tourists feel welcome. For the price you pay, the rooms feel a tad spartan, but they are warm, clean, & dry, & this is Iceland (all have private bathrooms with shower). If you plan your trip right, this makes a nice finale before your departure from the airport. The 'natural' restaurant is not the organic gourmet it professes to be, but the weekly vegetarian buffet is popular for a good reason. B/fast inc. **$$**

**Blue Lagoon Restaurant** Contact details above; 11.00–20.00 daily. The restaurant gets away with serving decadent food simply because it's located in a spa (if you're eating it here, it must be healthy). There's plenty of choices for all diets: lots of fresh fish & vegetarian dishes, a few truly Icelandic delicacies, & some staple, tasty European classics to keep the middle content. *Mains from 2,000ISK.* **$$$**

## GRINDAVÍK

The charm of Grindavík is that it will never change – this quiet harbour has always been a prize fishing village and always will be. Watching the boats sail in and out of the harbour and the cranes unload giant crates of cod is comforting given the number of similar places in Iceland that are now ghost towns. Grindavík even smells like fish (in a good way) and the people in the town dine on fish caught by their own family members who work on these very boats.

The success of Grindavík as a fishing station has made it a coveted piece of property ever since settlement. By the late 13th century, all the fishing rights of Grindavík had been bought up by the Bishop of Skálholt (see page 224) who collected tithes and rents in stacks of salted cod. In 1532, the culmination of the rivalry between the English and Hanseatic fishing companies was played out in the streets of Grindavík, when the English fisherman John the Broad was stabbed (see page 20). In 1627, the same Algerian pirates who laid waste to the Westmann Islands (see page 230) also made sure to pay a visit to Grindavík. The town led the rest of the country in new methods of finding and catching cod, even pioneering a system of nets that was adopted across the Atlantic.

This whole story is relayed in the **Saltfish Museum** (*Saltfisksetur; Hafnargata 12A;* ☎ *420 1190;* e *saltfisksetur@saltfisksetur.is; www.saltfisksetur.is;* ⏲ *09.00–18.00 daily; entrance 500ISK*). A reconverted warehouse shelters a path leading visitors along a chronological tour of Iceland from 1770 to 1965. Old-time photos, and old-time objects (including a full-size *knörr* fishing boat) explain the development of saltfish, the key role it plays in Iceland's economy, and its fascinating history (ie: the Cod Wars). As an aside, it's absolutely impossible to read all the exhibit labels and follow the audio guide at the same time.

Outside the museum, Grindavík is a good place to eat a piece of fish or visit the nearby Blue Lagoon. In the town's central garden, there's a touching **memorial** for the drowned men of Grindavík, depicting a mother, daughter and son waiting for their sailor husband/father to come home. Right next door is the handicrafts gallery inside the oldest house in Grindavík (*Gallerý Gesthús;* m *849 1703;* ⏲ *13.00–17.00 daily*). If you want to walk, head southeast to the point of Hópsnes and out to the **lighthouse** (built in 1928).

## WHERE TO STAY

Two guesthouses are open year-round.

**Borg** (4 rooms) Boragarhraun 2; m 895 8686; e bjorksv@simnet.is. A simple but friendly B&B in the centre of town. **$$**

**Fiskanes** (40 beds) Hafnargata 17–19; m 897 6388. A large hostel, mostly inhabited by seasonal workers & fishermen. The top floor has been remodelled into a nice guesthouse with clean & concise rooms & shared bathrooms. The campsite (☎ *420 1190*; **$**) on the town green is pretty bare, with toilets & a sheltered kitchen, but no showers. Pay at the Saltfish Museum (where there are showers). **$$**

## WHERE TO EAT

**Brim** Hafnargata 9; ☎ 426 8570; e brim@brim-veitingar.is; www.brim-veitingar.is; ⏲ 11.00–21.00 daily. Upmarket restaurant in the town centre serving seafood, steaks, burgers or vegetarian dishes. But you should really go for the seafood. *Mains from 1,800ISK.* **$$$**

**Salthúsið** Stamphólsvegur 9; ☎ 426 9700; e salthusid@salthusid.is; www.salthusid.is; ⏲ 11.00–21.00 daily. The 'salt house' is a congenial restaurant that's well worth the drive down to Grindavík. It's a large place, with lots of tables set out beneath the big wood beams & the big appetites of the fishermen who come here. If the museum whets your appetite, there's plenty of saltfish on their menu (nuggets, salad, soup, or au gratin), but the best choice is whatever came off the boat in Grindavík that day. They also do a filling & well-priced lunch & the chocolate delight makes a killer dessert. *Mains from 1,700ISK.* **$$$**

**Lukku Láki** Hafnargata 6; ☎ 426 9999; www.lukkulaki.is; ⏲ 12.00–22.00 Sun–Thu, 12.00–01.00 Fri/Sat. Named after the cartoon character Lucky Luke, this rowdy sports bar is the

## SALTFISH

*Lífið er saltfiskur* – 'Life is saltfish'. These were the words of Halldór Laxness (see page 197) in his feminist novel *Salka Valka*, in which the young woman Salka rejects the oppressive gender roles of an Icelandic fishing village and joins the men in the fishing boats. Read widely as a political novel, it is also the perfect photograph of daily life in so many of Iceland's saltfish communities. *Saltfiskur* is simply codfish that has been gutted, split and beheaded, flattened, heavily salted, then dried. It has been the staple food and export of Iceland for centuries to the extent that until independence, the country's coat of arms was a saltfish. Invented as a means of preservation, saltfish is now a delicacy in the Mediterranean world, namely Italy, Spain, and Portugal. Known as *bacalao*, the very salty dish is traditionally moistened in a tomato sauce or cooked into a soup. These recipes are now common on Iceland's restaurant menus and if you walk around any of the harbours, you might just get a peek of these splayed and salted cod, stacked for export. Today, the number-one importer of Icelandic *saltfiskur* is Nigeria.

town's main watering hole & a good place for a pub lunch. On weekends, it turns into a bit of a disco with lots of live music, more drinking, & dancing. *Mains from 900ISK.* $$

✕ **Mamma Mía** Víkurbraut 31; ☎ 426 7860; ⏲ 17.00–22.00 Mon–Thu, 11.30–23.30 Fri–Sun. The town's one & only pizzeria. Eat in or order out. *Mains from 1,400ISK.* $$

## REYKJANESTÁ

The Reykjanes 'toe' is the tiny cape that juts out to the southwest of the peninsula. From Grindavík, head west on Route 425. The road changes to unpaved and then changes to really bad as you drive through the sand and lava rock for which Reykjanes is known. This road brings you to the geothermal area of **Gunnuhver**, where gas fumaroles hiss into the air and mud pots plop away with their own lowly form of ferocity. As one of the less-visited geothermal areas in Iceland, observers get a full head-on dose of steam and sulphur. It's also one of the least guarded, with mud and gas shooting out of the ground all around. Watch your step and stay on the wooden path. The name 'Gunna hot spring' recalls a revenge killing when the accused woman (Gunna) was thrown into these hot springs without even the chance of a fair trial. The nearby opaque turquoise lake is the reservoir for the nearby power plant which is not the Blue Lagoon though it looks similar.

The **lighthouse** Reykjanesvíti sits atop a knoll near the point. This was the first lighthouse ever built on the Icelandic coast (back in 1878), guiding ships between Europe and America. The original lighthouse was an octagonal structure only 6m high, but it was knocked down in an earthquake. The new lighthouse stands at 73m above sea level, which is best appreciated if you hike up the sloping cliffs that take you to a dizzying height before dropping straight down to the sea. From the top of this slope you can see out to Eldey Island. In my view, the view from Reykjanestá is one of the most exhilarating in Iceland. A rough campsite near the lighthouse allows for caravans and tents, but has no amenities.

At this point Route 425 becomes paved again and takes you northwards, crossing right over the Mid-Atlantic Ridge. Here, plate tectonics and continental drift are expressed in no uncertain terms and you can plainly see the basalt cliff of the North

American plate diverging from the basalt cliff of the Eurasian side. In fact, the two plates are moving apart at about 2cm per year, one side pulling to the southeast, another to the northwest. The **intercontinental bridge** spans the 20m divide, with flags on either side to let you know exactly where you stand. Down below lies a perfect black-sand bottom where people shuffle their feet to form giant letters and hearts with arrows through them. If you walk out past the road and to the sea, you come upon the black-sand beach of **Sandvík**, a memorable place.

## ELDEY

Eldey, or 'fire island', is located some 15km (nine miles) southwest of Reykjanestá. The basalt cliffs reach up to 75m high but the surface area on top is quite small – only seven acres (3ha) – the equivalent of about four New York City blocks. Eldey is part of the same volcanic ridge that created all the lava fields in Reykjanes and the same hotspot that heats the Blue Lagoon. Tiny islands are created and destroyed all the time. The youngest of these is Nýey ('new island'), created in the undersea eruption of 1783. Several other islets have disappeared in the last century.

Today, Eldey is home to the largest colony of gannets in the world, with some 35,000 breeding pairs. The island is a protected bird refuge – perhaps it's out of concern for the gannets, or perhaps it stems from a centuries-old guilt complex about the great auk going extinct (see below), but all access is strictly prohibited. That doesn't mean you won't see the island – on a clear day it's quite visible from shore, and from the air. Up close, the island looks like a slanted cube of dark-grey rock – it's amazing that anyone could ever successfully climb to the top.

### LAST OF THE GREAT AUKS

Of all the tragedies in Iceland, the most tragic is the tale of the great auk. *Pinguinus impennis* was the largest bird in the auk family (the same as puffins), weighing 5–8kg (11–17lb) and standing quite tall at 75cm (2.5ft). They had black bodies with white tummies and they were flightless birds, with teeny tiny wings, but wide, webbed black feet and big, sharp bills. They were the most powerful diving bird in recorded history, swimming to depths of more than 110m (330ft)! Being flightless, they were easy prey for sailors and fishermen cruising the islands of the north Atlantic. Laying just one egg per year, the great auk was especially vulnerable to any drop in population. Bit by bit they disappeared from their former habitat: first Ireland, the Faroe Islands, then Scotland and Canada. In Iceland, the birds were most prominent in Reykjanes, especially on the rocks of Geirfuglaskér or 'Great Auk Skerry'. In 1808, a ship of British sailors raided the rocks and took a huge number of birds, but in 1830 an undersea eruption caused the rocks to disappear beneath the surface. By 1840, the world's last remaining great auks had flown to the island of Eldey. On 3 June 1844, a specimen collector hired four Icelandic fishermen (Jón Brandsson, Ketil Ketilsson, Sigurður Íslefsson, and Vilhjalmar Hakonarsson) to find a great auk. The four sailed to Eldey and chased down a nesting pair, then wrung their necks and accidentally broke the egg in the nest. From henceforth, the great auk was extinct; this final pair of auks from Eldey are now bottled in the Royal Museum of Copenhagen (*www.zoologi.snm.ku.dk*). In 1971, the National Museum of Iceland paid £9,000 (equivalent to £85,000 today) for a single stuffed great auk.

## THE REKJAVEGUR TRAIL

A fairly level, but truly fascinating, week-long walk across the peninsula. Start (or finish) at the lighthouse and follow the blue stakes in the ground.

Day 1: Reykjanesvíti–Blue Lagoon (19km)
Day 2: Blue Lagoon–Leirdalur (13km)
Day 3: Leirdalur–Djúpavatn (14km)
Day 4: Djúpavatn–Kaldársel (18km)
Day 5: Kaldársel–Mt Bláfjöll (16km)
Day 6: Mt Bláfjöll–Hamragil (20km)
Day 7: Hamragil–Thingvellir (14km)

## KRÝSUVÍK

Much of Reykjanes is off the beaten path, but if you want to test the limits, the abandoned settlement at Krýsuvík offers the same deathly silence of the interior, but it's right next to the sea. Next to the old farmhouse is the very simple church, built in 1857. Travelling the lava field between Grindavík and Krýsuvík is best left to 4x4s and mountain bikes. Otherwise, it's much quicker driving south from Hafnarfjörður. The unpaved section of Route 425 connects Krýsuvík to Thorlákshöfn, and Hveragerði. The bend around **Herdísarvík** and **Hlíðarvatn** is beyond description, especially when the wind is howling in full force. It's advisable to do this in a 4x4 – the road across the lava field is quite rough and quite beautiful.

## TREKKING IN REYKJANES

That mountain you keep seeing no matter where you go in Reykjanes is **Mt Keilir** (379m). The sloping triangle shape is compelling, and a climb to the top offers you the best view of the peninsula. To get there, take the lava rock road south from Route 41. There's a car park at Lambafell. Mt Keilir is also part of the Reykjavegur.

The **Reykjavegur** is a 1,000-year-old trail that winds through the lava from the Reykjanesvíti lighthouse all the way to Thingvellir (130km). Throughout history, Icelanders in Reykjavík used the path to go to and from the Althing in summer. For most people, the path takes seven days, so it's not a light endeavour. On the other hand, it takes you past the very best of Reykjanes: all the lava fields, the strange formations, numerous geothermal areas, low volcanic plugs, crater rows, and open fissures. Take a quality map with you, and a good tent. Low-impact, wild camping is permitted along this route, except at the Blue Lagoon, where campers congregate next to Mt Thórbjarnarfell (231m).

SEATTLE
HELSINKI
TRONDHEIM
STOCKHOLM
OSLO
ICELAND
BERGEN
GOTHENBURG
STAVANGER
COPENHAGEN
BERLIN
BILLUND
HAMBURG
FRANKFURT
REYKJAVIK
AMSTERDAM
MUNICH
MINNEAPOLIS / ST. PAUL
GLASGOW
MANCHESTER
BRUSSELS
MILAN
LONDON
PARIS
BARCELONA
TORONTO
ALICANTE
MADRID
NEW YORK
BOSTON
HALIFAX
WASHINGTON D.C.
ORLANDO
YOUR NATURAL CHOICE
TO ICELAND AND BEYOND
Icelandair, the national carrier of Iceland since 1937, offers three cabins of premium service featuring impressive new leather seats, personal in-flight entertainment and non-stop flights to Keflavik from North America, Scandinavia, The United Kingdom and Continental Europe.
+ To book tickets, contact your travel agent or go to www.icelandair.com
ICELANDAIR
WWW.ICELANDAIR.COM

# 7

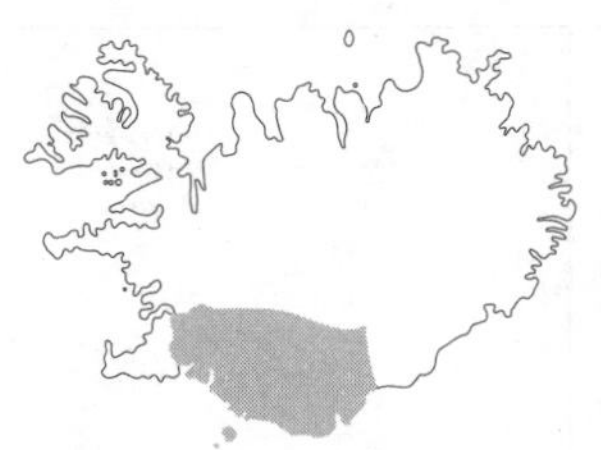

# Suðurland (South Iceland)

The beautiful south is the most developed and densely populated part of Iceland outside Reykjavík, which means it attracts the most tourists. Thankfully, that doesn't disqualify the region from feeling totally exotic in places. You don't have to go far to capture huge mountains, some of Iceland's great glaciers and Iceland's highly active volcanoes (Hekla and Katla). Powerful rivers pulse through bright-green valleys and scenic waterfalls break all along the coastal rim. With good reason, the south is popular among travellers, but don't be too much of a foreigner and assume 'south' means sunny. Truth be told, much of the region is flat farmland that suffers from bad weather. What's special about the south is the mix of square hayfields at the edge of volcanic wastelands and how such well-known sites like Thingvellir and Geysir are offset with unfamiliar hinterland the likes of Landmannalaugar and Thjórsdalur. Truly, the south is a wide and diverse region. If you think these views are spectacular, just keep going.

## GETTING AROUND

There are more roads in the south than in any other part of Iceland and they all connect to Route 1. Driving around is fairly easy and taking time to explore this part of Iceland is extremely rewarding. As always, buses are tricky, changing slightly with the season. The main bus routes (*www.bsi.is*) come and go from Reykjavík along three main trajectories: to Gullfoss (via Thingvellir and Geysir), to Skaftafell (all along Route 1) and southwest to Thórlaskhöfn (via Selfoss). In summer, highland buses connect the more obscure inland destinations like Thórsmörk.

## THINGVELLIR NATIONAL PARK

Thingvellir is only a mossy field outlined by a crumbling cliff at the edge of a pristine lake, yet the clefted landscape represents the birthplace of the Icelandic nation. As the country's first national park, Thingvellir commemorates both the political and natural foundations of Iceland. Historically, Thingvellir marks the spot where a horde of rogue settlers first gathered as the nation of Iceland and met as a democratic legislature for close to a millennium. Geologically, the valley floor marks the mid-Atlantic fault line from which the land of Iceland unfolded. Today, the valley is a run of small gorges, lumpy rocks covered with strange mosses and lichens, and a grassy plain interrupted only by spring-fed streams and the myriad pathways trodden for centuries by Viking ghosts. No other place in Iceland feels so solemn and ancient, and it is the colour and mood of the place that make Thingvellir the most visited natural attraction outside Reykjavík.

Most images of Thingvellir depict the epicentre cluster of houses and the church next to the imperial *lögberg* ('law rock'), but the sizeable national park encompasses

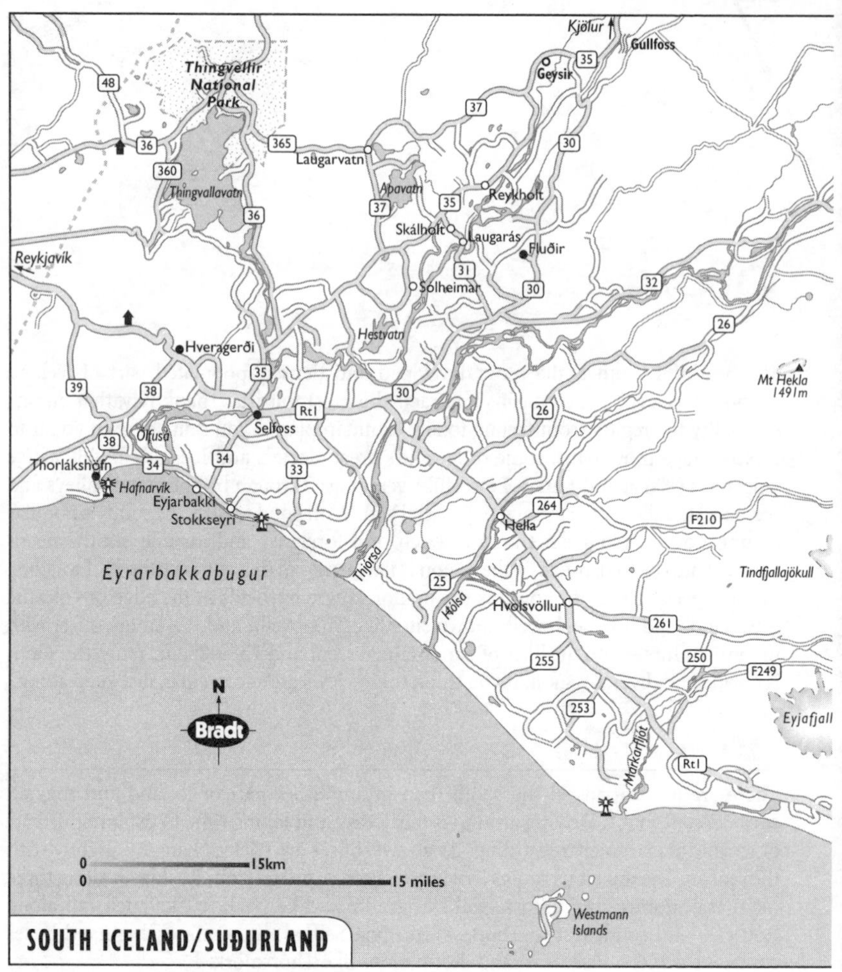


the entire northern half of the lake and all the mountains and lava fields beyond. Thingvallavatn (Thingvellir Lake) is the largest natural lake in Iceland (83km$^2$) and probably the most tranquil. Here the melting ice of faraway glaciers is filtered through miles and miles of volcanic rock before the purest water flows directly into the lake from underground springs. The result is a deep (over 100m), clear, body of water that supports a vibrant ecosystem like no other.

The significance of Thingvellir as a destination lies in its great symbolism and its serenity. It is commonly thought that if Reykjavík is the country's head then Thingvellir is its heart. Indeed there is poetry in the notion of a national congress at the edge of two continents and I doubt anyone can truly understand Iceland without visiting this spot. The natural panorama is equally important and Thingvellir is the rare Icelandic landscape where each of the four seasons is reflected so vividly and separately. Proximity to the capital helps – those lacking time but longing to escape the city can easily get to Thingvellir and 'see some of the country'. Alas, the popular tourist circuit treats the park as a two-hour layover to elsewhere, which is a pity. In the olden days, travellers came and stayed for six weeks.

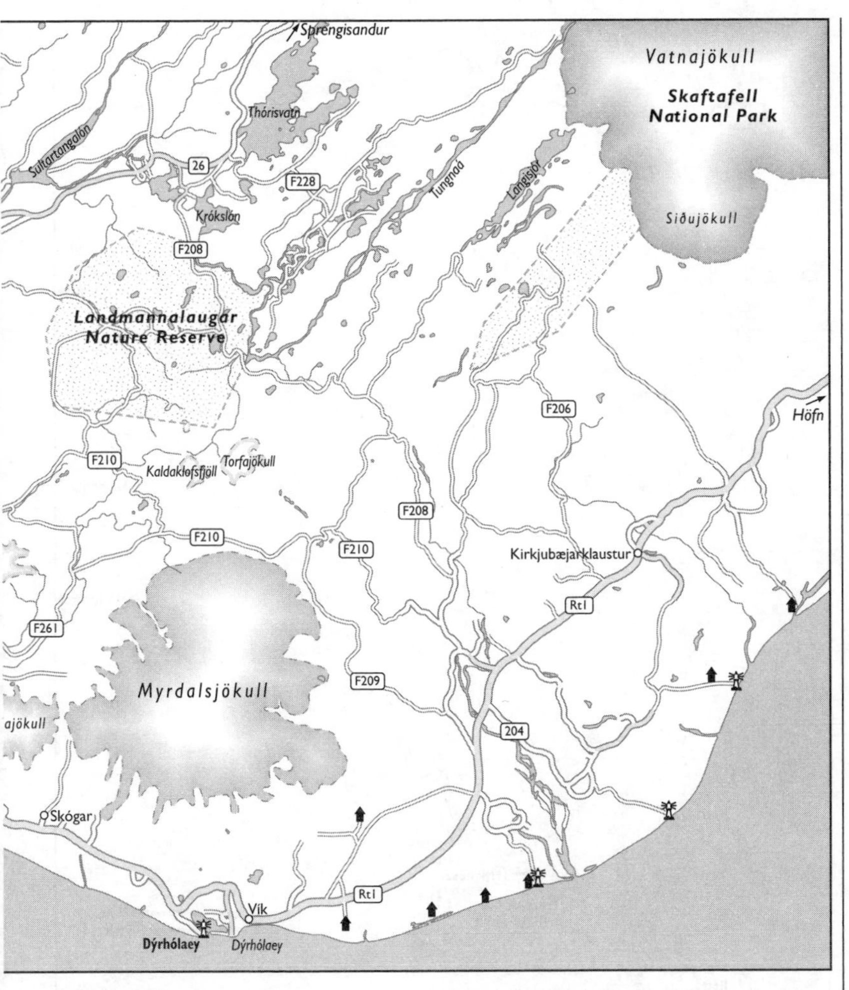


**HISTORY** Iceland's parliament, or Althing (see page 7) was founded at Thingvellir in AD930. The first gathering followed a mutual agreement by the earliest settlers that Iceland would not have a king or be a kingdom, but would take the form of a commonwealth (*Þjóðveldið*). All of the local councils, or 'things', would meet once a year to make judgements, discuss current events and pass new laws. Thingvellir became the chosen spot for this general assembly for several reasons – besides the conducive terrain, the valley lies at the crossroads at the south and west corners of Iceland and the overland Kjölur route. Summertime allowed for convenient travel from all over the country, and the Althing was typically held for a six-week period in June and July.

The outdoor setting did not prevent the Althing from developing into a very sophisticated government for Iceland. The *lögrétta* served as the Althing's active legislative council, comprising three *goðar* (chiefs) to represent each district – a total of 39 members. The *lögsögumaður* ('law-speaker') was elected by the council for a term of three years and was the only public official to receive payment for his services. It was his responsibility to know the law by heart, recite it out loud,

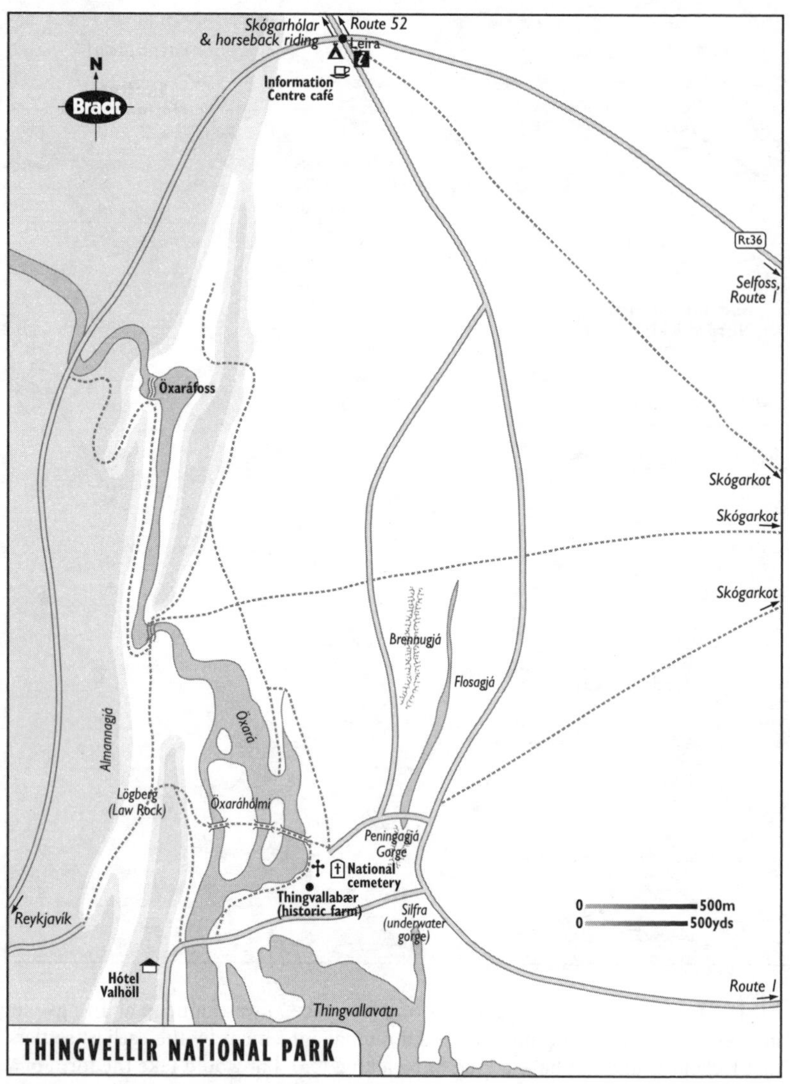


and lead the proceedings of each council meeting. Thingvellir represented total transparency in government as the hundreds of Althing attendees were allowed to listen freely to the council. Observers could not 'vote' on decisions, but everyone was allowed a chance to argue from the *lögberg* ('law rock'), the raised block of stone that overlooks the earthen amphitheatre. The system encouraged lively political debate, and the sagas are filled with tales of men who wait patiently for their turn to disagree or compromise. Women attended the Althing and could present cases before the body, but they were not active participants in the legislative process.

In a country divided by distance and difficult weather, the annual summer gathering at Thingvellir allowed universal interaction among otherwise disparate settlers. Marriages were negotiated, alliances were forged, business ventures were plotted and land and horses were traded. The people of Iceland became the nation of Iceland at Thingvellir. It was here that Icelandic became a standardised spoken language, the culture and customs of Iceland were established, and Icelanders first achieved self-determination.

That all changed after 1273, when Icelanders became subject to the King of Norway (see page 20) and adopted the Norwegian 'Ironside' codex. This altered the function of the Althing to some degree, but did not affect the spirit of the annual gathering. For the next 500 years the Althing met annually, despite their waning political authority. The last official Althing session at Thingvellir took place in 1798, after which the body was formally disbanded. It was re-established (albeit nominally) in 1848, and was moved to its present location in Reykjavík in 1874.

In celebration of the Althing's millennial anniversary, Thingvellir was made a national park in 1930 – the first such 'protected area' in Iceland. Reviews were mixed: some appreciated the special status the park afforded, others saw it as a lame consolation prize from a Danish crown that would never grant full independence. The more momentous occasion came on 17 June 1944, when close to 30,000 Icelanders gathered at Thingvellir to declare the independent Republic of Iceland. Ever since, Thingvellir has been the site of all sombre and sacred national commemorations, like the millennial celebration of Christianity in 2000. Thingvellir was christened a UNESCO World Heritage Site in 2004.

**GEOLOGY** Thingvellir represents a divergent rift valley within the Mid-Atlantic Ridge, where two plates are pulling apart in opposite directions. Other than the Great Rift Valley in east Africa, Thingvellir is the only place on earth where 'seafloor spreading' can be witnessed on land. The phenomenon is most evident when looking down into the valley from up high, with the flat lava plains laid out between the visible edges of each plate. At Thingvellir, the plates are moving apart at about 7mm per year – getting technical, the Eurasian plate is moving eastward at a rate of 3mm per year, and the American plate at 4mm per year. Over the past 10,000 years, the valley has expanded its width by 70m, while the valley floor has subsided some 40m. Continental drifts make for countless fissures that break up the otherwise flat valley. Also, despite its calm appearance, Thingvellir exhibits a violent volcanic past. The most prominent of these volcanoes is the ice-covered Mt Skjaldbreiður (1,060m) to the northeast.

**GETTING THERE AND AWAY** From Reykjavík, Route 36 takes you to the northern end of the park. There is no official public transportation to Thingvellir, but with all the tour groups that come year round, it's not too difficult to catch a bus.

## TOURIST INFORMATION

**Tourist information** Leirar, next to the campsite; 482 2660; e thingvellir@thingvellir.is; www.thingvellir.is; May–Oct 09.00–19.00 daily, Nov–Apr 09.00–17.00 daily

## WHERE TO STAY

**Hótel Valhöll** (30 rooms) Thingvellir; 480 7100; e hotelvalholl@hotelvalholl.is; www.hotelvalholl.is. Crafty businessmen wasted no time in opening an exclusive boutique hotel right next to the law rock. The sprawling country residence seems simply charming on the outside but is quite the luxury hideaway on the inside. Common spaces are sleek & modern, while the individual rooms feel intimate, dainty, & historic. Only some rooms have their own individual (but cramped) bathrooms with showers. Significant discounts available in winter. Amazing b/fast inc. **$$$$**

**Skógarhólar** Thingvellir; 566 7600; e trvhorse@centrum.is; www.centrum.is/travelhorse. Located about 3km north of the

Leira information centre, this age-old horse farm offers horseriding & spartan sleeping-bag accommodation. Priority is given to booked horseriders, though all are welcome. Showers & camping also available. **$**

**Camping** The park's main campsite is right across the car park from the information centre (*482 2660;* **$**). It is one of the largest campsites in the country, with plenty of space for tents and caravans. Showers, indoor laundry room, and semi-sanitary bathrooms.

**WHERE TO EAT** The in-house restaurant at **Hótel Valhöll** (*08.00–22.00 daily; mains from 2,500ISK;* **$$$$**) is home to a prize-winning chef who performs the basic duties of Icelandic cuisine with extraordinary finesse. The freshwater fish (salmon, trout, and char) are a noted speciality and the three-course chef's tasting menu is a must for gourmets.

The **information centre** runs a small café that serves coffee, pastries and sandwiches.

**WHAT TO SEE** Tourists at Thingvellir always seem to be in a bit of a daze, as if unsure about what it is they're supposed to be looking at. A constant barage of tour buses doesn't help the situation much, though the 'tour' that most experience is fairly straightforward: **Almannagjá** (or 'all man's gorge') is the tallest and most visible cliff face and the original backdrop to the Althing. This rock face is essentially the edge of the North American plate, viewed best up close. The Icelandic flag flies above the **lögberg** ('law rock'), surrounded by a 'look-but-don't touch' wooden walkway. Most visitors follow the path and the trail that links the shelf above with the plain below. The **Öxará** ('axe') River meanders over the lava field (Kerlingahraun) and then tumbles over the cliff's edge at the waterfall **Öxaráfoss**. Legend states that the river was diverted into the gorge to provide fresh-flowing water to attendees of the Althing – a believable tale given the landscape.

The cluster of buildings on the river's edge consists of the church and **Thingvallabær**, a five-gabled farmhouse designed (by Guðjón Samúelsson) as a nostalgic tribute for the 1930 celebrations. It is now the official summer residence of Iceland's sitting prime minister. The present-day Thingvellir **church** was built in 1859 on the same spot as the first church, constructed at the adoption of Christianity in AD1000. In moments of bad weather, the Althing would meet inside the church. Interestingly, the interior strays from some of the more traditional features of an Icelandic church (*summer 09.00–19.30*). Encircled by lava rock, Iceland's **national cemetery** (*Þjóðargrafreitur*) was added to the church grounds in 1939 as a final resting place for the country's heroes. Einar Benediktsson (see page 39) and Jónas Hallgrímsson (see page 39) are both buried there. Twice a day (on weekdays), park rangers give free guided tours (1 hour) in English explaining the history and natural world of Thingvellir. Groups gather by the church.

To capture the real sense of Thingvellir, it is imperative to wander among the gorges and fissures. Footbridges cross **Öxaráhólmi**, the flat, grassy island in the middle of the river. In the past, this was the approved site for duels, as neither party could run away (the old Icelandic word for 'duel', *hólmganga*, means 'march to the island'). **Flosagjá** ('Flosi's gorge') reveals groundwater just before it flows into the lake. An offshoot, **Peningagjá** ('penny gorge'), is filled with the pennies of well-wishers. A parallel gorge (without water) is **Brennugjá** ('burn gorge') where sorcerers were burned to death.

## DIVING AT THINGVELLIR

Exploring the underwater splendours of Thingvallavatn is an extraordinary adventure unlike any other. For starters, such pure, cool, and naturally filtered water offers incredible visibility – up to 150m. The view is far more lucid than any tropical sea and taking in the submerged scenery through such sunny blue water seems clearer than on land. Blocks of basalt walls and untouched sandy bottoms are decorated with the strangest algae growths in pink, purple and neon green. It is beautiful, if not slightly frigid, but where else can you pull your regulator out of your mouth and take such a refreshing drink at the bottom of a lake?

Water temperature at Thingvallavatn averages a chilly 3°C, so obviously a drysuit is necessary (the constant current prevents ice from forming). Diving below 30m is prohibited, but that poses no limitations on the experience. Iceland's premier diving spot is in the fissure of Silfra, the watery gap just within sight of the farm and church. Diving in the rocky channel takes you right inside the Mid-Atlantic Ridge. Swimming between two tectonic plates is pretty awesome. Another popular dive site is the fissure of Davíðsgjá, over on the northeast corner of the lake. This rift is equally beautiful, but a little more complex to access. For an all-inclusive (equipment, guide and transportation) organised tour, contact **Dive Iceland** (*699 3000; e hedinn@kafarinn.is; www.kafarinn.is*). Their two-tank dive package is pricey (about US$400) but it's definitely the experience of a lifetime (for non-divers, snorkelling tours are available at half the cost). The summertime midnight dive at Silfra is otherworldly.

Hikers will quickly appreciate the peculiarities of this landscape. Small lumpy knolls rise up out of the flat lava, and 100 or so open rock fissures make you watch your step (try not to fall inside). Foot trails criss-cross the valley floor and are wonderful for the most casual hiker. Walkers can easily reach the abandoned **farm ruins** of Skógarkot, Hrauntún, and Vatnskot. Another trail follows the north shore of the lake around the point at **Lambhagi**.

The greater portion of Thingvellir National Park lies outside the tourist hubbub and is well worth exploring. Climbers should go in for the accessible mountains, all of them volcanic ridges. **Mt Syðstasúla** (1,085m) forms the northern edge of the park and is the tallest and easiest to ascend. **Mt Ármansfell** (765m) offers less of a view, but holds great importance as the legendary home of Árman, a lost shepherd and the guardian spirit of Thingvellir. The ridge at the east end of the park is 'mount raven' or **Mt Hrafnabörg** (765m).

**WHAT TO DO** The Thingvellir interpretive centre offers an interactive multimedia display on the park and its history (*1 Apr–1 Nov 09.00–17.00*), and the adjoining information office offers local hiking maps. Walking through the deep gorges, across the lava landscape and around the lake should all take priority. No boating is allowed on the lake, but **fishing** permits are sold at the information centre. Arctic char and brown trout are your best bet.

Thingvellir is also a popular place for **horseriding**, with several day trails that offer the chance to explore some of the more dramatic areas of the park. Most tours cost just under US$100. Contact the horse farm at Skógarhólar (*Thingvellir; 566 7600; e trvhorse@centrum.is; www.centrum.is/travelhorse*) for further information.

## HVERAGERÐI

The signs for Hveragerði are the first ones travellers see after leaving Reykjavík, less than 40km west of the capital. The small, unaffected Icelandic town happens to lie next to the Varmá River and right on top of a highly active geothermal zone. Free heat and low-cost living made this an artists' haven after World War II, and there was a time when any Icelandic poet, musician, or painter of note was spending time in Hveragerði. Natural heat also enables a bunch of steamy greenhouses where vegetables and flowers grow in a manmade tropical cocoon. Today, indoor agriculture is a major earner in the town. For its proximity, its nature, and its great geothermal springs, Hveragerði makes a soothing year-round destination – especially for those who enjoy a good soak. It's also fast becoming a base from which to explore the 'golden circle', as well as a convenient last-night stay for travellers wanting to wind down before their next-day departure.

**TOURIST INFORMATION** Hveragerði is home to the south Iceland regional information centre, located at Sunnumörk, right off Route 1 (*483 4601; e tourinfo@hveragerdi.is; www.southiceland.is; 09.00–17.00 Mon–Fri, 12.00–16.00 Sat/Sun*). Even if you're on your way to somewhere else, it's not a bad place to stop; & there are a number of ways to enjoy the abundant hot water. The outdoor swimming pool is tempting, as is the natural steam bath & the bubbling hot pot right next to the river.

### WHERE TO STAY

**Hótel Örk** (85 rooms) Breiðamörk 1C; 483 7000; e info@hotel-ork.is; www.hotel-ork.is. This sprawling, new 'country' hotel touts itself as the chosen weekend getaway for city-dwellers, but feels a lot like most family holiday hangouts. Rooms are sizeable & private, & a large staff takes care of all your requests. The hotel also features a geothermal resort, with a number of hot pools, waterslides, & spas. A 9-hole golf course & tennis courts round off the ensemble. B/fast inc. **$$$$**

**Frost & Fire** (14 rooms) Hverahvammur; 483 4959; e info@frostogfuni.is; www.frostogfuni.is. This friendly & high-quality boutique hotel stands out for its dedication to comfort & good taste. Luxury beds grace the light-filled rooms (all with private showers) Recommended. B/fast (fresh & organic) inc. **$$$**

**Frumskógar** (25 rooms) Frumskógar 3; m 896 2780; e gisting@frumskogar.is; www.frumskogar.is. Located on the 'street of the poets' (just blocks from the ring road) Frumskógar is a happy collection of houses & apartments that offer clean & reliable accommodation. Each is fitted out to ensure optimal relaxation for tired drivers. Some are self-contained, others offer more of a communal feel (though all apartments have private bathrooms). Kitchen use available & breakfast is served for a cost. **$$**

**Camping** (*Reykjamörk; 483 4605; e tourinfo@hveragerdi.is; www.hveragerdi.is;* **$**) Big, sprawling campsite among the steamy banks of the Varmá River. Convenient amenities, clean, and not so crowded.

### WHERE TO EAT

**Hótel Örk** Breiðamörk 1C; 483 7000; e info@hotel-ork.is; www.hotel-ork.is; 08.00–22.00 daily. The hotel restaurant does Icelandic specialties with banquet-style flair. Flavourful soups are prominent & the main dishes represent a florid tribute to fish, lamb, & more. *Mains from 1,800ISK.* **$$$**

**Kjöt og Kúnst** Breiðamörk 21; 483 5010; e heilsuk@eyjar.is; 11.00–21.00 Sun–Thu, 11.00–midnight Fri/Sat. Artsy café in town with a festive atmosphere & food to match. A wide variety of cuisine, but the meat & veggie plates are the most trustworthy. *Mains from 1,600ISK.* **$$$**

**Kidda Rót** Sunnumörk 2; 552 8002; e rotarinn@simnet.is; 11.00–22.00 daily. Inside the shopping plaza, this casual café serves surprisingly good food. Besides the typical pizza & burgers, the lamb steak & a few Chinese dishes are a pleasant change from more average menus. *Mains from 1,700ISK.* $$

**Self-catering** Try the **Bonus** grocery store (*Sunnumörk 2; 482 1818; e hvera@bonus.is; www.bonus.is; 10.00–18.30 daily*), or **Hverabakarí Bakery** (*Breiðamörk 10; 483 4879; 10.00–20.00 daily*). Also, the health clinic (*www.hnlfi.is*) serves an amazing vegetarian spread (see following section).

**WHAT TO SEE AND DO** Hot springs! That's why people come to Hveragerði and why any kind of weather is fine. The main **geothermal area** is located right in the town centre, but for safety reasons is only open at certain times (*Hveramörk 13; 09.00–11.00 & 17.00–20.00 Mon–Thu, 14.00–16.00 Sat/Sun*). A path treads lightly between the colourful hot pools, fumaroles, and small geysers – all of which are too hot for bathing (60–95°C). Instead, enjoy the hot water at the town's public outdoor **swimming pool** (*Laugaskarð; 483 4113; summer 08.00–20.00, winter 14.00–18.00*), or for something more medical, try the **spa** at the NLFÍ Health and Rehabilitation Clinic (*Grænumörk 10; 483 0300; e heilsu@hnlfi.is; www.hnlfi.is*). Holistic health care treatments range from mud and herbal baths, acupuncture, and massage. If natural, outdoor springs are what you're looking for, then follow Breiðamörk out of town and continue on the trail northwards. Once the road ends (about 2km), it's another 3km into **Reykjadalir** ('smoky valley')

## THE GOLDEN CIRCLE

The most touted tour in all Iceland is the 'golden circle', a well-trodden path from Reykjavík to the highlights of south Iceland, namely **Thingvellir**, the waterfall at **Gullfoss**, and the geysers of **Geysir**. The tour was likely invented around the same time as the motor car showed up in Iceland – it seems the perfect group of attractions to squeeze into a single day's drive and make it back to the capital in time for dinner. If you're on your own and without plans, it is quite simple to just show up at the bus station (BSÍ) in Reykjavík on any given morning and join one of the independent bus tours. Otherwise, tours can be arranged online or through your hotel or travel agent. Most organised packages offer transportation and guides and cost anywhere from US$60 to US$100 (depending on what's being offered). The journey lasts from five to nine hours, half of which is driving time. With so many tour operators competing for the same tour, variations are frequent. Common add-ons include places like Skálholt or Hveragerði, but that doesn't change the fact that this is the number-one day trip outside Reykjavík and that everybody's doing the same thing. While the golden circle is definitely a great introduction to Iceland's natural wonders, it pays to question tradition. Driving the circle yourself allows you to break away from the crowds and buses and add your own variations (like Laugarvatn, Flúðir, or anywhere else in the countryside). Plus two can do it on their own for less than going with an organised tour. There are plenty of different routes to choose. From Thingvellir, I suggest taking the unpaved overland Route 365 to Laugarvatn, or else drive the tour in reverse (take Route 1 past Selfoss, then turn off and follow Route 30 to Gullfoss, and track back on Route 35 via Geysir to Thingvellir.

where there are plenty of tempting pools to bathe in, all along the trail. Several national tour operators will advertise 'hot spring hunts' from Reykijavík and this is the area they visit. Several exciting and invigorating trails track through these highlands between Hveragerði and Thingvallavatn, and are known as Hengill. **Mt Hengill** (803m) offers a rare view of the volcanic landscape with its active (read hot!) landscape – stick to the trail. The volcanic craters are the most active spots, and probably the most beautiful is Nesjavellir – a colourful valley of hot springs and steam, best accessed from the southern shores of Thingvellir. If you yearn to explore the true wilds of Iceland and your time is severely limited, Hengill is the place to roam.

## GULLFOSS

The magnificent waterfall of Gullfoss marks the edge of the highland shelf, over which tumbles the roaring Hvíta River. The 'white' river seems a fitting name, given the boisterous white water, but the colour of the water dallies in between deep aquamarine to a translucent grey (from the glacial runoff), not to mention the bright rainbows in the mist. Also, Gullfoss means 'golden falls', although nobody really knows why except that out of all the falls in Iceland, they are the most highly prized.

Gullfoss is totally unique in its shape and form, with three separate levels of water divided by two separate cascades that fall perpendicular to one another, like a set of diagonal right angles in the middle of the river. The upper falls are 11m high, the lower 21m. At its peak (from July to August), some 130m$^3$/second of water is rushing over the ridge, and the earth-shaking din makes you feel utterly minuscule. The 70m-deep gorge is similar to those at Thingvellir with the exception of gushing water. A wet trail connects the lower end with the upper falls and forces you to walk through a cloud of thundering mist. Note that you'll get a better picture from faraway than up close, especially when the wind is eager to get you soaked.

The affection that Icelanders feel towards Gullfoss was heightened by the threat of losing it and the long fight that ensued to preserve this natural wonder. At the turn of the last century, British developers sought to harness the energy of the falls for its hydro-electric potential. When offered an outlandish sum for the rights to do so, the farmer who owned the land at the time, Tómas Tómasson, responded 'I won't sell my friend'. His daughter Sigriður Tómassdóttir spent the rest of her life protesting the government and hiring lawyers to combat developers. In 1939, she sold the farm to her foster brother Einar, who waited 40 more years before gifting the falls to the state as a protected area. A memorial to Sigriður now stands above the falls, showing a very serious pout on her face. For her unrelenting vision to preserve nature, she is considered a hero by conservationists worldwide.

Another great thing about Gullfoss is that you are about as close as you can get to the interior and still be on a paved road. From Gullfoss you can see the light-blue ice shield of Langjökull and the great mountain pass of Kjölur. **Mt Bláfell** (1,222m; see page 377) is the most visible peak and an impending flat table mountain in the distance.

**GETTING THERE AND AWAY** From the ring road, Route 35 goes directly to Gullfoss (about 2½ hours from Reykjavík). Bus company SBA-Norðurleið (*www.sba.is*) makes a daily stop to and from Gullfoss on its cross-country Kjölur route, while Trex (*www.trex.is*) makes as many stops as they have tours for the day.

**WHERE TO STAY AND EAT** The tourist information centre at the falls has an informative exhibit on the geology of the falls and surrounding area. Next door is the recommended **Gulfoss Café** (*Gulfosskaffi;* ☎ *486 6500;* e *gulfoss@gulfoss.is; www.gulfoss.is;* ⏲ *summer 09.00–21.00, winter 09.00–18.00 daily; mains from 1,400 ISK;* **$$**). Catering to the tourist palate, the menu features a robust Icelandic meat soup, lamb steak, sandwiches, coffee, and cakes, served by a friendly and good-natured staff. **Hótel Gulfoss** (*16 rooms;* ☎ *486 8979;* e *info@hotelgulfoss.is; www.hotelgulfoss.is;* **$$$$**) is located at the beginning of the gorge (before the falls). Situated in a remote but peaceful area, the farm-like atmosphere is conducive to those headed across the interior and those who simply enjoy the seclusion of the unadulterated countryside. Rooms are quite plush and well furnished, all with private bathrooms. A hot tub out back is a plus, as is the dependable restaurant and cool antler keyrings. In nearby Myrkholt, *Skalínn Guesthouse* (*32 beds;* m *895 9500; www.gljasteinn.is;* **$**) offers sleeping-bag accommodation only, hot showers, discounted prices for children, laundry facilities, housing for horses, and a guest kitchen for ridiculously low prices.

## GEYSIR

When you visit Geysir, you are visiting the very first recognised tourist attraction in Iceland (a travellers' guide published in the late 1700s gives an exhilarating account of the eruption and it is early British tourists who introduced the word into English). The world's original geyser was formed at the end of the 13th century, when earthquakes jumbled up the underground channels of hot springs, causing them 'to gush' or *gjósa*. A geyser is quite literally 'a gusher', and the great geyser of Geysir has been known to shoot boiling water more than 70m high. Still, it is a somewhat unreliable phenomenon, most active following an earthquake. For centuries, the surges have increased or decreased, and in 1915 the main geyser simply stopped. Over the years, attempts were made to provoke an eruption, digging tunnels and pouring soap into the pool to cause it to bubble over. Fortunately, all that nonsense stopped when the earthquake of 2000 kicked natural processes back into gear. Geysir was erupting with regularity until around 2005, when it again waned significantly. At the moment it is dormant (just a giant, quivering, circular pool) but that could change at any moment.

Today's ultimate Iceland geyser photo-op is **Strokkur**, or 'churn', which erupts at a height of under 20m every seven to eight minutes. The bubbling turquoise pool and churning gush of hot water *is* impressive. Trails meander through the surrounding geothermal field, a compact collection of hot pools, fumaroles and geysers. The hot pools of **Blesi** (one turquoise and clear and another milky blue) are truly beautiful, but devilishly hot like everything else. Stay on the trail and don't get burned. As expected, there's a good deal of tourist fanfare around Geysir, with large groups coming and going non-stop in summer. Few stay for more than 30 minutes, so it is definitely worth spending a little longer and following the trails up into the hillsides. Look closely so as not to miss all the hissing cracks in the ground, and the boiling water trickling through mineral-streaked streambeds.

**GETTING THERE AND AWAY** From Reykjavík, Route 1 then Route 35 take you straight to Geysir (2 hours), a mere 20 minutes away from Gullfoss. SBA-Norðurleið (*www.sba.is*) makes a 20-minute stop on its highland route (just enough time for a picture), while Trex (*www.trex.is*) makes as many stops as they have tours for the day.

 **WHERE TO STAY AND EAT** All activity centres on the **Geysir Hotel** (*24 rooms; Geysir;* ☎ *480 6800;* e *geysir@geysircenter.is; www.geysircenter.is*), right across the street from the geysers. Non-guests can get tourist information, gas, food, and anything else at the travel centre next to the car park. The hotel's well-dressed rooms are situated inside duplex cabins that are private and cosy, but less special when it's drizzling and you have to trek up a hillside in the mud. The luxury suites (**$$$$**) include gigantic jacuzzi tubs and rich, queen-size beds. The regular rooms are still quite nice and priced quite reasonably – for Iceland (**$$$**). An outdoor swimming pool and hot tub are open to hotel guests. The big breakfast buffet costs extra. The central **Geysir Hotel Restaurant** (◷ *08.00–22.00 daily*) is a large, atmospheric tourist eatery that behaves much like a frilly gourmet. Dishes are Icelandic, somewhat extravagant, but very delicious. The popular lunch buffet is yet another spread of Icelandic delicacies (not so delicately) aimed at tour buses. For dinner, the three-course set menu is a very good deal (about US$45) considering the high quality of the food. **Camping** is also permitted in the designated area. **Guesthouse Geysir** (*24 beds;* ☎ *486 8733;* e *agustath@visir.is, www.geysirgolf.is;* **$$$**) is a bit further down the road, offers sleeping-bag accommodation, is cheaper, newly renovated and a little more personable. Plus, it comes with a nine-hole golf course.

## SKÁLHOLT

Iceland's very own 'Vatican' is no more than a simple white church atop a lonely country hill, and yet the bulk of Icelandic history is tied up in this one quiet spot. The bishop's 'see' for the whole of Iceland was set up in Skálholt in 1056 and for the next 100 years, Skálholt held the record for the largest town in Iceland. In 1109, Iceland was divided into two dioceses, the north being led by a second bishop at Hólar (see page 323). Still, Skálholt remained the central office for all ecclesiastical (and some political) affairs for over seven centuries. Until the Reformation, 32 Catholic bishops served at Skálholt. After inciting a civil war and fighting Protestantism by

### ST THORLÁKUR (1133–93): PATRON SAINT OF ICELAND

Born to a family of landowners facing financial ruin, Thorlákur Thórhallson was still educated by the most learned men of the commonwealth. At the age of 18, he was ordained a priest for the parish of Kirkubæjarklaustur and later travelled to France and England to study theology. Upon returning to Iceland, he refused an arranged marriage and the fortune it would bring, founding instead an Augustinian monastery on the south coast. The literalist monk followed a rigorous daily regime and ruffled the feathers of the rest of the clergy by demanding total celibacy (a new concept at the time). In 1174, The Althing elected Thorlákur as Bishop of Skálholt. In his 20 years of office, he fought against the practice of individual Church-ownership, the buying and selling of offices, and aristocratic patronage. Thus he managed to consolidate the nation's wealth and set the ball rolling for the Church's later domination of Iceland. He died on the evening of 23 December 1193, a night that is now celebrated throughout Iceland as St Thorlákur's Feast, or Þorláksmessa (see page 37). His skull was encased in a silver trophy and kept at Skálholt for centuries, and the Althing canonised him immediately. Only in 1984 did Pope John Paul II approve the ruling and designate Thorlákur the Patron Saint of Iceland.

*above left* The cotton flower, or *fífa*, grows in great abundance in valleys and on islands (B/D) page 50

*above right* Iceland's fields of purple lupins (*Lupinus nootkanensis*), or *lúpína*, are beautiful but controversial, as they are considered an invasive weed from Alaska (So/D) page 50

*below left* Lichen – a few hundred species of moss cover the hills and valleys of Iceland with their densely packed leaves (CC) page 49

*below right* Lava rocks and Icelandic moss (*Cetraria islandica*), Reykjanes; Icelandic moss is the commonest type of brown-green lichen that grows everywhere and anywhere (CC) page 49

*above left* Kittiwakes (*Rissa tridactyla*) nest right in the middle of the cliffs and hatch the fluffiest, all-white babies of any bird in Iceland (R/D) page 56

*above right* The great skua (*Catharacta skua*) is the bully of the seabird schoolyard (KK/D) page 54

*left* The Arctic tern (*Sterna paradisaea*) migrates huge distances – more than any other bird in the world (CC) page 53

*below left* Snow buntings (*Plectrophenax nivalis*) are quite common in the highlands and you will hear them chirping a song before you see them (M/D) page 58

*below right* Bird cliffs in the midnight sun, Látrabjarg; more than one million birds will cling to the sheer and vertical surface (AE) page 296

*above right* More than 80,000 Icelandic horses live in Iceland today, all of them descended from a controlled group first carried over by the settlers (Re/D) page 60

*right* The harbour seal (*Phoca vitulina*) is the most common species of seal in Iceland (SS) page 62

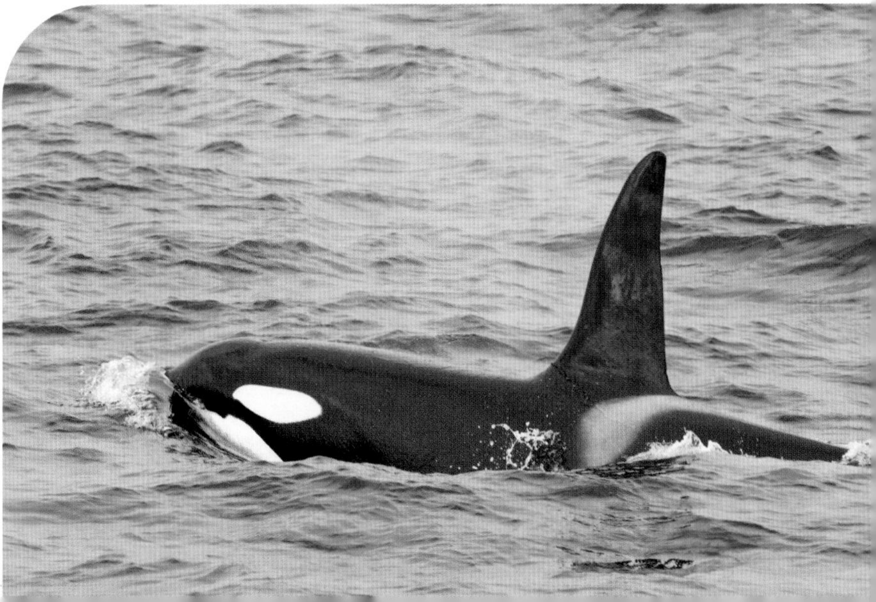

*below* Orcas (*Orcinus orca*), or killer whales, are traditionally most likely to be seen in the East Fjords (SS) page 63

*above* Village church, Flatey – visitors must see the church's amazing ceiling, which has a dark and splendid mural depicting the island's history (SS) page 304

*left* The picturesque city of Akureyri is a great place to visit, either as a destination in and of itself or as a home base from which to explore some of Iceland's wildest landscapes (SS) page 332

*below* Puffin signposts on Heimaey in the Westmann Islands; with about 5,000 people, Heimaey is one of the largest 'cities' outside Reykjavík (AC/A) page 229

*above* **Húsavík has a fair claim to being Iceland's first settlement** (MT/D) page 377

*right* **The town of Ísafjörður has an old-fashioned appeal that sets it apart** (SS) page 281

*below* **Sauðárkrókur – the town's name means 'sheep's corner', a reference to the name of the river (Sauðá) that passes by the harbour on the base of the fjord** (SS) page 319

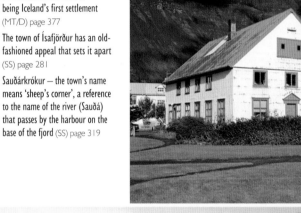

*above* Iceland's east coast is a rugged fringe of long, V-shaped fjords in between rows of layered, pointed mountains (So/D) page 405

*left* Nobody should miss the wonders of Jökulsárlón, the only place in Iceland where you are guaranteed to see icebergs up close (Np/A) page 421

*below* The strange pseudo-craters at Skútustaðir are all that's left of early volcanic lakes that were vaporised by the same eruption that created the present-day Lake Mývatn (CC) page 374

*right* The perfectly straight Skógarfoss waterfall drops 60m over a green cliff after tumbling all the way down from the glacier above (SS) page 246

*below* The perfect row of square, rock pillars known as Gerðuberg, at Ytri-Rauðamelur, is an example of columnar basalt at its finest (AE) page 264

*above left* The Northern Lights (*norðurljós*) are just one of Iceland's many outstanding natural phenomena and reason enough to travel there in wintertime (Sol/D) page 44

*above right* The mountains, ice and steam at Kerlingarfjöll make it a remarkable hiking destination (SS) page 434

*left* Pedalling around Iceland is a totally thrilling endeavour (SS) page 98

*below* Wildlife watching at Vigur Island; birds are always close by, including the few thousand eider ducks which nest there year after year (SS) page 286

the book and the sword, Jón Arason (see page 21) was beheaded at Skálholt with two of his sons. A stone memorial marks the spot where his head left his shoulders. Today, a sarcastic and commonly used rebuttal in Icelandic is *Veit ég það, Sveinki* ('I know that, little Svein!'). Legend claims these were the last words of Jón Arason in response to a young priest (Svein) who tried to comfort the condemned bishop by reminding him that there was life after death. From 1540 to 1796, Skálholt served as the southern headquarters of the Lutheran Church in Iceland, during which time 13 Protestant bishops served. In 1801, a single diocese was formed in Reykjavík for the whole of Iceland and Skálholt became a centre for spiritual education.

Ten different churches have stood at Skálholt – the first, a simple turf-style *hof*, later replaced with a gigantic wooden cathedral imported by ship from Norway (which later burned down). The slender white structure you see today was built in 1963 and somehow manages to win the affections of even the staunchest critics of modern architecture. The minimalist forms, straight vertical lines, and an overwhelming devotion to white and black might seem austere, but inside, the church is totally calm and compelling in its beauty. Visiting Skálholt is an easy detour from the golden circle route (just off Route 35). A museum of sorts recounts Church history, and the crypt beneath the church displays the sarcophagus of Bishop Páll Jónsson, the 7th Bishop of Iceland (from 1195 to 1215) whose skeleton was accidentally discovered in the digging of these foundations. For incredible summer concerts, visit the choir's website (*www.sumartonleikar.is*).

## LAUGARVATN

'Bathing waters' is a hot spring and lake halfway between Thingvellir and the geothermal fields of Geysir. For its proximity to the Althing, the warm waters were a traditional bathing stop for delegates travelling across Iceland. The lake's water temperature is around 15°C, which by foreigners' standards, makes it the only 'swimmable' lake in Iceland. That fact opens up possibilities for otherwise non-existent activities like windsurfing, though the highlight is the **Old Steam Bath** (*Gufubaðið; Lindarbraut 1; ☎ 486 1235; e gufan@gamlagufan.is; www.gamlagufan.is; ⏲ Jun–Aug 12.00–21.00 daily, winter 14.00–18.00 Sat/Sun; entrance 350ISK*). Built in 1930, the wooden enclave captures the sulphuric steam as it hisses out of the earth, creating a natural sauna and steam bath. Beloved by locals, tradition dictates sweating your lungs out in the dark cubicle before running headlong into the balmy lake. It's definitely worth the stop, and for backpackers, there are several buses every day from Reykjavík (on their way to Geysir).

### WHERE TO STAY AND EAT

**Efsti-Dalur** (14 rooms) ☎ 486 1186; e efstadal@yjar.is; www.efstadal.is. This modern sheep farm is set in some truly wondrous countryside. The family home is clean & well kept, with several large, furnished rooms (some with private bath). A great base for anyone doing the golden circle route. B/fast inc. **$$$**

**Hótel Edda** Manages 2 separate locations in Laugarvatn (e edda@hoteledda.is; www.hoteledda.is).

**IKI Laugarvatn** (26 rooms) ☎ 444 4820; ⏲ summer only. In a calm setting right on the lake, this school/hotel is frequently used as a quiet base from which to explore the south by car. All rooms have private bathrooms & the temporary restaurant is surprisingly good. **$$$**

**ML Laugarvatn** (99 rooms) ☎ 444 4810. Refitted school in the town, not far from the lake & steam baths. True to the Functionalist creed of Edda, one-third of the rooms have private showers, the rest share. A big dining hall/kitchen serves guests well-planned meals & you will likely be rubbing shoulders with large groups. **$$$**

**Dalsel** (70 beds) ☎ 486 1215; e laugarvatn@simnet.is; www.laugarvatnhostel.is; ⏲ all year. Probably the best youth hostel in south Iceland, Dalsel is within walking distance of the lake & the old steam bath. The insightful management accommodates every kind of traveller (from single backpackers to big groups to families with young children). Rooms house 1–6 people & are kept spotless; 10 rooms feature private bathrooms, the rest share. Kitchen & laundry facilities available & there's a hot tub out back. Recommended. **$$**

**Camping** On the north end of town by the mountains (☎ *486 1155;* **$**). Hot showers, laundry and caravan space aplenty.

## WHERE TO EAT

**Linden** Lindarbraut 2; ☎ 486 1262; e lindin@laugarvatn.is; www.laugarvatn.is; ⏲ summer 11.00–23.00 daily. How wonderful it is to happen upon such a perfect little place as this! This summery restaurant features a light interior of lace tablecloths, fresh flowers & dainty curtains with a menu that knocks the socks off most tourist restaurants. It specialises in wild fish & game, hungry patrons choosing from fresh trout out of the lake, or dishes like reindeer, guillemot, veal & lamb, each in some creative sauce. The drinks & desserts menu, as well as the ambiance of the place, is fitting for afternoon tea. *Mains from 2,200ISK.* **$$$**

**N1** Laugarvatn; ☎ 440 1000; e n1@n1.is; www.n1.is; ⏲ 09.00–22.00. Attached to the petrol station is this small fast-food restaurant & grocery store: pizza, hot dogs & great hamburgers. *Mains from 700ISK.* **$**

## SELFOSS

As the main 'city' of south Iceland, Selfoss offers a functional but pleasant base for travellers to go anywhere else in the region. The sizeable population (6,000) offers visitors a number of high-quality hotel rooms, fine eating establishments, and the necessities of fuel stations, grocery stores, and banks. The 'foss' of Selfoss are the combined rapids and waterfall on the Ölfúsá River, where one of the first bridges in the country was built – spend any time in Selfoss and it's hard to rid your head of the sound of rushing water. Today, Selfoss seems an OK place to stop and re-energise before a major adventure, but just outside the town lie some welcome diversions.

A short drive south of Selfoss brings you to a curious bit of coastline and with it a number of intriguing choices. Travellers heading to the Westmann Islands (see page 228) catch the ferry at **Thorlákshöfn**, but besides the dock there's not much there. Far more interesting is the quaint seaside village of **Eyjarbakki**. With its rows of well-preserved 19th-century houses and its unhurried pace, it's a fun place to stop off – notably the regional **Folk Museum** (*Húsið;* ☎ *483 1504;* e *husid@south.is; www.husid.com;* ⏲ *Apr–Oct 11.00–17.00 daily*; *entrance 600ISK*). Built in 1765, this 'kit' house was one of the first in Iceland, home to the local Danish merchant and his large family and business. Today, the many rooms reflect Iceland in the 1870s. Next door is the **Maritime Museum** (*Sjóminjasafnið; Túngata;* ☎ *483 1504;* e *sjominjasafnid@arborg.is; www.arborg.is/sjominjasafnid;* ⏲ *Apr–Oct 11.00–17.00 daily*), although frankly it's a lot like every other maritime museum in Iceland.

Five minutes away brings you to the seaside village of **Stokkseyri**, known for its famous restaurant and the new **Ghost Centre** (*Draugasetrið; Stokkseyri; Hafnarga 9;* m *895 0020;* e *draugasetrid@draugasetrid.is;* ⏲ *summer 14.00–21.00 daily*). The ghost stories are cool, the exhibits are a little hokey, but it's all in good fun.

**GETTING THERE AND AWAY** Several buses service Selfoss from Reykjavík (1 hour) every day. To drive, simply take Route 1. The buses all stop and pick up near the main circle (Austurvegur) at the library.

## TOURIST INFORMATION

**Tourist information** Austurvegur 2; 480 1990; e info@arborg.is; www.arborg.is; Jun–Aug 10.00–19.00 daily

**WHERE TO STAY** When choosing your accommodation, be aware that that many rural guesthouses and farms that list Selfoss as an address are actually located quite far away from the town.

### In Selfoss

**Hótel Selfoss** (99 rooms) Eyrarvegur 2; 480 2500; e hotelselfoss@hotelselfoss.is; www.hotelselfoss.is. An amazingly swish & sleek Modernist hotel, the Selfoss ranks among Iceland's top-tier large-scale accommodations. Focused on design & comfort, the rooms are huge & sprawling, with ritzy bathrooms, & closet space galore. The Selfoss, with a stunning atrium and glass lift, has become the new corporate conference centre outside Reykjavík & is one of the most wheelchair-friendly hotels in the country. Despite the very aloof feel of the place, service is personable, down to earth & friendly. The restaurant is definitely worthy of mention, as is the recently opened luxury Northern Light Spa. B/fast inc. **$$$$**

**Fosstún** (32 rooms) Eyrarvegur 26; 480 1200; e fosstun@fosstun.is; www.fosstun.is. Fairly new & very sensible, this 2-storey apartment house offers travelling families & couples both independence & privacy. Each unit has a full kitchen & a bathroom with shower, with beds (sleeps 2–4); 4 rooms have been especially equipped for disabled travellers. **$$$**

**Gesthus** (22 rooms) Tjaldsvæðið; 482 3585; e gesthus@gesthus.is; www.gesthus.is. A bundle of bungalows near the town centre; each self-contained unit offers guests their own bathroom, kitchen & beds for 2–4 people. They also offer cheap camping with all the amenities you could want. **$$$**

**Menam Guesthouse** (9 rooms) Eyrarvegur 8; 482 4099; e menam@menam.is; www.menam.is. The Menam ('by the river') is above the restaurant of the same name & across the street from Hótel Selfoss. The Thai theme is soothing, the beds are comfortable, the lamps are cool, but there's no breakfast. Rooms are for 2–3 people & the staff are friendly. **$$**

**Selfoss Hostel** (60 beds) Austurvegur 28; 660 6999; e selfoss@hostel.is. Hospital-turned hostel, this place is the bomb. It's head & shoulders above other Icelandic hostels, with large rooms, a laundry, guest kitchen, hot tub, & mini gym, & a jovial staff. Private, double, & dorm rooms (sheets included). There's also a wheelchair lift. Recommended. **$$**

**Sólbakki** (4 rooms) Thórsmörk 2; 483 4212. Homely, suburban guesthouse with comfy beds & a nice attitude. Shared bathrooms. **$$**

### Outside Selfoss

**Kvóldstjarnan** (5 rooms) Eyjarbakki; m 896 6307. Clean & new looking, this guesthouse has a perfect balcony view of Mt Hekla & the infamous volcano Eyjafjallajökull. Rooms sleep 1 or 2, plus a 4-person apartment with full kitchen. B/fast is on the house. **$$$**

**Suðurgata** (3 rooms) Eyjarbakki, Eyrargata 37A; m 898 1197. Quaint, quiet, & off the beaten path. Shared bathrooms. **$$$**

**WHERE TO EAT** The culinary spirit of Selfoss relies heavily on fast food and big stores. Walking or driving up and down Austurvegur (Route 1) offers you every choice available (fried chicken, hot dogs, etc).

## In Selfoss

**Riverside** (at Hótel Selfoss) 480 2500; e hotelselfoss@hotelselfoss.is; www.hotelselfoss.is; kitchen 07.00–22.00, closes when you're gone. Chic dining in an upmarket hotel restaurant, with a spectacular view of the river. Expect Icelandic nouvelle cuisine: tiny pieces of fish, creamy risotto, intricate salads, & artsy presentation (if it didn't taste so good you'd think it was pretentious). For something more lowly, try their gourmet burgers or imaginative vegetarian ensembles. *Mains from 2,900ISK.* $$$$

**Menam** Eyrarvegur 8; 482 4099; 11.00–14.00 & 17.00–22.30 daily. Delightful Thai restaurant serving everyone's favourites, minus the MSG. *Mains from 2,190ISK.* $$$

**Pizza Islandia** Eyrarvegur 5; 486 6600; 11.00–21.00 Mon–Thu, 11.00–22.00 Fri–Sun. Far-out pizza for eat in or take out, with crazy toppings, like the Detox (chilli peppers, jalepeños, pepperoni, etc). The restaurant doubles as a local hangout during football season. *Mains from 1,180ISK.* $

## By the sea

**Hafið Bláá** Thorlákshöfn; 483 1000; e info@hafidblaa.is; www.hafidblaa.is; 11.00–22.00 daily. 'The Blue Sea' is a wistful little café overlooking the constant waves of the sea. Enjoy a cup of coffee & the view, or relax with a warming meal. Various fish soups & lobster dishes are on offer, as well as a reliable 'catch of the day' & bacalao salted cod. *Mains from 1,500ISK.* $$$

**Rauða húsið** Eyjarbakki; Buðarstígur 12; 483 3330; 11.30–23.30 Sun–Thu, 11.30–02.00 Fri/Sat. 'Red house' is another great restaurant that's famous all over Iceland. The lively café & bar offers delicious salt cod, & is known for its ability to please vegetarians. *Mains from 2,000ISK.* $$$

**Við Fjöruborðid** Stokkseyri, Eyjarbraut 3A; 483 1550; e info@fjorubordid.is; www.fjorubordid.is; summer 12.00–21.00 Sun–Thu, 12.00–22.00 Fri/Sat, winter 17.00–21.00 daily. How far will you drive for a bowl of soup? Just 15mins from Selfoss brings you to the seaside village of Stokkseyri & its outstanding gourmet restaurant, world famous & easily one of the very best in Iceland. 'By the sea' does indeed look out over the sea & provides relaxing deck chairs for you to enjoy the beach, & bonfires to keep you warm. The indoor atmosphere is entirely warm, with all energy focused on people enjoying good food. The restaurant's winning formula is simplicity & the clever Icelandic lobster (a slimmer version of the yummy crustacean). The menu is short but eloquent: a pot of lobster tails grilled in garlic butter & local herbs, served with fresh-baked bread & ingenious dipping sauces. It's heavenly & filling, yes, but don't leave without trying the creamy lobster soup – for this is nothing less than a bowl full of velvety perfection (bliss!). You can also order lamb or steak, but why? With Icelanders driving all day to eat here, it does help to book ahead. *Mains from 1,550ISK.* $

**Self-catering** Visit **Bonus** (*Austurvegur 42; 12.00–18.30*) or the delicious little **bakery** at the end of Tryggvagata.

## VESTMANNAEYJAR (THE WESTMANN ISLANDS)

A mere 10km (5.4 miles) from the southern mainland, the Westmann Islands are a pretty little world still in the making. Every newborn island represents a different stage in a staggered chain of volcanic events. The dramatic result is a row of lumpy mountains in the middle of a not-so-gentle ocean, the largest of which is home to a pile of people. Life on the edge makes Vestmannaeyjar an interesting place and quite different from Iceland's other offshore islands. For one, these are the very youngest landscapes around, right on the diagonal line of fire with Mt Hekla and Krafla at Mývatn. The chocolate-coloured basalt cliffs are the most recent; the lighter 'tuff' dates from the last ice age. Grassy-green pastures grow right up to the most challenging peaks but end abruptly at the scorched, still-cooling red and black lava rock. On days without storms, the coves and inlets reflect a bottomless aquamarine right next to the empty charcoal beaches. Lichens, moss, and seaweed cover almost every rock and the bravest sheep in the world know no limits.

The jury is still out as to how many 'islands' there actually are, though official maps label 18 separate outcrops. Several smaller skerries and stacks exist – as the wind and sea beat the rocks back underwater, new volcanoes build up new islands. Each bit of land is the remnant edge of a separate volcanic eruption – or else the culmination of several. The largest and only inhabited island is Heimaey ('home island'), compiled from nine major eruptions. The most prominent of these occurred just 5,000 years ago, when the volcano Helgafell surfaced and conveniently bridged two older islands with a lava field. The most recent was the eruption of Eldfell in 1973 – an event that traumatised the local population and made their island famous.

With about 5,000 people, Heimaey is one of the largest 'cities' outside Reykjavík. The harbour is the most picturesque in Iceland, with perfect rows of what look like bright toy boats, and a lively town centre known for its vibrant colour and fun-loving citizens. Farther out, the right-angled street corners and cute matching houses contrast the very shifty landscape. It feels both odd and endearing to saunter down these orderly suburban lanes only just laid down over cooled pyroclastic flow and giant pumice clusters. I think this is the only city in the world with a neighbourhood called 'new lava'.

In the near distance looms the snowy cap of Mýrdalsjökull glacier and the rest of Iceland. Separated by the sea, the Westmann islanders endorse a strong self-government and follow their own unique traditions: fishing is the main job, puffins are the main pastime. For their daring beauty and close proximity, the islands are a popular holiday spot for mainland Icelanders, not to mention an obvious cruise destination and an easy but rewarding trip for independent travellers. The wild volcanic terrain, the poetic mountains, and the surrounding ocean are something to experience in full, be it winter or summer.

## TYRKJA-GUDDA (1598–1682)

Born and raised on Heimaey, Guðriður Símonardóttir lived the typical life of a fisherman's wife until the fateful summer day of the Algerian pirate attack. As a young woman of 29, she was captured with her young son Sölmundur and sold as a concubine in Algiers. It took the King of Denmark ten years to finally pay the proposed ransom to the Ottomans, after which she was separated from her son and sent to Copenhagen with the other Westmann islanders. To re-acquaint these blonde 'barbarians' with the ways of Christianity and civilisation, the Danish government tracked down a local Icelandic theology student. That man was Hallgrímur Petursson (see page 39), the poet and lyricist for whom Hallgrímskirkja (see page 174) in Reykjavík is named. He fell in love with Guðriður and took her back to Iceland where they married and gave birth to a son. Of the 242 Westmann islanders who were captured from Heimaey, Guðriður was the only one to return home. Her adjustment was not easy – she was constantly teased and given the nickname Tyrkja-Gudda or 'Gudda the Turk'. She was buried with her husband in Hvalfjörður (see page 254), but a statue of Tyrkja-Gudda now stands in the town of Heimaey, on the green below the library and folk museum.

**HISTORY** The Westmann Islands are filled with some amazing stories. Today's islanders are quite proud of the fact that their history pre-dates the settlement of the mainland and its capital. By AD800, there were already many Irish monks or *papar* living on the islands. Before Ingólfur Arnason set off to found Reykjavík (see page 124), his brother Hjörleifur had already headed west and founded a farm below Mýrdalsjökull (near Vík). Hjörleifur's slaves (captured from Ireland) conspired against their master and killed him, then stole his boat and rowed off to the nearby cluster of islands. Ingólfur's own Irish slaves discovered the body and informed their master of his brother's death. True to the Viking spirit of vengeance, Ingólfur tracked down his brother's slaves and surprised them while they were eating their dinner. He killed them all, either with his own sword or by chasing them over the edge of a cliff. A few of these cliffs still bear the names of the unlucky slaves and the group of islands were named after these Irishmen, or 'men of the west' (*vestmenn*). Ingólfur took the surviving widows and married them off to his own men. Irish blood still runs strong.

The first Norse settler was Herjólfur Bárðarson, who arrived in AD900 and gave his name to his farm (Herjólfsdalur) and to the ferry that services the islands today. A wooden church was imported from Norway in 1000, and by 1200 the entire island group became the personal property of the Bishop of Skálholt. Heimaey's perfect natural harbour was the best in Iceland and generated a lot of wealth from fishing and trade. In the early 1400s, during the English–German struggle for fishing rights in Iceland (see page 20), the English claimed the Westmann Islands and built a fort at the harbour's entrance (Skansinn). This did absolutely nothing to deter the King of Denmark's personal claim on the island in 1609, nor did it protect Heimaey from foreign attacks. On 16 July 1627, three Algerian pirate ships sailed to the islands, noticed the fort and landed instead on the southern end of the island. Thirty-four islanders were burned to death and 242 more were captured and taken away as slaves. The 200 or so who did escape only did so by climbing over the edges of the sea cliffs and hiding on the steep ledges. Losing half the island's population was a traumatic event. In spite of Danish army reinforcements, the islanders organised their own lookout points to keep watch over incoming ships – a programme that continued well into the next century.

In August 1874, King Christian IX of Denmark came to Reykjavík to celebrate the country's millennium and to grant Icelanders their very own constitution. The whole country was invited to the celebration. Alas, the weather was not co-operating (some things never change), the sea was too rough, and the islanders were unable to travel to the mainland. In self-consolation, they held their own national festival, or 'Thjóðhátíð', an historic event in its own right that confirmed the separate identity of the Westmann Islands. The festival is now the major event of the year, attended in large part by mainland Icelanders.

After the islands received their town charter in 1919, the harbour at Heimaey became the largest fishing port in Iceland in terms of fish catch and numbers of boats. Compared with the rest of Iceland, the people of the Westmann Islands were quite well off, though they have always suffered the added challenge of living on an active volcanic fault. On 14 November 1963, a new eruption shook the islands and steam was seen rising from the sea. In the country's longest recorded eruption ever (five years), a volcano grew up from 130m below the sea's surface into a 4km$^2$ mountain that reached 174m above sea level. The eruption ended on June 1967 and the new island was named Surtsey after Surtur, the Old Norse god of fire. By that time, there were already plants growing and birds had taken up permanent residence on the newest part of Iceland.

## MAN VERSUS NATURE: COOLING THE LAVA

At the onset of the 1973 Heimaey eruption, two Icelandic geologists theorised that one might redirect the volcano's lava flow by cooling certain sections and creating 'dams'. Specialists from England and America laughed at the concept and even appeared on TV, calling the Icelanders 'amateurs'. But when the lava threatened to close off the mouth of the island's harbour (and render the town useless), the geologists led the local firemen in pumping water directly onto the lava to repress the flow. Their hoses sprayed only 400 litres of water per second – not enough to slow the advancing fire. Diplomatic interventions finally convinced the United States Army Corps of Engineers to lend them much more powerful pumps that were quickly flown in from the NATO base at Keflavík. The firemen worked around the clock for months, spraying 6.2 million tons of seawater into the volcano. As theorised, the cooling caused an outer crust to form, forcing the flow eastwards into the sea. The harbour was saved and even improved – the channel was doubled in length and narrowed down to less than 200m wide.

In the early morning hours of 23 January 1973, another famous eruption shook Heimaey. With little warning, a one-mile-long (1.6km) fissure split down the northeast side of the island and began spewing out gas, hot ash, rock, and molten lava. Fortunately, a bad winter storm had brought in the island's entire fishing fleet the night before and the town's leaders were quick to respond with an evacuation. The volcano was discovered at 01.58, and by 02.30, most of the island's 5,000 residents were leaving the island on fishing boats. About 200 residents stayed behind to help and try to save the town.

Within the first week of the eruption, most buildings were buried under 4m of ash. Several dams were constructed to stop the lava flow, but all of them broke – nearly 400 homes were either burned or buried. Miraculously, the only death attributed to the volcano was a rescue worker who died from inhalation of poisonous gasses. The emergency relief effort was amazing – within a month, the entire island population was provided with housing, food, jobs, and childcare on the mainland. The eruption ended five months later on 3 July – still celebrated as the day the volcano stopped.

The Heimaey eruption had a pronounced effect on the islanders and the whole of Iceland. Nearly every Icelander had a friend or relative involved in the evacuation and so many Westmann islanders are now scattered across the rest of the country. Less than two-thirds of the islanders returned, when they discovered a third of the town was destroyed and the island was now 2.2km² larger. They quickly set to work salvaging their homes, digging out a huge amount of ash and using it to pave new roads and cover the airstrip. A competition was held to name the new mountain in their midst, with a winning vote for the apt but uncreative Eldfell, or 'fire mountain'.

The islanders today show few qualms about living on a ticking time bomb ('this is our home') and now strive for normality and redevelopment. Fresh water is pumped to the island in a submarine pipe from the mainland, and electricity comes through a single submerged cable. When Keiko the killer whale (see page 65) was returned to Iceland, he was given to the Westmann Islands where he lived from 1998 to 2003. Such schemes don't soften the daily blows of difficult island life – the highest wind speed ever recorded in Iceland was in the Westmann Islands – 119 knots (220km/h or 137mph)!

**GETTING THERE AND AWAY** The Westmann Islands are the easiest of Iceland's islands to visit, with frequent transportation links.

**By air** The airport is located in the heart of the island (at the end of Dalavegur), with an airfield that looks a lot like an 'X marks the spot' on a treasure map. Frequent flights take off and land all day long. **Air Iceland** (☎ *481 3300; www.airiceland.is*) flies to and from Reykjavík City Airport (20 minutes) three times a day (around US$120). They also offer packaged day trips with bus and boat tours on the island. Cheaper and more convenient is the smaller **Westmann Airlines** (*Flugfélag Vestmannaeyja;* ☎ *481 3255;* e *eyjaflug@eyjar.is; www.eyjaflug.is*). The planes seat four–six persons but fly back and forth from the tiny beachside airport of Bakki (☎ *487 8415*) (5 minutes) and Selfoss (10 minutes). Bear in mind that all flights are dependent on the weather, and that creeping fog and high winds are quite common. Also, the Westmann Islands lie right below the flight path of all flights to Europe. On a clear day, you can get a good look coming in and out of Keflavík.

**By sea** The Eimskip car ferry *Herjólfur* sails twice daily to and from **Thorlákshöfn** (2 hours 45 minutes); **Heimaey harbour** (☎ *481 2800;* e *info@eimskip.is; www.herjolfur.is*). The cost is around US$30 per person, and berths are available. Vehicles cost more, but if you already have a rental car, then it's definitely worth bringing it to the island. From Reykjavík, there is a direct bus to Thorláksöfn (45 minutes) and the ferry office there (☎ *483 3413*).

## TOURIST INFORMATION

**Tourist information** Ráðhúströð; ☎ 481 3555; e tourinfo@vestmannaeyjar; www.vestmannaeyjar.is; ⌚ 09.00–17.00. The main office (open year-round) is located on the ground floor of the library, beneath the museum. Smaller offices are located at Vestmannabraut 38 & Strandvegur 51.

**TOUR OPERATORS** Viking Tours (*Suðurgerði 4;* ☎ *488 4884;* e *viking@vikingtours.is; www.vikingtours.is*) is the main company on the island and offers scheduled tours around Heimaey by boat or bus. The general 2–3-hour 'circle tour' sails all the way around the main island (dress warmly!) and costs about US$40. Other trips sail close to the other islands for birdwatching, whale-watching or fishing. The main building is right near the harbour and includes a thriving little coffee shop and internet café.

For details of other tour operators, see *Chapter 4*, page 72.

**WHERE TO STAY** Heimaey is one of the few places in Iceland with plenty of affordable accommodation for all. The handful of big hotels/guesthouses are owned and managed by the same people, but there are plenty of other islanders who are up for hosting tourists. If you're coming for the festival (first week of August), book ahead.

## Hotels

**Hótel Eyjar** (14 rooms) Bárustígur 2; ☎ 481 3636; e hoteleyjar@eyjar.is; www.hoteleyjar.eyjar.is. The town's 'other' hotel is a distinguished & modern block of rooms in the town centre. All rooms are spacious & well maintained with private bathrooms. Breakfast (& kitchen use) is available in the all-glass rooftop dining hall. **$$$**

**Hótel Thórshamar** (21 rooms) Vestmannabraut 28; ☎ 481 2900; e thorshamar@eyjar.is; http://hotel.eyjar.is. This well-managed 'upmarket' hotel is near the town

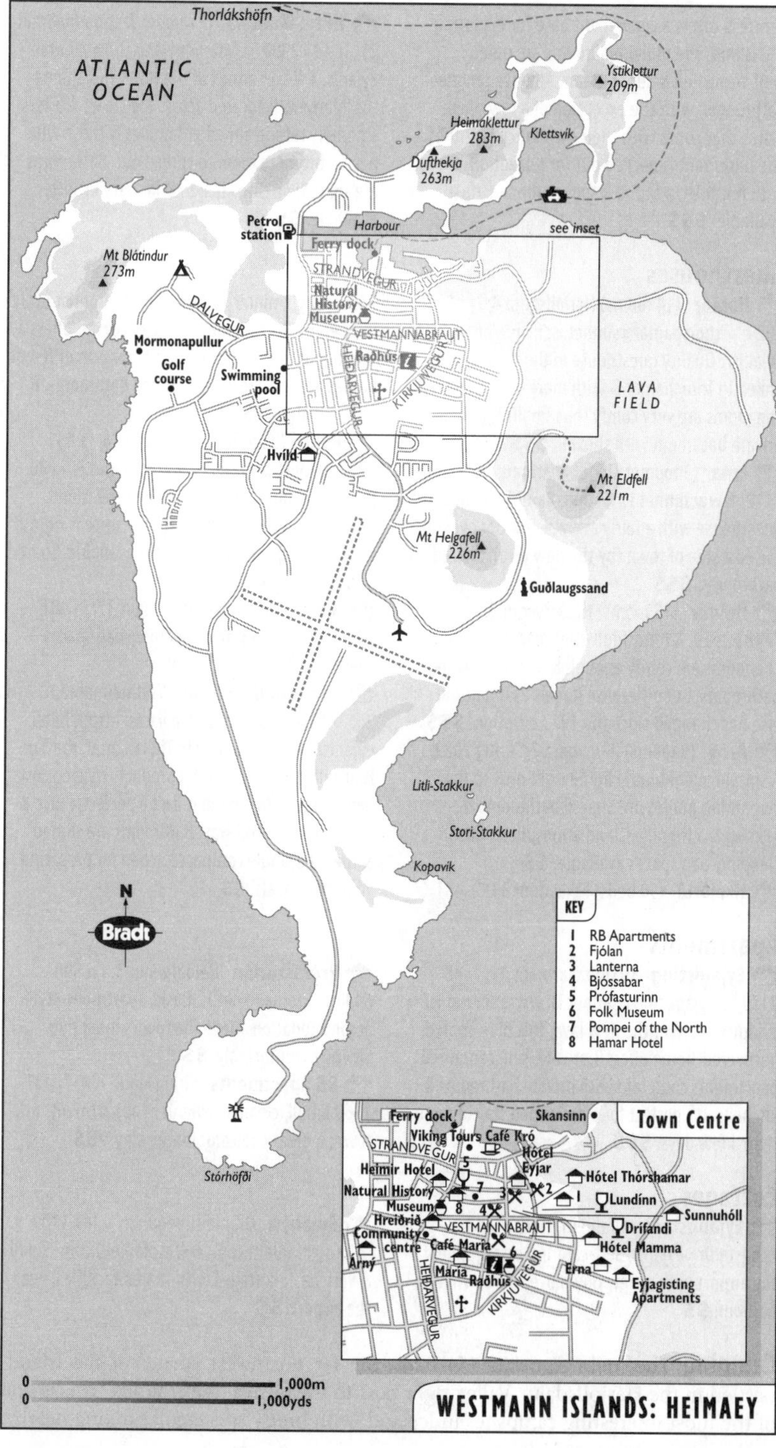

Thorlákshöfn
ATLANTIC OCEAN
Ystiklettur 209m
Heimaklettur 283m
Klettsvík
Dufthekja 263m
Petrol station
Harbour
see inset
Ferry dock
Mt Blátindur 273m
STRANDVEGUR
Natural History Museum
DALVEGUR
VESTMANNABRAUT
Mormonapullur
Raðhús
Golf course
Swimming pool
HEIÐARVEGUR
KIRKJUVEGUR
LAVA FIELD
Hvíld
Mt Eldfell 221m
Mt Helgafell 226m
Guðlaugssand
Litli-Stakkur
Stori-Stakkur
Kopavík
N
Bradt
Stórhöfði
KEY
1 RB Apartments
2 Fjólan
3 Lanterna
4 Bjóssabar
5 Prófasturinn
6 Folk Museum
7 Pompei of the North
8 Hamar Hotel
Town Centre
Ferry dock
Skansinn
Viking Tours
Café Kró
STRANDVEGUR
Hótel Eyjar
Heimir Hotel
Hótel Thórshamar
Natural History Museum
Lundínn
Sunnuhóll
Hreiðrið
VESTMANNABRAUT
Drífandi
Community centre
Café María
Hótel Mamma
Árný
María
Raðhús
Erna
Eyjagisting Apartments
HEIÐARVEGUR
KIRKJUVEGUR
0 1,000m
0 1,000yds

WESTMANN ISLANDS: HEIMAEY

centre & offers a convenient base for exploring the island. The individual rooms are quiet, well-furnished & super-clean. All have private bathrooms, with the exception of a few plush suites that come with their own fancy bathtubs. The basement is decked out for relaxation with hot tubs, a sauna & games room. B/fast available. **$$$**

**Hótel Mamma** (7 rooms) Vestmannabraut 25; ☎ 481 2900; e hotel@eyjar.is; http://hotel.eyjar.is. A lesser annex of the Hótel Thórshamar, the 'Mamma' is located across the street & offers a homely refuge aimed at families & those who need a bit more room to spread out. Bathrooms are shared; on-site kitchen & laundry facilities available. **$$**

## Guesthouses

**Hamar** (14 rooms) Herjólfsgata 4; ☎ 481 2929; e thorshamar@simnet.is; http://hotel.eyjar.is/. Quality guesthouse in the town centre, linked to Thórshamar & with more of a hotel feel. The rooms are very comfy (but small) & have a private bathroom with shower. **$$$**

**Erna** (5 rooms) Kirkjubæjarbraut 15; ☎ 481 2112; www.simnet.is/gisting. Rambling, modern guesthouse with a fairly average interior over on the east side of town (by the new lava). Shared bathrooms. **$$$**

**Heimir** (15 rooms) Heiðarvegur 1; ☎ 481 2929. A retro 'high-rise' near the harbour. The rooms are comfy enough & all have private bathrooms, but otherwise it feels as if nothing else has changed since the 1973 eruption. **$$$**

**Árný** (8 rooms) Illugagata 7; ☎ 481 2082. A simple, neighbourly home right next to the swimming pool/gym. Shared bathrooms & kitchen & a friendly island atmosphere. Cheap sleeping-bag spaces available. **$$**

**Hreiðrið** (50 beds) Faxastígur 33; ☎ 481 1045; e eyjamindir@isholf.is; http://tourist.eyjar.is. Friendly & exuberant tour service that offers a number of recently refurbished rooms in different homes around the island. Shared bathrooms. B/fast available. **$$**

**Hvíld** (9 rooms) Höfðavegur 16; ☎ 481 1230; e hvild@simnet.is; www.simnet.is/hvild. Basic guesthouse in the middle of the island. Rooms feel a bit cramped, but the price is right & sleeping-bag accommodation is available. Shared bathrooms. **$$**

**María** (8 rooms) Brekastígur 37; ☎ 481 2744; e breko@eyjar.is. Sleeping-bag spaces available. **$$**

**Sunnuhóll** (8 rooms) Vestmannabraut 26; ☎ 481 2900; e hotel@eyjar.is; http://hotel.eyjar.is/. Another annex to Thórshamar, the 'Sun Hall' relies heavily on IKEA products to keep costs low. That doesn't mean it isn't a perfectly nice & inexpensive island stay. Bathrooms are shared & there's a single compact kitchen for preparing your own meals. **$$**

## Apartments

**Eyjagisting** Kirkjubæjarbraut 17; ☎ 481 2159; e eyjagisting@simnet.is; www.simnet.is/eyjagisting. Near the new lava, this blue-roofed 'recovered' home offers 3 private, self-contained apartments complete with private bathrooms & kitchens. It's perfect for a prolonged stay of more than a few days. **$$$**

**Prófasturinn** Heiðarvegur 3; m 898 6448; e steina@xnet.is. Basic, apartment-style accommodation above the town's main pub. Sleeps 7 comfortably. **$$**

**RB Apartments** Kirkjuvegur 10A; ☎ 481 1569.Small, clean, convienient appartments in town; a great choicefor longer stays. **$$**

## Cottages

**Eyjabústaðir** Ofanleiti; ☎ 481 1664; e bustadir@eyjar.is. Self-catering cottages near the airport with a view down over the town & harbour. **$$**

**Smáhýsi** Ofanleitisvegur 2; ☎ 481 1109; e info@ofanleiti.com; www.ofanleiti.com. Small & very basic cottages with shared facilities, near the airport. **$$**

**Camping** The main campsite (**$**) is on the far northwest corner of the island, nestled in the Herjólfsdalur Valley right next to the festival fairgrounds. This is one of the most interesting campsites in Iceland, with pretty spectacular hiking nearby.

The central shelter has showers, a large kitchen, laundry facilities (use hot water sparingly), and a drying room. In summer, someone will come by to collect payment.

## WHERE TO EAT

### Restaurants

**Café María** Skólavegur 1; 481 3160; 11.30–23.30 Sun–Thu, 11.00–01.00 Fri/Sat. 'The restaurant' for the whole island, cherished by locals & crowded by tourists who want to try the house special: pan-fried puffin. Other choices are diverse – fresh seafood (grilled monkfish, lobster, & halibut) sweet & savoury crêpes, great soup, salads, & of course, pizza. Finish it off with sticky, gooey desserts or ice-cream sundaes. The upstairs bar is a town favourite. Recommended. *Mains from 2,600ISK.* $$$$

**Fjólan** Vestmannabraut 28; 481 3663; 08.00–22.00 daily. The fancy in-house restaurant for the island's largest hotel & the top spot for business dinners. Banquet-style seafood & saucy meat dishes served with flourish & by candlelight. *Mains from 2,500ISK.* $$$$

**Lanterna** Bárustígur 11; 481 3393; 11.00–22.30 daily. Italian cuisine & distinctive seafood, with an allegiance to fresh ingredients & classy presentation. *Mains from 1,750ISK.* $$$

**Bjóssabar** Bárustígur 1; 481 3940; 17.00–21.00 Tue–Sun. Where the Westmann islanders come to get their fast-food fix: dressed-up hamburgers, fried chicken, pizza with everything, & Chinese take-away in tiny cardboard boxes. It's comfort food served in a friendly window-front restaurant with high-back chairs. *Mains from 600ISK.* $$

### Cafés and bars

**Prófasturinn** Heiðarvegur 3; 481 3700; 12.00–22.00 Mon–Thu, 12.00–03.00 Fri/Sat, 13.00–19.00 Sun. Although this is really just a nice restaurant with good food, the locals come here to drink & dance up a storm. The menu is fish, lamb, & puffin; the music is pop rock. *Mains from 1,600ISK.* $$$

**Café Kró** Smábátabryggja; 488 4884; 10.00–18.00 daily. Viking Tours office/café that functions as a living museum of the island complete with regular showings of the volcano documentary. A good place to meet fellow travellers & have a cup of coffee with kleinur. Light meals also available. *Mains from 1,000ISK.* $$

**Café Skans** Skansinn; 481 1194; summer 11.00–17.00, winter 15.00–17.00 Sat/Sun. Simple museum café inside the old fort. *Mains from 1,000ISK.* $$

**Drífandi** Bárustígur 2; 481 3636; 10.00–22.00 Sun–Thu, 11.00–01.00 Fri/Sat. Upstairs bar with coffee, sandwiches, & cakes by day – ale, cocktails & live local music by night. *Mains from 400ISK.* $

**Lundínn** Kirkjuvegur 21; 481 3412; 21.00–01.00 daily , summer 14.00–05.00 Fri/Sat. Crazy, noisy pub with live music; close to the new lava.

**Self-catering** A large grocery store, the **11-11** (*Goðahrauni 11; 585 7580; 09.00–23.00 Mon–Fri, 11.00–23.00 Sat, 12.00–23.00 Sun*). There's another convenience store in the geodesic dome, **Vöruval** (*Vestruvegur 18; 481 3184; 10.00–18.00)* and the typical hot-dog/ice-cream fare at **Skylið**, at the end of the port (*Friðarhöfn; 481 1445; 08.00–21.00 daily*). The town's cheery **bakery** makes filling sandwiches to order, as well as a lot of other tasty things (*Vilberg-Kökuhús; Bárustígur 7; 481 2664; 08.00–16.00 Tue–Sat, 10.00–16.00 Sun*).

## WHAT TO SEE

**In town** For all your questions and travel needs, head to the main tourist information office, located on the main floor of the library (*bókasafn*), next door to the town hall. The second floor houses the island's **Folk Museum** (*Safnahús Vestmannaeyjar; Ráðhúströð; 481 1194; e byggdasafn@vestmannaeyjar.is; www.*

*vestmannaeyjar.is/safnahus;* ⌚ *May–Sep 11.00–17.00 daily; entrance 400ISK*). The exhibit takes visitors through some of the island's history (whaling boats, fishing implements, old paintings and photographs) and traditions (puffin hunting, festival tents), an extensive re-telling of the 1973 eruption and rescue efforts, along with a sobering display regarding all the Vestmannaeyjar ships and sailors lost at sea. Time is, however, better spent at the island's top-notch **Natural History Museum** (*Náttúrugripasafn Vestmannaeyja; Heiðavegur 12;* ☎ *481 1997;* e *natturu@vestmannaeyjar.is; www.vestmannaeyjar.is/safnahus;* ⌚ *1 May–15 Sep 11.00–17.00 daily, winter 15.00–17.00 Sat/Sun; entrance 500ISK*). A comprehensive collection with a professional touch, this museum is one of Iceland's very best, thanks to extensive scientific displays on island wildlife (lots of eggs, nests, and mounted birds), minerals (lava pearls from Surtsey and local geomorphology), plants, and fish. The in-house aquarium features all the local species that the fishermen catch, but swimming live in sizeable tanks – eg: cod, Arctic char, haddock, and a rare albino catfish (NB: visitors can buy an 'island pass' to both museums and the swimming pool for 900ISK, quite a bargain). If natural history feels too much like school, the cheesy alternative is the fire-and-brimstone **volcano show** (*Community Centre; Faxastígur 33;* ☎ *481 1045; www.tourist.eyjar.is;* ⌚ *15 Jun–20 Aug 11.00–21.00; entrance 600ISK*). Various documentaries on the eruption and other island oddities are best saved for foggy days.

The ferry and boat tours originate at the dock and the **harbour** area is a busy little place all year round and worth exploring. The oldest house on the island is located near the harbour's entrance – **Landlyst** was built in 1847 as the first maternity hospital in Iceland. Throughout the 19th century, the Westmann Islands suffered from an ongoing tetanus epidemic and it was this Danish doctor's office that stopped the spread of the disease. The house is now part of the **Skansinn** complex, the 17th-century fort built to protect the harbour from invasion. Both English and Danish troops were stationed at this spot, and today it's become the point where children wait for their fathers to return from fishing trips. The old wood clapboard **stave church** next door is a replica presented to the islands from Norway in 2000 to commemorate the first church 1,000 years earlier. One fun little street to walk down just below the harbour is called **Skvísusund** (the actual street name is Norðursund, in between Heiðarvegur and Græðisbraut). Once upon a time, these brightly painted warehouses were home to various island fishing co-operatives (eg: Erlingskró and Baldurskró). Today, the peach, purple, orange, green, yellow, and pink houses are homes to clubs that 'compete' with their parties during the July celebration. Also, on the corner of Bárustígur and Miðstræti is the **mural** of the 'tunnel to the mainland' – wishful thinking for some islanders and a joke to others. At the end of Skólavegur sits the bas-relief *Birth of a Soul* (*Fæðing sálar*) by the Icelandic sculptor Einar Jónsson (see page 183). The island's main church is the black-and-white **landkirkja**, built in 1955 to replace a smaller 18th-century structure. Right behind the church stands the island's **cemetery** with its iconic gate and the inscription: *'Ég Lifi Og Þér Munið Lifa'* ('I live and you shall live'). In the 1973 eruption, when the town was buried under ash, this archway was still visible and became the islanders' inspirational slogan. A documentary account of the event (*Ég Lifi*) is shown regularly at Café Kró.

**The island** Despite appearances, hiking around the peaks of Heimaey is a fairly simple activity for most physical abilities. The highest point on the island is **Heimaklettur** (283m), a rugged mountain that provides a perfect shelter above the harbour – the steep and stocky terrain curves around the cove of **Klettsvík** (former

## GUÐLAUGSSAND

On 11 March 1984, the fishing trawler *Hellisey* capsized and sank within a few minutes. Of the five crew, only one survived – deck officer Guðlaugar Friðthórsson, aged 23. Despite rough seas and a water temperature of only 6ºC, the young man aimed for the shore of Heimaey and swam. Guided by the lighthouse and a fulmar flying overhead, he swam 6km (3.2 miles) in seven hours. Barefoot and exhausted, he landed on the new lava, climbed over the mountains and discovered an old bathtub used as a watering trough. He broke the ice with his hands and drank the water, then walked to the closest farm and collapsed. His heroic feat is revered throughout Iceland and Guðlaugar continues to serve as a respected leader on Heimaey. The bathtub is now part of an island memorial honouring his feat and those fishermen who perished.

home to Keiko the whale) to **Ystiklettur** (209m). The views of the island and mainland are spectacular. The northwest corner of the island is another pointed shield of mountains, with a number of great trails that lead up to **Mt Blátindur** (273m) and its severe drop-offs on either side. The ultimate pinnacle is a one-person perch, but a lofty and contemplative spot. Then follow the sheep trails to the next peak **Dufthekja** (263m), named after the Irish slave Dufthakur who perished from this ledge. These rugged mountaintops expose the oldest part of the island, formed in the first eruption. On the opposite side rises the green volcanic cone of **Mt Helgafell** (226m), or 'holy mountain', which accounts for the creation of the island's middle 5,000 years ago. Almost in exact parallel sits **Mt Eldfell** (221m), the youngest volcanic cone (c1973), made of red-black scoria. The *Ný Hraun* ('new lava') manifests itself in colour and appearance and this scorched northeast section of the island is still a no-man's-land of sorts (NB: there's no mobile-phone reception on the new lava). One trail leads into the centre of the crater, where (if you crouch down) you can still feel the heat radiating from the red-orange rocks. The ground is often too hot to touch and it's not a good idea to linger, especially if you are wearing rubber-soled shoes. Just 1m below this spot, the temperature rises to 470°C and baking bread in the rocks is now a common island gimmick. A pointed **silver cross** memorial raised in 1998 commemorates the 25th anniversary of the eruption, and one of the original green pumps used to stop the lava is still on display. At the base of the new lava is the excavation/museum now known as **Pompei of the North** (*www.pompeiofthenorth.com*). Since 2005, volunteers have performed an archaeological dig on the sections of the town that were buried in the 1973 eruption. Several homes have now been uncovered, and visitors can walk down the former street of Suðurvegur to understand the sheer scale of destruction and get a sense of how tremendously deep the ash fell.

The greener and more rural parts of the island are definitely worth wandering through. The entire west coast is low and rocky, with a nice long path from the golf course that grants a good view of some of the other islands. Near the shore lies the **mormónapollur** ('Mormon puddle'), a natural rock pool where new converts were baptised in 1853. A memorial was raised in 2000 to commemorate the group of Westmann islanders who joined the Mormon faith and emigrated to Utah. The beach at Vík is one of a kind, with strange volcanic formations created by hardened layers of ash now eroded away. The same goes for the bays on the other side, though the mountains become higher and more impressive towards the airport. The southern tip at **Stórhöfði** was once a separate island and now home to a 100-year-old **lighthouse**. The slopes are quite steep but this is definitely the best place to see puffins in the summer.

**WHAT TO DO** Boat tours take visitors all around Heimaey and sometimes pass by the smaller islands, like Elliðaey, Bjarnarey, and Faxasker towards the east, and Grasleysa and Hrauney in the west. There really is no better way to see the tan, pock-marked cliffs up close and to capture the full force of the land versus the sea. Birdwatching and whale-watching trips are also quite rewarding if you are lucky. Setting foot on the other islands is far more difficult – you have to make your own contacts and arrange private transport, typically through the hunting clubs. The island of **Surtsey** is off-limits in order to protect new vegetation and bird communities, but you can easily see it from the air, by land, or by sea. The island's very own national festival, or '**Thjóðhátíð**', takes place the first weekend in August. This is quite a huge affair, with over 10,000 guests. Westmann tradition calls for each family to decorate their own tent, fitted out with full tea services, carpets, beds, and music. The more lavish and extravagant, the better. This all happens at the fairgrounds in Herjólfsdalur and the party goes on non-stop for at least four days. There is much music, much drinking, and lots of bonfires and fireworks. The 3 July celebration is also quite a joyous occasion with much fanfare but fewer people. **Golf** is to Heimaey as chess is to Grímsey (see page 362), with the added handicap of high winds that carry balls off into the stormy Atlantic. The 18-hole course occupies a ridiculous amount of the island, complete with imported white-sand traps (*Vestmannaeyjar Golf Club; Torfmýrarvegur;* ☎ *481 2363;* e *golf@eyjar.is; www.eyjar.is/golf*). Also nearby is the town's gym and indoor **swimming pool** (*Brimhólabraut;* ☎ *481 2401;* ⌚ *07.00–21.00 Mon–Fri, 09.00–17.00 Sat/Sun*), and Heimaey provides a romantic backdrop for **horseriding** (*Hestaleiga í Vestmannaeyjum; Gunnar Árnason;* ☎ *481 1478;* e *hestaleigave@simnet.is*). An afternoon ride along the beaches and inland pastures normally costs around 2,000ISK per person.

**BIRDS** The many bird cliffs around the islands are quite amazing. Besides the southern tip of the island, try the cliffs on the ocean side of the northwest

### SPRANGAN

Among the many wonderful contributions of Vestmannaeyjar culture comes the thrilling sport of not falling to one's death. *Sprangan* was invented by egg collectors who in springtime, would dangle themselves from long ropes over the many cliffs, swinging from side to side as they gathered eggs. The more nimble collectors outdid one another with competing tricks until official competitions were held at the annual festival. 'Athletes' wear no harness and merely hang from the rope with their very strong arms. The real 'sport' involves twisting, flipping, turning and bouncing off the face of the cliffs, even switching from one rope to another. *Sprangan* is now common among the hunting clubs on all the islands but the most common place to see the practice is on the cliffs above Herjólfsdalur – notably **skipahlettur**. Visitors are often given a chance to try it out on a low rope – to do it right, keep your legs bent at the knees and point your toes upwards so that your feet hit the wall flat and soften the impact; then 'spring' off the walls, bounding back and forth. It helps to have huge biceps.

mountains. Fulmar are especially plentiful. The Westmann Islands are also well known for getting lots of vagrant species, blown over from both sides of the Atlantic. Be on the lookout for the unexpected. On the more predictable front, the Westmann Islands are home to an estimated two million puffins and despite the whole of Iceland claiming the bird as their own, Vestmannaeyjar has made it their mascot. The bird is integral to the islands' personality, culture and economy. If you haven't noticed, the islanders also enjoy eating puffins and there is not a single restaurant that doesn't carry the bird on its menu. Hunting the birds is a highly regulated practice – only adolescent birds are taken, and only between 1 July and 15 August. Elaborate **hunting clubs** (complete with crests) keep their own lodges. There are 15 in all (one club per island), where they practise the centuries-old ritual of netting puffins and collecting eggs using flimsy ladders and long ropes. Though all is not death and destruction. On the contrary, Heimaey is home to the official **Puffling Patrol** (Psyjueftirlitíð). At the end of the breeding season (mid-August), a few hundred thousand baby puffins make their way from the cliffs to the sea. Disoriented by the town's lights, they descend onto the busy streets instead of the ocean. An island tradition is for the local children to go out with flashlights and 'rescue' the birds. Children catch a dozen or so per night, keep them warm and fed through the night and then release them from the cliff's edge the next morning. This is the only time and place where you can legally handle baby puffins and it's great fun – especially if you are travelling with children. The puffling rescue is now a serious scientific study – volunteers are asked to keep track of the birds they catch and release, and to weigh them. For more information, contact Psyjueftirlitíð (*481 111; pmj@eyjar.is; www.lundi.is*). The official weigh station is located at the **natural history museum**.

## MT HEKLA (1,491m)

The great volcano of Hekla is the most active in Iceland today, having erupted five times in the last century and more than 20 times since Iceland's settlement. Hekla is known for its spectacular explosions that come in noisy, violent bursts and for the havoc wreaked upon the land. The early settlers were quite surprised by the devastating explosion of 1104, after which Hekla was considered the gateway to hell. During another memorable eruption in 1766, Hekla spat out the largest lava eruption in the history of Iceland. Hekla last erupted in 2000, which meant it was due for a repeat sometime around 2010; however, nearby Eyjafjallajökull erupted instead. This is one reason why there is so little around Hekla today – over time, enough farmers saw their farms get buried and their sheep die from the poisonous gases emitted.

The name 'Hekla' means 'cloak' or 'hood' because it is always covered up in the clouds (so feel fortunate if you see the top). Hekla is a traditional cone volcano, a rarity among Iceland's more common fissure volcanoes, though long fissures do line the base of the mountain. Impossible lava fields prevent casual strolls around the base. Getting across the lumpy furrows takes some concentrated effort. The closer you get to the summit, the newer the lava; it is quite easy to tell how recent the lava is, based on the shape of the pumice and the amount of moss growing on it. Most of what you see has fallen in the last 20–30 years.

Climbing to the summit of Mt Hekla is fairly straightforward, especially if you have a car. The F255 mountain road (just off Route 26) takes you to a gravelly turn-off (heading south) that crosses the Nýjahraun (new lava) field and heads a good way up the peak. From the makeshift parking area, it's another 7km trail to the summit, which takes most people three or more hours to climb. There is a snowy

> **GO TO HEL**
>
> Icelanders have considered Mt Hekla the gateway to hell ever since the 1104 eruption that buried half the country in noxious ash and car-sized chunks of flaming pumice. The belief quickly spread among medieval Europeans, who offered Christian believers two options for going to hell: Italy's Stromboli or Iceland's Hekla. However, long before there was hell, there was *Hel*, the dour and misunderstood daughter of Loki, Norse god of fire and mischief. Hel lived in *Helheim* ('Hel's home') where she welcomed all humans who died from sickness or old age, the weakest and most cowardly form of Viking death. In contrast, Odin's realm Valhalla was an ongoing party for the heroic dead who had perished in battle. Valhalla had a constant fire glowing in the hearth, whereas the Icelandic *Hel* was a cold and dreary place where sleet fell without cease (where did they come up with an idea like that?). It's likely that Hel took after her mother Angrboða, the frost giant. Her house was cold and dark, she appeared as a sickly, half-decomposed woman, and she was quite possessive of the souls she claimed. Obviously, the English word 'hell' derives from Hel, as does the name of the nearby town Hella. Icelandic mythology spelled out precise directions for going to hell: enter at Mt Hekla and follow the *Helvegur* until the gate of corpses (beware the bloodthirsty watchdog Garmur). Hel is beneath the third root to the left under the tree of life, Yggdrasil (see page 32). If you're driving on the ring road, just follow the signs to Hella.

cap at the top, but Hekla is the rare case where crampons are not usually necessary. The best time to make an ascent is late summer (August–September) when snow is minimal, but for Hekla, it's very important to have good weather conditions. Check in with the **tourist information office** in Hella (*487 5165*).

**GETTING THERE AND AWAY** Hekla is visible from many different directions, but also easy to miss on a cloudy day.

Take Route 26 from the ring road (near Hella). After some 30km it becomes a dirt road that circles the base of the mountain. Also, **Hekluferðir** (*Hella; Heiðvangur 18; 487 6611*) offers bus trips to the base trail from Hella, and **Toptours** (*Hella; Thrúðvangur 39; 487 5530; e toppferðir@mmedia.is*) offers exciting snowmobile trips to the summit.

**WHERE TO STAY AND EAT** The town of **Hella** is the point on the ring road closest to the volcano, though it is not much more than a crossroads surrounded by hayfields and farms. There's a petrol station and *sjoppa* for food and fuel, as well as a few hotels.

## Near Hella

**Hótel Rangá** (50 rooms) Suðurlandsvegur; 487 5700; e icehotels@icehotels.is; www.icehotels.is. A luxury country hotel located just off the ring road. The deluxe timber rooms are especially cosy in wintertime & you've always got a nice view of the mountain. Hot tubs & good fishing add to the attractions. B/fast buffet inc. **$$$$**

**Árhús** Rangárbakkar (28 rooms); 487 5477; e arhus@arhus.is; www.arhus.is. A quiet collection of cottages on the riverbank just outside Hella. Each room is an individual cottage with private bathroom, though it can feel a bit like camping. Actual camping & sleeping-bag spaces are also available & meals are served in the dining room. **$$$**

### Near the mountain

**Leirubakki** (14 rooms) www.leirubakki.is. This is all about location. From this historic farm, the view of the rivers, fields, & volcano are all unbeatable. The clean & well-kept guesthouse isn't bad either (some shared bathrooms) & it's also home to the 'Hekla Centre'. What's even better is that this is a horse farm that does horseback rides near Mt Hekla. Recommended. **$$$**

## THJÓRSÁRDALUR

Tracing the Thjórsá upriver (Route 32) takes you into the rocky highland gorges and the exciting white-water rapids of Iceland's longest river. The valley deepens into a gorge while the horizon opens up to some picturesque mountains, like **Mt Búrfell** (669m). After finishing the dam, the Búrfell hydro-electric station used their leftover cement to build an open-air swimming pool at **Thjórsárdalslaug** (*summer 10.00–21.00 Wed–Sun*). Nearby is the settlement-age farm Stöng that was completely buried by Mt Hekla's eruption of 1104. Unearthed by archaeologists, the reconstructed 11th-century longhouse was placed in this protected valley (*Þjóðveldisbær; 488 7713; thjodveldisbaer@thjodveldisbaer.is; www.thjodveldisbaer.is; Jun–Aug 10.00–18.00*). In the whole of Iceland, this is the only traditional turf home from the Viking era, offering a rare chance to walk inside and get a glimpse of how Iceland began. This particular farm is believed to have been the home of Gaukur á Stöng from Njáls saga (a fierce warrior later killed in a duel for love). Nearby **Gjáin** is one of those places you hesitate putting in a guidebook for fear that too many people will find out about it. With a simple name like 'gorge', one expects little and yet the Rauða (red) River splashes down over the moss and stone in the most gorgeous arrangement of waterfalls and pools. To call it idyllic is a start – if anywhere resembles the 'Middle Earth' of Old Norse legend, this is it. To get to Gjáin, follow Route 32 to the end, then continue on the dirt path (Route 327) past the original Stöng, and go to the riverbank. You'll know when you get to Gjáin because you'll want to stop and get out to have a look around.

## LANDMANNALAUGAR

Hot springs and volcanoes are found just about everywhere in Iceland, but nothing compares to the wild wonderland that is Landmannalaugar (pronounced *lahnd-mahn-a-loy-gahr*). Halfway between the volcanoes of Laki and Mt Hekla, this polygon-shaped nature reserve encloses a mysterious landscape made from the many forms of water and lava. Pictured in almost every travel brochure out there, the mountains of Landmannalaugar are pure rhyolite (see page 42) – a crystallised, slow-forming igneous rock that is far more interesting than the basic basalt blocks seen everywhere else in Iceland. The colourful stone forms smooth, pyramid-shaped peaks, with slopes that lie somewhere between gentle and unforgiving. Depending on the weather and the light, the rocks and sand shine yellow and reddish-brown, streaked with blue, green, and purple ash impacted from ancient eruptions. On other days, the earth seems scorched and lifeless. In fact, much of Landmannalaugar is dead, the desert wake of volcanic destruction. The steam rising up from each valley adds a mystical sense and leads to the hidden lives of all the rivers, pools and springs that mark the land. Each is a private oasis where green marshes flourish in spite of the cold.

The name 'Landmannalaugar' simply means 'bath of the land's men', which points to a long history of travellers who liked to come here for a warm dip in the

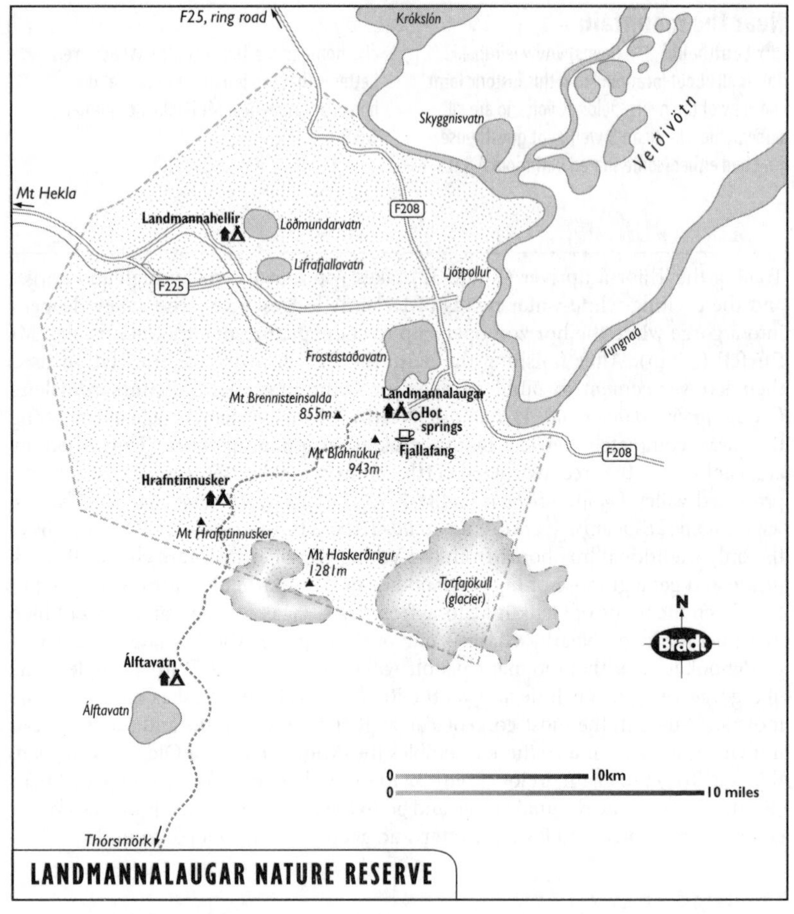

LANDMANNALAUGAR NATURE RESERVE

many springs. Some things never change, and this is still the number-one spot in Iceland for all-natural, outdoor bathing. Unpredictable rivers and the tricky lava fields around Mt Hekla have prevented mass tourist development, but for hikers, Landmannalaugar is now the ultimate destination. Like all beautiful, remote places that become extremely popular, the scene at the main camp flips from a chaos of caravans one minute to ghostly emptiness the next. From mid-July to mid-August, the place is a jam-packed hiking hell, not bad if you don't mind having your wilderness with a side of civilisation. If things are busy when you arrive, do not despair, as it's quite easy to step off the beaten path (just don't step too far away). Just climb to the top of a hill and in every direction, the mountains go on for ever.

**GETTING THERE AND AWAY** If you are driving and unsure of your vehicle's ability, take the 'high' road – continue on Route 26 past Hekla, then turn south on Route F208. That way you'll avoid any fords. If you've got a good 4x4, then it's quicker taking Route F225 but you must ford a number of rivers. It's also possible to take Route F208 from the ring road (by Kirkjubæjarklaustur), which is an extremely beautiful route but also the most difficult (try shaking your head vigorously for two hours). There is an unending argument about whether or not you need a 4x4 to get to Landmannalaugar. Honestly, a normal car can make it there with little trouble (via Route 26), but why risk it? Car-rental companies will not insure you there. Keep in mind that once you get to Landmannalaugar, you are 50km from the nearest petrol station.

Highland **buses** service Landmannalaugar from June to mid-September, with a daily bus to and from BSÍ in Reykjavík (4 hours) that continues on to Kirkjubæjarklaustur (4 hours) and Skaftafell (5 hours); Reykjavík Excursions (*562 1011; e main@re.is; www.re.is*). In either direction, the bus makes a two-hour stop in Landmannalaugar.

Plenty of people hike into Landmannalaugar, or else ride their bike, motorcycle, or horse. Bike and motorcycle riders should take the high road to avoid impassable rivers. Horses can go pretty much anywhere they like.

**WHERE TO STAY AND EAT** The main site at Landmannalaugar is home to a popular **mountain hut** (*100 beds; m 854 1192; e fi@fi.is; www.fi.is*) that gets booked out well before the summer season begins. There's a good kitchen, hot showers, but sleeping-bag spaces only. **Fjallafang Café** (*m 853 7828; www.landmannalaugar.info; 11.30–20.00 daily*) is the shop/restaurant that occupies a pair of green buses and sells an astounding amount of equipment and maps for hikers, along with groceries and hearty hiking food (mainly sandwiches and pastry). The other main campsite is at **Landmannahellir** (*m 893 8407; e info@landmannahellir.is; www.landmannahellir.is; Jun–Sep*). Used most often as a stop for organised horse treks, there are several cosy cottages for sleeping bags: Gil (24 beds), Fell (18 beds), Höfði (18 beds), and Hlið (12). Each has its own bathroom and kitchen facilities. To protect the landscape, pitching tents is prohibited outside designated campsites in the nature reserve. Both Landmannalaugar and Landmannahellir have hot showers and toilets, with charges per person (not per tent or caravan). Because the hard ground is impenetrable, experienced campers hold their tents in place with rocks and it's a common courtesy to put the rocks back into the allotted box when you are finished. If the elements have you craving comforts, just outside the reserve (on Route 26) is the sprawling highland hotel of **Hrauneyjar** (see page 435), a great base from which to explore the area.

**WHAT TO SEE AND DO** The main **bathing pool** is right near the campsite and is quite shallow (and hot!), but with icy-cold water running in from the river. Keep your toes pointed upward to avoid getting burned. For this one spot, Icelandic tradition dictates nude bathing, though the influx of group tours now supports an equal balance between clothed and unclothed. Please note that using soap is prohibited in any of the hot springs; also, a few springs are home to a biting parasite – quite harmless but still annoying.

The main camp sits in the middle of several beautiful sites: the peaceful lake of **Frostastaðavatn**, the bright-green bogs of **Grænagil** ('green gully'), the obsidian lava field of **Laugahraun** and the active volcano **Mt Brennisteinsalda** (855m). The mountain is extremely colourful (and climbable), with bright-red, black, blue, and grey streaks amid the yellow sulphur. **Mt Bláhnúkur** (943m) or 'blue peak' is the blue-grey mountain directly south from the camp. The panorama from the top is wondrous, but the hike is much steeper than it looks – only do it in decent weather. The crater **Ljótpollur** ('ugly puddle') is another must-see highlight: a clear pool set within a crater of black and red earth.

Outside the main camp, the world is your oyster. The hordes of hikers come here to trek the **Laugavegurinn** trail, which is truly rewarding. Still, the rest of

## LAUGAVEGURINN: THE LAUGAVEGUR TRAIL

The highland trek between Landmannalaugar and Thórsmörk is one that every Icelander walks at least once in their lifetime. Crossing such primitive terrain is truly invigorating, and the overall experience is also exhilarating. The fact that this is a busy and well-trodden route doesn't make it any less beautiful. The marked trail is 56km long and fluctuates a good 1,000m in altitude. Warm (and dry!) mountain huts are situated all along the way – if hiking in July–August, book all your accommodation beforehand with the Iceland Touring Association (see page 114) (*568 2533; e fi@fi.is; www.fi.is*). You may also camp with tents at each designated stop. Several maps are sold for the route – the 'best' (the most accurate and comprehensive) is the *Landmælingar Íslands Sérkort: Thórsmörk-Landmannalaugar* (1:100,000) because it marks the trail and every single hot spring in the reserve. You can also just follow the trail posts with yellow tips.

To avoid wasting car-rental days on hiking, outside visitors can take the daily highland bus to Landmannalaugar and pick up another from Thórsmörk (or vice versa). Obviously, the trek can be done in either direction. From Landmannalaugar, the first two days are considered the most difficult, after which it gets easier. It is also quite possible to speed things up and hike it through in three–four days, but that takes all the fun out of it.

**DAY 1: LANDMANNALAUGAR TO HRAFNTINNUSKER** (12km) Cross the Laugahraun lava field then ascend the southern slope of Mt Brennisteinsalda and continue on the plateau to the bubbling hot springs of Stórihver. Cross the 'saddle' (*söðull*) between mountains to the hut at Mt Hrafntinnusker (1,128m). Geothermal activity and the nearby ice caves are popular, but use extreme caution.

**DAY 2: HRAFNTINNUSKER TO ÁLFTAVATN** (12km) Descend southwards into the valley and continue to the glacier at Mt Háskerðingur, then walk down the steep slopes of Jökultungur and into the valley of streams called Gráshagi. Continue southwest towards the pair of huts on the heavenly shores of Álftavatn ('swan lake'; 537m).

**DAY 3: ÁLFTAVATN TO EMSTRUR** (15km) A day to get wet: wade the first river at Bratthálskvísi then pass south by the huts at the Hvanngil Gorge. Take the footbridge across the Kaldaklofskvísi River and take the less-travelled path (not the jeep track F261); wade another river (Bláfjallakvísi) and then cross the bridge at Nyrðri Emstruá. Continue across the rock flats to the pair of huts at Botnar (617m).

**DAY 4: EMSTRUR TO THÓRSMÖRK** (15km) Go around the top of the Emstruá Gorge, descend (steep!) to the footbridge, then loop back around to the top of Markarfljótsgljúfur. Follow the edge of this 'canyon' in which you must ford a number of streams, the largest of which is the last, Thrónga. Then enter into the valley at Thórsmörk (310m).

Die-hards often tack on another day of hiking to take them across the final mountain pass between Thórsmörk and Skógar, though this is periodically closed owing to the volcanic activity of Eyjafjallajökull (see page 43).

the reserve is huge, empty, and wonderful. Good maps are sold in the shop, but given the number of hot springs and hot ground, it's important to stick to the paths. Before heading off, let others know of your plans.

## HVOLSVÖLLUR

Nestled between the rivers Thverá and Hólsa, Hvolsvöllur is the epicentre of one of Iceland's most well-known tales, **Njáls saga**. Njál's is the very definition of *saga* with its generations of bloody family feuds, legal wrangling at the Althing, and bitter Viking divorces. Njál's is the longest and most complex of the sagas: the introduction alone is a whopping 17 chapters long, the paperback version is almost 400 pages (even longer on calfskin), and there are more plot lines than there are streams in Thórsmörk. The central conflict of Njáls saga begins with the wives of two friends (Njál and Gunnar) who argue about seating arrangements at a feast. This turns into a series of contract killings that eventually leads to the innocent Njál getting burned to death in a farm at **Bergthórshvoll**, near present-day Hvolsvöllur (hence the Icelandic name for the saga *Brennu-Njáls* or Burning Njál).

Tourist information about the saga sites is available at the Saga Centre (*Sögusetrið; Hlíðarvegur 14; 487 8781; e njala@njala.is; www.njala.is; May–Sep 09.00–18.00 Mon–Fri, 10.00–18.00 Sat/Sun, winter 10.00–17.00 Fri/Sat & by appointment*). Dedicated to the intricacies of Njáls saga, this high-quality, multimedia museum has three permanent exhibitions: one on Njáls saga, another on the history of the sagas themselves, and a display on the world of the Vikings. In some ways, this is a typical museum of reading, old artefacts, wax models, and the like, but also provides rich context for the surrounding landscapes. That makes it a good visit for those who know nothing about the sagas, as well as those who think they know everything. Maps and information are available for a driving tour to all the sites of Njáls saga, including the medieval turf house at Keldur. You are also just a hop, skip and a jump from Oddi, a prominent church and farm for much of Iceland's history, and the former home of Sæmundur the Learned (see page 170).

Hvolsvöllur is a good base from which to explore the country's history and also home to a good **swimming pool** (*Vallabraut; 487 8607; 08.00–20.00*). Also, the turn-off at Route 253 goes to the hamlet of **Bakki** and the airport (*487 8043*) for a quick flight to the Westmann Islands (see page 228).

### WHERE TO STAY AND EAT

**Hótel Ránga** (51 rooms) 487 5700; e hotelranga@hotelaranga.is; www.hotelranga.is. 8km east of Hvolsvöllur, the Ránga is a 4-star mega-cabin. The rooms are just right, & hot tubs are out back. The in-house bar stocks every liquor imaginable & the polar bear guarding the doorway is pretty cool too. The rooms each have their own theme. The hotel serves many large corporations for rustic-lodge-meets-ritzy-hotel retreats. **$$$$$**

**Hótel Hvolsvöllur** (59 rooms) Hliðarvegur 7; 487 8050; e info@hotelhvolsvollur.is; www.hotelhvolsvollur.is. Modern construction. For the most part, rooms are very spacious, well furnished, clean, comfortable, & wheelchair-accessible. All rooms have their own private bathroom, which are bigger than usual for European countries. The in-house restaurant is the best around, if not slightly predictable. B/fast inc. **$$$$**

**Ásgarður** (50 beds) 487 1440; e asgardur@travelsouth.is; www.asgardurinn.is. This primly painted schoolhouse turned youth hostel is a nice detour from the ring road, just outside the town itself. A few private cottages are available, but the cheery main house provides everything a traveller could want (kitchen, a spacious living room, & a hearth). Shared bathrooms, but no Wi-Fi. **$$**

**Fljótsdalur** (15 beds) 487 8498; Apr–Oct. Halfway between Hvolsvöllur &

Thórsmörk, this turf-covered hut is beloved by travellers who yearn for tradition & the true spirit of place. Nestled in one of south Iceland's more remote areas, the down-to-earth hostel feels a lot like camping, so bring your own food & sleeping bag. To get there, take Route 261 from Hvolsvöllur. **$$**

**Goðaland Guesthouse** (21 beds) 618 2400; e godalandguesthouse@gmail.com; www.godaland-guesthouse.com. Located just outside Hvolsvöllur, 'God's Land' is probably the most aptly named guesthouse in Iceland. Run by a saintly husband-&-wife team, the former school is a heavenly haven right in the middle of Fljótshlið farmland. Everything in southern Iceland is easily accessible from Goðaland, with incredible views in every direction. Wi-Fi, books, movies, a pool table, bookshop & other entertainments are available, & free parking abounds around the splendid courtyard. The guesthouse has single, double, & triple rooms, with a kitchen for guests' use. Recommended. B/fast inc. **$$**

**Smártún** (60+ beds) 487 8471; e smaratun@simnet.is; www.smaratun.is. An uber-complex of vacation housing, Smáratún was once a farm, 13km outside Hvolsvöllur. Today, the barn is a Green Globe-certified hotel. The restaurant-worthy staff serve 3 meals a day, & the 14 rooms are American-sized, with luxurious bathrooms, and wheelchair-accessible. The hotel has a ballroom for large gatherings, & a bar for late-night drinks. Across the car park is the guesthouse, with beds for 13 people. It feels like you're staying in a family friend's house. While there's no b/fast & some of the beds are narrow, the homely feel makes up for it. You can also rent horses. The walls are covered in cool photo murals. There's also a guest kitchen, big enough for 40 people, which is also shared by the campsite (which means 100–200 people). The hot tub can be in high demand, but the garden/patio area gives a stellar view of the beautiful night sky. Smártún also has 5 cabins, each with individual bathrooms & TVs, & several summerhouses, with space showers, fully equipped kitchens, 6 beds, & a big loft each, as well as a patio with grill (Iceland has recently caught on to the barbecue party idea). Whatever accommodation you're looking for, it's safe to say you'll find it at Smártún.

## SKÓGAR

Alas, the ancient farm known as 'forest' has no trees today. Instead, this spot is well known for the number of drivers who slam on their brakes once they spot the idyllic waterfall of **Skógarfoss**. Here is a postcard picture not to be missed: the perfectly straight waterfall drops a good 60m over the green cliff after tumbling all the way down from the glacier above. A wide path goes up to the base of the falls and allows you a peek behind the roaring echo. It's believed that the first farmer to live here (Thrasi Thórolfsson) hid a chest of gold coins behind the falls. For tour buses and ring-roaders, the hamlet represents an obligatory stop at the **Skógar Folk Museum** (*Skógasafn; 487 8845; e skogasafn@skogasafn.is; www.skogasafn.is; summer 09.00–18.00 daily; entrance 450ISK*). Surely an impressive and exhaustive exhibit, the various displays focus on rural development in Iceland through the ages. You'll find schools, churches, and homes of old (including several turf-roofed buildings), as well as the tools, boats, crafts, and artwork of the local populace. Even if it's not the first of its kind, this is one museum that's not to be rushed through. A small café and gift shop aims to collect the rest of your money. Putting aside the commercial destination, Skógar is an ideal stop if you're hiking in and out of Thórsmörk. It represents a beautiful back door into the untouched highlands.

### WHERE TO STAY AND EAT

**Hótel Anna** (5 rooms) Moldnúpur; 487 8950; e hotelanna@hotelanna.is; www.hotelanna.is. Right off the ring road (20km from Skógar), this boutique, country hotel offers a unique, pastoral setting for weary drivers. Located on a traditional horse farm, the generation-to-generation owners brandish a theatrical appreciation for Icelandic culture, seen in the décor of every private bedroom (with bathroom – which includes plenty of towels) to the folksy (but authentic) meals served. Part of the hotel is a museum dedicated to the life of Anna of Moldnúpur. Summer **$$$**; winter **$$**

**Hótel Edda Skógar** (34 rooms) 444 4830; edda@hoteledda.is; www.hoteledda.is; summer only. This concrete school is a tried & trusted travellers' lodge. After a long day's drive, it's a good place to come & rest. They also offer cheap sleeping-bag spaces. Outdoor hot tub, some bathrooms shared. B/fast available. **$$$**

**Skógar Youth Hostel** (30 beds) 487 8801; skogar@hostel.is; www.hostel.is. A reconverted old school that's perfect for hikers, drivers, & bikers alike. Bathrooms are shared. It's small & a little bit remote (bring food), but well clear of the riff-raff. **$$**

## THÓRSMÖRK

'Thór's woods' is renowned for its stunning nature, a transcendent, hidden valley beneath a romantic breadth of volcanic mountains. Hundreds of glacial streams pour down the mountainsides and combine into an immense swathe of braided rivers that rush through the valley's shifting bed of black sand. Thórsmörk also wows its visitors with all the great colours of Iceland: shiny, moss-green mountains, volcanic black pumice, the brown of aged basalt, steely-blue water, and snow-white glaciers whose long, icy tongues flow down into the valley. The tremendous scale of the place sets it apart from anything else and that is exactly why anyone with even a mild case of wanderlust should hurry there. Alas, only a few can make it given that unless you're hiking over the mountains, the only way in and out of the valley is along the banks of the very turbulent Krossá River. Driving to Thórsmörk becomes an amphibious activity, and those who actually get this far tend to bask in the light of their own bravado. And yet, to experience this corner of Iceland is something far bigger than machismo.

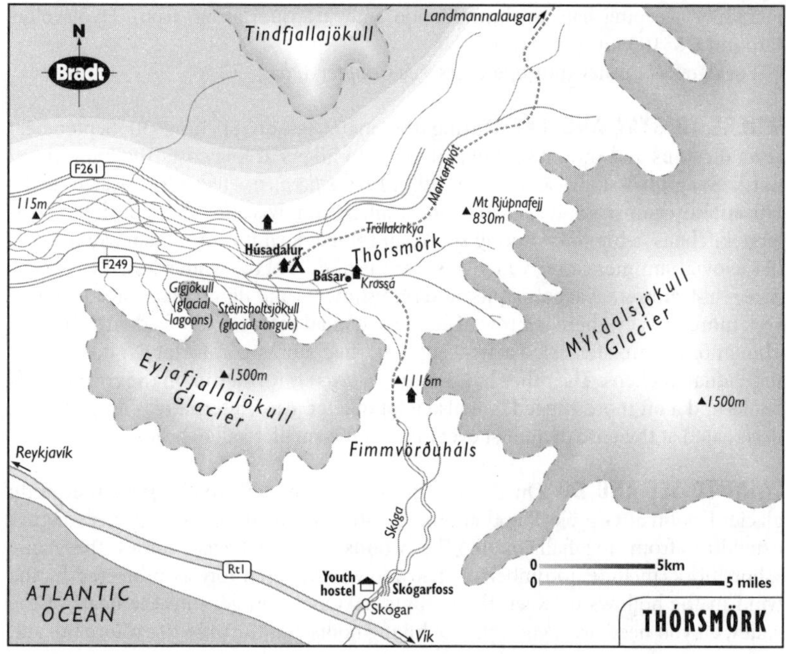

## HIKING INTO THÓRSMÖRK

The mountain pass from the ring road (at Skógar) into Thórsmörk is a popular and beautiful trek, typically added as the fifth day on the famous Laugavegurinn walk (see page 244). The trail originates at the Skógar Waterfall and ascends between the two glaciers (Mýrdalsjökull and Eyjafjallajökull), through the pass known as Fimmvörðuháls ('five cairn hill'). The five cairns are there for a reason, as it is very easy to lose sight of anything in a dense fog. Fimmvörðuháls (1,116m) is highly elevated and cold; it is rare for there not to be substantial snow cover in the pass, and the wind can be murderous – it's worth waiting for good weather. At about 20km, most hikers complete the trek in a day, though one may break it up into two by stopping at either of the huts in the pass. Dress warmly – walking between two giant glaciers has a cooling effect. Icelandic tradition motivates first-timers to hike the pass on the night of 21 June to experience the full summer solstice.

**GETTING THERE AND AWAY** Inaccessibility is a large part of Thórsmörk's appeal. The landscape is untarnished and the numbers of tourists are relatively few. The jeep track from the ring road (Route 249), is for hefty 4x4 vehicles only. Drivers must cross no fewer than 20 rivers, some of which rise to depths of more than 1m. If you don't know what you're doing, don't chance it. In summer, a highland bus runs twice a day between Reykjavík and Thórsmörk (3½ hours) via Hella and Hvolsvöllur; Thórsmörk Kynnisferðir (for contact information, see following section).

**TOUR OPERATORS** Thórsmörk Kynnisferðir (*☎ 580 5400; e thorsmork@thorsmork.is; www.thorsmork.is*) offers several affordable, short, summer trips into Thórsmörk, including sleeping-bag accommodation and transportation from Hvölsvollur (around US$100 for four days).

For details of other tour operators, see *Chapter 4*, page 72.

**WHERE TO STAY AND EAT** During the main season (1 June–30 September) several cabins and mountain huts are open to hikers at low cost. The main travel hut is **Skagfjörðsskali** (*75 beds; m 893 1191; e fi@fi.is; www.fi.is*), located at the **Húsadalur** campsite and known by most hikers simply as the Thórsmörk hut. Two large kitchens, a big open dining space, and three dormitory rooms make this feel like a jovial summer camp, which it is. For the middle of the wilderness, life is pretty nice – hot showers, barbecue pits, and refreshments and light meals for sale. If you seek more privacy, there is a row of eight individual **cottages** (booked only through Thórsmörk Kynnisferðir). Each sleeps four–five adults comfortably and features individual kitchens. The other hut, **Básar** (*16 beds*) is further in on the river's south banks and a bit more rugged, but also a lot quieter. Also, alternative **campsites** are designated at the base of almost every one of the smaller valley heads.

**WHAT TO SEE AND DO** On the way into the valley, the road passes the pretty glacier lagoon at **Gígjökull** and another at **Steinsholtsjökull**, both glacier tongues extending from Eyjafjallajökull. The **woods**, from whence comes the name 'Thórsmörk', include a number of shady, low-lying birch forests protected by the wind in the hollows between the mountains. Once you get into the heart of the valley, all you need are a good pair of hiking boots and the urge to explore hill and dale. A popular trail goes to the top of **Mt Rjúpnafell** (830m) and another ascends to the icy edges of Mýrdalsjökull. Also, take a look at the telltale rock formations of **Tröllakirkja** ('troll's church'). The trail to Skógar passes the southern uplands of the valley, known as **Goðaland** or 'God's land'. After a day's hiking, have a good, hot soak in **Thórslaug**, a manmade but naturally heated wading pool near Húsadalur.

## VÍK

The pretty meadows of Mýrdalur ('marsh valley') are wedged between the sea and the towering glacier Mýrdalsjökull. Iceland's southernmost village is this forgotten collection of homes known simply as 'bay'. The area was first settled in the 9th century by Hjörleif, the unfortunate brother of Ingólfur Arnason (see page 124) who was mercilessly killed by his own slaves (see page 230). Owing to the impending volcano Katla, the area remained uninhabited until the last 100 years or so, when new lava created enough flat space for the buildings seen today, including the traditional church. For ring-road tourists, Vík has become a popular south Iceland stop, although it is quite small and not known to be a thrilling destination. Nearby however, one can easily explore both mountain and sea.

**GETTING THERE AND AWAY** Vík represents the point on the ring road when you've gone beyond the comfortable 'day trip' distance from Reykjavík and are now entering the domain of the wilder parts of east Iceland. Drivers need only follow the ring road in either direction. Daily buses service Vík on the way between Reykjavík (4 hours) and Skaftafell (2 hours).

### TOURIST INFORMATION

**Tourist information** Vikurbraut 28; 487 1395; e info@vik.is; www.vik.is; summer 09.00–18.00 daily

### WHERE TO STAY AND EAT

**Hótel Edda** (32 rooms, 10 summer houses) Klettsvegur; 487 1480; e edda@edda.is; www.hoteledda.is. With its 'plus' distinction, this Hótel Edda outshines the rest on account of its upmarket attitude that gets reflected in both the rooms & service. Each room has its own bathroom (with bath) & the restaurant serves meals with a view of the blue sea. **$$$**

**Hótel Höfðabrekka** (62 rooms) 487 1208; e info@hofdabrekka.is; www.hofdabrekka.is. Just outside Vík, this open 'ranch' of a hotel is the ultimate traveller's rest on the ring road. Clean & open (yet private), nearly every spacious room has its own bathroom (with shower) & the buffet meals are a well-known treat among seasoned travellers. Cheaper sleeping-bag spaces are also available & there are 4 hot tubs out back. Recommended. **$$$**

**Hótel Lundi** (22 rooms) Víkurbraut 24A; 487 1212; e hotellundi@islandia.is; www.hotelpuffin.is. Quirky hotel in town managed by great hosts with a personal touch. Rooms are comfortable & clean, with some bathrooms shared. Non-guests might want to try out the restaurant's well-meaning cuisine (*mains from 2,490ISK*). The Lundi also operates a 12-room guesthouse. B/fast inc. *Sleeping-bag accommodation 3,100ISK*. **$$$**

**Camping** (*Klettsvegur; 487 1345;* **$$**) Next to the Edda, with average amenities.

**WHAT TO SEE** The southernmost point of mainland Iceland is the cape at Dýrhólaey (the 'hole in the door'), where the sea erodes the 100m-high lava cliffs into weird and wonderful shapes. The namesake rock is a natural arch formed by wave erosion, and many more stacks and rock pinnacles poke up from the point at Reynisdrangar. These are all remnants of volcanic islands, some broken into smaller islets, others joined to the land with black-sand beaches. It is definitely a windswept place and in July, the area is teeming with puffins and guillemots. For a more intimate look, book an amphibious tour (*Dyrhólaeyjarferðir;* ☎ *487 8500;* e *info@dyrholaey.com; www.dyrholaey.com*) on one of the car/boats that gets a lot closer to the geology on offer. To be frank though, a walk along the very wide beach is just as amazing, unless you are eager to ride a boat through the hole in the rock. Inland takes you to the icy shield of Mýrdalsjökull glacier (almost 600km² of ice). The glacier covers Katla, probably the most horrific volcano in the country and the cause of much grief and suffering throughout Iceland's history. The mountain is now a sleeping giant, allowing tourists to trek around on glacier trips (*Arcanum;* ☎ *487 1500;* e *snow@snow.is; www.snow.is*). The company can arrange to pick up guests at both Skógar and Vík, offering tours on the ice with snowmobiles, jeeps, or crampons. A typical two-hour tour costs around US$288.

## KIRKJUBÆJARKLAUSTUR

The 'church farm cloister' sits at the edge of Eldhraun ('fire lava'), the impressive lava field laid out during the 1783 Lakí eruption. The village's name denotes an ecclesiastical past, starting with those early Irish monks and then a 12th-century Benedictine convent, hence the many place names that begin with *systra*, or sister – Systrastapi or 'the sisters' rock' marks the spot where two nuns were burned to death; the lake Systravatn is where they bathed. Although this is quite a small village, Kirkjubæjarklaustur is an important travellers' junction, with amenities including an active fuel station and *sjoppa*, and some good hotels. From here, one can head into the interior (Landmannalaugar) or visit the nether regions of Skaftafell (Lakagígar).

**GETTING THERE AND AWAY** There is a bus from Reykjavík (5+ hours) via Vík (1 hour) that continues on to Skaftafell (1 hour). Another bus connects Kirkjubæjarklaustur to Landmannalaugar (4 hours) via Eldgjá (2 hours) (e *info@re.is; www.re.is*).

### TOURIST INFORMATION

**Tourist information** Located inside the Skaftárskaáli; ☎ 487 4620; e klaustur@klaustur.is; www.klaustur.is; ⏲ 09.00–17.00 daily

### A FIERY SERMON

When Lakí erupted in 1783, local pastor Jón Steingrímsson kept a good diary of the events, describing the sulphur raining down, ash falling from the sky, and poisoned sheep. After months of terrible destruction, the lava began flowing into Kirkjubæjarklaustur. Jón then gathered his congregation to the church and delivered his infamous Eldmessa ('fire sermon'), in which he reproached the crowd for their sins and laziness. The penitent believers became even more believing when the creeping lava stopped right at the edge of the church (next to the sisters' rock) and all were spared.

## WHERE TO STAY

**Hótel Klaustur** (25 rooms) 487 4900; e icehotels@icehotels.is; www.icehotels.is. A classy, upmarket Icelandair hotel with private rooms (& showers) & a grand restaurant. B/fast inc. **$$$$**

**Geirland** (28 rooms) 487 4677; e geirland@centrum.is; www.geirland.is. Clean, decent 'travel centre' just outside the town that caters to groups. Most rooms (some in separate cottages) have their own bath, but not all. **$$$**

**Hótel Lakí** (16 rooms); 487 4694; e efrivik@simnet.is; www.efrivik.is. This new hotel has a very good vibe & is strange in that gracious Icelandic kind of way. Located just outside the village, the compound comprises individual cabins with private kitchens & bathrooms. A dining room feeds guests from morning to evening & there's a nice sauna & hot tub. **$$$**

**Hvoll Youth Hostel** (70 beds) Skaftárhreppur; 484 4785; e hvoll@hostel.is; www.simnet.is/nupsstadarskogur; Mar–Nov. A renovated farm school, this very large youth hostel is located about 5mins off the ring road as you head east from Kirkjubæjarklaustur; caters to hikers. **$**

**Camping** A well-managed site in the village centre (*487 4612;* **$**). With all amenities.

**WHERE TO EAT** The **Hótel Klaustur** (see above) has the nicest restaurant in town, although most travellers tend to make a pit stop at the petrol station/fast-food joint **Skaftárskali** (*487 4628; 08.00–23.00*). Both Laki and Geirland have so-so dining halls.

**WHAT TO SEE** A modern church commemorating the faith of Jón Steingrímmson stands near the spot of his famous sermon, **Kirkjubæjarstofa** (*487 4645; e kbstofa@simnet.is; kbkl.is*). The deceiving 'church floor', or **Kirkjugólf**, is the curious basalt crystals formed in that same eruption, laying out a flat, hexagonal pattern on the ground.

From the village there are a number of easy and interesting hikes up into the mountains, namely Kaldbakur. The ring road west to Skaftafell takes you past the ancient farm of **Núpsstaður** where a very old turf church remains. Continue up the valley to Núpsstaðskógar, a wooded area on the edge of Vatnajökull glacier.

## LAKAGÍGAR

The epicentre of Iceland's deadliest volcano (see *A Fiery Sermon*, opposite) is a rare and fragile landscape, recently made a part of Skaftafell National Park (see page 422). The central highlight is the ominous Lakí crater (818m). From the car park, several trails explore the region; the longest (the yellow one), goes all the way around the base, and the shortest (marked blue), which descends into the crater row itself. Another good hike follows the broken ridge of the Tjarnargígur crater.

As it becomes more popular, getting to Lakí is becoming easier. In a 4x4, take the F206 northwards. Be warned that this is a VERY rough road with several fords along the way. In summer (July/August), bus tours to Lakí leave from Kirkjubæjarklaustur (2.5 hours) and Skaftafell (3.5 hours) (*545 1717; e info@austurleid.is; www.austurleid.is*). No camping is allowed inside the park's boundaries, but there are comfortable mountain huts at Blagi and Skælingur (*e fi@fi.is; www.fi.is*). It is nearly impossible to reach, but those who make it to Langisjór are met with a most heavenly view.

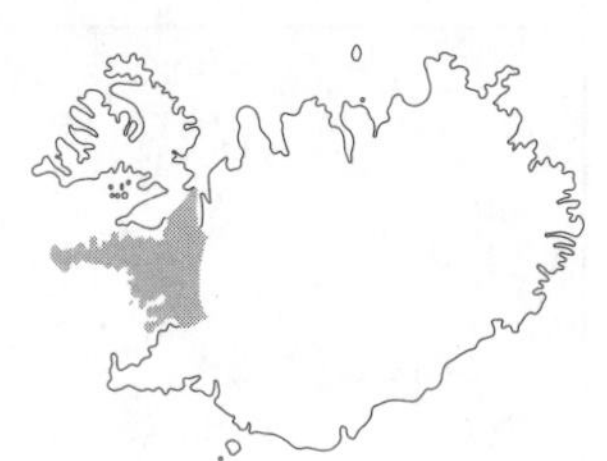

# Vesturland (West Iceland)

Icelanders maintain that the west represents the whole of Iceland in miniature. How true that is, for everything that Iceland has – mountains, glaciers, hot springs, black-sand beaches, rapid rivers, wistful churches, sleepy fishing villages – all of it is packed tightly into this one little robust stretch on the west side of the country. That is why travellers love it so much and precisely why the west is best for those with very limited time.

You will see some astounding things with each passing mile, scenes that demand frequent stops and long stares. An hour or so outside the capital, the land starts to change into something quite extraordinary. Beyond the plotted hayfields and working farms lies a volcanic landscape that does whatever it wants. Visitors are surprised to find out that mountains come in these shapes, that cows graze at the edge of gigantic craters, and that no matter where you wander, the mystical ice cap on Snæfellsnes is always looming back at you.

On maps, the west shows up as the far fringe of a round country, but for Icelanders this is the heartland. The earliest settlers congregated on these rivers, fjords and mountainsides, and there is not a spot of rock or land that hasn't been touched by their folklore. The west was home to Snorri Sturluson (wily author of so many sagas) along with thick-skulled Viking Egil Skallagrímsson (see page 258) and a whole cast of Iceland's heroes. A trio of classic western towns (Ólafsvík, Grundarfjörður, and Stykkishólmur) set the stage for some of Iceland's greatest fishing ventures, and even today Vesturland has a peculiar hold on national politics. Of course, the casual observer is more privy to the natural world: the seals, the whales, and a lovely barage of birds. The sea is also more prominent and part of the open emotion of this western peninsula.

The ultimate finale comes at the end in a beautifully barren national park, a reward for those who go the distance.

## GETTING AROUND

Route 54 diverges from the ring road at Borg, after which it circles the Snæfellsnes Peninsula, with all paths leading to Stykkishólmur in one way or another. The three roads that cut across the centre each provide a scenic interlude.

**Trex** (*www.trex.is*) offers bus links from Reykjavík, and has several routes that are conducive to sightseeing (around the peninsula, inside the national park, and to the bigger towns); however, note that outside summertime, these links are greatly reduced.

As a resut of its concise highlights and short distances, west Iceland is a real hit among cyclists.

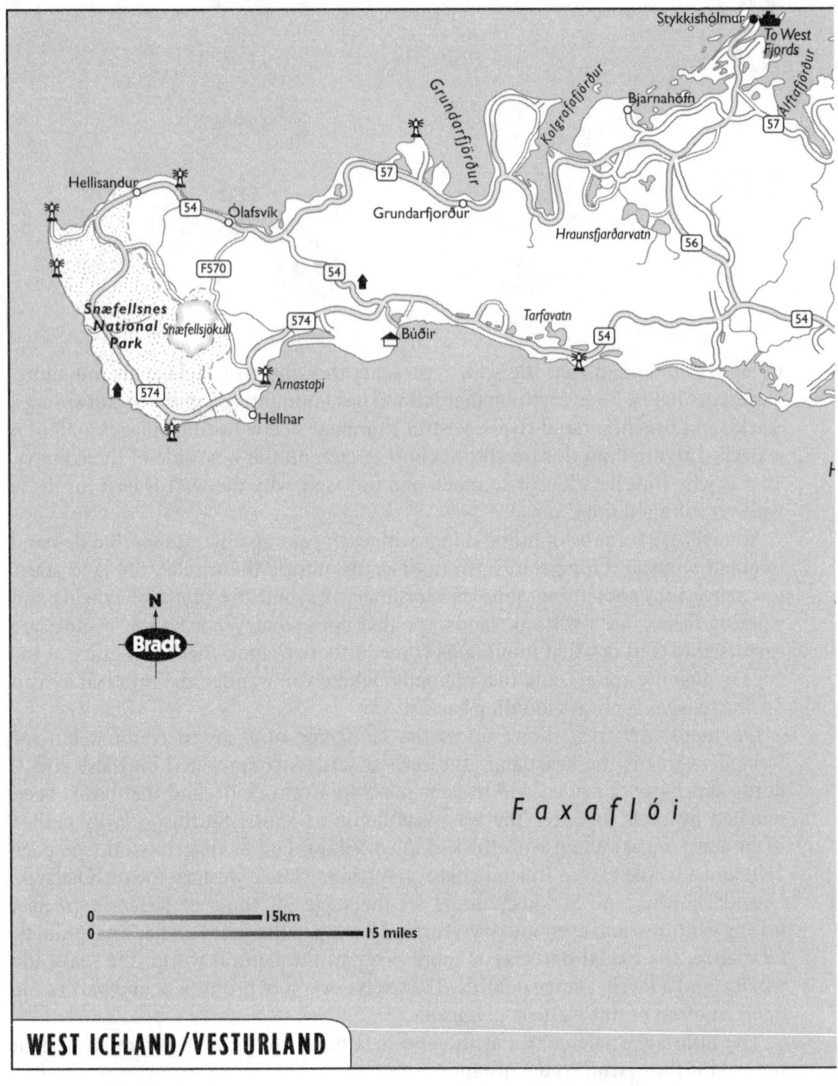


## HVALFJÖRÐUR

'Whale fjord' is the long hooked finger of a fjord curving in beyond the uplands of Mt Esja and dividing the west from the rest of the country. Abundant whales once lived in the fjord (note the local whaling station), but the name comes from the Eddic legend of Ruðhöfði, the red-headed whale. The road around the fjord (Route 47) offers a scenic prelude to what lies ahead and is known for its stillness and isolated mountain views. For its secrecy and proximity to the capital, Hvalfjörður was a base of operations for the British RAF in World War II. A number of barracks are still standing at the base of the fjord, some of which have been converted into summer homes. The trail of the 'herringmen', or **Síldurmannagöngur**, follows the old path that fishermen once used to and from the fjord to net herring. Few people hike the path today, although the cairns are still there all the way across Botnsheiði

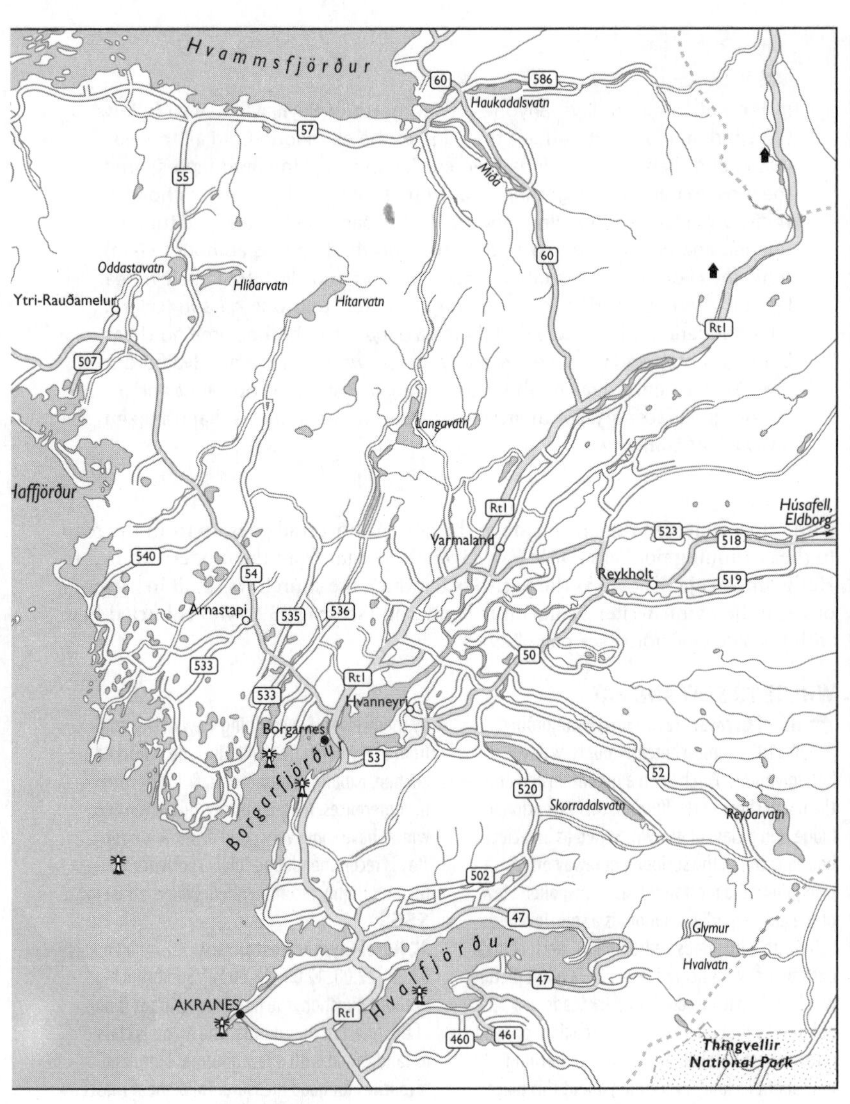


(note that it is very steep and leads you into a pretty but empty valley that's not close to anything). The more obvious highlight is **Glymur**, the tallest waterfall in Iceland at 200m. The name 'ringing' falls comes from the natural acoustics of so much water falling so far into a narrow chasm that's been cut from the volcano **Mt Hvalfell** (848m) or 'whale mountain'. Surely, this is a breathtaking sight, but hiking up to Glymur is not some effortless jaunt and there's a reason why so few travellers go there. From the road at the very back of the fjord, the hike to the waterfall takes about three hours, following the Botnsá streambed up a very narrow 'canyon'. Hikers must cross the river many times, sometimes on boards balanced on boulders with just a rope to guide you. Because you are essentially trekking up the narrow gorge of a powerful river with a waterfall at the end, the path is best avoided if it's raining or recently been raining – an inch of rainfall can make the

## HVALFJARÐARGÖNG

In the not-so-olden days, anyone driving north of Reykjavík had to follow the winding road as it hugged the edge of the extra-long fjord all the way inland and then all the way back again. For so many, the fjord represented the most tedious part of getting away from the city, and weekend or holiday traffic only made it worse. In 1998, the Hvalfjarðargöng ('whale fjord tunnel') opened and drivers cheered as they sped north, dropping an hour (65km) from their journey. The tunnel is 5,770m long and dips 165ft below sea level; it's an engineering feat and one of the few tolls one pays in Iceland (at a staggering price!). Now that there's a bypass, the 'bothersome' fjord has been forgotten and yet there are a few people who miss the old Hvalfjörður road. They've started taking the long way again just for the nostalgia and for the gorgeous scenery. For them, the best part of the tunnel is that it's taken away all the traffic.

path impassable. On the north side of the fjord a short trail goes up from the road to the swimming pool at **Hlaðir** (☎ *433 9890*), not far from the modern church of **Hallgrímskirkja**. Known as the parish of Saurbær, the church was built in memory of Icelandic hymn-writer Hallgrímur Pétursson (see page 39) who is buried here with his wife Guðriður (see page 229).

### WHERE TO STAY AND EAT

**Hótel Glymur** (22 rooms) Hvalfjörður; ☎ 430 3100; e info@hotelglymur.is; www.hotelglymur.is. Perched on a mountainside on the north shore of Hvalfjörður, this exceptional lodge is in a class of its own. Styled as an eclectic boutique hotel, the secluded getaway offers tranquillity & a most fabulous & unspoiled view of the entire fjord. Each room is a split-levelled suite with a luxurious bedroom loft, perfect little bathrooms (with heated floors!) & a giant picture window. A spacious outdoor deck leads to a set of hot tubs that offers reflective soaking, or head into the vast hotel library & learn something new about Iceland. Everything about this place just makes good sense, including the art on the walls. There are also 6 villas on the property, each an exercise in modern splendour and comfort: acrylic furniture, personal hot tubs, bedrooms that could pass as upmarket hotel rooms all by themselves, & a stunning view of the fjord from every porch. The villas include a stocked kitchen, expanded bathrooms, & 1 is devoted to conferences. Alas, it's pricey, but autumn & winter have some very good deals. A longer stay is recommended to fully experience Glymur. Highly recommended. Divine b/fast inc. **$$$$**

**Hótel Glymur Restaurant** ⌚ for all meals: 07.00–22.00, 12.00–18.00 Sat/Sun brunch. Without question, the hotel's restaurant is one of the finest in the country. The menu is classic Icelandic food with a few gourmet European favourites for good measure. Think meat roasts & good fish with lots of fresh sides (eg: home-baked bread, smoked Icelandic lamb, etc), made by the 3 full-time chefs. Evening & brunch buffets make this a popular dining destination from Reykjavík. *Mains from 2,650ISK.* **$$$$**

## AKRANES

Akranes is turning into a bit of a bedroom community for Reykjavík, with commuters zipping to and from the capital through the new tunnel in under 30 minutes. For the 6,000 people who live here, life is good – the streets are laid out in practical square blocks and behind the smokestacks and harbour cranes, there's a popular grey-sand beach that only Icelanders could love. The *Landnámabók* claims Akranes was settled in the 9th century by Irish immigrants, now the basis for the town's annual 'Irish Days' celebration. Following the general evolution of Icelandic settlements, Akranes grew into a major fishing port and then a major centre of industry by the mid 1940s. Today, Akranes exudes the enthusiastic tone of post-war industrial films, a town that's 'on the move' with industry and healthy living and a giant aluminium smelter that employs thousands. It's the kind of place that gets advertised as a 'good place to raise kids' and the kind of town that takes pride in having had the first paved streets in Iceland. Despite worthy attempts by the town council and big industry, Akranes holds practically zero tourist appeal. Unless you're visiting friends, on a business trip, or caught in a blizzard, there are far more exciting places to be exploring in Iceland. Icelanders themselves only care about Akranes for one reason – the Akranes football team is the best in the country, having won the Iceland Cup again and again. Known simply as **ÍA** (*www.ia.is*), the yellow and black play all over Europe and repeatedly bring shame to Reykjavík.

**GETTING THERE AND AWAY** From the ring road, take a turn on Route 51. Akranes is halfway between Reykjavík (30 minutes) and Borgarnes (30 minutes). Akranes is close enough to Reykjavík to take the city bus with a transfer at Háholt, but it takes twice as long (1 hour).

### TOURIST INFORMATION

**Tourist information office** e info@visitakranes.is; www.visitakranes.is. Located at the Folk Museum.

**WHERE TO STAY** For such a big city, guest beds are in short supply. Besides the nearby Hótel Glymur, there's a handful of bed and breakfasts: the small guesthouse **Móar** (*4 rooms; Innri Akraneshreppur;* ☎ *431 1389;* e *sollajo@simnet.is;* **$$**); in summer, you can stay at the home of Ólina Jónsdóttir (*Háholt 11;* ☎ *431 1408;* **$$**). For something more fancy, try the **Hótel Barbró** (*16 rooms; Kirkjubraut 11;* ☎ *431 4240;* e *barbro@internet.is; www.barbro.is;* **$$$**). The town's **campsite** (**$**) is on the bay Kalmansvík up on the north side of the peninsula.

**WHERE TO EAT** Akranes is not known for fine dining, but there are plenty of casual places to grab a bite. Hótel Barbró features the best cuisine in town and the biggest dining space. Another town favourite is **Café Mörk** (*Skólabraut 14;* ☎ *431 5030;* ⌚ *10.00–22.00 daily*), a relaxed diner. Also, the pizza joint **Hrói Höttur** (*Stillholt 23;* ☎ *431 1200;* ⌚ *11.00–23.00 daily*) who do deliver. There's more fast food to be had across the street at **Café 67** (*Stillholt 16–18;* ☎ *430 6767;* ⌚ *09.00–21.30 Sun–Thu, 10.00–midnight Fri/Sat*). On your own, head to the grocery store **10-11** (*Skagabraut 43;* ☎ *431 2592;* ⌚ *10.00–23.00 daily*) or the **bakery Harðarbakarí** (Kirkjubraut 54; ☎ 431 2399; ⌚ *08.00–18.00 Mon–Fri, 08.00–16.00 Sat/Sun*).

**WHAT TO SEE AND DO** The **Folk Museum** (*Safnasvæðið á Akranesi; Garðar;* ☎ *431 5566;* e *info@museum.is; www.museum.is;* ⌚ *summer 10.00–18.00 daily, winter 13.00–18.00 daily; entrance 500ISK*) has a huge display that comprises several buildings and so many different attractions that it feels like a ploy. Still, anyone who likes technology, old boats, or history will enjoy a lazy wander through the grounds and exhibits. Geirsstaðir is the local school built in 1903, next to the red house **Neðri-Sýrupartur** (built 1875), considered the oldest wooden house in the town. A boatyard displays a history of fishing boats in Akranes, the prize of which is the English cutter *Sigurfari* (built in 1885). There's also an art museum, a sport museum, and a scattering of other diversions. The truly exceptional exhibit is the mineral museum in the largest building. Here visitors can become acquainted with every kind of stone that occurs in Iceland – the most exhaustive collection in the country. Akranes also takes great pride in its huge sport complex at Jaðarsbakkar, the highlight of which is the spectacular **swimming pool** (☎ *413 3112;* 🕒 *year-round 06.45–21.00 Mon–Fri, 09.00–18.00 Sat/Sun*). If you're feeling brave, try swimming at the beach of Langisandur, on the south bay of Krossvík.

## EGILS SAGA

Egil Skallagrímsson (AD910–90) was the younger son of Skalla-Grímur, the man who founded Borg, the town of Borgarnes, and all the farms around Borgarfjörður. The sagas describe Egil's older brother Thorolf as handsome, gifted, and likeable. Egil, on the other hand, is described as ugly, difficult, and talkative. At age three, Egil crashed a drinking party and surprised the guests with his improvised poetry. At age six, he committed his first murder when he drove a battleaxe into the brains of a bully who was teasing him in a ball game (his mother smiled proudly and told Egil that he'd grow up to be a great Viking). At age 12, Egil developed a tit-for-tat rivalry with his father. First Skalla-Grímur grew so enraged that he killed Egil's best friend, then drowned Egil's favourite nanny. That night at dinner, Egil retaliated by killing his father's favourite farmhand. Thus began his long and prosperous (and violent career) as an Icelandic Viking.

Egils saga describes countless wars, raids, trades, and exploits all over Europe. His life personified the ultimate image of what makes a good Viking: a man who is fierce, strong, sometimes fair, and always poetic. For one, Egil was a highly accomplished drinker who consistently out-drank his friends and enemies – there is a good reason why Iceland's most popular beer is named Egils. He was unbelievably strong – often defending himself against ten or 20 men. Also, his violent outbursts were legendary. In one duel, Egil throws down his sword and shield, rushes his opponent and kills him by biting his throat with his teeth. In the course of the saga, he murders and maims hundreds, and kills a wild bull with his bare hands. For Egil, the show of courage was key – one time his men robbed a farm in the dead of night, walking away unnoticed. Troubled by this show of cowardice, Egil goes back to the farm, wakes everyone up, burns down the farmhouse and kills everyone inside.

Fortunately, poetry softened Egil's animal instincts, and his words won him great respect. Facing an early morning execution at the hands of King Eric Bloodaxe, Egil spent a whole night composing *Höfuðlausn* ('Head Ransom'), a clever, 20-stanza poem in praise of the king that won him a pardon. Back at Borg, after one son was killed and another drowned in an accident, Egil composed the 25-stanza poem *Sonatorrek* (Loss of Sons'), a thoughtful reflection on the emptiness he felt. Egil went on to live a long life, ending his days at his daughter-in-law's home at Mosfellsbær (see page 197), where he buried his famous treasure of silver. Egils saga is one of the longer tales among those of the Icelanders (almost 200 pages in print). If you don't have the patience to read it all, visit the Settlement Centre in Borgarnes – it's as good as watching a film, if there was a film.

## BORGARFJÖRÐUR

Borgarfjörður is the heart of Iceland's 'Viking country', the peaceful green homeland of the very same scary band of marauders who once terrorised Europeans. It makes sense why they picked this place – a land of salmon-filled rivers, open valleys for grazing, and easy access for boats. The first settler to the fjord was Skalla-Grímur Kveldúlfsson, who had fled the ire of King Harald the Fair-haired of Norway at the end of the 9th century. Skalla-Grímur claimed the land from the sea all the way up to the mountains, and named practically everything that you see on the map today. The largest 'white' river he called Hvíta, and the river that crosses it he called Thverá ('cross'). He made his home at Borg ('fortress') the beautiful 'marshland' Mýrar. Today, one of the best views of the fjord is from the bridge of Route 1 as it crosses into Borgarnes below the stunning sharp mountains of Hafnarfjall. As friends and relatives followed Skalla-Grímur, the number of Viking farms spread all the way upriver, from Hvanneyri to Húsafell. This is still one of the most densely populated valleys in the country outside Reykjavík.

Borgarfjörður is an easy and very interesting region to visit. All sorts of organised tours offer 'saga trail' excursions, revisiting the sites of the most well-known sagas, especially Reykholt. Anyone can drive, bike, or hike through these farms (most of which offer accommodation) and enjoy the historical landscape. Route 1 skims over the top of the valley as it heads to Brú (see page 313) and the northwest, but Route 50 takes you along the same route that Skalla-Grímur explored 1,100 years ago.

## BORGARNES

The first farm in west Iceland was at Borg, after which the nearby *nes*, or peninsula, was named Borgarnes. Pay attention to place names, as so many of them come right out of Egils saga. The town occupies a narrow spit of hilly land that juts out into the fjord, connected to the ring road by one of the longest bridges in the country. The view from town over the water to the Hafnarfjall Mountains is captivating. Despite all the history and activity in these parts, Borgarnes only became a town in 1861 and later had its own stake in Iceland's co-operative movement. Today, it's a town of 2,000 people and a convenient travel stop on the ring road, with much to see and do in the close vicinity.

**GETTING THERE AND AWAY** Borgarnes is about an hour from Reykjavík on Route 1. A number of **Trex** (*www.trex.is*) buses travel to and from Reykjavík on their way to Snæfellsnes, Reykhólar, Reykholt and Brú. The bus station is at the Hyrnan travel centre.

**TOURIST INFORMATION** A comprehensive travel centre is located in the Hyrnan complex, just off the ring road (after the bridge) (*Brúartorg; 437 2214; e tourinfo@vesturland.is; www.borgarfjordur.com; 08.00–23.30 daily*).

### WHERE TO STAY

#### In town

**Hótel Borganes** (75 rooms) Egilsgata 16; 437 1119; e hotelbo@centrum.is; www.hotelborgarnes.is. Modern, functional, travellers' hotel with plain rooms but decent service. More than half the rooms have private showers, the rest share. Located in the town centre on the top of a hill, it's a short walk to the pool & the museum. B/fast inc. *Sleeping-bag accommodation 3,000ISK.* **$$$**

**Bjarg** (14 beds) 437 1925; e bjarg@

simnet.is. A down-to-earth farmhouse just on the outskirts of town but with great prices. Sleeping-bag accommodation available; shared bathrooms. Bjarg is in the midst of an expansion, so be ready to be dazzled... in a low-key, homely Icelandic way. Recommended. **$$**

**Borganes Hostel** (52 beds) Borgarbraut 9–13; ☎ 695 3366; e borgarnes@hostel.is; www.borganeshostel.com. This new hostel used to be the town hall, & before that was a centre-of-town factory. Accordingly, it's large, spacious, & perfectly located. Guests have access to 2 kitchens & a large commonunal area. From the front door, it's a quick walk to the pier looking over the fjord, the Settlement Centre, or the popular World of Puppets (see *What to see & do*, opposite). **$$**

**Lækjarkot** (20 beds) ☎ 551 9590; e laekjarkot@laekjarkot.is; www.laekjarkot.is. 6km outside town are 4 cabins (5 beds each) with kitchens, shower/WC, & additional space for campers. Contact for pricing.

**Camping** The campsite is located right at the edge of the fjord, looking out towards the mountains (☎ *437 2214;* e *upplysinagar@vesturland.is; www.borgarbyggd.is;* ⏲ *25 May–20 Sep;* **$**). Pay at the information centre at Hyrnan. Note that this place is always fairly crowded and noisy in summer. For facilities available, see Borganes Hostel above.

## Outside town

**Hótel Hamar** (30 rooms) ☎ 433 6600; e hamar@icehotels.is; www.icehotels.is, www.hotelhamar.is. A little way outside town, this contemporary, ranch-style country hotel caters to conference visitors with a focus on the nearby golf course, & a luxury in-house restaurant. All rooms have private bathrooms & big windows that look out over the landscape. 3 geothermal hot tubs make it even nicer. B/fast inc. **$$$$**

**Hamar Youth Hostel** (18 beds) ☎ 437 2000; e hamar@hostel.is; www.hostel.is; ⏲ May–Sep. Big country villa with a stunning view of the fjord & mountains. A shuttle goes back & forth to the bus stop & town centre (4km away). The golf course nearby can be booked through the hostel as well, Mon–Fri. Shared bathrooms, sleeping-bag spots available. Summer **$$$**; winter **$$**

**Motel Venus** (8 rooms) ☎ 437 2345; e motel@centrum.is; www.motelvenus.net. In the shadow of the mountain before you cross the bridge into Borgarnes, this gritty little lodge is a slightly less expensive option to staying in the town itself. Rooms are fairly average & badly decorated, a few of which have their own bathrooms. A popular travellers' café serves greasy food & pizza. Overall, not as innocent as it might seem. *Sleeping-bag accommodation under 3,000ISK; 1,500ISK to pitch a tent (which includes fishing rights)*. **$$$**

**Old English Lodge** (10 rooms) ☎ 437 1725; e enskuhusin@simnet.is; www.enskuhusin.is. *Ensku húsin* is a misnomer, given the master of the lodge was not *Ensku*, but Scottish – a Lord Campbell who used this faraway cottage as his own private fishing hideaway. Situated among the waterfalls of the Lángá River, great efforts have been made to preserve the original early 1900s feel of the place. Rooms are small but steeped in history & authentic antiques. For real effect, stay in the upstairs loft, or rent one of the separate cottages. A jewel of a B&B in the gorgeous Icelandic countryside. **$$$**

**WHERE TO EAT** All the hotels have their own restaurants, and the youth hostel serves meals. Hótel Borgarnes caters to the tourist palate (trusty fish and lamb), while Hótel Hamar is more gourmet (eg: grilled salmon in reduction sauce). A more honest and original dining experience is found at Buðarklettur (*Brákarbraut 13;* ⏲ *11.00–21.00 daily*), and if you're seeing a show you get a special price. Dedicated to fresh and organic ingredients, the menu pays tribute to Viking times with healthy alternatives (and lots of vegetarian dishes). There's also a nice café to enjoy coffee and cakes.

## SNORRI STURLUSON (1179–1241)

Iceland's ultimate 'Renaissance man' was born into a powerful family, the Sturlungs (see page 20). On his mother's side he was descended from Egil Skallagrímsson of Borg. As a child, Snorri was educated at Oddi in south Iceland (see page 245). He married a wealthy widow and established himself at Reykholt in 1206. There he began his prolific writing career – the greatest of all the saga writers. He wrote the *Heimskringla* (History of Kings), the poetic *Edda*, and many sagas, including (some believe) Egils saga. He was known to write all through the long winters, but scholars are still amazed by his output. He twice served as the law-speaker at the Althing, where he was respected as a talented leader. His fatal flaw was his dealing with King Håkon of Norway who tried to use Snorri to bring the whole of Iceland under his control. Such was the beginning of Iceland's civil war, but Snorri attempted to play all sides and lost on all fronts. Eventually tiring of Snorri's antics, the king dispatched a rival clan to Reykholt to get rid of him. Snorri was killed in his basement by the axe of Árni Beiskur ('the bitter'). Snorri's famous last words? 'Don't strike!'

Unique for Iceland is the Filipino restaurant Matstofan (*Brákarbraut 3; ☎ 437 2017; ⌚ 11.00–23.00 daily*) – it's kind of amazing to find rice this good way out here. The bulk of the population feed at Hyrnan (*Brúartorg; ☎ 430 5550; ⌚ 08.30–23.30 daily*), a grocery store/fast-food paradise of soft-serve ice cream, hot dogs, overflowing sandwiches, and pizza, of course.

**WHAT TO SEE AND DO** The farm of **Borg** lies on top of the rocky rise just outside town, after the junction with Route 54. Borg á Myram is where it all began – Egils saga and the many adventures that followed. Today it is a quiet, black-and-white church (built in 1880) with a monument to Egil's epic poem *Sonatorrek* (see next section). A trail ventures up to the outcrop behind the church where a stone pillar shows the exact location of the famous ruins. Walking in the footsteps of all these characters from Egils saga can feel stirring.

Back in Borgarnes, the main street is called Brákarbruat (Brák's Way), which was the path along which Egil's nanny Thorgerður Brák was chased before jumping off a cliff and getting pummelled with a boulder thrown by Skalla-Grímur. She drowned in Brákarsund (Brák's Sound), and the gigantic stone cairn memorial (tied with chains) reads 'here Skalla-Grímur drowned Brák'. Likewise, the park **Skallagrímsgarður** was the location of Skalla-Grímur's burial mound, near the town's swimming pool (*Thorsteinsgata 1; ☎ 437 1444; ⌚ 07.00–22.00 Mon–Fri, 09.00–18.00 Sat/Sun*).

You find out all these details and more at the **Settlement Centre** (*Landnámssetur Íslands; Brákarbraut 13–15; ☎ 437 1600; e landma@landnam.is; www.landnam.is; ⌚ summer 10.00–19.00 daily, winter 11.00–17.00 daily, closed Tue; entrance 800ISK*). No other museum in Iceland explains the settlement of Iceland in a more entertaining and educated fashion. Audio narratives explain each separate exhibit, one of which focuses solely on the story of Egils saga. Anyone setting off on a 'saga' tour would be well advised to get their bearings and some context here before starting.

The **World of Puppets** (*Skúlagata 17; ☎ 530 5000; e bruduheimar@bruduheimar.is; www.bruduheimar.is; ⌚ 11.00–18.00 daily)* has a museum and theatre and is also popular.

## THE SAGA CIRCLE

The knot of rivers and roads beyond Borg offer easy access to a number of natural and historical sites. Aside from all the 'saga circle' package tours available, a daily bus travels from Borg to Reykholt via Hvanneyri with stops at most of the attractions. From Hvanneyri (one of Skalla-Grímur's first sheep farms), follow Route 50 to the village of Kleppjárnsreykir and the nearby hot springs of **Deildartunguhver**. A guarded path takes you through the largest geothermal area in Iceland, in terms of volume of hot water that gets pumped to all the cities in Vesturland. If you take a shower anywhere within a 100km radius, you've already bathed in it. Also, look for the bright-green *skollakampi* or hard fern (*Blechnum spicant*) – quite common in England, this is the only place it grows in Iceland, thanks to the permanent warmth and humidity. Another 6km up the road brings you to the historic hamlet of **Reykholt**. The private estate of saga author Snorri Sturluson is now the celebrated compound of all things relating to the sagas. His statue stands at the centre of it all: the literary institutes, educational exhibits, libraries, farm ruins and the old and new churches that comprise **Snorrastofa** (*433 8000; gestastofa@snorrastofa.is; www.snorrastofa.is*). Part-museum, part-memorial, and part-institute, Reyholt is a pilgrimage site not just for Icelanders, but also for all Scandinavians. Most visitors simply want to visit the place where so many sagas were written, others are there to study, and the local church pays eternal tribute to the father of medieval Scandinavian culture. Foreign tourists usually find a stronger attraction towards **Snorralaug**, the 13th-century natural hot tub where Snorri used to bathe. When it's not closed for 'research', visitors are welcome to take a hot dip.

### WHERE TO STAY AND EAT

**Fosshótel Reykholt** (54 rooms) 435 1260; reykholt@fosshotel.is; www.fosshotel.is. In spite of its matching white concrete exterior, this themed-Fosshótel is rich in medieval Scandinavian imagery. A popular location for conferences, guests are just steps away from Snorrastofa. Rooms are large & modern & all feature private bathrooms (with bath or shower). The restaurant is excellent. B/fast inc. **$$$**

**Camping** On the road to Reykholt, **Fossatún** country farm (*433 5800; info@steinsnar.is; www.steinsnar.is; summer only;* **$**) is a popular country farm campsite for tents and caravans, with great facilities, a sauna and hot tub, and a unique restaurant, Time and Water. Specialising in big Icelandic buffets, it's become a common stop for tour groups.

## HÚSAFELL

Húsafell is mentioned in several sagas, and sets the stage for a huge portion of the Eyjarbyggja saga. The end of the Hvíta River valley marks the western gateway into the highlands, a remote and distant hideaway. On the way there, travellers pass two sets of waterfalls: **Hraunfossar** ('lava falls') and **Barnafoss** ('children's falls'). The latter takes its name from the children who disappeared from a nearby farm – their grieving mother put a curse on the falls that nobody should ever cross the river alive, so don't even try. Upriver and once inside the valley, it is understandable why Húsafell was a popular artists' colony that boasted the likes of Jóhannes Kjarval (see page 183) and Ásgrímur Jónsson (see page 182). The inspiring landscapes still look like paintings – the hills, the heath and the backdrop of glaciers. Húsafell is best for those who want to relax, camp, and be outdoors. If you felt tortured going past all those hot springs that you can't swim in, try the local multi-level **swimming pool** (🕒 *Jun–Sep 10.00–22.00 daily, winter 13.00–16.00 daily*).

Hiking in Húsafell is rewarding, with a number of good trails into the wild beyond. The simplest is right up to the top of **Mt Bæjarfell** (578m) with a wide view from the top of all of Vesturland. A bit more complex is the track up to the glacier-capped **Mt Ok** (1,141m), as in 'oak', not 'OK'. Crampons are normally not necessary, but this still represents a good five hours' walk. More intensive 'fire and ice' destinations are just a short drive outside the valley. **Surtshellir** is a lava cave once inhabited by outlaws and sheep rustlers that looks like an open tear in the ground. The nearby farm at **Fljótstunga** allows access to **Viðgelmir** lava cave, a weird cavern of dripping lava rock versus dripping icicles and the largest in Iceland. This is a beautiful and highly dangerous place with a history of accidents – visitors are only allowed to enter with a licensed guide (*www.fljotstunga.is*). One of the least-visited and least-known regions of the country is **Arnarvatnsheiði**, a barren heath that's spotted with hundreds and hundreds of lakes. Tiny streams and rushing highland rivers connect them all together – an exclusive fisherman's paradise. There's a dirt road (4x4 only) from Húsafell that takes you up to the largest lake, **Úlfsvatn**. It's lovely because there is nothing out here at all. Another rough mountain road (F35) takes you to the west side of **Langjökull** glacier, about 20km east of Húsafell.

**WHERE TO STAY AND EAT** Try to stay at the time- and weather-beaten **old farm** (*Gamli Bær; 5 rooms;* ☎ *435 1550;* ✉ *info@husafell.is; www.husafell.is;* 🕒 *summer only;* **$$**). This bed and breakfast feels like going back in time and has a contemplative atmosphere that matches the natural surroundings (breakfast included). One can also rent a number of small **cabins** with sleeping-bag space for two adults each, or pitch a tent or caravan in the extensive campsite, with hot showers and kitchen space aplenty. For nourishment, you're relegated to the summer *sjoppa* at the petrol station. The farm at **Fljótstunga** (*50 beds;* ☎ *435 1198;* ✉ *fljotstunga@fljotstunga.is; www.fljotstunga.is;* **$$**) is a super-remote but super-popular accommodation, with heavy bookings in summer. Comfy made-up beds are on offer inside the big house and sleeping-bag spaces are available in several smaller shelters; these are excellent facilities for campers.

## SNÆFELLSNES

*Snæ-fells-nes* merely means 'snow mountain peninsula', which it clearly is. Covered in a permanent shield of lumpy ice, **Mt Snæfellsjökull** (1,446m) is the tallest mountain in the long row of grey peaks that divides the sea between Breiðafjörður and Faxaflói. Rising alone from the water, no other point is so visible from the rest of Iceland as this one majestic volcano. Be you in Reykjavík or in the West Fjords, a sunny day will grant you a vision of the mountain and its glacier. As you approach the peninsula the view becomes even more astounding, but once you arrive at the base, the mountain disappears – it is too big to see up close. The mystique of Snæfellsnes lies in its remarkable terrain, the energy of the mountains and the legends connected to this place.

Snæfellsnes seems a determined detour that might feel like going way out on a limb. Anxious tourists often bypass the whole area just to make good distance on the ring road. That is a big mistake, since they are missing a most magnificent place. This long volcanic ridge is a natural paradise with very few people and memorable landscapes. Serious hikers will want to trek any of the many trails, especially those that cross the peninsula – a short distance that ascends some mighty mountains. Everyone should feel encouraged to experience the national park.

**SOUTHERN SHORE** Route 54 crosses a rough lava field before turning into the peninsula. **Eldborg** is the circular crater remaining from a volcanic eruption of 5,000 years ago, although the *Landnámabók* describes a devilish character who caused the eruption by digging into the earth at midnight. As far back as the late 1700s, travelogues have described hiking up to the rim and looking down into the perfect stone circle (well, it's really more of an oval). Its dimensions are 200m in diameter, 50m deep inside, and a rim that's 100m above sea level. Various trails link to the crater, but the most straightforward is from the south at the farm Snorrastaðir. Those who try to cross the lava rock elsewhere give up once they figure how impossible it is. A few miles north and on the opposite side is the turn-off to **Ytri-Rauðamelur**. Here the road passes the most perfect row of square, rock pillars in the whole country, known as **Gerðuberg**. This is columnar basalt at its finest. Further on brings you to the old farm of Réttarskarð and the cute, tin-sided **church** of Ytri-Rauðamelur. A typical country chapel, the red and white exterior sits on a lava rock foundation. Inside, there is room enough for only six benches. At this point the road gets steeper (it helps to have a 4x4) and passes by the namesake **Mt Ytri-Rauðamelskúla** (222m), a bright black and red hill made of scoria, pumice, and sand. It's both astounding and foreboding, as is the surrounding volcanic landscape. The road ends at a dirt car park, near the springs of **Rauðamesölkelda**. This is a very special place, where a clear waterfall tumbles over the basalt cliffs into a myriad pools. A hike to the falls is nice, but Icelanders make the journey to this spot to drink from the spring, where naturally carbonated water gurgles out of the ground, filled with gas bubbling up from the earth. The water has healing qualities and tastes delicious. The spring is marked with an orange flag to let you know where to drink. Please be courteous and do not soil the source.

Route 54 continues along the southern coast and into the heart of the peninsula, with big, flat plains between the black mountains and the sea. The brown-sand beach at **Ytrí-Tunga** is a well-known stop for its seal colony. Don't walk away too quickly; the seals are friendly and curious and will climb up on the rocks near the beach. The best time to see the pups is in June and July. Up on the mountainside is the one-of-a-kind mineral swimming pool **Lýsuhólslaug** (*433 9917; 14.00–20.00 Mon–Sat, 13.00–18.00 Sun*). The popular outdoor baths are filled with naturally carbonated, geothermal water. This is also the start of a great hiking trail up over the mountains to Grundarfjörður (see page 27). The flat plains end at the bumpy lava fields of **Buðahraun**, where a rope lava flowed out of the volcanic fissure of **Buðarklettur**. A single trail traverses this protected nature reserve, passing right next to the crater of Buðahellir. Another trail follows along the wild shore, known for its pure olivine sand (magnesium iron silicate).

## WHERE TO STAY AND EAT

**Hótel Búðir** (20 rooms) 435 6700; e budir@budir.is; www.hotelbudir.is. A boutique hotel without any guile, the Búðir embraces the very mood of the secluded beach upon which it is set. Each room breathes an air of distinction & calm; guests can feel confident that nothing's been overdone. Alas, such soothing taste & effortless charm comes at a staggering price – the 'standard rooms' are less expensive. *Standard rooms around US$250/night.* **$$$$**

**Hótel Eldborg** (26 rooms) 435 6602; e hoteleldborg@hoteleldborg.is; www.hoteleldborg.is; summer only. Very functional, concrete family hotel near Eldborg. Rooms are spacious, clean & warm & the management particularly open & accommodating. Shared bathrooms for all & camping also available. Meals that fill tummies are served in the dining room, including a well-rounded, all-you-can eat dinner buffet. Added bonuses include the geothermal swimming pool & horseriding tours. *Sleeping-bag accommodation under 3,000ISK.* **$$$**

**Snorrastaðir** (50 beds) 435 6627; e snorrastadir@simnet.is; www.snorrastadir.com. This traditional, working, west Icelandic farm welcomes travellers year-round. Located near the trail to Eldborg, group excursions often book out the big 'white house' hostel (sleeps 24), while smaller groups & families can have their own, self-contained summerhouses with kitchenette & bathroom. There's a hot tub & horseriding, too. **$$**

**Hótel Búðir Restaurant** See above; 16.00–22.00 daily. Top of Iceland's gourmet circuit. Serene to the point of sanctimony, everything on your plate is entirely fresh. The menu changes daily, depending on season & the local catch, but there's a strong focus on keeping things local, even serving local birds. The chef's 5-course menu (US$100 pp) is an artistic endeavour. Plan on seeing truffles & double the price for wine pairings. **$$$$$**

## SNÆFELLSJÖKULL NATIONAL PARK

Snæfellsjökull is the youngest (opened in 2001) and smallest of Iceland's four national parks. It might also be the most fascinating, for the twisted lava shapes, its compact size, and the contrast from sea to icy summit. The park centres on the imposing volcano **Mt Snæfellsjökull** (1,446m). Geologists consider Snæfellsjökull dormant but Icelanders insist the mountain is very much alive – the last eruption took place 1,800 years ago, but the previous 10,000-year period saw some 20 different eruptions. The volcano is the best-known Icelandic mountain outside Iceland, thanks to the adventure novelist Jules Verne, whose tale *Journey to the Centre of the Earth* takes its protagonists into the earth through the Snæfellsjökull volcano. Although he never travelled to Iceland, Verne aptly described the top of the mountain as a 'vast dome of white'. In actuality, the summit is a deep 300m crater surrounded by three separate peaks. That means the glacier takes the shape of a lens filling the hollow of the volcano with a globe of ice. As a national park, Snæfellsjökull offers a tranquil escape with powerful views. Below the white cap, the sloping lava descends into a rough and desolate landscape of grey-black hills, craters, cliffs, and fields of broken lava rock. This is not some kind of action-packed adventure land at the edge of a volcano. On the contrary, wandering through this lost world feels meditative and ethereal. If anything, Snæfellsjökull is pure silence.

**GETTING AROUND** Snæfellsjökull features its very own 'ring road': Route 574 skirts the shoreline all the way around the park. The paved Route 54 connects the loop between Búðir and Ólafsvík, while the scenic but more difficult unpaved Route 570 crosses quite close to the mountain's summit. In summer, a number of **Trex** (*www.trex.is*) buses travel in both directions, from Arnastapi to Ólafsvík and beyond, with stops at all the major 'attractions' in the park. The ring loop is perfect for mountain bikers, but note that Route 574 is unpaved through much of the park, so road bikes are not the best.

**WHERE TO STAY AND EAT** With the exception of hikers and bikers in tents, camping inside the national park is strictly prohibited; all other forms of accommodation are located outside the park. The park's main gateway is at Hellnar, home to **Hótel Hellnar** (*20 rooms; 435 6820; e hotel@hellnar.is; www.hotelhellnar.is; May–Oct;* **$$$**). As a certified 'Green Globe 21' (*www.greenglobe21.com*) sustainable tourist destination, the hotel is dedicated to the highest environmental principles.

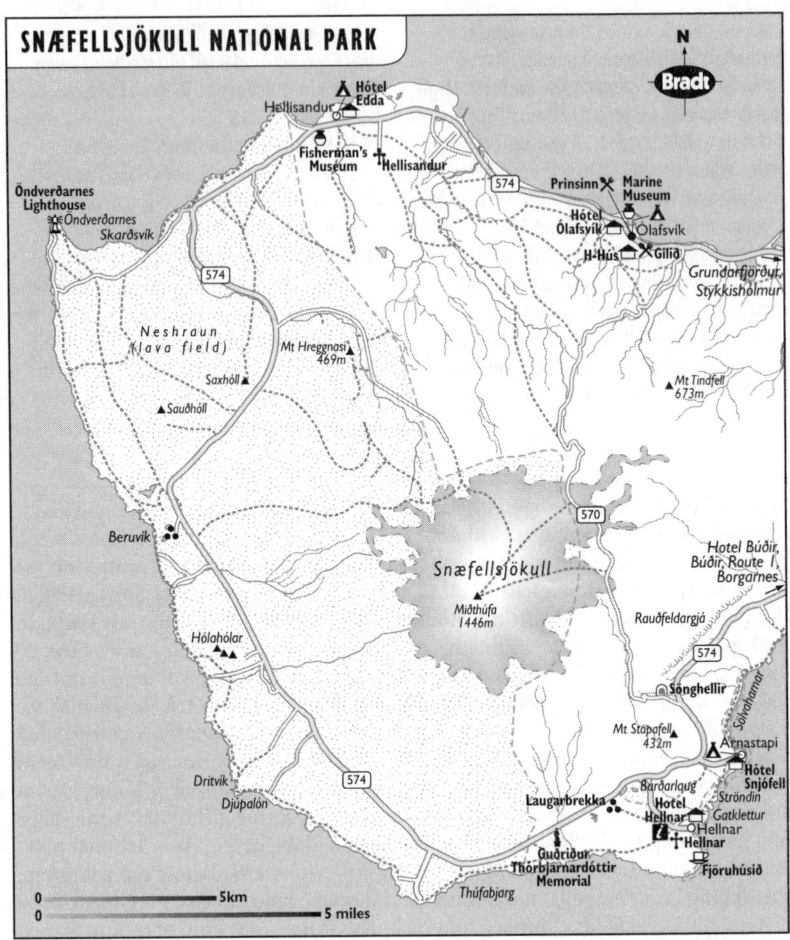


The beauty of this country resort is in the detail, like fresh mountain flowers in every room and the broad range of services. Large, clean, rooms offer lots of light, each with private bathroom (with showers). A few separate cottages offer greater privacy and wonderful views out over the bay Hellnavík. Of equal high standard is the **restaurant** (🕒 *08.00–09.30, 12.00–14.00 & 19.00–21.00 daily; mains from 1,600ISK;* $$$). Order the catch of the day and you won't be disappointed. The talented chef offers a diverse menu to please both carnivores and vegetarians.

From Hellnar, the trail down the hillside to the natural harbour takes you past the tiny cottage of **Fjöruhúsið** (☎ *435 6844;* 🕒 *summer only; mains from 1,000ISK;* $$). It's a cute little place, and the rocky shore with all these birds is lovely, but the café also happens to serve the most famous bowl of soup in Iceland. You can smell it cooking from far away, and 'going to get soup' is a common pastime. Coffee, cakes and sandwiches are also available.

Just up the coast lies the tiny village of **Arnastapi**, home to many summer houses and the compound of **Hótel Snjófell** (*16 rooms;* ☎ *435 6783;* e *snjofell@snjofell.is; www.snjofell.is;* **$$**). The main guesthouse has decent beds at great prices – sleeping-bag spaces are under 2,600ISK; bathrooms are shared. Within walking distance is the restaurant, housed in a red, twin-gabled, turf-roofed dwelling. Expect great seafood, good soup and the famous afternoon coffee and cakes buffet. This is also the base of operations for Snjófell, who conduct tours up on the glacier. The campsite is managed by the hotel and offers bathrooms with hot showers, as well as a playground.

## WHAT TO SEE

**Near the park** Before entering, get acquainted with what's on offer at the official **Snæfellsjökull National Park Visitors Centre** at Hellnar (*☎ 436 6860; e snaefellsjokull@ust.is; www.ust.is; ⏲ summer 09.00–16.00 daily*). Exhibits give in-depth information (in English) on the history, geology, and wildlife that's in the park. Nearby is the peaceful little **Hellnar church** and the old farmstead of **Laugarbrekka**. The heated pool of **Bárðalaug** is the ancient bath of saga hero Bárðar Snæfellsás. The **Ströndin trail** is a stunning but easy walk from the bay at Hellnar all the way to Arnastapi (2.5km), a must-see. The cliff with a hole in it is called **Gatklettur**, or 'hole-cliff'. These rocks are a nature preserve unto themselves, with incredible birdlife and distinctive wave action that has eroded the rocks into swirled patterns and arches. Another easy but steep hike mounts **Mt Stapafell** (432m), with a great view over the bay. Hikers can enter a cave – **Ytri Knarratunga** – at the front of the mountain. A more sweat-inducing trek starts right off the road (Route 574) at **Rauðfeldargjá**. This is the gorge where Bárðar's nephew made his exit from this world – a narrow and very deep chasm that rises up right inside a set of very high cliffs. You're walking right up the streambed, a secret world of 100 little waterfalls and pools that keeps going up and up. A few notes of caution – the chasm is often barely 2m wide so the hike is not recommended for claustrophobes. Also, it's a lot easier to climb up than it is to climb down, and if it's been raining, the stream will be higher and impassable. Lastly (in summer), there's an unbelievably high number of dead birds and bird droppings all over. Don't let that deter you, but don't drink the water either.

**Inside the park** Don't get caught in the trap of 'doing' Snæfellsjökull by driving around the circle. It's quite possible to zip through the park in 30 minutes and be done with it. Turning off the main road takes you to the most interesting thing. The south shore of the park ends in a series of steep bird cliffs, the largest of which

### BÁRÐAR SNÆFELLSÁS

The Bárðar Snæfellsás saga is one of the lesser-known tales outside Iceland, perhaps because some feel it tastes of fiction. Bárðar was a mighty man, fathered by a giant and a human mother. He landed at Dritvík and worshipped at Tröllakirkja ('troll's church'), bathed at his own pool (Barðalaug) and spent a good deal of time in the singing cave Sönghellir. On one occasion, his two nephews Sölvis and Rauðfeldar played a prank on his daughter, in which she was swept away on a piece of drift ice. She went on to land safely in Greenland, but Bárðar was so enraged that he took the boys and threw one of them over a cliff – Sölvahamar ('Sölvis's cliff') – and threw the other one into the gorge Rauðfeldargjá ('Rauðfeldar's gorge'). Deeply troubled, he then simply walked 'into' the glacier, disappearing for ever. Bárðar is now considered the 'man of the mountain' and guardian spirit to Snæfellsjökull. A rough-hewn rock monument to Barðar stands at Arnastapi.

is **Thúfabjarg**. The trail continues to the lighthouse at Malariff, which marks the southernmost point of the peninsula. The next detour takes you to **Djúpalón**, or 'deep pools', where the lava shoreline has eroded into many different puddles. The trail descends to the beach at **Djúpalónssandur**, where there seem to be more rocks than sand. Among them sit four gigantic boulders, known as testing rocks. Back when this was a fishing station (a ruined hut is still visible), local fishermen lifted the rocks to determine their level of strength: *Fullsterkur* (fully strong: 145kg); *Hálfsterkur* (half-strong: 100kg); *Hálfdrættingur* (half as good: 54kg); and *Amlóði* (weak: 23kg) (NB: Amlóði is the hero in the Icelandic version of *Hamlet*; in the 16th century, the name was a common insult when calling someone a weakling). To be hired as an oarsman, a man had to be able to lift the *Hálfsterkur* (in trying to duplicate this medieval test, please don't break your back, and do replace the stone). A popular trail follows the shoreline into the cove of **Dritvík**, or 'dung bay'. In the saga of Barðar Snæfellsás, the Viking and his friends defecate over the side of their ship on the approach to Snæfellsjökull. The effluent washed ashore at this bay, where they later landed. From 1550 to 1850, Dritvík was an important commercial fishing station – the buildings have all washed away, but the foundations remain. At the top of the point is **Suðarbarði**, a maze of rocks made by the early fishermen as a means of entertainment. **Tröllakirkja** ('troll's church') is the pillared complex of lava rock. Down in the cove, visitors enjoy hunting the abundant 'lava pearls' on the beach – the small, smooth, and shiny stones of pure lava that appear tear drop in shape. The pebbles are considered good-luck charms, but not every black pebble

## A MAGIC GLACIER

The supposed supernatural qualities of Snæfellsjökull are based in the belief that the glacier is a powerful source of energy, one of the seven such energy wells in the world. New Age gurus go a step further, explaining that it represents the heart chakra of planet earth. To support that idea, they draw a line from the pyramids of Giza to the magnetic North Pole, which crosses Iceland precisely at Snæfellsjökull. What does that mean for you? Believers claim the glacier works like a magnet, pulling people in closer with its incredibly high energy. Proximity to the glacier magnifies your emotions, so whatever it is you are feeling, you will feel it with much greater intensity at Snæfellsjökull. Other beliefs range from the subtle (the glacier reveals insights) to the not-so-subtle (the glacier acting like a gigantic crystal to UFOs hovering overhead).

These are not new ideas. In his novel *Under the Glacier* (*Kristnihald Undir Jökli*), Nobel laureate Halldór Laxness (see page 197) ponders the Icelanders' reverence to the glacier, its supernatural forces, and their propensity towards pagan beliefs. The story is narrated by a young theology student who is sent by the Bishop of Iceland to investigate strange reports regarding the rogue pastor at Snæfellsjökull. The book is told in a series of official reports back to the bishop, in which the young emissary becomes increasingly alarmed at the pastor's strange beliefs. After deciding that the pastor 'is not even a Unitarian', he sees how the dead are not buried, but merely put up on the glacier, and that the local populace considers their mountain the centre of the earth. That concept has carried over to the 21st century, and today Snæfellsjökull attracts a fair number of people in search of positive energy. You'll find that no matter what your beliefs, the glacier is mesmerising.

you see is a lava pearl (the pearls weigh more). Continue up the coast to **Hólahólar** (113m), a very gentle sloping lava hill, next to an ancient farmstead. The hike to the top is easy and fun.

Other forgotten fishing stations line the coast, the largest of which is at **Beruvík**, where there are a number of remains. The entire northwest corner of the park is covered in volcanic craters, known simply as **Neshraun** or 'lava point'. The hiking is rewarding but long and desolate. It's easier to simply drive or ride right up to the base of **Saxhóll**. A trudge up the spiral trail takes you right to the top of this awesome black crater, shaped by pure ash. The sweeping peak to the east is **Mt Hreggnas** (469m), a side vent for the volcano. Of the several trails to the top, the one from the north is the least troublesome. The highlight of the park's northern shore is at **Skarðsvík**, a white-sand beach guarded by a band of rough lava rock. Sit and watch the waves roll in – this is quite a pretty bit of sea. A trail leads all the way to the lighthouse and old fishing station of **Öndverðarnes**.

**WHAT TO DO** The first people to climb to the top of Snæfellsjökull were Icelanders Eggert Oláfsson and Bjarn Pálsson, who in 1754 launched an expedition after locals called them 'absolutely foolhardy'. Reaching the summit is also absolutely extraordinary – it's a shame to come this far and not get up on the summit of the great glacier. How you do it depends greatly on the season, as the ice changes by the day. Earlier is better for hiking, when there are fewer crevasses; July and August demand extra caution on the ice; and autumn (September–October) is optimal for snowmobiles. The company **Snjófell** (*✆ 435 6783; e snjofell@snjofell.is; www.snjofall.is*) in Arnastapi offers several different tours of the summit, the most popular on snowmobiles. That's the quick and easy way, and riding up to the top in summer at midnight with all the pink and yellow light and the view over to the West Fjords – well, it's pretty unforgettable. If you choose to hike on your own, use extreme caution. The most tried approach is from where the road (Route 570) almost touches the glacier. From here, it's best to follow the tried-and-trusted tracks of the snowmobiles uphill to Vesturthúfa. From the summit, on a clear day, you can see Greenland. The three 'peaks' up on the ice are known as Þúfa, where a giant chunk of stone is lifted up by the ice and permanently frozen into place. Of these, Miðthúfa is the tallest.

**Hiking** Snæfellsjökull is best for open scampering. Great, simple, and mostly level trails criss-cross the lava fields, others wander around the wild coast, and others go right up to the ice. Longer treks through the park can range from two to three days. Most hikers follow the coast, between Hellnar and Hellisandur. Take drinking water with you, as large expanses of the park do not have dependable streams flowing throughout the year. Guided hiking tours, both long and short, are available from the visitor centre at Hellnar. In summer, they also do special wildlife walks to visit the dens of Arctic foxes – very cool if you can see them.

**HELLISANDUR** Hellisandur is a speck of a village on the north side of the park and home to the **Fisherman's Museum** (*Sjómanagarður; Útnesvegur; ⏲ Jun–Aug 09.30–18.00 Tue–Sun; entrance 700ISK*).The outdoor compound includes the old turf dwellings of early fishermen, a trawler from the 1950s and the oldest intact rowboat from c1826. Besides fish, the history of Hellisandur rests in the **Hellisandur church**, perched up on a hill beyond a field of lupins beneath the glacier. The vantage point from the church is remarkable, with a bold panorama of the national park. Known locally as Ingjaldshóll, the church site dates back to 1317. According to the diary of Christopher Columbus, the Italian explorer travelled to Iceland in 1477 to consult

## A WELL-TRAVELLED WOMAN

The most widely travelled woman of medieval times was an Icelander, **Guðriður Thórbjarnardóttir**. The sagas describe her as a woman who was very attractive, very wise, and who 'knew how to behave among strangers'. Born in Laugarbrekka (near Hellnar), her family moved to Greenland around AD985 when she was just a teenager. She travelled with one of the first expeditions to North America, where her first husband Thórir died of the plague. Back in Greenland, she was remarried to Thórstein (brother to Leifur Eiríksson). He too died of plague, but sat up in his coffin to tell his wife that she would marry yet again and travel widely. Thórfinnur Karlsefni was her third husband, and he took him with her back to America (Vinland) to try to establish a settlement. They stayed three years, during which time Guðriður gave birth to a son named Snorri – the first 'white man' ever born on American soil. Restless natives forced them back to Greenland, and then later to Iceland. After the death of her third husband, Guðriður made a pilgrimage to Rome and took vows as a nun. Her son built a church for her in Glaumbær (see page 322), and the Icelandic sculptor Ásmundur Sveinsson raised a memorial in her honour, seen on the road just after entering the park from the south.

with those Icelanders descended from the Viking explorers who had travelled to the new world. A mural of Columbus and the Icelanders is in the basement of the current church, built in 1903 as the first concrete church in Iceland. In case you're wondering, the long-wave radio tower at Hellsiandur is the tallest manmade structure in Iceland.

### Where to stay and eat

**Hótel Edda** (20 rooms) Klettsbúð 9; 444 4940; e edda@hoteledda.is; www.hoteledda.is; May–Sep. Another school turned summer hotel, with modern structure, linoleum floors, & a high standard of cleanliness. Rooms are big with private bathrooms & nice beds, & there is disabled access available on both floors. A reasonable restaurant serves OK meals. **$$$**

**NORTH SHORE** The north shore of the Snæfellsnes Peninsula is much more populated and greener (the odd effect of a rain shadow on the other side). Route 54 travels directly across the top of the shore. A daily bus travels to and from Ólafsvík and Reykjavík (3 hours) via Grundarfjörður (30 minutes). The drive along the north shore is magnificent, for the green mountains set in the silver fjords and the tiny ribbon of road that winds across all of the undisturbed landscape.

## ÓLAFSVÍK

'Olaf's bay' is a town that's still firmly dedicated to fishing and the sea in general. If you had a piece of fish anywhere in west Iceland, it's likely that it came from Ólafsvík, and all it takes is standing near the harbour for five minutes to figure out what people wake up for around here. All of that is explained in the **Marine Museum** (*Sjávarsafn; 436 1491; May–Oct 10.00–18.00 daily; entrance 350ISK*). Housed inside an old fishing warehouse, the exhibit ranges from seafaring to ocean life, with a nifty aquarium and lots of fishing implements. Behind the water and cute houses flows the town's waterfall that flows down from the glacier. As the largest and closest town to the national park, travellers often make Ólafsvík their base of operations. It is quite possible to hike right into the back of the park from trails in town. Otherwise, people come to Ólafsvík for its unrivalled **whale-watching** (*Sæferðir;* ☎ *438 1450;* e *seatours@seatour.is; www.seatours.is*). If you're looking for blue whales, this is one place where you might see them. The area is also renowned for its sightings of sperm whales. The whale-watching operations are based in Stykkishólmur but the ships leave from this port, so it is possible to book a tour from here. For more information, check out the **visitors centre** at the old wooden building by the harbour (built 1848) (*Gamla Thakkhúsið;* ☎ *433 6930;* e *info@snb.is; www.snb.is*).

### WHERE TO STAY

**Hótel Ólafsvík** (48 rooms) Ólafsbraut 20; ☎ 436 1650; e hotel.olafsvik@simnet.is; www.hotelolafsvik.is. Right in the town centre, near the harbour, this sizeable hotel offers big, clean rooms & copes well with groups. They also offer wide-open studio apartments – most rooms have private bathrooms with shower. Good b/fast inc. **$$$**

**H-Hús** (6 rooms) Ennisbraut 2; ☎ 436 6925; e hhusin@simnet.is; www.hhusin.is. Quaint, tin-sided guesthouse in a quieter part of town. Prices are fair & the atmosphere wonderfully homely & convivial. Shared kitchen & bathroom facilities. **$$**

**WHERE TO EAT** The main fine-dining spot is the restaurant at **Hótel Ólafsvík**, where very fresh, banquet-style meals are presented with real feeling. The fish is flawless. You can also just settle for a burger, though for that sort of thing the locals prefer **Prinsinn** (*Ólafsbraut 19;* ☎ *436 1632;* ⏲ *10.00–23.30 Mon–Fri, 11.30–23.30 Sat/Sun; mains from 800ISK; $$*). Primarily pizza and ice cream, they do brilliant grilled sandwiches and hot dogs. Another new café/bar is **Gilið** (*Grúndarbraut 2;* ☎ *436 1501;* ⏲ *11.00–23.00 Sun–Thu, 11.00–03.00 Fri/Sat; mains from 650ISK; $$*). This is probably the best place for coffee and cakes, but their fresh fish is worth shouting about too, and the beer flows freely on weekends.

## GRUNDARFJÖRÐUR

A phenomenal spread of mountains surrounds this bright-blue cove, as if guarding the unique seaside town of Grundarfjörður from the outside world. This lovely little place hasn't an ounce of pretence about it, a fact that's kept it off the beaten path. There is no room for show – those who live here catch, clean, and pack fish. What's most ironic is that the townspeople seem half-oblivious to the overpowering beauty of their home. The crowning glory is the towering Kirkjufell ('church mountain'), a cathedral of stone that rises up in the middle of the fjord. It's a stunning postcard vision, printed in ads and brochures but often without any acknowledgement. Granted their first view, travellers on wheels are compelled to stop and exclaim 'wow'. Cruise ships are only just now discovering what a special place it is.

This region is the setting of the Eyrarbyggja saga – the fjord was once known as Eyrarfjord, and *grundar*, or 'field', basically means the same thing. Ruins of a Viking homestead are still visible near the shore, but the true 'scenes' are the row of mountains behind it. The harbour, town, and businesses in Grundarfjörður were founded by French fishermen in 1786. Today, the inhabitants have a very strong connection with France, and French yachtspeople are keen summer visitors. About 1,000 people live here, half of whom are employed on the fishing boats or in the three fish factories. Every week, after a two–three-day stint, the boats come in and unload, and this is definitely a sight to see. In Grundarfjörður, visitors can feel confident that there is no dressing up for tourists.

## TOURIST INFORMATION

**Tourist information** Grundargata 35; 438 1881; e info@grundarfjordur.is; www.grundarfjordur.is; 10.00–18.00 daily. Inside the town museum.

## WHERE TO STAY

**Hótel Framnes** (29 rooms) Nesvegur 8; 438 6930; e framnes@hotelframnes.is; www.hotelframnes.is. As a converted fisherman's hostel, this harbourside hotel has an authentic, tavern-like feel to it, mixed with modern, convenient accommodation. All rooms are newly refurbished with private bathrooms & a sauna is soothing on the odd blustery day. Their motto 'your home on holiday' sums it up perfectly. Recommended. Summer **$$$**; winter **$$$**

**Youth Hostel** (24 beds) Hlíðarvegur 15; 562 6533; e grundarfjordur@hostel.is; www.hostel.is. In a cherry-red building with white painted trim, this happy little youth hostel has everything just right, & it's right in the middle of the town. Owned & managed by well-travelled travellers, the rooms are very comfy. If you're looking to chill out & take Iceland in as it happens, this is the place to do it. Significant discounts available to students & in winter. Shared kitchen & bathrooms. **$$**

## WHERE TO EAT

**Hótel Framnes** Nesvegur 8; 438 6930; e framnes@hotelframnes.is; www.hotelframnes.is; 07.00–10.00 & 17.00–21.00 daily. A well-known restaurant throughout the peninsula, the Framnes has a reputation for fancy but well-priced seafood dishes. They cater equally well to vegetarians & the b/fast buffet goes above & beyond anything else you've eaten in Iceland. *Mains from 1,100ISK.* **$$$**

**Kaffi 59** Grundargata 59; 438 6446; 10.00–22.00 Mon–Thu, 10.00–01.00 Fri/Sat, 12.00–22.00 Sun. Cod, lobster, & lamb dishes plus a good deal of beer on tap & a wide selection of wines in a hotel dining-room atmosphere. No points for service (read shabby). Being the only restaurant in town, it sees a lot of traffic on weekends. *Mains from 1,800ISK.* **$$$**

**WHAT TO SEE AND DO** The 463m-high **Mt Kirkjufell** is beckoning from the moment you arrive. With sheer rock walls that slope steeper and steeper, it might seem impossible to climb, but it's really quite a cinch. Anyone can do it, but given a few complex situations near the top, it's imperative that you take a guide with you. In summer, that's easily arranged at the tourist information centre. Off season, it's still a nice walk around the base of the mountain. Other hikes take you up **Mt Klakkur** (380m) and **Mt Eyrarfjall** (352m) at the far eastern point of the fjord. Both allow a grand panorama back over the peninsula, across to Faxaflói and over to the West Fjords. A popular hike also crosses the peninsula to the south side of Snæfellsnes (see page 263), which takes about five hours. The **Town Museum** (*Grundargata 35; 438 1881; 10.00–18.00 daily*) is dedicated to the events of the Eyjarbyggja saga, but also the rural development of Iceland. With a most passionate historian as curator, this is a delightful orientation to the town and all of its idiosyncrasies. The old ruins of the former homestead and 'camp' **Grundarkampur** lie on the far eastern edge of the village. Visitors are free to explore, but note that this is an active archaeological dig. Grundarfjörður was home to the original '**village walk**' where a local guide took visitors on a walking tour of the town to explain the daily life of those who live here. Highlights included the docks, the fish factories, the historical streets, some of the old homes and the town's modern church with its resounding acoustics. It's all in English, all quite clever, and a great way to learn about life in present-day Iceland. Sign up for the walk at the youth hostel or at the information centre. When all else fails, there's always the **swimming pool** (*Borgarbraut; 430 8564; 08.00–19.00 daily*).

## BJARNAHÖFN

The road between Grundarfjörður and Stykkishólmur crosses some truly barren seashore next to amazing mountains. The point at Bjarnahöfn is named after the Norse settler Björn Ketillson Austræni, who established his farm on the shores overlooking several small islands in Breiðafjörður. To get there, one must drive across **Berserkjahraun**, or the 'berserkers' lava'. Berserkers were fierce, possessed warriors of superhuman strength who fought like madmen. The Viking chieftain Viga-Styr ordered two of his berserkers to clear a path through the difficult lava field, a clearing now known as the 'berserker's way', or **Berserkjagata**. Alas, once he finished the job, Viga-Styr killed them and buried them in the two hills you pass on the way to the farm. Today, the Bjarnahöfn farm (*Hákarlsverkun Ferðaþjónustan; ☎ 438 1581; ⏲ 09.00–19.00 daily; entrance 500ISK*) is dedicated to the making of the Icelandic delicacy *hákarl* (see page 106). Known everywhere as the 'shark guy', the salty owner takes visitors through the whole process – from catching the shark to butchering it and curing it. Tons of meat are often curing out back and the smell is almost unbearable, but it's a unique insight into the ways of old. Not only is this man one of the few who carries on this important Icelandic tradition, his collection of 'sharking' implements and curiosities is also mind-boggling. Of the many exhibits, the 'things I've pulled out of a shark's stomach' is the most interesting. If you're not too disgusted by the free sample, be sure to take a peek inside the cute little **church**, a historic relic that marks the spot of many goings-on in the sagas.

## STYKKISHÓLMUR

Stykkishólmur is how you always imagined Scandinavia: a shimmering harbour surrounded by rocky ledges and outcrops, and every perfect antique house painted a different bright colour. It almost makes you wish the women were wearing bonnets and carrying baskets, for the town's so darned quaint, it feels like a period piece. It's also one of the few Icelandic town names that looks like a tongue twister, but isn't.

The Thórsnes Peninsula was the farthest point of land sticking out into Breiðafjörður, just begging to be settled. It was the Norseman Thórólfur Mostrarskegg who claimed the land after following an omen to this point in the late 9th century. His farm was important – before there was Thingvellir (see page 213), the Althing met at Thórsnes. Then the monastery from Flatey Island (see page 302) was moved to nearby Helgafell ('holy mountain'), and traffic to the harbour increased. *Stykkishólmur* literally means 'a piece of island', which it is, considering how the direction and geology of the land lines up with the other tiny islands in Breiðafjörður. The actual town dates back to the trade war of the Hanseatic League (see page 20), when various German monopolies sought a hold on different Icelandic harbours. At the height of the subsequent Danish trade monopoly, there was an ongoing rivalry between Stykkishólmur and Grundarfjörður as to which should be granted rights to trade. Thanks to a vindictive sheriff, Stykkishólmur was opened to trade (though the rivalry continues to this day). Eventually, the local industry fell into the hands of Icelandic merchant Árni Thorlacius. Known as a generous and peculiar citizen, he founded the first official weather station and gave daily reports for more than 50 years. Stykkishólmur's charming nature stems from this rich era of Scandinavian trade, when Norwegians, Danes, and Swedes, as well as Dutch, German, and English ships, would sail in and out. The colourful wooden homes reflect wealth and status that rivalled that of the capital.

Today, Stykkishólmur is the major gateway to Breiðafjörður (see page 301) and its nearly 3,000 islands, as well as the main transportation hub for western Iceland. As a picturesque town that's not so far from Reykjavík, it makes sense that Stykkishólmur tastes just a little bit like a tourist town. If you come in summer, you won't be alone since the tour buses treat this place as a jaunty day trip. Indeed, as far as post-industrial Icelandic fishing towns are concerned, Stykkishólmur does have a merry mood.

**GETTING THERE AND AWAY** The amazing thing is that Stykkishólmur is just a little over two hours away from Reykjavík. **Trex** (*www.trex.is*) offers a daily bus to and from the capital, as well as a number of summer buses all the way around the Snæfellsnes Peninsula. Year-round, the ferry *Baldur* (see page 301) crosses Breiðafjörður between Stykkishólmur and Brjánslækur via Flatey. The journey takes about three hours; purchase tickets at Seatours (*Sæferðir; Smiðjustígur 3; ☎ 438 1450; e seatours@seatours.is; www.seatours.is*).

### TOURIST INFORMATION

**Tourist information** Egilshús, Aðalgata 2; ☎ 438 1750; e stykkisholmur@stykkisholmur; www.stykkisholmur.is; ⌚ 10.00–17.00 daily

### WHERE TO STAY

**Hótel Breiðafjörður** (11 rooms) Aðalgata 8; ☎ 438 1417; e hotelbreidafjordur@prinsvaliant.is; www.prinsvaliant.is. A plain & simple refuge for the tired traveller. Rooms are rich with IKEA accoutrements & good lighting (all have their own private showers). Otherwise, it can feel a bit blasé. B/fast available. **$$$**

**Hótel Stykkishólmur** (80 rooms) Borgarbraut 8; ☎ 430 2100; e hotelstykkisholmur@simnet.is; www.hotelstykkisholmur.is. Don't be fooled by the dour concrete exterior. Inside, this healthy-sized hotel brandishes a classy demeanour. Hotel rooms are nice, new, modern, & well furnished – all with private bathrooms. B/fast buffet inc. **$$$**

**María** (4 rooms) Höfðagata 11; ☎ 438 1258. Personal B&B run by a very nice woman. Shared bathrooms. B/fast inc. **$$**

**Sjónarholl Youth Hostel** (50 beds) Höfðagata 1; ☎ 438 1417; www.hostel.is; ⌚ May–Sep. A hostel on a hill, so there's a great view over the town & harbour. Overall, there's a relaxed, family-oriented atmosphere, though the impeccably clean rooms can feel a bit monastic with so many bunks crammed together. The deck & breakfast room are also unique, plus the price is right, & cheaper sleeping-bag spaces are available. No shoes allowed inside! **$$**

### WHERE TO EAT

**Ocean View** Borgarbraut 8; ☎ 430 2100; e hotelstykkisholmur@simnet.is; www.hotelstykkisholmur.is; ⌚ 07.00–10.00 & 18.00–22.00 daily. Thankfully, Hótel Stykkishólmur's 'executive' restaurant is dressed down enough to avoid pretence; alas the food is not. Admittedly, the Asian-meets-Icelandic cuisine feels a little tired, though a gourmet attitude bears tasty results. The grilled fish is a hit & the vegetable sides are unique. Not the place to come feeling famished. *Mains from 2,800ISK.* **$$$$**

**Fimm Fiskar** Frúarstígur 1; ☎ 436 1600; e fimmfiskar@simnet.is; www.simnet.is/fimmfiskar; ⌚ summer 11.00–22.00 Sun–Thu, 11.30–01.00 Fri/Sat. 'Five fish' serves 5 different kinds of fish. Well, actually, even more than that. The point is, the seafood is good & so is the pizza. On stormy evenings when the town seems dead, you can find them in this bar. *Mains from 1,650ISK.* **$$$**

**Narfeyrarstofa** Aðalgata 3; ☎ 438 1119; e steina@narfeyrarstofa.is; www.narfeyrarstofa.is; ⌚ 11.00–22.30 daily. This green, historic home is a classy, local eatery known for high service, delicious comfort food, & a relatively healthy menu. Besides the typical hamburgers & fried fish, there are meal-size salads & great big plates of 'local' cooking. That means birds out of

Breiðafjörður, lamb from the hills, & fish from the fjord. The US$75 piece of steak isn't bad either. *Mains from 2,000ISK.* $$$

✕ **Nesbrauð** Nesvegur 1; ☎ 438 1830; ⏲ summer 08.00–10.00, winter 09.00–16.00 daily. A great little bakery on the edge of town. The best *kleinur* in Iceland, easily. *Mains from 200ISK.* $

**WHAT TO SEE** Stykkishólmur is the kind of tourist town that's good for walking around if you can stand the hills and the weather's right. When it's not, there's plenty to see inside, starting with the **Norwegian House** (*Norska húsið; Hafnargata 5; ☎ 438 1640; e norskhus@simnet.is; www.norskhusid.is; ⏲ Jun–Aug 11.00–17.00 daily; entrance 500ISK*). Built in 1832 out of timber shipped from Norway, the black with white-trim building was the very first two-storey home in Iceland. It began as the residence of local trader Árni Thorlacius. The ground floor is set up as a typical merchant's shop of the time, especially nice if you like antiques. As the local museum of Snæfellsnes, historic exhibits come and go, but the upstairs is a meticulous re-creation of an era (the 1870s) and a class – the merchant upper crust versus Iceland's farmers and fishermen. The attention to detail and authenticity in each room is absolutely amazing. Also, take a peek in the attic to see the collection of local bird eggs and check out the gift shop's dainty souvenirs like lace, cloth, porcelain and traditional Scandinavian crafts and design. If old houses are your thing, Stykkishólmur will keep you busy. Start by going down Aðalgata: number 2 is **Egilshús**, a red warehouse built in 1887 that now houses the tourist information centre. Across the street stands the old grey-blue **church** (Stykkishólmskirkja) built in 1878, and at number 7, the old **Læknishús** (or doctor's office), built in 1896. Also, take a walk down Skólastigur, with almost every home here built between the 1890s and 1910s. You really can't run out of houses to look at.

A walk around the **harbour** brings you past the lighthouse, as well as the **monument** to Árni Thorlacius and another to those seafarers who have been lost at sea. The most popular 'city hike' follows the ridge of the island **Súgandisey** (next to the harbour), up above the columnar basalt cliffs and its many birds.

**WHAT TO DO** Getting out on the water (Breiðafjörður) is simple and encouraged. The main tour operator in town is **Seatours** (*Sæferðir; Smiðjustígur 3; ☎ 438 1450; e seatours@seatours.is; www.seatours.is*), who also run the ferry to Flatey and the West Fjords. Their most popular trip is the **wildlife tour** (about 2 hours) that takes in the nearest islands of Breiðafjörður. Besides birds (mainly puffins, guillemots, fulmar, and eider ducks), you'll see seals, a lot of rocky cliffs, and shellfish. Breiðafjörður is a well-known hotspot for birdwatchers since more than half of Iceland's birds live in this region. If you haven't already seen these birds or done a boat tour, then it's definitely worth the cost (around US$70 per person). But know that for the same price, you can go on a chaperoned **fishing** trip, catch giant cod to your heart's delight and see the very same birds. Or you could simply sail to **Flatey Island** (see page 302) and see it all yourself. The **whale-watching trip** is a major attraction, as it should be, seeing as in summertime you have a 50/50 chance of spotting a blue whale. The ship departs from Ólafsvík, but transportation is provided from Stykkishólmur. The islands of Breiðafjörður are also perfect for **kayaking** (*☎ 690 3877; e info@seakayakiceland.com; www.seakayakiceland.com*). The Seatours office manages a retail-intensive souvenir shop. For hot tubs and swimming, visit the town's outdoor **swimming pool** (*Borgarbraut 4; ☎ 438 1150; ⏲ 07.00–22.00 Mon–Fri, 09.00–19.00 Sat/Sun*). Outside town, it's an easy trip to the top of **Mt Helgafell** (73m), where there's a historic church and a heart-swelling view over the fjord.

## BÚÐARDALUR

Iceland's 'valleys' region, or the dales (Dalir), is a sparsely populated area at the base of Hvammsfjörður. The scenery is that of pleasant Icelandic nature, but it is the rich history of these valleys and shores that puts it on the map. First, this is the setting of the Laxdæla saga, a tale of love, romance, jealousies and vengeance. Much of it takes place in **Laxardalur**, or 'salmon valley'. More renowned is Iceland's great hero Leifur Eiríksson, known around here as Leif the Lucky. His father Eirík the Red settled on the nearby farm of **Eiríksstaðir**, which is where the young explorer was raised. The remains of this farm are now a **museum** (*Eiríksstaðir; ☎ 434 1118; e vatna@ismennt.is; www.leif.is; ⌚ Jun–Aug 09.00–18.00 daily; entrance 600ISK*). The exhibit focuses on a replica of the turf-and-driftwood longhouse in which Leif was born, and guides dressed as Vikings bring it all to life. Ever since all the real Vikings left for Greenland and America, the only real village in the area is Buðardalur. It's a stopping point for those travelling to and from the West Fjords on Route 60. There's not much here, though history buffs should want to have a look around at all the saga sites. One noted exception is the bare coastline of Fellsströnd and Skarðsströnd. Unpaved Route 590 follows the eastern shore of Breiðafjörður along some very remote areas, best explored by 4x4 and crazy mountain bikers. For more information, contact the tourist information office (for contact information, see below).

### TOURIST INFORMATION

**Tourist information** Búðardalur, Vesturbraut 2C; ☎ 434 1410; e dalir@dalir.is; www.dalir.is

### WHERE TO STAY AND EAT

**Hótel Edda Laugar** (22 rooms; 60 beds) ☎ 444 4930; e edda@hoteledda.is; www.hoteledda.is. This hearty outdoor complex is located near the old Viking hot spring at Laugar, a place where the lovers in the Laxdæla saga would often meet up for a chat. Today, the hotel in its place has a great big outdoor swimming pool. Individual rooms are very nice (all with private shower), & the large amount of sleeping-bag space caters well to big groups; there's also a good campsite for tents & caravans. The in-house fish & lamb restaurant does well for being the only place around. B/fast inc. **$$$**

**Bjarg** (10 rooms) Dalbraut 2; ☎ 434 1644; www.aknet.is/bjarg. Peaceful roadside guesthouse & café. Rooms are basic but have what you need in them. Bathrooms are shared. Camping for tents & caravans. *B/fast inc (other meals also available)*. **$$**

# 9

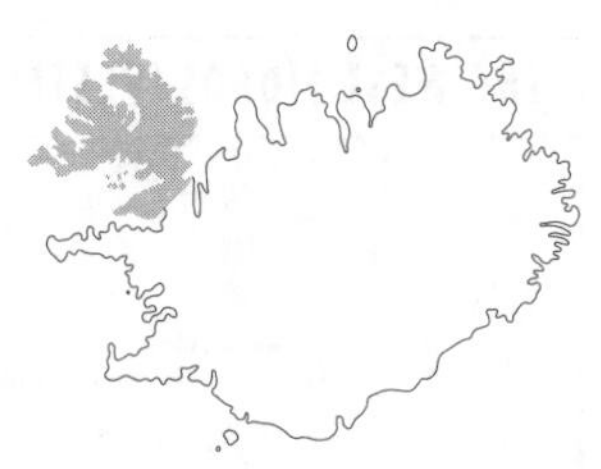

# Vestfirðir (The West Fjords)

Every country has that one quirky region that's far away from anywhere else. It's hard to reach and there's really not much there besides the land and the sea. Nature is vibrant and tradition strong. The people are fiercely independent and just a little suspicious of their countrymen back in the cities. All the children dream of leaving one day, and once they do, they all dream of coming back. It tends to be a place of remarkable beauty that gets completely overlooked. In Iceland, that one place is the West Fjords.

The peninsula is best known for its amazingly intricate coast (medieval mapmakers said it resembled the head of a dragon). The West Fjords occupies less than 10% of Iceland's landmass but represents 50% of the country's coastline – more than half the fjords in Iceland. And what stunning fjords they are: absolutely huge and impressively silent. You could spend a day just watching the water change colours. The mountains also look different – they are more uniform and block-like, rising right up from the sea and becoming vertical cliffs right at the top. Their summits are flat so that a West Fjords horizon is always marked by a row of long and level shadows.

Geologically speaking, the West Fjords is the oldest part of Iceland, built from basalt strata laid down some 14 million years ago. On the surface, this is one of the youngest landscapes in the country – the ice only disappeared a few thousand years ago, and in the case of Drangajökull, it is still there. Every hillside is marked with the grooves of spring waterfalls. Temperatures are cooler and the weather far more treacherous. In summer, the snow and ice linger a little longer and it was here in the West Fjords that Iceland was given the name 'ice-land'. Altogether, it is a land of extremes: the cliffs are higher, the wind blows harder, and the sunbeams shine more intensely – everything seems more beautiful.

As a region, the West Fjords represents a nostalgia that Iceland has for itself. It is the birthplace of Icelandic national hero Jon Sigurðsson (as well as the current president), and the homeland of so many artists and poets. It is why so many Icelandic films are filmed here and why Icelanders would rather holiday in the West Fjords than get sunburned in Spain. It seems somehow that every Icelander has an elderly relative who lives in the West Fjords. Today, fewer than 8,000 people live here and they all know one another (really). Indeed, Vestfirðir is such a marvellous place because it is so entirely empty. Everything manmade is reduced to miniature and the tall, barren landscapes induce an odd emotion of being the only human on earth. This is true wilderness, cut off from the body of Iceland by sheer distance and difference.

Even so, the West Fjords is the least-visited region in all of Iceland – more people travel through the country's desert interior than up into this wayward corner. Getting there is a one-day detour from the more accessible ring road, and so the

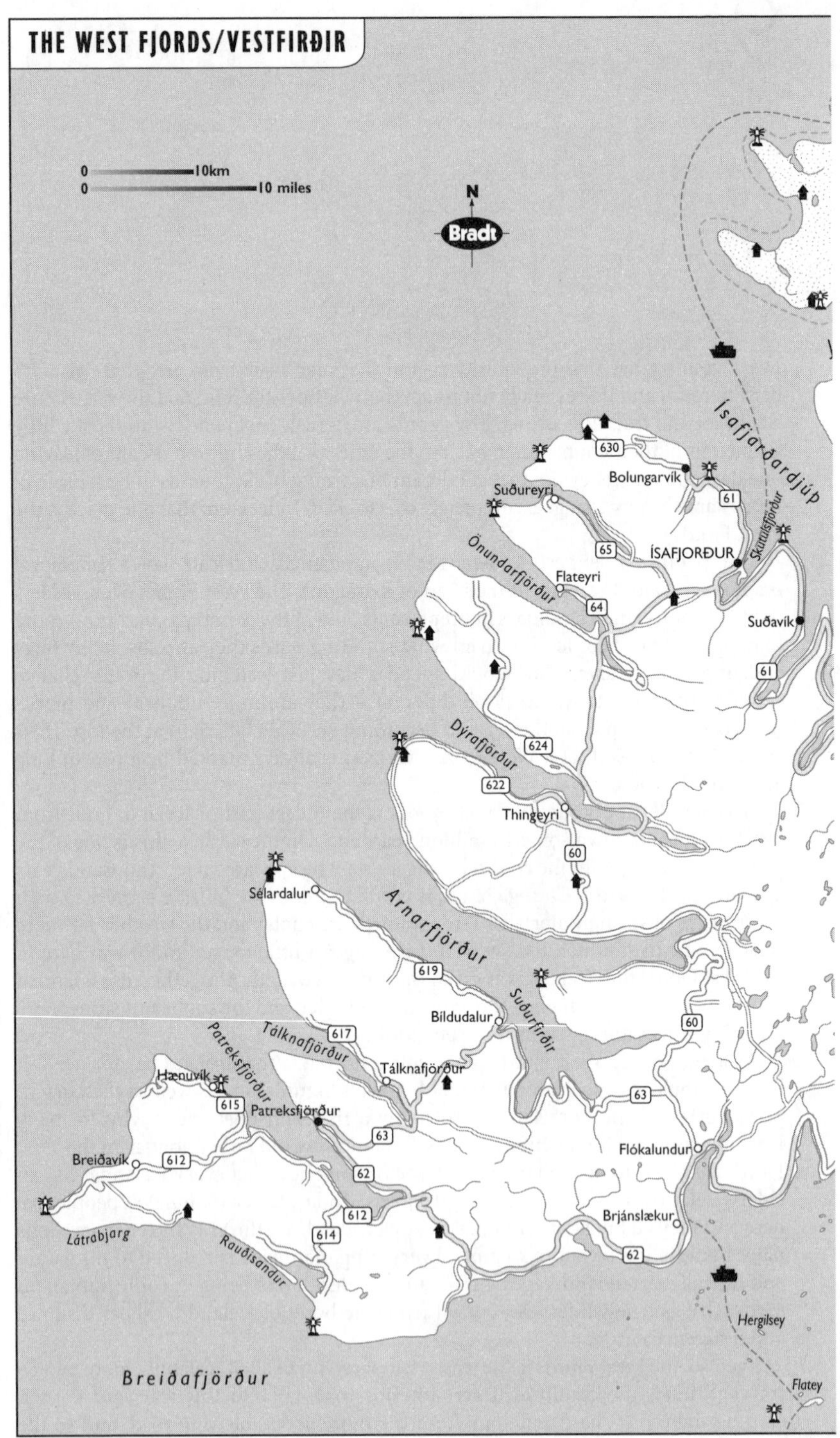

THE WEST FJORDS/VESTFIRÐIR
0 10km
0 10 miles
N
Bradt
Ísafjarðardjúp
Bolungarvík
630
61
Suðureyri
Skutulsfjörður
Önundarfjörður
65
ÍSAFJORÐUR
Flateyri
64
Suðavík
61
Dýrafjörður
624
622
Thingeyri
60
Sélardalur
Arnarfjörður
619
Suðurfirðir
Bíldudalur
60
Tálknafjörður
617
Patreksfjörður
Hænuvík
Tálknafjörður
615
Patreksfjörður
63
63
Flókalundur
Breiðavík
612
62
612
Brjánslækur
614
Látrabjarg
Rauðisandur
62
Hergilsey
Breiðafjörður
Flatey

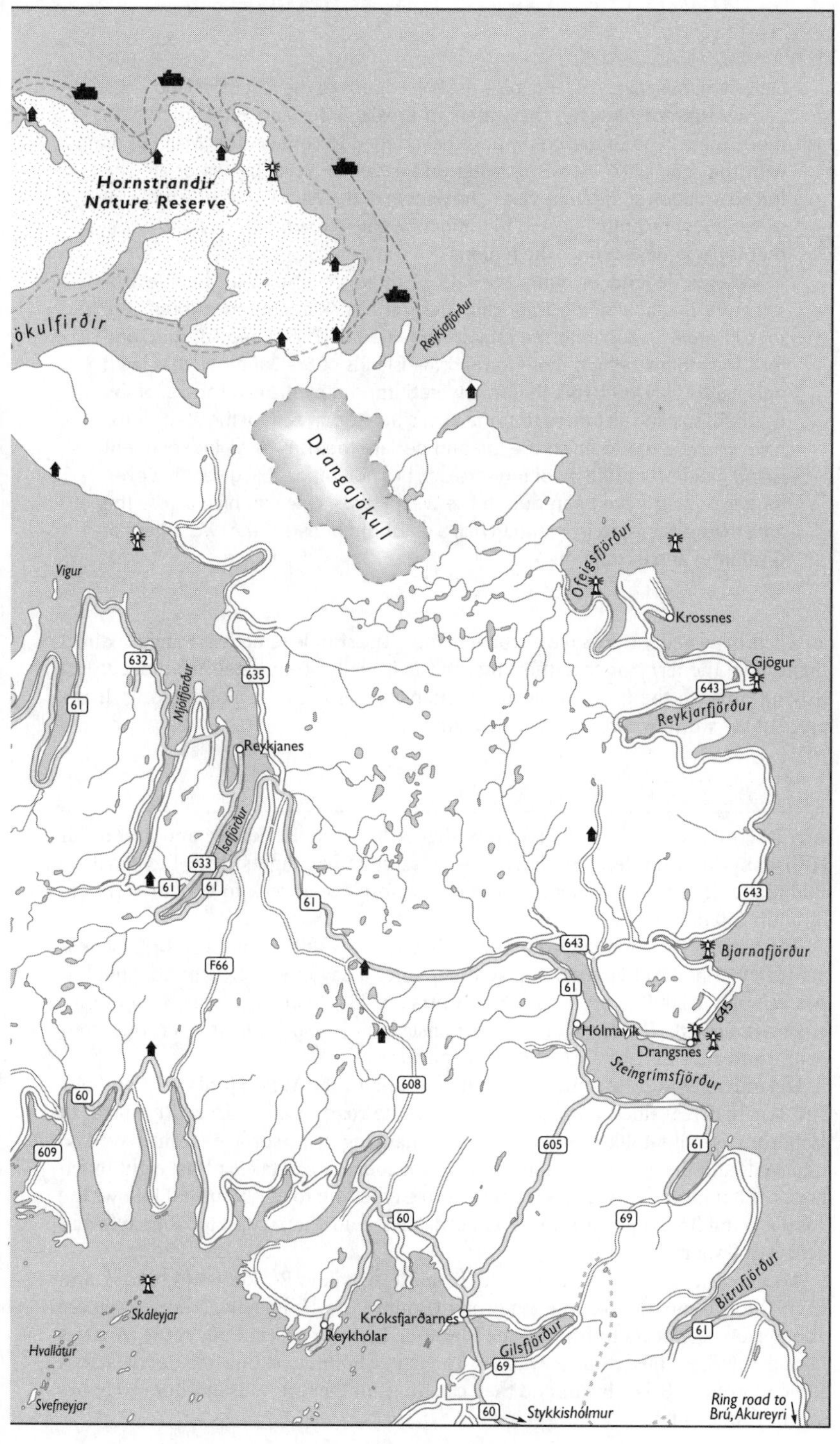

Hornstrandir
Nature Reserve
ökulfirðir
Reykjafjörður
Drangajökull
Ófeigsfjörður
Vigur
Krossnes
Gjögur
643
Reykjarfjörður
632
635
Mjóifjörður
61
Reykjanes
Ísafjörður
633
61
61
61
F66
643
Bjarnafjörður
61
645
Hólmavík
Drangsnes
Steingrímsfjörður
643
60
608
609
605
61
69
60
Bitrufjörður
Skáleyjar
Króksfjarðarnes
Reykhólar
Gilsfjörður
69
61
Hvallátur
Svefneyjar
60
Stykkishólmur
Ring road to
Brú, Akureyri

## ALMOST AN ISLAND

Only 8km (five miles) of land joins the West Fjords to the rest of Iceland – the narrow isthmus between the waters of Breiðafjörður and Húnaflói. What's more, there is no single, continuous paved road to connect the West Fjords with the 'mainland' – it is still faster and easier to travel by sea or air. The forced isolation sometimes vexes the people of the West Fjords (the national government recently rejected funding for a paved road) but they also know that separateness defines the region.

Icelandic legend recounts the tale of three trolls who, in a contest of strength, began digging frantically from either side, cutting through the rock in order to separate the region from Iceland. The clumps of mud and rock they threw behind them formed the islands of Breiðafjörður. Alas, with only a little way left to go, the trolls were surprised by the early arrival of the northern sun and all turned to stone. Ever since, the citizens of the West Fjords have volunteered to finish the job and declare themselves an independent island nation. It's just a bit of fun sarcasm, but not impossible given that even longer tunnels have been dug in the West Fjords. One can hike across the area the trolls missed in less than half a day; right between the two valleys of Gilsfjörður and Bitrufjörður.

area gets bypassed for the sake of convenience. The simple remedy is to take a direct flight, take the ferry or take the time. But is it really so unique? Yes indeed. Just driving through the fjords is an unforgettable experience, let alone hiking. It is a piece of the world where seeing is believing.

## GETTING THERE AND AWAY

**Air Iceland** (*www.airiceland.is*) runs flights between Reykjavík and Ísafjörður (IFJ) daily (45 minutes). **Eagle Air** (*www.ernir.is*) has flights from Reykjavík to Bíldudalur (BIU) once a day (40 minutes), and twice a week to Gjögur (GJR) in Strandir (40 minutes).

The ferry across Breiðafjörður travels between Stykkishólmur and Brjánslækur via Flatey (3 hours) twice daily in summer, once a day in winter; around 2,600ISK per car plus 2,500ISK per adult; **Sea Tours** (☎ *438 1450;* e *seatours@seatours.is; www.seatours.is*). The ferry office in Brjánslækur (☎ *456 2020*) is open one hour before and after the ferry arrivals and departures.

Icelanders tend to murmur about travel time to the West Fjords – it is a long and lonely drive, albeit a breathtaking one. The road distance from Reykjavík to Ísafjörður is only 460km, but given the changing road surface (from paved to unpaved) and the meandering fjord roads, the journey can take at least eight to ten hours, if not more. Two routes branch off from the ring road – Route 60 follows the coast around Breiðafjörður; Route 61 heads up the northern coast to Hólmavík and across to Ísafjörður.

**Trex** (*www.trex.is*) offers bus routes from Reykjavík to Reykhólar (4 hours), and from the Brú junction on the ring road (Route 1) to Hólmavík (2 hours), where another bus connects to Ísafjörður (4 hours). The more scenic bus route involves taking the Trex bus from Reykjavík to Stykkishólmur, riding the ferry across Breiðafjörður to Brjánslækur and then catching another bus to Ísafjörður (10 hours journey time in total).

## GETTING AROUND

Icelanders typically divide the West Fjords into three main areas – the 'capital' Ísafjörður and central group of fjords in the middle, the southern tier including Látrabjarg and the Breiðafjörður coast, and the spectacular northern coast of Strandir. There are no commercial flights within the West Fjords.

In summer, ferries sail to and from the bays of Strandir from Ísafjörður and Norðurfjörður. The West Fjords can try the patience of speedy drivers but also tends to appease with heavenly landscapes. There are no shortcuts – only scenic routes – and if there is a road, there is always the chance that part of it will be unpaved. Use extra care when driving here: the roads are narrow and the drop-offs much steeper than elsewhere in Iceland. High winds and fog can be dangerous. Also, the tunnels will be longer than those to which you might be accustomed – slow down and be prepared to yield to oncoming traffic. Keep in mind that distances between farms and villages are much more disparate and petrol stations can be scarce in number. As a precaution, plan your fuel wisely and always top up your tank.

Riding the bus around the West Fjords is not exactly user-friendly, but quite possible. Ísafjörður is the main hub for travel, with regular buses to and from Látrabjarg via Patreksfjörður and Brjánslækur, another to Hólmavík (☎ *456 3518*) and another to Thingeyri via Flateyri (m *893 1058*). Some travellers find it easier to hire a car or hitch.

## ÍSAFJÖRÐUR

'Ice fjord' is the largest city and de facto capital of the West Fjords. Nearly half the region's population live in the area (around 4,000), so the infrastructure makes it a convenient base from which to travel to the rest of the region. Yet this fearless northern town has an old-fashioned appeal that sets it apart – an island frontier in the midst of a grand wilderness.

The quaint streets of Ísafjörður are laid out upon a flat, hook-shaped peninsula that juts out into the middle of Skutulsfjörður. Massive mountains surround the town on all sides like the high castle walls around a moat. The only way in and out is through the narrow tunnel or the open sea. Depending on the weather, the enclosure engenders a sense of protection or that of being completely cut off from the rest of the world.

The area was first settled in the 10th century by Helgi 'the lean' Hrólfsson who left Norway for Iceland only to discover the favourable properties in Eyjafjörður had already been taken. By and by he made his way to a solitary fjord in the West Fjords where he found a harpoon (*skutul*) lying on the shore. Such a good omen convinced him to stick around and he named the place Skutulsfjörður.

The town of Ísafjörður was only founded in 1569 as a salting station for fish. Proximity to the cod-rich waters of the Greenland current helped make this the largest city in Iceland during the 18th century. The town received its official charter in 1786 (the same year as Reykjavík), at which point the wealthy Danish trading post was far more established than the future capital. The frigid name derives from the drift ice that once floated down the long channel of Ísafjarðardjup. Spring ice could make life difficult, closing off the port for months. Today, the icebergs are no more, but local temperatures never get too high.

No other town in Iceland expresses the kind of intense loyalty and pride for which Ísafjörður is known. There is a strong bond among its citizens, no matter where they may roam in the world. This might go back to the nationalist movement that was born here, or it could just be the town's one-of-a-kind personality. Over the centuries, Ísafjörður has preserved more than just its old-world architecture and sense of style; it remains a dynamic outpost in spite of its latitude.

**GETTING THERE AND AWAY** Flights with **Air Iceland** (*www.airiceland.is*) run between Reykjavík and Ísafjörður (IFJ) twice a day in winter (45 minutes), and several times more in spring and summer. Flying into Ísafjörður is considered an extreme sport, as planes drop right down into the fjord and land at the edge of an impressive mountain. Ísafjörður Airport is on the opposite side of the fjord (*456 3000*). An airport shuttle drives to and from the town centre; pickup is in front of Hótel Ísafjörður (*456 7195*).

By car, one can follow the north coast to and from Ísafjörður on Route 61, which leads to Hólmavík (4 hours). The shortcut is through the tunnel on Route 60, which connects to the ferry port at Brjánslækur (approximately 3+ hours).

Buses travel from Ísafjörður to Holmavík (4 hours) and to Brjánslækur (3 hours). The bus station is on Pollgata, right next to the tourist information centre. For its scenery and wonderful, walkable streets, Ísafjörður is becoming Iceland's elite cruise-ship destination. Most ships anchor at least 1km from the city and ferry passengers to shore on smaller motor boats.

## TOURIST INFORMATION

**Tourist information** Aðalstræti 7; 456 5121; e info@vestfirdir.is; www.vestfirdir.is; 08.00–18.00 Mon–Fri, 10.00–15.00 Sat/Sun, Sep–May weekdays only. Highly informative & a great base to start your West Fjords adventure. Rent bikes & camping gear, or join up for hiking groups & local tours. Depending on quality, bikes rent for about US$20–50/day.

## TOUR OPERATORS

**Sjóferðir** Sjóferðir Hafsteins og Kiddýjar; 456 3879; e sjoferdir@sjoferdir.is; www.sjoferdir.is. This local ferry company is what links Ísafjörður to the isolated islands in the bay (Vigur, Æðey), as well as the barren coasts of Jökulfirðir & Hornstrandir. All tourist bookings are made through West Tours, but private trips can be organised directly.

**West Tours** Vesturferðir; Aðalstræti 7; 456 5111; e vesturferdir@vesturferdir.is; www.vesturferdir.is. The largest & most comprehensive tour services company covering the entire West Fjords, located in the same building as tourist information. They offer everything from organised hiking trips to Strandir, ski tours, boat trips to Vigur, walking tours around Ísafjörður, to kayaking in the fjords.

## WHERE TO STAY

**Hótel Ísafjörður** (36 rooms) Silfurtogr 2; 456 4111; e info@hotelisafjordur.is; www.hotelisafjordur.is. Unsurprisingly, the city's namesake & centremost hotel is also the most lavish place in town. The sturdy concrete construction seems a tad austere & functional, but the rooms inside are snug & dry & provide a warm haven from the outdoor elements. All rooms have private bathrooms – some are more compact than others. Guests can walk to most everything in town & the attentive service makes life pleasant. Sleeping-bag spaces are available off season. **$$$$**

**Hótel Edda Ísafjörður** (40 rooms) Menntaskólinn; 444 4960; e info@hoteledda.is/en; http://www.hoteledda.is/en; Jun–Aug. Managed by the Hótel Ísafjörður for the busy summer season, this Hótel Edda caters to the tour-bus & the proletariat traveller who needs a place to sleep & wash. It all feels like a university dorm hall, with beds & desks in each room & a bathroom down the hall. The exception is a handful of doubles with private bathroom. A nice living room space allows for relaxation & the kitchen serves a solid b/fast buffet for extra. If you don't have your own car or bike, going to &

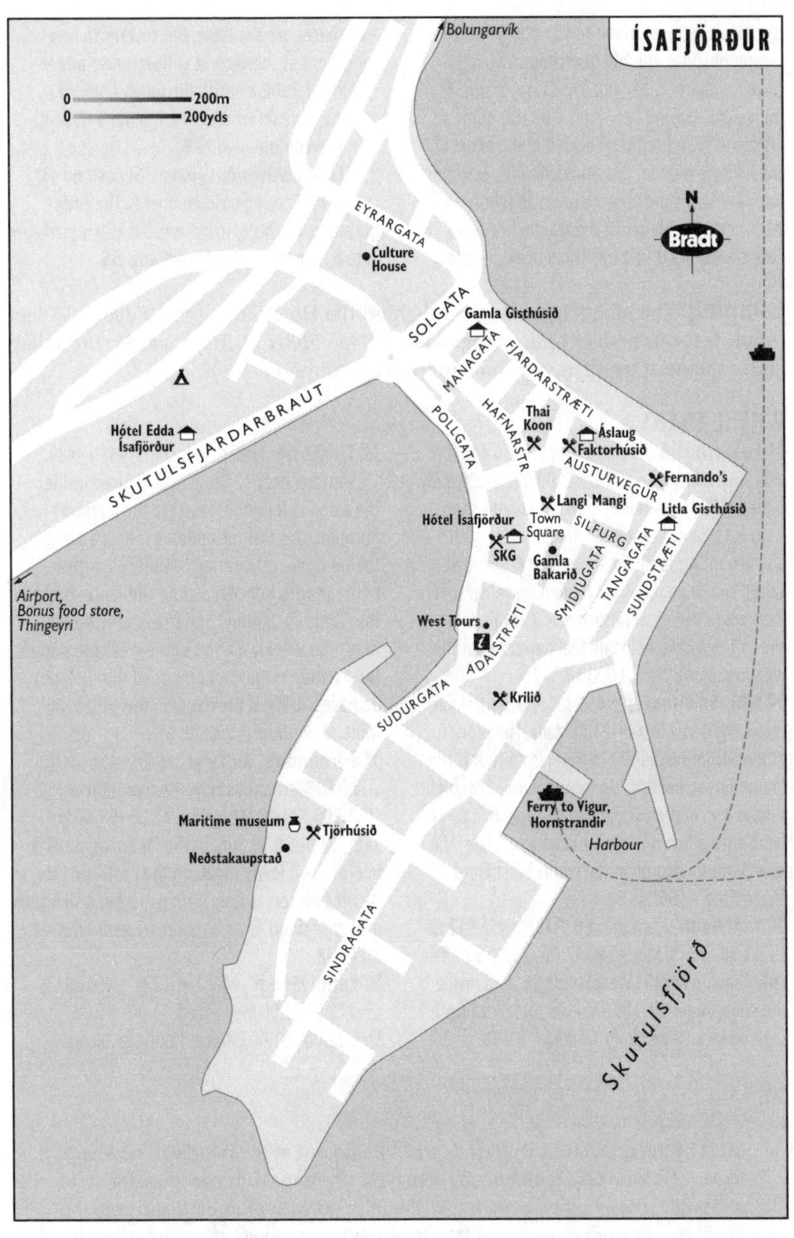


from the town centre can be a hassle. *Sleeping-bag space under 2,500ISK pp in private rooms, less for hostel-style classroom at 1,500ISK pp; camping out back is much less.* **$$$**

**Áslaug** (6 rooms) Austurvegur 7; ☎ 456 3868; e gistias@snerpa.is; www.randburg.com/is/aslaug.html. Another small & historic home open to tired travellers in the old town. The rooms are eclectic, the kitchen & bathrooms are shared, & there is a family suite. Some rooms are available for long-term renters only. *Suite around 16,000ISK per night per group of 4.* **$$**

**Gamla Gisthúsið** (9 rooms) Mánagata 5; ☎ 456 4146; e gistihus@gistihus.is; www.

gistihus.is. Housed in the town's 100-year-old former hospital, the 'old guesthouse' wins the prize for charm & personality. Clean, warm, & individual, staying here feels a bit like going to visit your grandmother. Located in the heart of the historic section, the single, double, & triple rooms are all done up with great affection – bathrooms are shared & there are a few nice, cosy nooks for curling up with a book. Sleeping bag spaces are available, but cost much less for groups at the second 'yellow house' annex (around 1,700ISK each). Kitchen & laundry facilities; breakfast served for under 1,000ISK. Highly recommended. **$$**

**Litla Gisthúsið** (5 rooms) Sundstræti 43; 474 1455; e reginasc@simnet.is. The 'little guesthouse' is little, to be sure, but also remarkably cute & friendly. Shared bathrooms. **$$**

**Camping** The main city campsite is behind the Hótel Edda (*444 4960*). A less urban feel can be had up in Tungudalur (*456 5081*; *May–Sep*; **$**), the valley above the fjord (right as you come in from the tunnel).

## WHERE TO EAT

**Faktorhúsið** Aðalstræti 42; 456 1414; e hrafn@fvi.is; www.fvi.is; 09.00–22.00 daily. Built in 1788, this Norwegian merchant's shop is now a quaint Scandinavian restaurant with a penchant for lamb, fresh seafood & of course, salted cod. It's a popular hangout for rainy/snowy days when there's not much else you can do – the coffee & cake help one feel better about the weather. *Mains from 2,000ISK.* **$$$**

**SKG** Silfurtorg 2; 456 3360; e skg@skg.is; www.skg.is; 07.00–23.30 daily. The precise, ground-floor restaurant in Hótel Ísafjörður is the town's finest, hosting big events & quiet candlelit soirées for couples. The menu is staple fish & lamb with a luxurious twist of banquet fare. The only place to splurge in the whole West Fjords. *Mains from 1,900ISK.* **$$$**

**Thai Koon** Hafnarstræti 9-13; 456 0123; 11.30–21.00 Mon–Sat, 17.00–21.00 Sun. The only Thai food in the West Fjords, located inside the 'shopping mall'. Pad Thai has that extra fresh seafood kick. *Mains from 1,500ISK.* **$$$**

**Tjörhúsið** Neðstakaupstað; 456 4489; summer only 12.00–22.00. Housed inside the wooden longhouse next to the Maritime Museum, this historic building is now a popular theme venue celebrating Ísafjörður's saltfish heritage with lots of old-time ambiance. Besides the staple (& yummy) *plokkfiskur* or fish soup, they offer weekly all-you-can-eat saltfish buffets (which may or may not be a good thing). If not, do have a drink at the bar or in the garden out front. *Mains from 2,000ISK.* **$$$**

**Fernando's** Austurvegur 1; 456 5001; e shiran@fernandos.is; www.fernandos.is; 12.00–22.00 Mon–Thu, 12.00–01.00 Fri/Sat, 12.00–20.00 Sun. In the far north, pizza & beer is not a lowly meal. On the contrary, this classic pub serves it up with panache, & delicious grilled seafood as an alternative. *Mains from 1,200ISK.* **$$**

**Langi Mangi** Aðalstræti 22; 456 3022; 11.00–23.00 Mon–Wed, 11.00–01.00 Thu, 12.00–03.00 Fri/Sat, 12.00–23.00 Sun.

### A ROOM WITH A VIEW: SUMMER COTTAGES

Most of the appeal in the West Fjords is being out in the middle of nowhere. Icelanders who take their holiday here typically rent a summerhouse for up to a month. These homes are often well equipped with plumbing and cooking facilities but are far, far away from the madding crowd. It's a great way to enjoy the surrounding nature, to enjoy unhurried walks in the mountains and wake up to breathtaking views of the fjords. It's also a great deal for Iceland. Renting a remote cottage in the West Fjords runs from around 40,000ISK per week for up to four guests. For more information, contact the West Fjords Tourism Office (*www.westfjords.is*), West Tours (*www.westtours.is*) in Ísafjörður, or Súdavík Summer Houses (*www.sumarbyggd.is*).

Ísafjörður's number-one hipster hangout, with a strong punk vibe, live music & 'healthy' foreign food. Choose from Tex-Mex (burritos for under 1,500ISK), steaming bowls of soup, sandwiches or the more substantial mains (ie: pasta & meat). When evening comes, the pub atmosphere erupts – & the whole town turns out for a rousing time. *Mains from 650ISK.* $$

**Krilið** Sindragata 6; 456 3556; 09.30–23.30 Mon–Thu, 09.30–03.00 Fri/Sat, 11.00–23.30 Sun. Everything you need for your late-night fast-food fix. Pizza, fried chicken, burgers, hot dogs & soft-serve ice cream galore. *Mains from 900ISK.* $

**Self-catering** The **Bonus** food store is right at the T-junction at the base of the fjord (*Skeiði 1; 456 3230; 12.00–19.30 Mon–Sat, 12.00–18.00 Sun*). In the centre of town, pay a visit to the bakery **Gamla Bakarið** (*Aðalstræti 24; 456 3226; 07.00–16.00 Mon–Sat*).

**WHAT TO SEE AND DO** Ísafjörður is a good place to walk and watch. It is also a historic town with the most well-preserved houses in the country. The old harbour complex towards the end of the peninsula is **Neðstakaupstað**, comprising the oldest buildings in Iceland, dating back to the mid 18th century. Turnhús (built in 1744) is now home to the **Maritime Museum** (*Sjóminjasafn Vestfjarða; Neðstakaupstaður; 456 4418; 1 Jun–1 Sep 10.00–17.00 daily; entrance 1,200ISK*). Here the bygone era of salt cod is commemorated with passion - anyone who loves boats or fishing should enjoy the museum. There are a lot of old fishing implements (hooks, ropes, harpoons, sinkers, nets, oilskins and lanterns), informative displays and documentaries about life in the old fishing stations of Iceland, and plenty of intricate ship models (probably assembled during the long winter nights). Also, don't miss the driftwood carpentry exhibit up on the third floor, all about building homes in the West Fjords. The longhouse Tjörhúsið (built 1742) offers periodic summer feasts with saltfish and shrimp and in the evening, there are illustrated lectures (in English) and dramatic re-enactments at the museum; check with the tourist office to see what's on at present (*www.aneveninginisafjordur.com*). Several old-time 'museum boats' are tied up in the harbour - most are undergoing renovation but some allow tourists to have a look around.

The new **harbour** (Sundahöfn) is much more alive with its run of fishing boats and the active ferry dock. This is the main embarkation point for trips to Vigur Island and Hornstrandir - both priorities if you have the chance. The tourist information booth is located just two blocks away in the middle of the town, from whence begins Aðalstræti. The main street leads to the **town square**, Silfurtorg or 'silver square'. The historic bookshop on the corner was built in 1930 (*Bókhlaðanl; Hafnarstræti 2; 456 3123*) and just a taste of Ísafjörður's architectural wonders. Simply walking down the side streets is pleasant, especially among the old homes and bright little gardens. The buildings on the corner of Silfurgata and Smiðjugata reflect a boom from the early 20th century, and the picket fences and windows are a delight. When you're done exploring, there's an indoor **swimming pool** (*Austurvegur 9; 456 3200; 07.00–21.00 Mon–Fri, 10.00–17.00 Sat/Sun*).

The most prominent building in town is the stately white **Culture House** (*Safnahúsið; Eyrartún; 456 3296; e myndassafn@isafjordur.is; www.safn.isafjordur.is; 13.00–19.00 Mon–Fri & Sun, 13.00–16.00 Sat; entrance free*). Built in 1925 as the regional hospital (*sjúkrahús*), the Modernist design is that of Iceland's one and only state architect Guðjon Samúelsson (see page 176). Today, it is home to the town's library, photo archives, art collection, and free internet portals. There is quite a lot of history stored on these shelves, not to be overlooked by the non-Icelandic speaker (especially on cold, foggy days or if you like to look at old pictures). The memorial on the green outside the library is to the seamen of Ísafjörður with the inscription: 'To honour those who were lost and to remind those who have been warned.'

**Hiking** When the weather co-operates, several hikes offer a grand view of the town and its remarkable setting. Right across the fjord stands the imposing cliff of Kirkjubólshlíð and the summit of Mt Kirkjubólsfjall (731m). The perfectly formed glacier bowl **Naustahvilft** (225m) sits right above the town, almost begging you to climb up inside. The 500m trail begins just after the airport, and it is a fairly easy ascent but not without some huffing and puffing near the top. Just follow the pair of babbling streams up to the bottom lip of the bowl. Be sure to sign the guestbook and if you venture into the base of the bowl, watch for tumbling rocks.

Longer and more adventurous is the walk to Bolungarvík. One trail goes up around the base of Mt Eyrarfjall (724m), the mountain to the west of Ísafjörður. The second one (recommended for its beauty) follows the streambed along Hnífsdalur ('knife valley') then heads uphill, after which it veers right (north). Both trails pick up on the dirt road that goes into Bólungarvík. Either route takes about half a day to complete.

## VIGUR

Vigur Island is the humble exception to the colossal landscapes of the West Fjords. The flat speck of bright-green earth is small (only 2km long and 400m wide) but offers a wonderful duck's-eye view of this, the largest fjord in the region. The shore is gradual and covered with small, rounded stones (no sharp cliffs), so the birds are always close by: tetchy Arctic terns, plentiful puffins, a hearty colony of black guillemots, and the few thousand eider ducks which nest here year after year (see box on page 54).

Like all of Iceland's offshore islands, Vigur was settled early on (about AD1000), and has always been a coveted property for its abundant natural wealth – namely birds, seals, and fish. You can still see all three, along with the occasional whale out in the fjord. The current owners came here four generations ago and still live off the land, hunting puffin, gathering guillemot eggs and eider down, and raising cows and sheep.

Besides the island's obvious beauty, what makes Vigur so special is the preservation of a way of life that has disappeared elsewhere in Iceland. Island traditions are still the daily routine – livestock is carried in open rowboats and the eider down is collected out of stone walls several centuries old. The little box windmill (built in 1830) is the last of its kind in Iceland and with its millstone intact. The main house (Viktoríahús) was built in 1862, to which a further building was added as the family grew. Several barns and warehouses round off the 'inhabited' part of the island and a side building houses 'the smallest post office in Europe'. Managed by one of the island aunties, sending postcards from this remotest of outposts is a tourist stipulation.

Visits to Vigur Island must be arranged as a guided tour from Ísafjörður (*West Tours; www.vesturferdir.is; summer only*). A ferry takes you to Vigur for an informative walking tour around the island, covering its history and splendid nature. It all ends with the farmer's wife putting out a healthy spread of coffee and Icelandic cakes. The two- to three-hour trips cost from about US$65 per person. The experience of Icelandic tradition, the quality of the tour, and just the chance to set foot on this island, all make it well worth the price.

## ÆÐEY

'Eider Island' takes its name from the 6,000 eider nests upon its shores, which represent a huge amount of annual income. To avoid disturbing the ducks the family who lives here has kept their island private and off-limits to outsiders. However, twice a week the mail boat makes a stop at both Vigur and Æðey. Year-round, visitors can go along for the ride but are not allowed to disembark. Alternately, one can get a good look at Æðey from the coast – especially Snæfjallaströnd.

## BOLUNGARVÍK

The next bay up from Ísafjörður is a quiet, secluded inlet marked by an impressively sharp peak. Bolungarvík is one of the first permanent fishing stations in the West Fjords and one of the most isolated (the road to the outside world only came in 1950). The tiny village gained celebrity status as the location for the award-winning film *Nói Albínói*, but fame is a two-edged sword. Now people know the place exists, but that's based on the story of a hopeless adolescent trapped inside a depressed, lifeless village on the verge of nowhere. And yet the village itself (and what lies beyond) holds a deeper, inexplicable attraction.

**GETTING THERE AND AWAY** The airport bus from Ísafjörður goes back and forth to Bolungarvík in conjunction with the flight schedule (*456 7195*). The drive/walk/ride to Bolungarvík is quite beautiful as you pass big cliffs with seabirds circling up above and waterfalls that gush right out onto the road. From Ísafjörður in a car takes about 20 minutes.

**WHERE TO STAY AND EAT** Choices are limited: spacious apartments (with private bathroom) are available at **Hafðu það gott** (*Holtastígurf 11; m 893 6860; e inga@bolungarvik.com; www.bolungarvik.com;* **$$**). The **campsite** is next to the swimming pool with hot showers and toilets (*456 7381;* **$**). The town bar/coffeehouse is **Kjallarinn** (*Hafnargata 41; 456 7901; 13.00–18.00 daily, also 22.00–03.00 Sat/Sun;* **$$**). Otherwise, it's hot dogs, pizza, pitas, and ice cream at the **Shell Skálinn** (*Thuríðarbraut 7; 456 7554; 09.00–23.00 Mon–Fri, 10.00–23.00 Sat/Sun*). The grocery store is at **Samkaup Úrval** (*Vitastígur 1; 456 7000; 09.00–19.00 Mon–Fri, 09.00–18.00 Sat/Sun*).

**WHAT TO SEE AND DO** Across the bay from the town lies the **Ósvör Fishing Museum** (*Sjóminjasafnið Ósvör; 450 7000; May–Sep 10.00–17.00 daily; entrance 500ISK*). The reconstructed fishing village on the shore harks back to the early seasonal fishing stations that once dotted the West Fjords (and much of Iceland). A bearded guide in a sealskin outfit takes visitors through the fisherman's hut, a salting house, and the drying hut, telling of the lifestyle lived by so many Icelanders for centuries. The overall effect is to leave feeling very sorry for the fishermen. The town's **Natural History Museum** (*Náttúrugripasafn Bolungarvíkur; Aðalstræti 21; 456 7005; e nagr@nave.is; www.nave.is; summer 09.00–17.00 daily, winter 13.00–17.00 daily; entrance free*) is filled with all the stuffed species of the region, including a lone polar bear (the town's pride and joy) and an admirable collection of minerals. And don't forget the **swimming pool** (*Höfðastígur 1; 456 7381; e sundlaug@bolungarvik.is; 08.00–11.00 & 13.00–21.00 Mon, Wed & Fri, 10.00–18.00 Tue & Thu, 10.00–16.00 Sat/Sun*).

A ridge of steep mountain peaks defines the rest of the coast – for an outstanding

## THE BREIÐADALS AND BOTNSHEIÐAR TUNNEL

Until recently, the heavy snows of the West Fjords winter cut off so many of the fishing villages in the surrounding fjords. For months, whole communities were left isolated until the high mountain passes opened up. In 1995, the problem was finally addressed with a Y-shaped tunnel system connecting Suðureyri, Flateyri and Ísafjörður. The three tunnels boast a collective distance of 9,120m, the longest road tunnel in Iceland (though longer tunnels are now under construction). Truly, this was an engineering feat – to cut through miles and miles of hard basalt, some of it still 'hot' with volcanic warmth. At one point, tunnel diggers unleashed an underground waterfall which had to be diverted. The main throughway is two lanes wide, but the two side tunnels are only the width of a single car. Use general tunnel precautions (slow right down, use your lights, and pull off into the passing places to let others pass).

panorama of the entire fjord and distant Hornstrandir, head to the top of **Mt Bolafjall** (638m). The road to the top is very narrow and steep and it's only free of snow for about six weeks out of the year (July/August). Otherwise, hike all the way up (about 1 hour). Standing at the edge of these cliffs allows a remarkable view – up here, one really is at the top of the world looking down on Creation. The big radar ball was part of the American Cold War defence system to keep track of the Soviets – it's been rusting away unmanned ever since 1992.

The long and glorious valley below is filled with streams and waterfalls – the farms in the area were abandoned some 50 years ago owing to the isolation and year-round snow. A nice hike (or drive) takes you all the way up to the undisturbed bay of **Skálavík**. A trail continues down the beach and up to the lonely lighthouse of **Galtarvití** (*www.galtarviti.com*), which guests can rent for an unconventional escape.

## SUÐUREYRI

Like a deep cleft in the mountain, Sugandafjörður may well be the narrowest fjord in all Iceland. The narrow road clings to one mountainside and leads from the tunnel almost to the mouth of the fjord, where lies the settlement of Suðureyri: it is a fishing village that smells like fish. Ordinary homes are bunched up along a single street near the busy fish-processing plant.

To lure outsiders all this way, villagers now market the destination as Iceland's 'original fishing village'. The truth behind the slogan is that Suðureyri has kept its small industry alive when others have closed down, preserving a way of life that is dying elsewhere in Iceland. Fish is now the heart of tourist activity: guided tours of the fish factory are informative (and fun), the local shop sells fish food so that you can 'feed the wild cod', visitors can rent boats and angling equipment or you can go out with the fishermen for a day at sea. Whatever your bliss, it's a one-stop shop at the village (VEG) guesthouse, whose managers organise all local activities and run the highly original and only café in town. Suðureyri is also home to the rare (for these parts) outdoor **swimming pool** (*Túngata 4; ☎ 456 6121; ⌚ 10.00–21.00 Mon–Fri, 10.00–19.00 Sat/Sun*).

**GETTING THERE AND AWAY** On weekdays, a bus runs back and forth to Ísafjörður (20 minutes) three times a day. The bus station is at the post office.

**WHERE TO STAY AND EAT** For a bed, meal, or an excursion, come to **Fisherman Hotel Veg** (*12 rooms; Aðalgata 14;* ☎ *456 6666;* e *guesthouse@sudureyri.is; www.sudureyri.is/guesthouse;* ). Efficient, homely and user-friendly, the guesthouse has a modern and comfortable feel with staff who care. Rooms come with or without private bathrooms and sleeping-bag spaces are available, along with kitchen and laundry facilities and the option of breakfast. They also have a strong environmental policy that's reflected in everything they do. The ultra-hip **café** on the main floor warrants the drive out here (🕒 *summer 08.00–23.00, dinner 18.00–21.00 daily*). The menus are bound in fish skin, and every dish that's listed is made from food harvested fresh in this fjord. Options range from the simple and delicious (fish stew, wild mountain lamb) to the more exotic (haddock carpaccio, catfish cheeks in cream). Dessert is rhubarb tart or the outstanding hand-picked blueberry soup with fresh cream. Plus there's coffee and cake all day long. You can't go wrong.

## FLATEYRI

Önundarfjörður is your standard issue Nordic fjord, V-shaped and without any irregularities. It was first settled by Önundar Vikingson, whose ambiguous patronymic was meant to mask that he was in fact the illegitimate son of King Harald of Norway. He farmed the only flat piece of land available, and that '*eyri*' eventually became the village of Flateyri. The local Norwegian whaling station began to wane in the early 1900s, but the fishing industry stayed fairly strong until only recently. In October 1995, a gigantic avalanche buried the town beneath one million tons of snow, killing 20 people and destroying dozens of homes. The calamity was a shock from which the town has never fully recovered. Although an avalanche barrier was built and the town was shifted a few blocks, nearly one-third of the population has picked up and left. It is a tragedy that has permanently marked the place and affected the whole country.

**GETTING THERE AND AWAY** A bus runs back and forth to Ísafjörður (30 minutes) three times a day. The bus station is at the post office.

### WHERE TO STAY

**Grænhöfði** (3 rooms) ☎ 456 7762; e jens@snerpa.is. Self-catering luxury apartments in town for up to 6 people. All-inclusive, this is a great deal for families or groups. **$$**

**Korpudalur** (24 beds) ☎ 456 7808; e korpudalru@centrum.is; www.superhighway.is/travel/korpudalur. Located at the base of the fjord, this cottage-style youth hostel has simple rooms, which are furnished with bunks, & bathrooms are shared. Kitchen & laundry facilities are available, & horseriding can be arranged. Book ahead, as the house is sometimes rented out as a whole for groups. **$$**

### WHERE TO EAT

**Vagninn** Hafnarstræti 19; ☎ 456 7751; e info@vagninn.is, www.vaginn.is; 🕒 11.00–23.00 Sun–Thu, 12.00–02.00 Fri/Sat. The village pub & tavern is one of the most lively in the West Fjords & people travel a great distance just to have an evening drink. Fish & lamb meals are served, as well as lighter sandwiches & fast food, plus live music on weekends. *Mains from 1,000ISK.* **$$**

**WHAT TO SEE AND DO** The fjord is especially apt for **kayaking**, which can be arranged at Grænhöfði guesthouse. A great experience is to arrange a longer trip that travels for over a week or more from fjord to fjord. With its hot tub and sauna, a popular attraction is the town **swimming pool** (*Tjarnagata;* ☎ *456 7738;* 🕒 *10.00–12.00 & 16.00–21.00 Mon–Fri, 16.00–21.00 Sat/Sun*). The extensive beach makes a nice walk, and fishing fish for trout from the bridge is popular.

**OVERLAND HIKES** It is possible to explore the northwest coast of the West Fjords more intimately by walking overland between the villages of Flateyri, Suðureyri and Bolungarvík. This is rugged territory and a hike of three to four days allows a unique view. Watch the weather and carry a good map.

## THINGEYRI

Thingeryi is the largest settlement on Dýrafjörður, which says less about the village and a lot more about the barren and beautiful area that this is. Fewer than 300 people live here, and every morning they all wake up to a view that much of the rest of the world only dreams of: the silver-grey water, long entrenched valleys, and the tallest mountain in the West Fjords, **Mt Kaldbakur** (998m). The fjord takes its name from its first settler, a wealthy Norseman by the name of Dýra (which also means 'animal') – Thingeyri claims to be the first trading post in the whole West Fjords, though today it's known as the place where the scenic yet difficult unpaved road suddenly becomes paved and civilised for the rest of the way towards Ísafjörður. The bridge allows the rare feeling of driving over a fjord and also saves a good 15km.

**GETTING THERE AND AWAY** The bus (m *893 1058*) travels twice daily to and from Ísafjörður (1 hour) via Flateyri. The bus stop is at the Esso petrol station in the centre of the town.

### TOURIST INFORMATION

**Tourist information** Fjarðargata 24 (inside the woollen goods gallery); ☎ 456 8304; e umthingeyri@snerpa.is; www.thingeyri.is; 🕒 Jun–Aug 10.00–18.00 Mon–Fri, 11.00–18.00 Sat/Sun, Sep–May 15.00–18.00 Thu

### WHERE TO STAY

**Alvidra** (22 beds) ☎ 456 8229; e avidra@snerpa.is; www.veidkortid.is. An old farm on the north side of the fjord, which offers seclusion & tremendous views of the water but is close enough to town (25km) to make it accessible. Rooms are clean & proper but all bathrooms are shared. They also offer a studio apartment & a cute separate cottage that's a great deal. B/fast inc. **$$$**

**Hótel Núpur** (40 rooms) Dýrafjörður ☎ 456 8235; e info@hotelnupur.is; www.hotelnupur.is. A reconverted rural school building, this fjord-side compound offers an added degree of seclusion & quiet with the benefit of a nice in-house restaurant. Rooms are tight but tidy; bathrooms are shared. The beach, mountains, & church are all lovely, but there's not much to do apart from quiet evening walks in the historic Skrúður gardens. **$$$**

**Vera** (4 rooms) Hlíðargata 22; ☎ 456 8232; e skuli@snerpa.is. Basic apartments in a simple house with all the amenities, as well as sleeping-bag spaces for a very reasonable cost; shared bathrooms. **$$**

**Við Fjörðinn** (8 rooms) Aðalstræti 26; m 847 0285; e vidfjordinn@vidfjordinn.is; www.vidfjordinn.is. 'On the fjord' guesthouse is a rather plain travellers' refuge but comfortable as they come. Bathrooms are shared. They also have 2 fully furnished apartments with private bathroom, of which one is fitted out for wheelchair access. B/fast is available for a cost. *Sleeping-bag spaces 2,100ISK, made-up rooms around 3,500ISK.* **$$**

**Camping** Located right next to the town swimming pool, with toilets and sinks available (shower at the pool) (*456 8225;* **$**). Rather compact, but with grounded wind protection for tents.

**WHERE TO EAT** Your best option is **Dúddakaffi** (*Hafnarstræti 2; 456 8415; 10.00–21.00 daily*), the one-stop pizzeria/coffeehouse in the town centre. Otherwise, there is food at the Esso station (*456 8380; 09.00–22.00*). You can also head all the way out to the fancy restaurant at **Hótel Núpur** (*456 8235; e info@hotelnupur.is; www.hotelnupur.is/restaurant; 12.00–21.00 daily;* $$$). In search of haute cuisine that pays tribute to the region, expect salt cod with a twist and fresh favourites like homemade bread and butter-churned ice cream.

**WHAT TO SEE AND DO** Thingeyri is rightfully proud of its **swimming pool** next to the campsite (*456 8375; 07.45–21.00 Mon–Fri, 10.00–18.00 Sat, 10.00–17.00 Sun*). Otherwise, enjoy the fjord and head into the hills. Trails run up each of the valleys, all of which are laden with saga-era history. Thingeyri is also the de facto base for anyone attempting the Svalvogar circle. On foot or bike, the simplest way to the top of Mt Kaldbakur is through Kirkjubólsdalur (follow the bicycle dirt path, then turn off for the last few hundred metres to the summit). On a clear day, the view is overwhelming. Add a stone to the cairn and sign the guestbook. Follow the road up the opposite side of Dýrafjörður to the petite church at Núpur and the century-old botanical garden of **Skrúður**, maintained by the local school students.

## ARNARFJÖRÐUR

Arnarfjörður is simply gorgeous. There's no better way to explain the power and beauty of this amazing fjord – one of the largest in the whole West Fjords, shaped by formidable black mountainsides and coloured with golden sand and crystal-blue waters. The odd-shape of the fjord is what grants such a dramatic perspective – long and narrow by the entrance, it branches off into a wide panorama of smaller fjords and bays. Some of the best views are from behind, on routes 63 and 60 as you drive over the higher mountains. Because the fjord is so steep, travel along its sides can be cumbersome. Look out for seals – they like to slide up on the beaches.

The tick-list highlight for most who pass should be the tumbling white waters of **Dynjandi** ('thundering') Waterfall. Truly a deafening sight, the series of waterfalls tumbles stepladder-fashion down a 100m-long descent, following the natural contour of the layers of basalt underneath. In staircase perspective, the bottom of the falls is twice as wide as the top, making it all the more impressive. Trails on both sides allow you to clamber up higher, and a long drink from the falls can help clear the head. Near the base of the falls is a good campsite (free) with showers and toilets, which is relatively empty on account of its isolation.

The only town on the fjord is tiny Bíldudalur. Continuing on the road that runs along the southern coast of the fjord (Route 619) takes you to its remote outer edge. The road is unpaved, narrow, rough, and prone to slow sheep and falling rocks – but it's all about the beautiful scenes you can see across the water. It can take a good while to make it out to the lonely farm of **Selárdalur**, a strange place on many counts. What you can see is the lifeless farmhouse of celebrated Icelandic folk artist Samúel Jónsson. Living in total isolation, the farmer spent his spare time creating fanciful sculptures with concrete, hay, glass, and paint. Examples of his menagerie still remain (eg: walruses, lions, seals and horses). Just across the way is the 19th-century church that marks the spot of the original Selárdalur farm. In

## THE OUTLAW: THE SAGA OF GÍSLI SÚRSSON

The waters of Dýrafjörður may appear calm and unwavering but this scenic fjord is the opening scene for one of the most celebrated sagas in Iceland. The tale is rich with imagery of the West Fjords, including powerful sorcerers, snow avalanches and strong winds that blow away the roofs of houses. It has the plotline of a Shakespearean tragedy, the melodrama of a soap opera, and more fights than a Jerry Springer show – truly, it is an amazing story (and it all really happened, between AD940 and AD980).

Once upon a time lived the hero Gísli, a strong and wise man who was known throughout Iceland for being a skilled craftsman and fighter. It was said that no matter what he aimed at, he hit the target dead-on. He settled in Haukadalur ('hawk valley') in Dýrafjörður after escaping the law in Norway where he had killed his sister's ex-boyfriend, maimed the man who wanted to marry her and threatened another. In retaliation, the injured family burned down the farm of Gísli's father. The old man narrowly escaped the flames with his sons by covering up with goatskins dipped in whey, hence Gísli's patronymic nickname 'Súrsson' (*súr* means 'whey').

Once safe in Iceland, Gísli and his brother Thorkel build a successful farm and try to enter an oath of protection with their two brothers-in-law, Verstein (brother to Gísli's wife) and Thorgrim (husband to their sister Thordis). Only after the men cut their arms and the blood is mixed into the earth does Thorkel back out, refusing to vouch for Verstein. A while later, Thorkel overhears his wife Asgerd gossiping with his sister-in-law (Gísli's wife) Aud. He discovers that prior to their marriages, both of these women were romantically linked to one another's brothers-in-law – Aud (Gísli's wife) once had eyes for Thorgrim, and Asgerd (Thorkel's wife) used to date Verstein. That night, Thorkel tells his wife to sleep on the couch but takes it back when she threatens to divorce him.

Later, in the midst of a vicious storm, Verstein is stabbed through the heart with a spear and dies. The spearhead is made from a piece of the powerful ancient sword ('grey blade'), once owned by Gísli's grandfather who had stolen the sword from his slave before bludgeoning him to death. Thorkel and Thorgrim hired a

spite of abundant yellow flowers and the radiant sunbeams that may shine from above, the farm and church hold an eerie past. Evil spirits are said to roam freely, making the area uninhabitable. In 1669, a wife to the local pastor fell ill and blamed it on their farmhand's alleged dabbling in black magic. The farmhand was burned to death, as were five more unassuming 'witches' – one for every subsequent time the pastor's wife fell ill.

The north coast of Arnarfjörður takes you past the birthplace of Jón Sigurðsson at **Hrafnseyri** (☎ *456 8260;* e *hrafnseyri@hrafnseyri.is; www.hrafnseyri.is;* 🕒 *1 Jun–31 Aug 13.00–20.00 daily; entrance 500ISK*). The humble, three-gabled turf home has been restored and is now a quaint and under-appreciated museum dedicated to the man behind the Icelandic independence movement. The actual museum (photos and paper) is perhaps less interesting than the whole of the traditional Icelandic homestead that's on display (complete with a red and white church). It is exactly the kind of dreamy, faraway memory-laden landscape that befits a homesick nationalist. There's a small café on the premises that serves soup, sandwiches, coffee, and cake.

For those who prefer the road much less travelled, just follow the fjord (the main road heads up over the mountains to and from Thingeyri). The **Svalvogar circle** is a

local sorcerer to fashion the magical spearhead, thus Gísli implicates Thorgrim for the murder of his friend. When the two are playing at sport, Gísli forewarns Thorgrim by throwing a ball at his back and knocking him to the ground. Then Gísli bribes Thorgrim's servant to unbolt the doors at his master's farm and that night, he sneaks in and plunges the spear right through Thorgrim so that he is pinned to the bed and dies – Gísli gets away because all the farmhands are drunk and cannot identify him in the darkness. As revenge, Thorgrim's brother pays the same sorcerer to put a curse on anyone who gives help to Thorgrim's killer. That winter, Gísli tracks down the sorcerer, stones him to death, and buries him in the muddy shores of the fjord.

Eventually, Gísli is found out and pronounced an outlaw by the West Fjords assembly. He goes into hiding – first in a hut in Arnarfjörður, then in the underground passage of an old widow's house, and finally at his cousin's farm on the island of Hergilsey. Thorgrim's family are also out to kill him, but Gísli evades them with cunning and skill. He fakes his own death by capsizing his boat, and changes clothes with his servant to create a mistaken identity. When a spear is finally thrown at him, he catches it mid air and tosses it back, killing the aggressor. All the while Gísli is troubled by dreams that foretell his own death. He finally meets his end when Thorgirm's gang catches up with him on the shores of Hjarðarnes. When his wife Aud brandishes a club and fights beside him, Gísli delivers a classic one-liner: 'I always knew I married well, but only just realised what a great couple we make.' Gísli defends himself with incredible strength, using rocks, axe, and his sword to kill eight out of the 12 men, but finally succumbs to his wounds.

Today, Gísli remains the homegrown hero of the West Fjords and it's fairly easy to follow his own travels as an outlaw. The south coast of Dýrafjörður takes you into his farmland at Haukadalur (which you can hike through), and the Svalvogur road (Route 622) brings you around to Arnarfjörður where he spent three long winters. The ferry across Breiðarfjörður passes right by the island of Hergilsey (where he spent many summers), and Hjarðanes (where he died and was buried) is the mountain right across the fjord from the ferry dock at Bjarnslækur.

route well known for its jaw-dropping scenery (but still a well-kept secret). Here the mountains and sea are gargantuan to the point of oblivion, with just the ribbon of dirt road to skirt around the peninsula. A few brave souls have attempted the drive in a 4x4 but most of them have destroyed their axles in the process (unadvisable). Hence the area being claimed by cyclists – in fact, Svalvogar has become a sort of pilgrimage for those who travel Iceland on two wheels. The road is driveable by normal car up until Fossdalur, where you must ford a stream and then ride along the most unbelievable bike path in the world. Certain areas along the coast are steep to the point of vertigo, and you cross several-dozen streams which may or may not be filled with rushing water. It is a land of audible 'wows' and childlike wonder – favourite spots along the way include Lokinhamrar (and the vertical cliffs behind it), the lighthouse point at Svalvogar, and the deep valley of Keldudalur. One can easily hike the coast as well, but plan carefully. It is possible to walk the 20km or so between car-accessible spots, but you'll need a designated driver or pickup service at the other end. The full 'circle' as depicted on local hiking maps heads up Kirkjubólsdalur (from Thingeryi), around the summit of Mt Kaldbakur, down Fossdalur then all the way around the coast.

## BÍLDUDALUR

The only village for the whole of Arnarfjörður is just a speck of a place right on the edge of the fjord. Only 200 souls live beneath these shadowy mountains, but the local airstrip makes this a new gateway in and out of the West Fjords, with easy access to Látrabjarg. The town is also home to the **Melodía Music Museum** (*Tjarnarbraut 5; ☎ 456 2186; ⏲ summer 14.00–18.00 Mon–Fri; entrance 500ISK*). It is the only monument to the heyday of Icelandic pop orchestras and jazz music from the 1950s onwards. Icelandic star Jón Ólafsson still manages the fervent display of musical paraphernalia, including dazzling costumes and worn album covers.

**GETTING THERE AND AWAY** Bíldudalur Airport (BIU) offers an alternative access to the West Fjords (☎ *456* 2152). **Eagle Air** (*www.ernir.is*) offers daily flights to and from Reykjavík (40 minutes), which can also be booked through **Air Iceland** (*www.airiceland.is*). There is an airport bus that visits Talknafjörður and Patreksfjörður once a day.

**WHERE TO STAY AND EAT** The town's only guesthouse is **Kaupfélagíð** (*11 rooms; Hafnarbraut 2; ☎ 456 2100; e kaupfelagid@simnet.is; www.lokinhamrar.is;* **$$**). The main floor houses a restaurant and tavern, as well as a multi-purpose shop. Food is soup, burgers and fries, all for under 1,000ISK. Upstairs lie a number of clean, nice-smelling rooms, decked out with IKEA staples. Two double rooms have private bathrooms, the rest share, and the largest room accommodates sleeping bags. The campsite (by the football field) has limited services. The town restaurant is the veggie-friendly **Vegamót** (☎ *456 2232; e birna@vegamot.biz; www.vegamot.biz; ⏲ 09.00–21.00 Mon–Thu, 10.00–22.00 Fri/Sat, 11.00–21.00 Sun; mains from 1,200ISK;* **$$**). It's a cute café with lots of light, strong hippie vibes, and plenty of healthy (and unhealthy) lunch and dinner choices. For a little more peace and quiet, stay at the **Otradalur farm** just down the road (*2 rooms; ☎ 456 2073; e otradalur@simnet.is; www.otradalur.is;* **$$$**).

## PATREKSFJÖRÐUR

Patreksfjörður is a small fishing town that's evolved into 'the town' for the entire Látrabjarg Peninsula. The fjord was first settled by a single boatload of men who sailed from Norway at the behest of Örlygur in the 9th century. As a Christian among old-school pagans, Örlygur rejected heathen omens and instead consulted his bishop Patrick about the upcoming journey to Iceland. The bishop prophesied of the fjord where he should land and settle, loading up Örlygur's ship with enough wood and a bell to build a church. The men lost their way and Örlygur prayed to St Patrick to find land, promising to name the site after him. Hence 'Patrick's fjord' and the inlet of 'Örlyg's harbour'. The most exciting and beautiful parts of the fjord are well outside the town, but this is a very good base from which to explore the region, as well as stock up on petrol, food, etc, as you journey into the uncivilised wilderness. There's also a fabulous swimming pool (with indoor gym, steam bath and hot tubs) for dull, wintry days (*Brattahlíð; Aðalstræti 55; ☎ 456 1301; ⏲ 09.00–21.00 Mon–Fri, 10.00–18.00 Sat/Sun*).

**WHERE TO STAY**

**Eyrar** (8 rooms) Aðalstræti 8; ☎ 456 4565; e handradinn@simnet.is. Endearing & earnest family guesthouse in the town centre; doubles with bathrooms, singles without, &

## JÓN SIGURÐSSON (1811–79)

Iceland is a nation of many heroes, but one man stands above them all. A life-size statue of Jón Sigurðsson faces the parliament building in Reykjavík, his face is on the 500 krónur note, and his birthday (17 June) is Iceland's national holiday. Jón was born at the parish farm of Hrafnseyri where his father served as the local pastor. Like most semi-privileged Icelanders of the time, he was sent away to Denmark to be educated at the national university. Living in Copenhagen, he earned his keep by working in the library, managing the prized *Arnamagnæan Codex* – the only academic collection of Icelandic sagas and literature in the world. He never did finish a degree, spending all his time reading the history and stories of his country. A meeting of like-minded expat Icelanders led to the founding of the Icelandic romantic journal *Fjölnir*, followed by Jón's founding of the more academic *Ný félagsrit* ('New Society Writings') in 1841. This annual journal became the political vehicle for the Icelandic independence movement. Though many Icelanders longed for economic and political liberation from Denmark, it was Jón Sigurðsson who built a sound intellectual and historical argument for independence, based on Danish documentation. Jón declared the illegality of the Kópavogur Meeting of 1662 (when Iceland 'agreed' to absolute rule by the King of Denmark) and picked apart other fateful events that led to Iceland's eventual lack of self-determination. His case was convincing to many Danes and led to the re-establishment of the Icelandic Althing in 1845. Jón was elected MP for Ísafjörður and twice served as the president of the legislative body but still lived most of his life in Denmark. As the leader of the Icelandic intelligentsia in Copenhagen, he continued to push for total independence. In 1874, the year after he ended publication of his journal, Iceland received its own constitution and limited self-rule. It was the beginning of the end of Danish subjugation. The path to complete independence was protracted, but unlike the bloody revolutions of so many nations, this was a struggle borne from literature. Jón Sigurðsson died in Copenhagen in 1879, having lived to see some of the fruits of his labours.

plenty of inexpensive spaces for sleeping-bag accommodation. B/fast is available in the downstairs café, which serves coffee & cake (*09.00–18.00*). **$$$**

**Erla** (7 rooms) Brunnar 14; 456 1227. Simple B&B with sleeping-bag accommodation, shared bathrooms & kitchen. **$$**

**Stekkaból** (18 rooms) Stekkum 19; 456 1675; e stekkabok@snerpa.is. A rambling sort of travellers' guesthouse – rooms vary (some are small) & all bathrooms are shared. Sleeping-bag spaces available; communal kitchen, laundry & living room. **$$**

### WHERE TO EAT

**Thorpið** Aðalstræti 73; 456 1667; e thorpid@simnet.is; 11.00–22.00 Mon–Thu, 12.30–01.00 Fri/Sat, 13.30–21.00 Sun. The town's main café, bar & restaurant resting on the hillside. The glass walls guard you from the elements while allowing a great view of the fjord. Specialities are local trout, plokkfiskur, crêpes, fish soup & hamburgers. Drinking, music & good times on the weekend. *Mains from 700ISK*. **$$**

**Self-catering** The best place to stock up on groceries is at **Smáalind** (*Aðalstræti 110; 456 1599; 10.00–22.00 daily*).

## LÁTRABJARG

The great cliffs of Látrabjarg are one of the great natural wonders of Iceland. The vertical wall of layered basalt drops straight down into the waters of Breiðafjörður from such dizzying heights that the human eye fails to take it all in. It is impossible to exaggerate the sheer size of these cliffs: well over 400m (1,200ft) high (twice the height of Ireland's cliffs of Moher) and more than 14km (8.6 miles) long. Equally impressive is the massive bird population that make this their summer home. Látrabjarg is the largest bird cliff in Iceland and also in the entire northern hemisphere. Nobody's had the patience to take an official count, but we know there are several million birds – enough to completely cover the cliff from one end to the other. It is a unique habitat and on such a massive scale that several seabird species sustain their population at this one spot. From May to August, expect puffins, guillemots, razorbills, and fulmar in overwhelming numbers. The birds love the cliff for its perfect nesting spots and the abundant food below. The violent current that swirls off the tip of this peninsula is rich with fish – hence the birds, fishing boats, and a long history of shipwrecks.

Látrabjarg is also the westernmost point of Iceland and Europe (24° 32'W). On a clear, sunny day it is sometimes possible to see the glare from the ice cap in nearby Greenland, only 278km (173 miles) away. The cliff's highest point is known as **Heiðnakinn** at 441m(1,447ft), or the 'heathen wall'. The abrupt peak hints at the malevolent spirit said to reside here – a devil that cuts the ropes of the climbers gathering bird eggs. Such was the livelihood of locals who rappelled (abseiled) down the rock face, sending up flat baskets filled with guillemot eggs for food and sale. It is a sport of great agility and nerve, still practised in other parts of Iceland (see box on page 238).

Crazily enough, Látrabjarg is not an officially protected nature reserve (yet), perhaps in part because so few travellers make it out this far. It takes some patience and effort to get here, but the experience is a powerful one.

**GETTING THERE AND AWAY** The only road to Látrabjarg (Route 612) is unpaved, bumpy, and quite steep in places. Be prepared, as the closest fuel stop is in

### THE REMARKABLE RAZORBILL: *ALCA TORDA*

Látrabjarg is home to the largest razorbill colony in the world, with an estimated cliff population close to half a million. The notable birds are all black except for their white tummies, and a distinctive white line on their beak and nose. Though they do resemble small penguins (their French name is *petit pinguoin*), razorbills are a member of the auk family (eg: puffins, guillemots), the only living species of the *Alca* genus, and the closest relative to the now-extinct great auk (see page 210). They are very fun birds to watch as they are quite active little creatures. Except for their time nesting in the cliffs, they spend their entire lives at sea and are fantastic swimmers and divers. Flying is a little harder so they tend to stumble across the water to get airborne. Razorbills stake out spots all along the cliff, but the largest concentration is near Stóruð, about 3.5km east of Bjargtangar lighthouse. With binoculars you can sometimes spot their unique eggs: cream-coloured with black granite-like specks. Their eggs hatch after a month, but the babies hit the sea in just two weeks, long before they can fly.

## HIGH-RISE HOTEL

Birds of a feather flock together, birds with different feathers do not. So many different birds live on Látrabjarg, and yet they co-exist with far more harmony than humans have ever achieved. This phenomenon of sharing the rock face is often compared to a high-rise apartment building, where distinct communities occupy different 'floors'. Among the broken scree and fallen boulders at the bottom of the cliff live the razorbills. The fulmar live just above on the grassy lower ledges. The next layer is occupied by the kittiwakes, and in the steepest (almost vertical) section of the higher cliff live the guillemots. At Látrabjarg, you'll find Brünnich's guillemot occupying the lower tier, and common guillemot the upper. Neither species makes a nest but lay their conical, roll-proof eggs on the most precarious rock ledges. In Látrabjarg, there's another layer of razorbills and fulmar closer to the top of the cliff (above the guillemots), after which you reach the puffins. Puffins rule the roost, occupying the very top tier of the cliff and digging their holes among the turf and tufts of grass. The same natural order exists elsewhere, but nowhere is it more pronounced than at Látrabjarg.

Patreksfjörður, 60km away. In summer, there is a bus (☎ *456 3518*) that travels between Látrabjarg and Brjánslækur (2 hours) via Örlygshöfn and Patreksfjörður. From Brjánslækur, a corresponding bus travels to and from Ísafjörður (3 hours).

**VISITING THE CLIFFS** The cliffs of Látrabjarg are so tremendous that it's hard to take it all in. The road ends at the car park next to the Bjartangar lighthouse, the westernmost point in Europe. You can see a lot from this point, but the really big cliffs are accessible only on foot. A trail follows the top of the ledge all the way to the descent into the low bay (and former fishing station) of Keflavík, 14km away. The ultimate viewpoint is at Heiðnakinn (about 6km in), after which another trail loops back to the lighthouse overland. If staying at Breiðavík, it is possible to arrange a car pickup and drop-off to facilitate a one-way hike in either direction. Further east, it is possible to descend to lower points, but be careful. Remember that you are standing at the top of a 1,000ft drop with the potential for high winds – use common sense and pay attention to your instinctive fear of heights. Most people lie down on their stomachs and peer over the side. For birdwatching, it's best to find a spot where the cliff face turns in so that you are facing the birds somewhat directly – binoculars should be mandatory.

In my view, Látrabjarg is the very best spot to encounter puffins in Iceland, if not the entire world. Because hunting is prohibited on the cliffs, the birds are fearless and allow you to get within a few inches of them, even touch them gently (although you probably should not). At the height of summer, when the birds (and tourists) are in full force, the real secret is to go to the cliffs at night. The tour groups and caravans will come and go all day long, but few realise that the puffins only start returning from the sea after 22.00. They flutter up to the tufts at the top of the cliff and preen or relax before retiring to their holes. This is the time when the birds are the least jittery and the most apt at posing for pictures. If you can, take an early-evening nap and then head out quite late. In the midnight light, one can sit quietly in the midst of a few hundred thousand puffins. Later in the summer, when it's darker, come at sunrise (03.00 or 04.00) and watch as they take off *en masse* for their day of work.

## WHERE TO STAY AND EAT

**Breiðavík** (52 rooms) ☎ 456 1575; e breidavik@patro.is; www.breidavik.is; ⏲ 15 May–15 Sep. The closest accommodation/campsite to the great cliffs is about 12km away. Feeling much like the end of the world, Breiðavík could very well be the most inspiring & least pretentious 'hotel' in the world. Until 1980, it was a reform school for wayward boys – the most criminal-minded adolescent didn't stand a chance against the starkness & isolation of this beautiful bay. There's nowhere to run away to, but lots of great places to explore. As the only guesthouse in the area, Breiðavík caters to all tastes & degrees of independence. Cosy, prefabricated double rooms (with private bathroom) cost the most; made-up beds with shared bathrooms are less expensive & the dormitory-style sleeping-bag accommodation is a bargain. With racks of muddy hiking boots & people making soup in the kitchen, the atmosphere is one of a busy travellers' refuge. There's also a huge & popular campsite with hot showers (1,000ISK per tent) with their own separate toilets & kitchen facilities. Visitors are offered full-pension meals options – eating in the dining hall/restaurant feels like having dinner at your mother's house. Expect hearty, home-cooked meals from the lovely owner who bakes all her own bread fresh every day; a 3-course meal costs around 3,200ISK. **$$$**

**Hótel Látrabjarg** (12 rooms) ☎ 456 1500; e info@latrabjarg.com; www.latrabjarg.com; ⏲ May–Sep. This reconverted boarding school is now a lovely boutique-style B&B, offering a slightly more upmarket stay for this area. Built on the mountainside above Örlygshöfn, the giant windows offer a fantastic view of the fjord, about 24km away from the cliffs. The well-decorated rooms are super-clean & a little retro (on purpose); private bathrooms are available. Off season, they do take large groups. B/fast inc (other meals available). **$$$**

**Hænuvík** ☎ 456 1574; e haenuvik@mi.is. The most authentic farm experience in the West Fjords. The Icelandic family who live here look after 1,000 sheep & also man the nearby lighthouse. They offer 2 historic, self-catering cottages (sleeps 6–8 people); 1 is right next to the sea, the other looks out on to the valley. Amenities are somewhat primitive (you need your own bedding), but the solitude is total & the nature absolute. You can also choose to eat or stay with the family. **$$**

**Camping** A semi-official campsite, **Látravík** (**$**) can be found at Hvallátrar near the bay closest to the cliffs. Very basic, with toilets and sinks only; often taken over by caravans.

## AROUND LÁTRABJARG

The southwest peninsula around Látrabjarg is another one of Iceland's hidden gems. The landscape is somewhat severe in its beauty, with grey clumps of basalt and olive-coloured moss that run across high plateaux and break into cliffs, steep slopes and gigantic empty bays. The weather can become so hideous it's comedic and the winter population drops down to the four families who each occupy their 1,000-year-old farms. Even if you choose not to stay there, the bay at **Breiðavík** makes for an inspiring visit. The awesome scale of this deep, bowl-shaped valley and the beach that goes on for ever is great for long, undisturbed walks or longer overland hikes. The current church was built in 1960 but is the third to stand on this spot since AD1200. Another key highlight is the **Hnjótur Folk Museum** (*Minjasafn Egils Ólafssonar; ☎ 456 1511; e museum@hnjotur.is; www.hnjotur.is; ⏲ 1 Jun–15 Sep 09.00–18.00 daily; entrance 500ISK*). The farmer who started this eclectic collection never threw anything away. As a result, this museum has lots of character – selected objects have been polished and arranged to document the everyday life of the inhabitants of this far-off corner of the West Fjords. Learn about the art of collecting bird eggs from the cliffs and see what's been salvaged from all the shipwrecks, then go out back to see all his old

### THE *DHOON*

On 12 December 1947, the British fishing trawler *Dhoon* was caught up in a violent winter squall and wrecked against the rocks at Látrabjarg. Three of the crew perished in the gigantic waves and the remaining sailors found themselves trapped 70m offshore, right beneath a 200m-high vertical cliff. News of the shipwreck spread swiftly from farm to farm, and 12 local men quickly formed a daring rescue operation. Despite high winds and deep snow, the stalwarts travelled a good 15km by horse and foot to the top of the cliff. With ropes they lowered themselves down the cliff wall to the bottom of the shore, then climbed another kilometre over wet rocks to get as close to the ship as possible. The farmers strung up a line between boat and shore, using a 'breeches buoy' to pull the sailors off the ship one by one. The survivors were then pulled to the top of the cliff, where the rescue team spent another freezing night waiting for the weather to calm. After a four-day rescue, they made it back to their farms – 12 of the 15 crew were saved. The Icelandic farmers earned medals of honour from Queen Elizabeth.

Hoping to recreate the dramatic Látrabjarg rescue for a broad audience, Icelandic filmmaker Oscar Gíslasson head out to the cliffs with his crew only to witness another ship as it wrecked in nearly the exact same spot as the *Dhoon*. With cameras rolling, Oscar captured an identical rescue with a number of remarkable real-life scenes. Visitors can now watch the entire film at the Egils Ólafssonar Folk Museum in Hnjótur where a whole room is dedicated to the wreck and the rescue.

planes – quirky but cool. The natural history section and a great little coffee shop have made this museum the de facto visitors' centre for Látrabjarg. The long blue bay down below is called **Örlygshöfn**, named after Örlygur, the first Viking settler in Patreksfjörður. Close by is a farm noted for its horseriding excursions (m *894 1587;* e *vesturfari@internet.is; www.internet.is/vesturfari*). Following the dirt road up the southern coast of Patreksfjörður brings you to **Hænuvík**. The bay was first named after an Irish monk (Hænnir) who lived here before the Vikings arrived but eventually took on the Icelandic synonym 'bay of hens'. It is a vast and lonely valley – quite beautiful and quite empty. The road winds down to the sea at Kollsvík where you can see the ruins of the old farm. Further down Patreksfjörður takes you past the valley and church of **Sauðlauksdalur**. Here in the 18th century, the impassioned Reverend Björn Halldórsson carried out his experiments with crops and agriculture, founding a convict colony to acquire the necessary labour to build a retaining sea wall (still visible) to prevent erosion (be careful driving in the sand dunes). The next road down (Route 614) leads to Saurbær and the tremendous beach of **Rauðisandur**. 'Red sand' is just that – a vast stretch of bright-red sand that extends for some 10km along the shore of Breiðafjörður. To get there, you must have a 4x4 to continue after the road ends or else you can hike. There is a long trail that connects Rauðisandur to Látrabjarg via Keflavík – good if you can arrange a pickup at either end.



## VATNSFJÖRÐUR

'Water fjord' is home to the famous site of **Flókalundur** where the explorer Flóki-Raven (see page 16) first landed in the late 9th century. After a disastrous winter he climbed to the top of Mt Lómfell only to see the next fjord over filled with ice, inspiring him to name the country 'Iceland'. In a like manner, this particular fjord takes its name from the abundant water all around. The young glacial landscape features hundreds of kettle lakes, tarns, clear pools, trickling brooks, streams, waterfalls, and a single gushing river that pours through the valley and into the fjord. It is a magnificent place and very wet, with lots of mist in the highlands and fantastic light that pours through the clouds. To bask in the heavenly scene, take a drive (or a walk) through the **Vatnsfjörður Nature Reserve** which incorporates the coast, valley and upper plateau of the fjord. So much water means everything is a vibrant green in summer and there are a number of native trees and plants. Expect seals in the fjord, be on the lookout for white-tailed eagles and ravens, and the secretive Arctic fox (also, beware of the nasty wasps).

Hótel Flókalundur is the location of the tourist information office and a petrol station with a small shop. Across the road is their campsite with full amenities and an outdoor **swimming pool** (*456 2044; 10.00–12.00 & 16.00–19.00 daily*). The nearby summerhouses are popular among Icelanders and make a nice retreat (check with the hotel).

**GETTING THERE AND AWAY** One of the main entry points into the West Fjords is at nearby Brjánslækur; 5km from Flókalundur. Twice a day the ferry travels to Stykkishólmur via Flatey. Take Route 612 to Látrabjarg (1½ hours); another incredibly scenic drive is on Route 60 over the highlands and on to Thingeyri (1½ hours). This is a steep, very high and totally unpaved road – you'll be fine in a regular car but only with patience and careful attention. The Brjánslækur–Ísafjörður bus (3 hours) follows this route with a stop in Flókalundur.

**WHERE TO STAY AND EAT**

**Hótel Flókalundur** (15 rooms) 456 2011; flokalundur@flokalundur.is; www.flokalundur.is; 15 May–30 Sep. This single-storey, ranch-style hotel is the central travellers' station in the area & makes a nice jumping-off point to or from the ferry. Rooms are compact, but very clean & carpeted, & all have their own private bathrooms (with notably good showers). One room is fitted out exclusively for wheelchair access. The big, open living room contributes to a very homely atmosphere & the friendly staff make an effort to ensure a nice stay. B/fast buffet inc. **$$$**

**Hótel Flókalundur Restaurant** 08.00–22.00 daily. The in-house restaurant features delicious local fare with a heady gourmet attitude. Although the menu appears small, the food tastes a step above the hotel it serves – the fresh trout is fished right out of these lakes. An out-of-hours grill serves basics (hamburgers, sandwiches & soup). *Mains from 2,000ISK.* **$$$**

**WHAT TO SEE AND DO** The great thing about the nature reserve is that you can drive to a number of short, convenient hiking trails. Enjoy the gorgeous views but use caution when crossing rivers which fluctuate greatly. If there's not a trail or a bridge, that's a clue. The three main 'canyons' are actually U-shaped valleys carved out by the now-obsolete glacier Gláma – the towering basalt substrate reveals the ice's last stand. A road, then trail, follows all the way up Vatnsdalur, past the lake Vatnsdalsvatn, and through the braided river. Alternatively, the main road (Route 60) follows the Penná River valley and leads to a trail that takes you to the top of historic Mt Lómfell (850m). Weather permitting, the climb is not arduous and the view over all the pools is amazing. Thingmnnadalur is the least-visited valley but renowned for its waterfalls, and has a short trail near its entrance. A popular trail ascends the slope behind Flókalundur up to the beautiful Helluvatn. Hörgsnes is the right-angled peninsula on the fjord's southeast coast, renowned for the cave (where saga hero Gísli hid out) and its seals.

## BREIÐAFJÖRÐUR

'Broad fjord' is what separates the West Fjords from the rest of Iceland – a 50km-wide watery gap that looks like a giant bay but is still very much a fjord by definition and formation. The Old Norse explanation goes back to the three trolls who dug frantically to separate the region from Iceland – the rocks flung between their legs became the scattered islands that characterise the fjord. Seeing as some rocks are semi-submerged and less than 1m wide, there's no telling how many islands exist, but the last person who counted came up with more than 3,000. As compelling as the trolls sound, geologists attribute this great bay of islands to active eruptions of ancient times. The rims of sub-glacial volcanoes were ground down by the retreating ice cap, forming the telltale *roches moutonnée* of glacial landscapes – or rather, a glacial seascape. The islands follow the grain of this prehistoric ice flow, and you can still see the scratches and cracks where the rocks were smoothed down into paisley-shaped islands. Much of the fjord is remarkably shallow and the islands low, like silver drops on a sheet of steely blue. Thus, tides are felt very strongly, so much so that three or four 'islands' may become a single island at low tide, and certain broad channels suddenly become impassable. A few of the islands are still 'hot', namely Hrauneyjar ('lava islands') and Drápsker ('killer skerry').

The very first settlers rushed to Breiðafjörður because it was filled with so much quick and accessible food (seals, fish, birds, eggs, and whales). In summer, seabirds still dominate the sea and sky – expect cormorants, shags, lone puffins and eider ducks galore, perhaps even the rare and endangered sea eagle (this is where most of them live). Harbour seals also love these islands, but normally keep to the rock skerries farther out. The waters are still the home of many spawning fish and the entire eastern half of the fjord is a protected nature reserve.

### THE BREIÐAFJÖRÐUR FERRY

The best way to experience Iceland's broadest fjord is to take the ferry **Baldur** (*438 1450; e info@seatours.is; www.seatours.is*). As the ship crosses Breiðafjörður, it manoeuvres through thousands of tiny islands. Obviously, the birdlife all around the boat is superb and will keep you busy watching. Also look for the giant white and orange jellyfish in the water, all the seals on the rocks, and the occasional whale or dolphin. The ferry runs between Stykkishólmur and Brjánslækur once a day in winter and twice a day in summer via Flatey Island. The entire journey takes about three hours and costs around US$50 one-way per person. Vehicles are an extra charge (US$50 each-way for a normal car) – if taking a car in summer, it is imperative to book ahead. If you're travelling on foot or bike, it's not so hard to get a place.

In the West Fjords, the ferry office in **Brjánslækur** (*456 2020*) is open one hour before and after ever ferry landing and departure. It also plays the role of bus stop and coffee shop. The bus between Brjánslækur and Ísafjörður (3 hours) coincides with the ferry schedule. Brjánslækur is a stop-and-go kind of place, but while you're stopping, check out the cute, tin-sided white and red church at the base of the oversized cliff-mountain, next to the babbling brook. Further down the coast brings you to **Krossholt** where natural hot springs have been diverted to a pair of hot swimming pools, one of which sits right on the rocky beach. There is a local guesthouse with sleeping-bag accommodation, but it's only so-so.

## THE ISLES OF BREIÐAFJÖRÐUR

Eight main island groups make up the 'west islands' of Breiðafjörður – the 600 or so that lie closest to the West Fjords. Each group has a unique history and its own peculiarities:

**BJARNEYJAR** (bear islands); an old-time fishing station, now uninhabited. The last bear was spotted some 1,100 years ago.
**FLATEY** (flat island); the largest and most inhabited with a winter population of 15.
**HERGILSEY** (Hergil's island); settled by Hergil, son of Thrándur of Flatey. Summer hideout of Gísli the outlaw.
**HVALLÁTUR** (whale rest); comprising 250 separate islets.
**SVIÐNUR** (burnt island); no connection to the farm that burned down here. Fantastic wildlife.
**SAUÐEYAR** (sheep islands); abandoned for lack of water but still used for sheep grazing.
**SKÁLEYJAR** (bowl islands); supposedly haunted by a friendly population of *húldufolk*.
**SVEFNEYJAR** (sleep islands); named in the 10th century when the local landowner/chieftain found his slaves sleeping instead of working – he sailed them to Sviðnur and hung them from the tall rocks.

Trade has always been key in these parts and the islands are close enough to each other to facilitate trade on the typical small boats built by the islanders. Yet life out here is difficult. Lack of fresh water and unpredictable weather is why so many island farms were finally abandoned. A popular legend tells of a homesick Icelandic horse that swam from island to island all the way across the fjord in order to get back to his old farm.

Today, nearly all the islands in Breiðafjörður are privately owned. Some families use them as summer holiday homes, others for fishing, grazing or collecting eider duck down. One can arrange a visit to any of them, usually through a personal contact or by taking your own boat and stepping lightly (and respectfully) wherever you land. The islands are perfect for kayaks, and kayak rentals are becoming more and more popular. Use caution – there's always an island close by but the weather changes quickly; you are principally in the middle of the ocean and currents are very strong. By far the simplest island to visit is Flatey, which is large enough to host a small village, a big history, and a public ferry dock.

## FLATEY

The largest and most populated island in Breiðafjörður is Flatey, the hearth of a low-lying island cluster whose beauty is found in its simplicity and total rejection of anything frantic or fake. Here lies a separate existence, where time is distinguished not by sunlight and clocks, but tides, the flowers in bloom and which birds are hatching that week. Colourful old houses brighten the wistful landscape, where the grass is always blowing and the waves keep lapping away at the rocky shore. If you are in search of 'the real Iceland', this is one of them.

Flatey was formed from the collapsed caldera of a sub-glacial volcano, hence the presence of both columnar basalt and some lighter pyroclastic clumps. The ice age nearly ground the island out of existence, pushing it down to just a few metres above sea level and making it as flat as its name. The island was first settled in the 10th century by a man named Thrándur ('skinny bones') whose descendants moved on to settle the other islands in the fjord. In 1172, an Augustinian monastery was built, marking the island as a centre of learning and literature. The German Hanseatic League showed up in 1569 and began trading, after which Flatey became a rather wealthy place – the island received its town charter in 1777 – nine years before Reykjavík. The 19th century saw the island boom – there was a time when several hundred people lived here all year round. There were a lot of fish, a lot of money, and a lot of building. The Flatey Progressive Establishment (Flateyjar Framfarastiftunar Bréflegafélagíð) was set up to benefit the large populace, and in 1864 Iceland's first-ever public library was opened on Flatey. Only after the two world wars did islanders begin leaving for the city. By the 1930s, the old fish-freezing plant was shut down simply because there were not enough people on the island to run it. A few stalwarts continued to graze sheep over the years, but it was only very recently that a kind of renaissance took place. Nearly all the old houses have been refurbished to their original glory, and today the picturesque isle is a favourite retreat for artists and writers. Despite the obvious appeal, the island remains wonderfully untainted with fewer than 2,000 visitors per year.

**GETTING THERE AND AWAY** The only commercial transport to Flatey is on the ferry ***Baldur*** (*438 1450; e info@seatours.is; www.seatours.is*). The boat travels to Flatey from Stykkishólmur (1 hour 35 minutes) and then on to Brjánslækur (1 hour) and back again. In summer, the ferry schedule offers a few different options for short-term visitors. You can take the first boat in one direction and catch the second, allowing you six hours to explore the island; or wait for the same boat to loop around (in about 2 hours). Best of course is to spend one or several nights on the island and just take a later boat. There are no cars on Flatey, but if you are taking one on the ferry, the company will simply take your keys and leave the car for you at the terminus on either shore.

## WHERE TO STAY

**Hótel Flatey** (13 rooms) 422 7610; e info@hotelflatey.is; www.hotelflatey.is; 1 Jun–31 Aug. The magic of Flatey Island is aptly expressed in this thoughtful boutique hotel, made up of several 19th-century homes that have been poetically redesigned. True to Scandinavian style, every space is immaculate – white, plain, clean & cosy – & the details are charming. Each room is named after a different island bird, & although there are a few tight corners, the beds are heavenly. It's all been ripped right from the pages of a too-good-to-be-true glossy magazine with prices to match. A worthy splurge. B/fast inc. **$$$$**

**The Farmhouse** (8 beds) Home of Ólina Jónsdóttir; 438 1476. This friendly island farmer & his wife take in guests at a reasonable price in this low-key B&B. It's preferable if you have your own sleeping bag, but not necessary as made-up beds are available. Bathrooms are shared. B/fast inc. **$$**

**Camping** A small campsite is available on the southern shore of the island, between the church and the farmhouse (pay at the house). There are no amenities, and worse, no shelter. Check the weather forecast and be warned: several diehard campers have given up halfway through the night and run to the farmhouse.

**Note:** if all other options are full, there are other houses on the island that will host you for about 1,500ISK per person. Just ask at the hotel.

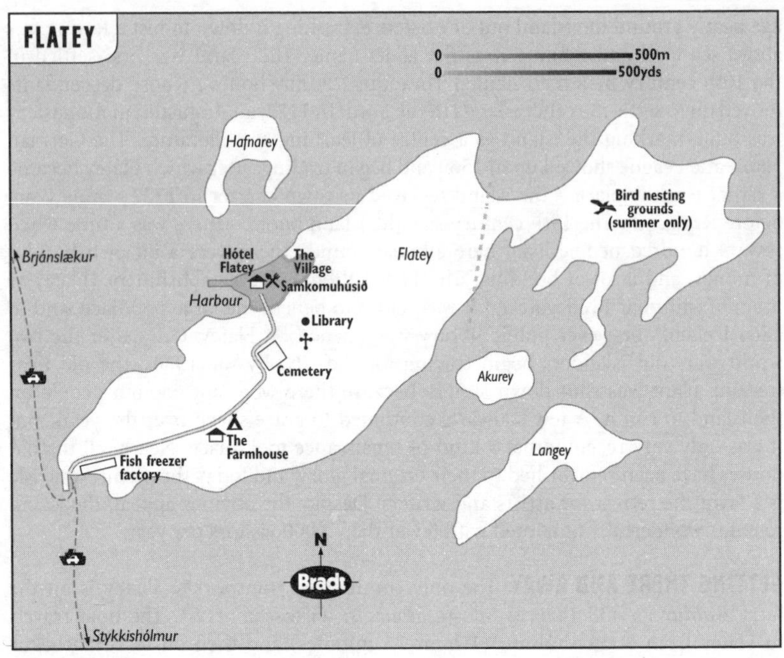


## WHERE TO EAT

**Samkomuhúsið** 422 7610; e info@hotelflatey.is; www.hotelflatey.is; 08.30–22.00 Sun–Thu, 08.30–midnight Fri/Sat. The restaurant at Hótel Flatey serves as the island's kitchen & lounge – it is the place where islanders gather in the evening to listen to music, to tell stories & simply to be with one another. The menu strikes a lovely balance of something delicious & almost gourmet but entirely unpretentious – this is true-to-life Icelandic cuisine without any gimmicks. Try the *plokkfiskur* or the cod balls with herb sauce. The smoked seabird salad (guillemot) is an island speciality & there are always big, lovely hunks of moist, home-baked bread to go with it. For day visitors, the restaurant serves a lovely spread for lunch. *Mains from 2,600ISK.* $$$

**Note:** there are no shops on Flatey – just a small booth at the hotel that sells toiletries, postcards, stamps and sweets. Also, the water on Flatey is not potable – only drink bottled or boiled water, and if you are coming for a longer stay, be sure to bring some along.

**WHAT TO SEE AND DO** Flatey Island fosters a contemplative mood and is best enjoyed in several quiet walks. The ferry stops at the old freezer factory and the dirt road connects to the village. The 'village' is a cluster of a dozen or so houses near the old harbour which at low tide is a tangled mess of purple kelp. The current island **church** (Hjallsvíkskirkja) was built in 1926 and stands at the island's highest point. The door is always open and visitors must see the church's amazing ceiling – a dark and splendid mural depicting the island's history. It is the work of Catalan artist Baltasar Samper (renowned in Iceland) who did the painting in exchange for a place to stay on the island (note the white-tailed eagle above the altar). Across the path is the island **cemetery**, with graves dating back several hundred years.

### THE FLATEYJARBÓK

The *Flateyjarbók* is the largest illuminated medieval manuscript to be written in Icelandic. The book was transcribed at the end of the 14th century by a pair of priests on 225 sheets of calfskin vellum. The book's pages contain the sagas of the Old Norse kings, the history of the Viking explorers to Greenland, the settlement of the Orkney and Faroe islands, and a few more sagas. When the King of Denmark requisitioned all Icelandic manuscripts, Flatey resident and churchman Jón Torfason refused. The *Flateyjarbók* had been in his family for several generations, and was prized not only for its great stories, but also for its colour and beauty. In 1654, after three years of coaxing and bribing from the bishop, Jón finally turned the book over in exchange for a piece of land several times larger than Flatey Island. The country's most valuable history ended up in a museum in Copenhagen where it stayed for 300 years. Although most of the sagas are recounted in several books, the *Flateyjarbók* is the most complete version and has been acclaimed as the key text in Old Norse studies. Denmark finally returned the manuscript to Iceland in 1971, and today you can see the original (an excerpt) at the Culture House in Reykjavík (see page 181).

Right next to the church stands the little yellow **library** (Bókhlaðan) – the oldest in Iceland and open to visitors occasionally.

From 15 May to 15 July, a large section of the eastern half of the island is off-limits in order to protect the large number of nesting birds there. There are plenty of puffins, oystercatchers, gulls, and especially Arctic terns – if you're there in summer, be prepared to get attacked. There are trails around the coast on all sides, one of which passes by the 'ghost ship', an old trawler that met its end here. When walking about, be wary of tides, which can leave you stranded for half a day (just because the sheep are out there doesn't mean that you can get back). By far the best way to explore the intricacies of the area is by kayak. The hotel offers two–three-hour guided kayak excursions (*kayakleigan*) to the nearby islands of Svefneyjar for around US$90 per person.

## REYKHÓLAR

The countryside around Reykhólar is the closest one gets to Reykjavík in the West Fjords – if you're driving from the capital, this marks your arrival. Despite being on a main road, Reykhólar feels a bit off the beaten path since so few people make the stop. The village of 200 residents is situated at the bottom of the Reykjanesfjall Peninsula, an area of beautiful mountains, gently sloping shores and some geothermal activity. People stop in this area on their way in or out, or else to take a break and do some hiking (Vaðalfjöll is the pair of volcanic rock pillars above the pass in the road).

Also popular are the outdoor **swimming pool** and **hot tubs** (*Grettislaug;* 🕒 *10.00–22.00 daily*), if not the local seaweed factory, where the easiest by-product in Breiðafjörður is turned into all sorts of useful things (as displayed at the information centre). The many fjords just north of Reykhólar are quite beautiful and totally devoid of civilisation, with the exception of a few picturesque churches. In summer, it is possible to catch a boat to the Skáleyjar Islands (☎ *434 7841;* e *skaleyjaferdi@hotmail.com*).

## TOURIST INFORMATION

**Tourist information** 434 7830; reykholar@simnet.is; www.reykholar.is; Jun–Sep 09.00–17.00 daily. Be sure to catch the old boats exhibition.

## WHERE TO STAY

**Hótel Bjarkalundur** (11 rooms) 434 7762; bjarkalundur@bjarkalundur.is; www.bjarkalundur.is; May–Oct. An isolated road stop on Route 60, this average hotel complex includes a petrol station, shop, & popular restaurant. Recent improvements have spruced up the experience just a little. Bathrooms are shared & a number of sleeping-bag spaces are available. B/fast inc. **$$$**

**Álftaland Hostel** (10 rooms) Barðastrandssýslu; 434 7878; reykholar@hostel.is; www.alftaland.is. A modern, efficient hostel on the verge of a vast & boundless landscape. Bathrooms (& the kitchen) are shared, they've gone to extra efforts to make things wheelchair-friendly, & there's a nice hot tub & steam bath out back. Sleeping-bag spaces are available for less. **$$**

**Camping** Right next to the swimming pool (*434 7738; reykjolar@simnet.is; www.reykholar.is;* **$**). Amenities are limited.

## WHERE TO EAT

**Hótel Bjarkalundur** 434 7762; bjarkalundur@bjarkalundur.is; www.bjarkalundur.is; 07.00-22.00 daily. The biggest restaurant in the area is at the hotel. The menu is a fairly eclectic, albeit typical, mix of fish & lamb with a few international staples (lasagne, Tex-Mex, burgers, soup, etc) – the fish gratin is a popular choice with good reason. *Mains from 2,000ISK. Fixed-menu 3-course meal 3,000ISK.* $$

**Jónsbúð** 434 7890; 09.00–21.00 daily. The town *sjoppa* with hot dogs, ice cream, & a few shelves of groceries. *Mains from 300ISK.* $

## STRANDIR

The hooked peninsula at the top of the West Fjords is known simply as Strandir, an ancient name that means simply 'coast'. And what a coast it is – an exquisite shore furrowed by unknown fjords and anvil-shaped mountains. Indeed, the scenic contrast is quite remarkable: the harshest of cliffs break into breathless, open valleys; long piles of dead wood stand out against the millions of yellow summertime flowers, and the colours shine brighter against the white nothingness of the Drangajökull glacier. For many, Strandir feels like the most 'Arctic' place in Iceland, not for the lingering snow but for the raw and relentless landscape, not to mention that hardly a soul lives up here.

From the beginning, Icelanders have felt both reverence and intrigue towards the great beauty and dangers in Strandir. The most rugged types tried to settle here and found creative ways to survive the climate and isolation. Farming was impossible and fishing was too short-lived, so the only towns that lasted are those that stem from old whaling ventures. The weather aims to be the most horrific and frightening in Iceland. Catching a storm in Strandir is definitely the best in show. An added dimension is the local reputation for mysterious happenings and the supernatural. You're unlikely to find a farm that isn't haunted (allegedly).

Needless to say, Strandir is not an easy place to get around – there's a reason why it's mostly uninhabited today. There are basically no roads, and any roads that do exist are unpaved and often closed owing to the heavy snow. It might take some necessary planning to travel here but it's worth every second. Once a deprived backwater to be pitied, Strandir is now the ultimate destination for outdoor enthusiasts. Most hikers head straight to the wonders of Hornstrandir, an area reached only by boat. Those who want a heated hotel room come up via Holmavík and work their way northwards along the coast.

**HOLMAVÍK** This pleasant northern town is no more than a tiny cluster of well-heated homes at the base of Steingrímsfjörður. There is very little else besides the curved shores of the fjord and the whales that swim in it, but those who live here seem to like it that way. Hólmavík is now the major stopping point coming in and out of the Strandir coast so, if you're travelling overland you are likely to make a pit stop.

**Getting there and getting away** Route 61 connects Holmavík to the ring road (2 hours+) and Ísafjörður. Regardless of where you're headed, be sure to fill up with fuel. The closest petrol station is another two hours away in any direction. From the ring road, there's a bus that stops in Holmavík on its way between Bru (2 hours) and Drangnes (30 minutes). Another bus runs three times a week from Ísafjörður to Holmavík (4 hours) by way of Reykjanes (1 hour 15 minutes) (*456 3518; www.stornubilar.is*).

## Tourist Information

**Tourist information** 451 3111; e info@holmavik.is; www.holmavik.is; 09.00–20.00 daily

## Where to stay and eat

**Borgarbraut** (7 rooms) Borgarbraut 4; 451 3136; e borgarbraut@simnet.is. The town's one & only guesthouse, with shared bathrooms & sleeping-bag spaces. Open kitchen, a nice living area, & a kindly management. **$$**

**Kirkjuból** (5 rooms) 451 3474; e kirkjubol@strandir.is; www.strandir.is/kirkjubol. A charming private country home on the south end of the fjord. Bathrooms & kitchen are shared, b/fast available. The location is a bit out in the middle of nowhere – about 12km from Holmavík. It is also possible to rent out the entire house. **$$**

**Café Riis** Hafnarbraut 39; 451 3567; e caferiis@caferiis.is; Jun–Sep 11.00–23.00 Sun–Thu, 11.00–03.00 Fri/Sat. Built in 1897, the town's tavern keeps the locals busy with big pizzas & the like. The wonderful exception to the rule is their equal devotion to Icelandic cuisine: locally caught shrimp, grilled sandwiches, traditional flatkaka, & their own homemade smoked lamb. Wild times on the weekend. *Mains for 1,000ISK.* **$$**

**Esso station** 455 3107; summer 09.00–23.30 daily, winter 11.00–22.00 daily. The town's *sjoppa* for all your hot-dog needs; also lots of groceries. *Mains from 250ISK.* **$**

***Camping*** A very good campsite (*451 3111;* **$**) is sectioned off into various protected zones and is right next to the swimming pool in town. Pay at the information centre across the street.

**What to see and do** People also make the voyage to Holmavík to see the **Museum of Sorcery and Witchcraft** (*Galdrasýning á Ströndum; Höfðargata 8–10; 451 3525; e galdrasyning@holmavik.is; www.galdrasyning.is; Jun–Sep 10.00–18.00 daily; entrance 500ISK*). The only one of its kind in Iceland, the exhibit is built on the spot of the country's most famous witch trial. Running over two floors, the displays take visitors through the magical traditions that go back to medieval Iceland. Beyond the expected runes, spells, and grimoires (and the spooky interactive histories), the museum does a great job spelling out a narrative of the times and circumstances surrounding Iceland's biggest witch hunts (the 17th century). The informative audio tour is available in English, and the museum gift shop is anything but typical. The sorcerer's cottage at Kluka is a separate annex (see below). Holmavík is also the proud owner of the newest swimming pool in the West Fjords (☎ *451 3560;* e *sundlaug@holmavik.is;* ⏲ *09.00–21.00 daily*). A steam bath and several hot tubs make it a popular soaking spot for campers.

**BJARNAFJÖRÐUR** The next 'village' up from Hólmavík is **Drangnes**, which sits beneath a striking rock pillar, said to be one of the three trolls that helped dig out the West Fjords. This marks the end of the line for public transportation – a bus comes once a week) (*www.hopferd.is*). There's a single small guesthouse (*Sunnu; 6 beds; Holtagata 10;* ☎ *451 3230;* e *holtag10@snepra.is;* **$$**), a campsite with showers, new outdoor swimming pool, good grocery store (*Borgargata 2;* ☎ *451 3325;* ⏲ *09.00–19.00 Mon–Fri*), and a petrol station. A better holiday option is the self-contained summer cottages overlooking the fjord (*Bær III;* ☎ *453 6999;* e *info@this.is/baer; www.this.is/baer;* **$$**). There's a great view of tiny **Grímsey** Island (not to be confused with the Arctic Circle Grímsey), and it is possible to catch a boat out there in summer to see the puffins or go fishing (*Sundhani; Ásbjörn Magnússon;* ☎ *451 3238;* e *sundhani@simnet.is*).

**Bjarnafjörður** is the next fjord north, known for its witchcraft past – the **sorcerer's cottage** at Kluka is a recreated, 17th-century, turf-covered witch's hovel and the annex to the museum in Homavík (*Kotbýli kuklarans;* ☎ *451 3524;* e *galdrasyning@holmavik.is; www.galdarasyning.is;* ⏲ *10.00–18.00 daily; entrance 300ISK*). The hotel in **Laugarholl** (*Hótel Laugarholl; 16 rooms; Bjarnafjörður;* ☎ *451 3380;* e *matti@snerpa.is; www.strandir.is/laugarholl;* **$$$**) is new and modern, with bright IKEA interiors, a fantastic swimming pool and geothermal hot tub. Most rooms have their own bathroom, some do not. All meals are served at extra cost in the adjoining dining area – the food is not bad. Camping is also available.

**THE STRANDIR COAST** Route 643 continues northwards as a narrow dirt road that winds its way around the beautiful Strandir coast. A few remote travellers' rests allow one to migrate in short hops, starting with the former herring station of **Djúpavík**. The present hotel is a cheery frontier outpost, open year, round, well-known and highly regarded among hikers (*10 rooms;* ☎ *451 4037;* e *djupavik@snerpa.is; www.djupavik.com;* **$$$**). All rooms have private bathrooms with showers, and cheaper sleeping-bag accommodation is available. The restaurant is open all day and there's also a small shop, petrol station, kayak rentals and guided tours in the old herring station. On the other side of the fjord lies tiny **Gjögur** Airport with twice-weekly flights to and from Reykjavík (☎ *562 2640;* e *ernir@ernir.is; www.ernir.is*).

The next fjord up is **Nordurfjörður**, another small station of fishermen, outdoorsmen and hardy hikers. Besides an average guesthouse (*Norðurfjarðar;* ☎ *554 4089;* e *gulledda@simnet.is*) with kitchen and shared bathrooms, there's another for sleeping bags only (*Bergistranga;* ☎ *451 4003;* **$$**), and a very nice summer mountain hut (*20 beds; www.fi.is*). The campsite, grocery store, petrol station, and bank are a clue that this is your last stop before all civilisation ends. Renowned throughout all of Iceland is the **hot pool** that's built right into the stone beach of Krossness. The ice-cold seawater splashes into the natural geothermal water. The **ferry** to Hornstrandir departs from Norðurfjörður (*Sædís;* m *852 9367;* e *freydis@freydis.is; www.freydis.is*). The boat makes a stop at **Reykjarfjörður** where there is a small shelter (*22 beds;* ☎ *456 7215;* e *reykjarfjordur@simnet.is*), and a natural outdoor swimming pool.

**HORNSTRANDIR** The purest part of Strandir is the 'horn' – the final peninsula that juts over the top of the West Fjords. It is a daunting place for its intense beauty and extreme nature. The mountains are pyramid-shaped, sharpened by constant ice and wind. The cliffs stand up like defiant walls against the sea, and the intermittent valleys are lush green places of rare plants and flowers. It is a place to enjoy silence – a place where you actually notice the sound of a bird's wings, the wind, the trickle of a stream or the hum of a very distant boat engine. Other than Iceland's desert interior, Hornstrandir is the best place to feel completely alone on planet earth.

Once upon a time, Hornstrandir was an idyllic land of tiny farms hidden among these gargantuan rocks. At its height (about 1930) about 500 people called the valley home, but life was very difficult. Extreme weather aside, there were no roads, no electricity, and limited outside contact. Winters were long and impossible and the war years caused many to leave for the capital. By 1952, the area was permanently evacuated.

Today, wildlife thrives unmolested. The bird cliffs are a crazy echo of several million seabirds and Honrstrandir is the number-one spot in Iceland to see an Arctic fox. You are almost guaranteed a sighting if you come hiking here in the summer. Also, watch out for trolls. As the 'mainland' was covered with churches, the bothered trolls headed further and further north, finally ending up here. It's thought that there are more trolls in Hornstrandir than anywhere else in Iceland.

Today, the **Hornstrandir Nature Reserve** occupies the northernmost section of the peninsula, with the highest cliffs and some of the most striking terrain in Iceland. The park was established in 1975 and is now the most protected part of the country. All cars (and horses) are banned, fishing and hunting are illegal, you must carry out whatever you bring in, and travel is somewhat regulated. Most of the land in the park here is private property (those who left have kept it in the family), and the plants and animals are protected – you must tread lightly. Thus, Hornstrandir is best for serious hikers who know what they are doing and have a sound plan. This is one place where you must have appropriate gear (especially warm, waterproof clothing, good boots and a strong tent). Hornstrandir is also a little bit colder than

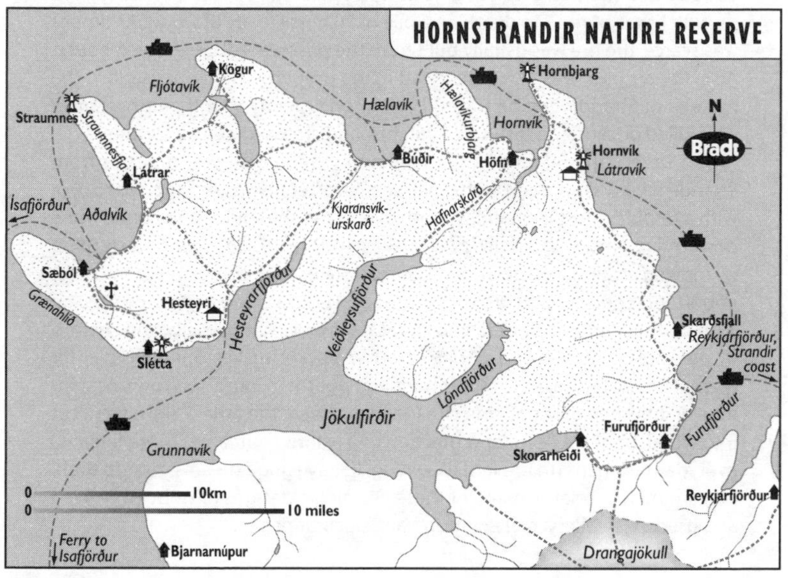

the rest of Iceland – you are farther north, there's a large piece of permanent ice on top of the mountains and you're getting hit with the brunt of the Arctic wind. Snow lingers in the shadows all year long, bays get closed off by drift ice, and some areas are only accessible for about six weeks of summer. All this should not foster discouragement though (on the contrary), but the intense circumstances support a kind of rugged elitism among those who make it out here, because so few actually do. A simpler approach is to go with an organised group tour.

**Getting there and away** The main travel season is from mid-June to mid-August. Outside that time, weather and ice are unpredictable. The quickest way to get there is to fly direct from Reykjavík to either Ísafjörður or Gjögur, from where you can take a ferry into Hornstrandir. From Ísafjörður, there's regular passage on **Sjóferðir** (*456 5111; sjoferdir@sjoferdir.is; www.sjoferdir.is*). The main boat goes to Hornvík (2–3 hours) with stops on request in the other northern bays (Aðalvík, Hælavík). Return boat passage is about US$100 (any gear you bring with you is free). They also make regular trips to Hesteyri and Veiðileysufjörður. It is best for hikers to plan a hiking route that corresponds with a boat drop-off and pickup – merely communicate what you want with the boat captain. **West Tours** (*www.*

## GALDRASÝNING: WITCHCRAFT IN STRANDIR

Like dentists, actors, and mechanics – some witches are better than others. In Iceland, the most talented sorcerers lived in the West Fjords and most notably in Strandir. Witches might cause dense fogs that make you lose your way, a fox to kill your sheep, some strange sickness to befall you, or your cow to give sour milk. Other spells could help you secure love or find money.

In the 17th century, Strandir was the epicentre of a widespread witch-hunt and pointing a finger at a neighbour was enough to get him killed (most witches in Iceland were men). To be cleared of any wrongdoing, the condemned had to find 12 peers who could testify to his innocence and good nature (quite difficult in a sparsely populated region). If unsuccessful, the witch was burned to death on a pile of 20 horse loads of wood. As timber was scarce, the fire was usually built from the prisoner's disassembled house. Also, the accuser was given the dead man's property as compensation. The hysteria in Strandir can be traced back to one greedy sheriff and his family who killed dozens and dozens of 'witches' and amassed quite a fortune.

Jón 'lærði' ('the learned') Guðmundsson (1574–1658) was a pastor from Strandir who was charged with devil worship after he was summoned to deal with a terrible ghost in Snæfellströnd. To exorcise the spirit, Jón penned three powerful poems, or *fjandafæla* ('to make fiends fear'). He escaped execution by moving around Iceland and to Denmark, later to become one of the most important scholars of the time. The most powerful Icelandic grimoire was the 17th-century *Galdrabók*, detailing magical symbols, runes, spells, and charms. (A piece of lignite cached in one's trouser pocket makes one invisible; for eternal friendship, take two silver rings and put them into a sparrow's nest for nine nights, then give one ring to a friend and wear the other.) Signs were cut into wood, bone, or flesh for protection or a wanted outcome. These became everyday talismans (to prevent drowning, to have good dreams, to stop theft, etc). In today's Iceland, many of these Old Norse designs have been revived and used in jewellery, crafts, tattoos, and decorations.

## DRIFTWOOD

Giant piles of driftwood line the coast of Strandir, most of it heavy, white logs of Siberian pine. The wood has been carried a few thousand miles from the Arctic shores of Russia where the timber escapes from loose northern river mills. After several years of soaking in salty brine, the logs are deposited on these flat beaches where the coast catches the current. Places like Reykjavík ('driftwood bay') take their name from the phenomenon and despite Iceland's great need for wood, the driftwood is not particularly useful. The salt ruins woodworking tools and the wood itself is often cracked or extremely hard. You will find that the wood is useful for benches to sit on or bridges across streams.

*vesturferdir.is*) offers a number of guided day trips and multi-day hiking trips all over Hornstrandir, which eliminates some of the hassle of organising things yourself.

If coming from the east side of Strandir, you can catch the ferry from Norðurfjörður on **Sædís** (m *893 9367;* e *freydis@freydis.is; www.freydis.is*). Boats travel westward to Hornvík (4 hours) with stops (on request) at Drangar, Reykjarfjörður and Látravík. The ultimate hike might include getting dropped off by one boat company and hiking all the way to the next (ie: Aðalvík to Reykjarfjörður).

**Where to stay** There are several cottages in the park, most of them refitted farmhouses now used as summer homes for private Icelandic owners. Sleeping-bag accommodation is available at Heysteri and Grunnavík, but these are exclusive to organised trips. One option that is open to the general public is the **old Hornvík lighthouse** at Látravík (*Hornbjargsviti;* *566 6752;* e *ovissuferdir@ovissuferdir.net; www.ovissuferdir.net*). A sleeping-bag space indoors costs around 2,400ISK and I can't think of a better location from which to be based. Most hikers bring their own sturdy tents. When pitching tents, be respectful of summer residents – if you can see them, you are on their property. There are eight emergency shelters located in the park and several more throughout the rest of Hornstrandir, all equipped with provisions and radios.

**What to see** Only come to Hornstrandir if you enjoy solitude, birds, and the wilderness. The northern coast takes you past a number of amazing bird cliffs. **Grænahlíð** (green cliff) is a long and furrowed bird cliff with a jagged finale at Riturinn. On the other side lies the gentle bay of **Aðalvík** and the cluster of huts at Sæból. The next mountain over is **Straumnesfjall**, which falls straight into the sea, but is not as high or impressive as the bird cliff of **Hælavíkurbjarg**. This is probably the best place to watch birds – mainly guillemots, puffins, fulmar and kittiwakes. A water approach allows you to pass through the stacks of rock and get up right beneath the sheer wall as it curves around into the silent bay of Hornvík. A long sand beach curves around to the fairy-tale picture of **Hornbjarg** (534m). This is the tallest cliff in Iceland, though not the 'biggest', standing like a jagged crown with a constant swirl of birds on all sides. Ascending to the peak is as easy as climbing a staircase but feels like some epic feat. The view is beyond description, unless you are terrified. Right around the corner sits the abandoned **Hornbjarg lighthouse**, built in 1930. On the shores of Jökulfirðir (on the other side of the park) lies **Hesteryi**, now known as the abandoned village. This was once the main habitation in the area, with about 80 residents.

**Hiking** The best map for the area is the *Landmælingar Íslands Hornstrandir Göngukort* (1: 100,000), which you can buy in any of the cities. Also make sure you have appropriate gear. Hornstrandir is a remote wilderness area, so plan well and use extra caution. There's plenty of water, but it's a good idea to have some extra food. In spring and summer, there's a huge number of rushing streams and rivers that you must cross – most trails will indicate an appropriate ford, but use common sense. Also pay attention to tides – sometimes you may have to wait for the water to recede. The same caution applies to ice – if you have no experience or are without crampons, don't do it. The glacier Drangajökull (200km²) lies outside the park and there's a 'trail' that crosses the ice from Reykjarfjörður. In the park, most hikes lead from one bay or fjord to the next, often over a very barren (but beautiful) mountain pass. Most routes are meant to last half a day (4–5 hours) so that you can configure your itinerary to match. The most popular day hike is between Hesteyri and Aðalvík; there's an old church (Staður) right above Sæból. A good multi-day tour starts in Aðalvík and jumps from bay to bay all the way to Hornvík (2–3 days) and then down to Furufjörður (2–3 days). The two main mountain passes include Hafnarskarð and Kjaransvíkurskarð.

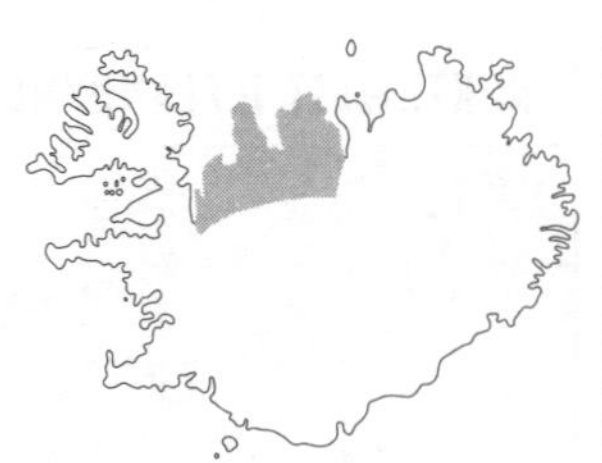

# Norðurland vestra (The Northwest)

The northwest is a bit of a misunderstood corner of Iceland, even among Icelanders. This is sparsely populated farm country, dotted with fog-laden fishing villages and secluded homesteads with pronounced histories. Beneath the layered landscapes lie deep-rooted tales that domino back through time. Three of Iceland's most renowned sagas were lived out in these valleys and fjords – those of Grettir the Strong, the people of Vatnsdalur, and the Sturlunga civil war. For nearly 900 years, the Church of Iceland was headquartered at Hólar, and the whole northwest region is dotted with traditional churches from every era. The fishing villages of the northwest took a strong hit in recent times, and some of them have never recovered – the population is sparse, which makes it a perfect escape. Seals, seabirds, and whales have found a safe haven along these coasts, and the Icelandic horse has claimed the northwest as its very own, especially the open terrain of Skagafjörður.

As a whole, the northwest is shaped by three distinct peninsulas divided by three distinct fjords. The ring road races across the bottom of each of these without thinking much about what lies north or south of the car-window view. An hour in either direction takes you to the tumbling waterfalls of Víðidalsá, to dreamy towns like Siglufjörður, or the barren seaside of Skagi. No doubt, the northwest is only as simple as one's imagination.

## GETTING AROUND

From the capital, the gateway to the northwest is the travel station at **Brú**, right at the base of Hrútafjörður. As the main junction for north and west Iceland, the bus links to Reykjavík (2 hours 30 minutes), and Hólmavík (2 hours) in the West Fjords, as well as all the other northwestern cities on the ring road (Hvammstangi, Blönduós, and Varmahlíð). The ultimate roadside service centre is just up the road at **Staðarskali** (*451 1150;* e *stadur@stadarskali.is; www.stadarskali.is;* *24hrs*). Anyone driving around the ring road is bound to make a stop. The complex includes a large grocery store, a big fast-food café, a motor and petrol service station, and a country hotel. The adjoining guesthouse (*26 rooms;* **$$$**) offers typical motel-style accommodation with private bathrooms and breakfast included. The central bus junction is at Varmahlíð, with connections to all major towns in the northwest and links to both Reykjavík and Akureyri.

## VATSNES

The forgotten peninsula of Vatsnes is a point of windswept hills and empty valleys jutting out into the cold waters of Húnaflói. The dirt road that goes around the coast (Route 711) is quite scenic, known best for its rocky shoreline and a great

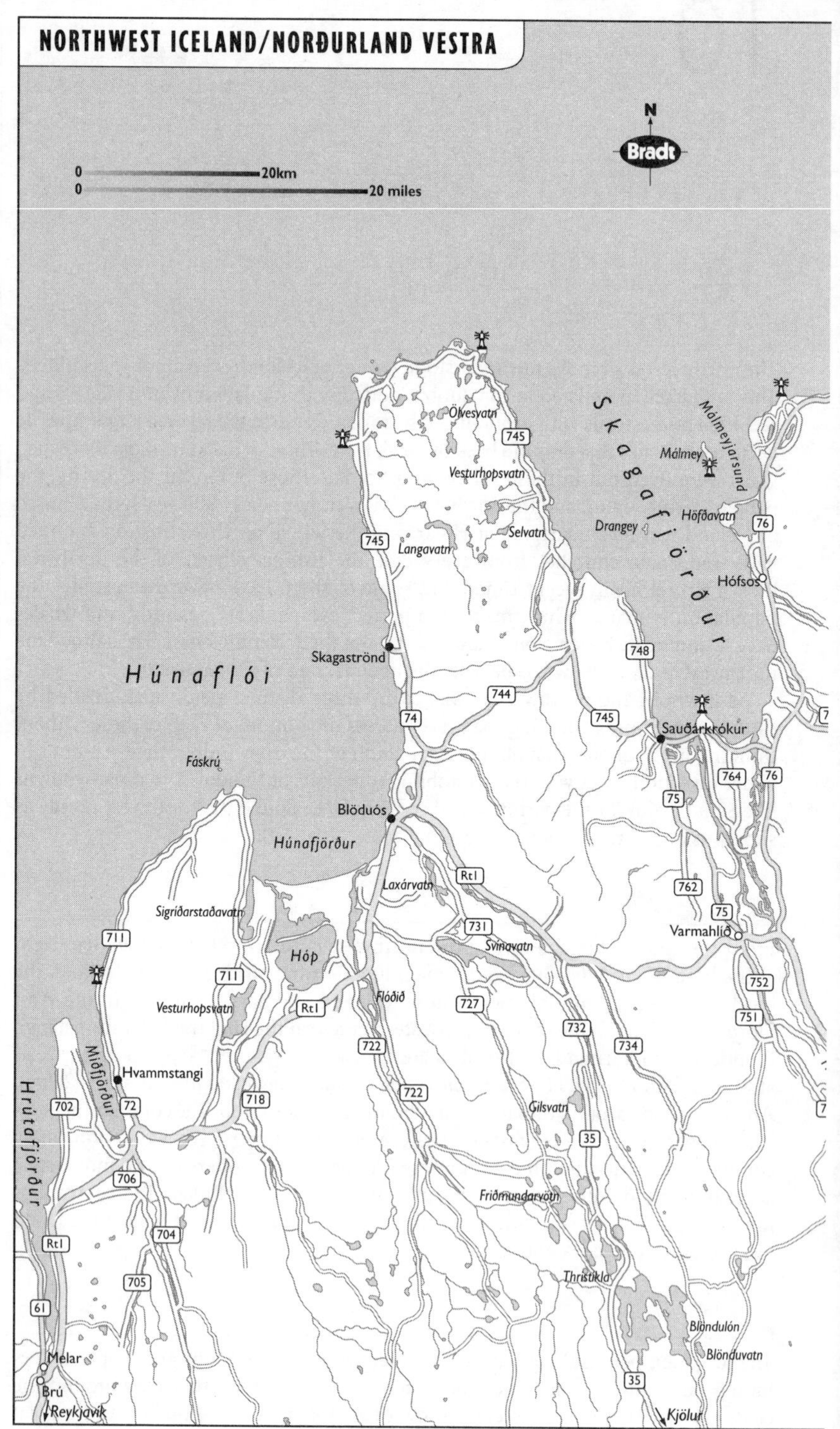
NORTHWEST ICELAND/NORÐURLAND VESTRA
N
Bradt
0 20km
0 20 miles
Skagafjörður
Málmeyjarsund
Málmey
Ölvesyatn
745
Vesturhopsvatn
Höfðavatn
Drangey
Selvatn
76
745
Langavatn
Hófsos
Skagaströnd
748
Húnaflói
744
74
745
Sauðárkrókur
Fáskrú
764
76
75
Blöduós
Húnafjörður
Rt1
Laxárvatn
762
Sigríðarstaðavatn
75
731
Varmahlíð
711
Svínavatn
Hóp
711
752
Vesturhopsvatn
Flóðið
727
Rt1
751
732
734
722
Miðfjörður
Hvammstangi
722
Hrútafjörður
702
72
718
Gilsvatn
35
706
Friðmundarvötn
704
Rt1
705
Thristikla
61
Blöndulón
Blönduvatn
Melar
35
Brú
Reykjavík
Kjölur

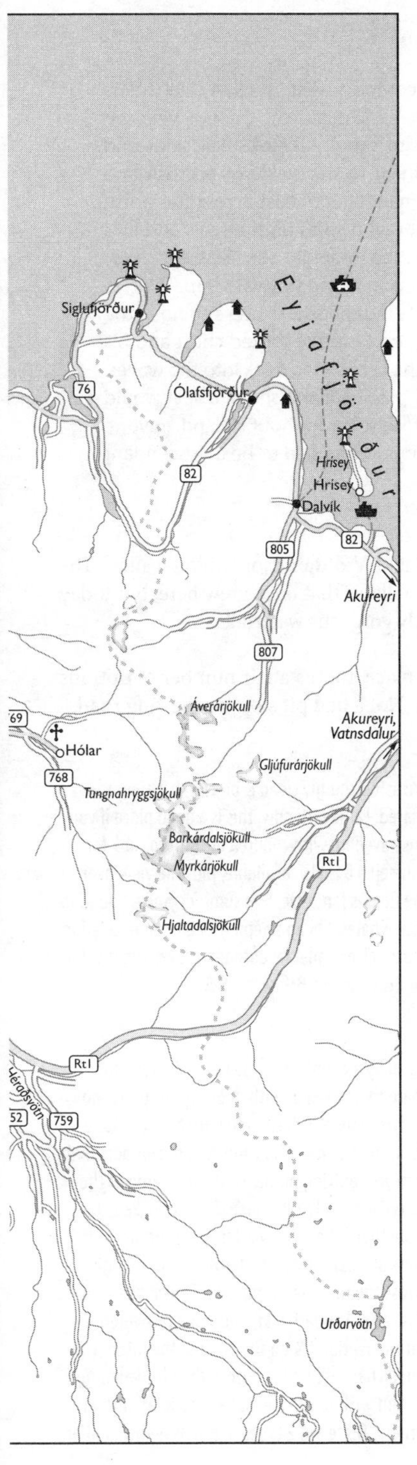


abundance of seals. Now protected by law, Iceland's most densely populated seal colony resides at the northernmost point of **Hindisvík**. This is the only spot in the country where you are almost guaranteed a sighting of both grey and harbour seals. Profiting from that phenomenon is the steadfast village of **Hvammstangi**, home to Iceland's one and only **Seal Centre** (*Selasetur Íslands; Brekkugata 2; 451 2345; selasetur@selasetur.is; www.selasetur.is; 3 Jun–31 Aug 09.00–18.00 daily, 1 Sep–15 Oct 10.00–16.00 Mon–Fri, call in winter*). Once a manufacturer of seal oil, the comprehensive museum now instructs guests on all the different species of Icelandic seals, their biology and behaviour, and a history of seal hunting and subsequent conservation. Heavy on interactive displays, this is a great place for younger children. Afterwards, join one of the centre's seal safaris on a refitted fishing boat. The tour lasts about two hours and sails out into Miðfjörður. Pottering around the shoreline gets you up close and personal with the seals. The centre also offers popular angling trips for people wanting to catch some cod. Right next door is the historical **Merchant Museum** (*Verslunarminjarsafn Bardúsa; Brekkugata 4; 451 2747; 11.00–18.00 daily*), a quirky old-time shop that's frozen in the early 1900s. The owner has kept one room exactly as it was, including all the old merchandise (china, rope, pharmaceuticals, etc). Antique-lovers will be kicking themselves that none of it is for sale, but the shop out front offers all kinds of curious Icelandic craft. After the seals, most people cut across the ring road with a potential pit stop at the birdwatching pond of **Gauksmýri**, known for the occasional rare grebe. Those who drive around the Vatsnes Peninsula will pass the oft-photographed rock stacks of **Hvítserkur**. Here the basalt bedrock sticks up from the sea some 16m, with two holes eroded in the middle that facilitate the troll image. Beloved by birds, the black outcrop is appropriately named 'white stack'. Those who venture below the peninsula (south

## THE SEAL WOMAN

Because of their warm eyes and friendly comportment, the early Icelanders believed that seals were drowned humans lost at sea. Once a year, on midsummer's eve, the seals would swim to shore, take off their skins and walk on land. These *sæfólkið* are very similar to the selkie of Scottish and Irish folkore, and versions of the seal woman legend exist across the north Atlantic. In Iceland, it is the tale of a farmer who spies on the seals and falls in love with a beautiful woman dancing in the midnight sun. He steals away her sealskin and locks it away in a chest, forcing her to stay with him. The two marry and have many children, but the wife is unhappy, always staring at the sea. One day, the farmer forgets to hide the key to the locked chest and his wife recovers her sealskin. All he hears is the seal diving back into the waves. Years later, whenever the children would play near the shore, a seal would swim up to them and watch over them closely. Throughout Iceland, anyone who could swim well or who had short fingers was said to be a descendant of the seal woman.

of the ring road) come to the under-appreciated **Viðidalur**, or 'willow valley'. The early explorers eagerly chopped down all the willows that once grew here, but today one may drive on the dirt roads past some truly gorgeous waterfalls.

**WHERE TO STAY AND EAT** For such a small place, there's a fair number of options for accommodation, all of them fairly priced. Not a bad pit stop for the ring road.

### In Hvammstangi

**Thinghús** (6 rooms) Norðurbraut 1; 451 2630; e thinghus-bar@simnet.is. Pub & restaurant with rooms attached (with private bathrooms). The menu is typical (fish, pizza, burgers, & sandwiches), as are the drinks (beer). **$$$**

**Hanna Siggi** (6 rooms) Garðavegur 26; 451 2407; e gistihs@simnet.is. A most hospitable B&B inside a local home. Rooms are astonishingly clean & precise; bathrooms shared. Family friendly, this is a good place if you are travelling with children or want to cook for yourself. FB is also available, plus the view over the fjord is fantastic, & in summer you're bound to spot whales. Cheap sleeping-bag accommodation spaces also available; outdoor jacuzzi. Great value for little money. B/fast inc. **$$**

### South of Hvammstangi

**Dæli** (40 beds) Viðidalur; 451 2566; e daeli@centrum.is; www.centrum.is/daeli. Embrace the Icelandic countryside on this cheerful valley homestead near the Vððdalsá River. The farm comprises a large lodge, several smaller farmhouses, cabins, huts, & a campsite. Visitors have a wide choice of varying degrees of comfort & price (with cheap camping or sleeping-bag accommodation available). The restaurant feels like your own mother is cooking for you. Hot tub & sauna, horse rentals also available. **$$$**

**Gauksmýri** (27 rooms) 451 2927; e gauksmyri@gauksmyri.is; www.gauksmyri.is. Calling all horse lovers – this country lodge is run by a couple of horse nuts who love to share their passion with guests. The sprawling frontier 'ranch' is decorated with a rustic stone floor, rough-wooden furniture & lots of personal artwork centring on the constant theme of the marvellous Icelandic horse. The stable keeps more than 60 horses & offers great riding tours all year round. The farm is situated right across the ring road from Lake Gauksmýri (just after Laugarbakki), among a recovered natural wetland & on the edge of the interior. A wheelchair-accessible path & the birdwatching station with telescope make it popular among birders. There are 2 types of rooms – the smaller doubles have shared bathrooms but at a great price. The rooms upstairs are much larger & nicer, with new beds, big fluffy duvets, & spotless private bathrooms. The best feature is the giant picture windows with an explanation of your view & a name for each room based on what you can see. There's a hot pot too, but watch out, sometimes it's too hot. Obviously, recommended. b/fast inc. **$$$**

**Laugarbakki** (28 rooms) 444 4920; e edda@hoteledda.is; www.hoteledda.is; summer only. One of the nicer Hótel Eddas. This school-turned-hotel is quite spacious & clean, with big rooms & comfy beds. All bathrooms are shared, & cheaper sleeping-bag spaces are possible. The hot tubs are a nice touch. Plus, the very good hotel restaurant serves an ample breakfast, lunch, & dinner with a few gourmet surprises up the chef's proverbial sleeve. **$$**

**Gauksmýri restaurant** 07.00–22.00 daily. The in-house restaurant is dedicated to all things local: trout caught on a line, rhubarb from the garden, & fantastic Icelandic lamb stew. Good eating. *Mains from 2,600ISK.* **$$$**

### In Vatsnes

**Ósar Youth Hostel** (40 beds) near Hvítserkur; 451 2678; e osar@simnet.is; www.hostel.is. New hostel on the edge of the sea with super-clean living spaces. Staying here is a conscious decision to get away from it all (but not really, seeing as you're only 20mins from the ring road). Private rooms with private bathrooms are available. **$$**

## HÚNAFJÖRÐUR

After his first winter shivering in Iceland, the 9th-century Viking settler Ingimundur Thorsteinsson hiked out to the shores of this fjord and found it covered in drift ice. Staring back at him from the ice was a dazed mother polar bear with her two cubs, so he named the place 'Húnafjörður', or 'bear cub fjord'. That scene is now the town crest for Blönduós. The fjord shapes the west coast of the Skagi Peninsula and the mouth of the Vatnsdalur Valley. It is essentially what separates the West Fjords from the northern part of Iceland.

## VATNSDALUR

'Water dale' is a wide, magical valley just south of the ring road. Unpaved roads venture up either side of the Vatnsdalsá estuary, with a grand view over the many waterfalls, and streams and the emerald-green hillsides on either side. When the sun is shining, this is a magnificent, glorious hideaway – one of those average areas that suddenly seems extraordinary. Vatnsdalur is the eponymous setting for the Vatnsdalur saga, the tale of Ingimundur Thorsteinsson and his many descendants who made this valley their home and then fought over it for the next five generations. Ingimundur founded the farm at **Hof**, which is still in business today, 1,100 years later. The saga was said to be written at the nearby monastery of **Thingeyrar**. The current church was built in 1877, a rare example of stonemasonry. If you have the time, try to count the 1,000 gold stars painted on the ceiling.

### WHERE TO STAY

**Hof í Vatnsdal** (28 beds) 452 4077; e hof@simnet.is; www.hof-is.com. A truly historic farm, Hof is a pleasant country getaway well off the beaten track. Only 15mins south of the ring road, visitors are housed in a working sheep & horse farm (rides available). A few rooms have bathrooms, the rest are shared. Outdoor jacuzzi. B/fast inc, other meals available. **$$$**

**Thingeyrar** (30 beds) 452 4365; e thingeyrar@thingeyrar.is; www.thingeyrar.is. A serious horse farm for people who are serious about horses. A personal touch & very nice amenities help guests feel welcome. Shared bathrooms. B/fast inc. **$$$**

**Stóra Gilјá** (12 beds) 452 4294. A farm that's right on the ring road, the 'big gully' is renowned for its legend of Christian conversion. The farm is convenient because it is close, with ample affordable accommodation. Shared bathrooms; sleeping-bag accommodation available. **$$**

## BLÖNDUÓS

Blönduós means the 'mouth of the river Blanda', a word that means 'mix' from the same root of the English 'blend'. The town was built up around the bridge that crosses the river and comprises several small shops and disparate houses. It's a diffuse little place, but large enough and convenient enough (on Route 1), that it's become a somewhat major stop for ring-road travellers. The town's main claim to fame is Halldóra Bjaradóttir (1873–1981), who was the oldest living citizen in Iceland's history. As of yet, nobody has linked her record longevity to the general lack of excitement in Blönduós, but there just might be a correlation.

### WHERE TO STAY

**Hótel Blönduós** (16 rooms) Aðalgata 6; 452 4205; e gladheimar@gladheimar.is; www.gladheimar.is. The town's best hotel is luxury in that each room is pristine & thoughtfully decorated, (if you like pink). The colourful rooms have bathrooms with showers, but can feel a bit dated, as does the disco lobby. B/fast inc. **$$$$**

**Gladheimar Guesthouse** (12 rooms) Blöndubyggð 10; 452 4205; e gladheimar@gladheimar.is; www.gladheimar.is. A lower-cost alternative to the hotel, the guesthouse occupies the old post office but exudes a hospital-like mood. Bathrooms are shared. They also offer cheaper, self-contained cottages (near the campsite) replete with outdoor hot tubs. These are a bargain if you've got 3 or more travelling. B/fast inc (guesthouse only). **$$$**

**Camping** A very large and spacious field, right next to Route 1, and in summer always jam-packed full of cars and caravans (*452 4520;* **$**). Decent amenities; hot showers.

### WHERE TO EAT

**Sjoðathjófurinn** Aðalgata 6; 452 4205; e gladheimar@gladheimar.is; www.gladheimar.is; 08.00–22.30 Mon–Thu, 08.00–01.00 Fri/Sat. 'Innovative Icelandic cuisine' means a mix of hearty sandwiches, fish & lamb, a few fancy tourist specialities, & home cooking for all the local farmers who come here to kick back & eat up. *Mains from 1,650ISK.* **$$$**

**Árbakki** Húnabraut 2; 452 4678; e arbakkin@islandia.is; www.islandia.is/arbakkinn; 11.00–17.00 Mon–Thu, 12.00–20.00 Fri, 12.30–17.00 & 23.00–03.00 Sat, 13.30–18.00 Sun. The town's main café with coffee, pastries, sandwiches & bigger meals (fish & lamb) according to the chef's discretion. There's always a nice vibe here, & sometimes live music. *Mains from 1,000ISK.* **$$**

**Bakarí-Konditori** Húnabraut 4; 452 4500; e vardberg@simnet.is; 08.00–16.00 Tue–Sun. A trustworthy Icelandic village bakery (what a relief!). Pastries, light meals, & fabulous bread. **$$**

**WHAT TO SEE AND DO** Visitors are immediately propositioned with the town's **Textile Museum** (*Heimilisiðnarsafnið; Árbraut 29; 452 4067; e textile@simnet.is; www.simnet.is/textile; Jun–Aug 10.00–17.00 daily; entrance 700ISK*). The history of all things threaded means old looms, how wool is processed, national costumes, and local crafts. If you're just looking for quality woollen goods (sweaters, scarves, and mittens), go straight to the gift shop. Several Danish-era buildings are worth checking out, including the **church** (built 1894) and the 18th-century **Hillebrandtshús**. At present, it is home to an exhibit on sea ice (*Hafíssetrið; 455*

*4710;* ⏲ *summer 09.00–17.00 daily*). The island of **Hrútey** is the nature preserve in the middle of the island that's a nice walk in nice weather. When it rains, go to the town **swimming pool** (*Húnabraut;* ☎ *452 4451;* ⏲ *08.00–21.00 Mon–Fri, 09.00–17.00 Sat/Sun*).

Blönduós is also a great place to take a detour up north and explore Skagi. The 'cape' exhibits an extraordinary coastline of great geology and few people. A popular hiking trail crosses from the town of Skagaströnd through the protected reserve of **Spákonufellsborg**. For the same view but less effort, simply drive Route 744 from Blönduós to Sauðakrókur. The wildest and most awesome parts of Skagi are near the top. The bay of **Kálfshamarsvík** is enclosed by cliffs of towering columnar basalt that almost look manmade. The rest of the peninsula is a protected area connected only by a singular dirt road. The driving is rough going and the weather rarely co-operates,

## SKAGAFJÖRÐUR

For its combination of hilly farm country and sweeping seascapes, Skagafjörður is one of the most romantic regions in Iceland. At first glance you might think you've seen it all before, but a more intimate prodding opens up a world of horse farms, holy men, and deep mountains. First and foremost, this is horse country. The brooding animals are part of the landscape and with so many farms and breeders, Skagafjörður's horse to human ratio is the highest in Iceland. The country's history was forged among the ancient churches of this district, and every village, valley and island has a curious tale behind it. The fjord is named after the two 'capes' of Skagi on either shore, to the west is simply Skagi, and to the east (with mountains three times as high) is Tröllaskagi, the cape of trolls. The region's natural beauty is in the contrast of raw coastline and weathered farms. Back in the age of settlement, these were coveted properties and some of the first to be picked up by the Vikings. As time wore on, Skagafjörður became the stronghold of the Sturlung clan, who were the cause of Iceland's drawn-out civil war (see page 20). To this day, Skagafjörður is still known for its strong regional identity and fierce allegiance – forgive the metaphor, but this really is the Texas of Iceland. Today, Skagafjörður reaches from the tips of both northern shores down to the Route 1 junction at Varmahlíð and all the way to the Austurdalur Valley and the interior.

## SAUÐÁRKRÓKUR

Skagafjörður's largest town is still just a one-street kind of place where nightlife and daylife both centre on a few short blocks. The town's name means 'sheep's corner' a reference to the name of the river (Sauðá) that passes by the harbour on the base of the fjord. Today, everyone who lives here (about 3,000) prefers fishing to sheep herding, with a scent from the nearby shrimp factory wafting through the air. In other ways, this is a typical modern Icelandic town complete with the scent from the factory. Despite its small size, Sauðárkrókur is an important transportation hub for the north and well equipped for travellers to easily explore the more remote hinterlands of Skagafjörður.

**GETTING THERE AND AWAY** Flights back and forth between Sauðárkrókur Airport (SAK) (☎ *453 6888*) and Reykjavík are run by **Eagle Air** (*www.eagleair.is*) five times a week (40 minutes). To drive, take Route 75 or 76 from the ring road. From Sauðárkrókur, there's a daily bus back and forth to Varmahlíð (30 minutes) and another to Siglufjörður (1 hour 15 minutes) via Hólar (15 minutes) and Hofsós (45 minutes).

## WHERE TO STAY

**Hótel Tindastóll** (10 rooms) Lindargata 3; ☎ 453 5002; e sml@simnet.is; www.hoteltindastoll.com. Built in 1884, this very historic boutique hotel has individual rooms, each with private bathroom & each named after a historic Icelandic hero. Truly a tribute to the past, the natural-stone hot pool mimics nearby Grettislaug. B/fast inc. **$$**

**Fosshótel Áning** (71 rooms) Sæmundarhlíð; ☎ 453 6717; e bokun@fosshotel.is; www.fosshotel.is; ⌚ Jun–Aug. This new tourist hotel is of top quality, with a better standard of comfort & efficiency compared with most. Rooms (with or without private bathroom) are large & modern (almost flashy) & the restaurant is a favourite among large groups. Sleeping-bag accommodation available. B/fast inc. **$$$**

**Mikligarður** (4 rooms) Kirkjutorg 3; ☎ 453 6880; e gistiheimilid550@simnet.is; www.skagafjordur.com/mikligardur. A humble, homely guesthouse with lots of motherly care. Cosy rooms, convenient location & shared bathroom with showers. B/fast is available. (NB: 'Mikligarður' was the Vikings' name for Russia.) **$$$**

**Camping** By the swimming pool, with shared amenities (☎ 453 5226; **$**).

## WHERE TO EAT

Walking up and down Aðalgata will present plenty of eating options. The restaurant at Fosshótel is also very good.

**Ólafshús Aðalgata** 15; ☎ 453 6454; ⌚ 11.00–15.00 & 17.00–23.30 daily. This 100-year-old restaurant is one of those nice surprises that you remember long after you get home. An inspired chef takes the freshest fish around & comes up with some dishes like cod gratinée, honey-roasted catfish, Arctic char, etc. If you are on a budget, then order any number of quick pasta dishes for under 1,000ISK, as well as pizza. The building itself represents the entire history of this town, from a saddle-making shop to the priest's home. Recommended. *Mains from 1,800ISK.* **$$$**

**Kaffi Krókur** Aðalgata 16; ☎ 453 6299; ⌚ 11.00–22.30 Sun–Thu, 11.00–03.00 Fri/Sat. This city café advertises itself as a European Brasserie that seems to be a carbon copy of Ólafshús across the street. Nevertheless, the menu oscillates between nachos & burgers & things like halibut steaks & marinated horse meat. It's also a bit of a teen hangout, with loud, live music on the weekends. Also good for afternoon coffee. *Mains from 1,900ISK.* **$$**

**Sauðárkróksbakarí** Aðalgata 5; ☎ 455 5000; ⌚ 08.00–18.00 Mon–Fri, 08.30–16.00 Sat/Sun. The town's lovable bakery.

**WHAT TO SEE AND DO** The information centre is located at the **Town Museum** (*Minjahúsið; Aðalgata 16B; ☎ 453 6870; ⌚ 13.00–18.00 Mon–Fri; entrance 300ISK*), which is your typical historical museum. The real highlight of the exhibits is the restored turf-roofed farm of nearby **Glaumbær** (see page 322). To appreciate the town's sense of humour, go up to the harbour and the town's shrimp factory, painted with the giant mural of a shrimp with the phrase '*Ceci n'est pas une crevette*' (This is not a shrimp), a tribute to Belgian Surrealist Magritte. Beyond the fish-drying racks lies **Reykjaströnd** ('smoky shore'), an ancient farm mentioned in Grettis saga. To get there from Sauðárkrókur, take Route 748 north until the end of the dirt road (about 30 minutes). Be courteous as you are crossing onto private property: close and secure all sheep gates behind you. The finale takes you to a rocky shore and the famous hot pool of **Grettislaug**. Filled with a flow of 40°C water, this is the very spring in which saga hero Grettir the Strong warmed himself after swimming across the freezing fjord in the dead of night (a journey of four miles/6.5km) all the way from Drangey. You can see the island from this point and shiver at the thought, then jump in his ancient pool and have a nice warm soak. Do try to keep it clean and contribute some coins for the pool's upkeep. If the algae are too much for you, then go for a dip in Sauðárkrókur's town **swimming pool** (*Skagfirðingabraut*; ☎ *453 5226*; ⏲ *08.00–20.00 daily*).

## DRANGEY

The lone island of Drangey rises straight up from the waters of Skagafjöúrður like the most impossible island in the world. Sheer cliffs of 180m surround all sides of the island, so that even from far away it looks a bit like a giant brown block with tufts of green on top. The single stack of rocks sticking out of the water is the widowed trollwoman whose troll husband fell into the sea during an earthquake two centuries ago. It is possible to sail to Drangey (on a sailboat) from the farm at Grettislaug (*Jón Eiríksson*; ☎ *453 6503*; *about 5,500ISK pp*), or you can take a tour from the harbour at Sauðárkrókur (☎ *453 8245*; *www.skagafjordur.com/eyjaskip/trips*). There is only one place to land a boat and only one way to get up to the top of the island – a narrow and steep pass that requires a ladder. Once up top, you can stare over the precipice, enjoy all the birds and visit the foundations of the hut where Grettir lived more than 1,000 years ago. Another hut, *Drangeyjarskáli*, is still used by egg gatherers and bird hunters.

## VARMAHLÍÐ

This is not a town, but rather a crossroads – the sensible result of Route 1 intersecting with all of the other interesting paths into Skagafjörður. There is nothing very special to see or do right at this junction, but plenty just outside. For this one convenience, Varmahlíð has become the adventure travel centre for northwest Iceland and the place for a pit stop.

### GRETTIS SAGA

The best-known saga of northwest Iceland is that of **Grettir Ásmundsson**. Grettir was a troubled youth, and had there been a reform school in 10th-century Iceland, he would have been sent there. At age ten, his father tried to teach him the value of work by assigning him the chore of watching over the geese. Grettir got bored and wrung all their necks. In his teen years, he physically abused his father and was known to beat up his opponents on the playing field. On his first trip to the Althing, a fellow traveller stole his luggage. Grettir responded by sticking a battleaxe into his head (though it was actually in self-defence). At first, Grettir blamed the murder on a female troll, but then he confessed and got away with a three-year banishment. He went off to Norway, where he gained a reputation for strength, first by killing 12 berserkers (warriors), then stabbing a bear through the heart, and committing several more murders. Back in Skagafjörður, Grettir was the only one brave enough to handle an evil ghost causing mischief, but the ghost cursed Grettir to lose half his strength. In the end, Grettir is re-sentenced as an outlaw for his many other crimes and with so many people seeking vengeance, he is forced into hiding out on the lonely isle of Drangey (see page 321). When his fire goes out, he performs the impossible by swimming to the mainland from the island. His enemies eventually track him down on Drangey and kill him. The saga claims that Grettir's grip was so tight on his sword that his killers had to cut off his hand to take it away from him.

**GETTING THERE AND AWAY** Varmahlíð represents the main transportation hub for the northwest, with a daily bus service to and from Reykjavík (3 hours), via Brú, Akureyri (1 hour), and Sauðárkrókur (35 minutes). This is also an important junction between the ring road and the two main roads of the interior: the Kjölur route and Route 752 to Sprengisandur.

**TOURIST INFORMATION**

**Tourist information** ☎ 455 6161; e info@skagafjordur.is; www.visitskagafjordur.is; ⌚ summer 09.00–21.00 daily, winter 09.00–16.00 Mon–Fri, 13.00–18.00 Sat/Sun. The official Skagafjörður tourist office with everything a traveller could want.

**WHERE TO STAY AND EAT** The best and most obvious choice is the upright **Hótel Varmahlíð** (*19 rooms; ☎ 453 8170; e info@hotelvarmahlid.is; www.hotelvarmahlid.is;* **$$$$**). The rooms are modern and elegant, the staff are inviting and friendly, and at the end of a long day no place is more welcoming. All rooms have private bathrooms and televisions, and the five-person apartment is a good deal for families. A breakfast buffet is included in the very original restaurant which focuses on local fish and produce, and features the classic, wholesome Icelandic soup. The classic, old-time Icelandic menu attracts a lot of locals. Across from the hotel car park is the petrol station and **grocery store** (*KS-Varmahlíð; ☎ 455 4680; ⌚ 09.00–23.30 daily*). The main campsite is at **Lauftún** (*☎ 453 8133;* **$$**), which offers all amenities for tents and caravans, as well as a number of comfy cottages offering both made-up beds and sleeping-bag spaces – truly a good deal.

**WHAT TO SEE AND DO** Less than five minutes from Varmahlíð stands the old turf church of **Víðimýrarkirkja** (*☎ 453 5095; ⌚ 09.00–18.00 Mon–Sat, for services only Sun; entrance 250ISK*). Fashioned from thick turf walls and a frame made entirely of driftwood, the church was built in 1834 to replace an older medieval-era structure. This is still a working church, and the two bells hanging outside ring with each service every Sunday. The interior grants some insight into the politics and social standing of the early 19th century, namely how the farmers sat on benches in the front, the landowners and merchants in the closed choir, and the poorest people in the back. Víðimýri is unusual in that it predates the vast majority of churches one sees in Iceland.

The **Skagafjörður Folk Museum** includes three main sites, the most popular being the old farm of **Glaumbær** (*☎ 453 6173; e glaumb@krokur.is; www.krokur.is/glaumb; ⌚ summer 09.00–18.00 daily, winter by appointment; entrance 500ISK*) – some 8km north on Route 75. Iceland was not born of large cities or grand ports – it is a nation of stalwart farms, and nowhere else grants visitors a better understanding than this, the most well-preserved turf dwelling in the country. Like stepping back in time, this six-gabled compound is a labyrinth of dry and cosy corridors and small rooms. If you ever wondered how Icelanders have survived the last 1,200 Arctic winters, this is how. The turf insulation is thick – some 2–3m, and the roomy pantries stored food for a whole season. The oldest room is the kitchen (built in 1760) and the youngest is the main room, or *baðstofa* (built in 1876), with its line of beds and their original *rumfjöl* (see page 34). Great care has been taken to preserve the original character and purpose of each of the 13 rooms and walking through the house appeals to all senses: the touch of the rough, patterned walls of turf, the faint light coming in through the tiny windows, and the smell of the earth itself.

The farm at Glaumbær was founded by Snorri Thorfinsson, the first European child born on the American continent (see page 270) who brought his well-travelled mother to finish her days at this quiet spot (the original site is under excavation). The old farmhouse was inhabited between 1760 and 1947; at one time there were 22 people living in this one complex. The grey wooden house Gilsstofa (1849) represents the transition to life above ground, and the bright-yellow Áshús (1886) was moved from another Skagafjörður farm to represent a latter farmhouse. Glaumbær owes its preservation to the English nobleman Mark Watson, who began travelling to Iceland in the 1930s. He came to Glaumbær and was so impressed that he donated £200 for it to be refurbished and turned into a museum. Guided tours in English are available throughout the day all summer long. Next door stands the Glaumbær church, built in 1926 to replace the previous church that was blown away in a wind storm. A museum gift shop and café, **Áskaffi** (🕒 *summer 09.00–18.00 daily*) offers coffee and Icelandic cakes, as well as light meals (fish soup, open-faced sandwiches, etc), and a full-spread 'Icelandic dinner'. Needless to say, Glaumbær should be a priority for anyone travelling around the ring road.

For something more thrilling and less educational, the rivers south of Varmahlíð are renowned for **white-water rafting** (*Activity Tours;* ☎ *453 8383;* e *info@rafting.is; www.rafting.is;* 🕒 *May–Sep*). The two Jökulsá rivers (east and west) flow down from Hofsjökull glacier in the highlands. Both offer incredible rafting over serious rapids, but the west (Vestari–Jökulsá) is slightly tamer than the class four and five rapids of the east (Austari–Jökulsá). To prevent a perhaps sudden death, participants are fitted with dry suits and helmets; trips range from two to three hours to six to seven hours, as well as an ultimate three-day journey that begins in the highlands at Laugafell (see page 436) before rafting all the way back. Besides the adrenalin rush, this is a great way to see Iceland's interior and a virtually unknown river system from a wild perspective.

In the grand tradition of Skagafjörður, the same company/different name offers offers all sorts of **horseriding** tours (*Hestasport; Vegamót;* ☎ *453 8383;* e *info@riding.is; www.riding.is*). To house the guests on their tour, they've built a small village of very nice cottages which include private bathrooms, kitchen facilities and outdoor 'natural' hot pool (**$$$**), all just off the ring road near Varmahlíð. With hundreds of beautiful horses, it's hard to say no to travelling across the rugged landscape on horseback. Short tours are offered, and day tours start at around US$100. The longer voyages offer the experience of a lifetime – the ultimate is their cross-Iceland tour on the Kjölur route (see page 432), which either starts or finishes in Varmahlíð. Another popular tour is participation in the sheep roundup, or *réttir* (see page 37) in the autumn. For something more personal, try the horse farm **Lýtingsstaðir** (*4 rooms;* m *853 3817;* e *info@lythorse.com; www.lythorse.com;* **$$$**). Located about 15 minutes from Varmahlíð, their excursions tend to be smaller and more authentic, as this is a working sheep farm. Horse lovers will want to stay at this bed and breakfast place.

## HÓLAR

Iceland's 'other' Vatican is the northern alternative to Skálholt (see page 224). The tiny hamlet is set inside an alpine-like backdrop of mountain meadows, and in summer endless fields of purple lupins. It doesn't give the impression of being the epicentre of Iceland's Lutheran Church, but once upon a time, it was. Hólar was the northern see of the Icelandic Church from 1106 until 1801, after which the seat was abolished in favour of a single bishopric for the whole of Iceland. Today, Icelanders and foreigners alike come to take in the mighty **Hóladomkirkja** (☎ *453 6300;* e *biskup@holar.is; www.holar.is;* 🕒 *summer 10.00–18.00, winter by appointment*). The cathedral at

Hólar is a special church, quite unique for Iceland. It was designed by the famous 18th-century Danish architect Lauritz de Thurah who died before it was completed. Much larger than Iceland's traditional churches, Hólar is built from red sandstone that has been taken from the nearby mountains. Since Icelanders knew nothing about working with stone, the church commissioned Polish mason Sabinsky in 1757 to direct the construction. He found the local farmers reluctant stonemasons, and although his contract was originally for three years, it took him almost seven years to complete. During the process, Sabinsky's two-week-old daughter died and as a memorial he buried her in the wall of the church (marked by the epitaph near the entrance). The adjacent 27m-high square tower was added in 1950 in honour of slain Bishop of Iceland Jón Arason, and is built of reinforced concrete made to look like hand-hewn timber, a luxury in Iceland. The climb to the top grants an open view of the mountains and down the valley. The relics inside the church tell of a long and treasured history, starting with the altarpiece from 1450 and the 300-year-old crucifix hanging from the wall. The baptismal font was carved in 1674 from a single piece of rare soapstone that had drifted to Iceland from Greenland on a piece of ice. There were no trained craftsmen at the time, so a local Skagafjörður farmer was sent to Denmark for the express purpose of learning how to carve this stone. Aside from the magnificent bronze bells, and the silver organ pipes, the church is fairly plain and simple (notice that there are no images inside the church).

A church and farm have stood on this spot from well before the 1100s and visitors can peek into the ongoing archaeological excavation of these early buildings. A well-marked 'history' walk takes you through some of the sites from Iceland's ecclesiastical past. Today, Hólar is home to Iceland's agricultural college that specialises in horse breeding. Hence a passionate body of students and the local **Icelandic Horse History Centre** (*Sögusetur Íslenska Hestsins; ☎ 455 6300; e sogusetur@sogusetur.is; www.sogusetur.is*). In summer, this is a happy place of families on holiday, whose children splash about in the local **swimming pool** (*⊙ summer 07.00–21.00 daily*). Serious hikers also come and leave from Hólar, as this valley of Hjaltadalur is a great base to venture into the mountains of Tröllaskagi.

**GETTING THERE AND AWAY** Take Route 767 from Route 76. A daily bus goes to and from Siglufjörður (1 hour) and Sauðárkrókur (30 minutes).

**WHERE TO STAY AND EAT** The college's dormitory doubles as a hotel in summer (*30 rooms; ☎ 455 6333; e booking@holar.is; www.holar.is;* **$$**). Rooms are smallish, but clean, with shared bathrooms down the hall. A nearby campsite is a very popular holiday spot in summer. Everyone is welcome to try out the local restaurant **Undir Byrðunni** (*☎ 455 6333; ⊙ summer 07.00–22.00 daily; mains from 2,600ISK;* **$$$$**). Catering to upmarket travellers and tour groups, the kitchen dishes out gourmet surprises like local-caught Arctic char, shrimp, and lots of red meat (ie: lamb, veal, and horse). Everything (soup, bread, cakes, and the paté) is homemade and the chefs have a distinct style all their own, which is refreshing.

## HÓFSOS

This scant collection of prim Scandinavian houses relays an earlier time, when the Danes and their ships were busy in this harbour. There was a time when the farmers and fishermen of Skagafjörður gathered on this pier and among these warehouses to sell their goods to the rest of the world. Today, Hófsos has a slightly melancholy feel that is common in very small, quiet places. The Hófsá River splashes down

## GUÐBRANDUR'S BIBLE

While mainland Europe was in the throes of the Reformation, Bishop Jón Arason had a printing press shipped to Iceland, in hope that one day the Bible could exist in the Icelandic vernacular. A few 'illegal' translations had already been finished prior to the Reformation, including one by a daring monk who worked for years in a cowshed by candlelight, but none of these had been distributed. In 1584, the new Bishop of Hólar, Guðbrandur Thorláksson (1541–1627) was able to print 500 copies of the Bible in Icelandic; about 35 known copies of Guðbrandur's Bible remain in Iceland today. To pay for the printing, every church in Iceland had to purchase one copy and it took seven men two years to complete the actual physical printing of all those pages. It seems that the talented bishop carved his own woodcuts that were used to illuminate the headings. Guðbrandur was also an accomplished cartographer – he drew the first known map of Iceland in 1590.

the mountainsides before flowing into the sea, and the dull grey-and-black sand contrasts the red-brown scree of the hills. The village is now home to the **Icelandic Emigration Centre** (*Vesturfarasetrið; 453 7935; e hofsos@hofsos.is; www.hofsos.is; Jun–Sep 11.00–18.00 daily*). Part museum, part research institution, the very moving exhibit recounts the story of the 20,000 Icelanders who emigrated to North America between 1870 and 1914. What makes it relevant is that during that same era, 1,420 people left Hófsos; today it's a village of only 150 people (in summer). Three historic buildings house very different displays and each explores different aspects of the emigration phenomenon: why people left, where they went, and the changes that followed. At a time of great poverty and oppression, emigration was important for Iceland, leading to an influx of cash and an exchange of ideas and new technology. If you've got Icelandic blood running through your veins, the centre is extremely helpful in trying to locate your ancestors, or at least their records. Family history is a major draw for the tens of thousands of visitors who come by here every year, and for the rest of us, it's just interesting.

Driving up the coast from Hófsos takes you past the island of Malmey (and Drangey in the distance), as well as the peninsula of **Thórðarhöfði**. The sandbar has built up into a natural bridge out to the rocky outcrop where there's a world of puffins in the summer.

**WHERE TO STAY AND EAT** The only place to stay in the village is the guesthouse up at the top of the hill, **Sunnuberg** (*5 rooms; 453 7310*). Basically, it's like staying at your grandmother's. The cheery blue house by the harbour is the café **Sólvík** (*453 7930; May–Sep 10.00–22.00 daily; mains from 2,100ISK; $$$*). Their speciality is Icelandic pancakes and coffee, but for something more filling, go for the honey-glazed lamb or the hearty meatballs. The only other bona fide restaurant is the fish and lamb joint (and bar) **Sigtún** (*Suðarbraut; 453 7393; 18.00–22.30 daily; mains from 1,500ISK; $$*).

## SIGLUFJÖRÐUR

Isolated from the whole of Iceland, Siglufjörður grips the edge of the most amazing fjord as if it might disappear in the fog. Never bustling, the town feels like a dream sequence without any sound. Maybe it's the Arctic lighting, but there's a technicolour feel to the painted warehouses and rusting ships reflected in the still harbour. Time and nature are equally still, especially the chiselled mountains that hide this world from the rest of the world. This is a place where people have got by on their own for 600 years, the kind of town where nobody locks their doors, where everyone knows each other, but where outsiders are as welcome as the sun.

Siglufjörður claims to be the northernmost town in Iceland, but that's misleading; the largest town this far north is more correct. It all began with a fishing station at the tip of the fjord, Siglunes or 'sail point', where shark was the main catch. Denmark's demand for shark oil instigated larger sailing ships and a move to a new harbour inside 'sail fjord', where a town sprawled out on the *eyri* or flat bank along the shore. The inscrutable herring, or *slíð*, is what put this town on the map. The Depression of the 1930s and the subsequent war years of the 1940s fed a global demand for conserved food. Iceland's herring fisheries boomed. By the 1950s, Siglufjörður was the largest port in Iceland, with over 500 active boats motoring out to the summer migration of herring schools. It was herring that modernised Iceland, bringing in the latest technology and lots of cash. At the time, herring made up 25% of Iceland's export earnings and most historians agree it was herring exports that underwrote Iceland's independence in 1944. Early photos of Siglufjörður show the docks piled high with barrels of smoked and pickled herring. Seasonal workers from all over Iceland, Scandinavia and beyond all came to Siglufjörður for the good pay and the good times connected with the herring run. This was a golden age, a time when a person could walk the streets with money in their pocket and hear a dozen different languages being spoken. All was grand until the mid 1960s, when the herring simply disappeared. Either they were overfished or else they decided to stop swimming in Icelandic waters. In just a few years, Siglufjörður shut down completely. Today, the town numbers 1,500, less than half the population of 50 years ago. There is a real pride for the past and what Siglufjörður meant for Iceland, along with a wistful longing for something that will never be again. Luckily, the townspeople get all the catharsis they need at the outstanding herring museum.

**GETTING THERE AND AWAY** Siglufjörður is special because getting there seems precarious. The mountain road turn-off at Route 82 is a shortcut to Akureyri (almost 2 hours), but is closed in winter due to heavy snows. The new tunnel system links Siglufjörður, Olafsfjörður, and Dalvík. Driving Route 76 from Akureyri to Siglufjörður takes less than an hour. The road hugs a steep cliff around several tight bends before going through several sections of tunnel (the first is 4km, the second 5km, with a short stretch of open road in between) and suddenly you're there. Enjoy the novelty of Icelandic tunnels and the 'Hall of the Mountain King' feel as you drive under the mountains. A daily bus connects with Varmahlíð (1 hour 30 minutes) and another 'airbus' connects to the airport at Sauðárkrókur (1 hour).

## WHERE TO STAY

**Hvanneyri Guesthouse** (23 rooms) Aðalgata 10; ☎ 467 1378; e hvanneyri@hvanneyri.net; www.hvanneyri.net. This big, warm, 4-storeyed guesthouse is the town's haven from the storm, built in 1935. Every room is decorated with love (flouncy beds, lacy pillows & frilly curtains), & the living-room atmosphere is both mature & relaxed. A few rooms have their own bathrooms, the rest share. A big downstairs kitchen is a warm place for swapping stories. Sleeping-bag spaces also available. **$$**

**Iþróttamiðstöðiri Höll** (30 beds) The 'Sports House' is owned by the Sports Society of Fjallabyggð, & is great for those visiting for snowsports, given its proximity to the ski runs. During the summer, soccer fields & a golf course are also available. As well as the 30 beds, there are an additional 20 spaces (the sleeping spaces are for sleeping bags only). A large, well-equipped kitchen is provided for guest usage, as well as a large dining area. The couple who manage the house are very sweet & helpful. **$**

**Camping** On the green in the town square (*460 5600;* **$**). Bathrooms with hot showers.

## WHERE TO EAT

**Allin Aðalgata** 36; 467 1169; 11.00–22.00 Mon–Fri, 11.00–01.00 Sat/Sun. The town's gritty little sports bar. Hamburgers, fries, beer & football, plus a dance floor & 3 group rooms. The place to go. *Mains from 1,200ISK.* $$

**Torgið** Aðalgata 32; 11.00–19.00 but 'we try not to leave anyone hungry'. A well-lit, football-watching eatery, specialising in American-style food like pizza, hamburgers, & sandwiches, but with an Icelandic seafood slant. *Mains from 1,500ISK.* $$

**Aðalbakarí** Aðalgata 28; 467 1720; 07.00–17.00 Tue–Sun. Siglufjörður's busy town bakery. Try the liquorice-flavour *Síropskaka*. Recommended. *Mains from 250ISK.* $

**Samkaup Úrval** Suðurgata 2–4; 467 1201; 09.00–19.00 daily. The grocery store, on the corner with Aðalgata & within walking distance of the campsite.

**WHAT TO SEE AND DO** Start with the prize-winning **Herring Museum** (*Síldarminjasafnið; Snorragata; 467 1604; www.sild.is; Jun–Sep 10.00–18.00 daily; entrance 1,200ISK*), even if you think you will have no interest in it. You'll be glad you went. The main exhibit is housed in the red warehouse building Róaldsbrakki (built 1907), where a visual narrative recounts the rise and fall of the herring era. Upstairs are the recreated dormitories of the seasonal workers – perhaps the most touching aspect is the glass cabinet filled with all the little objects found hidden in the walls during the remodelling. A guided tour takes about one hour. The museum also includes two other buildings that bring the herring era back to life – the boathouse (where visitors can clamber about a pair of old herring boats) and the salting station (where the machinery of yesteryear is still functioning). There is also a gift shop (see the unique hand-painted postcards). Every Saturday there's a salting show, demonstrating the process of salting fish, and groups can request one at a different time. The museum also hosts concerts. The town's other indoor delight is the **Folk Music Centre** (*Þjóðlagasetur; Norðurgata 1; 467 2300; e setur@siglo.is; www.siglo.is/setur; summer 10.00–18.00 daily, winter by appointment*). With the strong musical traditions of Iceland, it's a wonder there are not more places like this. The former home of folklorist Reverend Bjarni Thorsteinsson (1861–1938) now exhibits his lifelong collection of Icelandic folk songs. Each room is dedicated to a different form of music (*rímur*, *tvísöngur*, nursery rhymes and hymns) sampled on television screens, sound recordings, or live performance. The monument in the grassy square commemorates all the town's fishermen and sailors lost at sea.

Walking the streets of Siglufjörður is an insightful exercise for the boom-town remnants that linger. The harbour is still a colourful place with some endearing bits of Nordic wooden architecture near the docks. I can also recommend a dip at the old-fashioned **swimming pool** (*Hvanneyrarbraut 52; 467 1352; 07.00–21.00 Mon–Fri, 10.00–17.00 Sat/Sun*). The weather is tricky up here, so it pays to follow the rule about sun meaning fun. If it's a clear day, then hit the trail. These mountains are ideal for broad hikes over hill and dale, with unspoiled views of the sea and the whole northern shore. A most remarkable trek crosses the eastern mountains at the Hestskarð Pass (580m) and down into the untouched **Héðinsfjörður** or 'heathen's fjord'. Free of roads, traffic, people, and towns, this may very well be the most pristine fjord in the country. The hike takes about five hours each way and is of medium difficulty. Another trek crosses halfway up the eastern mountains and then descends into the gorgeous valley of Nesdalur, continuing all the way out to the tip of the coast to the lighthouse at **Siglunes**. Almost all year around, the high mountains surrounding the town are optimal for **skiing** with a view; contact the local ski club (*Skíðafélag Siglufjarðar; Tjarnargata 14; ☎ 467 2120; e skisigl@simnet.is; www.siglo.is/sss*).

## ÓLAFSFJÖRÐUR

Between the tiny village of Siglufjörður and the small town of Dalvík lies Ólafsfjörður. Following the long-awaited construction of a tunnel between the two towns, Siglufjörður and Ólafsfjörður have incorporated themselves into Fjallabyggð. Whilst now operating under a single government, both are still autonomous. Fjallabyggð is almost solely dedicated to tourism, as evidenced by the nine festivals it holds during the summer months. Alongside these festivals, there are also tournaments for tourists and locals alike, such as a floor hockey competition between local companies. Awards such as 'complained the most' and 'most foul words' are handed out at these games. The Nicholas tournament features children's soccer, and snowsledding and snowmobiling have their own competitions as well.

A rarely visited region, Ólafsfjörður offers remarkable views of the surrounding sea and mountains and is one of the prettier spots along Iceland's northern coast. If you're not in a rush and want to experience the fullness of small-town Iceland, this is it.

**GETTING THERE AND AWAY** Route 82 runs into town as a mountain road from the west and exits on the east as the main road leading down the coast to Dalvík. Route 76 leaves from the north of town heading for Siglufjörður, which is only a few minutes away, thanks to the new tunnel system. Open roads between Siglufjörður and Akureyri can be especially treacherous during the winter, given the proximity to the sea and mountains... like the rest of Iceland.

### WHERE TO STAY AND EAT

**Hótel Brimnes** (11 rooms, 8 cabins) Bylgjubyggð 2; ☎ 466 2400; e hotel@brimnes.is; www.brimnes.is. The hotel in Ólafsfjörður. The staff are welcoming & accommodating, & the rooms are like really nice college dorms complete with private bathrooms. The cabins (**$$$**) are clean & cosy & are wheelchair-accessible. The hotel restaurant is a good place to get a meal. Summer **$$$**; winter **$$**

As for dining, pickings are slim here, with the **Brimnes Restaurant** (*see above for contact details; ⏲ 12.00–14.00 & 17.00–22.00 daily; mains from 1,890ISK; $$$*) serving grilled lamb, chicken pasta and salted cod. Originally a pizza place, **Höllin** (*Hafnargata 16; ☎ 466 4000; ⏲ 11.30–13.30 & 18.00–21.00 Mon–Fri, 14.00–02.00 Sat, 16.00–21.00 Sun; mains from 550ISK; $*) has expanded to serving hamburgers and steaks too. Still known for its pizza, it's the (only) local hangout.

## DALVÍK

The medium-sized fishing village of Dalvík marks the border between northeast and northwest Iceland. Facing the opening of Eyjafjörður, this harbour offers an alternative view from that of Akureyri. It's a nice combination of the fjord and the deep mountain valleys nearby. Dalvík is also the embarkation point for the ferry to Hrísey Island and Grímsey (see page 354), but for hikers and bikers, the real attraction lies in the hills. Dalvík is a great place for delving into Tröllaskagi and experiencing a world that few know.

**GETTING THERE AND AWAY** Three buses a day travel to and from Akureyri (35 minutes) and Ólafsfjörður (15 minutes). It takes about an hour to drive here from Siglufjörður on the mountain road (Route 82).

## WHERE TO STAY

### In town

**Fosshótel** (32 rooms) Skíðabraut 18; ☎ 466 3395; e dalvik@fosshotel.is; www.fosshotel.is. This bright, new yellow hotel is truly 'sunny', completely refurbished in 2006. Situated right near the town centre, all rooms are spacious with lots of light & private bathrooms, as well as a guest kitchen. A cheery atmosphere & attentive staff. The hotel also functions as a travel centre that can arrange all kinds of local activities (ie: biking, whale-watching, horseriding, skiing, & fishing). Be sure to check out the mural on the breakfast room window; it's a labelled map of the mountains seen from the same window. Dorm-style & sleeping-bag rooms are also available. **$$**

**Camping** Next to the swimming pool (*Svarfaðarbraut; ☎ 466 3233; e sundlaugdalvikur@simnet.is;* **$**). All amenities. Prices: 1,000ISK for a tent; 1,500ISK for a camper spot the first night. The second and third nights are half price, and any days after that are free.

### In the valleys

**Ytri-Vík** (30+ beds) Árskógsströnd; ☎ 466 1982; e sporttours@sporttours.is; www.sporttours.is. A group of 5 cottages that are perfect for rural getaways & outdoor activities. Full services, with self-catering & private hot tubs. **$$$**

**Dæli** (10 beds) Skíðadalur; ☎ 466 1658; e daeli@islandia.is; www.internet.is/daeli. A sprawling renovated farm fitted out for groups of hikers, with kitchen, bathroom, & plenty of space, all in the middle of a hiking paradise. **$$**

**Klængshóll** (5 rooms) Skíðadalur; ☎ 466 1519; e skidadalur.is; www.skidadalur.is; ⏱ summer only. This is how you wish it could always be: an honest country guesthouse on the verge of a gorgeous wilderness. Hike all day, & relax at night. About 20km from Dalvík, this is a great escape & a good deal. Rooms are cosy & clean; bathrooms shared. Recommended. B/fast inc. **$$**

**Skeið** ☎ 466 1636; e md@thule-tours.com; www.thule-tours.com. Remote cottage in the valley just outside Dalvík. Shared bathrooms; sleeping-bag spaces available. **$$**

**WHERE TO EAT** Besides the hotel, the petrol stations on the main road, and the bakery (*Hafnarbraut 5; ☎ 466 1012*), pickings are slim. **Tomman** (*Hafnarbraut 21; ☎ 466 1559; ⏱ 18.00–22.00 Sun–Thu, 18.00–23.30 Fri/Sat*) is the main restaurant, while **Veró** (*Goðabraut 3; ☎ 466 1040*), is the town's pizza place and bar, where the locals go at weekends. **Kaffihúsið** (*Goðabraut 2; ☎ 466 3330; ⏱ 12.00–18.00 Mon–Fri, 14.00–17.00 Sat/Sun; mains from 1,000ISK;* **$$**) is part of the local museum, town hall, and hangout for brunches, sandwiches, light meals, and long coffee dates.

**WHAT TO SEE AND DO** In a heartfelt attempt to lure tourists up off the ring road, Dalvík hosts the annual Fiskidagur or 'fish day' festival in mid-August, which involves the townspeople stuffing you with copious amounts of seafood (for free). Other diversions include the **swimming pool** (*Svarfaðarbraut; ☎ 466 3233; ⏱ 07.00–20.00 Mon–Fri, 10.00–19.00 Sat/Sun*) and local **whale-watching** (*Ásvegur 6;*

☎ *466 3212;* e *hvalaskodun@hvalaskodun.ic; www.hvalaskodun.is*), with daily tours of three hours for around US$75 per person. They have better luck than most with finding killer whales, but humpbacks are the most commonly spotted. From Dalvík, the ferry company **Sæfari** (*www.saefari.is*) provides daily passage to the islands of Eyjafjörður, namely **Grímsey** (3½ hours) and nearby **Hrísey** (30 minutes).

Right outside the town is the entrance into the valley of the **Svarfadardalur Nature Reserve**. A rare combination of high mountains and low wetlands make for fantastic summer birding. The mountains beyond are a hiker's dream. The best trail map is *Gönguleiðir á Tröllaskaga,* with infinite routes. The treks up Thórvaldsdalur are equally incredible as you pass through rugged and raw territory that's almost completely uninhabited. If driving from Route 1, you cannot miss the jagged fairytale peak that sticks out against the sky. **Hraundrangi** (lava column) is part of the range in **Hörgárdalur**. In this valley lies the farm of Möðruvellir where Iceland's very first prime minister, Hannes Hafstein (see page 23), was born in 1861. At the mouth of the valley is the ancient trading post of Gásir (*www.gasir.is*) which is currently undergoing archaeological analysis, where a jubilant, Renaissance-type festival takes place every year.

## HRÍSEY

This flat, green island in the middle of the fjord is what inspired the name 'island fjord' for Eyjafjörður. These are some of the best panoramas of this beautiful area, and out of all the offshore islands in Iceland, this is the easiest one to get to. Like Siglufjörður, Hrísey was a Norwegian herring station for much of the 19th century. Hrísey is a big island, the second largest in Iceland after Heimaey (see page 229). The village and harbour are located at the island's southeast corner. The ultimate day-long walk crosses to the other side and follows the northern coast all the way up to the cliffs and beyond to the lighthouse (built in 1920), then back down the centre of the island. A shorter half-day walk loops around the coast and back again. If you have tired legs, try the tractor tour (☎ *699 0077*), which covers a good amount of distance.

Tourists and townspeople eat together at the restaurant **Brekka** (☎ *466 1751;* ⌚ *11.00–20.00 daily*). Their combination of fancy seafood and Icelandic farm cuisine attracts Icelanders from all over, along with all the day trippers who want to dine on the isle. Brekka also offers decent accommodation (sleeping bag) in their upstairs rooms. Otherwise, Hrísey is one place where camping seems *á propos*. The **campsite** is next to the **swimming pool** (☎ *466 3012*). For real seclusion and something different, rent a summer cottage on the island (☎ *466 1079*).

**GETTING THERE AND AWAY** Besides the boat from Dalvík (*Sæfari;* ☎ *461 3600;* e *saefari@landflutningar.is; www.landflutningar.is/saefari*), the ferry ***Sævar*** (☎ *695 5544*) sails between the island and the nearby village at Árskógsssandur (15 minutes) at least ten times a day.

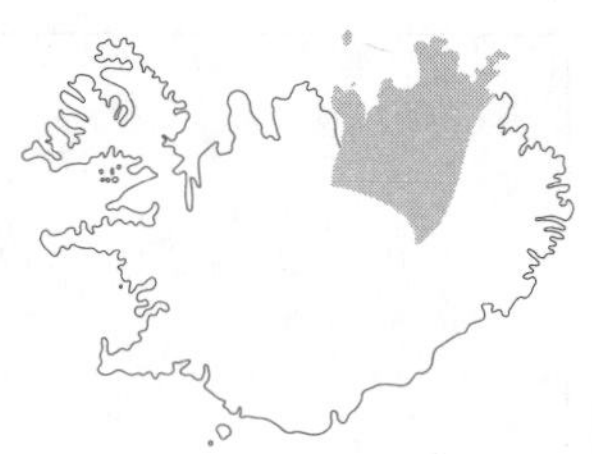

# Norðurland eystra (The Northeast)

The country's northeast corner offers such a diverse experience that it's fast becoming the new magnet for travellers to Iceland. Just beyond the town of Akureyri lie some of the country's highest peaks and the flattest plains, the longest fjord, wide empty bays, and the remotest but unforgettable island of Grímsey. Venturing inland takes you to Lake Mývatn and its very distinct environment, past the steamy lava fields of Krafla and on to the majestic Dettifoss Waterfall in Jökulsárgljúfur National Park. Travels along the coast take in the hinterlands of north Thingeyjarsýsla (one of the most traditional but least-populated areas of the country) and finishing off with the solitary peninsula of Langanes. The natural element is particularly unrivalled and such an all-encompassing region is a priority for every interest and type: the outdoorsmen and the seeker of comforts, birders and rock hounds, and above all – the adventurous.

## GETTING AROUND

The ring road cuts across the northern end of the interior, connecting Mývatn to Akuryeri and crossing the plains and valleys to the east. A much longer but arguably more interesting route follows the northeast coast (Route 85) to Húsavík and beyond. Travellers' bus services between towns and attractions are frequent and reliable, and a good amount of local air service helps shorten the distance. The hiking is fabulous.

## EYJAFJÖRÐUR

'Island fjord' is one of the longest, narrowest, and straightest fjords in Iceland, not to mention one of the most beautiful. The island after which the fjord is named is Hrísey (see page 330), a flattened hillock that contrasts the stunning mountains on both shores. Travelling inward, one follows the gentle path of the glacier that gouged out this landscape about 12,000 years ago. From its mouth on the Arctic Ocean to its base at Akureyri, the fjord measures some 60km (37 miles) long. The valley of Eyjafjarðardalur continues another 100km (62 miles) into the interior. The rich soil deposits of Eyjafjarðarsveit make this some of the most fertile land in all of Iceland and a number of working farms dot both sides of the river.

Eyjafjörður was first settled around AD890 by Helgi 'the lean' Eyvindarson and his wife Thórunn Hyrna. Helgi was the half-Norse, half-Irish Viking who professed to believe in Christ on land, but prayed to Thor when at sea. He spent his youth at the monastery of Iona (in Scotland) where his ascetic lifestyle reduced his stature to 'the lean'. When he announced his intention to relocate in Iceland his father-in-law denounced his idea to live in 'that fishing camp'. Helgi came anyway, and as the west of the country was taken, he headed up north and then into the fjord, claiming all

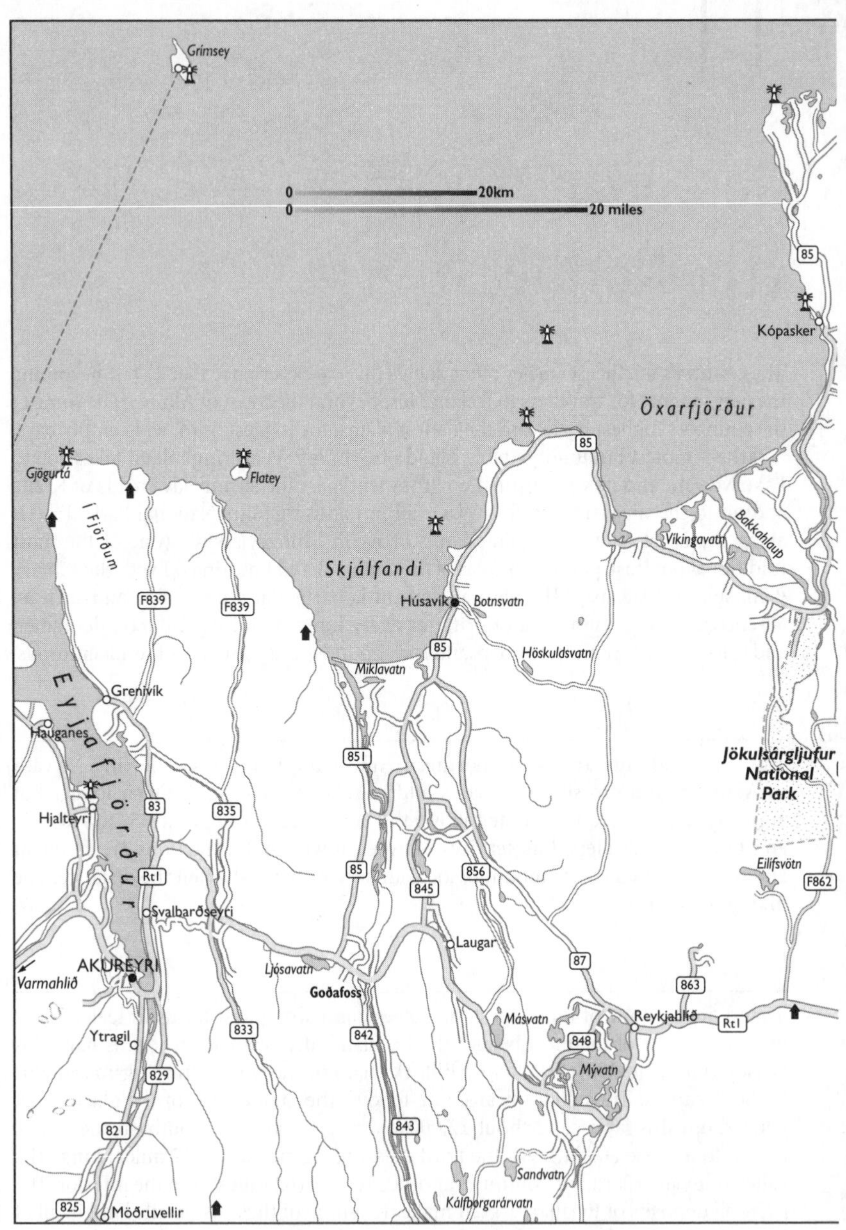


the land he saw, but settling in the valley at the nearby farm of Kristnes. The history of Eyjafjörður is detailed in several sagas, particularly that of Viga-Glúm.

## AKUREYRI

Akureyri might be the most civilised place in Iceland, insisting on normality despite its Arctic reputation. Nowhere else are gardens planted with such gusto: there's a

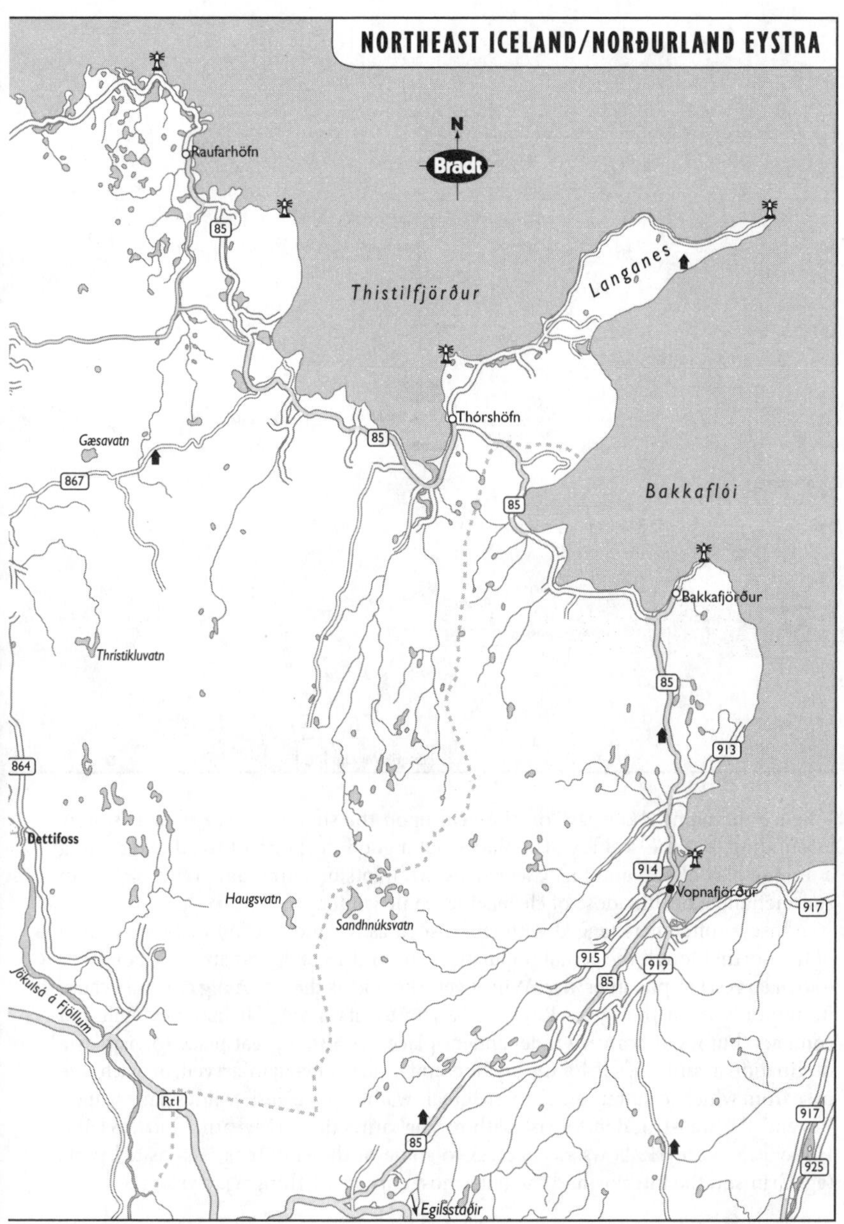


white picket fence around every well-kept 'gingerbread' house, and sailboats glide up and down the fjord all day long. Church bells chime the hour, the streets are lined with tall trees and someone sweeps the town square with a broom. There are days when the town feels a bit like a child's drawing.

Akureyri lies at the base of Eyjafjörður, surrounded on either side by a sloping wall of snow-capped mountains. The determined town clings to one hillside before spilling onto a small stretch of land that seems to float upon the shimmering water

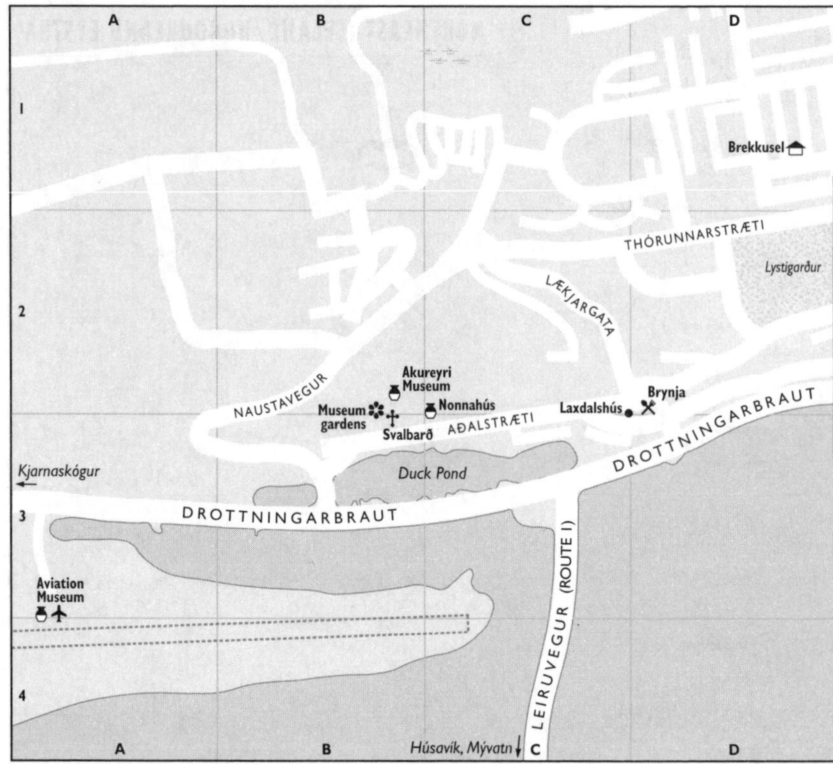


– hence the name *Akur-eyri*, or 'the field upon the shoreline'. The view is simply astounding, but the scenery also blocks out a good deal of bad weather, granting a unique play of sun and fog. Clear skies mean lots of sunny days (and nights) in summer and a healthy dose of clean snow come winter.

Akureyri often gets tagged with labels such as Iceland's 'second city' or 'capital of the north', though the actual population (around 18,000) and size (the country's fourth largest) imply otherwise. Why it gets the nod as the 'other big city' is because it's the only town that gives Reykjavík a run for its money. It may be small and compact, but it's also a very independent place. It's also a great place to visit, as a destination in and of itself, for the idyllic countryside of Eyjafjarðarsveit, or as a home base from which to suit up and explore great swathes of Iceland's wildest landscapes. Beyond the well-trodden tourist path to 'big' attractions (Mývatn, Goðafoss and Húsavík), Akureyri allows easy access to some of the country's less-visited parts (eg: Grímsey, the interior, and the outermost corners of Thingeyjarsýsla).

**HISTORY** Before Akureyri there was Oddeyri, the point of land that forms the industrial port of the town. The sagas tell of important Viking councils and light-hearted brawls, and the court that found a guilty verdict after Jón Arason's execution (see page 21). As the population and industry of Eyjafjörður grew, an important market was established farther north at Gásir (see page 330) which lasted throughout the medieval period. The name 'Akureyri' was first mentioned as the scene of a crime in a sheriff's report dated 1562 (the offence was adultery) and the Danish merchants arrived shortly thereafter. They only stayed for the short

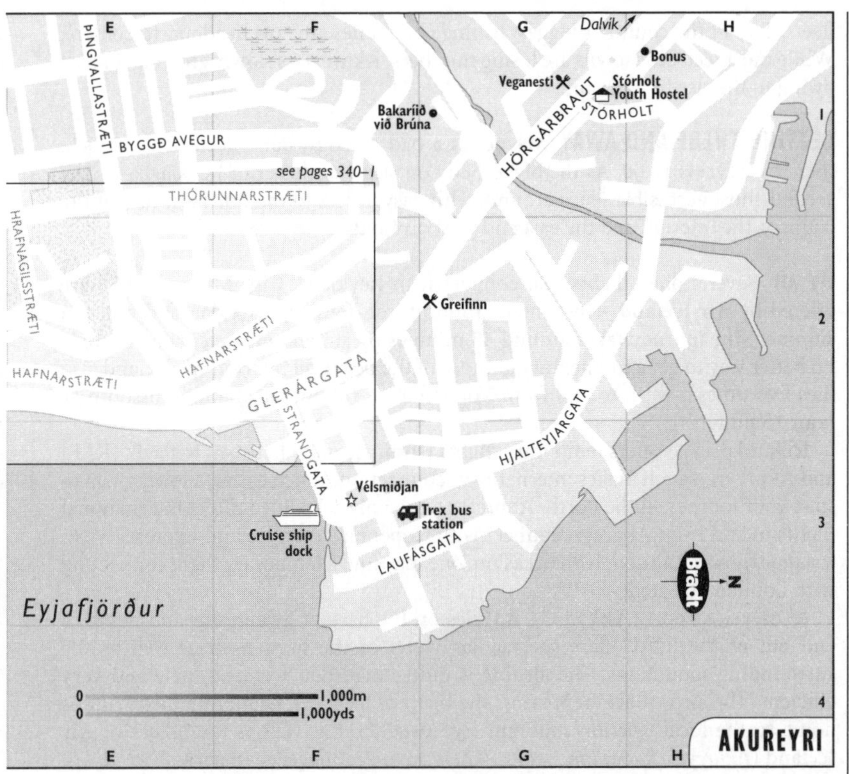


summer, and it was not until 1777 that a wooden house was built on site to house the shopkeeper Friðrik Lynge. Akureyri was granted its charter in 1786 (the same year as Reykjavík) but lost it in 1836 because of the small population, bothersome ice flows and bad business. In 1862, the 300 inhabitants were granted a second attempt at making a city and the Grána Trading Company was formed to profit from the produce of Eyjafjarðarsveit farmers. They built their warehouses and port at Oddeyri and soon the strength of local agriculture was felt throughout all of Iceland. Eventually the houses and shops of Akureyri met up with the industry of Oddeyri, becoming the city of Akureyri (you can still see the marked differences between the two ends of town).

Upstaged by Reykjavík in size, Akureyri has always sought to outpace the capital in business and social progress. The first woman to vote in Iceland voted in Akureyri. Not long after, the Grána company became the KEA co-operative (Kaupfélag Eyfirðinga), the first farm-owned company in Iceland and the birth of the Icelandic co-operative movement. KEA still owns a significant number of national holdings (as well as all their namesake hotels). As the money poured in, Akureyri adopted with fervour the aesthetic movement of the early 20th century – the flowered walkways, green lawns and tall trees are all the city's trademarks. This was also the first city in Iceland to welcome a scheduled flight: Akureyri Airlines was founded in 1937 and later became Icelandair (see page 75). In World War II, Akureyri became an important base for the British RAF, who used a fleet of seaplanes to protect the north Atlantic shipping lanes (the fjord makes a perfect runway). The 1950s and 1960s saw Akureyri lead the country's northern fishing fleets. Two of the country's biggest fishing companies are now headquartered here. While most Icelandic towns are losing numbers, Akureyri is slowly growing, in part owing to the rise in tourism.

**GETTING THERE AND AWAY** Maybe it's a bad analogy, but if Iceland is a clock, then Akureyri is 12.00. As the biggest city outside the cluster of Reykjavík, it's the second-most accessible place around, with easy access to the northern half of the country, the interior, and the east and west on Route 1.

**By air** Several daily flights that connect with Reykjavík City Airport (REK) are offered by **Air Iceland** – in winter, around three–four flights a day, and more in summer. The journey takes around 45 minutes by air, and on a clear day, there is no better way to get a momentary glimpse of the beautiful interior. Air Iceland also flies five times a week to and from Vopnafjörður (45 minutes) and Thórshöfn (1 hour 15 minutes).

**Icelandair** also offers temporary flights (summer only) between Keflavík (KEF) and Akureyri, which makes international connections much easier, allowing you to start your journey in the north. At present, the only scheduled direct international flights to and from Akureyri connect with Copenhagen on Iceland Express (*www.icelandexpress.is*) although on occasion, one may find a temporary flight connecting with London Stansted.

Akureyri Airport (AEY) [334 A3] lies on the base of Eyjafjörður and flying in and out of the fjord offers spectacular views of the fjord itself as well as the surrounding mountains. The airport is quite small but it is neat, new and very efficient. The airport also represents the birth of Iceland's aviation industry and is home to the local aviation museum (see page 351) as well as the offices of **Air Iceland** (*Akureyrarflugvöllur;* ☏ *460 7000;* e *websales@flugfelag.is; www.airiceland.is;* 🕒 *09.00–17.00 daily*).

**By car** Route 1 finds its apex at Akureyri, second only to Reykjavík when it comes to numbered road signs. Icelanders judge one another's ability at the wheel by how quickly someone can drive between Reykjavík and Akureyri. At 389km (243 miles) on a fairly flat road (for Iceland), some do it in under four hours but with a good chance of a speeding ticket showing up in their mailbox. From Reykjavík you'll enter Akureyri from the north, while the road from the east crosses a causeway on the fjord on the southern end of town. There's a cluster of petrol stations at the junction.

**By bus** Year-round, the bus company **Trex** offers a daily service to and from Reykjavík (6 hours) and Egilsstaðir (4 hours), as well as Húsavík (1 hour 15 minutes) and Ólafsfjörður (1 hour 15 minutes) via Dalvík (45 minutes). In summer, each line increases to two–three trips a day. The downside is that Trex has a more secluded bus station in Akureyri, near the port [335 F3] (*Kaldbaksgata 1;* ☏ *461 1106;* e *info@trex.is; www.trex.is*).

The city's main bus terminal is located at Hafnarstræti 82 [340 B5]. The private bus line **SBA-Norðuleið** is based here and caters specifically to tourists, but only in summer (*Hafnarstræti 82;* ☏ *462 3510;* e *sba@sba.is; www.sba.is*). That means driving daily across the interior to and from Reykjavík between 18 June and 7 September on the scenic Kjölur route (9 hours). Between 16 June and 31 August they also offer a daily service between Akureyri and Húsavík (2 hours), Ásbyrgi (3.5 hours), and Dettifoss (5 hours).

**By boat** Sailing the length of Eyjafjörður is probably the best way to come and go. Cruise ships tend to dock at Strandgata [335 F3] so that most passengers can simply walk the few blocks into the city centre. Yachts tie up at the smaller nearby port, which is even closer.

**GETTING AROUND** Akureyri is a great walking town. Sensible outdoor paths connect everything and make the city very open and accessible. It's also fairly compact, so that a circle of five or six city blocks takes in the crux of the town. Driving on your own makes the hills more manageable, but pay special attention to parking (see page 345). Akureyri's city **bus** line is not terrifically convenient but certainly does try (*Strætisvagnar Akureyrar; Strandgata 6; ☎ 462 4020; e svak@akmennt.is; fares 600ISK*). Buses run from 06.20 to 22.40 Monday to Friday, 12.20 to 17.20 Saturday, and pick up and drop off in front of the restaurant Nætursalan. Akureyri also boasts a **taxi** monopoly and all the cabs hang out by the cruise ships [335 F3] (*BSO taxi station; Strandgata; ☎ 461 1010*).

**Car hire** Most companies at least have a desk at the airport with a shuttle to the cars.

**Avis** Freyjunes 2; ☎ 461 2428; e avis@avis.is; www.avis.is
**Bílaleiga Akureyrar** Tryggvabraut 12; ☎ 461 6000; e holdur@holdur.is; www.eurorent.is
**Budget** Laufásgata 9; ☎ 462 3400; e budget@budget.is; www.budget.is
**Hertz** Akureyri Airport; ☎ 461 1005; e hertz@hertz.is; www.hertz.is

**TOURIST INFORMATION** The **tourist information office** [341 F5] (☎ *460 1199; e info@visitakureyri.is; www.visitakureyri.is;* 🕒 *10.00–17.00*) is located at the Hof, in the centre of town; you can't miss it. Built to resemble the saga-period *hofs* (temples) the cylindrical structure is an all-in-one home to the local cultural centre, with a large theatre for performances, a ballroom, art gallery, the Music School of Akureyri, café and gift shop (check out the rooster-skin bracelets).

## WHERE TO STAY

### Hotels

**Hótel Íbúðir** [341 G3] (6 apts) Geislagata 10; m 892 9838; e hotelibudir@hotelibudir.is; www.hotelibudir.is. Lush self-catering apartments in the city centre: big wooden beds, great mattresses, & shiny kitchenettes & bathrooms. Wooden floors & lots of light make this one of the nicer places to stay in town. Sizes range from studios to 3 bedrooms & if you're a group of 2 couples, the price is the same as what you'd pay for a nice guesthouse. Individual rooms are available at the guesthouse (for further information, see following section). **$$$$**

**Hótel Akureyri** [340 B4] (19 rooms) Hafnarstræti 67; ☎ 462 5600; e hotelakureyri@hotelakureyri.is; www.hotelakureyri.is. The city's fancy boutique hotel, just steps away from the bus station. The black-&-white building is fairly simple & quaint, while every room features a very cosy but elegant quality. Most rooms offer a nice view of the fjord & you get lots of personal attention. Beautiful b/fast buffet inc. **$$$**

**Hótel Edda** [340 A1] (204 rooms) Thórunnarstræti; ☎ 444 4000; e edda@hoteledda.is; www.hoteledda.is; 🕒 14 Jun–27 Aug). Come autumn, this is a college dorm, albeit a very posh one. The hotel makes very good use of the building & this is not a bad option at all. About a third of the rooms have sinks only (with shared baths on the floor); the rest all feature private in-room showers. *Sleeping-bag accommodation under 2,500ISK pp available.* **$$$**

***KEA hotels*** A local company, KEA owns and manages hotels KEA, Norðurland, and Harpa. Although each offers a different degree of luxury, the weird pricing structure means rooms can cost within US$10–20 of each other. Check their website for details (www.keahotels.is).

**Hótel KEA** [340 D5] (73 rooms) Hafnarstræti 87–89; ☎ 460 2000; e kea@keahotels.is; www.keahotels.is. Akureyri's leading luxury hotel complete with red carpet, faux marble floors, & well-groomed staff. The attractive building was one of the first 'Functionalist' concrete constructions in Akureyri. Rooms are of ample size with private bathroom, big windows & big solid beds, with a fantastic view of the city & the fjord (just like every room in town). The location is also ideal, at the main crossroads & the base of the steps beneath the church. B/fast inc. **$$$$**

**Hótel Norðurland** [341 G4] (34 rooms) Geislagata 7; ☎ 462 2600; e kea@keahotels.is; www.keahotels.is. Located on a quiet street just a block from the main action, this hotel is pleasantly quiet & family friendly. Regarding rooms, the Norðurland fits somewhere between Hótel KEA & Harpa: a bit small, but very clean & cosy. The attentive staff are quite helpful. Good with groups. Private bathrooms. During the winter, the hotel is closed; all reservations are transferred to Hótel KEA. B/fast inc. **$$$$**

**Hótel Harpa** [340 D5] (26 rooms) Hafnarstræti 83–85; ☎ 460 2000; e kea@keahotels.is; www.keahotels.is. These are just the cheap seats for Hótel KEA – a separate wing without the pomp & without the view (you still check in & eat breakfast at Hótel KEA). The main difference is the rooms, which are a little more modern & a lot more working class, although honestly the beds feel much the same. Smaller private bathrooms. B/fast inc. **$$$**

## Guesthouses

**Hallandsnes** (5 rooms) Bravo; m 895 6049; e hallandsnes@hallandsnes.is; www.hallandsnes.is. A peaceful cottage 5mins' drive outside Akureyri. White walls & black leather furniture. The owners also run a stylish boutique in town. A guest kitchen is available for use, but the renter must be over 30 & there's a 2-night minimum booking. **$$$$$**

**Akureyrar** [341 E4] (19 rooms) Hafnarstræti 104; ☎ 461 5588; e guest@nett.is. Because it's within walking distance of everything, this is fairly coveted accommodation. Shared bathrooms & rooms that sleep 1–4 people. They also rent bicycles. B/fast inc. **$$$**

**Íbúðir** [341 G3] (6 rooms) Brekkugata 4; m 892 9838; e hotelibudir@hotelibudir.is; www.hotelibudir.is. The guesthouse annex of the hotel apartments, the Íbúðir is by far the fanciest guesthouse in Akureyri. All rooms have their own private bathrooms with shower, the beds are simply exquisite, & there's an unrivalled sense of style. Open kitchen for guests. **$$$**

**Natur** (24 rooms) Thorisstaðir (across the fjord); ☎ 467 1070; e nature@hotelnatur.com; www.hotelnatur.com. Icelandic barns make great hotels, & Natur is an especially nice one. Each room has a TV & private bathroom, & the yoga classes & outdoor hot tub are nice too. The farm is located 10mins away from Akureyri on the opposite side of Eyjafjörður. Look for the green tower. B/fast inc (& dinner for groups; they also get a discount). **$$$**

**Akur Inn** [341 G2] (8 rooms) Brekkugata 27A; ☎ 461 2500; e akurinn@akurinn.is; www.akurinn.is. Built in 1930, this home's charming exterior gives way to a comfy & practical interior. The neighbourhood is nice & central, & the stay made better by the affections of the kindly couple who run the place. Shared bathrooms & breakfast costs extra (no kitchen available). **$$**

**Brekkusel** [334 D1] (6 rooms) Byggðarvegur 97; m 895 1260; e info@brekkusel.is; www.brekkusel.is. This lovely house & garden is exactly what most travellers want. Fairly unbeatable on all counts (location, price, & quality); be sure to book ahead to get in. The spacious rooms sleep 1–3 people & about half have private bathrooms. The atmosphere is family friendly & everything is kept spotless. Open kitchen & sleeping-bag accommodation available. **$$**

**Gula Villan** [340 C2] (9 rooms) Thingvallastræti 14; m 896 8464; e gulavillan@nett.is; www.gulavillan.is. The 'yellow villa' is indeed yellow & cheery. It's also right next to the swimming pool, which is truly a nice feature. Rooms are a bit cramped, though they are well furnished & comfortable. All bathrooms are

are shared. B/fast costs extra; open kitchen & sleeping-bag accommodation available. (Gula Villan manages another location at Brekkugata 8 in the city centre, along the same lines as the larger house). **$$**

**Salka** [341 E4] (8 rooms) Skipagata 1; 461 2340; salka@nett.is. In the heart of the city, with inexpensive but warm & comfortable rooms. Shared bathrooms & open kitchen. *Sleeping-bag accommodation 2,100ISK.* **$$**

**Sólgarðar** [341 G3] (6 rooms) Brekkugata 6; 461 1133; solgardar@simnet.is. Close to the library, this grandmotherly home is quite reserved & comfortable. There's lots of light in the upstairs rooms & the neighbourhood is just as quaint. B/fast costs extra; sleeping-bag accommodation & open kitchens available. **$$**

**Súlur** [340 A1] (20 rooms) Thórunnarstræti 93; 461 1160; sulur@islandia.is; summer only. Next to the swimming pool & campsites, this concrete guesthouse offers the basics, & by so doing, attracts those who need a cheap break from camping. Simple rooms with made-up beds, bathrooms down the hall, & a kitchen for your use. Súlur also manages an annex house (*Klettastígur 6; m 863 1400; sulur@islandia.is;* **$$**). The house is a bit nicer & more personal, but ranges from nice, big family-style rooms to more dormitory, sleeping-bag bunk beds. It's also a fair walk into the city centre. **$$**

## Youth hostel

**Stórholt Youth Hostel** [335 G1] (50 beds) Stórholt 1; 462 3657; akureyri@hostel.is; www.hostel.is. This incredibly well-managed hostel challenges all the negative stereotypes usually associated with hostel accommodation. In spite of the many muddy, exhausted travellers who pass through here, everything is kept religiously clean & the silence is golden. Guests share 3 very large kitchens & a number of small (but very clean) bathrooms, as well as a great laundry room. They've also gone to great lengths to make everything on the first floor wheelchair-accessible. Located on the far north side of the city, it is an advantage if you have a car although the city bus does stop very close by (& it's a 45min walk to the airport). You're also within fair walking distance of food stores (Bónus) & fast-food shops. Costs are low (around 2,000ISK pp in a sleeping bag) which means the hostel is about 95% booked in advance before the summer season even begins. For overflow, the hostel manages a couple of cosy log cabins that are great for groups (fireplaces, barbecue grills, & porches). **$**

**Camping** Akureyri offers two separate campsites. The first (and more common choice) is located by the garden complex next to the swimming pool: **Thórunnarstræti Camping** [340 B1] (*Hafnarstræti 49; 462 3379; hamrar@hamrar.is; www.hamrar.is; 1 May–30 Sep;* **$**). Typical of urban camping, things can get crowded, but there's the added convenience of good facilities and access to everything, from the swimming pool to local restaurants. Showers, bathrooms, and kitchen sinks.

Akureyri's other campsite is out near the manmade forest of Kjarnaskógur (see page 348): **Hamrar Camping** (*Kjarnaskógur; 461 2264; hamrar@hamrar.is; www.hamrar.is; 1 May–30 Sep;* **$**). To get there from the city, just take Drottningarbraut south for a good 2km, then turn right at the sign. Hamrar is farther in, up on the slope overlooking the woods. This is one of Iceland's better large-scale campsites in terms of amenities (hot showers, clean-ish bathrooms, and decent kitchen space), and the fact that it's in a very natural area. The location is great for accessing the nearby trails and wilderness, but not so great if you are keen to visit the centre of Akureyri.

**WHERE TO EAT** No it's not the capital, but Akureyri does not disappoint when it comes to variety and availability of dining options. You'll also find that your money buys more food up here.

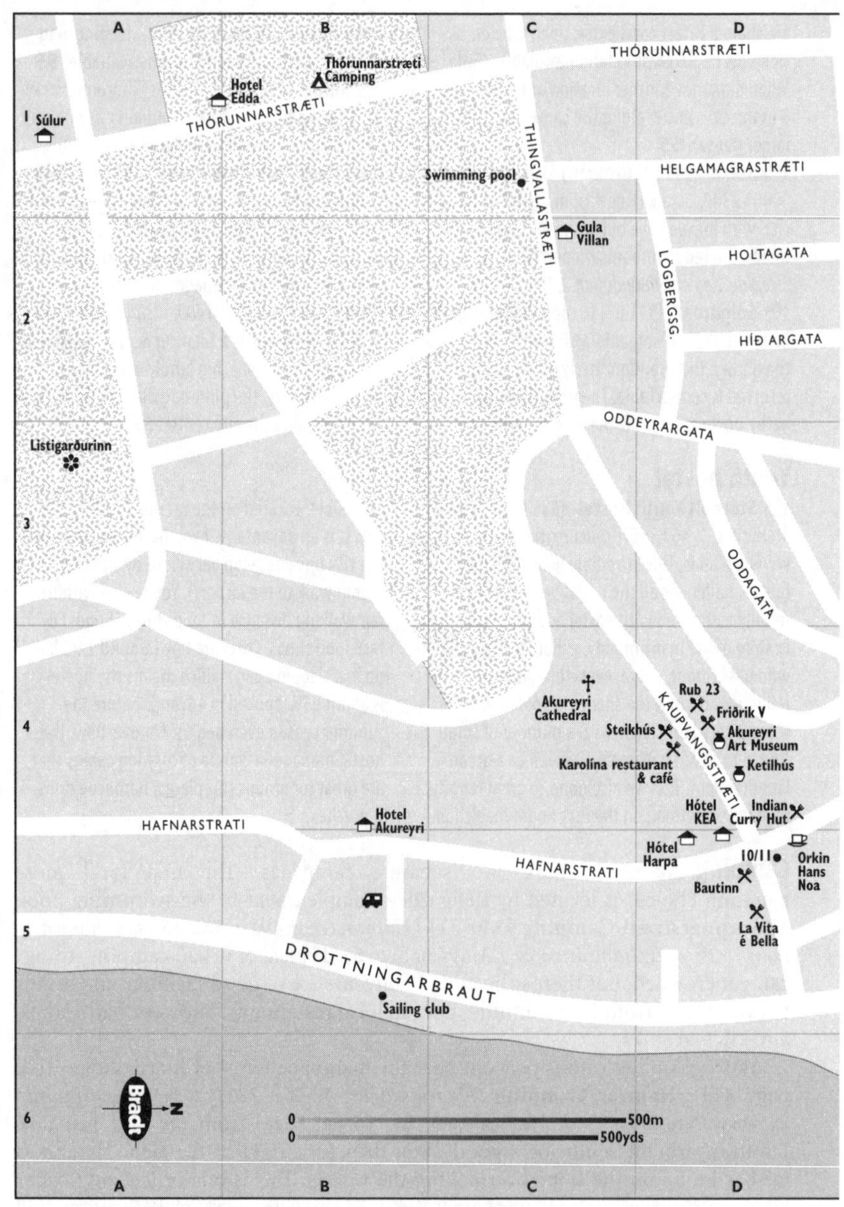


## Very Akureyri

**Karolína** [340 D4] Kaupvangsstræti 23; 461 2755; karolina@islandia.is; www.karolina.is; 18.00–23.00 daily. This leading local gourmet has outlived the changing trends & is still turning out highly creative dishes that are both beautiful & tasty. The serene dining room offers a worthy haven to investigate this modern & slightly Mediterranean menu. The chef has a small penchant for exotica (horse, seabird, whale, etc), but there's enough focus on local products to step away from clichés. The set 5-course meal is recommended, as is the prize-winning chocolate

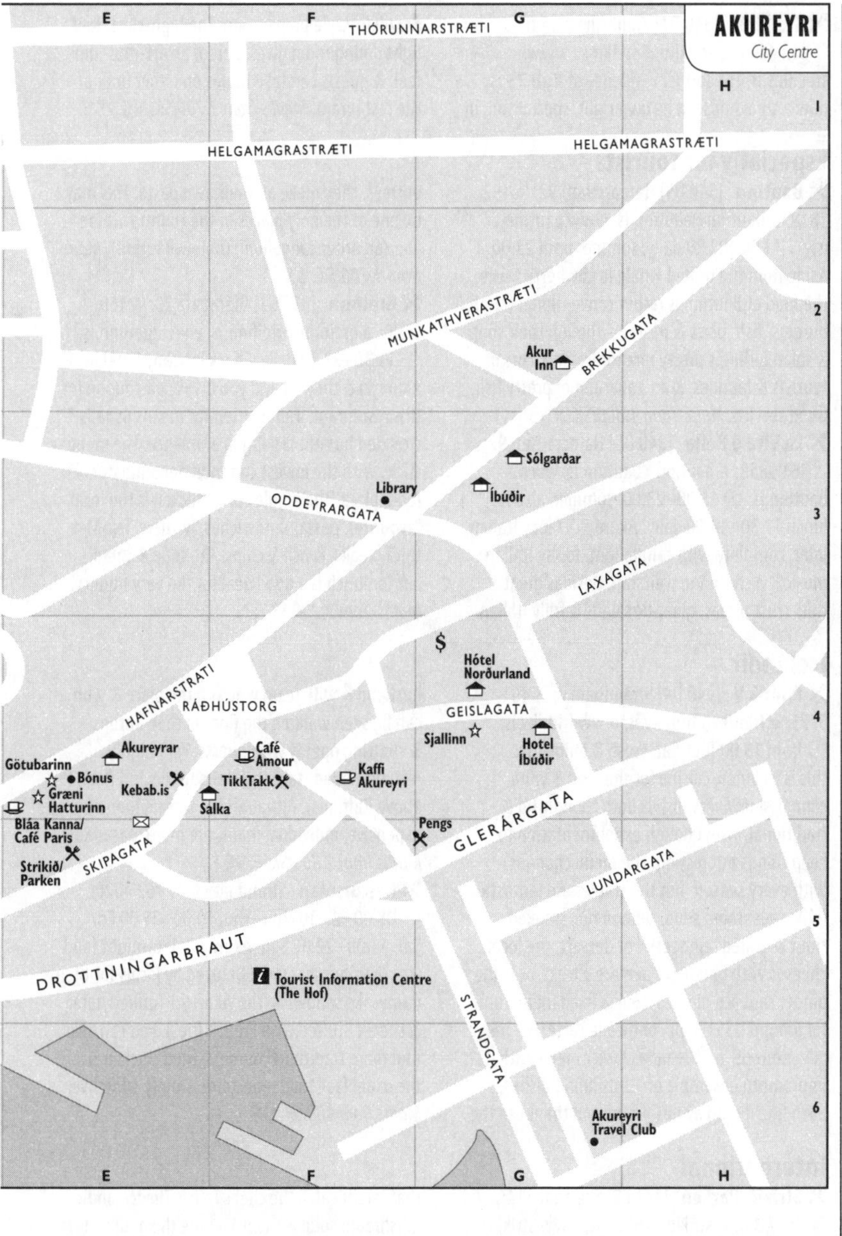


soufflé. If you want to tone it down, try out their downstairs café. *Mains from 4,000ISK.* $$$$$

**Rub 23** [340 D4] Kaupvangsstræti 6; 462 2223; www.rub23.is; 17.30–22.00; daily. Possibily the poshest dining experience in town. One of the most famous steakhouses in Akureyri, Rub is big on fish & sushi, but also serves chicken, lamb, & kangaroo. There are lots of *National Geographic*-like photo murals. The local practice is to arrive & head up to the cosy 2nd-floor lounge for a pre-dinner drink, then head to the dining room for a scrumptious, fine-dining meal of yummy food in tiny portions. It's comfortable, classy, & costly. *Mains from 3,750ISK.* $$$$$

✕ **Steikhús** [340 D4] Kaupvangsstræti 23; ☏ 462 4423; ✉ steikhus@steikhus; www.steikhus.is. The former residence of **Rub 23** is now a steakhouse in its own right, specialising in Brazilian-style preparation. The high-class, low-light dining room gives a bit of an art-museum feel, & guests can take tables on either floor of the restaurant. *Steaks from 2,700ISK.* $$$$$

## Especially for tourists

✕ **Bautinn** [340 D5] Hafnarstræti 92; ☏ 462 1818; ✉ bautinn@bautinn.is; www.bautinn.is; 🕒 11.30–22.30 daily, summer until 23.00. Aside from the grilled whale in cowberry sauce, the food at Bautinn is rather conventional (lamb, burgers, fish, pizza & pasta) – though their soup & salad buffet is pretty rare for Iceland. Lots of tourists & families, & an aquarium of pretty fish. Good service. *Mains from 1,800ISK.* $$$

✕ **La Vita é Bella** [340 D5] Hafnarstræti 92; ☏ 461 5858; ✉ bautinn@bautinn.is; www.bautinn.is; 🕒 18.00–23.00, summer, also for lunch 11.30–14.00 daily. Akureyri's fancy Italian joint, complete with candlelight, folksy Italian music & a charming waitstaff. Besides great thin-crust pizzas, gigantic salads & frilly Italian entrées, they make all their own pasta. This may be one of the only places in the country where you can order cannelloni; (below Bautinn). *Mains from 1,700ISK.* $$$

✕ **Greifinn** [335 G2] Gléragata 20; ☏ 460 1600; ✉ greifinn@greifinn.is; www.greifinn.is; 🕒 11.30–23.30 daily. Check into any hotel in Akureyri & they'll hand you a 15% off coupon for this restaurant. 'Family friendly' means usually crowded but not lacking in ambiance. The menu sticks with the lowest common denominators in food: pizza (the jungle curry chicken is the local favourite), pasta, sandwiches, burgers, Tex-Mex, thick steaks, & fish & chips. The soup & salad bar for lunch is a good deal for the very hungry. *Mains from 2,200ISK.* $$

## Icelandic

✕ **Friðrik V** [340 D4] Strandgata 7; ☏ 461 5775; ✉ fridrikv@fridrikv.is; www.fridrikv.is; 🕒 from 18.00 Tue–Sat. Fresh & innovative, this is Icelandic cuisine for the food & wine connoisseur. Every dish is both thoughtful & traditional, with enough experimentation to keep things interesting. The menu changes with every season, but the staples are fantastic (wild mushroom soup, salmon roe, smoked trout & grilled reindeer). For dessert, the local cheeses with blueberry jam are a treat, as is the ginger rhubarb pie. A 5-course fixed menu runs for around US$120 pp, or go à la carte. For the adventurous, try the tapas taster menu with its impromptu ensemble of 10 stunning dishes. Such fine dining avoids pretension thanks to the husband & wife team who run the place & who can be seen walking the floor in their aprons & chatting openly with guests. Very highly recommended (take the stairs to the 2nd floor above Kaffíhus). Although the tasting menu is expensive, individual mains are more reasonable. *Mains from 2,800ISK.* $$$$

✕ **Nætursalan** Strandgata 6; ☏ 462 4020; 🕒 08.00–23.30 Mon–Thu, 10.00–05.00 Fri/Sat, 11.00–22.00 Sun. Akureyri's late-night food stop/hamburger stand. Beloved by locals for their namesake sandwich, the 'Akureyri' (grilled ham & cheese stuffed with French fries), you can also find more traditional burgers, fried chicken & the usual fast-food repertoire. Simply addictive. *Mains from 900ISK.* **$$**

## International

✕ **Strikið/Parken** [341 E5] Skipagata 14; ☏ 462 7100; ✉ strikid@strikid.is; www.strikid.is; 🕒 11.30–22.30 daily. No matter the weather, there will always be some light up here, the top floor of one of the city's tallest buildings. With all glass walls, Strikið offers a wonderful view of the city & the fjord. This upbeat modern brasserie is all about global fusion, which means a bit of Asian, Italian, Middle Eastern & anything else that might catch the chef's fancy. The Icelandic mushroom soup is superb, as are the gourmet burgers & tender fish dishes. Good for business lunches. *Mains from 2,600ISK.* $$$$

✕ **Pengs** [341 G5] Gléragata 36; ☏ 466 3800; 🕒 11.30– 23.00 Sun–Thu, 11.30–midnight Fri/Sat. The Chinese lanterns, fortune cookies, & soy sauce on the tables may give the wrong impression, as this restaurant is far from average Chinese. The atmosphere is light & friendly, & the food is delicate & cooked with care (not greasy). Pengs specialises in southern Chinese food, which can mean very hot but not always – the ginger salmon has a nice local flavour. For the hungry traveller, there's a 15-course buffet lunch from 11.30 to 14.00 for only 1,000ISK. Definitely one of Iceland's better Chinese restaurants. *Mains from 1,000ISK.* $$

## Quick

**Indian Curry Hut** [340 D4] Hafnarstræti 100b; 461 4242; 16.30–23.00. Mostly chicken & lamb with Indian spices, but the chicken massala is a big hit. *Mains from 1,595ISK.* $$

**TikkTakk** [341 F4] Strandgata 6; 461 1300; 17.30–21.00 daily, also midnight–05.00 Fri/Sat. The regular fast food along with boxed pizzas & sloppy submarine sandwiches. Best at night. *Mains from 700ISK.* $$

**Kebab.is** [341 E4] Skipagata 2; 461 1615; www.kebab.is; 17.00–midnight daily. Akureyri's salute to healthy chic, specialising in wraps. All food on the premises, down to the sauces, is made from scratch. *Mains from 975ISK.* $

**Veganesti** [335 G1] corner of Hörgárbraut & Stórholt; 461 3012; 08.00–23.30 Mon–Fri, 09.00–23.30 Sat/Sun. The kind of food one finds at petrol stations (grilled & greasy) along with pizzas, ice cream, & sweets. Very popular among those who stay at the hostel. *Mains from 450ISK.* $

## Cafés

An acute café culture distinguishes Akureyri from the design-ridden shop fronts back in Reykjavík. With lighter summers and darker winters, people spend long hours sipping caffeine indoors and out (stopping for a latte on a sunny patio at 23.00 is fashionable). Most cafés serve light meals.

**Café Amour** [341 F4] Ráðhústorg 9; 461 3030; amour@cafeamour.is; www.cafeamour.is; summer 11.00–01.00 Sun–Thu, 11.00–04.00 Fri/Sat, winter 14.00–01.00 Sun–Thu, 14.00–04.00 Fri/Sat. By day, this corner café offers great people-watching on the city's main square. Step inside & see the work of local artists decorating the walls & ceiling. Intense conversations occur over rich coffee or colourful cocktails, along with 5 beers on tap & a variety of cakes. By night, & especially on weekends, it's lounging room only & it gets pretty smoky on the ground floor. The upstairs bar & dance floor are a lot more mellow. *Mains from 650ISK.* $$

**Café Karolína** [340 D4] Kaupvangsstræti 23; 461 2755; karolina@karolina.is; www.karolina.is; 17.00–01.00 Sun–Thu, 17.00–04.00 Fri/Sat. Laid-back little sister to the big gourmet restaurant upstairs, the café version is just as pleasant & more peaceful. All day & into the night you'll find delicious fresh-roasted coffees, grilled sandwiches, fresh salads, & heart-warming soups. *Mains from 700ISK.* $$

**Kaffi Akureyri** [341 F4] Strandgata 7; 461 3999; kaffiakureyri@islandia.is; www.kaffiakureyryi.is; 11.00–01.00 Mon–Thu, 11.00–04.00 Fri/Sat. A nice, open coffee shop with huge windows that let you check out who's inside before deciding to enter. At weekends, the mild-mannered pub turns into the craziest club in town with lots of loud music, alcohol & dancing youth. Quite smoky. *Mains from 1,000ISK.* $$

**Bláa Kanna/Café Paris** [341 E4] Hafnarstræti 96; 461 4600; summer 08.30–midnight daily, winter 09.00–23.30 daily. With bright-blue metal walls & twin red turrets, you can't miss this place. Not only is the 'blue pot' one of the oldest houses in town, it's also smoke-free. The front half is decorated in traditional Icelandic style, while the back is eclectic bohemian. They bake their own bread, pastries, & Icelandic cakes, & serve it with great coffee, tea & hot chocolate. You can also buy sandwiches any time of day, but soup is only served at lunchtime. The painted tables & crystal chandeliers add to the artsy flavour, & in summer there's a big outdoor patio to enjoy the sunshine. *Mains from 500ISK.* $

**Orkin Hans Noa** [340 D5] Glerárgötu 32; 11.00–18.00 daily. 'Noah's Ark' is part coffee house, part art gallery, part furniture store. It is bright & happy, with hot drinks, eclectic modern art on the walls (including Cat in a Bath, which is exactly what it sounds like), & comfy seats. If you like the chair you're sitting on, you can pay for it with your coffee & take it home. *Mains from 900ISK.* $

**Self-catering** The most convenient food shop is the **10/11** on the corner of Hafnarstræti and Kaupvangsstræti [340 D5] (🕒 *08.00–23.00 Mon–Fri, 09.00–midnight Sat/Sun*). In addition to staples like bread, cheese, veggies, meat and drinks, they have their own soup and salad bar (very cheap) and a trusty hot-dog stand. For heftier purchases, head out to **Bónus** [335 H1] (*Longholt 1;* ☎ *466 3500*). The bakeries of Akureyri are all quite tempting. The most central is at **Kristjáns** (*Hafnarstræti 108;* 🕒 *08.00–17.30 Mon–Fri, 10.00–14.00 Sat*). You'll find American doughnuts, Icelandic *kleina*, abundant pastries, bread, soups, rolls, sandwiches, coffee and tea. A much larger bread factory runs an on-site shop **Bakaríið við Brúna** [335 G1] on your way out of town towards Dalvík (*Dalsbruat 1;* ☎ *461 2700;* 🕒 *07.00–18.00 Mon–Fri, 07.00–16.00 Sat/Sun*).

**Ice cream** Founded in 1939, **Brynja** [334 D2] (*Aðalstræti 3;* ☎ *462 4478;* e *brynja@simnet.is;* 🕒 *09.00–23.30*) is Akureyri's most famous ice-cream parlour. Serving up Iceland's favourite ice cream since 1942. In summer or winter, the shop is packed full with a line coming out the door. The owners claim a special ingredient makes their homemade ice cream taste better than anyone else's. It could also be that they simply use fresh local dairy produce. Residents of Reykjavík often have friends flying to the capital from Akureyri stop by at Brynja's before flying down, to bring them a treat. A must.

While **Benni og Bára** (*Hafnarstræti 95;* e *gersemi@simnet.is*) is not Brynja, this ice-cream parlour certainly deserves mention. Located in House París, a nationally protected Akureyri landmark in the middle of town, it serves up cold treats all year round.

**ENTERTAINMENT AND NIGHTLIFE** On weekends, Akureyri makes up for its small size with a show of intense energy on the streets and inside a handful of clubs. The *runtur* is performed with vigour and cars clog the circuit well into the early morning hours, almost forcing you to pick a club just to get away from the exhaust fumes. **Café Amour** [341 F4] and **Kaffi Akureyri** [341 F4] are favourite nightspots for drinking/dancing. Other hotspots include:

☆ **Götubarinn** [341 E4] Hafnarstræti 94; ☎ 462 4747; 🕒 17.00–01.00 Sun–Thu, 17.00–03.00 Fri/Sat. One of the more popular bars, given its central location, Götubarinn is also looking to establish itself as a reputable winehouse. Housed in the historical House París, the areas of the bar are named after Akureyri's streets, there's a free-for-all piano, & the décor (including cow pelts & the front of a Fiat) is both unusual & friendly. So is the resident ghost, so no worries.

☆ **Græni Hatturinn** [341 E4] Hafnarstræti 96 (beneath Bláa Kanna); ☎ 461 4646; 🕒 (typically) 20.00–03.00 Fri/Sat. The 'green hat' is a wild pub/disco with lively events, but open sporadically. Check local listings or ask around.

☆ **Sjallinn** [341 G4] Geislagata 14; ☎ 462 2770; e sjallinn@sjallinn.is; www.sjallinn.is; 🕒 19.30–01.00 Sun–Thu, 19.30–04.00 Fri/Sat. The biggest of Akureyri's clubs, featuring live music, big banquets, dancing, lots of young teenagers & a healthy party atmosphere on all counts. Usually a cover price for events.

☆ **Vélsmiðjan** [335 F3] Strandgata 49; ☎ 461 7710; 🕒 22.00–04.00 Fri/Sat. Popular weekend pub with a Viking theme. Jazz & rock bands & slow dancing with a slightly older (30+) sophisticated crowd. Free until midnight, then 1,000ISK cover price.

**SHOPPING** Residents of Akureyri have debated which route to take in attracting tourism: is it food, sites, or shopping? **Centro** (*Hafnarstræti 97;* e *centro@centro.is;* 🕒 *10.00–18.00 Mon–Fri, 10.00–16.00 Sat*) is certainly making the argument for shopping. It's a girl's shopping dream, and while not cheap, the bang-for-buck ratio is pretty good. The shop stocks a wide variety of trendy boots and, in true Icelandic fashion, black everything.

**Frúin í Hamborg** (*Hafnarstræti 90;* ☎ *461 5577;* e *fruinihamborg@fruinihamborg.is; www.fruinihamborg.is;* ⏲ *10.00–18.00 Mon–Fri*) is a great little secondhand shop, complete with a shrine to old records. The owner loves to sew and resurrects cast-offs into stylish clothes.

## OTHER PRACTICALITIES

**Banks and changing money** There's a 24 hour-ATM at Landsbankinn (*Strandgata 1*) and quite a few at KB Bank (*Geislagata 5*). Both banks exchange currency during opening hours (⏲ *09.00–17.00*).

### Bookshops

**Eymundsson** Hafnarstræti 91–93; ☎ 540 2180; www.eymundsson.is; ⏲ 09.00–22.00 Mon–Fri, 10.00–22.00 Sat/Sun. Your standard mega-bookstore, complete with cafe & Starbucks-like coffee bar. Popular with tourists – if you need a quick 'visit' home. Free Wi-Fi.

**Froði** Kaupvangsstræti 19; ☎ 462 6345; ⏲ 11.00–18.00 daily, although it's pretty much closed in the winter. An unforgettable secondhand bookshop beneath the church, if you love old books no matter what the language.

**Penninn** Hafnarsstræti 91-93; ☎ 461 5050; e akureyri@pennin.is; ⏲ 09.00–22.00 Mon–Fri, 10.00–22.00 Sat/Sun. The town's main bookshop & a de facto souvenir stop for cruise-ship passengers & coach tourists. A great collection of postcards & photo books, along with a wide variety of English-language publications on Iceland.

**Communications** The **post office** is at Skipagata 10 [341 E5] (☎ *580 1000;* ⏲ *09.00–17.00*) and sells sell international calling cards, as do most petrol stations and small shops. There's a pay **phone** at the tourist information office. For mobile phones, prepaid cards, and new chips, the Síminn office is at Hafnarstræti 102 (☎ *460 6700*).

**Parking** Akureyri must earn a good deal of its town budget by dishing out parking tickets to unassuming tourists as this is a fairly common complaint. Space in the town centre is tight, and even the big hotels may not offer parking for your rental car. To avoid the hassle (worse than the expense), pick up the free little cardboard dial clock tag at the tourist information office. Pay attention to signs and restrictions. Once you've found a spot you think is safe, move the little hands on the clock to show the current time and display it prominently on the dashboard. If the parking attendant doesn't see the clock, they'll issue a flat US$100 fine.

**WHAT TO SEE AND DO** The town of Akureyri is pleasantly small but with much to enjoy. Take in the many views, wander through the small gardens, have a swim at the fabulous pool, definitely see the church, and then head out into the breathtaking landscapes. Orient yourself at the main intersection of Hafnarstræti and Kaupvangsstræti. **Akureyri Cathedral** [340 C4] is on top of the hill and the town spreads out from the **Raðhústorg** [341 F4], the paved town square (that's really a circle).

**Innbær** (inner town) is the thin strip of flat land that hugs the coast of the fjord towards the south. The fact that **Aðalstræti** (Main Street) is nowhere near the city centre says something about how Akureyri is the combination of several different settlements. At the bottom of the street is the standard Icelandic **duck pond** [334

**LAUFABRAUÐ** *Nathan Evans*

Born in the north of Iceland, Akureyri is the cradle of this Icelandic tradition. The first mention of *laufabrauð* is from 1730, where it is referred to as a sweet, despite it being blatantly un-sweet. Notwithstanding its scarcity and cost in the olden days, wheat was a Christmas speciality. Icelanders would roll the dough out into extremely thin bread, almost like a cracker. Once flattened to the size of a dinner plate (so everyone could have a piece), they would carve intricate designs into the bread to make up for the small portions.

Today, *laufabrauð* remains a Christmas tradition, and everybody holds big parties to prepare and eat it. *Laufabrauð* has come to be a symbolic tale of Iceland: hardy, beautiful people eking out a life in a hard, beautiful land.

B3], where you can see plenty of ducks, oystercatchers and terns, as well as whatever else is stopping over while you're there. In summertime, a good number of pink-footed geese add their own colour to the display. Right across sits the black-and-white **Nonnahús** [334 C2] (see page 350), childhood home to Jón Sveinsson, identified by his kindly statue. Next door is the **Svalbarð church**, built in 1846 on a farm in Eyjafjarðarsveit and transported to this spot in 1970 to replace the original Akureyri church (built in 1862). During World War II, the British Forces used the Akureyri church as a military post, after which it had to be torn down. The trail leading up the hill from Nonnahús and the church leads to the **Akureyri Museum** [334 B2] (see page 350).

Heading up or down the Aðalstræti/Hafnarstræti stretch takes in many of the **historic houses** that characterise the town. The old hospital (*Aðalstræti 14*) was built as a private home in 1835 and donated by the merchant Friðrik Guðmann to improve the health of the townspeople. Besides surgery, there were hot-water baths open free to the public once a week. The old pharmacy (*Aðalstræti 4*) was built in 1859 and may be the most photographed house in town. Officially the oldest building in town is **Laxdalshús** [334 C2] (*Hafnarstræti 11*) constructed in 1795 as the private home of the Danish merchant family Kyhn. (The ravine that opens up behind the house is **Buðargil**, named after the medieval *buð* or trading booths that once stood there, now marked by Lækjargata. This was also the birthplace of Akureyri's first vegetable gardens, watered by the flowing brook (*lækjar*).

Yachts, fishing boats, cruises, and some hefty cargo ships all compete for the port of Akureyri, which can be an exciting place to explore. The little industrial stretch from Strandgata is slowly getting gentrified into offices and bars, but is not entirely picturesque. The north side of town lies above the Gléra (glass) River, hence the surrounding neighbourhood of Glérahverfi, which is residential and modern. What lies just outside Akureyri holds far more pull and several amazing spots are all within an hour's drive.

**Akureyri Cathedral** [340 C4] (*Akureyrarkirkja; Eyrarlandsvegur; ☎ 462 7700; e akirkja@akirkja.is; www.akirkja.is*) The town's centrepiece is the pair of rectangular steeples on top of the steep green hill in the city centre. Akureyrikirkja is the work of Iceland's one and only state architect Guðjón Samuelson (see page 176) and may be the best example of his departure from classic Art Deco in search of something unique and Icelandic. Even the diehard traditionalist can be intrigued by the repeated square forms in the striking façade, though perhaps the real beauty of Akureyri's church is found inside.

Clear and simple, visitors are often surprised by the very warm light inside the church. An original window from Coventry Cathedral decorates the far back wall, though the other stained glass is some of the very best in Iceland so try to visit on a sunny day. The scenes from the life of Christ reflect a truly emotive Modernist style (he wears the same bright scarlet in each). The windows on the sides of the church depict important moments in local church history: a converted Thorgeir dumping his pagan idols into Goðafoss, Iceland's last Catholic bishop Jón Arason (who was tried and found guilty at the court in Akureyri after his beheading), and the Reverend Matthías Jochumsson (see page 35), poet and author of Iceland's national anthem – Akureyikirkja is dedicated in his honour.

The angel baptismal font is a copy of the Bertel Thorvaldsen original at the Vor Fruhe Kirke in Copenhagen, the sculpted balcony is the work of Ásmundur

## THE COVENTRY WINDOW

It's no secret that Akureyri's stained-glass altarpiece comes from England's Coventry Cathedral, though how it got there is a little less straightforward. In 1939, the fear of German air raids led to the removal of all of Coventry's stained-glass windows and their careful placement among the farms of Warwickshire. Such foresight paid off on 14 November 1940, when the Luftwaffe bombed Coventry and burned its historic cathedral in the notorious Operation Moonlight Sonata. Just a few months later, three stunning pieces of stained glass popped up in the back room of a London antique shop where they caught the eye of a window-shopping tourist from Iceland, Helgi Zoéga. Helgi also happened to work as an antiques dealer in Reykjavík, so he bought all three windows and carried them back with him to Iceland. Meanwhile, KEA chairman and Akureyri Town Council member Jakob Frímannsson just happened to be in the capital on business and heard of the windows at Zoéga's shop. At their last meeting in Akureyri, the town council had discussed decorations for their new cathedral – Jakob made a few quick calls home to check for measurements and then headed to Zoéga's. Only one of the three windows was the correct width and Jakob bought it on the spot (the other two windows remained in Reykjavík, one in a modern church and another in a private home). Jakob presented his find as a personal gift to the city and the church, and the window was installed in the apse in 1943.

The Coventry Window depicts the Nunc dimittis or Canticle of Simeon, when Mary and Joseph presented the baby Jesus at the temple in Jerusalem and where the Christ child was blessed by Simeon (Luke 2: 25-34). Although the stained glass fits perfectly inside the narrow width of the apse's back wall, the window was much shorter than needed, so modern glass was used to add length (the violet pieces you see today). Some of the window was actually cut out and suspended within the larger window (note the lamb and the St George's Cross of England). This is quite a feat, considering the original window is at least 200 years old. The surrounding windows in the apse were also artfully designed to match the style and depiction in the Coventry Window.

Nobody in Iceland ever admitted to knowing that the window came from Coventry – the discovery was made in the recent past by some English visitors who swore that they'd seen that window somewhere before. Now the only part of the story that's missing is how the window made it from a hayloft in the West Midlands to an antique dealer in wartime London. Puzzling.

Sveinsson (see page 183), and the model ship hanging from the ceiling is the *Samson*, a gift to commemorate the first pastor of the cathedral, Friðrik Rafnar.

In summer, the church is open to the public from 10.00 to 12.00 and 14.00 to 17.00 daily. Otherwise, you can catch a Sunday service at 11.00 or an organ recital at the times listed on the door. For some odd reason, fewer people climb up the massive stairs than those who climb down. One can skip the steps by walking the gentler slope of Kaupvangsstræti or driving up behind the church. There's also a cute little path that leads from the front of the church down to Sigurhæðir (see page 351) and the older houses on Hafnarstræti.

**Gardens** In 1808, the Danish merchant Hans Lever began planting potatoes in his backyard in the centre of Akureyri. After two edible crops, he published a pamphlet entitled '*Instructions in potato cultivation for the common people of Iceland*'. Soon after, every household in Akureyri was growing potatoes, then other vegetables and then flowers. Just over 200 years later, the trend continues with a flourish. Akureyri is famous for its serious vegetable plots and optimistic flower gardens, as well as its orderly public greens. The most historic example is the **museum garden** [334 B2] in front of the town museum at the end of Aðalstræti. This 'plant nursery' dates back to 1899, though in 1912, an Akureyri women's co-operative started the much larger

### A FOREST FOR THE TREES

In the 1870s, there were only five trees in Akureyri. They were most likely planted by homesick Danes who refused to accept a treeless landscape and gave extra special care to ensure the survival of the hapless seedlings. For the townspeople, the novelty of these few trees fuelled a trend: in 1882, a maple tree was planted, and in 1899, a nursery was founded in Akureyri for the express purpose of growing trees. Birch seeds were collected at Fnjóskadalur (on the east side of Eyjafjörður) and other tree species were imported from Norway – mostly rowan trees. In 1909, Iceland's first apple tree was planted and produced fruit. The nursery garden is now part of the town museum and boasts the very tallest birch and rowan trees in all Iceland, some of them reaching over 30m. Take a good look and be amazed at how tall and straight these trees are, considering the ankle-high bushes that grow everywhere else in Iceland. The rare sight is due to Akureyri's mild climate, the sheltered hillside, and several generations of caring hands.

As confirmed tree huggers, the people of Akureyri took on an intensive planting campaign – to grow a manmade forest that would encircle the whole town. In 1952, the first tree was planted in **Kjarnaskógur**, a designated recreational zone just south of the airport. Tens of thousands of trees were added, and limb by limb, the 'nuclear woods' took root (that's really what they're called). Today, most of the trees appear as overgrown bushes, with a few noted exceptions. Birch trees are predominant and the coniferous trees you see are mostly European larch (*Larix europaea*) imported from Scandinavia. To some of us the woods seem fairly ordinary, but for Icelanders this is a real jungle and you'll find excited families tearing through the trees on an extensive network of hiking trails. Several children's parks, barbecue pits and shelters, and a campsite make this a popular holiday destination. There's also a lit outdoor running/skiing path for darker months (*Kjarnaskógur; ☎ 462 4047; ⌚ year-round*).

**Listigarðurinn** [334 D2] (*Eyrarlandsvegur;* ☎ *462 7487;* ⏲ *1 Jun–30 Sep 08.00–22.00 Mon–Fri, 09.00–22.00 Sat/Sun*). Today this bona fide botanical garden fills a very large city block. It's a great place to get acquainted with Icelandic flora: they've got at least one of everything that grows in the country, although what you actually see depends on when you come. Summer is spectacular with the many flowers that blossom here, but winter is still educational. Several other small gardens are planted throughout the town, most of which are connected by walking paths. It's also a lot of fun just to peek into the gardens of private homes. Someone's always planting or digging something and you may get some ideas for back home.

**Swimming** Akureyri boasts what is arguably the best swimming pool in the country or at least the most visited [340 C1] (*Sundlaug Akureyrar;* ☎ *461 4455;* e *sund@akureyri.is;* ⏲ *07.00–21.00 Mon–Fri, 08.00–18.30 Sat/Sun; entrance 300ISK*). The new complex includes two huge outdoor pools, several children's wading and play areas, fanciful water slides, a steam room and sauna, and a sunbathing area that's heated with warm water. It's difficult not to want to spend a large chunk of the day here.

**Hiking** A steady pace out of Akureyri will take you into some great scenery within minutes. Glerárdalur (see page 352) and Eyjafjarðardalur (see page 352) are some of the closest. Pick up some good trail maps at the tourist information centre, or for even more detailed information contact the **Akureyri Travel Club** (*Ferðafélag Akureyrar; Strandgata 23;* ☎ *462 2720;* e *ffa@li.is; www.ffa.est.is*). They are the pros when it comes to walking beyond the beyond. They also organise several group hikes of various lengths and often venture into the highlands.

**Boating** In summer, small boat trips leave from the main dock by the waterfront, normally on the refurbished fishing ship the *Huni II* (m *848 4864;* ⏲ *13.00–17.00*). You can also arrange for day trips in the fjord with the local **Nökkvi sailing club** [340 B5] (*off Drottningarbraut;* ☎ *462 7488;* e *nokkvi_siglingar@nett.is; www.est.is/~siglingar*).

**Skiing** The wonderful thing about Akureyri is that within ten minutes you can be sitting on a brand-new ski lift in your skis, climbing to the top of **Mt Hlíðjarfjall**. Not only is the **Hlíðjarfjall ski station** (☎ *462 2280;* e *hlidjarfjall@hlidjarfjall.is; www.hlidjarfjall.is*) close, the skiing is open for much of the year, weather permitting (⏲ *spring & autumn 13.00–19.00 Mon/Wed, 13.00–21.00 Tue/Fri, 13.00–17.00 Sat/Sun, winter 14.00–19.00 daily*). A dozen trails are all quite low (around 1,000m) but there's always snow because you're actually skiing on two tiny specks of glacier. Lift tickets run to about US$20 a day; the on-site equipment rentals cost more. A 'skibus' runs back and forth from the tourist information office in Akureyri; otherwise take the road that goes past the swimming pool.

**Ice skating** By the airport (*Naustavegur 1;* ☎ *461 2440;* ⏲ *10.00–19.00 daily*).

**Beer** If you head up to Oddeyri and the port, you can smell the local brewery that makes Viking Beer (*Vífilfell; Furuvellir 18;* ☎ *462 1444;* e *info@vifilfell.is; www.vifilfell.is*). Tours are available, although these are typically arranged for larger groups. The going rate for a pint of beer in Iceland is 800ISK.

## Museums

***Akureyri Museum*** [334 B2] (*Minjasafnið; Aðalstræti 58; www.akmus.is;* ☎ *462 4162;* 🕒 *summer 1 Jun–15 Sep 10.00–17.00 daily, winter 16 Sep–31 May 14.00–16.00 Sat only; entrance 450ISK/concessions 250ISK*) Definitely one of the town's highlights, 'the museum' is housed in a unique home on the upward slope of Innbær. The merchant Baldvin Ryel built the Villa Kirkjuhvoll in 1934 and the wonderful design is a site to behold. The permanent exhibit in the basement offers a folksy rendition of the history of both Akureyri and Eyjafjörður. This starts with the geological background, saga references and the contents of a local Viking burial mound. A chronological exhibit continues, with archaeological finds of Gásir, the founding of the town, and a mocked-up 19th-century Akureyri street (including the standard-issue turf dwelling). It's great for children who can go in and out of all the various shops, most of which once belonged to Akureyri citizens. The exhibit also pays great attention to the town's architecture, detailing the individual stories of so many homes and businesses. The main floor holds the temporary exhibits, which are always highly creative and provide a fascinating slice of insight into local culture.

***Nonnahús*** [334 C2] (*Aðalstræti 54;* ☎ *462 3555;* e *nonni@nonni.is; www.nonni.is;* 🕒 *Jun–Sep 10.00–17.00 daily; entrance 300ISK*) The childhood home of children's author Jón Sveinsson sits at the end of Aðalstræti, next to the town museum and Svalbard church. The small black wooden house was built in 1850 and now commemorates the life and literature of Akureyri's most famous resident. On the first floor you'll find a monumental display of Nonni books in dozens of different languages, along with large illustrated prints and Nonni's personal effects (vestments, crucifix, clothes chest, and desk). The upstairs favours very short people, but still offers a peek into the lifestyle of mid 19th-century Iceland, as well as the very bedroom where young Nonni once slept.

**Note:** visitors may purchase a combined ticket for Nonnahús and the Akureyri Museum for a discount.

***Sigurhæðir*** (*Hafnarstræti;* ☎ *466 2609;* ☎ *466 2609;* e *skald@nett.is;* 🕒 *open to the public Jun–Aug 15.00–17.00 daily; entrance 700ISK*) The final home of national poet Matthías Jochumsson, who wrote the lyrics to Iceland's national anthem (see page 35). It was built in 1903 and now houses a cultural centre, literary library, and the offices of creative writing fellows. For tourists, the outside holds the same attraction as the inside.

***Aviation Museum*** [334 A3] (*Flugsafn Íslands; Akureyri Airport;* m *863 2835;* e *flugsafn@flugsafn.is; www.flugsafn.is;* 🕒 *1 Jun–31 Aug 14.00–17.00 daily, 1 Sep–31 May 14.00–17.00 Sat only; entrance 300ISK*) Iceland's aviation industry took off in Akureyri with the creation of Icelandair. Flights allowed quick connections among the more remote areas of the north. The museum offers a historic play-by-play of aviation's advancement in Iceland with several restored examples, including the first gliders and aircraft, the first flying ambulance, and a few mementos from World War II. A fairly small museum just south of the airport, it really just caters to more serious fans of old planes and machines.

***Industry Museum*** (*Iðnaðarsafn; Krókeyri 2;* ☎ *462 3600;* e *idnadarsafn@simnet.is;* 🕒 *1 Jun–31 Aug 13.00–17.00 daily, 1 Sep–31 May 14.00–16.00 Sat only; entrance*

## JÓN SVEINSSON (1857–1944)

Jón 'Nonni' Sveinsson was born in the nearby hamlet of Möðruvellir but moved with his family to Akureyri when he was seven years old. A few years later his father died, and at age 13 Nonni was sent away to Europe under the auspices of a wealthy French benefactor. He made it as far as Copenhagen before running away with a Gypsy caravan. He finally did make it to France where he converted to Catholicism, graduated from university and became a Jesuit priest. For over 20 years, he taught at a boys' school in Denmark, and only in his fifties did he begin to write the children's stories that would make him famous. Each 'Nonni' book recounts the madcap adventures of a young boy (named Nonni) and his close friend, who most likely represents Jón's real-life younger brother Manni (who died in his twenties). In all, Nonni wrote 12 books, with titles such as *Lost in the Arctic: the Adventures of Two Boys* (1927). Though he wrote primarily in Danish and German, Nonni books are recognised as Icelandic literature for their constant reference to Iceland in theme and plot, as well as the memories of Nonni's youth in Akureyri. Extremely popular among children for decades, the books have sold over ten million copies in more than 40 languages. Early illustrated editions are now collectors' items and a visit to the museum at Nonnahús shows just how far-reaching is the influence of 'Nonni' in the world.

*300ISK*) A walk through Akureyri's manufacturing past with all the many products that have been, and still are, produced in this town. Good for rainy days, but probably not why you came to Iceland. To get there, drive south on Drottingarbruat, turn right before the airport.

**Art in Akureyri** A fiercely independent art scene sets Akureyri apart from the everyday creativity you can find throughout the rest of Iceland. The town's artsy epicentre is **Grófargil**, a series of art museums, galleries, and studios that are housed among the abandoned industries along Kaupvangsstræti. The artists' co-operative **Gilfélagið** (*466 2609; listagil@listagil.is; www.listagil.is*) oversees the collective and manages the yearly Akureyri summer arts festival. The main attraction is the **Akureyri Art Museum** [340 D4] (*Listasafnið á Akureyri; Kaupvangsstræti 12; 462 2619 listasafn@akureyri.is; www.listasafn.akureyri.is; 12.00–17.00 Tue–Sun; entrance free*), which was opened in 1993 as the country's youngest art museum. The sheer Bauhaus façade was built as the city dairy but now houses a small but effective exhibition space for Icelandic artists, both classic and progressive. A new exhibition is unveiled every eight weeks. Next door is the Akureyri Art School, as well as the gallery **Ketilhús** [340 D4] which always has some curious little show going on. The open, outdoor spaces on Kaupvangsstræti are also used for photography shows and installations – follow the path and alleyways (or the staircase around the corner on Hafnarstræti) to catch some ingenious street art. Another interesting detour is the nearby **Museum of Icelandic Folk Art** (*Safnasafnið; Svalbarðsstrond; 461 4066; safnasafnid@simnet.is; summer 12.00–18.00 daily; entrance 600ISK*) which is in the midst of renovations, but worth checking out for its fantastical collection of local sculpture and painting. The museum is on the other side of the fjord, a good ten-minute drive from Akureyri (before the turn-off of Highway 1).

## AKUREYRI'S BIG HEART

*Nathan Evans*

When the 2008 financial crisis hit Iceland, Akureyri was mauled like the rest of the country. In an attempt to lighten the mood, the city began a campaign to transform the town with the new slogan 'Smile with your heart'. Schoolchildren wrote down thoughts from their hearts and each week a few of these are printed up in brochures that circulate through town. Each business was given a heart sticker to display in their windows and encouraged to do something with the heart theme. Bakeries cooked heart-shaped cookies. The red stoplights were all changed to be heart-shaped, and the electric company put up a blinking red heart on the mountainside across the fjord from Akureyri. Dísa Óskardóttir, who played a big part in the campaign, and also designed the heart decals (the hearts are made from forget-me-nots, in memory of better times), says: 'We are thinking of our children… and all the things that are more important than money.'

The mood is certainly lighter in Akureyri; scores of hotels and restaurants are opening, the people are optimistic and generous and in a land renowned for its friendliness, they are smiling with their hearts.

## GLERÁRDALUR

The Gléra River gorge cuts deeply into the high mountains to the southwest of Akureyri. The quick ascent from sea level (and city) to the absolutely still glacier level means a lush variety of vegetation and diverse birds. Trails follow both banks of the stream uphill to the base of the mountains, and if you want a quiet day's walking out of Akureyri, this is it. For longer treks, the Lambi mountain hut (sleeps 6) is the base camp at the end of the valley trail about 10km from Akureyri. From here you can head up several peaks, the highest of which is **Mt Kerling** (1,536m). Some trails are more innocent than others – have a good map and take crampons for glaciers.

## EYJAFJARÐARSVEIT

The long valley due south of Akureyri is some of the richest farm country in Iceland thanks to the settling of glacial sediments all along the Eyjafjarðará estuary. The valley floor is quite narrow (never wider than 7km) and every flat piece of land is cultivated for haymaking or animal grazing. Mountains sweep upwards on either side and make it all the more picturesque – hike the slopes and you quickly drop into the oblivion of the northern wilderness. A number of deep glacial valleys branch away from the main vale and for those with the stamina to venture off into any of them – or better yet, climb the nearby hills and look down over them – the most dramatic views await.

The mouth of the Eyjafjarðará estuary is now best seen from the airport and the Route 1 causeway that crosses it. Despite its urban proximity, the birdlife is excellent, and further inland, the low-lying islands and marshes are popular breeding grounds in spring and summer. You can travel up and down Eyjafjarðarsveit on either side of the river, though the road is longer and much better paved along Route 821 (left bank). Nearly every place name you pass is a farm that is mentioned in the sagas, such as Kristnes (home of Eyjafjörður's first settler Helgi the lean) and Munkathverá (birthplace of the fierce Viking Killer-Glum and where Sighvatur Sturluson is buried) (see opposite).

Fewer than 1,000 people live in the valley today, which means that very little has changed over the past ten centuries. In between the battles of the sagas, the tired heroes are always stopping here for a bath – nearby Laugaland ('Bath land') is an important geothermal source that still feeds hot water to Akureyri. **Hrafnagil** is the largest outpost in the area, founded as an ancient farm that later gained fame in the Age of the Sturlungs (see page 20). By 1258, the popularity of Thorgils the hair-lipped (emissary of King Hakon of Norway) earned the jealousies of rival families so much that after a Christmas celebration at Hrafnagil he was betrayed and bludgeoned to death in his sleep. Today, nearly every tour bus stops for a lunch here in the renovated, turf-covered **Iceland farm** (see *Where to stay*, page 354) before heading to the area's biggest tourist trap, the **Jólagarðurinn** on Route 821 (*463 1433; summer 10.00–22.00, winter 14.00–18.00*). The 'Christmas garden' was founded by a man who just happens to look a lot like Santa Claus and bears no intended connection to the famous Christmas murder 800 years ago. As if Iceland did not get enough snow, they've added some painted icicles to this Disney-esque reconstruction of the North Pole. Beneath the gaudy décor are shelves and tables filled with gaudy holiday knick-knacks that sell for high prices, along with something more traditional – food.

Besides the rich history and beautiful scenery, Eyjarfjarðasveit is home to some of the country's oldest churches, each relaying a distinct look and past. The black-and-white church at **Munkathverá** (built 1844) replaces a 12th-century monastery. **Grund** was another important hideout in Iceland's 13th-century civil war, now known for its fanciful red-and-white church (built 1905) that's topped with a unique onion-shaped steeple. **Möðruvellir** (not to be confused with the many other farms by the same name) was the home of saga hero Guðmundur the Powerful, so named for his immense wealth and for the fact that he held great sway at the Althing. The tiny country church of St Martin (built 1848) pales in comparison with the goings on of 1,000 years ago, when this was a coveted travellers' rest. The church was blown off its foundations in the 1970s but patiently rebuilt by the farmer's family, who still maintain the property. Perhaps the best preserved and most interesting to see up close is **Saurbær** (built 1858), one of six remaining turf-covered churches in Iceland. This is the one on all the postcards in Akureyri and the view from the front seems to take you back a century or two.

Just behind the church lies the quirky museum of small things, **Smámunasafn** (*Sólgarður; 461 1261; e smamunir@esveit.is; www.smamunasafnid.is; 15 May–30 Sep 13.00–18.00 Mon–Fri; entrance 500ISK*). A local carpenter, Sverrir Hermansson, collected small objects for nearly 80 years, which are now on display here. What's so wonderful about the random collection of nails, keys, hammers, gramophone needles, doorknobs, and everything else is that it all comes from Eyjafjarðarsveit. The drawers and panels packed full of tiny things says much about daily life in this particular region of Iceland, as well as revealing the Icelanders' fondness for collecting stuff.

Keep heading inland and things become a lot more rugged and remote. The farm at **Hólar** is ancient, but still working. A few of the buildings are still covered with turf and the small white church was built in 1853. Beyond Hólar, the road becomes unpaved and starts crossing rushing streams and curving upwards. Keep going and you'll end up in Laugafell (see page 436), way up in the highlands.

**WHERE TO STAY AND EAT** Most people opt to stay in Akureyri, but a night in the country of Eyjarfjarðarsveit is nice too, especially if you desire some tranquillity and easy access to the hills. There's also camping at Hrafnagil.

**Hótel Vin** (45 beds) 463 1400; e vin@est.is; www.vin.nett.is. The biggest hotel around, with dormitory-style rooms (some with private bathrooms), a heated swimming pool & hot tub, & lots of tourists. Their main attraction is the Icelandic farm (Íslandsbærinn), a recreated turf dwelling for meals & parties. They also run the campsites. **$$$**

**Leifsstaðir** (10 rooms) Eyjarfjarðarsveit; 462 1610; e leifsstadir@sveit.is; www.leifsstadir.is. Golf course & guesthouse on the right bank, south on Route 828. Rooms are big enough, with wooden floors & comfy single or double beds; many feature private bathrooms. B/fast inc. **$$$**

**Fellshlíð** (4 rooms) Eyjarfjarðarsveit; 461 2491; e fellshlid@hostel.is; www.hostel.is. A wonderful country hostel & working farm, about 25km south of Akureyri. Best for those who enjoy being in the middle of nowhere surrounded by cows & sheep. The location is quite historic, in the midst of several saga-era farms. Pack your own food. **$$**

## Í FJÖRÐUM

The east side of Eyjafjörður forms a mountainous curved peninsula that is a barren region of outstanding beauty. Very few travellers ever venture into this northern territory for the difficulty in getting around and for the limited amenities, though the truly adventurous should be racing to the spot, hiking boots and camera in hand. These empty, quiet spaces of wild coastline are incomparable to anything else in Iceland.

Heading north from Akureyri on Route 83, one arrives first at the ancient farm of **Laufás** (*463 3196; e akmus@akmus.is; www.akmus.is; 15 May–15 Sep 10.00–18.00 daily; entrance 450ISK*). The turf-covered gables you now see were panelled up in the mid 19th century, though the farm dates back to the settlement period, and pieces of the house are at least 500 years old. In its heyday, over 30 people lived and worked here. Stand beneath the earthy eaves and gain a better understanding of a few centuries of indoor living. The current church was built in 1855, the same year in which the 'ancient' rowan tree in the back was planted. The old vicarage is now a café that serves old-fashioned Icelandic lunches and coffee.

The only human civilisation around is tiny **Grenivík**, a speck of a fishing village right on Eyjafjörður at the end of Route 83 (population 300). A delightful little place, Grenivík provides travellers with the basics before they head off on some great expedition northwards. A popular climb ascends any number of trails to the top of **Mt Kaldbakur** (1,167m) from which you get a wondrous view of the peninsula, Eyjafjörður, and Hrísey Island. The slightly taller **Mt Blámannshattur** (1,201m) is a more difficult climb because it is quite steep in places with lots of loose rock at the top.

North of Grenivík lies **Látraströnd**, a 20-odd kilometre stretch of steep coastline with an angled slope that drops right into the fjord. The name (*látra* = 'litter'; *strönd* = 'coast') denotes a place where seals and whales come to give birth to their young, which is still a fitting title in the late spring. On a fair day you can see the island of Grímsey from the northernmost point at **Gjögur**, and to the west lie the open cove-size fjords that give Í Fjörðum its name. Big, dramatic peaks slope down to an abrupt edge, and waterfalls tumble over the edge of cliffs and into the open sea. Once upon a time, a few stalwart farmers managed homesteads up here, but they finally gave up after World War II because access by sea or land was never guaranteed. The same was true for the remote offshore island of **Flatey**, inhabited up until the 1960s and now a private summer property. The island is short, stocky and flat (only 22m high), but covered with birds in summer. There is no public access to the island, but day excursions sail from Húsavík (see page 377). A pair of rough-and-tumble 4x4 trails trace the two valley beds from the main road at Grenivík, but water levels and/or snow can impede access. This is exactly why the area is deathly quiet and such a popular place for hardcore hikers. The most popular trek originates in Grenivík, follows the coast to the lighthouse Gjögurtá around Fjörðum to Bjarnarfell (from which you can make the bumpy 4x4 return drive). For most, that's a three–four-day leisure hike with some truly marvellous moments. Other treks in can divert to a number of trails that head inland to explore the pristine valleys and untouched peaks.

There's no question that this is a wild, magical place. Given the total isolation and sheer coastline, it is also quite dangerous. Steep cliffs, sudden drop-offs, and high winds demand that no journey be undertaken without proper planning and the right equipment. Bring your own tent, carry enough food (there are plenty of freshwater streams), and let others know where you are going and when you expect to return. Also, pay close attention to weather reports and when crossing streams. Emergency huts are spaced out along the northern shore.

**TOURIST INFORMATION AND TOUR OPERATORS** Several national and area tour groups will offer adventure treks in Í Fjörðum. In Grenivík, the company **Fjörðungar** (*Túngata 3; ☎ 463 3236; www.fjordungar.com*) knows the area best, specialising in short and long treks, horseback rides, cruises in the fjord and occasional whale-watching trips. **Kaldbaksferðir** (*☎ 463 3172; e info@kaldbaksferdir.com; www.kaldbaksferdir.com*) offers snowmobile tours up to the top of Mt Kaldbakur, along with skiing and sledding.

**WHERE TO STAY AND EAT** In Grenivík, **Jónsabuð** (*'John's shop'; Túngata 3; ☎ 463 3236*) fills the role of food shop/post office/tourist information bureau. The guesthouse **Miðgarðar** (*9 rooms; Miðgarðar 4; ☎ 463 3223;* **$$**) offers comfortable dormitory-style accommodation in town, a café with lacy tablecloths for meals, becoming the local bar after 21.00. There's also a swimming pool and **campsite** next to the school (*☎ 463 3218; e itrottamidstod@grenivik.is; tents 800ISK*). Closer to Akureyri (5km outside Grenivík) sits the farm **Hléskogar** (*6 rooms; ☎ 463 3112; e hleskogar@hleskogar.is; www.hleskogar.is;* **$$**). Open year-round, rooms are basic but clean, and the surrounding hills very inviting. They also offer horseriding tours and instruction.

## GRÍMSEY

The tiny isle of Grímsey is an utterly pure and separate world from the rest of Iceland, 40km (24.5 miles) off the northern coast. As the country's remotest (inhabited) offshore island, Grímsey grants the traveller the gift of isolation and windswept beauty. On one side, a mighty wall of basalt cliffs stands firm against the open sea – from these great heights the island descends in a slope of green lumpy fields to the opposite shore with its lowly coves and harbour. The island is pleasantly small (5.3km$^2$ or 2 square miles), like a punctuation mark for the whole of Iceland. Besides a handful of resolute islanders and a few million seabirds, there are only rocks, grass, the wind and the sea.

Just being on Grímsey feels like stepping off the edge of the earth. The next stop north is the North Pole and when the sky is clear, locals point south to 'Iceland': the jagged line of grey-ish mountains that stretch from Skagafjörður to Melrakkasletta. Exposed as it is, Grímsey gets hit with the full force of Iceland's terrific weather. Things are always a bit blustery, the fog rolls in and out and then the wind picks up. There's sudden rain, sleet, hail, or snow – huge waves crash on all sides and then, total

## THE ARCTIC CIRCLE: NORÐURHEIMSKAUTSBAUGUR

You might feel like an Arctic explorer in Iceland but that doesn't change the fact that only the most frightfully minuscule piece of Iceland actually lies above the Arctic Circle. For all the excitement of travelling to the top of the world, less than one mile (1.6km) of the Arctic Circle ever crosses the country – here at the northern end of Grímsey. The imaginary line is a wonderful tourist attraction for those of us who like to say we crossed it, but did we really?

How convenient that the Arctic Circle monument (and the circle itself) should be right next to the baggage claim of Grímsey Airport! The metal staircase lets you walk up one side and pause right over the metal pipe marking the polar circle before stepping back down onto the 'Arctic' side. Painted wooden arrows point to faraway London, Reykjavík, and New York, and a locked coin box asks that you tip for the privilege of a quick and easy photo op. Follow the protocol and you'll get a certificate of achievement for crossing the Arctic Circle. It's a nice souvenir, but don't rush home and frame it.

Getting technical, the monument cannot coincide with the actual Arctic Circle because the circle is never fixed. The real location of the polar latitude depends on the angle of axis on which the earth rotates, an angle that changes because the earth wobbles. On the ground, the shifting tilt of the earth's axis equals a fluctuation of about nine latitudinal seconds (about 300m). Right now on Grímsey, the Arctic Circle is moving slightly north (around 15m per year) although that distance will correct itself over a short-term cycle of 18.6 years. The actual astronomy gets far more complex, but this explains why the line is always drawn in different places on different maps. What is certain is that the Arctic Circle does indeed cross the island of Grímsey, most likely at some point on the airport's runway. If you want to be absolutely certain that you've crossed the line, then walk all the way up to Básavík. A less scientific approach to finding the exact point is to arrive in Grímsey on 21 June and walk backwards at midnight (wear sunglasses). The second that any portion of the sun disappears from view, you've just crossed the Arctic Circle.

A local island legend (with a few-dozen variations) places a house and its master bedroom right on the Arctic Circle, with the actual line bisecting the marriage bed. Insert a punch line about the cold side of the bed and then run with the joke.

silence. On those days, Grímsey feels like the most peaceful place on earth. On other days, watching the sky is sheer entertainment. Grímsey is also one of the few spots in Iceland where you can see the entire 'midnight sun' above the horizon, and in winter's months of darkness the Northern Lights streak a bright blue, green and red.

One cannot help but feel a fascination for those who live their lives in such seclusion. The entire listing for Grímsey fills up just half a page in the national phone book. Ask any islander how many people live here and they'll give you an exact number for that day – the population fluctuates above and below 100 depending on the school season and which fishing boats are out at sea. Some 50 sheep and 20 horses live here too, but absolutely no cats or dogs (the birds prefer it that way). First and foremost, the island is a fishing community. The 20-odd boats that you see in the harbour catch around 3,000 tons of fish per year, all of which get processed in the island's own plant – you can find boxes of Grímsey salted cod almost anywhere in the world.

Tourism to the island has recently become a significant source of cash, though it's mostly in the form of day trippers eager for an Arctic Circle certificate. Indeed, the Arctic Circle does cross Grímsey, but that is such a small part of what makes this island such a unique destination. Few travellers ever make it out here, and only the very lucky get to stay for any length of time. A half-day trip by plane or ferry does give a taste of freedom, after which most rush back to civilisation and a tight tourist agenda. For anyone else – for those who love birds, who embrace solitude, and who seek close encounters with the elements – Grímsey demands a lingering stay.

**HISTORY** The small islands of Iceland have always been coveted property for their abundant birdlife and fish stocks. Grímsey is no exception, and from the beginning, explorers and settlers have been drawn to the riches of such an isolated spot. Grímsey translates as 'Grímur's isle', and although you'll find a number of Grímseys across the Nordic world, this one is named after Grímur Sigurdsson (in Old Icelandic, *Grímur* means 'masked man'). The Viking lived in the West Fjords sometime in the 10th century and was the first to talk openly of the island. His tales proved tempting – in 1024, the King of Norway Ólafur Haraldsson (St Ólaf) tried to convince the Althing to give him Grímsey as a token of friendship. Only one Einar Thveræingur (a farmer from Eyjafjarðarsveit) spoke out against the king's request, arguing that although this particular king was good, to give in to his request would begin a tradition of bondage to future, less benevolent foreign monarchs. Thus Grímsey remained independent, later becoming the offshore haven of medieval Iceland. In 1222, after murdering the member of a rival clan in Skagafjörður, Bishop Guðmundur Arason escaped to Grímsey, only to be captured and sent to Norway for trial. Around the same time, a permanent settlement evolved on the island, including a church and small monastery.

Life has never been too easy here. The weather and isolation offset the island's riches, and those who live here must be totally self-sufficient. Traditionally, the islanders have made a fairly good living by fishing and collecting the birds and bird eggs from the cliffs. Every spring (to this day), a few brave souls are lowered over the edges of Miðgarðabjarg where they collect thousands of eggs. In the past, getting the valuable product to market proved the difficult part – the 40km trip in an open boat was always unpredictable and perilous. At the end of the 18th century, nearly all the men of Grímsey succumbed to a deadly smallpox epidemic. The six survivors sailed to the mainland in the hope of replenishing the island's population but their boat capsized and all were drowned.

New men arrived and since the early 19th century, Grímsey has been divided into 11 properties shared by 11 families. Some reshuffling has occurred since, but there is a general understanding on the island about which land belongs to whom and how it is to be used. Most of the island is inter-related, but the common practice is to lure a spouse from the mainland. To this day, the island council governs all island affairs and all major decisions are decided by vote. In that way, Grímsey's isolation has granted the islanders an edge. They are both democratic and self-sufficient, and unlike the rest of rural Iceland, Grímsey has a cosmopolitan side. In the past, whenever storms were brewing, fishing fleets from all over the world sought refuge in Grímsey harbour. The present-day tradition for hospitality stems from centuries of taking care of travellers, both intentional and stranded.

**GETTING THERE AND AWAY** Grímsey is not good for tight schedules. The uncertainty of getting on and off the island is exactly why this island is such a

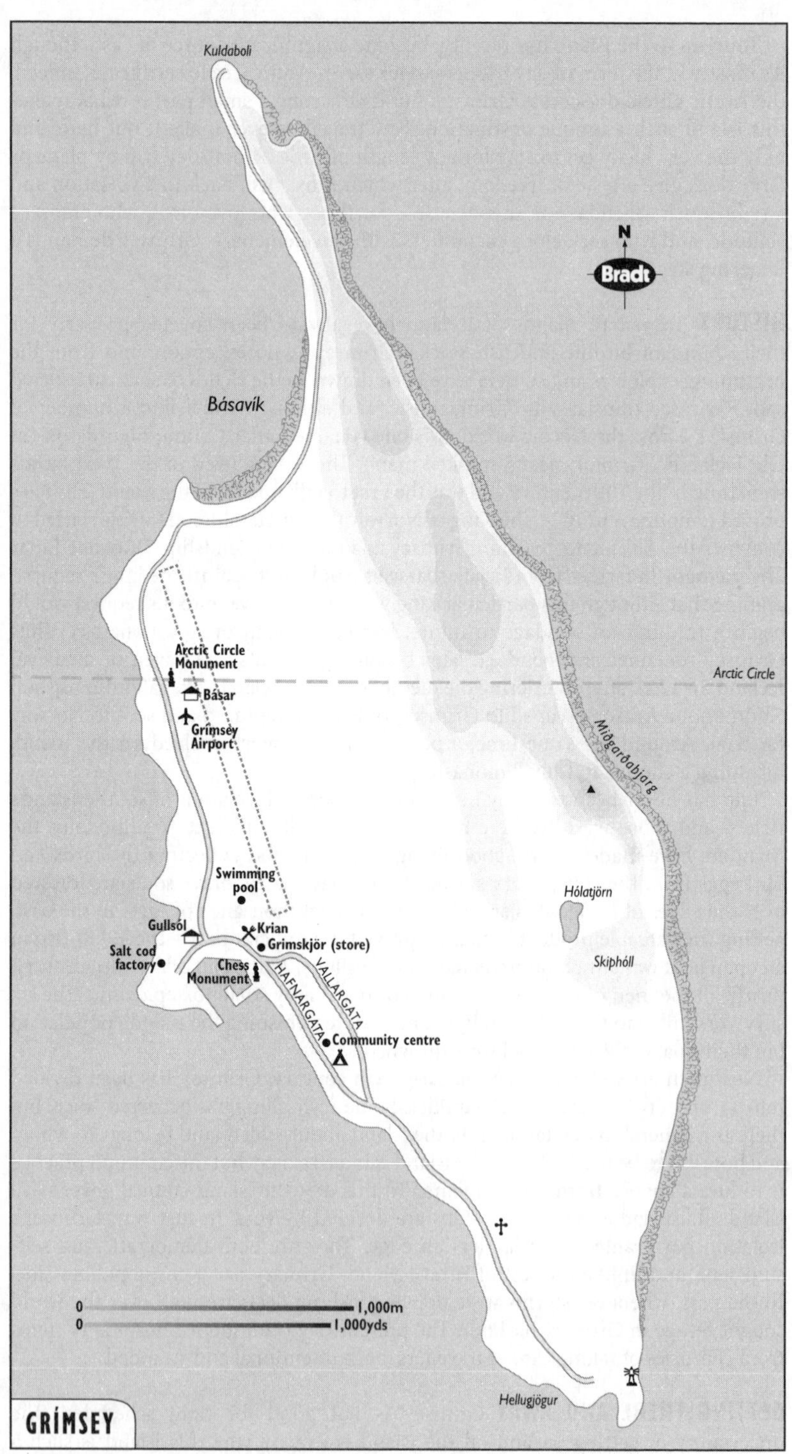
Kuldaboli
N
Bradt
Básavík
Arctic Circle Monument
Básar
Grímsey Airport
Arctic Circle
Miðgarðabjarg
Swimming pool
Hólatjörn
Gullsól
Krian
Grimskjör (store)
Salt cod factory
Chess Monument
HAFNARGATA
VALLARGATA
Skiphóll
Community centre
0
1,000m
0
1,000yds
Hellugjögur
GRÍMSEY

special place. Yes, flights and ferries are scheduled to be frequent and regular but everything depends on the severe mood swings of island weather. A slight fog or wind is enough to cancel a trip for the day – when you see the tiny island from the air, it makes perfect sense that a sane pilot would not want to try to land a plane in the haze.

**By air** The flight between Grímsey and Akureyri is a magnificent experience and the plane small enough for everyone to get a window seat from every angle. The whole trip takes less than 20 minutes, but passes over the spectacular mountains of Látraströnd, then across the empty sea before dropping into the middle of an empty sea and landing on the strip of rock and grass. In summer, the runway is white with birds (mostly terns and gulls) and the aircraft controller must drive up and down the runway to clear them all away.

**Air Iceland** (*www.airiceland.is*) offers regular flights to Grímsey from Akureyri: every day in summer and three times a week in winter. Prices vary, but a good deal is about US$100 return. Buy tickets online, at Akureyri Airport or at the one-room Grímsey Airport (GRY). In summer (10 June–20 August), Air Iceland offers a package tour from Akureyri to Grímsey. The two-hour trip includes return flights to the island, a quick run up and down the only road, and just enough time to wish that you were staying longer (around US$200). The charter airline **Mýflug Air** (*www.myflug.is*) can also be hired for flights to Grímsey from either Mývatn or Akureyri.

**By sea** The boat to Grímsey is less influenced by the weather, which makes it a more reliable (albeit slower) method of getting out to the island. All year round, the **Sæferi** ferry (*Dalvík, Ránarbruat 2b; ☎ 458 8970; e jonarnar@samskip.is; www.landflutningar.is/saefari_ferry_english*) runs back and forth between Dalvík and Grímsey three times a week (Monday, Wednesday, and Friday); the cost of this trip is around US$50 return. Sæfari. The journey takes about 3½ hours each way and passes through the whole length of Eyjafjörður. Buy tickets online, in Dalvík, at the port in Grímsey (*☎ 467 3110*) or in Akureyri at the shipping office (*Tryggvabraut 5; ☎ 458 8900*) or the local travel agency, **Nonni Travel** (*Brekkugata 3; ☎ 461 1841; e nonni@nonnitravel.is; www.nonnitravel.is*).

It is possible to buy a ticket in Akureyri that includes a chauffeured bus up to Dalvík to get on the ferry (arriving one hour before departure). Usually, the boat leaves Dalvík in the morning, arriving at Grímsey around lunchtime. The boat stays in Grímsey harbour for three–four hours before heading back to Dalvík for an evening arrival. If you want more than the three hours allotted, it is quite possible to take the ferry to Grímsey and fly back, or vice versa.

**GETTING AROUND** There are only a few streets on Grímsey, and only one road that follows the western coast of the island. The majority of the islanders have cars and use them to run up and down the 4km stretch of road, but visitors usually have to walk or hitch a ride to get around. When the ferry is in dock, there's normally a small bus or van that takes visitors down to the southern end of the island and the lighthouse.

Taking a boat trip around the island is the very best way to capture the glory of the bird cliffs. You can make informal arrangements with a local fisherman who will charge you a fair price calculated on his time (1 hour) and the necessary fuel. As with everything on this island, contact **Binni** (e *binni@grimsey.is*) for further information.

## WHERE TO STAY

**Básar** (5 rooms) ☎ 467 3103; e sigrun@konica.is; ⌚ 15 May–31 Aug. Right next to the airport, Básar is a private home that caters to the pre-arranged group tours that zip in & out in the summer. The location is not optimal as you are quite isolated from the rest of the village & its amenities. **$$$**

**Gullsól** (8 rooms) ☎ 467 3190; e binni@grimsey.is; www.grimsey.is. 'The Guesthouse' is open year-round & houses most visitors who arrive on Grímsey. The wooden building is one of the oldest on the island (from 1928), now shielded in aluminium plates to protect it from the constant salt spray of the harbour. Inside, the rooms are quaint, cosy & warm, with a nifty trapdoor to the upstairs. Bathrooms are shared & there's a sunny kitchen where you can prepare your own food. **$$**

For larger groups, sleeping-bag accommodation and food can be arranged (in advance) at the **community centre** (*Kvenfélagið Baugur;* ☎ *467 3115*). The **campsite** is behind the community centre/school so as to protect you from the wind. For that reason, wild camping elsewhere on the island is discouraged. Camping is free, but you must have a tent and there is only an outdoor sink and toilets for your use. Be courteous to the islanders, keep quiet and don't litter. If the weather worsens, you might find yourself knocking on their door for shelter.

**WHERE TO EAT** The island's only restaurant and pub is **Krian** (*Hafnargata 3;* ☎ *467 3112;* e *binni@grimsey.is; www.grimsey.is;* ⌚ *18.00–midnight daily, summer 12.00–midnight when the ferry comes;* **$$**). The fare is pretty standard (baconburgers and fries) with a few island specials like fresh cod or pan-fried puffin. Otherwise, you can find practically anything on the well-stocked shelves of Grímskjör. It is also possible to arrange breakfast in a private home, normally for a comparable charge; just ask.

**OTHER PRACTICALITIES** Grímsey is a very small and isolated place, blissfully free of the tawdry developments that tourism can bring. Once you've landed, the distinction between traveller and host is often blurred. One cannot emphasise enough the need to tread lightly and keep Grímsey the very special place that it is. For general information and questions, check the island website (*www.grimsey.is*). Otherwise, keep in mind that you are travelling to a very remote island with certain limitations.

The island's one and only real store is **Grimskjör** (*Hafnargata 3;* ☎ *467 3110;* ⌚ *10.00–12.30 & 14.00–17.00 Mon–Fri*). It's truly amazing how much the shop carries, and this is the one place where the public can access the internet. There are no pay phones on the island, but you can purchase phonecards at the store and use them from one of the islanders' private home phones. The island **'bank'** is the kitchen inside a private home at Vallargata 11 (☎ *467 3148*). Visitors may draw cash from a debit card or change foreign currency. A doctor visits the island only once every three weeks. All other medical emergencies are flown to the mainland on the 'ambulance plane'.

The school house and library are part of the community centre, the de facto venue for gatherings and celebrations. The only place to buy locally made souvenirs is at **Gallery Sól** beneath the guesthouse Gullsól (☎ *467 3190;* ⌚ *with the ferry landing 12.30–16.00 Mon, Wed & Fri*). The shop is owned and managed by the island's women's co-operative who make many of the things sold there: T-shirts, Grímsey postcards, maps, woollen socks and framed pictures. They also run a small café that serves coffee, tea, hot chocolate, sandwiches and delicious waffles (made with eggs collected from the island).

**Safety** A lack of crime means there are no police stationed on Grímsey. Rather, one contends with nature: the wind can be very strong, the water freezing, and colossal island waves are known to rise up and out of nowhere. For that reason, use caution along any shoreline. By island law, all children under the age of 14 must wear a lifejacket when in the harbour area (note the posted signs), even if they are simply walking or playing on land. Be careful when walking along the edge of cliffs, especially the high ledges along the east side – the uneven turf and puffin holes can make walking precarious and it's a deadly drop to the rocky bottom. Elsewhere on the island, be careful where you choose to descend. Several shallow inlets and coves appear easily accessible from the top (and they are), but getting back out can be impossible. Changing tides, sudden storms and fog will impede your exit. Be smart.

**WHAT TO SEE AND DO** The southern end of the island descends in a chain of broken rocks and skerries, and it's a good place to (safely) watch the furious sea. The fluorescent-orange **Grímsey lighthouse** sits square and squat at the edge of the southernmost cliff, built in 1937 and still functioning in winter. On a clear day, the view of the mainland from the lighthouse deck is magnificent. Moving up the road takes you past several old farms up to **Grímseyarkirkja**. The island church was built in 1867 out of driftwood, replacing a turf church dating from 1254. The white -and-red exterior is classic for Iceland, as is the cerulean roof and gold stars indoors. The church is usually open (sign the guestbook). The schoolhouse and **community centre** is further up, also housing the city library and the island museum.

Most of the 'town' is in the middle of the island next to the harbour. Vallargata is the residential street that looks incredibly suburban; Hafnargata is the street by the **harbour**. There's always something going on by the water, and it can be interesting to watch the fishermen unloading their catch, typically in the afternoon. The large building on the hill above the harbour is the island's **salt cod factory** where the fish is cleaned, salted, and packed for shipment. Someone's always working here, but you can normally take a peek or else arrange for an informal tour (it smells awful). Past the town and up the road are the airport and the **Arctic Circle monument**, complete with the photogenic 'Grímsey' sign. Cross the imaginary line and pick up your certificate at the local airport or from the ferry administrator. Beyond the human elements, Grímsey is ripe for exploring. The most rewarding sites involve birds and the dramatic coastline.

**Walking** Several dirt roads and paths criss-cross the island, and smaller sheep trails connect these. Be careful as the lumpy turf on Grímsey is a recipe for a twisted ankle – the best way to get around is to hop from tuft to tuft. Also, look out for puffin holes (don't trip) and in spring, bird eggs.

A common walk follows the length of the island from its southernmost point at the lighthouse up to the northernmost end (about 5.5km). The panorama from the northern point is a sight to behold, taking in the whole island with the sea on both sides and the marked slope of the landscape. Walking along the cliffs on the east side is a little more difficult, given there is no definite path that follows the entire length. The birds are worth the effort though.

Overall, it's pretty much impossible to get lost on Grímsey, but keep in mind that the island is wider than it looks. Skiphóll, or 'ship hill', is the small knoll in the middle that does indeed look like an overturned ship's hull, right next to the still pond Hólatjörn.

**Rocks** Grímsey is the remaining shard of volcanic rim on this, the rumbling Mid-Atlantic Ridge that extends northwards from Mývatn area. In the last ice age, glaciers pushed the island deeper into the sea, which explains why the island is so small and why you can find sedimentary rock (sandstone) right next to the basalt – the island comprises two geological pieces. At the southern end of the island, the cliffs have been eroded from underneath, leaving a ledge of hanging basalt

## DANIEL WILLARD FISKE (1831–1904): THE CHESS PLAYER

Grímsey islanders have a reputation as cunning players in the game of chess, or *skák* in Icelandic. Dark winters and total isolation may have something to do with it, but it is true that historically, chess has been a major pastime. One popular legend speaks of the islanders taking chess so seriously that the loser of the game throws himself over the high cliffs at Miðgarðabjarg, although if it really did happen, the incident was singular and the loser otherwise deranged. The main point is that chess is key to Grímsey's identity.

That fact was brought to the attention of one travelling professor, Daniel Willard Fiske, who saw the rocks of Grímsey from the deck of his ship. Born in New England, Fiske left school early 'to travel' and ended up in Germany and Denmark, where he learned to speak German, Danish, and Icelandic. He showed a keen interest in Icelandic literature and read as much as he could on Iceland in the libraries of Copenhagen. He then moved to Sweden, picked up Swedish and became a professor of British and American history at the University of Uppsala. He also learned to speak French, Italian, Russian and Persian, before returning to become a professor at the newly founded Cornell University in Ithaca, New York. A true 'Renaissance man', Mr Fiske has been called many things – a geographer, journalist, linguist, and librarian – but he was also an avid chess player who belonged to several prominent chess clubs and edited an American chess journal. Only in 1879 did he finally make it to Iceland, and when he heard of Grímsey and their love of chess, he felt compassion for their isolated lifestyle.

The following year, Fiske married the millionaire heiress Jennie McGraw, who died of consumption within a year of their wedding. Having inherited a fortune, he spent the rest of his life travelling and buying up books and precious manuscripts (the bulk of which is now known as the Fiske Collection at Cornell University). Although he never set foot on Grímsey, he left the islanders a sum of US$12,000 for a library along with a few thousand books to fill the shelves. His generous gift also included 12 marble chessboards – one for each family on the island plus one extra. A single remaining board is still kept in a locked cabinet at the community centre (along with another board signed by Bobby Fischer and Boris Spassky from the 'Match of the Century' held in Reykjavík in 1972).

Needless to say, the islanders were touched by the stranger's concern and generosity. Today, the birthday of Daniel Fiske (11 November) is Grímsey's 'national' celebration, when school is let out and there's a big party at the community centre. You will also notice a monument to the man next to the flagpole above the harbour. Right next to it sits a permanent stone table with a chess set and two stools. Chess is still an important pastime and is taught as an obligatory course at Grímsey school. If you happen to be wonderful at chess, don't swagger too much. Some six year-old might tell you *mát* (checkmate).

columns. Another mystical little spot is the cove at **Hellugjögur**, on the island's lower southwest corner. Here, the columnar basalt has broken away from the top in pieces, creating a series of hexagonal steps down to the sea. The honeycomb rock beach is a beautiful and quiet little place; it's also fairly easy to climb around.

The long line of cliffs on Grímsey's east side rise straight up from the sea to staggering heights. **Miðgarðabjarg** is the longest and tallest cliff and Vænghóll is the tallest point on the island at 105m, although the cliffs at the northern end are more accessible and visible. From above or below, **Básavík** is the largest bay on the island (above the airport). The trail circles around the top and up to the northern cliffs, allowing a grand view of the sandy beach and all the lively bird colonies. If tempted to climb down into the cove, don't – this is one place that's safer from up high. The northernmost tip of Grímsey drops off in a cliff known as **Kuldabolí**, a rock face that looks like the profile of an old man with a crooked, frosty nose. A legend tells of a troll caught in the glare of the midnight sun, but the likeness can only be seen from a boat.

**Wildlife** The wildest life on Grímsey takes the form of a few million birds that make the island a summer home. There are no cats, dogs, rats, or mice (every year the island council takes a vote to maintain the status quo and protect the birds) – though children are allowed pet rabbits kept in cages. Once upon a time, Grímsey was a paradise for seals, but over the years they've learnt to keep away from the islanders. The whales are still learning, and it is quite possible to see them from the shore, spouting in the air, arching their backs or splashing their tails (minke are commonly seen). In an oft-remembered and oft-recounted incident, a young boy herding sheep on Grímsey spotted a polar bear in 1969. At first he thought it was a lost white horse, but quickly discovered otherwise and ran away. Nearly every man on Grímsey fired a shot and the stuffed bear skin is now on display at the museum at Húsavík (see page 380). It was suspected that the bear had drifted over to Grímsey on an ice floe from Greenland.

**Birds** Birds own the whole of Grímsey, but they allow a limited number of humans to squat as long as you stay out of their way. What sets the island apart from other birding spots is how severely outnumbered you are – the huge crowd of birds can be delightfully overwhelming, and you are always surrounded. In winter, the eider ducks tend to stick around, as do one pair of ravens and a lot of cute little snow buntings. The spring and certainly the summer are the best for catching the full glory of Grímsey with all of the squawks, squeaks, chirps and cries. March and April see a fair number of arrivals every day; in June Grímsey becomes a throbbing nursery.

By far the best thing to do on the island is to plant yourself at some decent vantage point with a good view of a bird cliff. Bring a decent pair of binoculars and enjoy the non-stop show, be it guillemots feeding their confused babies or puffins dive bombing for fish. The bird cliffs of Grímsey's east side are the most densely populated, but they are also fairly high and quite steep. A few spots curve inwards to allow you a better view, namely at the northeast end of the island. Up here, when the wind blows from the east, you can see the puffins gliding motionless against the updraft. The photogenic pose is totally uncharacteristic for a bird that flaps its wings so furiously.

All the puffins disappear together on one night, typically between 15 and 20 August.

Besides the ubiquitous puffin, Grímsey is home to the rest of Iceland's auk family, including the black, common, and Brünnich's guillemot, as well as a healthy number of razorbill. A few pairs of the rare little auk (*Alle alle*) have been known to appear on Grímsey in winter, although they have not been spotted here for a few years now.

The Arctic terns dominate the flat areas along the runway but can attack you almost anywhere. Grímsey is also the earliest recorded fulmar colony in the world, and the gulls and kittiwakes abound on all sides. The fishermen often look to the gulls to find the fish, dropping their hooks where the birds are diving. Don't be afraid to tap into the locals' amazing knowledge about the birds that live here. They are just as passionate about the different species and their latest antics. Simply ask, and you will probably learn something new, or get pointed to a spot that you may have missed otherwise.

**Plants** Look for scurvy grass (see page 106) as there is plenty that grows all over the island, still picked and chewed by fishermen. In spring, the indented valleys in the island's middle blossom into a million little yellow flowers, which are mostly buttercups and dandelions. Closer to the shoreline you will find a lot more colour, including the little blue stars of the forget-me-not. Grímsey is also a great place to inspect the seaweed up close, with lots of Irish moss, the purple-brown dulse, and rockweed.

**Swimming** The pool is the slant-roofed building before the airport (*467 3155; 14.00–17.00 3 times a week*). The rule on the island is that if more than three people want to go swimming, they'll open up the pool.

## KOLBEINSEY

The northernmost tip of Iceland's mainland is at Melrakkasletta (see page 389) and the island of Grímsey is one step closer to the Arctic. Technically though, the northernmost point of Iceland is the faraway island of Kolbeinsey, a broken slap of basalt that sits slightly higher than the crashing waves of the Arctic Ocean. The rocks lie 107km off the coast of the mainland (75km from Grímsey) and are inhabited solely by birds, mainly fulmars.

Kolbeinsey is first mentioned in the opening paragraphs of the settlement saga *Landnámabók* where it is said to be one day's sailing from Greenland. The Svarfdæla saga reports how the political games of the Sturlung era (13th century) caused the man Kolbeinn Sigmundarson to be so disgusted as to sail out to sea and be shipwrecked on the rocks north of Grímsey. Since then, 'Kolbein's isle' has gained a mythical status, improved over time by the vague reports of fishermen and lost sailors. In 1580, Bishop Guðbrandur Thorláksson (see page 325) of Bible fame – but also a keen cartographer – hired three brothers (Brjarni, Einar, and Jón Tómasson) to find the islands. They sailed for two days before spotting the white streaks of bird guano on the rocky peak through the fog. Overcome by the abundance of birds and seals for the taking, the brothers were almost stranded when their boat drifted away, then drifted back. After a week, the three men returned to the mainland with over 1,000 birds and reports that Kolbeinsey was 'buried in eider down'. To Icelandic ears, that sounded like the 'streets are paved with gold' and adventurous souls have been attempting voyages ever since.

Born from volcanic activity in the ice age, the island is breaking apart from the constant wave erosion, ice floes, little earthquakes and underwater geothermal eruptions. In the 16th century, the Tómasson brothers measured Kolbeinsey to be 400 fathoms long and 60 fathoms high (about 700m by 90m high). Some 300 years later, French sailors reported an island of only 500m and after another 100 years (in 1970) Kolbeinsey was only 40m long by 5m high. By that time, the riches gathered on the rocks paled in comparison with the riches promised by the rocks just being there – as the starting measure for Iceland's coastal baseline, Kolbeinsey greatly extends the country's Exclusive Economic Zone (EEZ) for control of fishing rights. Eager to keep the island on the map, Iceland enlisted the help of the American air force who in 1989 poured a concrete landing pad for helicopters. The attempt was short-lived, as the whole thing simply washed away in a storm in 2006. Today, it's less of an island and more of a skerry, with the largest remaining rock less than 10m across and 4m high. Most geologists predict that Kolbeinsey will disappear completely by 2020.

The only way to get to Kolbeinsey is on your own boat or by hitching a ride with any of the local fishermen (who still swear by the rich cod stocks). For the curious, the island's official GPS co-ordinates are 67°08'09"N, 18°40'08"W. Obviously, no-one should attempt to land on the rocks – history has shown this to be a very bad idea.

## THINGEYJARSVEIT

The region between Eyjafjörður and Mývatn is known as Thingeyjarsveit, characterised by the long and wide Skjálfandafljót River, the low valley Aðaldalur and the beautiful Skjálfandi Bay in the north. It is a pretty and peaceful bit of Icelandic farmland, undisturbed and largely unvisited with the exception of the waterfalls at Goðafoss. Here the Sprengisandur highland route (see page 435) joins up with Route 1.

## GOÐAFOSS

The wide white waterfalls of Goðafoss come as a bit of a surprise, even if you can see the mist rising from a distance. In the midst of the flat, rocky landscape, a gorge of columnar basalt suddenly opens up, causing the Skjálfandafljót River to tumble in a loud rush. The semicircular falls are not only impressive for their height (only 12m), but also for their width (over 30m) and the massive volume of clear water that shoots from the edge.

The main bridge of Route 1 is the only place to cross the gorge, but hiking trails follow upstream on either side. Most of the gorge features the very straight basalt columns seen throughout Iceland, but the closer you get to the falls, the more weird and twisted they become. Rough pumice stones surround both sides and allow plenty of nice spots to sit and observe the powerful spectacle.

The falls take their name from a momentous occasion in Icelandic history, when in AD1000, the Althing debated the virtues of Iceland becoming a Christian nation. The lawmaker of the time was Thorgeir Thorkelsson Ljósvetningagoði (see page 19), who after a day and night of meditation decided that Iceland would adopt Christianity, but that believers in the pagan traditions could still worship their gods in private. A converted Thorgeir returned to his home in the north, and threw his pagan idols over this waterfall, hence the name 'God falls'. You can still visit the place of Thorgeir's farm at Ljósavatn, the church at the turn-off right before Goðafoss (coming from Akureyri).

### WHERE TO STAY AND EAT

**Fóssholl** (26 rooms) 464 3108; e fossholl@nett.is; www.nett.is/fossholl. This cheery yellow house is within walking distance of the falls & functions as a B&B, guesthouse, & campsite. It's also your only option near Goðafoss. Most rooms come with private shower; a few rooms must share. The hotel also features a small souvenir shop, bank, & information office. The new, separate annex of rooms in the back has been built with larger (but more expensive) rooms. **$$$**

**Restaurant Fosshóli** 464 3108; summer 07.30–22.00, winter at mealtimes only. On the first floor of the Fóssholl, complete with checked tablecloths & candles. Catering solely to tourists, the establishment sticks to basic fish & lamb tourist fare, with a few cheaper options like hamburgers & sandwiches. *Mains from 1,750ISK.* $$$

## LAUGAR

The closest village to Goðafoss is 'bath', named after the many geothermal springs in the surrounding Reykjadalur Valley. As the prime junction between Akureyri, Mývatn, and Húsavík, the town plays the role of travellers' rest stop, with a big, user-friendly hotel, a number of outlying farms and a petrol station/restaurant.

### WHERE TO STAY

**Fosshótel Laugar** (75 rooms) 464 6300; bokun@fosshotel.is; www.fosshotel.is; 1 Jun–23 Aug. In winter, Laugar is one of the largest boarding schools catering to the children of farmers in northeast Iceland. In summer, this is a popular stop for tourists in cars as they move between the natural delights of Mývatn & the whales of Húsavík. Rooms are basic but clean with varying degrees of luxury & price. Choosing a room without a shared bathroom drops the price significantly. Sleeping-bag accommodation is also available. Heated indoor pool, a functional in-house restaurant. B/fast inc. $$$

**Narfastaðir** (43 rooms) 464 3300; farmhotel@farmhotel.is; www.farmhotel.is. A rambling country hotel in the middle of Reykjadalur, with beautiful views & a great location (if you have a car) right off the main road to and from Mývatn. The restaurant & natural-fed hot-tub help the stay feel more self-contained. Most rooms have their own bathrooms; about a dozen share down the hall. Larger family-sized rooms are also available. $$$

**WHERE TO EAT** Besides the summer-only restaurant at Fosshótel (which is not bad at all) and the kitchen at the farm, the best chance for a bite to eat is at **Laugasel**, the food shop/convenience store/restaurant/petrol station in Laugar (*Laugabær; 464 2021; 10.00–22.00 Mon–Fri, 12.00–22.00 Sat, 12.00–20.00 Sun; mains from 1,300ISK;* $$). Food is pizzas, giant cheeseburgers, steak and fries.

## MÝVATN

The volcanic wonderland of Mývatn is a bright oasis at the edge of Iceland's desert highlands. Black lava fields give way to young mountains, interesting crater circles, and a flow of inland streams and lakes. The largest of these is Lake Mývatn, whose myriad pools and archipelagos are laid out with all the precision of a golf course. Yet only nature is to blame for the vivid colours and sublime contrast on offer: one hillside might be carpeted in grassy green, but the next is likely to be scorched white and dusted with yellow sulphur.

It is the famous Krafla hotspot that transforms a beautiful lake into an extraordinary landscape. The magma reservoir sits less than two miles beneath the surface – a literal bubble of volcanic activity that keeps things bubbling. Between the hot springs and mud pots the crusted ground is cracked and bulging. The most innocent outdoor stroll takes one past cones and calderas right out of a textbook. If anything, Mývatn inspires reflection about how the rest of the earth was made.

The lake of today was formed about 2,300 years ago in a routine eruption of one of the Krafla fissures. Often mistaken for a crater, Lake Mývatn is actually a very flat lava field that was dammed in around the edges by subsequent flows – that explains the vague shoreline, the size (more than 12km in length), the 40-odd islands in the

## THE MIDGES OF MÝVATN

In summertime, the 'Lake of Midges' is just that: a beautiful lake decorated by cloudy pillars of tiny, black specks. Millions of midges love Mývatn because the lake is shallow, calm, and filled with rich nutrients. They are an essential part of the ecosystem – the ducks and fish (Arctic char and brown trout) love Mývatn because the lake is filled with midges and their larvae.

The tiny insects are part of the Chironimidae family, a subgroup of gnats. The most common midge in Mývatn is *Tanytarsus gracilentus* which is non-biting (unlike their sabre-toothed cousins in Scotland). The life cycle of the midge entails four phases: eggs are laid in a gelatinous mass on the surface of the water, near the shore. Slowly, the eggs sink to the bottom of the lake, where they hatch into clear larvae called 'bloodworms' because of the bright-red colour that develops from their haemoglobin. The larvae burrow into the mud or attach themselves to the lake floor by a self-made tube and then feed off the organic matter around them. Over time the pupa evolves and swims up to the surface – in just a few hours, the adult fly (about 2mm long) crawls out of its 'shell' and takes wing.

The length of the entire cycle varies, but in summer it makes a complete round in about three weeks – an adult midge lives for less than a week. In autumn and winter the cycle takes a long pause at the larva stage and the tiny adolescent worms stay under the ice, only to be released *en masse* in spring. That's why May is such a crazy time in Mývatn – the midges emerge and so does everything that wants to eat them. Still, the midge population in Mývatn fluctuates wildly from year to year, affected by a number of factors that include weather and lake chemistry.

The best place to examine a midge up close is squashed across the front bumper of your car (or on your face if you're biking). Second best is within the buzzing columns on and around the lake. You can also find them in the water and the tiny larva are visible to the naked eye.

Luckily, the midges of Mývatn do not bite, choosing to annoy humans instead by swarming at head level. Perhaps instinctively, the little bugs aim for your eyes, ears, and nostrils. A good insect repellent may not do the trick – protective face nets are sold in local shops but you have to ask yourself if obstructing your view is worth it. Instead, pray for a clear, sunny day – midges hate direct light.

middle and why the lake is so shallow (only 2–4m deep). The eruption disrupted the flow of the Laxá River and the new lake was filled with underground spring water. The two main basins of the lake were created separately and are fed by separate springs – in Syðriflói (the larger section) the water temperature averages 5°C; in Ytriflói (the northern end) the water gets up to 30°C.

Such a complex environment represents a delicate and totally unique ecosystem. Sunny skies and mineral-rich spring water mean lots of algae and lots more midges which eat the algae – hence the name *Mý-vatn* ('midge-lake'). The bountiful midges attract a bounty of ducks and it is commonly said that more species of duck breed in Mývatn than anywhere else on earth. That could very well be true – around here, the tufted ducks, teal and harlequins are more common than mallards. For serious birders, Mývatn is a site of pilgrimage; the rest are converted upon arrival. One-third of the lakefront is a protected nature reserve for nesting waterbirds.

In summer, life centres on thousands of fuzzy ducklings, and in winter a few hearty birds keep a few inlets free from ice.

The 'Mývatn' of travel brochures and road signs refers to the entire area: the lake, volcanoes, lava fields and steamy landscapes. As a destination, it's right at the top of the list – stunning and easy to get to. Relatively speaking though, Mývatn remains gloriously undeveloped with just a handful of hotels and restaurants. Fewer than 500 people live here, on lakeside farms or in the village of Reykjahlið. When not catering to summer tourists, locals farm or work in one of two industries: the Krafla geothermal power plant and the local diatomite mine (taken from the lake's fossilised algae deposits and used to make filters and abrasives). Recent fears of pollution have sparked a shift towards tourist-oriented businesses like the Mývatn baths and the Mývatn marathon. The plan is working, but that doesn't change the main attraction of the lake and the incredible nature on display.

**GETTING THERE AND AWAY** Mývatn is an important crossroads between Iceland's vast interior, the east coast, and the north, which makes it a convenient destination for both overland excursions and travellers following the ring road. Route 1 skirts the southern and eastern sides of the lake between Akureyri (1 hour) and Egilsstaðir (2 hours 15 minutes). The junction at Reykjahlíð connects to Route 848 that follows the lake's northern side. An unpaved turn-off on Route 87 to Húsavík (1 hour) carries a lot less traffic and is good for motorcycles and mountain bikes. Route 862 connects the ring road to Jökulsárgljúfur National Park, although this is a very bumpy option. **Trex** (*www.trex.is*) offers a daily bus service to Mývatn between Akureyri (1 hour) and Egilsstaðir (2 hours) with a stop at Skútustaðir and Reykjahlíð. In summer, **SBA-Norðurleið** (*www.sba.is*) offers a direct daily service between Mývatn and Húsavík (45 minutes) and Dettifoss (1 hour 30 minutes).

The quickest way to get to Mývatn is by air – most fly directly to Akureyri and then drive the rest of the way. There's also a small airport just above Reykjahlíð that services private and charter aircraft. For more information, contact **Mýflug** (see page 370).

**GETTING AROUND** A well-paved road circles the lake with marked turn-offs to all the local attractions. In summer, **SBA-Norðurleið** (*www.sba.is*) offers a tour service that starts at Hótel Reynihlíð and terminates at Skútustaðir (or vice versa), making short stops at Höfði, Dimmuborgir, and Hverfjall. There are three buses a day in either direction, so it's quite possible to hop on and off for short walks. On its way elsewhere, the **Trex** bus also passes between Reykjahlíð and Skútustaðir (10 minutes) twice a day.

Because there is only one road circling the lake, Mývatn is an easy place to hitch a ride. Also, the short distances and diverse attractions make biking one of the best ways to explore the area (weather permitting). Nearly every local hotel offers bike rentals, and in summer there seems to be more bikes than cars on the road. Some of the most impressive sites are seen on foot, namely Námaskarð, Krafla, and Dimmuborgir. Well-maintained paths grant hikers a complete view – for your own safety, stick to the trail.

Because Mývatn is a protected nature reserve with a fragile ecology, commercial boat tours are not permitted. Smaller rowboats can be rented in Reykjahlíð.

**TOURIST INFORMATION** The official Mývatn tourist office is next to the **Strax** food shop (*Hraunvegi 8;* ☎ *464 4460;* e *bergthorak@ust.is; www.ust.is;* ⌚ *year-round*

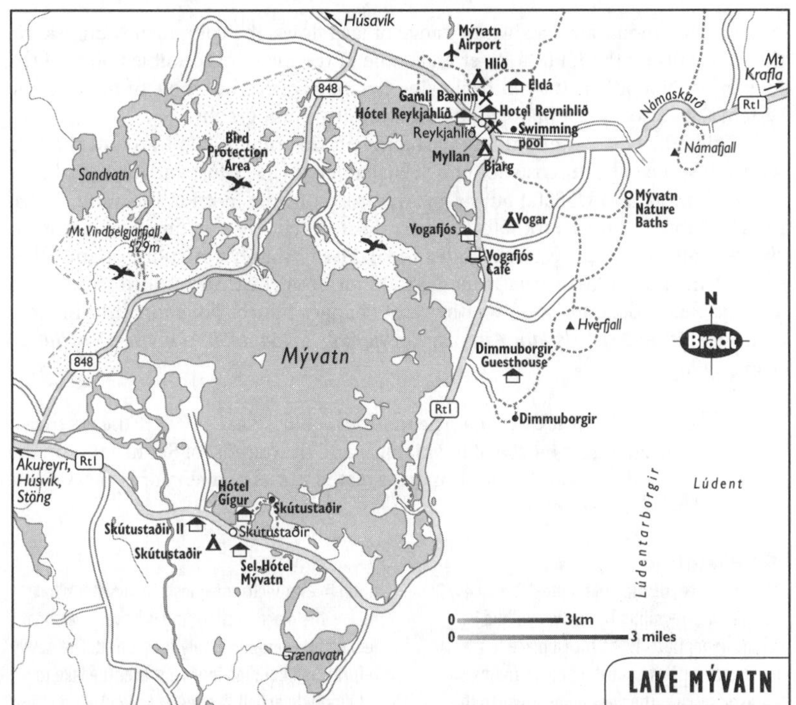


*09.00–17.00 daily*). The shops at Skútustaðir also carry plenty of helpful information and provide some of the same services. The **Mývatn marathon** usually takes place in June around the summer solstice to allow for a midnight race (the road distance around the lake is a bit longer than a perfect 26.2 miles). For more information, email or see the website (e *myvatn@myvatn.is; www.myvatn.is*).

**TOUR OPERATORS** Every hotel organises its own excursions for the area, the largest of which are Sel-Hótel Mývatn in Skútustaðir and Hótel Reynihlíð in Reykjahlíð. The hotel offices organise everything from snowmobiling and cross-country skiing to horseriding and the Mývatn marathon. **Mývatn Tours** (☎ *464 4196;* e *myvatntours@emax.is; www.askjatours.is*) offers little by the lake, but is quite reputable for venturing across the barren interior to Askja (see page 436) – definitely worth it if you have a day to spare.

**Hótel Reykjahlíð** goes one step further with a number of super jeep tours that leave every morning at 08.00 and cost around US$100–230 per person. Destinations include Krafla, Lake Elífsvötn, Dettifoss, Mt Herðubreið, and Askja. Their most unique tour heads out to the ice caves of Lofthellir, but all of their trips are good in that they get way off the beaten path and into some of the really wonderful lava fields.

For details of other tour operators, see *Chapter 4*, page 72.

**Air tours** With landscape as the main attraction, a bird's-eye view is no doubt the best way to take in all of Mývatn. The charter airline Mýflug flies out of the tiny airport in Reykjahlíð offering short to longish tours of the area. Their small planes (3–8 passengers) fly low enough to capture some incredible sights: the lake and the surrounding mountains, a gigantic range of lava flows, the colours of Namarskarð, the waterfalls on the Jökulsá River and some of the most inaccessible points of the highlands. Not only is it a mind-blowing perspective on the whole of the volcanic system – it's also a great opportunity for stunning photography.

Luckily, the cost is not entirely prohibitive: a 25-minute flight around the lake with a close-up of Krafla costs about US$90 per person. Dettifoss and Jökulsárgljúfur cost a bit more and US$300 buys a two-hour tour of the interior, including Askja, Mt Herðubreið, and Kverkfjöll. If you're in a group, then it might be easier to charter your own tour. Charter flights to Grímsey, Akureyri Airport, or any other outpost in the country costs from US$500 an hour. Bear in mind that all tours are completely dependent on weather that changes hourly. For more information, contact **Mýflug Air** (*Mývatn Airport; Reykjahlíð; ☎ 464 4400; e myflug@myflug.is; www.myflug.is*).

**WHERE TO STAY** There are two main habitations around Lake Mývatn: the northeast corner (in the emerging village of Reykjahlíð) and the outpost of Skútustaðir on the south side. The latter can feel a bit more isolated but also opens up a marvellous section of southern shore.

## In Reykjahlið

**Hótel Reynihlið** (41 rooms) ☎ 464 4170; e bookings@reynihlid.is; www.reynihlid.is. This designer hotel is the nicest place to stay in Mývatn, with big, plush, modern rooms & fantastic service. The view alone is worth the price (so request a window facing the lake). The only downside is that the bathrooms are rather small & the internet is spotty. The whole operation started as an old farm & mill. The hotel organises plenty of local excursions & most bus tours originate here. B/fast inc. **$$$$**

**Dimmuborgir Guesthouse** (7 rooms) Geiteyjarströnd 1; ☎ 464 4210; e geitey@simnet.is; www.dimmuborgir.is. The farm at Dimmuborgir feels small & secluded despite being right off the main path to the lava formations. Sleeping-bag accommodation is offered at a very low rate, & some of the new smaller cottages offer private bathrooms. B/fast inc. **$$$**

**Eldá** (50 beds) Helluhraun 15; ☎ 464 4200; e info@elda.is. A collection of small, local houses in the village which offers B&B-style accommodation (all within walking distance of the main house). Some houses can be rented as a whole (with private kitchens & bathrooms), others offer rooms only. B/fast buffet inc. **$$$**

**Reykjahlíð** (9 rooms) m 845 2424; e reykjahlid@islandia.is; www.reykajlid.is. Fresh, clean & intimate, the Reykyahlíð was the first hotel to ever welcome guests in Mývatn. What makes the place so charming is its very personal feel & the energetic family that runs it. The newly refurbished building looks out over the lake to Mt Vindbelgjarfjall, & guests can walk along the shore to the village in about 5mins. All rooms get lots of light & have their own private bathroom – the rooms up top tend to be larger & better quality, opening into a nice TV lounge/library. A decent dining room restaurant is open in summer & the hotel also offers interesting tours to the interior. B/fast inc. **$$$**

**Vogafjós** (20 rooms) ☎ 464 4303; e vogar@emax.is; www.vogafjos.net. Vogafjós stands above the rest of the farms in the district simply because of all the little 'extras' they offer their guests. Owned by the same family for more than 100 years, guests are sucked right into the atmosphere of Mývatn & the working, on-site dairy. 2 very new 'longhouses' offer motel-style private rooms (with private bathroom) that are clean & nicely furnished. High standards, sincere hospitality, & the ambiant setting make Vogafjós extremely popular, especially among bikers who want to treat themselves – it's a good idea to book ahead, even if you plan on camping here (which is allowed). Breakfast included at the feel-good 'cowshed' café; highly recommended. **$$$**

## In Skútasataðir

**Hótel Gígur** (37 rooms) Skútustaðir; 464 4455; e gigur@keahotels.is; www.keahotels.is. As an old school that's undergone extensive redesign, the Gigur is pleasantly posh but with smallish rooms, albeit very private & 'luxurious'. Most windows are situated to offer a gorgeous view of the lake & there's a progressive policy to keep tour groups separate from individual travellers. Not terribly inexpensive, but clean, smart, & modern. B/fast inc. **$$$$**

**Sel-Hótel Mývatn** (35 rooms) Skútustaðir; 464 4164; e myvatn@myvatn.is; www.myvatn.is. This modern, family-friendly hotel, on the south side of the lake, is right across the street from the trail around the pseudo-craters. The cosy interior is newly redecorated & every room has its own bathroom. The hotel functions as a regular travel haven with a campsite, restaurant, café, petrol station & a shop that sells everything from souvenirs to insect netting (*summer 08.00–22.00 daily, winter 14.00–18.00 Mon, Wed & Fri*). B/fast inc. **$$$**

**Skútustaðir II** (11 rooms) 464 4212; 1 Jun–1 Sep. The namesake farmhouse now welcomes a number of guests into an array of accommodation choices. Smaller 'cottages' offer private baths; rooms with shared bath cost considerably less. Affordable sleeping-bag accommodation is available & the campsites are right next door. The farm is part of the rest of the complex, so you have access to the shop & the other hotel restaurants. **$$$**

**Stöng** (21 rooms) 464 4252; e stongmy@simnet.is. A large but rural farm guesthouse about 10km southwest of the lake (best if you have your own transport – follow the signs from Route 1). All rooms sleep 1–3 & have sinks, but bathrooms are shared. There's also a good dining room & a hot pot for guests. This is at the cheaper end of local guesthouses & best for groups & those who don't mind a bit of isolation. **$$$**

**Camping** There are several good campsites around Mývatn – each is unique in size, facilities, and atmosphere. All of them fill up in summer. Camping rough is also permitted, but remember that this is a rare ecosystem and to tread lightly.

**Bjarg** 464 4240; e ferdabjarg@simnet.is; 20 May–20 Sep. This large, private campsite is right on the lakeshore by Reykjahlíð, next to shops, restaurants, & transportation. It also functions as the most user-friendly (& most popular) place for extended stays in the area. Camping costs 1,200ISK pp & includes hot showers & use of the kitchen. The cabin offers a limited number of spots for sleeping-bag accommodation at around 3,500ISK. Rowboats & mountain bikes are available for rental. **$**

**Hlíð** 464 4103; e hlid@ishold.is; 1 May–15 Sep. The 'town' campsite is up on the hillside next to Reykjahlíð Airport & more conducive to those with cars & caravans. Hot showers & kitchens are available; 600ISK pp. **$**

**Vogar** 464 4399. The Vogar farm will let you camp there, but remember this is a private working farm with a high amount of traffic. **$**

**WHERE TO EAT** The farms around Mývatn prize their native ingredients, so expect something with a bit of a local twist. A lot of the fish and lamb is smoked in sheep dung, which offers as peculiar flavour as any (hey, there's no wood!). The fresh salmon and Arctic char fished out of the nearby lakes and rivers are worth the healthy price you'll pay, and you should definitely try the paté. Another Mývatn tourist staple is the delicious 'hot spring bread' – a kind of dense rye cake that's baked (or rather, steamed) in the nearby hot springs. The most popular brand is Bjarnaflags brauð and it's sold in all the local shops.

**Sel Mývatn Restaurant** Skútustaðir; 464 4164; e myvatn@myvatn.is; www.myvatn.is; summer 08.00–23.30, winter 10.00–21.00. A nice & well-run hotel restaurant, this country dining room pays special attention to presentation & introducing guests to local flavours. They offer a great all-you-can eat buffet of Icelandic specialities (shark, sheep's head, reindeer paté, smoked lamb, & fish) for about US$25 (lunch) or US$50 (dinner), & don't worry, there are other choices besides the weird stuff (lamb roast, river trout, catfish, & delicious local desserts). *Mains from 1,600ISK.* $$$

**Sel Café** summer 08.00–23.30, winter 10.00–21.00. For something less sophisticated, you can try this café, next door to Sel Mývatn Restaurant, which sells soup, grilled sandwiches, pizza, hot dogs, coffee, & ice cream. *Mains from 700ISK.* $$

**Gamli Bærinn Reykjahlíð** Hótel Reynihlíð; 464 4170; e bookings@reynihlid.is; www.reynihlid.is; 10.00–22.00 daily. As a bona fide old farm, the 'Old Farm' is the closest thing to a pub in the whole of north Iceland. Low, wooden ceiling beams, live local music & the lager on tap are all part of this traditional tavern's atmosphere. By day, the kitchen serves up café fare: coffee, tea, cakes & waffles, along with hearty pub lunches, sandwiches on hot spring bread, & a very authentic *plottfiskur*. The outdoor seating makes it a great resting spot, & by night you'll meet everyone who lives by the lake. *Mains from 1,800ISK.* $$$

**Myllan Reykjahlíð** Hótel Reynihlíð; 464 4170; e bookings@reynihlid.is; www.reynihlid.is; 11.00–midnight daily. 'The Mill' is the more intimate, upmarket dining alternative for those visiting the lake's northern rim. The cool décor is balanced by a distinguished fixed menu of 2 or 3 courses. Expect glazed fish & roasted lamb or beef, served with style. *Mains from 3,200ISK.* $$$$

**Gigur** Skútustaðir; 464 4455; e gigur@keahotels.is; www.keahotels.is; 08.00–22.00 daily. The dining room of the Hótel Gigur treats busloads of tourists to an Icelandic meal with a view. Large glass walls & spacious outdoor seating offer a gorgeous view of the lake, & the menu is a dedicated review of fish & lamb. No matter the time or day, the atmosphere is not unlike a Sun afternoon lunch. *Mains from 1,600ISK.* $$$

**Vogafjós Café** Vogar; 464 4303; e hraunberg@simnet.is; www.vogarholidays.is; summer 07.00–23.30 daily , winter 09.00–19.00 daily. The earnest little 'Cowshed' café is legendary: set inside a dairy barn, a thick glass wall is all that separates you & your meal from the cows getting milked. Watch the process & then order the milk, fresh mozzarella & feta cheese, or ice cream that is made from the cows' milk. The menu is affordable & healthy – all meals are prepared right in front of you, the portions are generous, & the salads are some of the best you'll have in Iceland. It's all very sanitary & quite quaint, really. Milkings are at 07.00 & at 18.00. *Mains from 850ISK.* $$

**Reykjahlíð** 464 4142; e reykjahlid@islandia.is; www.reykajlid.is; May–Sep 12.00–14.00 & 18.00–22.00 daily. Small & schnazzy dining room at the hotel specialising in local dishes like Arctic char in lemon butter sauce & smoked lamb & fish. *Mains from 1,600ISK.* $$$

**Kaffi Borgir** 698 6810; e freddi@kaffiborgir.is; www.kaffiborgir.is; summer 09.00–midnight, winter 12.00–22.00. Located at the Mývatn Nature Baths, this café caters to the dehydrated & hungry. It's your basic cafeteria serving hot food, drinks, & pastry. *Mains from 1,200ISK.* $$

**Self-catering** For basic groceries, try **Strax** (*Hlíðarvegur 6; 464 4466; 08.00–19.00*), a tiny but convenient grocery store in Reykjahlíð that caters to the needs of travellers and campers.

## WHAT TO SEE AND DO

**Birds** Mývatn is home to healthy numbers of a few distinct species, which makes it great for passionate birders as well as those who don't know the difference between two kinds of pretty ducks. Certain ducks that are quite rare for Iceland are only seen around Mývatn – namely the common scoter (*Melanita nigra*), gadwall (*Anas strepera*), and shoveler (*Anus clypeata*).

The tufted duck (*Aythya fuligula*) is the commonest duck in Mývatn, followed by the somewhat similar-looking scaup (*Aythya marila*) and Barrow's goldeneye (*Bucephala islandica*). You'll also see plenty of wigeon, mallard, teal and perhaps pintail and long-tailed ducks (*Clangula hyemalis*). A common site (but rare for

## GOLDEN EYE

The lake might be full of ducks, but **Barrow's goldeneye** (*Bucephala islandica*) is the official mascot – Mývatn is the only place in Europe where the remarkable duck breeds. The species' Latin name indicates Iceland because it is here that the species was first discovered by Europeans. The rest of the world population (more than 95%) live in the mountains of the Pacific northwest coast (from California to Alaska), spending winter at sea and summer breeding in high mountain lakes. In Mývatn, the population of about 1,000 regular pairs arrive in late spring and fly away by the end of August, except for a few stragglers who stay through the winter.

The smallish ducks have odd-shaped heads and shiny golden eyes that seem to glow. Males feature distinctive white marks on their cheeks and the front of the wing; females are mottled grey with rich brown heads. You can see them anywhere on the main lake or along the Laxá River – in July, they are a sure thing in the lake's shallow northern pools, diving for midges. The very cute ducklings arrive at the same time, but by human standards, goldeneyes are not great parents. It is quite typical for a female goldeneye to simply abandon her newly hatched babies and run off. Childcare is often left to a single 'foster mother' duck who watches over a few-dozen ducklings. Giant clusters of baby ducks are a common sight in Mývatn – with a half-interested female watching from the bank.

The duck's common name honours **Sir John Barrow** (1764–1848), a British mathematics tutor turned civil servant turned admiral turned baron. He lived a very adventurous life: he learnt to speak Chinese fluently, helped settle the Cape of Good Hope, worked on a whaling ship in Greenland and authored the official report to the British government detailing the mutiny of the *Bounty* (which he entitled *Causes and Consequences*). Because of his strong support for Arctic exploration, expeditions gave his name to places like Point Barrow in Alaska and to this newly discovered duck species. In almost every other language, the duck's common name is a reference to Iceland. In Icelandic, however, the name *húsönd* simply means 'house duck'. The farmers of Mývatn have always enjoyed easy access to the indiscreet nest of the goldeneye, collecting their eggs as if they were house pets – today the practice is strictly regulated.

Europe) is the abundance of harlequin ducks (*Histrionicus histrionicus*), of which the face of the male looks painted. The Laxá River is one of their favourite abodes and a casual walk along the stream will lead you to them (this is always on private property, so be respectful).

The fanciful Slavonian (or horned) grebe (*Podiceps auritus*) is another waterbird that's common for Mývatn but rare for the rest of Iceland. Other rare waterbirds include the great northern diver, red-throated diver, red-breasted merganser and the whooper swan. Bird 'twitchers' come here to see what's in the water, but don't forget to check the land (where you'll spot red-necked phalarope and ptarmigan) and the sky (lots of geese and maybe even an owl).

All kinds of special birding tours are advertised, but there really is no magic to accessing the birds seeing as they dominate the whole of the Mývatn/Laxá system. As long as you have some binoculars and can get down to the water (and you're patient), you'll see some remarkable things. The Mývatn protected natural area

## MARIMO

Lake Mývatn is home to one of the rarest forms of algae in the world: the *marimo* or lake ball. These strange underwater growths form a perfect sphere of spongy moss that pile up on the bottom of the lake. Mývatn's *marimo* were only discovered in 1978 and are formed by the algae *A. linnaei*, whose green strings radiate out from the centre in a densely packed bunch. The balls can only occur under highly specific conditions of lighting, lake current, and just the right amount of soft sediments. Small waves cause the balls to roll gently back and forth, constantly exposing different sides to sunlight and forcing all sides to photosynthesise. In Mývatn, the *marimo* can only be found at depths of 2–2.5m and they never grow larger than 12cm in diameter. You are not likely to see one unless you happen to hook one on a fishing line or if you're part of a registered diving operation. In recent years, the *marimo* of Mývatn have begun to decline rapidly, although no-one seems to know why.

Outside Mývatn, *marimo* exist in only three other locations in the world, the most prominent site being Lake Akan in Hokkaido, Japan – hence the Japanese name *mari-* ('ball') *mo* ('water plant'). In Icelandic, the term is less endearing: *kúluskítur* translates literally as 'ball of shit'.

is a good place to start, up on the northwest side of the lake. The entire lake is protected, but here the shore is off-limits to people, cars, and buildings, and it's in these pockets of pools that most of the ducks spend the very long summer days. For birds, the heat of the moment is from May to mid-August, but early spring and late autumn sees the migration and there's a growing camp of devoted winter inhabitants, mainly geese.

**Mt Vindbelgjarfjall** (529m) Despite its haunting, conical shape, the mountain on the lake's west side is not a volcano but a hyaloclastite ridge. That means rapid-cooling lava beneath the ice was shattered into millions of tiny pieces. When you climb to the top, you're actually walking on rough fragments of broken volcanic glass. A dirt trail crosses the cracked black mounds (from steam explosions) near Sandvatn before zig-zagging up the very steep, gravelly side to the top. The mountain's name translates as 'bellowing wind', which is what you hear up on top. The view is the best panorama for the lake, taking in all the ponds and islands. The hike from the road to the top takes about two hours.

**Skútustaðir** Some of the most pronounced pseudo-craters line the southern basin at Skútusatðir. The strange circles are all that's left of an earlier lake that was vaporised by the same eruption that created the present-day Lake Mývatn. When the lava flowed over the water, steam exploded from beneath, forming the stone 'bubbles' seen today. A trail circles the pond in the middle (Stakhólstjörn), and allows access to the inside of the many pseudo-craters. The longer route (1 hour) follows the lakeshore or there's a shorter detour back to the car park (25 minutes).

**Dimmuborgir** The 'dark castles' are a forest of black lava rock pillars on the lake's east side. The ghostly towers rise up and form a separate enclosure that does indeed resemble a fortress. Prior to the creation of Lake Mývatn, lava flowed out of the crater row at Lúdentarborgir and formed a giant lava lake that was more than a mile across. Steam bubbles popped up to the surface and formed cooling vents that hardened into the 'chimneys' you see today. The rest of the lava slowly leaked into Mývatn, coating the pillars with a layer of scoria stone. This is the only spot on earth where such formations exist on land. Dimmuborgir is a highlight for casual walkers and geology buffs; a circular trail leaves from the car park and explores most of the features. Rock climbing is not permitted.

**Hverfjall** Hverfjall (or Hverfell) is the largest and best-preserved tephra crater (made of volcanic debris) in Mývatn and one of the best examples of such in the world. This classic volcanic vent is ash grey and completely devoid of life, but as an almost perfect circle the sheer dimension of the crater is impressive: more than 1km across and 140m deep in the middle. The reason it looks so low and flat is because of the subsequent lava flows that encircled its exterior. Hverfjall itself was formed over the span of 200 years of volcanic eruptions, where lava and pumice piled up into the ridge of today. A desolate trail circles the top but bear in mind the distance is much longer than it looks. The ascent from the northern end (by the car park) is far easier than the steep zig-zag on the southern end (connecting to Dimmuborgir).

**Krafla** The Krafla system is one of Iceland's largest hotspots, comprising a fissure swarm that extends for 100km. The concentrated, active area is about 14km wide and offers a splendid mix of volcanic features formed from gas, water, and molten lava. Route 1 crosses the fissure at Námaskarð, and Route 863 branches north to the actual volcano of **Mt Krafla** (818m). The angled cone was one of the very first volcanoes to erupt in the region (over 100,000 years ago) and is still off-limits to hikers. The entire area is still highly active – the steam rising up from the silver chimneys are part of the **Krafla geothermal power station**, which feeds electricity to Akureyri and all of east Iceland. It is the warm, chalky blue run-off from this

## MÝVATN: A VOLCANIC TIMELINE

| | |
|---|---|
| **100,000 years ago** | Krafla volcano and caldera formed |
| **10,000 years ago** | Lúdent erupts, causing new lava fields in the southeast |
| **3,800 years ago** | Ludentarborgir crater row formed; first Lake Mývatn formed |
| **2,900 years ago** | Hverfjall (Hverfell) erupts, forming the tephra crater |
| **2,300 years ago** | Ludentarborgir erupts: the lava flow creates the present-day lakes Mývatn, Arnarvatn, Grænavatn, and Sandvatn. Skútustaðir pseudo-craters formed. Steam bubbling up through the pooling lava forms Dimmuborgir. |
| **AD900** | Lava flows surround Hverfjall crater |
| **1724** | The 'Mývatn fires' begin: Krafla erupts and forms the crater of Stóra-Víti; two farms are buried in lava |
| **1729** | Leirhnjúkur erupts; creation of the Eldhraun lava field |
| **1759** | The 'Mývatn fires' end |
| **1974** | First attempts to tap geothermal energy at Krafla |
| **1975** | Start of the 'Krafla fires': fissures around Krafla erupt |
| **1984** | After nine eruptions, the 'Krafla fires' end. Noted changes to the chemistry of Lake Mývatn. |

plant that fills the Mývatn Nature Baths. A more natural version can be viewed at the caldera of Stóra-Víti or simply **Víti** ('hell'). The beautiful turquoise and emerald pool in the middle fills the remaining crater of the famous 17 May 1724 eruption. A very nice trail circles the top of the circular ridge, with great views right into the pool (1 hour from the car park and back). Hikers can feel the heat rising up from the centre – the water temperature is close to 100ºC. A small detour leads towards the base of the Krafla volcano, past boiling mud pools and milky hot springs surrounded by lots of colourful sulphuric formations (stay on the light-brown clay).

At the other side of Krafla lies the post-apocalyptic landscape of **Leirhnjúkur** ('clay peak'). Steam plumes float up in every direction against the varied colour of stilled lava flows (the blackest and darkest date from 1984) – the youngest in Iceland. A fairly level trail passes several beautiful hot spring areas and enters the most recent craters. A longer circular tour (1 hour extra) heads up to the **Hófur** crater that dates from the Mývatn fires. Look, but don't climb (the fragile edges are eroding). To the southwest (and accessible only on foot) stands **Mt Hlíðarfjall** (771m). The trail ascends rapidly but is not too difficult, and the surrounding view of the interior is unique, especially Mt Herðubreið.

**Námarskarð** Námafjall is another hyaloclastite ridge, formed right along the Krafla fissure. The mountain pass across Námarskarð is one of the highlights on the ring road – depending on the direction of travel, visitors get hit with idyllic views of Mývatn or the intense smell of sulphur. The naturally heated foot trail around **Námafjall** allows a view from up high, but one might save time by going straight to the hot springs area at **Hverir** where on-the-spot parking allows easy vehicle access. '*Hverir*' denotes hot springs that are on the verge of boiling – most of the mud and water pools range from 80°C to 100°C. The desolate scenery of Námaskarð is streaked with the most striking colours: reddish-brown ochre and whitish dirt, bright sulphur-green crystals and purplish pools of boiling mud. When there's wind (which is most of the time), the hissing fumaroles feel positively ethereal.

**Swimming** Enjoy the natural heat of Krafla by having a long soak at the **Mývatn Nature Baths** (*464 4411; e info@jardbodin.is; www.jardbodin.is; summer 11.00–21.00 daily, winter 12.00–20.00 daily; entrance: adults 2,500ISK, seniors 2,000ISK, under 16 1,000ISK*). Milky blue geothermal runoff from the Námarskað/Krafla power station flows into this natural-looking reservoir *à la* Blue Lagoon (see

## WALKING ON FIRE

Humans have good survival instincts when it comes to avoiding dangerous heights or sharp objects, but few of us know the proper safety etiquette of coping with molten lava. The simple rule is always, always stick to the marked trail, even when the trail doesn't make sense. In highly active areas like Víti and Námarskarð, the crusty ground may appear uniform, but its depth might range from 100m deep to just 1cm. Below lie natural steam vents and underground pools of boiling water and mud. The hot dirt and stones can burn you or melt your shoes. Despite the temptation, don't reach out to 'test' the ground with your bare hand, or hold your face to the steam. Such foolish acts end with serious burns. Also use caution when walking across dormant lava fields – the terrain may not be active, but it can be slick (from rain or ice) and deeply cracked.

page 206). The bacteria- and salt-free water is kept at a temperature of 36°C (96.8°F) and is filled with healthful silicates but no salts, hence the blue colour. The baths claim the waters are especially soothing to those with skin and respiratory ailments, namely asthma. Bathers can also enjoy a number of hot pots, two natural steam baths, a children's shallow soaking area and a small spa that offers massage and other beauty treatments. Note that the presence of sulphur can damage silver and copper jewellery so take it off prior to soaking. Bring your own towel (renting a small one costs 400ISK) and be sure to take a look at some of the iridescent lava stone in the area surrounding the car park. If you prefer wading in something far less romantic, there's a **swimming pool** just outside Reykjahlið (*464 4225; 08.00–20.00 Mon–Fri, 10.00–19.00 Sat/Sun; entrance 250ISK*).

## BEYOND MÝVATN

Since the days of settlement, Mývatn has served as an important base from which journeys into the highlands begin and end. Wanderlust is a common ailment when travelling on the verge of such captivating, lifeless stretches of lava and desert, and the intrepid tourist will be eager to conquer the horizon. A prominent view (and frequently depicted in Mývatn hotel-room oil paintings) is the stalwart **Mt Bláfjall** (1,222m), a flat-topped table mountain due south from Krafla. The signature shape of 'blue mountain' – like many others in the area – dates back to the ice age, when volcanic cones erupted up until the top of the ice before levelling off in a pool of cooled lava. Hikes out to Bláfjall are popular but not to be underestimated. There is a mountain hut at Barð for overnight stays. Keep in mind that this is the interior – there are no roads, no water, and no people.

Longer treks or 4x4 trips head from Mývatn all the way to **Askja** (see page 436) and **Mt Herðubreið** (see page 437). Adventurous types can also hike north, from Mývatn, across Krafla and up to Jökúlsárgljúfur (see page 383), passing the beautiful spring-lake of **Eilifsvötn** ('eternal waters').

## HÚSAVÍK

The grand panorama of Skjálfandi Bay and the snow-dusted mountains of Náttfaravíkur grant Húsavík a wonderful calm, even if this is the biggest town in all of Thingeyjarsveit (population 2,500). Boats bob in the harbour below a handful of rooftops, a ring of trees and the shadow of another barren mountain – the humpbacked Búrfell. It may look a little average but Húsavík goes back to the beginning with a fair claim as the country's first settlement. After sailing all the way around Iceland, the Swedish Viking and early explorer Garðar Svavarasson (see page 15) landed in this bay in AD870. Anticipating the brisk winter, he built himself a house and named the spot *Húsavík* ('house bay') where he lived for a few months before returning to Sweden – the event is remembered each year with the town's 'Swedish Days' summer celebration. The bay only became a town 1,000 years later, when Iceland was exporting sulphur to make Europe's gunpowder and this was the port from whence it came. Weapons and a slaughterhouse for sheep kept the town buoyant until the mid 1960s, when fish stocks began to dwindle and locals began selling off their fish quotas. The end seemed nigh until Húsavík reinvented itself overnight: the townspeople refitted a couple of retired fishing boats and dubbed the town Iceland's whale-watching capital, after which the slaughterhouse turned into the internationally acclaimed whale museum. A local population of uninhibited whales play along willingly, coming to feed in the shallows of Skjálfandi Bay in summer and putting on quite a show if they're in the mood. Now it's one of the best spots to catch an up-close look at Iceland's biggest animals – definitely worth the northern detour.

Today, Húsavík has evolved into a fully fledged tourist town with several competing whale-watching ventures, and gift shops selling sundry whale trinkets. The downside is that for a month or so each summer, there's a bit of a mad tourist rush – the upshot is that Húsavík's natural small-town hospitality copes remarkably well. In spite of being added to the must-see spots on the all-around-Iceland circuit, the town has managed to keep its soul. The fanciful wooden church symbolises a town reborn and the locals' genuine fascination with whales is contagious.

**GETTING THERE AND AWAY** Húsavík is right on Route 85, a short drive from Akureyri (90km), Mývatn (60km), or Ásbyrgi (65km). The bus line **Trex** (e *info@trex.is; www.trex.is*) offers a daily service to and from Akureyri (1 hour 15 minutes) and Thórshöfn (2 hours 15 minutes), as does **SBA-Norðuleið** (e *sba@sba.is; www.sba.is*), which also connects to Ásbyrgi (1½ hours), and Dettifoss (3 hours), as well as a regular round trip to Mývatn (1 hour each way). The bus pickup and drop-off is in the town centre, above the harbour.

## TOURIST INFORMATION

**Tourist information** Garðarsbraut 5; ☎ 464 4300; e info@husavik.is; www.husavik.is. ⏲ 09.00–16.00 daily. Another information centre is located at the town's main grocery store.

## WHERE TO STAY

**Árból** (8 rooms) Ásgarðsvegur 2; ☎ 464 2220; e guest.hus@isl.is; www.arbol.1.is. A century-old home not far from the town centre, with a quaint wooden exterior & renovated interior; quite popular in summer. Shared bathrooms. B/fast inc. **$$$**

**Fosshótel Húsavík** (70 rooms) Ketilsbraut 22; ☎ 464 1220; e sales@fosshotel.is; www.fosshotel.is. Húsavík's largest & highest-quality hotel, with a whole wing that's been recently refurbished to international standards. Modern private bathrooms & nice big fluffy beds make this a comfortable stop, & you're within walking distance of the harbour & other attractions. They've also got the best restaurant in town. Admirable b/fast buffet inc. **$$$**

**Kaldbaks Kot Cottages** (12 cottages) Norðaustuvegur; ☎ 464 1504; e cottages@cottages.is; www.cottages.is. Family-sized private log cabins complete with kitchenette, private bathroom, & a front porch. They sleep up to 4 people comfortably, which is a great deal price-wise. They also rent horses. On your left before you come into town from Akureyri/Mývatn. **$$$**

**Emhild K Olsen** (4 rooms) Baldursbrekka 17; ☎ 464 1618. A cute & homely B&B in a residential area. No pretence but a lot of heart & a good price. Bathrooms are shared. B/fast inc. *Sleeping-bag accommodation around 2,000ISK.* **$$**

**Husavík Guesthouse** (7 rooms) Laugarbrekka 16; ☎ 463 3399; e info@husavikguesthouse.is; www.husavikguesthouse.is. Run by an ever-friendly man & just a few mins' walk from the harbour. The guesthouse is a textbook example of Scandinavian functionalism & warm Icelandic hospitality. Recommended. **$$**

**Vísir** (4 rooms) Garðarsbraut 14; m 856 5750; e dora@visirhf.is. Clean & sensible, this centrally located guesthouse offers simple but spacious rooms with double beds. Shared bathrooms, laundry & kitchen facilities. **$$**

**Camping** Húsavík's campsite (*Héðinsbraut;* m *845 0705;* e *info@markthing.is; www.markthing.is;* **$**) is considered one of the very best in all of Iceland and is spacious enough to accommodate its popularity. The hill protects it from the wind, and there are a number of great amenities (hot showers, kitchens, etc); you only pay 800ISK the first night; every additional night is free.

## WHERE TO EAT

### Restaurants

**Gamlí Baukur** ☎ 464 2442; e gamlibaukur@gamlibaukur.is; ⌚ 11.30–23.30 Sun–Wed (kitchen closes at 22.00), 11.30–01.00 Thu, 11.30–03.00 Fri/Sat. This wood-panelled, harbour-side restaurant is the town's number-one hangout for both tourists & locals any night of the week. Jolly platters of seafood are washed down by pints of beer at 'the Shipyard' bar. Other than the catch of the day, it's food as usual (fish & chips, burgers, etc). The seafaring theme is not a front – the pictures & objects form a bit of a town museum, & the whole place is built from driftwood. *Mains from 2,500ISK.* $$$$

**Terian** Ketilsbraut 22; ☎ 464 1220; e sales@fosshotel.is; www.fosshotel.is; ⌚ summer only 12.00–21.00. The city's newest restaurant can also be considered its best, housed at the local whale-themed Fosshótel. A diverse menu goes in for a gourmet appearance, but the food is fairly priced & delicious. *Mains from 2,000ISK.* $$$

**Salka** Garðarsbraut 4; ☎ 464 2551; ⌚ 11.30–23.30 daily (kitchen closes at 22.00). Across from the church, Salka is a popular café/diner serving a typical fish & lamb repertoire along with pizza & burgers. Customer service is blasé & the servings small. *Mains from 1,650ISK.* $$$

**Skold Café** Húsavík harbour; ⌚ 1 Jun–30 Sep 08.30–22.00 Mon–Fri, 09.00–19.00 Sat/Sun. Right above the whale-watching boats in the harbour, this summer-only café is perfect for small meals, if you just want tea & coffee, or sandwiches & cake. *Mains from 500ISK.* $$

**Kofinn** Húsavík harbour; m 868 9677; e gourmet@kofinn.com; www.kofinn.com; ⌚ summer 09.00–22.00 Mon–Fri, 10.00–18.00 Sat/Sun. Summer only, made-for-tourists food stand that sells 'gourmet' Icelandic dishes, including fish caught in the bay, local lamb &… hot dogs. Good coffee & reasonably priced meals make it a popular eatery, & when the sun is shining you can eat on the patio. *Mains from 600ISK.* $$

**Pronto Pizza** Ketilsbraut 22; ☎ 462 2333; ⌚ summer only 11.00–23.00 daily. The best place for getting pizza delivered to your hotel/guesthouse/campsite. *Mains from 2,000ISK.* $$$

**Note:** Salka and Gamli Baukur are owned by the same bunch, hence the almost identical menus.

**Self-catering** Besides the mini marts in the petrol stations, the largest food store is located on the east side of town at Stangarbakki (⌚ *09.00–23.00 daily*). Also, bread, cakes, sandwiches and soup can be had at the local bakery; **Bakari** (*Garðarsbraut 15;* ☎ *464 2900;* ⌚ *07.00–20.00 Mon–Fri, 10.00–16.00 Sat*).

**WHAT TO SEE AND DO** People come to Húsavík to see the whales, but there's a bit more to the town. The **Húsavík church** was built in 1907 and looks nothing like any other church in Iceland. Designed in the Sweitzer style, every piece of the church came from Norway already shaped and painted, ready for assembly. It is the masterpiece of Rögnvaldur Ólafsson, the very first 'modern' Icelandic architect who went to great lengths to create something original. Note the faux marble columns that are actually wood, the perfect-square floor plan, the angled Gothic windows, the lofty ceiling and wide balconies. The carved wooden font is a town treasure, as are the silver candlesticks which came from Denmark in 1640. The most renowned prize is the painting behind the altar, completed in 1931 by artist Sveinn Thórarinsson. The event portrayed is biblical (the resurrection of Lazarus), but the landscapes are clearly Icelandic, including scenes from the painter's home (Kelduhverfi), the mountains of nearby Öxarfjörður, and the misty spray rising from the gorge at Dettifoss. The masterpiece caused some distress as the townspeople of Húsavík recognised their faces in the painting.

Across the street is the harbour area and town centre, marked by the **Garðar Svavarasson monument** commemorating the town's founder. Down at the docks are the **whale-watching** boats and ticket booths where you can sign up for a tour, while just above the harbour sits the gigantic **Húsavík Whale Museum** (*Hvalsafnið á Húsavík; Hafnarstétt;* ☎ *464 2520;* e *info@icewhale.is; www.icehwale.is;* ⏲ *Jun–Aug 09.00–19.00 daily, May & Sep 10.00–17.00 daily; entrance 600ISK*), recognisable by the whale murals painted on its walls. Housed in a former sheep slaughterhouse, the museum is one of Iceland's very best, with over one square mile of captivating displays that cater equally to heady scientists and the youngest of children. The smart exhibits detail the history of whaling, the whale species that live around Iceland, the biology of whales, whale migration and current conservation efforts. Up on the second floor, you can get an up-close look at a large collection of whale skeletons (all extracted from beached whales), including the only full-size sperm whale skeleton in the world.

In contrast to the very professional and fascinating whale museum is the private collection of privates held at the **Icelandic Phallological Museum** (*Hið Íslenzka Reðasafn; Héðinsbraut 3A;* ☎ *561 6663;* e *phallus@phallus.is; www.phallus.is;* ⏲ *20 May–10 Sep 12.00–18.00 daily; entrance 500ISK*). With nearly 200 phallic specimens on display, visitors can contemplate the male organs of a seal, walrus, polar bear, a few whale species and a lot of very small rodents, as well as a number of more fanciful depictions in art and sculpture. What seeks to be edgy, scientific, or humorous actually comes across as a little creepy and eccentric, especially the lampshades made out of sheep scrotums and bullwhips made from a bull's penis. The eclectic **Húsavík Town Museum** (*Safnahúsið á Húsavík; Stórigarðar 17;* ☎ *464 1860;* e *safnahus@husmus.is; www.husmus.is;* ⏲ *Jun–Aug 10.00–18.00 daily, May & Sep 09.00–17.00 daily; entrance 500ISK*) tends to be less visited, but combines the town's folk and natural history museums. Overall it's a random collection of bits and bobs reflecting local fauna, history, folklore, photography, and art – the highlight of which is the stuffed polar bear that was shot on Grímsey (see page 363).

**Whale-watching** Whales show up in Skjálfandi Bay in mid-May and are gone by the end of October at the very latest, although you never can say what you might see in the water. Twelve species of whale have been identified in the bay – minke, humpback, porpoise and dolphin are almost a sure sight. Blue whales, fins, and orca have also been spotted here enough to be recognisable. The breadth of whale species in such a confined spot has much to do with the underwater landscape of the bay, which has a very shallow section (near Húsavík), and a fairly deep section below the steep mountains on the other side.

Scheduled whale-watching tours typically start in June and finish up around mid-September. Despite the commercialised process, the experience still feels adventurous. Most trips last two to three hours and typically circle the entire bay. The boats have a spotter in the crow's nest seeking out the whales, but you should

### GIVE SOMETHING BACK: FINGERPRINTING THE WHALES

A scientific team based at the Húsavík Whale Museum performs non-invasive research on the whales in Skjálfandi Bay by identifying individual animals and tracking their movements and activities. Reporting what you've seen and submitting photographs (humps, flukes, and heads) helps scientists manage and protect the local whale population. You may also contribute financially, which can help maintain the bay as a conservation area. To get involved, contact the following: ☎ 464 2520; e info@icewhale.is; www.icewhale.is.

try to bring your own binoculars. More often than not, you'll spot something first. Once found, there is a tendency for several boats to cluster around a whale or two, but for now there are plenty of whales to go around.

Two companies offer whale-watching trips. A healthy dose of competition keeps the quality high and the experience pretty much identical. Both claim a 98% success rate with a guarantee of an additional free tour should the whales not co-operate.

**Gentle Giants** Húsavík harbour; ☎ 464 1500; e info@gentlegiants.is; www.gentlegiants.is. A smaller fleet, but with smaller boats that can sometimes be better for getting closer to the whales. Blankets & refreshments are also provided. Gentle Giants is becoming renowned for its fishing trips in the bay. *Tickets under 4,000ISK, children under 15 free.*

**North Sailing** Hafnarstétt 9; ☎ 464 2350; e www.northsailing.is. A fleet of historic ships & an experienced crew who started the whale-watching phenomenon in Húsavík (the first in Iceland). On board they provide blankets, identification charts, rolls & hot cocoa. Their sailing ship *Haukur* ('The Hawk') is a popular boat that offers a number of tours (see below). *Tickets under 4,000ISK, children under 14 free.*

**Other trips** Both whale-watching companies offer a number of extended tours in the area: fishing, birdwatching on the local islands (Flatey, Lundey, and Grímsey), horseriding, or multi-day trips that combine several activities. The 'puffin trips' tend to go around **Lundey Island**, rising out of the sea just north of Húsavík. Over 200,000 puffins breed here every year, and the boats allow you close access to the low, flat cliffs. A **fishing** trip on the bay lasts three hours and costs US$50–85. A three-day, all-inclusive sailing trip (landing on Grímsey) costs around US$900 per person. It's also possible to design your own custom cruise with either company.

**Swimming** (*Héðinsbraut; ☎ 464 1144; ⏲ 09.00–19.00 Mon–Fri, 10.00–17.00 Sat/Sun; entrance 200ISK*) The pool and hot tubs are on Héðinsbraut, across from the campsites (on your left heading north towards Raufarhöfn).

## TJÖRNES

The Tjörnes Peninsula juts out northwards from Húsavík, offering a rare sea view of both Skjálfandi Bay and Öxarfjörður and featuring a very rare geology. Unlike the volcanic landscapes everywhere else in Iceland, Tjörnes is sedimentary, made from layers of organic deposits that date back to the Pliocene era. When the earth's crust last moved, the layers were pushed up from the seabed. The sandy sediments remain a small mystery, as the fossils found here represent warm sea organisms only known to have existed in the Pacific Ocean – various theories explain how the creation of the Bering Sea opened up the north Atlantic and how the earth's shift in magnetic poles meant that once upon a time, Iceland was quite warm and covered in trees. You can see the evidence at the **Tjörnes Fossil Museum** (*☎ 464 1968; ⏲ summer 10 Jun–31 Aug 10.00–18.00 daily; entrance 350ISK*). The small, one-room museum houses a diverse collection of locally found fossils, including petrified wood, fossilised crystalline, whale and shark bones, and lignite (coal). There are also a few rare stones that have drifted over from Greenland (like granite) on the sea ice. To find your own fossils, just turn left towards the shore at **Hallbjarnarstaðir** (about 10km north of Húsavík) near the blue sign that says 'fossils' (be sure to close the gate behind you). The very steep dirt road leads down to a beach of smooth, black stones. The odd mixture of white shell and black stone contributes to the unique salt-and-pepper sand and the brown cliffs are layered with millions of fossils. The farmer who owns the land asks that you don't take anything from these cliffs without permission (look but don't steal).

Route 85 continues to loop up around the peninsula and passes some wonderful scenery – don't speed through too quickly. The cliffs are low and horizontal and the hills sweep inland. From the point at **Voladalstorfa** (by the lighthouse) you can see the tiny speck of **Mánáeyjar** (Moon Island), the remnants of an underwater volcano that last erupted in the mid 19th century. A number of trails run along the edge of the cliffs from the small pull-off and parking area. This is a great spot for birdwatching – in summer, the gulls circle endlessly and the puffins claim the cliffs. The farm at **Mánárbakki** runs a 'museum' in a small turf dwelling. It's more of a private collection of old things, quite similar to what you'll see everywhere else in the country (*Minjasafnið á Mánárbakka; ☎ 464 1957; ⊕ upon request; entrance 400ISK*). Perhaps more interesting is the view just beyond the final point when the road turns in towards Öxarfjörður. The lookout point opens to the fjord, where the varied depths (from the shifting glacial deposits) give the water a dozen different shades of blue.

## KELDUHVERFI

Kelduhverfi literally translates as 'the bog district' – a lowland of moors, marshes, and the watery delta of the Jökulsá River. The region is the flattest in all Iceland, where the Vatnajökull meltwater deposits mud and silt before flowing into the shallows of Öxarfjörður. The landscape can seem so quiet and uneventful at first glance, although actually, things are extremely active. On the surface, the powerful glacial runoff diverges into hundreds of rivers and streams that feed the swampy grasslands and create a unique ecosystem for Iceland. Beneath Öxarfjörður lies a fissure swarm, along with two fault lines in what is essentially the Mid-Atlantic Ridge. That makes Kelduhverfi one of the most earthquake-prone places in Iceland. It also means that natural hot springs dot the region, raising the water temperature in the glacial streams to about 15°C (as opposed to the normal 3°C). **Skjálftavatn**, or 'earthquake lake', was born between 1975 and 1976 when a number of earthquakes caused the soft land to sink and the streams and estuaries flooded the depression.

Route 85 cuts across the flat plain, balanced between the swampy delta on one side and the edge of a vast lava field on the other, the lumpy no-man's-land that stretches all the way to Krafla and Mývatn (see page 366). It's not hard to find the actual cracks and faults in the surface. The scenery feels a little strange because unlike most of Iceland, there are no giant mountains or seascapes nearby. Instead, the view is plain and the colours muted – black sand, greyish rock, brownish grass and the turquoise fjord. A couple of farms break the isolation, but otherwise it's a very peaceful and mysterious place. All you hear is the wind and running water.

Kelduhverfi was first settled by a Viking named Skeggi Böðolfsson in the 9th century. The original estate included the dramatic geology of Jökulsárgljúfur National Park – namely Ásbyrgi and Dettifoss – which later became a number of farms. Over 1,000 years later, the area still hangs on to the local tradition of beekeeping thanks to a rich variety of flowers that grow in the wet soil. As a wetland, the area is unique for birding. The lake is a known moulting spot for the whooper swan (Cygnus cygnus), and throughout the region (in summer), you can spot odd-ish ducks like the common scoter (Melanita nigra) and gadwall (Anas strepera). The horned grebe (Podiceps auritus) and red-throated diver (Gavia stellata) are a bit rarer, but known to breed along the many riverbanks. Almost 300 pairs of great skua (Stercorarius skua) breed around Bakkaland, an island in the delta not easily accessed by foot.

## WHERE TO STAY AND EAT

**Skúlagarðar** (36 rooms) ☎ 465 2280; e skulagardur@simnet.is; www.kelduhverfi.is/skulagardur. Run by a busy beekeeper & his friendly wife, this guesthouse accommodates guests year-round. The main building was once a school (hence the name) & the quality of rooms varies widely, from cosy doubles (with shared bathrooms) to outdoor cabins for sleeping bags (**$**) & a large campsite. Hot showers, kitchens & hygienic bathrooms are open to all guests & camping is free. Meals are served in the dining hall restaurant-style; b/fast costs extra. The area is wonderful for birdwatching & wandering – the red-roofed church at Garðar (across the road & down a bit) was built in 1890 but replaces a number of churches going all the way back to the 13th century. **$$$**

**Hóll** (4 rooms) ☎ 465 2270; e hrunda@ismennt.is. Right next to the earthquake-formed lake, the farmhouse at Hóll is only about 5km from Ásbyrgi. Clean, hospitable, & remote, it's best for those who seek quiet & solitude. Bathrooms are shared, but the bedrooms are large. Horseriding available. B/fast costs extra. **$$$**

**Lundur** (8 rooms) ☎ 465 2247; e lundur@dettifoss.is; www.dettifoss.is; ⏲ summer only 15 Jun–20 Aug. The closest 'settlement' to Ásbyrgi comprises a primary school & the grassy campsite next to it. Basic made-up rooms sleep 1–3, & sleeping-bag accommodation is also available at the school building (shared bathrooms). Meals are available in the school cafeteria (ie: pizza, soup, stuffed crêpes, etc), & this is also the office for the campsite. Lundur is considered the overflow campsite for the national park – things can get crowded & facilities are somewhat limited (bathrooms & sinks); tents cost 650ISK. Guests can get a hot shower at the small swimming pool across the street (⏲ *10 Jun–18 Aug 09.00–19.00; entrance 250ISK*).

# JÖKULSÁRGLJÚFUR NATIONAL PARK

Of Iceland's four national parks, Jökulsárgljúfur is the least visited and the hardest to pronounce (*yuh-kul-sour-glyu-fur*). The word means 'glacier gorge' and describes the deep chasm formed by the Jökulsá á Fjöllum River. Often referred to as a 'canyon' in English, the term is a slight geological mismatch – real canyons take an exceptionally long time to form, whereas Jökulsárgljúfur is the outcome of a few thousand years of cooled lava and melted ice. Phenomenal glacial floods burst through the bedrock with such force that they blew a channel through the land (not unlike a child with a bucketful of water on the beach). The resulting topography is strange and gargantuan, a rough-and-tumble mix of rocks, water and sand. The last such flood occurred only 2,000 years ago but the massive scale of the formations makes Jökulsárgljúfur feel positively prehistoric. The present-day gorge is about 25km long, but narrow (500m wide) and fairly deep (100m).

The national park was created back in 1973 in order to protect the left bank (the right bank is a flat, grey desert). Highlights include the odd-shaped Ásbyrgi, the echo rocks at Hljóðaklettar, the springs of Hólmatungur, and the powerful waterfall Dettifoss. The line of attractions are connected by several hiking paths and a single dirt road (Route 862). Organised tour groups and rushed travellers can be guilty of skipping the park and speeding down the right bank (Route 864) for a hit and run at Dettifoss. They will be sure to get a nice picture of the falls but they will also miss all the cool landscapes the falls have created.

The main office and tourist information centre for Jökulsárgljúfur National Park is at Ásbyrgi (☎ *465 2195;* e *jokulsargljufur@ust.is; www.ust.is;* ⏲ *24hrs daily*). Jökulsárgljúfur is open year-round, but the roads beyond Ásbyrgi are closed whenever there's snow. Those who wish to hike in and experience a one-of-a-kind winter wonderland must first register at the office.

## JÖKULSÁ Á FJÖLLUM

The Jökulsá á Fjöllum is the second-longest river in Iceland at 206km (the Thjórsá is just 24km longer – see page 47). The source of the river is at Dyngjujökull, the topmost bulge of Vatnajökull glacier, after which the river cuts across the desert highlands and barren lava fields before it tumbles down into the gorge at Jökulsárgljúfur. The Jökulsá carries over 23,000 tons of glacial debris per day, most of which ends up in the shallows of Öxarfjörður.

**GETTING THERE AND AWAY** The main entrance to the park is just off Route 85. It is also possible to come up from Mývatn via Route 862 and enter at the southern end of the park but the dirt road is narrow, bumpy and unpredictable. If you are not driving or biking, you can catch a bus: **Trex** (*www.trex.is*) makes a stop at Ásbyrgi between Húsavík (1 hour 15 minutes) and Kópasker (30 minutes); **SBA-Norðuleið** (*www.sba.is*) travels from Akureyri to the park with stops at Húsavík (1 hour 45 minutes), Ásbyrgi (3 hours), Hljóðaklettar (4 hours) and Dettifoss (5 hours). You can also take the return journey as a day tour. Another SBA bus connects Dettifoss and Mývatn at Reykjahlið (1 hour 30 minutes).

**GETTING AROUND** Jökulsárgljúfur is made for those who love to hike (see *Walks in Jökulsárgljúfur*, page 388). You can also drive through the park along the dirt road (Route 862) but it's up on the plateau and avoids the main features of the area. Every 'attraction' has a nearby car park to allow for pinpointed walks, but the really fantastic landscapes are in between and close to the river – only accessible by foot.

**WHERE TO STAY** There are no guesthouses/hotels inside the park, but if you want a bed you can book at the nearby farms in Kelduhverfi. Otherwise the main **campsite** in the park is at Ásbyrgi, with plenty of space for tents and caravans (register at the office near the car park) (☎ *465 2391;* ⌚ *1 Jun–15 Sep; tent 650ISK*). The facilities are very good with a number of kitchens, bathrooms and hot showers (250ISK), and there's a shop selling camping goods and some food. Another smaller 'natural' campsite is situated in Vesturdalur, for tents only. Well outside the park limits is the very remote interior farm of **Grímsstaðir** (*9 rooms;* ☎ *464 4292;* e *djupadokk@simnet.is;* ⌚ *1 Jun–15 Sep;* **$$**). Bathrooms are shared; camping and sleeping-bag accommodation are also available. The landscape out here is completely unmarred – one is content simply looking at the horizon. It also makes a very convenient place to stop over on the way to Mývatn or the east.

**ÁSBYRGI** The gorge at Ásbyrgi represents one of only a very few geological phenomena of its kind in the world. The vertical rock walls form a rounded depression that is so precise, it seems almost surgical. These are not the after-effects of mere erosion, but a mysterious feature known throughout Iceland as a *byrgi*, which is caused by a *jökulhlaup* (see page 427) or catastrophic glacial flood. Following a volcanic eruption beneath Vatanjökull glacier, the sheer volume and pressure of melting water becomes so overwhelming that it finally breaks through the ice and unleashes a violent gush of water. In the case of Ásbyrgi, the meltwater from Vatnajökull glacier rushed over the land and seeped down into the bedrock, washing away the pumice and sand wedged in between the giant blocks of basalt. When the final wall of meltwater arrived (with unimaginable force), the unsteadied blocks were simply plucked out and pushed into Öxarfjörður. Studies have shown that there is no soil in the area that is more than

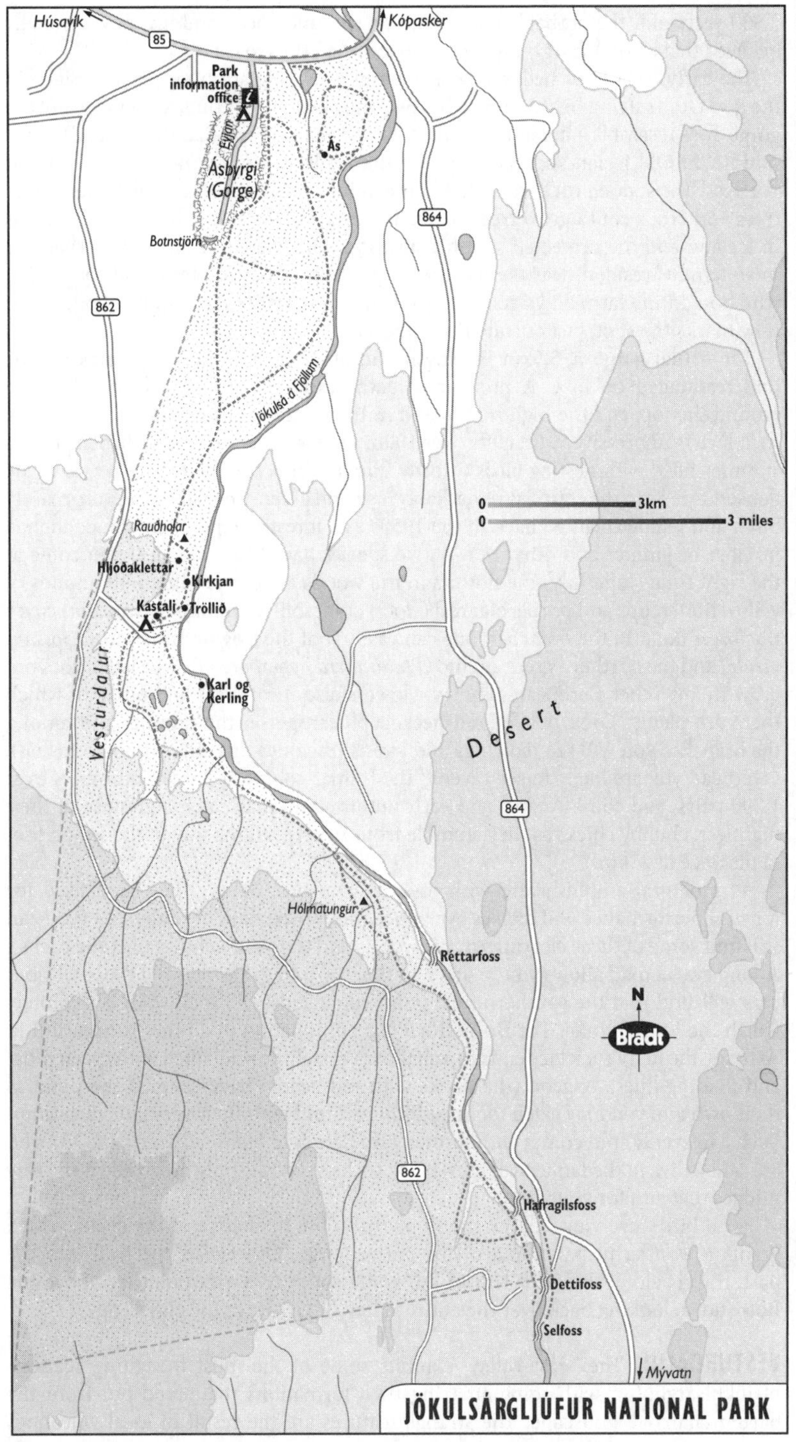
Húsavík
Kópasker
85
Park information office
Eyjan
Ás
Ásbyrgi (Gorge)
864
Botnstjörn
862
Jökulsá á Fjöllum
0 3km
0 3 miles
Rauðholar
Hljóðaklettar
Kirkjan
Kastali
Tröllið
Vesturdalur
Karl og Kerling
Desert
864
Hólmatungur
Réttarfoss
N
Bradt
862
Hafragilsfoss
Dettifoss
Selfoss
Mývatn
JÖKULSÁRGLJÚFUR NATIONAL PARK

2,500 years old (the probable date of the cataclysmic flood) and it is now generally believed that all of Ásbyrgi was created in less than three days.

The early Icelanders believed that Ásbyrgi was the giant hoof-print of Sleipnir, the god Odin's flying horse with eight legs. The allusion is fitting, as the shape of the gorge does resemble a horseshoe with its raised central plateau **Eyjan** (island) in the middle. In Old Icelandic, *Ás* denotes 'of the Gods' and *byrgi* means 'enclosure' or 'fortress'. The sudden rock walls shelter the hollow from the wind, which meant that trees and crops could grow freely here. The estate of **Ás** is one of the oldest farms in Iceland and the protected spot has always been coveted by farmers. Perhaps its most famous resident was the nationalist poet Einar Benediktsson (see page 172) who bought the farm and wrote a great deal of poetry here. A bundle of odd ruins now marks the spot, just outside the entrance.

The actual gorge is 3.5km in length and about 1km wide, an area not to be underestimated on foot. A number of paths explore the forested base, the rim around the top, and the high rock island in the middle. From inside the gorge, the rock face is impressive, with cliffs over 100m high that are covered in lichen, and in summer filled with nesting birds (mostly fulmar). This confined space is one of the densest forests in the country, remarkably lush and green. The tallest trees are mainly birch and willow, planted back in the 1950s as a forestry experiment. Since then, a number of juniper and other non-native species have been added. If you come at the right time (June/July) the flowers in the woods are outstanding – thousands of yellow buttercups and purple blágresi (wood cranesbill; *Geranium sylvaticum*) cover the forest floor. In the branches, one can easily spot the frog **orchids** (*Coeloglossum viride*) and the northern green orchid (*Platanthera hyperborean*) – the latter does not grow in any other European country. Flowers also mean bees and birds, of which there are plenty. Look out for red-necked phalarope on the ground, and among the branches you will see redwings and wrens (the ones that sing without ceasing). Overhead you are likely to see ravens. The fulmar colony at Ásbyrgi numbers over 1,200 pairs, and come August and early autumn you may catch a glimpse of their flightless, chubby chicks as they stumble from Ásbyrgi all the way to the sea on foot (a distance of 25km!).

As a natural amphitheatre with unique acoustics, Ásbyrgi has been used for musical performance and dances ever since the earliest days of settlement (you can still find some of these clearings in the woods and test your echo against the rocks). A long gravel road allows you to drive all the way into the gorge, and those without cars will find that the southernmost point (up against the rock wall) is definitely worth the longish hike. The **Botnstjörn** is a culmination of all that is beautiful in Ásbyrgi: the hefty rock face ends in a shallow, crystalline pool filled with green moss and floating lilies. Wigeon (the ducks with red heads) have claimed the pond as their own and you may catch them paddling around with their very cute ducklings. Such a heavenly spot comes with its own population of *húldufolk* (see page 33) who are said to live in the fantastical grey-black rocks. Alas, the only downside is the tiny midges that aim for your face.

For a bird's-eye view, follow the slope up to the final edge of the eyjan, which grants a wonderful panorama of the entire gorge. Otherwise, the trail into the park travels along the right rim of the gorge south to a viewpoint far above the Botnstjörn, looking back over the entire valley. Take care at the cliff's edge.

**VESTURDALUR** The 'west valley' exhibits some of the most intriguing sections of Jökulsárgljúfur, with some amazing rock formations that stand out from the barren charcoal landscape. The strange features are the result of local volcanoes that erupted from beneath the river, causing steam explosions and fast cooling. The immediate lava flow made the river even more narrow and increased the speed of the rapids. **Rauðholar** ('red hill') is the sloping pile of bright-red pebbled sand that sharply contrasts with the surrounding black landscape, evidence of iron oxides. Once upon a time, all of this area had the same red colour, but it was all washed away in the *jökulhlaup*.

A few of the volcanic craters are still visible as you move south to the **Hljóðaklettar**, or 'echo rocks'. Amidst the grey sand and birch scrub you'll find spectacular patterns of crystallised basalt – spirals, circles, twists, and hefty blocks. The rocks are the leftover cones of volcanoes, most of which have been eroded down to these harder 'plugs' of crystallised basalt that closed off the flow. There is a very distinct echo that resonates among the pinnacles, either from the sound of the rushing river or from you yelling. **Kirkjan**, or 'the church', is the impressive cave that looks like a stone wave. Once upon a time, this was a mound of sand over which a lava flow had hardened. During the *jökulhlaup*, the sand was washed away, leaving only the hollowed fold of basalt, which you see today. The cave reaches back a good 50m and displays a unique radial pattern of basalt cubes. The same formations are seen outside on the surface, showing the classic honeycomb pattern of weathering. Perfectly formed basalt stone steps make the path a lot easier to walk. **Tröllið**, or the troll, is a more recognisable volcanic plug that sticks straight up near the river. This particular troll was caught by the sun after trying to swallow a giant rock – a shepherd boy was eating his breakfast of bread by the river and the sorry troll tried to outdo him. The castle, or **Kastali**, is the closest feature to the car park and shows the incredible strength of the *jökulhlaup*. This single, castle-size rock was dropped here by the last flood when the river's volume was estimated to be over 1,000 times its current flow.

South of the car park stands the other **eyjan** (island) in the park, the raised cliffs of a rounded plateau with several small springs and ponds. A level trail circles the plateau, following the river past the two rock pillars of **Karl og Kerling**. Karl and Kerling are two unfortunate trolls who became petrified at the water's edge. Continuing south, the trail heads to Hólmatungur, or else loops back around to the Vesturdalur campsite.

## BRIDGE OVER TROUBLED WATERS

Seeing as the Jökulsá á Fjöllum flows from the biggest chunk of ice in the whole of Europe, compounded by the fact that the river's volume and speed is regulated by a number of highly volatile volcanoes (not to mention climate), it should really come as no surprise that for most of human history, the river was impossible to cross. In the past, travellers had one of two options: go out to sea and sail across Öxarfjörður, or take a very lengthy hike into the highlands and find a shallow ford. The Jökulsá is very wide in places, but the real difficulty is the speed of the rapids that prohibited any boats from making an attempt outside the frozen calm of winter. Today, only two one-lane bridges cross the river. The first successful span is where Route 185 crosses the river near Ásbyrgi (built in 1905 and replaced in 1958). The second is 50km upriver at Grimsstaðir (see page 384) where the ring road (Route 1) passes by without a hitch. The distance means that most visitors stick to one side of the river, though not so long ago you would have had to stick to one side of the country.

It takes about six hours to hike to Vesturdalur from Ásbyrgi, either over the top of the plateau at Klappir, or along the edge of the gorge. You can also drive there in about 20 minutes on Route 862, which crosses a rolling plain of birch scrubland before turning into the car park/campsite from which most trails originate.

**HÓLMATUNGUR** The 'tongues' of Hólmatungur are formed by a number of streams that trickle down into the Jökulsá. The car park is at the base of the mountain **Ytra-Thórunnarfjall**, one of the main volcanoes in Jökulsárgljúfur. The area represents one of the most canyon-like views in the park, with steep cliffs on the opposite side and the perfect right-angled waterfall **Réttarfoss** ('straight falls'). The narrowest section of the river is at Vígabjarg. Once upon a time, this too was a waterfall (where the trail is) until the Jökulsá changed course in the early 1950s.

**DETTIFOSS** The largest waterfall in all Iceland is also the largest waterfall in the whole of Europe. It's not so much the height (45m) or the width (100m) of the falls, but the sheer power and volume of water that comes shooting over its rough edge. On a 'slow' day, Dettifoss has an average flow of 200m³ of water per second, and in warm weather or rain, that figure bounces up to 500m³ per second (six times the average flow of the River Thames). To experience these falls is to feel the ground shake beneath your feet and to become deaf for a moment. It's no wonder that the early Icelanders considered this the 'king' of all waterfalls (whose queen is Mt Herðubreið; see page 437).

Dettifoss means 'tumble falls', which it most certainly does. The opaque grey-brown colour of the gushing water comes from all the rock, dust, and sand that gets picked up along the riverbed, as well as everything that's stuck inside the glacier when it melts at the river's source. The surrounding area is one of the driest in Iceland, with black sand dunes and desolate plains all around – the one exception is on the west side of the falls (in the park), where the constant spray has quenched a hillside oasis of green growth. That doesn't make the east side any drier. Depending on which way the wind is blowing, you may very well get drenched. What's more, there are no real guardrails – you are more than welcome to walk up to the very edge of the river at the top of the falls and test fate or the overwhelming pull of vertigo. The bottom of the falls is invisible from the mist, but there is an impressive range of columnar basalt that reaches all the way down to the rapids on either side.

Dettifoss marks the southern border of Jökulsárgljúfur National Park. There's a car park on the east side (Route 862), but the west side (Route 864) offers a better road with parking that's closer to the falls. The common opinion is that facilities are better on the east side, but if you are not hiking or driving, you can also opt to fly over the falls (see page 369), which lacks the thunder of being up close, but also grants a rare view. Just above Dettifoss is the jagged-edged **Selfoss** (10m high). Below Dettifoss is the waterfall **Hafragilsfoss** (27m high) from which a path continues upstream (but downhill) through some amazing basalt formations. At **Fossvogur** you can see the perfect vertical cut of a volcanic cone, although it's best viewed from the narrow path on the other side.

**WALKS IN JÖKULSÁRGLJÚFUR** The trails in Jökulsárgljúfur are well maintained and marked with signs or pegs in the ground – you can buy quality, detailed trail maps at the park office in Ásbyrgi. The most popular walk runs the length of the park, from Dettifoss to Ásbyrgi (or vice versa). Most hikers do it in two days, camping overnight in Vesturdalur. There are two main routes – either stick to the gorge for the whole way, or take the detours. At Dettifoss, this is the path at Hafragil which avoids the steep canyon edge. At Ásbyrgi, the path cuts across the top of the plateau, between the river and to the top of the plateau above Botnstjörn. It's an estimated three–four hours to hike from Ásbyrgi to Vesturdalur, and another six–eight hours between Vesturdalur and Dettifoss. The most dangerous part of the walk is the trail at Hafragilsundirlendi (along the canyon ledge) which is steep and single-file only (if you're afraid of heights, take the detour at Hafragil). The trail also crosses the Stallá, an ice-cold stream that can range from ankle to knee deep but which can only be crossed on foot. A number of shorter 'circuit' walks originate at each of the car parks, ranging from one to four hours' long. The most popular of these is at Hljóðaklettar.

## MELRAKASLÉTTA

The northeast peninsula of Melrakaslétta is a conscious step away from the beaten path that circles Iceland. There's not a lot up here, which is exactly what attracts the more rugged brand of traveller who seeks total solitude and a private view of the sea. The land is mostly flat and barren – a rock-strewn plain surrounded by the marshy coastline and a set of low, windswept hills. Beyond the saltwater ponds lies a stretch of silent, black beaches covered with driftwood, most of which floats here all the way from Russia.

The name means 'peninsula of the Arctic fox' – the animal is a little less elusive in these parts thanks to the utter absence of humans (if you're searching, go inland). Fewer than 800 people live among three minuscule villages (Kópasker, Raufarhöfn, and Thórshöfn) and a few weathered farms. Besides sheep, you are more likely to see a scarecrow than another person. For Icelanders, 'Slétta' is known as the home of a strong and resourceful bunch – driftwood is still prized property, and you don't take what isn't yours. Back in the early 19th century, a boatload of French fishermen landed on the peninsula and rustled up a few-dozen lambs to butcher. The local farmers banded together and caught the fishermen, marching them to Frakkagil ('Frenchman's gully') and hanging every one of them at Thjófaklettar ('the rock of thieves').

Farmers take more kindly to visitors these days and a series of flat trails open up the region to those who explore best on foot. The most popular inland trail connects Kópasker to Raufarhöfn and crosses a very stark landscape – the coast is a lot more interesting. For those with sturdy wheels, a number of detours venture out to the capes and lagoons. For their promise of peace and isolation, these areas are gaining a small following among free-wheeling caravans and 4x4s. **Rauðinupur** ('red knoll') is the 75m-high cliff that truly is red. Scoria stone and good lighting cause the bright hue – the path starts at the volcanic crater at Núpskatla and the path follows the cliff up to the lighthouse where the birds are especially active.

At the other end of the peninsula is the cape at **Hraunhafnartangi** ('lava harbour point'), the northernmost point in the whole of mainland Iceland, marked by the Modernist lighthouse of Grímshafnartangi. Standing here you really are just a stone's throw from the Arctic Circle. The stone cairn Thórgeirsdys marks the burial site of Thorgeir Hávarsson, a saga hero renowned for his utter fearlessness (he died at this spot after killing 14 men in battle, after which his foster brother Thórmoð sailed all the way to Greenland to kill his killer). South of the town Raufarhöfn is **Rauðanes** ('red point'), a smaller peninsula that is made up of seaside caves, rock stacks and hefty stone bridges. Some of the features are red, but most are the more ordinary grey and black basalt – a flat trail circles the point along the cliffs' edge.

### THE BIRDS OF MELRAKKASLÉTTA

Serious birders know that it's worth the journey to Melrakkaslétta for its rich diversity in habitat, its thorough lack of people, and the abundance of birds. The never-ending wetlands along the coast are filled with seabirds and waders like the purple sandpiper, red-throated diver, horned grebe, common teal and pintail. The gravel-strewn area inland sees a number of ptarmigan, and up in the sky you might spot a raptor, typically gyrfalcon (*Falco rusticolus*). **Rauðinúpur** (30km north of Kópasker) is arguably the best spot in Melrakkaslétta for seeing a little bit of everything. There's eider and Arctic tern, kittiwake and guillemot, puffin, and a well-known gannet colony that inhabits the rocks just beyond the point. Nearby **Hraunhafnartangi** is another great spot for seabirds. The pond of Kottjörn is a protected bird refuge next to the village of Raufarhöfn and is good for ducks and swans. **Rauðanes** (30km south of Raufarhöfn) was also once a great birdwatching area, but has become less so. The introduction of the mink (see page 59) has been detrimental to the peninsula's puffins, although passionate efforts by local hunters may reverse the trend.

**GETTING AROUND** Route 85 follows the coast all the way around the peninsula but most of the road is unpaved so 4x4s tend to manoeuvre better. **Trex** (*www.trex.is*) offers bus services year-round (Monday–Friday) between Húsavík and Kópasker (1 hour 15 minutes), Raufarhöfn (2 hours) and Thórsöfn (2 hours 45 minutes). A single dirt road (Route 867) crosses the middle of the peninsula, but note that this is a very bleak and isolated landscape (carry extra fuel).

## KÓPASKER

Kópasker was only founded in 1910 and almost got wiped off the map in 1980 after a series of intense earthquakes knocked down most of the houses. The name of the village denotes a rock skerry where seal pups live – if you walk along the coast in spring or summer you are likely to see pups, or just adult seals, lying among the rocks. The easiest place to see the seals is the **lighthouse** at the point. Kópasker resembles the Iceland of once upon a time with its picturesque duck pond and the bold red-and-white church of **Snartarstaðir**, built in 1928. Next door is the old schoolhouse that is now the **Book and Handicraft Museum** (*Bóka og Byggðasafn; Snatarstaði; ☎ 465 2171; e boknord@islandia.is; www.islandia.is/boknord; ⏲ 1 Jun–31 Aug 13.00–17.00 Tue–Sun; entrance 300ISK*). Housing one of the most random but captivating collections of folk memorabilia in Iceland, the museum is worth a stop, if not for the local history then for the chance to see some real Icelandic antiques. Dresses and christening gowns explore the local embroidery designs and the traditions of national costume, and the women of the district display a century of lace and crocheting. The most interesting part is the attic, where you can find just about anything: branding irons, napkin holders, jewellery, thimbles, butter churns, saddles, cane handles, carved bed boards, and the old typeset for a locally printed Bible.

**WHERE TO STAY AND EAT** Only 150 people live in Kópasker, but it's become a small haven for lonesome travellers with a well-stocked shop and a good youth hostel. The petrol station **Bakki** (*Bakkagata 10; ☎ 465 2122; ⏲ 09.30–21.00 Mon–Fri, 11.00–21.00 Sat/Sun*) carries some fast food, grocery staples, and a lot of do-it-yourself meals. The shop also offers two all-inclusive apartments (e *esso@kopasker.is;* **$$$**). Two separate buildings comprise the **hostel** (*14 beds; Akurgerði 7;* ☎ *465 2314;* e *hostel@kopasker.is; www.hostel.is;* ⏲ *May–Oct only;* **$$**). The first is right next to the shop, but the main building is a few blocks away. Both sites are kept very clean and cosy, with great kitchens and shared showers and bathtubs. Rooms have metal bunks, with a few doubles available. There is no public internet but lots of books to read; breakfast costs 900ISK extra. The **campsite** is on the small field next to the pond with only sinks and basic toilets.

## RAUFARHÖFN

The larger of Melrakkasléttа's only two towns, Raufarhöfn is still quite small, with around 250 people who live here on a good day. The villagers like to claim that this is the northernmost town in Iceland, which probably annoys the islanders on Grímsey (see page 354), although technically Raufarhöfn is the northernmost town on the mainland. People have been fishing near the 'harbour of holes' since Iceland's settlement. The town was officially founded in 1836, but had its real heyday during Iceland's herring boom (see page 326). After the fish left, things turned very quiet and they've stayed that way ever since. A pleasant walking tour takes in the historic church and the headland (höfði), around the harbour and above the bird cliffs, and back to the town's bird sanctuary at Kottjörn pond.

**WHERE TO STAY AND EAT** The biggest and best accommodation for the whole peninsula is at **Hótel Norðurljós** (*15 rooms; Aðalbraut 2;* ☎ *465 1233;* e *ebt@vortex.is; www.raufarhofn.is;* **$$$**). The metal-sided longhouse is built to keep out the cold, and all double rooms have private bathrooms. An in-house fish- and lamb-restaurant serves basic but filling meals. For blustery days, there's a swimming pool (*Skólabraut;* ☎ *465 1144;* ⏲ *Jun–Sep*) and the Raufarhöfn free **campsite** is next door. Amenities are basic with toilets and cold-water sinks. The shop (*Aðalbraut 26;* ☎ *465 1203;* ⏲ *09.00–21.00 daily*) carries basic groceries and supplies.

## THÓRSHÖFN

As a forgotten corner of the country, 'Thór's harbour' is anything but a tourist town. There's a fish-processing plant, some boats in the harbour, a lively bar and absolutely no pretence. The dose of reality is comforting. The view from the coast takes in the shining waters of Thistilfjörður ('thistle fjord') and the low hills of Melrakkaslétta, but winter sees choppy waves and a slight chance of drift ice. Early settlers believed that the god Thór slammed his hammer into the coast and gave the harbour its perfect shape (hence the name). Traders have docked here since the 16th century, but only in 1897 did a Danish fish company build a warehouse and open the town for business. Today, around 400 people live in the neighbourhood, most of whom follow the Icelandic custom of doing a little bit of everything, including fishing.

For most travellers, Thórshöfn is the gateway to Langanes, the last stop before the end of the road and the end of Iceland. The town makes a good base for an in-depth exploration of either peninsula (Langanes or Melrakkaslétta) or as a convenient stop along the northeast coast. It's also the biggest place for a very long way in any direction.

**GETTING THERE AND AWAY** Route 85 connects Thórshöfn with Húsavík and Vopnafjörður (1 hour 30 minutes). On weekdays, **Trex** (*www.trex.is*) offers a bus service to and from Húsavík (3 hours) via Raufarhöfn (45 minutes). Thórshöfn Airport (THO) lies just north of the town. **Air Iceland** (*www.airiceland.is*) flies five times a week to and from Akureyri during March–October only (about 1 hour).

## WHERE TO STAY

**Hótel Jórvík** (7 rooms) Langanesvegur 31; ☎ 468 1149; e jorvik@netfang.com; www.jorvik.vefur.com. This patriotic painted house/hotel seems a little zany – the 1960s vibe is unintentional but fun. Rooms are comfy enough, with shared bathrooms & kitchen facilities available. **$$$**

**Lyngholt** (7 rooms) Langanesvegur 12; m 897 5064; e lyngholt@lyngholt.is; www.lyngholt.is. This snug, log-sided guesthouse is a warm & welcome refuge within walking distance of the whole village & right across the street from the swimming pool. The owner is kind & understands the needs of travellers, taking special care with her guests. Double rooms with shared bathrooms, kitchen facilities (including outdoor barbecue). They also offer reasonably priced sleeping-bag accommodation, some of which is not on site. B/fast inc. **$$$**

**Ytra-Áland** (6 rooms) ☎ 468 1290; e ytra-aland@simnet.is; www.ytra-aland.is. This tidy farm rests right at the base of the fjord about 20km west of Thórshöfn, with open access to the shore & the bounding landscape. It makes a nice rural base from which to explore both Langanes & Melrakaslétta, & meals are available in the dining room. Half of the rooms have private bathrooms; the rest share. They also rent out a fully furnished 3-bedroom summer home (10,000ISK per night). Lastly, the farm offers affordable sleeping-bag accommodation at the school in **Svalbarð**. *Sleeping-bag accommodation from 2,200ISK. B/fast inc.* **$$$**

**Camping** The campsite (☎ *468 1220;* ⏲ *1 Jun–1 Oct daily;* **$**) is just north of the church (follow the signs). Next door is a surprisingly good gym and indoor **swimming pool** (☎ *468 1167;* ⏲ *16.00–20.00 Mon–Thu, 15.00–19.00 Fri, 11.00–14.00 Sat*).

## WHERE TO EAT

**Restaurant Eyrin** Eyrarvegur 3; ☎ 468 1250; e eyrin@eyrin.is; www.eyrin.is; ⏲ 10.00–22.00 Mon–Fri, until late Fri/Sat (around 01.30). The town pub & hangout, famous for its pool table. Expect fresh fish from off the boats in the harbour, but also realise that the pizza, steaks, & hamburgers are exactly what the fishermen want to eat. *Mains from 1,650ISK.* **$$$**

**Esso station** Fjarðarvegur 5; ☎ 468 1174; ⏲ 08.00–22.00 Sun–Thu, 09.00–23.00 Fri/Sat. Typical petrol-station fare but 'specialising' in fried chicken & with a number of sit-down dining booths. They're also famous for selling the cheapest hot dogs in all Iceland (175ISK with everything on it). *Mains from 450ISK.* **$**

# SAUÐANES

Sauðanes is the headland just north of Thórshöfn (7km away), right after the airport but just before turning off towards Langanes. Ever since the settlement of Iceland, there has been a church at Sauðanes. Apparently, this was a coveted parsonage because of its rights to great amounts of eider down, driftwood, and seals (you still see all three). What's more, the low tidal plains offered ample grazing room for sheep along the beach. The white stone house that stands there today was built by the social activist Reverend Vigfús Sigurðsson (1811–89), who moved to Sauðanes in 1869 with the hope of implementing his own brand of rural reforms. Vigfús believed that physical labour helped overcome sin and he prescribed the help of several local sinners to build a ship especially for transporting the stone necessary to build the rectory. Their general reluctance and constant yielding to the sin of drink delayed completion until 1880. One surprise is that the doors and doorframe are made from teak, cut from a tree trunk that somehow drifted from warmer climes to the north of Iceland. The tin-sided church was only built in 1889, after Vigfús had died. Sauðanes continued as a parish until 1958, when the farm was deserted along with the rest of Langanes.

Today, one can relive the past at the **Sauðanes Museum of Relics** (*Sauðaneshúsið; ☎ 468 1468; ⏲ 1 Jun–16 Aug daily, otherwise call; entrance 700ISK*). Besides their display of the past lives of Langanes, the rectory functions as the local **tourist information centre**. There's also a small café serving coffee and *kleinur* inside. Behind the church is the parish graveyard, a sobering resting place for the farmers, fishermen and drowned sailors who lived and died on Langanes. Despite its desertion, the hayfields are still planted and the farm is quite picturesque. One very nice walking trail follows the coast from the road to the lighthouse at Grenjanes (3km).

## LANGANES

Langanes feels like arriving at the end of the earth. For a good 40km, the grassy slopes roll on and on until finally giving way to the sea. At the end of Iceland's 'long peninsula' the waves crash on all sides, the whole country is at your back, and the wind is all you can hear. It's also completely uninhabited so there is nothing to disturb the beautiful, silent panorama before you.

Even the smallest maps of Iceland include Langanes as the stubborn point between Thistilfjörður (to the north) and Bakkaflói (to the south). That extra reach out to sea has always been good for fishermen, though small returns, perilous weather, and the modern age of convenience led to the total desertion of Langanes by 1960. Aside from some abandoned farms and a few adventurous sheep, you are the only civilisation around. The landscape is barren but relatively gentle with reddish dirt, long grass, and ash-coloured beaches that are covered in piles of driftwood. Larger boulders litter the smaller hills before they break into a few low, flat-topped peaks of basalt.

Desolation, however, does not mean boring. Langanes is remarkably peaceful and breathtaking, though it takes a special kind of traveller to appreciate the stark beauty of the place. It also takes some patience as the road on Langanes is rocky and quite difficult to drive on. A 4x4 is preferable for the first 20km and absolutely necessary if you intend to drive all the way to the end or ascend any of the hills. Mountain bikes fare well, but even then it's a bumpy ride and the distance long. Also note that because the peninsula is so narrow you are essentially driving or riding 'out at sea', and quite exposed to the weather.

The 'good' road was built by the American military and leads to the top of **Mt Heiðarfjall** (266m), where a defunct Cold War radar system has been rusting away since NATO built it in the late 1950s. From the gravel car park you get the best view of the whole peninsula. Directly south you can see the unspoiled bay of **Eiðisvík**, with a black-sand bar beach, a shimmering lake and the slanted cliffs of **Mt Naustinn** (382m). It looks beautiful and inaccessible, but there is a level path from the main road. Farther out on Langanes, the land flattens out but the road does not, approaching the bird cliffs just before **Skoruvík**. There's a gannet colony on the rock pillar Karl ('the man') and a mad number of gulls (beware of the Arctic terns). From Skoruvík, a hiking trail circles the point but the main road veers south, ending at **Skálar**. The ghostly remains of a tiny fishing village include stone foundations and the old cemetery. This is also the only emergency hut on the whole peninsula. About 2km back along the southern coast, you come to some

## THE SHIPWRECKS OF LANGANES

Peaceful as it can seem, the Langanes Peninsula has always proven treacherous for passing ships. High winds, stormy seas and potential drift ice make the long, rocky shallows even more dangerous. The lighthouse at Fontur marks the end of the narrow point, but many a sailor has been blown off course and many a fishing trip has ended as a battered wreck. On 5 October 1907, the Norwegian ship *Frithjof* went down right at the point, with 16 men drowned in the surf. One man survived – Johannes Larsen spent the night in a sea cave. The next day he climbed the 60m sea cliff and then walked 7km to a nearby farm. His fellow sailors are buried at the back of the graveyard in Sauðanes. A few decades later, an English fishing boat crashed on the north side of the point, where they were able to scramble up onto Engelskagjá ('English rift'). The men attempted to walk to Skálar, but they all died from exhaustion and exposure with the exception of the captain, who made it to the farm. A wooden cross marks their grave, halfway between Skoruvík and Skálar. The Icelandic text reads 'here lie 11 Englishmen'.

mighty bird cliffs where you can watch a mammoth-size nesting spectacle. **Fontur** is at the end of Langanes, and although the point holds no records (northernmost, easternmost, remotest, etc), it certainly feels like it should (perhaps a runner-up for least accessible). The **lighthouse** was first built in 1914, followed by the current structure in 1950. The view back over the peninsula 'to Iceland' is a little mind-bending and definitely worth the long journey out there. The 70m-high cliffs are also pretty fascinating, although you can't see much from up top. Expect puffins in summer and very high winds all year long.

## WHERE TO STAY

**Ytra-Lón** (18 beds) 468 1242; ytralon@simnet.is; www.hostel.is. This could very well be the most remote youth hostel in the country, a good 15km from Thórshöfn & a world apart from anything else. It's also your only choice. The owners have lived on Langanes for a long time & enjoy helping newcomers discover the peninsula. Ytra-Lón is a working farm, so it feels different from most hostels. You can saddle up a horse for a beautiful ride or go fishing for trout in the river at the back. Shared bathrooms & kitchen facilities; sleeping-bag accommodation available. Pickups in Thórshöfn are available for a fee. **$$**

12

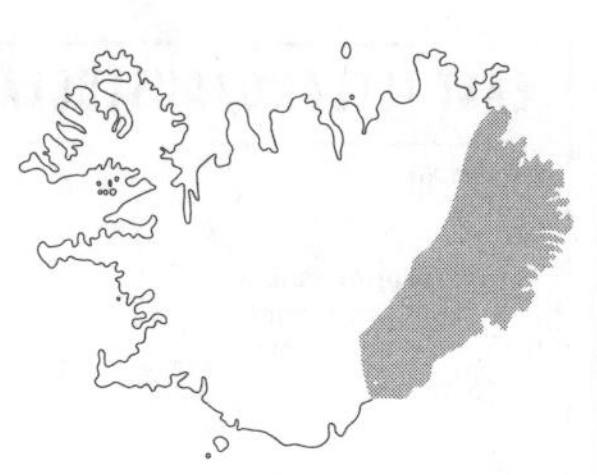

# Austurland (East Iceland)

Iceland's eastern edge is pleasantly untamed and far, far away from Reykjavík. Out here, everything looks and feels bigger: the mountains are the highest in the country, the fjords the steepest, and the land is pretty much devoid of people or buildings. The east is also where the real 'ice' of Iceland is – Vatnajökull glacier might be a huge white spot on the map, but the close-ups are truly captivating. You can drive or hike right up into the glacier's edge in the valleys of Skaftafell National Park, and with similar ease take in the floating blue icebergs of Jökulsárlón. Some of these areas get fairly crammed with tourists in summer, but it's nothing that a 15-minute detour can't fix. It's way up in the mist of the hard-to-get-to highlands that you'll spot the occasional reindeer.

The crowning glory of this region is the East Fjords, the very first part of Iceland to be discovered by the Vikings after sailing west from Norway. A thousand years ago, they commented on the never-ending view from these peaks and how surprised they were to find it so empty. Not much has changed since. The ring road careens around each and every inlet, taking you through deep-cut valleys, silent waterfronts and the perky little fishing villages of yesteryear.

The east tends to be treated as a through destination, rather than a to-and-from stop. Figure out whichever is more practical for your needs. The landscape prevents you from having too many options, but don't underestimate the time it will take to travel through. These are intricate parts with lots of curves in the road.

**Note:** winter tends to hamper travel in the area, especially the East Fjords, which means a lot of group tourist activities are limited. Unless otherwise noted, all museums in this chapter are open for summer only (1 June–15 August).

## VOPNAFJÖRÐUR

Somewhat off the beaten path, Vopnafjörður features the kind of simple, natural surroundings that too often go unnoticed. The quiet, V-shaped fjord divides the east from the north with a span of low cliffs, rocky beaches, and a wonderfully empty valley. So many rushing streams and rivers (namely the Selá, Hofsá and Vesturá) boast some of the best salmon fishing in Iceland, which explains why rights are so exclusive. Along the horizon stands the rising ridge of Smjörfjöll ('butter mountain'), so named after the shining dew on the grass. The protected topography makes this one of the warmest places in Iceland (after Akureyri) – in summer, the average temperature is above 20°C.

The legend of the *Landvættir* (see page 35) recounts how a malicious wizard first sailed into Vopnafjörður where his evil intentions were thwarted by a mighty poison-breathing dragon. Since then, the area has had a much quieter time of

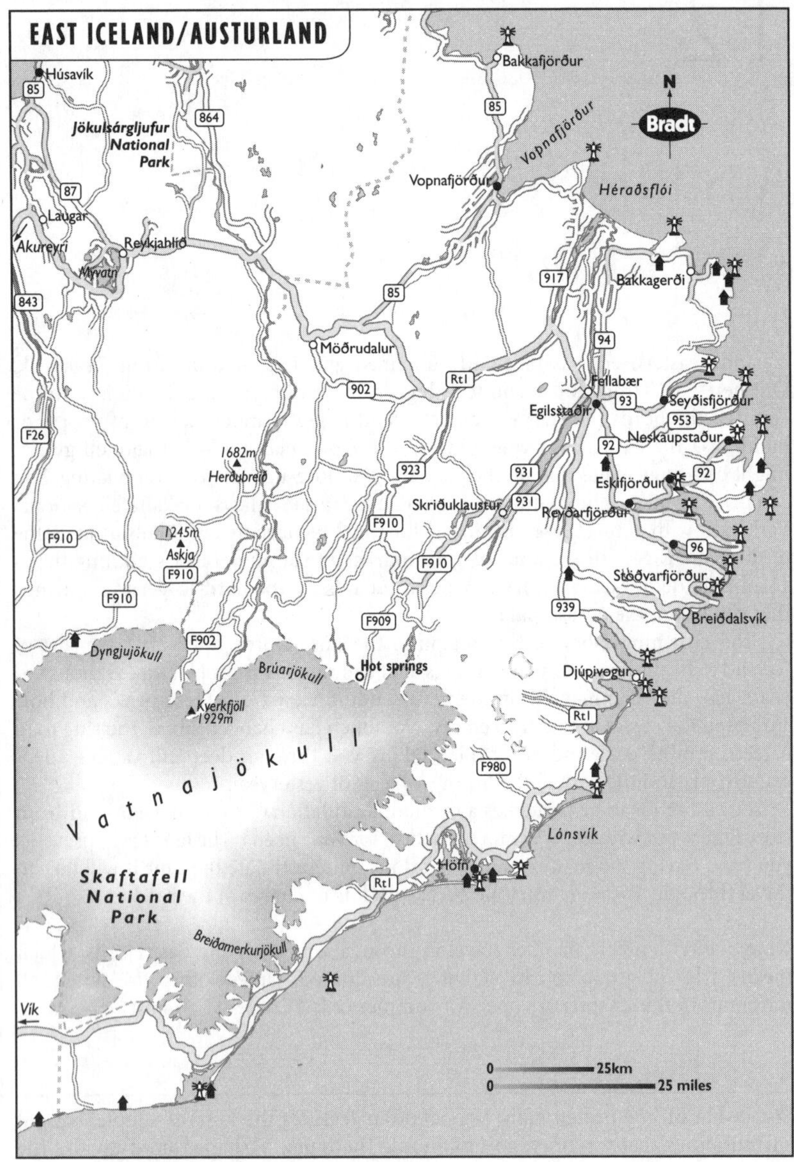


things, and has been pretty much been left alone. A handful of ancient farms dot the main valley and the town is home to around 500 people who still make their living from the land or the sea.

The name 'weapon fjord' derives from the Viking Eyvindur the Well-Armed or 'Weapon-ed' – who claimed the fjord and settled the valley. The names of the surrounding farms date back to the *Landnámabok,* and for centuries the pace of life in Vopnafjörður has changed little. That nostalgia is best reflected by the local writer Gunnar Gunnarsson, who set most of his novels among the bare hills of this unspoiled fjord.

**GETTING THERE AND AWAY** Daily flights travel to and from Akureyri (45 minutes) on Air Iceland at Vopnafjörður Airport (VPN), located at the very bottom of the fjord (*473 1121; airiceland@airiceland.is; www.airiceland.is*). Route 85 connects the town with Bakkafjörður (30 minutes) and Thórshavn (1 hour) in the north, or to Route 1 in the south, connecting to Egilsstaðir (1 hour 15 minutes). The very windy, unpaved road over the mountains (Route 917) takes in the most breathtaking view along with some treacherous hairpin curves.

**TOURIST INFORMATION** The big, yellow two-storey building is the food store, museum, and the town's information centre (*Hafnarbyggð 6; 473 1341; info@vopnafjardarhreppur.is; www.vopnafjardarhreppur.is; 10.00–17.00 Mon–Fri, 12.00–16.00 Sat/Sun*). The **Nema hvað?** ('Except what?') craft and souvenir shop across the street functions as a second information centre (*Hafnarbyggð; 473 1565 (if closed, call 473 1160); summer 13.30–17.30 Tue–Sat, winter 13.30–17.30 Fri*).

## WHERE TO STAY

**Hótel Edda** (17 rooms) Hafnarbyggð 17; 473 1840; edda@hoteledda.is; www.hoteledda.is. This newly refurbished, tourist-class hotel is always clean, dry & orderly, but the rooms can feel quite compact. Some offer lush private bathrooms, but most only contain a sink with shared facilities down the hall. The nicest place in town. B/fast buffet inc. **$$$**

**Syðri-Vík** (6 rooms) 473 1199; holmi56@vortex.is, ifh@farmholidays.is; www.farmholidays.is. This rural guesthouse embraces Vopnafjörður culture: a prim, working farm at the base of the fjord offering trout fishing & horseriding. 2 summer cottages can be rented out for families or groups. Kitchen, laundry, & camping facilities available; shared bathrooms. Recommended. **$$**

**WHERE TO EAT** Hótel Edda runs a good fish-and-lamb restaurant that's fresh and tidy, if not predictable (**$$$**). Otherwise, it's the Esso station (*Kolbeinsgata 35; 473 1204*). On your own, visit the Kauptún grocery store (*Hafnarbyggð 6; 473 1403; 13.30–17.30 daily*).

**WHAT TO SEE AND DO** Vopnafjörður's main attraction is the ancient farm of **Bustarfell** (*473 1466; 15 Jun–15 Sep 10.00–18.00 daily; entrance 500ISK*). The six-gabled, turf-covered farmhouse is one of the best preserved in Iceland, with much of the original 18th-century structure still in place. Perhaps most amazing is that the farm was inhabited by the same family for over 500 years: the land was purchased in 1532 by Árni Brandson, son of the vicar in Vopnafjörður. The original building fell victim to a summer fire in 1770, after which it was rebuilt. New generations have added new additions, and the last inhabitant – Methusalem Methusalemsson – furnished the entire home with family heirlooms. Visiting Bustarfell is like taking a step back in time to experience Icelandic farm life – to get there, you need to follow Route 85 all the way up into the beautiful valley of Hofsárdalur.

Finding other nice, pretty spots is a given in Vopnafjörður – just get out and explore. Favourites are the Selá River and the Selárdalur Valley. Besides hiking and fishing, there's a **swimming pool** (*Selárlaug; 473 1499; 10.00–19.00 daily*). A detour in the opposite direction takes you to the silent beach between Hámundarstaðir and Ljósaland. From this coast, hikers get a nice view of the cliffs, the town and the whole fjord. On the other side, Smjörfjöll Mountain is a hiker's paradise but with lots of tiny streams flowing down the sides of the hills. The surrounding heath is breathtaking and totally uninhabited. Most people settle

## GUNNAR GUNNARSSON (1889–1975)

It's no surprise that one of the most expressive and widely known writers in Iceland should be traced back to the lonesome climes of Vopnafjörður. Gunnar Gunnarsson was born in the valley of Fljótsdalur, but spent his childhood working on the family farm in Vopnafjörður. His mother died of pneumonia when he was only eight years old and he received virtually no education. Still, he was able to publish his first two collections of poems when he was only 17 years old (*Poems of Spring* and *Memories of My Mother*) and as a result, was accepted to a two-year 'folk high school' in Denmark. Seeking wider readership, he began writing in Danish but failed to publish. He only found success in 1912 with his second novel *Guest the One-Eyed* (*Borgslægtens Historie*), which grew into a multi-volume story detailing the lives and struggles of three generations of farmers. *Guest* was the first book written by an Icelander ever to be made into a film, and soon Gunnar was known throughout Germany and Denmark. Confident in his new-found fame, Gunnar began writing more autobiographically. *The Church on the Mountain* (*Kirkan á Fjallinu*) is considered his masterpiece – five volumes that are a direct reference to the author's own life in Vopnafjörður.

Just before World War II, Gunnar returned to Iceland and to writing in Icelandic. He strived politically for the unification of all Nordic countries which explains why some of his work was translated into Finnish, Faroese and Greenlandic. In English, his best-known work is probably *The Black Cliffs* (*Svartfugl*), whose plot and imagery deliver a dark tribute to east Iceland. Overall, he was very prolific with 24 novels in 20 languages and hundreds of poems. Three times he was nominated for the Nobel Prize for literature but lost to his more famous (and 'more Icelandic') contemporary Halldór Laxness (see page 197). Today, a statue memorial of Gunnar stands in the centre of Vopnafjörður. The author himself is buried in the cemetery at Viðey Island (see page 186), and his farm is now the Gunnar Gunnarsson Institute and Museum at Skriðuklaustur (*☎ 471 2990; e klaustur@skriduklaustur.is; www.skriduklaustur.is; ⌚ summer 10.00–18.00 daily; entrance 500ISK*).

for a rough drive through the mountain pass to the next valley over in Lagarfljót. The road (Route 917) passes a gorgeous two-level waterfall easily reached by hiking.

## MÖÐRUDALUR

In times of old, travellers on horses followed a dusty trail across the hinterland from the East fjords to Mývatn. The settlement at Möðrudalur was the journey's halfway mark, and to this day it is still the highest (469m) and driest farm in all Iceland. The grey sand dunes are the result of a rain shadow caused by Vatnajökull – on a clear day, one may look across the sand to the mountains of Herðubreið and Kverkfjöll, and even the glacier itself (100km away). The present-day church was built by local farmer Jón Stefánsson in loving memory of his devoted wife who died in 1949. Farmer Jón was known for his odd habits, like playing Bach backwards (note for note) on the church organ and forcing himself to sneeze (for a long life). The church he designed sticks to tradition on the outside but has a more individual interior – Jón painted the very unique altarpiece of Jesus Christ beneath a palm-covered Mt Herðubreið. Jón and his wife are buried in the churchyard.

Today, Möðrudalur is a busy little travellers' outpost in a beautiful but very empty part of the country. Technically, this is the vast highland interior, but it's also just ten minutes off the ring road. Visitors are welcome at the farm's **guesthouse and café** Fjalladýrð (*7 rooms;* ☎ *471 1858;* e *fjalladyrd@fjalladyrd.is; www.fjalladyrd.is;* **$$**). Overnight guests are put up in the *baðstofa* – a traditional, turf-covered farmhouse decorated down to every quaint detail (quite an experience). Camping is also available, with a full service for caravans. Aside from pastries and coffee, the café serves up a hearty lamb-and-vegetable stew and sandwiches (🕒 *11.00–20.00 daily*).

## EGILSSTAÐIR

The unofficial capital of the east only became a town for the sake of modern convenience. Not so long ago all that was here were a few stranded farms with a view. In 1944, the brand-new independent government of Iceland agreed that the big blank spot on the east side of the country would be problematic for development. Striving to unify the outlying parts of the country, they declared a great new high-tech city to co-ordinate nicely with the construction of Route 1. The ring road spanned the Lagafljót River at the narrow site of an ancient ferry and the city was laid out just beyond. In a bid for saga-age credentials, the project was christened 'Egilsstaðir' – a reference to the nearby farm 'Egil's stead' and named after Egil, a relative of Eyvindur of Vopnafjörður.

By 1947, the streets were paved, the houses were painted, and the town opened for business. Although it never came to resemble the great new dawn of a new Iceland, Egilsstaðir serves well its intended purpose as a crossroads and supply depot. For centuries, travellers came here just to take the ferry across the river. Today, Egilsstaðir is the de facto gateway for the tens of thousands who enter Iceland by ferry from the European continent. As it is the intersection of the port at Seyðisfjörður and the ring road, most visitors stop off for a rest before heading off or heading home. As a result, there's an excited energy that makes this town of 2,300 people feel a bit more adventurous than it probably is. Plus, the locals have learned how to make a living by catering to the demands of the over-tired and hyper-inquisitive.

**GETTING THERE AND AWAY** Egilsstaðir is the most easily accessible town in the east. Egilsstaðir Airport (EGS) is in the field just a short distance from the town – you can walk there from the town centre if needed, otherwise hitch or take a cab. **Air Iceland** (☎ *471 1210;* e *airiceland@airiceland.is; www.airiceland.is*) flies daily back and forth to Reykjavík City Airport (1 hour). Seasonal charter flights also link to other destinations, including Copenhagen (see *Tour operators*, page 72). If you're driving or riding, Route 1 connects Egilsstaðir with Akureyri (3 hours 30 minutes) and Höfn (4 hours).

The bus station is located right next to the tourist information centre at Kaupvangur 6 (☎ *471 2000*). **Trex** (*www.trex.is*) offers a daily bus service to and from Akureyri (4 hours) with stops in Grimsstaðir and Mývatn. **Austfjarðaleið** (*www.austfjardaleid.is*) connects daily with all the towns of the East Fjords, namely Reyðarfjörður, Eskifjörður, Neskaupstaður, Faskrúðsfjörður, Stöðvarfjörður, and Breiðdalsvík. A separate link connects several times a day to Seyðisfjörður, and in summer, **Austurleið-Kynnisferðir** (*www.austurleid.is*) connects to Höfn (4 hours 30 minutes).

## TOURIST INFORMATION

**Tourist information** Kaupvangur 10; 471 2320; e info@east.is; www.east.is; 15 May–15 Jun 08.00–22.00 daily, winter 09.00–18.00 Mon–Fri, 12.00–16.00 Sat/Sun. Hands down, Egilsstaðir has the busiest tourist centre in the entire country – in summer. As the welcome centre for everyone just coming off the boat or the ring road, things can get hectic. Besides the bus station, campsite, booking centre, & internet, there's a small café & a shop selling books, postcards, maps, & basic travel supplies.

**TOUR OPERATORS** The hiking and adventure tour company, **FA Travel** (*Miðvangur 2–4; 471 2000; e info@fatravel.is; www.fatravel.is*), offers a number of walks and horseriding options in the nearby mountains and fjords.

To rent bikes and camping gear, try **Skógar** (*Dynskógum 4; 471 1230; 10.00–18.00 Mon–Fri; 10.00–15.00 Sat*).

For details of other tour operators, see *Chapter 4*, page 72.

## WHERE TO STAY

**Egilsstaðir** (18 rooms) Fagradalsbraut; 471 1114; e egilsstadir@egilsstadir.com; www.isholf.is/egillstadir. Only 5mins outside the city; the real Egilsstaðir farm is still the quaint little place it was 1,000 years ago, with the addition of a friendly restaurant & a rambling 3-storey 'farmhouse' for guests. Small but clean non-smoking rooms (all with en-suite bathrooms) & the polite owners make this a very pleasant travellers' refuge. Recommended. Hearty b/fast inc. Summer **$$$$**, winter **$$**

**Fosshótel Valaskjálf** (39 rooms) Skógarlönd 3; 471 5050; e valaskjalf@fosshotel.is; www.fosshotel.is. This polished, user-friendly chain hotel offers guests a restful spot with a dash of style. All rooms are non-smoking with private bathrooms. B/fast inc. **$$$$**

**Hótel Herað** (60 rooms) Miðvangur 5–7; 471 1500; e herad@icehotels.is; www.icelandairhotels.is. Sleek new modern hotel, right in the town centre, within walking distance of most tourist amenities. The wooden floors & contemporary furnishings add a corporate flavour – all rooms have private bathrooms. Their in-house restaurant is stylish, expensive, & good. B/fast inc. **$$$$**

**Hótel Edda** (52 rooms) Menntaskólinn; 444 4880; e edda@hoteledda.is; www.hoteledda.is; 1 Jun–20 Aug. One of the nicer editions in the Functionalist Edda line, with all rooms having their own bathrooms, & a few larger split-level rooms for families with children. Good value yes, but the location is best for those travelling by car. **$$$**

**Lyngas Guesthouse** (6 rooms) 471 1310; e lyngas@lyngas.is. The small size of the guesthouse guarantees a quieter stay, while maintaining the signature Icelandic hospitality & cleanliness. **$$**

**Olga** (4 rooms) Tjarnabraut 3; m 860 2999; e gistihusolgu@simnet.is. Grandmotherly guesthouse in the town with shared bathrooms. B/fast inc. **$$**

**Camping** (*Kaupvangur 10; 471 2320; e info@east.is; www.east.is;* **$**) Quite an urban campsite, with more traffic than a summer fairground. Tents from 750ISK; includes access to hot showers and cooking facilities. Pay and register at the tourist information centre.

## WHERE TO EAT

**Herað** Miðvangur 5–7; 471 1500; e herad@icehotels.is; www.icehotels.is; 08.00–22.30 daily. Icelandair's swanky hotel restaurant stays true to nouvelle Icelandic tradition, with delicate & pretty meals. They've earned a reputation for thick reindeer steaks culled from those mountains just beyond the horizon, but the fish & lamb options are not bad at all. *Mains from 2,600ISK.* **$$$$**

**Egilsstaðir** Fagradalsbraut; 471 1114; e egilsstadir@egilsstadir.com; www.egilsstadir.com; 07.30–22.00 daily. The most original restaurant in town is none other than the classy & cosy dining room of the original Egilsstaðir farmhouse. The diverse & colourful menu takes its cue from east Iceland products; entrées range from pan-fried salt cod, perfect lamb fillets, & beef tenderloin raised right on the farm. Also, there are a lot of good vegetarian options & some unique desserts (eg: caramelised sweet potatoes). Highly recommended – this is a good place to splurge after a long journey. *Mains from 1,800ISK.* $$$

**Café Nielsen** Tjarnarbraut 1; ☎ 471 2626; e cafenielsen@simnet.is; ⏲ 09.00–21.00 Sun–Thu, 09.00–midnight Fri/Sat. Built in 1944, this is the very first house ever to be built in the town. The ground-floor café evokes a rich Scandinavian atmosphere with its coffee aromas & plethora of pastries. Choose from cakes, sandwiches, & soups, or from a limited option of hearty entrées. At weekends it feels a bit more like a bar. *Mains from 950ISK.* $$

**Söluskáli** Esso station; Kaupvangur 2; ☎ 471 1230; ⏲ 08.00–23.30 daily. The main petrol station is where all the action is. Fill up with fuel, clean off your car, grab a hot dog, or visit the cafeteria for some heavy-fried food. Sandwiches, hamburgers, pizza, & chicken. *Mains from 1,000ISK.* $$

**Self-catering** For food shopping needs, just head across the street from all the hubbub to the Samkaup grocery store (*Kaupvangur 6; ☎ 470 1210; ⏲ 09.00–19.00 daily*).

**WHAT TO SEE AND DO** Egilsstaðir's main attraction is the **East Iceland Heritage Museum** (*Minjasafn Austurlands; Laufskógar 1; ☎ 471 1412; e minjasafn@minjasafn.is; www.minjasafn.is; ⏲ 11.00–17.00 daily, 11.00–21.00 Wed, winter, closed Sun/Mon; entrance 500ISK*). What's unique about this 'how we used to live' display is not so much the objects, but the way in which the exhibits explore local themes of history and culture: farming, self-sufficiency, food preservation, livestock maintenance, family life, religion and industrialisation. This part of the country was especially slow to urbanise, portrayed in the fully framed restored farmhouse that makes up part of the educational display. Just down the street is the town's first-rate **swimming pool** (*Tjarnarbraut 26; ☎ 470 0777; ⏲ 07.00–21.30 Mon–Fri, 10.00–19.00 Sat/Sun*). Not a bad place to spend some time with a 50m laned pool, hot pots, waterslides, smaller pools and a great fitness centre/gym. Otherwise, there are very few pretences about Egilsstaðir – most of what you came for lies outside town – either in the fjords and valleys, or on the shores of Lagarfljót.

## FLJÓTSDALUR

Egilsstaðir lies in the middle of one of Iceland's longest glacial valleys, an area known traditionally as Fljótsdalshérað. In Icelandic, *fljót* means 'a large river' (similar to 'fleuve' in French), although Lagarfljót looks and acts more like a very young lake, extending the entire length of the valley. The sunken river basin collects the runoff of so many mountain rivers, the largest of which is the Jökulsá á Fljótsdal that flows all the way from the glaciers on Snæfell and Vatnajökull. The *fljót* itself is 92km long and is the widest (4km) and deepest (111m) 'river' in Iceland. A very special way of life has developed along its shores, known for its forthright beauty and a multitude of trees. The first bridge across was only completed in 1905 – before then this was a district of open boats and isolated farms. In World War II, British RAF pilots began landing seaplanes on Lagarfljót because there were no other airfields in the whole of east Iceland. Now there are good roads that run the length of the waterway, heading deep into the interior or all the way up north to the sandy shores of Hérað. In summer, riverboat trips are available on the *Lagarfljótsormurinn* (*☎ 471 2900; e ferja@ormur.is; www.ormur.is; fee 1,800ISK*). The boat typically sails between Egilsstaðir and Altavík, and is a relaxing way to take in a very long body of water.

## THE LAGARFLJÓTSORMUR

The gigantic monster that lives in Lagarfljót has mystified and terrified the poor souls of east Iceland for quite some time. The parallels to the Loch Ness Monster are uncanny, but Iceland claims theirs is much older and a lot less elusive. Sadly, there are no grainy photos, but there are enough eyewitnesses to sketch a convincing mugshot. *Ormur* means 'worm', and the Lagarfljótsormur is more or less a gargantuan worm – a creature of such incredible length that it could only live in Lagafljót.

The origins of the Lagarfljótsormur are believed to go back to a local milkmaid whose folk magic got a little out of hand. Trying for treasure, she placed a gold ring and tiny snail inside a box. When she opened the box later, instead of the promised gold, she discovered a giant snail had grown to fill the box. She tossed the freakish snail into the river where it continued to grow to fill the size of the lake. Another legend reports the Icelanders hiring a bunch of Finnish sorcerers who managed to subdue the monster by chaining him to the bottom of the lake. That seems unlikely given the many places the Lagafljótsormur has been spotted.

The first recorded sighting of Lagarfljótsormur was in the year 1345, when farmers noticed a row of rolling bumps moving across the water, but with such great length between each (fathoms!) that any natural explanation seemed impossible. Other sightings reported a colossal animal of greyish colour lacking head, tail or limb. Some claim to have seen the monster swimming upstream on the surface with humps slithering in the air. In the 18th century's Age of Reason, theoreticians explained how the ripples and 'humps' rose to the surface from gas bubbles down below. It's a very reasonable explanation given Iceland's volcanic activity, but not for this particular spot. Further sightings gave more credibility to the existence of a bona fide monster. One of the most recent eyewitnesses claimed the Lagarfljótsormur came to shore at the campsite in Atlavík and filled the sandy beach with its monstrous length.

In the past, a sighting of the Lagarfljótsormur was a bad omen – a premonition of harsh weather, dead livestock, or sickness. Today, the monster is a mascot for Fljótsdalur and often depicted as a smiling serpent or dragon. There is still a healthy reward for anyone who gets a good photograph of the animal. Should you capture the worm with your lens, do contact the museum in Egilsstaðir (see page 401).

*Thanks to Hrafnkell Lárusson of the East Iceland Heritage Museum in Egilsstaðir for his help with research.*

**HÉRAÐ** The lower (northern) river valley of Fljótsdalur flattens out into picturesque farmland marked by distant mountains and the parallel rivers of Lagarfljót and the Jökulsá á Dal. Between all the rushing water lie hayfields interspersed by wetlands. The combined estuaries culminate at the broad black sands of Héraðssandur, a very flat beach that is gargantuan and blissfully quiet. Out here seals are quite common, and the birds are anything but. Be mindful that this is most definitely the dirt road less travelled, but the scene is powerful and refreshing.

## Where to stay and eat

**Eiðar** (46 rooms) 444 4870; e edda@hoteledda.is; www.hoteledda.is. This settlement-era farm is now the district farm school turned summer hotel. Most rooms have shared bathrooms, & sleeping-bag accommodation & camping are available for much cheaper. OK meals served in the dining room/restaurant. **$$$**

**Svartiskógur** (15 rooms) 471 1030; e svartiskogur@mi.is. The 'black woods' country hotel is a nice & accessible residence right on the Jökulsá River & just off the ring road. All rooms have private bathrooms & the in-house fish & lamb restaurant isn't half bad. **$$$**

**Húsey** (20 beds) Hróastunga; 471 3010; e husey@simnet.is. Yet another very remote but very cool youth hostel, best for those who like to plant themselves in the middle of nowhere & connect with the environment. Clean & orderly on the inside, the outside offers some great seaside walks. There's a kitchen available, so bring your own food – this is the end of the road (Route 926), but they offer pickups from Egilsstaðir (25km away). **$**

## HALLORMSSTAÐUR

Iceland's largest forest grew up on the eastern banks of Lagarfljót, starting with a sizeable patch of native birch that had somehow survived the denuding of the rest of Iceland. It was here that Iceland's forestry service was founded in 1907 with conscious efforts to protect and expand a diminished resource (see box on page 48). To the native birch, rowan and willow were added about 50 different imported species.

The largest of these woods is the larch tree forest of Guttormslundur, named after Iceland's first forester Guttormur Pálsson. Icelanders make quite a big deal out of this spot, and the campsite in the middle of the Hallormsstaðarskógur woods is one of the busiest summer hangouts in the country. If you happen to be visiting from a country that has trees, you may find yourself wondering just exactly what all the fuss is about.

On the opposite side of the lake is the very tall (120m) waterfall of **Hengifoss**. A trail follows up from the road (Route 931), where you can see the upper layer of basalt above an ancient layer of petrified tree trunks. Further upriver is the farm of Skriðurklaustur, the last home of Icelandic writer Gunnar Gunnarsson (see page 398). The author's birthplace is the next farm upriver, marked by the church of Valthjófsstaður. The parish dates back to the 13th century, and the ornate wooden door is a replica of the original on display at the National Museum in Reykjavík (see page 180).

## WHERE TO STAY AND EAT

**Grái Hundurinn** (6 rooms) Hjalli; 471 2128; e graihundurinn@simnet.is. The 'greyhound' is a sophisticated cabin in the woods, with neat rooms & nice beds – most rooms have their own private bathroom. They also manage the **Hússtjórnarskólans** (*summer only;* **$$**), which is the very functional school/guesthouse just down the road. Made-up beds but shared bathrooms. The café is popular with campers. B/fast inc. **$$$**

**Camping** Iceland's most chaotic campsite by far, **Altavík** (*471 1774;* e *hallormsstadur@skogur.is; www.skogur.is;* **$**) is jam-packed with caravans, tents, cars and extensive Icelandic and German families on holiday. On the plus side are the lakeshore location and the many trails that allow exploration through the woods. Hot showers and kitchens are among the ameneties included, along with a small shop and café.

## VESTURÖRÆFI

Until quite recently, the barren highlands of the west Öræfi interior was off-limits to most travellers on account of the unforgiving terrain and a general lack of roads. That changed with the construction of the Kárahnjúkar Dam, which saw the opening of a first-rate paved road (Route 910) and new access to some incredible hiking spots. Both Icelanders and foreigners are only now discovering the rolling mountains, the virgin rivers, and the rock formations of this hidden corner of east Iceland. Such a far-flung destination has limited amenities, but exquisite sights.

**KÁRAHNJÚKAR** The Jökulsá á Dal is another glacier river that flows north from Vatnajökull all the way to the sea. The powerful water has ripped away a series of dramatic canyons like Hafrahvammagljúfur and Dimmugljúfur, which are both dark and imposing – amazing landscapes of sweeping desert mountains and black, grey and brown rock faces covered in moss, lichen, and ice. Kárahnjúkar now refers to this barren but beautiful highland area along the river. It is also home to one of Iceland's largest and most controversial industrial sites, the Kárahnjúkar Dams, which provide hydro-electric energy to the aluminium plants in Reyðarfjörður (see page 409). The two dams are quite large (193m and 60m high) and form a giant lake that only reached its peak level in the summer of 2007. The bad news is that a lot of wonderful wilderness area is now underwater. The good news, however, is that there is still a good deal left and a well-paved road getting there.

Obviously, the 'development' project is not without its discontents. Icelanders fear that their homeland is for sale and foreigners fear that a global push for clean energy will end in further destruction of Iceland. In an attempt to befriend the locals, there is now an informative and propaganda-laden **visitors centre** in Végarður (*471 2044; www.karahnjukar.is; Apr–Oct 09.00–17.00 daily*).

Controversy shouldn't stop you from heading into what is still a very remote area and enjoying the unrivalled nature. The weather can be spotty, but as long as you come prepared, the entire area is well worth exploring. One favourite hotspot is **Laugarvellir** in Laugarvalladalur, where a natural 'hot shower' of geothermal runoff falls from the rocks above. A dammed stream provides a natural hot-water pool for bathing. Other tracks head further into the highlands (see page 429), connecting with places like Herðubreið and Askja.

**MT SNÆFELL** (1,833m) 'Snow mountain' is the tallest mountain in Iceland that is not beneath a glacier. It is, however, covered with a patch of permanent snow on top, inspiring its name and preventing access outside the summer months. As a dormant volcano rising high above the rest of the highlands, the summit offers a terrific view of canyons, rivers, rocks and the 'backside' of Vatnajökull. The whole area feels rather exotic and pristine, seeing as it is so far away from anything else and the landscapes are so wild and rugged. Most people will tell you that this is the very best place to see reindeer herds (in summer), and there are a huge number of pink-footed geese that breed closer to the glacier.

To get to Snæfell, you need a pair of strong legs and good boots or else a 4x4. The newly paved Kárahnjúkar road (Route 910) takes you most of the way, but the unpaved Route 909 fords a few unpredictable streams before getting to the main station. It is also possible to take an organised bus tour from Egilsstaðir. Visitors can camp or grab a spot inside the Snæfell mountain hut (*sleeps 62; hot showers & toilets; 2,000ISK*).

A well-marked path ascends from the base station up to the peak of Snæfell. Also, an even rougher version of Route 909 continues across a few streams and up to the very edge of Vatnajökull at Eyjabakkar. This 'valley' is at the tongue of Eyjabakkarjökull glacier, renowned for its stunning ice caves. For the real hardcore trekkers out there, try the four–five-day hike which goes from Snæfell all the way to Lónsöræfi. There's a perfect row of cosy mountain huts to stay in all along the way.

## THE EAST FJORDS

Iceland's east coast is a rugged fringe of long, V-shaped fjords in between rows of layered, pointy mountains. There are 14 fjords in total (not counting the smaller bays) and each one cut out by the fast-moving glaciers of the ice age. These eastern fjords are said to be the oldest in Iceland, evident in the jagged peaks that time has sharpened – (younger fjords have flat-topped mountains). The most basic things make this area so extraordinary – the unnamed waterfalls, the single fishing village at the base of each fjord, and the way the sunlight hits the mountains from the east.

As an area, the East Fjords has always felt a little secluded from the rest of Iceland. The narrow fjords are a more dependable outlet than the barren highlands, and the ring road had no choice but to careen its way around each of the channels. For all those people whizzing past on Route 1, the East Fjords represents the part of the journey where most people wish they could stop and stay awhile, simply for the view. Every curve in the road is heightened by the surprise of the scene unveiled in the next fjord – it's no coincidence that so many travellers' tales begin with: 'We were driving in the East Fjords, when…'

Singular fishing villages cling to the base of each fjord – each is home to a few hundred souls, and each is totally different from the next one over. The isolation of these communities (and the recent drop in fishing) has contributed to their slowing down and general lack of cheer. Town museums aim to lure unsuspecting tourists (some are better than others) but the main attractions are the fjords, the people and birds who live there, the incredible rocks on the ground, and the extraordinary hiking.

**GETTING AROUND** Until the last 30 years or so, everyone in the East Fjords got from place to place by boat. Roads – either paved or unpaved – now reach all the inhabited towns, but it's still not an easy place to get around. There are regular buses to and from Egilsstaðir and Höfn that service all the towns in the fjords listed in this book; contact **Austfjarðarleið** (☎ *477 1713;* e *austfjardarleid@austfjardarleid.is; www.austfjardarleid.is*).

## BORGARFJÖRÐUR

The northernmost point of the East Fjords is terrifically beautiful and well out of the way of the tourist mob. If you like rocks and birds, this is heaven. Because there was already a much more famous 'town fjord' on the west side of the country, this one is known as Borgarfjörður eystri ('the east'). The best reason to head out to this abandoned little corner is to hike: the Dyfjöll Mountains are grand – the views feel almost alpine – and the trails are numerous and amazingly well kept. The ultimate walking experience is in the **Víknaslóðir**, or 'abandoned bays'. Take along the detailed map that's distributed locally, and note that most people venture into the region for several days. If you can, check out the lonely **wooden churches** at Húsavík and Klyppstaðir – truly the end of the earth. There are mountain huts and a campsite in the abandoned bays of Húsavík and Breiðavík.

More cushy travellers tend to base themselves in the barely there fishing village of **Bakkagerði** (population 100). Scattered loosely along the shore of the fjord, it makes perfect sense that this was the boyhood home of Iceland's best-known painter Johannes Kjarval (see page 183), who painted the altarpiece in the church. There's a so-so one-room museum dedicated to the painter's life; **Kjarvalsstofa** (*Fjarðarborg; ☎ 472 9950; e kjarvalsstofa@kjarvalsstofa.is; www.kjarvalsstofa.is; ⌚ 12.00–18.00 daily; entrance 500ISK*). Like Kjarval's paintings, there are a quite a few fairy folk and hidden people around, especially in the rocky hill behind the church, known as Álfaborg, or 'elf town' (hence the name of the fjord, really). For more information, see the website www.borgarfjordureystri.is.

**GETTING THERE AND AWAY** Route 94 connects to Egilsstaðir (1 hour+), from where there are daily buses in the summer only.

**WHERE TO STAY AND EAT** 'The inn' is Fjarðarborg (*12 rooms; ☎ 472 9962; e bergrunj@mi.is;* **$$$**) which offers a few private rooms/bathrooms, as well as sleeping-bag accommodation. Their in-house fish-and-lamb restaurant is the lifeblood of the town and your only option to eat out. Despite its remoteness, the youth hostel tends to be popular and is clean with good kitchen and laundry facilities (*18 beds; Ásbyrgi; ☎ 472 9962; e borgardjordur@hostel.is;* **$$**). Last but definitely not least is the friendly but simple Borg guesthouse (*6 rooms; ☎ 472 9870; e gisting-borg@visir.is;* **$$$**) which serves breakfast. There's also one small grocery store in town, the KHB (*⌚ 09.00–18.00 daily*).

## SEYÐISFJÖRÐUR

As the main ferry port to and from the continent, Seyðisfjörður plays back door to the whole of Iceland. Despite the crowds of travellers pouring in and out of the town, Seyðisfjörður remains a humble little place of 800 souls at the end of a long (18km), narrow, and slightly S-shaped fjord. Seyðisfjörður is irresistibly cute and yet so unaffected – as first impressions go, this may be one of the most fitting that Iceland can offer to a visitor.

The town was founded by a Norwegian fishing company in 1895, and functioned as a major herring port until the herring disappeared some 50-odd years later. Like many Icelandic towns at the time, Seyðisfjörður materialised overnight as a completely prefabricated town, shipped in boxes from Norway and nailed together before the winter snows arrived. It is one reason why Seyðisfjörður is such a clean-cut town today. The way that all the houses, warehouses, and church match one another is almost toy-like, especially against the background of a giant, ocean-going vessel, and the handsome pair of mountains on either side.

Because of the ferry schedules, a lot of travellers find themselves having to spend at least one night in Seyðisfjörður before or after taking the ferry. That's not a bad thing – you can either decompress among the turn-of-the-century homes, or head to the hills for the most stunning vista.

**GETTING THERE AND AWAY** There's only one road in and out of Seyðisfjörður (Route 93) that climbs up over the ridge and then back down to Egilsstaðir (25km). The bus goes back and forth twice a day from Egilsstaðir (*Ferðaþjónusta Austurlands; ☎ 472 1515*), with a convenient stop at the airport (55 minutes). The ferry to and from Denmark (*☎ 570 8600; www.smyril-line.com*) sails year-round (see page 78).

**TOURIST INFORMATION** Right after you get off the boat, you'll see the 'ferry house' on the harbour. The larger tourist centre is based here (*summer 09.00–17.00 daily, in winter, just when the boat is coming or going 09.00–17.00 Tue/Wed*) The other official information centre is located at the museum (*Hafnargata 44; 470 2308; ferdamenning@sfk.is; www.seydisfjordur.is; summer 11.00–17.00 daily, winter 13.00–16.00 daily*).

## WHERE TO STAY

**Hótel Aldan** (18 rooms) Norðurgata 2; 472 1277; info@hotelaldan.com; www.hotelaldan.com. Of all the hotels in the east, this is the one with the most character. Clean, fashionable rooms are offered in 2 separate boutiques: Aldan (the 'wave') was built as a bank in 1898 & exhibits true turn-of-the-century chic. Tasteful antique furniture, hand-woven linens, & lots of clean lines make this one of Iceland's most classic & celebrated hotels. B/fast inc. **$$$$**

**Hótel Snæfell** (12 rorooms) Austurvegur 3; for contact details, see Hótel Aldan above; spring–autumn). Built in 1908 & functioned as the town's post office. Rooms are a step down from the Aldan in terms of décor, price, & size, but the hotel is still a very nice place to stay. B/fast inc. **$$$**

**Hafaldan Youth Hostel** (38 beds) Ránargata 9; 472 1410; seydisfjordur@hostel.is; www.simnet.is/hafaldan. Modern but very laid-back, the town's hostel is a busy little place with lots of good vibes. Rooms are very basic (with sink), the location is a little farther than it should be, & the place is always packed with Germans drying out their clothes. Even so, it's a great hostel – spotlessly clean & superbly managed. The breakfast room overlooking the fjord is another great thing, & the Mongolian yurt in the back is hot property. **$**

**Camping** Near the town centre, at the end of Seyðisfjörður (*472 1551; ferdamenning@sfik.is; www.seydisfjordur.is;* **$**). With hot and cold running water, showers, and minimal kitchen facilities; a really crazy place in summertime.

## WHERE TO EAT

**Hótel Aldan** Norðurgata 2; 472 1277; info@hotelaldan.com; www.hotelaldan.com; 08.00–21.00 daily. Let finicky gourmets take note – this is a fish-&-lamb restaurant, but one that has a great sense of style. The dishes are classy & local (lobster, catfish, & salmon) with a continental twist. *Mains from 2,600ISK.* $$$$

**Kaffi Lára** Norðugata 3; 472 1703; 09.00–20.00 daily. Simple little old-fashioned café with soup, sandwiches, light meals, coffee, rolls & cakes. *Mains from 1,200ISK.* $$

**Skaftfell** Austurvegur 42; 472 1632; www.skaftfell.is; 10.00–22.00 daily. Cool, modish art bistro in the basement of the local artists' co-operative. Coffee & light meals served up with great panache & a wallfull of art to look at. *Mains from 1,100ISK.* $$

**Shell station** Hafnargata 2A; 472 1700; 09.00–21.00 daily. Hot dogs & hamburgers all around. $

**Self-catering** The grocery store **Strax** (*Vesturvegur; 472 1201; 10.00–18.00 daily*) is very well stocked and could very well be the busiest food shop this side of the Mid-Atlantic Ridge.

**WHAT TO SEE AND DO** Don't just 'pass through' Seyðisfjörður – if you can take the time, have a look around the town and the fjord. Start with the **wooden buildings**, each with its own unique history. Highlights include the warehouses by the harbour, the **Seyðisfjörður school** at Suðurgata 4 and the town's oldest home **Nóatún** (1871) at Bjólsfata 4. The pretty, pale-blue **church** was built in 1922 using timber rescued from the previous 19th-century church that was blown off its foundations.

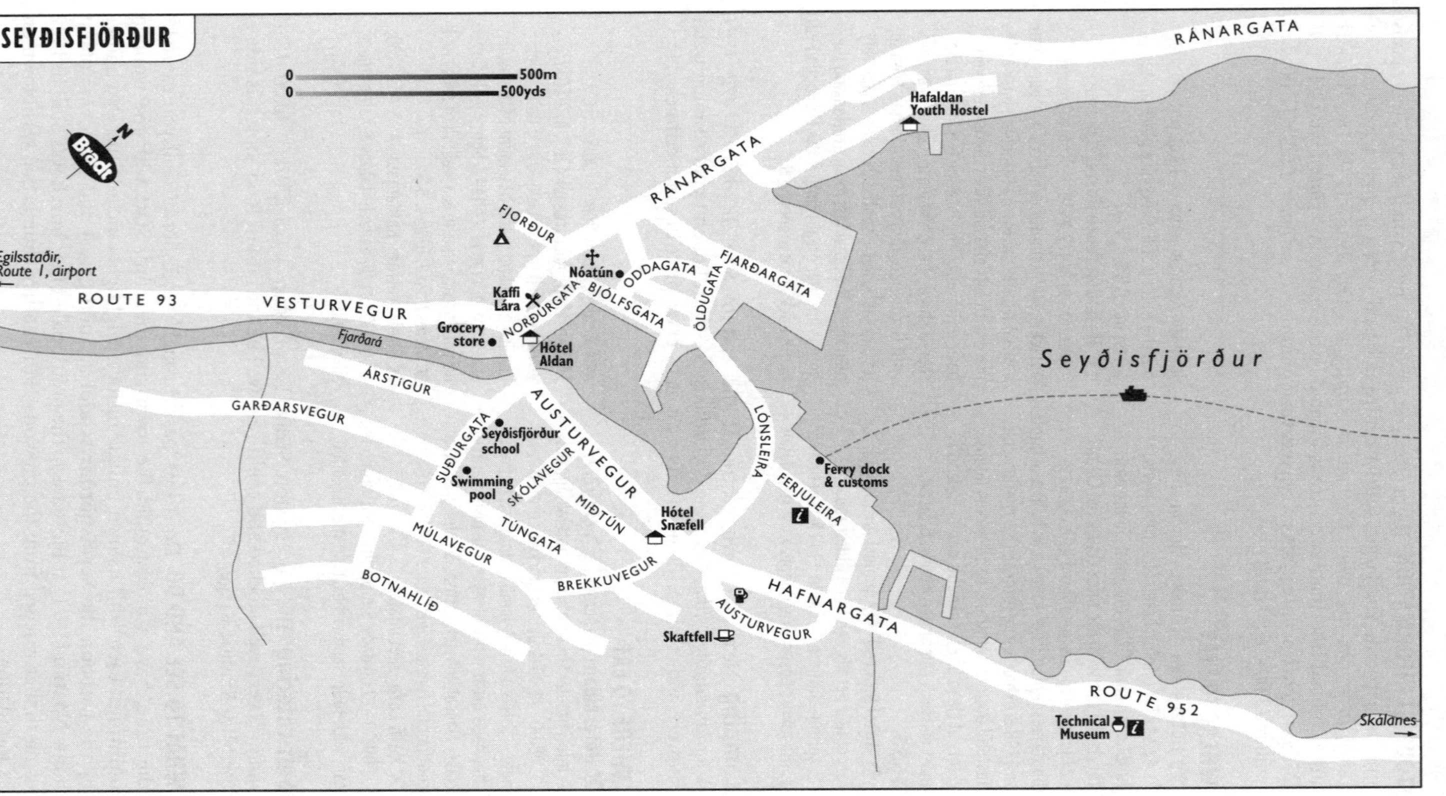
SEYÐISFJÖRÐUR
0 500m
0 500yds
Bradt
N
RÁNARGATA
Hafaldan Youth Hostel
FJORÐUR
Nóatún
ODDAGATA
FJARÐARGATA
ÖLDUGATA
BJÓLFSGATA
NORÐURGATA
Kaffi Lára
Egilsstaðir, Route 1, airport
ROUTE 93
VESTURVEGUR
Grocery store
Hótel Aldan
Fjarðará
ÁRSTÍGUR
GARÐARSVEGUR
Seyðisfjörður
AUSTURVEGUR
LÓNSLEIRA
SUÐURGATA
Seyðisfjörður school
Swimming pool
SKÓLAVEGUR
MIÐTÚN
Ferry dock & customs
FERJULEIRA
Hótel Snæfell
TÚNGATA
MÚLAVEGUR
BOTNAHLÍÐ
BREKKUVEGUR
HAFNARGATA
AUSTURVEGUR
Skaftfell
ROUTE 952
Technical Museum
Skálanes

## HIKING IN THE EAST FJORDS

A vast network of trails criss-cross the high mountains in between the many fjords, and weather permitting, the hiking is grand. Popular climbs include Goðaborg (1,132m) and Svartifjall (1,021m) and the ice cap of Fönn – as well as the beautiful coastline of Sandvík. Still, custom-designed treks are best, allowing for the independent traveller to walk his or her way from one fjord to the next.

The best hiking map for the area is ***Gönguleiðir á Fjarðasloðum*** (price 800ISK), which you can pick up at any information booth or petrol station.

Seyðisfjörður-ites also take great pride in the technological achievements of the past. For instance, the first telegraph machine in Iceland is on display at the **Technical Museum** (*Hafnargata 44; ☎ 472 1596; e tekmus@tekmus.is; www.tekmus.is; ⌚ summer 11.00–17.00 daily, winter 13.00–16.00 Mon–Fri; entrance 500ISK*). The exhibits visit the many feats of Iceland's delayed industrial advancement, with a few displays aimed expressly at children. If that's not enough, check Iceland's oldest electrical station (built in 1913) and now the **RARIK museum** on the river (*☎ 472 1122; www.fjardarsel.is; ⌚ summer only*).

On the opposite side is the artists' **cultural centre** of Skaftfell (*☎ 472 1632; e skaftfell@skaftfell.is; www.skaftfell.is; ⌚ 09.00–18.00 daily*) which may or may not be interesting, depending on what's going on at the time (art shows, programmes, etc). There's also the town **swimming pool** (*Suðurgata 5; ☎ 472 1414; ⌚ 10.00–19.00 daily*) which is small but warm and cosy (hot pots and sauna) on those bitterly cold days.

Visitors should be inclined to head up into the high mountains and wild landscapes in nearby Fjarðará. The high heathland is what kept this town isolated from the rest of Iceland for so long, and trails zig-zag their way up to the top and offer a great view of the fjord. **Mt Bjólfur** (1,085m) and **Mt Strandartindur** (1,010m) are the tallest peaks around, both of which can easily be ascended.

Those who yearn for distant climes should head to Skálanes at the very end of the fjord. A nature centre and ecotourist lodge have been established in the midst of the beach and rocky cliffs. A limited number of visitors may stay and get in touch with the very best of Icelandic wildlife (birds, seals, and whales). A number of graduate students conduct their research here and visitors are asked to help out with the tasks at hand. For longer stays, hostel-style accommodation is available (*Skálanes; ☎ 690 6966; e skalanes@skalanes.com; www.skalanes.com;* **$$**).

## REYÐARFJÖRÐUR

Reyðarfjörður was first discovered by Naddod the King, the Norse Viking who arrived in Iceland sometime in the 9th century and called the place 'snowland' (see page 15). Since he left, the fjord has remained a quiet place, with the exception of the country's largest aluminium-smelting plant that has opened recently (you can't miss the behemoth, mile-long building).

Reyðarfjörður's 1,500 residents are a little uncomfortable with all the attention and the fact that their town is beginning to grow in population and importance. Nobody quite knows what changes this new burst of business may bring to the town or the region.

## VÖLVULEIÐI

Route 92 swerves around the point at Hólmanes, where a tall cairn of rocks marks the burial spot of Völva, a local holy woman and 'good witch' for Reyðarfjörður. After a lifetime of service to the residents of the fjord, she asked that her bones be placed at the head of the fjord so that she could protect it from outside enemies. When a band of Algerian pirates began ransacking Iceland's coastal towns, a storm swept down from the mountain and blew their ship out of the fjord. In World War II, the Allied air force managed a base here and the only attempt at attack was thwarted when a spying Luftwaffe pilot got caught up in the fog and crashed into the mountainside. Outside travellers who pass by the point (even in cars) are supposed to add a small stone to the top of the cairn to show their intentions are not evil.

### WHERE TO STAY

**Hótel Reyðarfjörður** (21 rooms) Búðareyri 6; 474 1600; fjardarhotel@st.is. Modern & efficient, local business travellers have set the tone for the establishment. Rooms are small & cosy with private bathroom. B/fast inc. **$$$$**

**Tærgesen Guesthouse** (8 rooms) Buðargata 4; 470 4444; taergesen@taergesen.is; www.taergesen.is. A small but cheerful B&B in the town centre. A few rooms have their own private bath. B/fast inc. *Shared facilities only 7,000ISK per dbl.* **$$$**

**Camping** The **campsite** is next to the *tjrörnin* or 'duck pond' (*470 9090;* **$**). Hot showers available.

**WHERE TO EAT** Most people go in for the very civilised fish-and-lamb restaurant at **Hótel Reydarfjörður** (*12.00–22.00 daily; mains from 1,650ISK;* $$$). The **Tærgesen Guesthouse** (*12.00–21.30 daily; mains from 1,000ISK;* $$) serves up low-brow fast food (eg: pizza and hamburgers). The town hangout is **Café Kósý** (*Ægisgata; 474 1666; cosy@simnet.is; 09.00–20.00 daily; mains from 700ISK;* $) which is in fact, quite *kósý*. Choose from coffee, snacks, light meals or hearty comfort food. The grocery store is at **Krónan** (*471 2445; reydarfjordur@kronan.is; www.kronan.is; 09.00–19.00 daily*). As always, hot dogs and more at the Shell station (*474 1111; 08.00–21.00*).

## ESKIFJÖRÐUR

Eskifjörður is another Norwegian herring town turned post-industrial Icelandic fishing village. What makes it a worthwhile stop is how curious and simple a place it is today – a single road (Strandgata) runs through the town, past the harbour with its fishing boats, the marine museum, and the quiet, undisturbed lives of about 1,000 people. Since nobody else seems to stop here, the few foreigners who do are treated to a candid glimpse of everyday life in isolated Iceland – the only thing that's posing here is you.

### WHERE TO STAY AND EAT

**Guesthouse Mjóeyri** (5 rooms) Strandgata 120; 477 1247; mjoeyri@vortex.is; www.mjoeyri.is. The only place to stay in the whole town is near the end of Strandgata in the fjord. Built in 1895, the guesthouse is delightfully quaint, quiet, & remote. Rooms with made-up beds are available. Shared bathrooms. *Sleeping-bag spaces under 2,500ISK.* **$$**

**Pizza 67** Strandgata 49; 476 1767; 12.00–21.00 daily. Pizza delivered fresh or eaten in with all your favourite Icelandic toppings. *Mains from 1,000ISK;* **$$**.

**Self-catering** The grocery store **Strax** (*476 1580; 09.00–19.00*) is on the main road in town and the Shell station is at Strandgata 13 (*476 1383; 10.00–21.00 daily*).

**WHAT TO SEE AND DO** The **church** (*www.simnet.is/eskirkja*) in Eskifjörður is special – although it is of modern construction, the altarpiece has been replaced with a window that opens onto the boisterous waterfall behind it (a nice twist to an old Icelandic tradition). This marks the first 'independent' Christian church ever built in Iceland.

To celebrate the town's fishing history, there's also the **Maritime Museum** (*Sjóminjsafan Austurlands; 476 1605; e safn@fjardabyggd.is; Jun–Aug 14.00–17.00 daily; entrance 450ISK*). The black longhouse was put up in 1816 and it now houses a fascinating collection of old fishing artefacts. Make sure to also note the socialist-looking mosaic mural on the side of the harbour warehouse. A walk down the main street takes you past some very quaint wooden homes, well weathered but quite poetic all the same. Up at the guesthouse, they are warming to the idea of tourists and offer organised opportunities for hiking and kayaking.

## NESKAUPSTAÐUR

The most isolated town in all of the East Fjords only 'got connected' to the rest of the region in the 1970s, when a very long tunnel was built on Route 92 from Eskifjörður. The town is not that exciting, but it is right in the middle of four distinct fjords, and some remarkable scenery.

### WHERE TO STAY AND EAT

**Hótel Edda** Nesgata 40; 444 4860; e edda@hoteledda.is; summer only. The classic school-turned-hotel with shared bathrooms & proletariat rooms. The restaurant is pretty staple fish & lamb. **$$$**

**Egilsbúð** Egilsbraut 1; 477 1321; e egilsbud@egilsbud.is; www.egilsbud.is. The town's main establishment. They run a number of guesthouse locations, with both made-up beds & sleeping-bag spaces. They also have a good restaurant (**$$**), with lots of local fish that's affordable (1,300ISK) & the local pizza joint. **$$**

**Trölli Guesthouse** Hafnarbruat 50; 477 1800. Named after all the trolls that once roamed this area, the guesthouse is thankfully less frightening. *Sleeping-bag spaces under 3,000ISK.* **$$**

**Camping** The **campsite** (*470 9000;* **$**) can be found located on the far eastern side of town.

**WHAT TO SEE AND DO** In town, there's the slightly tired **Natural History Museum** (*Miðstræti 1; 477 1454; e na@na.is; www.na.is/safnid; Jun–Aug 13.00–17.00 daily; entrance free*). Expect lots of minerals and stuffed birds – not a bad thing if you can test your new-found knowledge with surrounding wilderness. The landscapes around **Barðsnes** and **Sandvík** are out of this world – both are not easy to get to without some determination and leg power, but definitely worth the struggle.

## FÁSKRÚÐSFJÖRÐUR

This East Fjords fishing station was founded by enterprising French fishermen in the early 19th century – a century later, there were over 5,000 Frenchmen living and working in the fjord. They built the local hospital and the church. The remaining Icelandic villagers in Fáskrúðsfjörður (population 500) still celebrate their Gallic semi-heritage with the museum **French Fishermen in Iceland** (*Fransmenn á Íslandi; Búðavegi 8; ☎ 475 1525; e fransmenn@fransmenn.net; www.fransmenn.is; ⏲ 1 Jun–17 Aug 10.00–17.00; entrance 600ISK*). The museum does tell a unique story and also has a great little French café, which is often packed with delighted French tourists.

## STÖÐVARFJÖRÐUR

This miniature fjord-side village is home to just 200 souls and a mere blink on the ring road. Other than the beauty of the fjord itself, with its layered mountains and waterfalls, the main attraction is the creative accommodation of **Kirkjubær** (*10 beds; Fjarðarbraut 37A; m 892 3319; e birgiral@simnet.is; www.simnet.is/birgiral;* **$$**). This refurbished church, built in 1925, wins the prize for the Icelandic hostel with the most character. It comes complete with pews and altar, and guests spend a night in the church, made more comfortable with beds, mattresses, a bathroom and kitchen. The owners offer fishing trips and there's a grill at the house to cook your catch.

The town's only restaurant, shop, and pub (rolled into one) is at **Brekkan** (*Fjarðarbraut 44; ☎ 475 8939; ⏲ 10.00–19.00 Mon–Thu, 10.00–23.00 Fri/Sat; mains from 900ISK;* $$).

## BREIÐDALSVÍK

'Broad valley bay' is an apt description for the sharp peaks and open water of this non-fjord of the East Fjords. The area is most popular for its great river fishing and as an unconventionally beautiful pit stop on the ring road. To embrace nature more fully, travel up the scenic Breiðdalur Valley; otherwise, enjoy the tiny town of 150 people. In summer, boat trips are offered out to the rocky skerries in the middle of the bay where there are likely to be seals basking. For more information, see the website www.breiddalshreppur.is.

### WHERE TO STAY AND EAT

**Hótel Bláfell** (24 rooms) ☎ 475 6770; e blafell@centrum.is; www.centrum.is/~blafell. The 'blue mountain' hotel has a blue roof to make it more recognisable & makes a nice place to stay. The wood-panelled rooms are comfy & big enough – most have their own bathroom; a few do not. There's a sound fish-&-lamb restaurant (they have great fish soup), & a nice sauna for those miserable days. **$$$**

**Hótel Staðarborg** (30 rooms) ☎ 475 6760; e stardarborg@simnet.is; www.stadarborg.is. The local schoolhouse is now a permanent 'upmarket' hotel catering to the ring-road crowd. Almost all rooms have private bathrooms, though some do not. There is also a campsite with access to showers. A jacuzzi makes it even nicer & the well-meaning restaurant serves up 3 meals a day. *Group sleeping-bag spaces 2,500ISK.* **$$$**

**Café Margrét** (6 rooms) Heimaleiti; ☎ 475 6625; e café.mar@mi.is. A cheerful mountain lodge known for its lively café & bar. Meals are sandwiches & Icelandic plates like *plottfiskur*. Made-up beds & sleeping-bag accommodation are available for overnight guests. **$$**

## DJÚPIVOGUR

'Deep bay' is the most picturesque town of all the East Fjords – from the tiny fishing boats in the harbour to the sweeping mountain peaks up above. Unlike the sheltered villages of the East Fjords, Djúpivogur lies out in the open, on the rocky point between two beautiful fjords, Berufjörður and Harnarsfjörður. The panorama is unforgettable and may very well explain the allure of this one spot above the many others along the coast.

Djúpivogur is one of the older towns in the East Fjords, founded by the Hanseatic League of Hamburg in 1589 as a trading post. The Danes arrived in the early 1700s, and took over the local fishing industry – theirs are still the largest buildings in town. Today, fishing is small but still important, as a walk around the harbour can attest. Only 375 people live here, but the town is very laid-back and tourist-friendly.

### TOURIST INFORMATION

**Tourist information** 478 8220; e info@djupivogur.is; www.djupivogur.is; Jun–Sep 10.00–18.00 daily

### WHERE TO STAY

#### In town

**Hótel Framtíð** (34 rooms) 478 8887; e framtid@simnet.is; www.simnet.is/framtid. This old house was shipped in pieces from Copenhagen & assembled in 1905 – prior to its life as a hotel, it was a merchant's shop & then the town post office. Today, it's the lifeblood of the town, with a merry little restaurant & nice, classic, wood-panelled rooms. About half the rooms have their own facilities; the rest are shared (which halves the cost). There's a good sauna in the basement. Recommended. *Sleeping-bag accommodation 3,300ISK.* **$$$**

**Camping** The campsite (*478 8887; e framtid@simnet.is; www.simnet.is/framtid;* **$**) is sheltered by a rocky outcrop on the hill – right around the corner from the Hótel Framtíð which manages the grounds (pay there). Caravans are favoured, and there are hot showers and good indoor kitchen facilities; 750ISK per person.

#### Out of town

**Berunes Hostel** (36 beds) Berufjörður; 478 8988; e berunes@hostel.is; www.hostel.is; May–Oct. Located across the fjord from Djúpivogur, this 100-year-old farmhouse-turned-hostel is an authentic little hamlet, complete with ancient Icelandic church & a fjord with a view. Right off the ring road, the Höfn–Egilsstaðir bus normally makes a stop here. Rooms are clean, spacious, & well furnished, & there are a few self-contained cottages (& camping) at the back; 30km from town. Meals are available in the simple nearby café **Gestastofan**. **$$**

**Eyjólfsstaðir** (20 beds) 478 8137; e foss@heima.is; www.djupivogur.is/eyjolfsstadir; Jun–Sep. Farm hostel with 20 sleeping-bag spaces, along with an open campsite (shared bathrooms). Located at the back end of Berufjörður, this is an ideal base for anyone looking to do some serious hiking up in the mountains; 20km from town. Bring your own food! **$**

**WHERE TO EAT** A café and exciting late-night bar, **Langabúð** (*468 8220; 09.00–21.00 Mon–Thu, 10.00–01.00 Fri/Sat; mains from 1,200ISK;* **$$**) runs all year round. The light meals are surprisingly traditional and yummy, with lots of local fish served – on nice days, one can eat outside overlooking the harbour. The town's only bona fide restaurant is in the **Hótel Framtið** (**$$$**).

The lacy tablecloths aspire to match the gourmet menu, which (thankfully) is an original take on the tired 'fish and lamb' staples. Only local seafood is served and this is one place where you will want to order dessert (with the fixed menu), though you can also get away with a fair-priced seafood soup-and-salad combo (1,700ISK). The bar is also a happening place all year round and a good place to connect with locals on dark, stormy nights.

Djúpivogur sports two food stores: the larger and more traditional grocery **Strax** (*Búland 1;* ☎ *478 8888;* 🕒 *10.00–18.00*) is conveniently located behind the campsite. **Við Voginn** (☎ *478 8860;* 🕒 *10.00–21.00; daily*) is above the harbour and serves fast food (hamburgers, pizza, etc).

**WHAT TO SEE AND DO** All the indoor action happens at the **Langabúð Folk Museum(s)** (☎ *478 8220;* e *langabud@djupivogur.is;* 🕒 *summer 10.00–18.00 daily; entrance 700ISK*), the red wooden longhouse above the harbour, built by the Danes in 1790. The building typifies Iceland's economic structure for so many centuries – a single warehouse owned by a single merchant where commerce for the entire district took place. Today, the building is divided into a confusing number of 'museums' with different subject matter and separate tickets (each between 250ISK and 500ISK).

The largest display is dedicated to Icelandic artist **Ríkarður Jónsson** (1888–1974) (*www.rikardssafn.is*). As founder of a national folk art movement in Iceland, Ríkarður's work portrays strong Icelandic themes in his portraiture and wood sculpture. The museum contains the contents of his workshop and a huge collection of his craft, including some truly beautiful carvings. The English narrative is limited, but the detailed artwork speaks for itself. Another room is dedicated to **Eysteinn Jónsson**, a local MP whose office has been recreated down to every last detail. Upstairs is the **Djúpivogur Folk Museum**, which is nothing more than a delightfully disorganised attic packed full of bizarre antiques. You'll find everything from whale harpoons to wagon parts and a coffin once used by a stowaway on a ship to Denmark.

Just as eclectic is the next-door **Nature Museum** (*Teigahorn;* ☎ *478 8905;* 🕒 *summer 10.00–16.00 daily: entrance 300ISK*). The amateur collection demands a little attention – stuffed displays of every local bird species (and some mammals) and a large number of rocks and minerals (jasper and obsidian) all found in the surrounding fjord and mountains.

If you've exhausted all town museums and the weather is still bad, then there's a nice set of hot pots to relax in at the indoor/outdoor **swimming pool** (*Varða 6;* ☎ *478 8999;* 🕒 *summer 07.00–21.00 Mon–Fri, 10.00–18.00 Sat/Sun, winter 10.00–16.00 daily*).

The mountains around Djúpivogur are a vast and splendid place, especially for those who are willing to explore freely. In town, there's a road and footpath that ascend to the highest point on the peninsula (**Búlandsnes**), where a directional dial identifies a 360° view. Don't miss the terrific black-sand dunes (**Sandey**) down by the beach (follow the signs to the airport).

Climbers should head up **Mt Búlandstindur** (1,069m) – the perfect pyramid-shaped mountain rising right above the town. The imposing peak is revered for its supernatural powers and the trail is easier than it looks. A little more than halfway up the mountain, the trail passes a cliff known as **Goðaborg** ('fortress of the gods') – after the Althing meeting where the decision was made to adopt Christianity (see page 19), the locals threw their pagan idols over the ledge. On the other side of the mountain is **Hálsfjall** or 'fairy-tale glade', which is another beautiful valley and ridge with mystical connotations.

## PAPEY

Papey lies about 10km off the point of Djúpivogur, and might very well be the first human habitation in Iceland. The island takes its name from the Irish monks (*papar*) who first lived here, most likely in the 8th and 9th centuries. Recent archaeological digs have uncovered a 10th-century Viking settlement, after which time Papey has always been a coveted property. Riches included seals, birds, and fish – the downside was the treacherous boat ride to the mainland and some fairly horrific storms. The smallest church in all Iceland is right here on Papey, first built in 1807 and then rebuilt in 1902 after it was destroyed by a storm. The black-and-white structure is chained down to cement anchors (as with all the buildings on the island), which keeps things sturdy in moments of hurricane-force winds.

On a sunny day, Papey is the most peaceful place on earth. The island is small – about 2km² – and has a strange, bumpy shape with lots of inlets and rounded, rocky peninsulas, along with a number of outlying islands. It is a very wet place, with lots of bogs, marshes, and soggy turf. In summer, the hillsides are covered with cotton grass and tiny yellow flowers. Írskuhólar ('Irish hill') rises up on the south end of the island and is named after the first residents. Hellisbjarg (58m) or 'cave cliff' is the highest point on the island – the narrowness of the cleft allows a great view across to the cliff; this is the best place on the island to see puffins and guillemots in huge numbers. The other rocky outcrop on the interior of the island is simply known as Kastali 'the castle' – an obvious home to the *huldufólk* (see page 33). Today the lighthouse (built in 1922) is automatic, but there is still one permanent inhabitant on the island. The descendant of the last owners spends the summers in the family home and visitors are allowed to hike on the island with the understanding that this is private property.

The ferry to Papey runs trips from May to October (*Papeyjarferðir; Hraun 3;* ☎ *479 8119;* e *papey@djupivogur.is*). Purchase tickets in the tiny shopfront beneath Langabúð (around 3,500ISK). The boat leaves right from the harbour. As a warning, this is a small boat heading out into the big ocean; the seas can get rough and even with the raincoats they provide, you are likely to get a little wet. On the way, the boat passes several rock skerries which are normally covered with a great number of lazy seals basking in the sun. Guides take groups all over the island – to the church and old farm and lighthouse, and to the cliffs and highpoints. The entire tour takes about four hours (including one hour's travel time).

## VATNAJÖKULL

Vatnajökull is the largest glacier in Europe and the third largest in the world (after the ice caps in Antarctica and Greenland). The glacier's entire surface area is 8,300km² (3,400 square miles), which covers roughly 8% of the country (about the size of Puerto Rico). The ice averages 500m thickness, but is more than 1,000m deep in some places. Scientists guess the volume of the ice to be around 3,300km³, which is a greater volume than Africa's Lake Victoria. The glacier is so massive that each of the many tongues have their own names and are referred to as separate glaciers. Unlike other glaciers that are formed by accumulated and firmly packed snow, Vatnajökull is a remaining piece of the last ice age – part of the polar ice cap that formed Iceland's coasts and terrain.

The name 'Vatnajökull' means either 'lake' or 'water glacier' – so many of the lakes and rivers you encounter in Iceland all originate from this one gigantic hunk of ice, but there are also a number of lakes beneath the ice, formed by the heat that wells up from the seven active volcanoes under the glacier. The most active is the fissure system near **Mt Grímsfjall** (1,719m) at **Grímsvötn**, the same name given to the many under-ice lakes that fill the calderas from previous eruptions. This strange phenomenon is truly the 'fire and ice' of travel-brochure headlines: regular bursts of magma from beneath several heated lakes beneath an even thicker layer of ice. The situation is quite unique and causes some amazing catastrophic events, like the *jökulhlaup*. **Mt Barðarbunga** (2,009m) is Iceland's second-highest mountain and another impressive volcano fissure that holds the world record for maximum lava flow in one eruption. **Mt Kverkfjöll** (1,929m) in the north shows the most visible signs of activity, with steam pouring up out of the ice. Iceland's tallest mountain, **Mt Hvannadalshnjúkur** (2,110m), lies beneath the southernmost section of the glacier (Oræfajökull) but has not erupted for almost 300 years. It is a classic 'cone' strato-volcano (see page 45) and is considered Iceland's most 'violent' volcano, despite its long era of peace and quiet.

Vatnajökull embodies all the extremes of Iceland – the highest elevation, the coldest temperatures, the biggest volcanic eruptions, the highest precipitation, and fastest winds. It is one of the most exotic things foreigners can experience in Iceland – there's something about driving along a ribbon of highway with giant licks of ice spilling down towards you. Up close, Vatnajökull can show itself as a snowy field of white, or expose all the gorgeous colours and strange shapes of compressed ice. Also, the view from the top – over the ocean or the mountainous interior – is superb.

Nobody can say who the first people to cross the glacier were, since the early Icelanders were known to have scoured every last bit of their country. The first recorded north–south crossing was in 1875 by Icelandic guide Páll Pálsson and the Scottish explorer W L Watts. This was followed by the 1932 'Cambridge Expedition' in which a few English students made a traverse journey across and back in just five days. Since then, the glacier has attracted the attention of several masochists: in 2004, explorer Cameron Smith completed the first solo east–west crossing in winter.

Of all the glaciers in Iceland, Vatnajökull is receding the fastest – every summer, locals can point to where the ice reached in the previous year. Pushing aside the uneasy jokes about global warming, there is a real urgency to visit – evident in the recent jump in European tourists who come specifically to see the ice.

## SIGURÐUR'S STORY: BENEATH THE GLACIER

Among the collection of tragic tales regarding the elements versus the Icelanders, there are a few happy endings that stand out. **Sigurður Björnsson** was a farmer from Kvísker (which you pass on Route 1 beneath Oræfajökull) who went out to round up his sheep in the autumn of 1936. Near the lip of the glacier he was swept from behind by an avalanche and thrown down backwards into the crevasse between the slick rock and the mass of ice. Sigurður found himself pinned beneath the glacier, lying upside down a good 30m beneath the surface. To comfort himself and to stay warm, he sang the Icelandic hymn *Praise to the Lord* over and over again. A day later, he was still singing and could be heard by those searching for their friend. He was rescued by means of ice picks and ropes and survived to have his story turned into a permanent display at the Glacier Museum in Höfn.

**VISITING THE GLACIER** Every large, nationwide tour operator in Iceland offers some sort of package trip to Vatnajökull, either a trip on the ice or a visit to the Jökulsárlón glacier lagoon, plus a number of ice-hiking options. The glacier tongue of Skálafelssjökull has been designated as the high-impact commercial tourist area (for jeeps and snowmobiles) and the lodge at **Jöklasel** is the largest base for 'action' tourism, with a small restaurant/café and hostel just steps away from the ice. Organised jeep caravans typically travel to Jöklasel direct from Höfn, with a few designated pickup spots along the way for outer hotel guests.

As exciting as snowmobiles might sound, it's not always the best way to connect with the glacier. Tours tend to run in big groups, led by one or two guides who are terrified of someone falling into a crevasse. The scenery is blinding and beautiful, but all the while you are being corralled, single-file like schoolchildren and breathing in exhaust fumes. The jeep allows a more tranquil mood, but the heated interior feels like cheating and the single side window inhibits the great white panorama of nothingness. The best way to take it all in, of course, would probably be to hike or ski across, although this is quite dangerous and should only be considered by experienced ice climbers. Less experienced people should stick to the edges.

The most accessible glacier tongues to reach on your own (by car) are Fláajökull and Höffellsjökull. Both stick straight out, perpendicular to Route 1, with small but slightly rough roads that lead right up to the ice's edge (Höffellsjökull is famous for its jasper and opal finds). With a few noted exceptions, the entire southern rim of the glacier now belongs to **Skaftafell National Park** (see page 422). The main area of the park is great for those who want to hike on good, sound trails right up to the glacier's edge. Nearly all organised hiking trips originate at the main entrance of the park, where there is close access to nearby glacier tongues. If you're backpacking and/or without wheels, you can either stay in Höfn and go on an organised trip, or simply bus/ride to Skaftafell and hike on your own.

## HÖFN

Höfn is the 'capital' of the southeast district of Iceland known as Hornafjörður. The area stretches all along the coast, from the glacial sands of Skeiðará all the way around to the East Fjords. The 'horns' are the two angled corner peninsulas that cut into the sea with a pair of exquisite, fairy-tale mountains – Eystrahorn and Vestrahorn. The sandy point of Stokksnes (just outside Höfn) grants a fabulous close-up view of the sharp rocks of Vestrahorn – though a faraway sunset view from the ring road is truly breathtaking. Eystrahorn is equally steep and picturesque and has the proud distinction of preventing a section of the ring road from being paved – the only section in the whole country. Here the cone-shaped gravel hills are in constant motion, and the rocks are sliding across the narrow lane of the road and down far below to the roaring sea (not a place to go whizzing around the corner).

Höfn simply means 'harbour' but sounds trickier – if you really want to impress the locals, say it like they do: *hup'n*. The town became a town by default in 1988 from all the people who had gathered around the harbour, though people have been fishing and farming the area for ever. What they lack in history they make up for in scenery – the town is laid out on a sandy hook that juts into the Hornafjörður lagoon. From any direction you can see the ocean, the bogs and shore farms, and then the backdrop of grey mountains and the glistening ice cap; that is, if it's not raining or foggy or snowing.

Today, Höfn is the de facto tourist base for venturing up, into, and around Vatnajökull glacier. The town is small (population 1,700) and accommodating, and they know their glacier quite well. There's a highly informative museum dedicated solely to Vatnajökull – the only thing like it in the country.

**GETTING THERE AND AWAY** One flight a day running to and from Reykjavík (1 hour) is managed by **Air Iceland** (*Landsflug; ☎ 481 3300; www.airiceland.is*). Hornafjörður Airport (HFN) is located just off Route 1, just outside the city. Höfn is an important **bus** stop, but it is a distant destination. There is one daily bus to and from Reykjavík (7–8 hours), and another that connects with Egilsstaðir (4 hours) via Djúpivogur.

## TOURIST INFORMATION

**Tourist information** Hafnarbraut 30; ☎ 479 1500; e tourinfo@hornafjordur.is; www.hornafjordur.is, www.visitvatnajokull.is. In the museum (see page opposite).

## TOUR OPERATORS

**Arctic Ice** Vesturbraut 21; ☎ 478 1731; e info@arctic-ice.is; www.arctic-ice.is. More of a specialised group that puts together custom-built ice tours for photographers/filmmakers.

**Glacier Jeeps** Hafnarbraut 15; ☎ 478 1000; e glacierjeeps@simnet.is; www.glacierjeeps.is; ⌚ year round. The largest company around – they run most of their trips from their mountain hut at Jöklasel on Skálafellsjökull. They offer several different 2–3hr tours, in the jeep, on snowmobiles, or skis. Every year they organise some pretty amazing expeditions to less accessible places on the glacier & also into the interior.

**Vatnajökull Travel** m 894 1616; e info@vatnajokull.is; www.vatnajokull.is; ⌚ summer only. Very professional company with trips to & from Reykjavík & Höfn to the glacier & the lagoon.

For details of other tour operators, see *Chapter 4*, page 72.

## WHERE TO STAY

### In town

**Hótel Höfn** (36 rooms) Víkurbraut 24; ☎ 478 1240; e hotelhofn@hotelhofn.is; www.hotelhofn.is. Höfn's only 'hotel' hotel is aimed at business travellers, with the same kind of standards you would find in a chain hotel – double beds with polyester bedspreads, nice private bathrooms, a cheery b/fast buffet & a slightly impersonal touch. **$$$$**

**Ásgarður** (36 rooms) Ránarslóð 3; ☎ 478 1365; e asgardur@eldhorn.is; www.horn.is/asgardur/. Concrete 'motel'-style guesthouse with a great view of the sea. The interior is very prim & orderly. Private bathrooms. B/fast inc. **$$$**

**Hvammur** (30 rooms) Ránarslóð 2; ☎ 478 1503; e hvammur3@simnet.is; www.hvammurinn.is. This practical, suburban-feeling guesthouse is within walking distance of the harbour & the waterfront trails. There are 2 separate locations: the main one is more convenient for those without cars. Bathrooms are shared. B/fast inc. **$$$**

**Nýlibær Youth Hostel** (34 beds) Hafnarbraut 8; ☎ 478 1736; e hofn@hostel.is; www.hostel.is. Conveniently central & clean. 2 rooms (for groups travelling together) have their own bathrooms. As the hostel is a popular stop for cyclists on the ring road, there's also a nice storage room for bikes. **$**

**Camping** (*Hafnarbraut 52; ☎ 478 1606; e camping@simnet.is; www.simnet.is/camping;* **$**) The well-kept campsite on the hillside has hot showers and kitchen facilities, and plenty of services for caravans. They also offer a number of private wooden cottages that sleep two–four people.

### Just outside

**Árnanes** (16 rooms) 478 1550; e arnanes@arnanes.is; www.arnanes.is. This idyllic farm hotel is far away from the madding crowd, but close enough to the town (& airport) to make it very convenient. Just off Route 1, this well-managed enclave has become the coveted stopover for anyone circling the country. Rooms are in comfortable private cabins (with private bathrooms), & meals are taken in the restaurant at the main lodge. The hotel also functions as a working horse ranch & offers great horseriding tours of the area. Highly recommended. *Sleeping-bag accommodation 3,000ISK.* **$$$**

**Fosshótel Vatnajökull** (26 rooms) Linderbakki; 478 2555; e bokun@fosshotel.is; www.fosshotel.is. About 10km from Höfn, this chain hotel offers nice rooms (all with private showers) with a nice view of the glacier. What it lacks in soul it makes up for at breakfast. **$$$**

**Hótel Edda Nesjaskóli** (31 rooms) Nesjar; 444 4850; e edda@hoteledda.is; www.hoteledda.is; summer only. Like all of the Edda hotels, these are school dormitories & classrooms refitted for your comfort. Showers are basic & shared, but the bedrooms are clean, orderly & comfortable. They also offer affordable sleeping-bag accommodation. **$$$**

**Jöklasel** (30 beds) e glacierjeeps@simnet.is; www.glacierjeeps.is. The mountain 'hut' hotel on the ice is owned & managed by the Glacier Jeeps company as a travel station & restaurant, & has the ambiance of a crowded ski lodge. Some sleeping-bag accommodation is available, though typically, you must first make a reservation with the travel company. *Sleeping-bag accommodation around 3,500ISK.* **$$**

**WHERE TO EAT** Höfn is trying to become famous for its lobster and has an annual lobster festival to prove it. All the hotels in Höfn keep their own restaurants to feed the guests; the nicest of these are in Hótel Höfn. The top floor houses the more refined dining room, which serves fantastic lobster and other seafood brought in at the local harbour ($$$$). The main-floor Restaurant Osínn is more casual, serving pizza and hamburgers ($$$). The restaurant at Árnanes (*May–Oct*) is quite original, with a regular evening buffet of Icelandic country specialities ($$$). Jöklasel does a popular all-you-can eat seafood buffet that rounds off a trip on the glacier ($$$).

In Höfn, there's a warm and cosy atmosphere at **Kaffi Hornið** (*Hafnarbraut 42; 478 2600; e ingo@eldhorn.is; 11.00–22.00 Mon–Thu, 11.00–01.00 Fri/Sat, 12.00–22.00 Sun; $$*). The menu is typical of a town restaurant (sandwiches, pasta, chicken and fish), along with cakes and coffee. The **Víkin Restaurant** qualifies as the town pub (*Víkurbraut 2; 478 2300; pub 09.00–01.00 Mon–Thu, 09.00–03.00 Fri/Sat; $$$*). If you want to meet hard-working local fishermen letting off steam, this is the place. They also serve great lobster and local fish. The local grocery store is part of the Miðbær shopping centre; on the corner of Hafnarbraut and Litlabrú (*09.00–18.00 daily*).

**WHAT TO SEE AND DO** **Vatnajökull** glacier trumps everything else. The tourist centre exists by booking tourists on glacier trips – from one-hour 'super-jeep' drives across the ice to snowmobiles and cross-country ski 'hikes'. The next-best option is to check out the **Glacier Exhibition** (*Jöklasýning; Hafnarbraut 30; 478 2665; e jokull@hornarfjordur.is; www.ice-land.is; Jun–Aug 09.00–21.00 daily, May & Sep 13.00–18.00 daily, Oct–Apr 13.00–16.00 Mon–Fri; entrance 500ISK*). The very well-planned museum explores the unique geology, ecology and history of the glacier and provides entertaining exhibits for all ages – definitely worth the time. They also show a short film about recent glacial eruptions and have a panoramic viewing platform up on top – a nice thing to do before or after visiting the ice itself. Other museums include the **Folk Museum** (*Gamlabúð; Hafnarbraut; 478 1733; May/Jun & Sep 13.00–18.00 daily, Jul/Aug 13.00–21.00 daily, entrance free*) and the **Nautical Museum** (*Pakkhúsið; Höfn harbour;* ☎ *478 1540;* ⏲ *Jun–Aug 13.00–18.00 daily; entrance 250ISK*). The former is a tribute to yesteryear – the latter is a craft and souvenir shop.

A walk around the **harbour** can also be entertaining – especially when the fish are being offloaded. **Ósland** is the bird refuge at the point just beyond the town – it is a good place for birdwatching, obviously, but also for sunsets. A marked path goes around the pond at the point. In case of bad weather, there's always the **swimming pool** (*Hafnarbraut 29;* ☎ *478 1157;* ⏲ *07.00–20.00 Mon–Fri, 09.00–18.00 Sat/Sun*) to fall back on.

## LÓNSÖRÆFI

The set of glacial valleys directly east of Vatnajökull display a colourful and desolate prehistoric landscape. This was all covered with ice at the time of settlement – over the past six million years, the continuous sub-glacial eruptions of the Kollumúli volcano led to a constant renewal of these mountains. The main difference is that with each new flow, the lava was cooled at a different temperature. The steep, conical slopes of Lónsöræfi are made from liparite that can only form when the cooling process is immediate. The slightest temperature variation causes a different colour (dark grey, blue-green, orange, purple, yellow and white) while the flash cooling of the ice is what causes entire mountains to shatter into a mound of sharp, tiny pieces that comprise these 1,000m+ high peaks. Rock hounds tend to fill their pockets here – for all the different colours and the tiny feldspar crystals visible in every stone.

To travel to Lónsöræfi is to enter a desolate and daunting world where everything feels as raw and empty as yesterday. The glacier river Jökulá í Lóni prevents any paved, permanent roads from entering and the rest of the landscape is a work in progress – that means unseen waterfalls, glacial moraines, and very little vegetation. Not enough people visit Lónsöræfi to make it a national park yet, but it is special enough to be the country's largest nature reserve. With increasing popularity, hikers are trekking the distance between Lónsöræfi and Mt Snæfell (see page 404) and staying in the mountain huts along the way. The trail follows up around the far northeast end of Vatnajökull – this is some of the best remote hiking out there and there's a good chance you'll spot some reindeer.

**GETTING THERE AND AWAY** Route 980 is the gravelled road that takes you up into the valley – it's the only way to drive there and you'll need a massive 4x4 that can push through a minimum of very fast, 1m-deep water. For those without trucks, the farmer at **Stafafell** makes his summer income by driving people (from Höfn) over the river and up the winding mountain road into Lónsöræfi with his monster-wheeled bus (3,000ISK one-way; 5,200ISK return). His day trips are great ventures into the highlands, with a guided hike to the first mountain hut (Múlaskáli) and the nearby waterfalls. Contact Stafafell (☎ *478 1717;* **m** *864 4215;* **e** *lon@lon.is; www.lon.is; available Jun–5 Sep*).

### WHERE TO STAY

**Stafafell** (18 rooms) ☎ 478 1717; **e** stafafell@eldhorn.is; www.stafafell.is. This private hostel is a bit of a hidden gem off the main road. Rustic & traditional, it's become a nice stop for bikers & hikers, especially for those heading into Lónsöræfi. Sleeping-bag spaces & made-up beds both available; shared bathrooms. **$$**

## SUÐURSVEIT

The 'southern district' marks the fairly empty stretch of coast between Höfn and Jökulsárlón. Isolated by the glacier and its floods, the local farmers and their families have a reputation for independence and strong imagination. These ideals are best portrayed in the new museum of **Thórbergur Thórðarson** (1888–1974), a noted Icelandic writer who was born and raised in Suðursveit (*Í slóð Þórbergs; Hali; ☎ 478 1073; www.thorbergur.is; ⏲ Oct–May 12.00–17.00, closed Mon, Jun–Sep 09.00–18.00 daily; entrance 400ISK*). Located near his boyhood farm, the museum takes visitors through a vivid 3D display of the author's life, with recreated scenes based on his memories of home. Some parts of the exhibit are in English, and it ends up being more interesting than it first appears (be sure to take a look at the back of the museum that pictures a line of leather-bound volumes on a bookshelf).

To go walking off into the great beautiful nothing of Suðursveit is also a wonderful thing. A series of good trails heads up into the grandiose glacier valley of **Kálfafellsdalur** all the way to the small remaining tongue of Brókarjöklull glacier. Another trail follows up from the tiny church at Kálfafellsstaður, up the mountainside and along the edge of the glacier Skálafellsjökull. You can pick up the free detailed hiking map (*Roots of Vatnajökull*) at any of the local information points.

### WHERE TO STAY

**Hali** (6 rooms) Suðursveit; ☎ 478 1073. The small farmhouse next to Thórbergur's museum feels a bit more suburban, despite its relative isolation. Guests are given a good deal of attention & have access to the shared kitchen & bathroom facilities. **$$$**

**Lækjarhús** (11 rooms) Suðursveit; ☎ 478 1517; e laekjarhus@simnet.is. The 'brook house' farm is a traditional Suðursveit homestead comprising 2 houses with comfortable rooms & kitchen facilities. This is a quiet & simple place out in the country, & a nice rest stop between Skaftafell & Höfn. Bathrooms are shared. *Sleeping-bag spaces under 3,000ISK.* **$$**

## JÖKULSÁRLÓN

The glacier lagoon of Breiðarmerkurjökull is the only place in Iceland where you are guaranteed to see icebergs up close. Only 50 years ago, the glacier reached all the way to the shore and the broken ice merely drifted away in the ocean waves. As the glacier recedes (100m per year) it gouges out a depression that is filled with melted water and giant chunks of ice. These icebergs collect at the lagoon's shallow exit until they melt down into smaller ice cubes that tumble out to sea. It makes for quite a dramatic scene, with icy blue and white shapes lingering gently before the glacial cliffs of Vatnajökull.

Jökulsárlón is also the lowest point in Iceland (technically), since the land beneath the ice is 200m below sea level due to the weight of the glacier. In warmer weather, the icebergs tumble off and melt quickly; in winter, the lagoon freezes and locks the icebergs in place until the following spring. The ice, sand, and water form a unique ecology – no fish live in the lagoon except for those that get pulled in from the sea by the tides. Happy seals congregate at the entrance to the lagoon to dive for fish among the icebergs – quite a sight to behold.

Jökulsárlón is the most photographed location in the whole of Iceland and has become the iconic Arctic backdrop for magazine covers and Hollywood (so far, five blockbusters have been filmed here). Nowhere else is such an exotic location so accessible – the ring road zips right by it and there's a huge car park on the edge of the lagoon to allow for maximum visitors. Since the 1970s, the lagoon has quadrupled in size.

**VISITING JÖKULSÁRLÓN** Nobody should miss the wonders of Jökulsárlón – this really is a spectacular and beautiful location. On that same note, the lagoon's popularity and convenience has turned it into a tourist conveyor belt: park your car, buy your ticket, ride the boat, snap a picture, and exit through the gift shop. In spite of the summer circus, rest assured, the icebergs are free and open to all any time of year.

You can't miss the lagoon, as Route 1 passes right next to it, and the traffic on the bridge will force you to stop and take a nice long look. Open-air tours are available on the amphibious boats of **Jökulsárlón** (*☎ 478 2122; e info@jokulsarlon.is; www.jokulsarlon.is; ⏲ 15 May–15 Sep, Jun–Aug 09.00–19.00, May & Sep 10.00–17.00 daily*). They also run a small café (sandwiches, coffee, and cakes) and gift shop. Tours last about 40 minutes – the boats drive into the lagoon and float among the icebergs. If you bring your own kayaks into the area, use caution. Launch on the left (opposite) side and try to avoid all the motorboats zipping back and forth. Admittedly, you can get just as close (if not closer) to the icebergs by simply standing on the shore; the broken ice tends to collect in the shallows. I also recommend taking a walk on the beach where big blocks of ice often get stranded on the black sand.

## SKAFTAFELL NATIONAL PARK

Skaftafell is a natural wonderland of ice, mountains, sand, and water. The sheer grandeur of the place lies in its massive size and the incredible glacial phenomena all around. Cradled in the valleys of Vatnajökull, the park and its geography embody all the processes of a living, breathing glacier – visitors can walk across moraines in the making, watch 'plucking' first-hand and witness features like crevasses and kettle lakes. Glacier tongues flow from the highest heights of the park all the way down to sea level, where the huge deposits of glacial sediments have spread out into the flat-sand delta of Skeiðarársandur. All in all, the gorgeous scenery is unrivalled – if you must choose only one national park to visit, this is the one.

Skaftafell was first designated a park in 1967 after the bridge near Jökulsárlón finally opened the area up to the rest of the country. In 2004, with the hope of protecting the glacier, the park was enlarged to its current (enormous) size of 4,807km$^2$ (about half of Vatnajökull). Today, Skaftafell is the largest national park in Europe and the most-visited campsite in Iceland. There really is nowhere else like it on earth, in terms of hiking trails and easy access to huge glaciers.

Much of the park is bowl-shaped, guarded from the elements by the surrounding ice. Some claim that's why there's good weather – it's also the reason the early Vikings gathered in Skaftafell for their *goðar* councils. The enclosed valley was first settled as a farm in the 13th century, but the onslaught of glacial sand eventually buried the original farm so that in 1850 it was finally moved up the hillside to its current location. Today, the main entrance to the park and the majority of the hiking trails are centred on these old farms – it is this core of glacier valleys that is known as 'Skaftafell', even though the entire southern rim of the glacier is part of the park.

Because Skaftafell is such an immense place, hit-and-run tourists fare badly. To capture the real magnitude of glacier morphology takes time – it is time that created everything in this park. That means more than a day or two, although if that's all you've got, so be it. It's just that visitors who can concentrate on the whole physical spectrum (from the mountains to the sea) will feel more fulfilled.

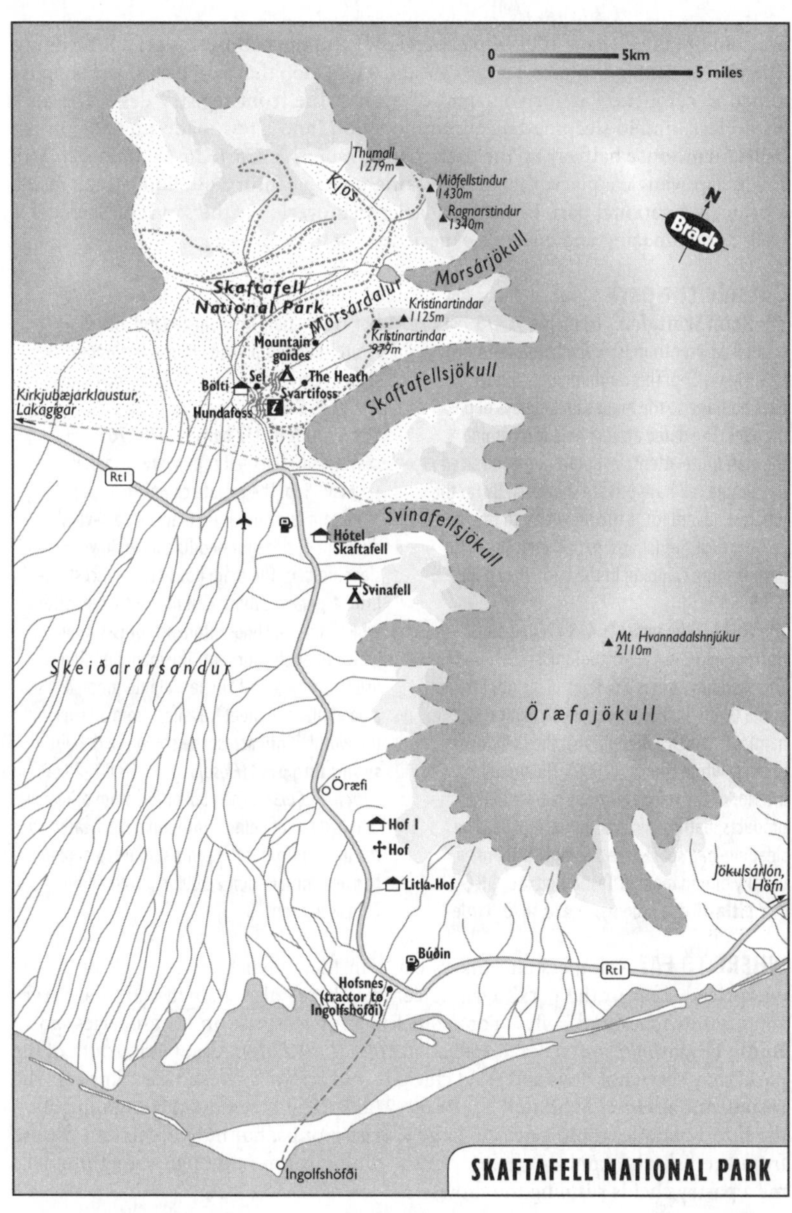


SKAFTAFELL NATIONAL PARK

**TOURIST INFORMATION** The **national park office** (☎ *478 1627;* e *skaftafell@ust.is; www.ust.is*) is located at the visitors centre (*www.umhverfisstofnun.is;* ⏲ *Jun–Aug 08.00–21.00, May/Sep 10.00–15.00 daily*), right near the entrance to the park.

## WHERE TO STAY

### In the park

The **campsite** in Skaftafell is one of the country's largest, comprising several long rectangular fields marked by tree lines that were planted as wind breaks. The facilities can be a good hike from where you pitch your camp. The hot showers are coin operated (have 100ISK pieces ready!) and the bathrooms get a little dingy. The **visitor centre** contains a large café and a gift shop that sells basic food supplies aimed at campers. Pay for your tent/caravan at the front registry desk. The park also offers limited sleeping-bag accommodation (and a few made-up beds) in the **Bölti farmhouse** halfway up the park road (*7 rooms;* ☎ *478 1626;* 🕒 *May–Oct;* **$$**). If you can wangle a place, then do – waking up in a century-old home that's inside a protected national park beneath a glacier that overlooks the sands of Skeiðará – well, its an amazing and enviable experience not to be missed.

## Outside the park

**Hótel Skaftafell** (63 rooms) ☎ 478 1945; e hotelskf@centrum.is; www.hotelskaftafell.is; 🕒 May–Sep. This rambling park lodge pays homage to the mountain holidays of past decades. The dated atmosphere is charming & the staff quite attentive. Rooms are good sized but simple (all have private showers). By far the greatest advantage is the proximity to the park & other facilities (shops, petrol, etc). They also permit some camping in the back. B/fast inc. **$$$**

**Hof I** (20 rooms) ☎ 478 2260; e hof@frostogfuni.is; www.frostogfuni.is; 🕒 Jun–Sep. This working farm is a delightful insight into life in the Öræfi district – even if you don't stay, the hamlet is worth a detour (visit the turf-covered green & white church, c1900). The modern interior of the rooms is a zany tribute to IKEA products; bathrooms are shared. Inexpensive sleeping-bag spaces are available & there's a worthy dining room. B/fast buffet inc. **$$$**

**Litla-Hof** (7 rooms) ☎ 478 1670. 'Little-Hof' is a friendly little sheep farm, newly refurbished but plain & simple; bathrooms are shared; kitchen facilities. *Sleeping-bag spaces 2,600ISK.* **$$**

**Svinafell** (32 beds) ☎ 478 1765; e svinafell@svinafell.com; www.svinafell.com; 🕒 May–Sep. The private campsite at 'pig mountain' is a busy little place, with several different options for bedding down in your own sleeping bag. The main house is the nicest, the little 4-person cabins a bit more spartan, after which you can choose from any grassy knoll on which to pitch your tent. The main building is used as a sheltered kitchen/dining room, & it's a good place to meet travellers from all over the world. Right across the street is a delightful **swimming pool** (*Flosalaug;* 🕒 *08.00–20.00; entrance 400ISK*). The pool differs from others in that instead of being geothermal, it's heated by the incinerator for the camp's refuse. Sleeping-bag accommodation 2,500ISK pp, camping 700ISK per tent. **$**

**WHERE TO EAT** Campers and hikers carry in their own food or stock up in the overpriced shop in the park's visitors centre. There's also a small café that serves soup, sandwiches and coffee. For a quick bite or to stock up on groceries, go to **Búðin** (*Fagurhólmsmýri;* ☎ *478 1603;* 🕒 *09.00–21.00 daily*). About 5km south of the park, they serve hot dogs and fried chicken, and are well stocked for campers. The **restaurant** at **Hótel Skaftafell** (🕒 *08.00–21.00;* **$$$**) is remarkably high quality – the florid banquet room caters to large tourist groups, but individuals can choose from the fish-and-lamb specialities in the dining room (although something tells me a pastry chef is running the show).

**WHAT TO SEE AND DO** The **visitor centre** manages the park's exhibits, which make a nice orientation to the area and its one-of-a-kind ecology (*entrance free*). When you're ready to hike, the Skaftafell farmhouses make a good place to start. The turf-covered gables of **Sel** are the oldest (from 1850) and have been renovated inside to portray the farm life of the time. To get there, you cross the Bæjargil ('farm gulch') with the three waterfalls Thjofafoss, Hundafoss, and Magnúsarfoss. These were the old fords for the farms and **hundafoss** ('hound falls') is so named after the many dogs that were swept over the edge. A walk upstream takes you to the

## SMALL THINGS IN A BIG PACKAGE: SKAFTAFELL'S WILDLIFE AND GEOLOGY

Skaftafell's gargantuan landscapes are its main selling point, but don't miss out on the small things. Start with the rocks in your boots: the round black pebbles come from more recent eruptions that have been carried over the ice; the sharp yellow-ish rocks are made from compound ash that fell in the 1362 eruption and were trapped under the ice. The 'sand' you see everywhere is not made of grains, but very tiny round pebbles of pumice. Inside the broken chunks of ice you'll find tiny bubbles of 10,000-year-old air. If you have a chance, take a nice long drink from the glacier and remember it.

On the ground you'll find an abundance of ferns, and dainty bluebells. Moths and butterflies are rare in Iceland, with the exception of Skaftafell, where the grey and white pretty pinion (*Perizoma blandiata*) flourishes. Also in summer, aside from regular breeders (ie: snipe, ptarmigan, and redwing), you'll spot tiny birds like the meadow pipit and the itsy, bitsy wren (Iceland's smallest bird). Field mice run about the valleys and the lower, wooded slopes and Skaftafell is the only place in Iceland where the Arctic fox is protected from hunters. Walk quietly and remotely and you just might see one.

more popular **Svartifoss** ('black falls') where gushing white water shoots out over an overhanging ridge of shiny black basalt columns. The rocks were formed from slow volcanic cooling, after which the water and ice broke down the cliff. The land beyond Svartifoss is 'the heath' or Skaftafellsheiði – it is a very gradual incline that rises up to the higher mountains in the park.

Start by checking out the glaciers – the bottom of the park's namesake glacier, **Skaftafellsjökull** is about a one-hour walk from the main office (there is also a wheelchair-accessible path). A sizeable glacier lagoon is forming at the base, and up on top of the glacier you can see all kinds of ice streams, ice formations like moulins, and rock boulders that have been 'plucked' onto the ice. The next glacier tongue down is the smaller but higher **Svinafellsjökull** ('pig mountain glacier') which curves upwards to the top of Mt Hvannadalshnjúkur. A large moraine is forming here, and there are trails on the rocky outside edges which allow you to look down over the glaciers or walk along their base. When hiking near the ice, use caution and be smart – the time of year and the air temperature can really affect the way the ice is behaving. The most 'active' glacier is that of **Morsárjökull** (in the back of the park) where you can actually see and hear the ice creaking and breaking as it grinds down the mountain. For more direct contact with the glaciers (ie: ice climbing, glacier walking, etc), book a tour with the local **Icelandic Mountain Guides** (m *587 9999;* e *mountainguide@mountainguide.is; www.mountainguide.is*). They have a base camp right in the park (near the visitors centre) and offer a number of guided treks on the glaciers, as well as training sessions for more high-tech adventure climbing.

For a longer half-day climb, head up to the twin peaks of **Kristínartindar** (979m and 1,125m). A narrow path connects the two summits along a jagged ridge that can feel a bit like tightrope walking – do not attempt to walk it in high winds. From here, one gets a grand view of the entire icy length of Skaftafellsjöúkull, the green valleys, the black-sand flats, and the great icy beyond of Vatnajökull.

**Morsárdalur** is a textbook glacial valley, ground out by Morsárjökull. Paths follow the far edges on both sides, as the centre of the valley is a shifting flat of lively braided rivers. Serious hikers will want to attempt tackling **Kjós**, a beautiful glacier valley, now free of ice. This is an all-day hike (12 hours) but definitely worth getting away from the summer crowds back at the main entrance. A decent trail ascends the side of the mountain ridge to three peaks – Thumall (1,279m) – the 'thumb'; Miðfellstindur (1,430m) – 'middle mountain summit'; and Ragnarstindur (1,340m) – 'Ragnar's summit'. From here, you can see up into the great expanse of Vatnajökull, and look back upon the park and the sea.

The lava craters of **Lakagígar** (see page 251) are another tremendous sight in the park, but are located in the highlands and quite inaccessible for much of the year. In summer, organised bus tours run from the park's main office.

Several magnificent **air tours** are available from Skaftafell Airport, located right across the entrance from the park (*Atlantsflug;* ☎ *478 2406;* e *info@atf.is; www.atf.is*). Their 90-minute sightseeing flight over and around Vatnajökull costs about US$250 – shorter flights cost about half that and take in Skaftafell and its glaciers.

**ÖRÆFI** Until very recently, the 'land between the sands' was the most isolated part of Iceland. On every side, these coastal farms were cut off: to the back stand Iceland's tallest mountain and the impassable ice of Vatnajökull to the north and east. To the south lies the sea (without any harbour) and to the west, the great sands of Skeiðará and its hundreds of raging glacier rivers. The resolute few who have lived here have always struggled to eke out a living in the narrow slope between mountain and sand, rarely venturing beyond the natural confines around them. At first, they affectionately called the area 'the little district' (Litla Hérað). That changed with the 1362 eruption of **Öræfajökull** – remembered as one of Iceland's deadliest volcanoes. The land was covered in ash and rendered uninhabitable for decades. The new name *Öræfi* means 'desolation' or 'wasteland'. Nowadays it seems to be dormant, and the caldera's high rim is **Mt Hvannadalshnjúkur** (2,110m), the country's highest mountain. The summit lies beneath the ice and out of view, but

## CLIMBING HVANNADALSHNJÚKUR – ICELAND'S HIGHEST PEAK

Out of sight is *not* out of mind when it comes to reaching the top of Iceland. Very few people try though – other mountains have less ice, are more popular and a lot easier to pronounce (*kvanna-dals-knyu-ker* can be a mouthful). Still, this is not a terribly difficult peak in terms of terrain. What matters is physical endurance, so a degree of fitness and hiking experience is required. The journey to the summit takes about 12–14 hours (there and back), ascends 2,000m (about 6,500ft), and covers a total distance of 22km. As with everything in Iceland – the weather affects everything, so don't plan your climb inside a tight schedule. Hopefuls normally stake out a week and set out the morning of a positive forecast. Early summer is best – after July there is an increased risk of crevasses.

The real 'man of the mountain' is Einar Sigurðsson – an experienced guide who grew up in its shadow and still lives in his farm at the base of the peak (his father and grandfather also climbed the mountain). He has made over 230 successful ascents in his lifetime (the world record) and now guides others year-round. He charges around US$250 for groups of two to eight people and provides the mountaineering gear you'll need (crampons, ice axe, etc); contact **Mountain Tour** (m *894 0894;* e *info@hofsnes.is; www.hofsnes.is*). The **Mountain Guides** (*www.mountainguides.is*) in Skaftafell also offer guided trips to the summit in summer.

## *JÖKULHLAUP!*

The whole world watched with great concern when the Grímsvötn volcano erupted in October 1996 – not only for the lava and ash that was contained by the ice cap, but also for the glacial outburst flood that was sure to follow. The mass of melted water increased in pressure, lifting the ice cap 10m before squeezing itself out over the mountains. It took a month to happen, but finally the gush of water broke through a 300m wall of ice. A 4m-high wall of water gushed across Skaftafell towards the sea. Fortunately, scientists had had enough warning to designate a predicted flood area and keep cars off the ring road – the bridge was washed away in less than an hour. At its height, the *jökulhlaup* was flowing at 50,000m$^3$ per second. Most of the sand you see today was covered with muddy grey water.

There's a film in the Skaftafell visitors centre that shows the incredible footage. No other *jökulhlaup* has been so well observed and documented as the Grímsvötn eruption of 1996. It is still very hard to predict details of future catastrophes, but for the record, Vatnajökull has produced a glacial outburst at least once every five years. Grímsvötn last erupted in 2004, but alas, there was no *jökulhlaup*.

you can at least get a sense of its imposing mass as you skirt around its edges.

Traditionally, Öræfi included about 24 farms, including Skaftafell, Svinafell, Hof, and Hofsnes. The people here mainly kept sheep and cows but were very limited in what produce they could send out and bring in. Hard winter freezes sometimes enabled travel while the glacial floods of spring and summer turned Öræfi into a distant island. Many Öræfi residents can still recall fording the glacier rivers and watching the water rise up through the floors of their trucks. Skeiðerársandur was the last great obstacle for Iceland's ring road – a bridge was finally completed in 1974.

**INGÓLFSHÖFÐI** Before founding his farm in Reykjavík, Ingólfur Arnason first set foot on land here at 'Ingólfur's cape'. He spent the winter of AD874 here, and 12 centuries later the farm still bears his name. The *höfði* or 'headland' is an important landmark in Iceland, where the great glacial sands of the south meet the mountainous ridge of Iceland's east. Although the area looks like a tidal flat – it is not. The geography is simply a huge expanse of black glacial sand covered with a few feet of water. The cape rises up from the sand in a slanted ridge of cliffs, the highest point being 78m. The view from here is astounding – back over the glossy black sand and up to Iceland's tallest mountain, capped with a giant white glacier – one can see a huge distance up and down the coast.

The cape is private land and a protected nature reserve. The puffins arrive in droves in summer, but more unique are the number of great skua (*Stercorarius skua*) which come to feed on them. These giant birds hatch their large chicks in July–August, and out on this island you can see them up close. The trip to Ingólfshöfði is a delightful family tradition that goes back many generations when the then farmer began piling visitors into his tractor and taking them out across the flats to the island. His descendants continue to share their impressive 'backyard' with people from all over the world. Groups still travel on the flatbed trailer pulled by the tractor. The very personal, organised tour lasts around 2½ hours. Visitors can enjoy the beautiful island and the black-sand dunes; have access to the great birds and see the stone pillar commemorating Ingólfur's first landing. Interested travellers should simply arrive at the farm at Hofsnes (e *info@hofsnes.is; www.hofsnes.is;* ⌚ *Apr–Oct morning & afternoon tours daily; cost 2,300ISK*)

**SKEIÐARÁRSANDUR** To comprehend the true size and power of Vatnajökull, one only needs to cross the sands and rivers of Skeiðarársandur. Over 100 glacier rivers flow out from beneath the glacier and wash out a huge amount of sediment. The 'sands' or *sandur* are vast and impressive – 50km across and 30km from shore to glacier. The area was impassable until 1974, and the bridge over Skeiðarársandur was a major engineering feat for Iceland, as it required dozens of separate spans. That same bridge suffered major damage in the 1996 *jökulhlaup* – the former iron struts (now twisted and bent) have been left as a testament to the glacier's power. Today, it is inadvisable to roam freely by foot or 4x4 out on Skeiðarársandur. Not only are the rivers fast and unpredictable – much of what you see is quicksand. There are a few marked turn-offs on Route 1 where you may pull over and enjoy the amazing view.

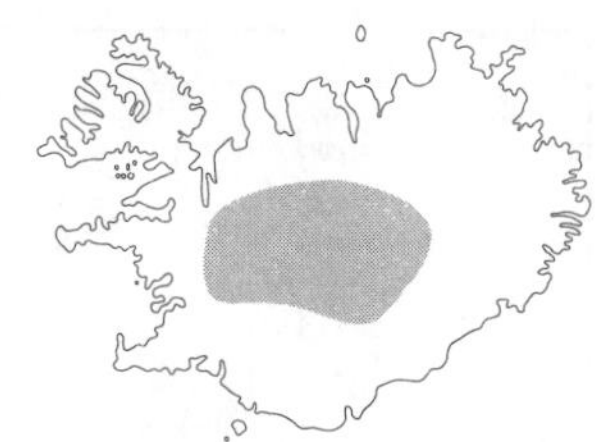

# Hálendið (The Highlands)

The middle of Iceland is a fabulous no-man's-land – a place that is so bleak and desperate that not a soul calls it home but everyone wants to visit. The reasons why the interior is uninhabited are plenty, starting with altitude. An average height of 500–1,000m means cold and crazy weather. Snow can fall on any day of the year and it often does – it was the snow that convinced the early settlers to give up and move back to the coast. Another problem is that most of the highlands consists of desert where there is not enough water to support life.

It's ironic, given that Iceland's largest glaciers (Langjökull, Hofskjökull, and Vatnajökull) make up the heart of this region. The lack of vegetation and a record for cataclysmic events have made any other attempts at settlement, even road building, impossible.

For the traveller, the highlands offers an endless display of raw and dramatic landscapes cut by ice, wind, and time. It is a joyously remote place where you can look in any direction and see not a sign of human existence. It is a place that accentuates all those feelings evoked by the Icelandic scenery: wonder, loneliness, desolation, grandeur, and inspiration.

It seems that every tourist wants to get into the highlands these days, either to say they did or to conquer the wilderness. It's a worthy ambition, but many travellers arrive in the country's centre only to realise that they have just exchanged Iceland's gorgeous green fjords for some dull black rocks. You have to like geology to be happy out here because there is not much else. The wildlife is remarkable because it is so scant and yet so colourful. This is the territory of the pink-footed goose and the purple sandpiper, both summertime breeders. There's dainty Arctic vegetation

### *VARUÐ!* – THE BIG DISCLAIMER

Travelling in the highlands is no cakewalk. Newcomers underestimate the region because it happens to be in Europe, but Iceland's interior feels more like a cross between the Gobi Desert and Antarctica. The wind is always strong and vicious sandstorms common. This is a very unpredictable place, which makes it both exciting and potentially hazardous. If you are driving, plan your fuel carefully because petrol stations are sparse. If you are entering a desert area, make sure you are carrying plenty of water (at least one litre per person per day). This is one part of Iceland where water is not readily available. Take a compass with you and very good maps that show all roads, all fords and potential river crossings, and all emergency huts (preferably with GPS markings). Knowing what you're up against, don't let paranoia ruin your adventure. Use common sense and have a good time.

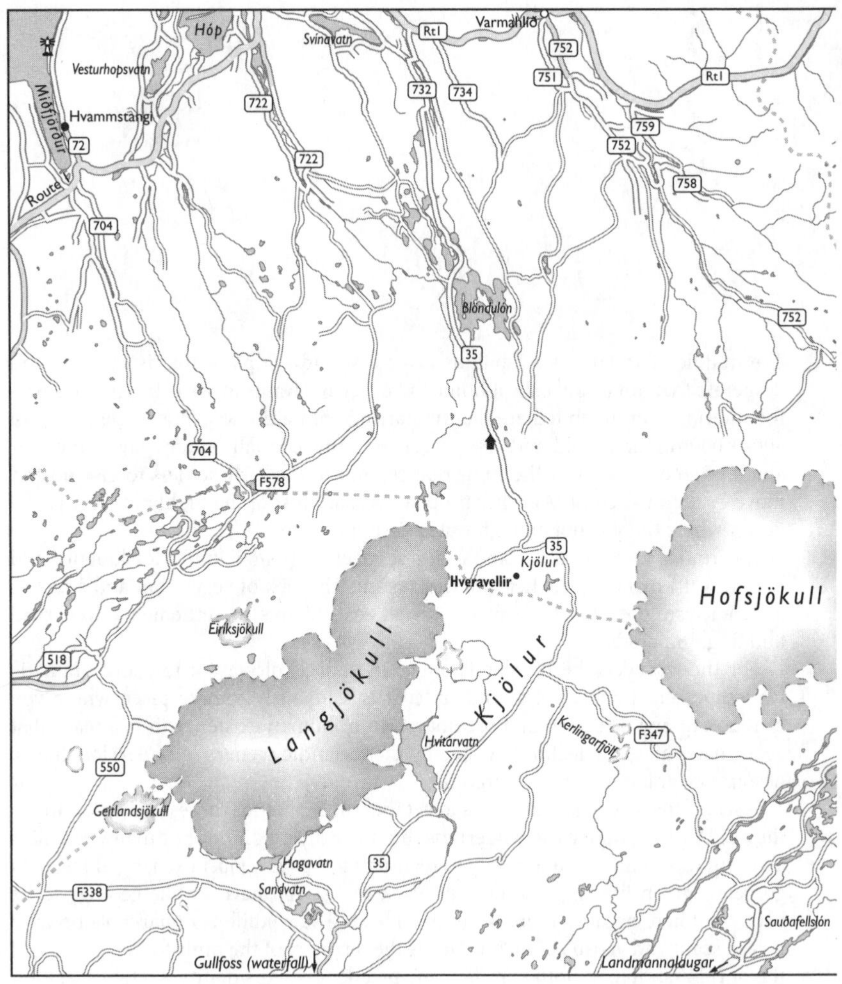


with pink and yellow flowers so minuscule they fit on your thumb, along with all kinds of strange moss and lichens. Everything else in the highlands is lava and ice or something in between those two.

On maps, the central highlands is an ill-defined region that is best defined as any place that's not on the coast where it's hard to access. The unpaved roads across the interior are only open for two to three months of the year. The two most prominent routes, Kjölur and Sprengisandur, are covered in this chapter. A few other traditional highland destinations, like Landmannalaugar (see page 241) and Snæfell (see page 404) are covered in their most proximate regional chapters.

## GETTING AROUND

Before you even consider a trip into the highlands, know that your window of opportunity is short and that the opening of roads is unpredictable. A late snowfall in June might keep a main route closed for an extra two weeks, and a sudden glacier flow

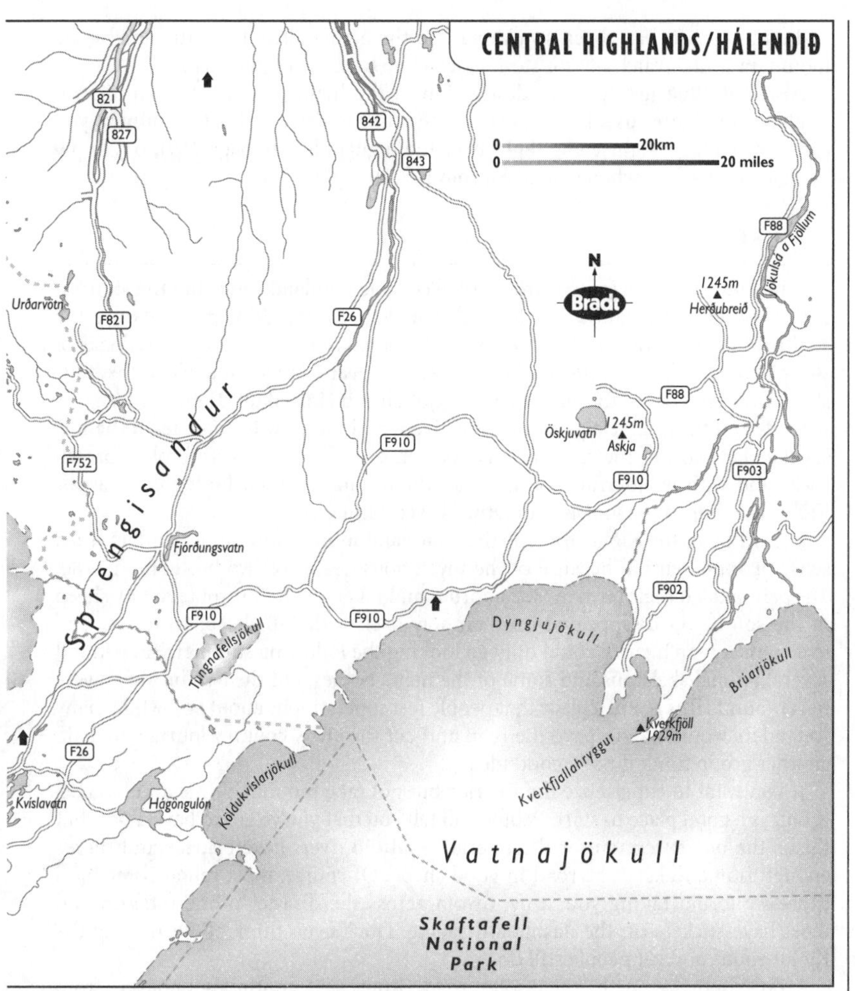


may cut off another road for however long it takes. Roads are officially open from June to August. To check expected opening times and current conditions, contact the **Icelandic Roads Association** (*Vegagerðin;* ☎ *1777;* e *vegagerdin@vegagerdin.is; www.vegagerdin.is/english*).

You should be driving a 4x4 in the highlands (the exception being the Kjölur route). The compact 4x4s offered by most car-rental companies do fine for the major routes, but the minute you start getting adventurous and crossing rivers, you really need something hefty (they don't call them super-jeeps for nothing). Well-equipped trucks include big, monster truck tyres and extra fuel tanks. Don't expect to average more than 45–50km/h.

In summer, buses cross the highlands daily, making regular stops at major camps and natural attractions. **SBA-Norðuleið** (*www.sba.is*) takes the Kjölur route between Reykjavík and Akureyri, via Gullfoss and with stops at the Kerlingarfjöll crossroads and Hveravellir. In the summer months, it is also possible to get a ride across Sprengisandur on the bus from Hella to Mývatn, via Nýidalur. Cyclists and motorcyclists have been swarming into the highlands of late, attracted by the mountain trails. Watch out for stones kicked up by vehicles that pass.

Also note that nearly every destination in the highlands has its own airstrip available for charter use. If you can't take the time to drive across the country, you can always take a sightseeing flight over the highlands (see page 369), or simply book a window seat when you take a commercial flight.

## KJÖLUR

The ancient Kjalvegur route is the most accessible highland route and the shortest path between north and south Iceland. For that reason, it's been used since the settlment era as a route to the Althing and as a passage for moving large flocks of sheep across the country. 'Kjölur' means 'keel', a clear Viking reference to the hull-shaped valley between the glaciers of Langjökull and Hofsjökull. These are Iceland's second- and third-largest glaciers respectively, and the view from beneath them is spectacular. Most of the route is a flat, barren plain, scattered with broken brown rocks and with wonderful mountains in the distance. Of all the highland areas, Kjölur is left open the longest, sometimes even until October.

Even though the Kjölur route is the easier and more common, Icelanders feel a sense of apprehension because of the mysterious deaths of two brothers in 1780. The pair had left their farm in Skagafjörður and taken the Kjölur route to buy sheep in the south, but disappeared on their way back with 180 sheep, 16 horses and five men. A search party could only go looking the following summer. They found several animal skeletons and some of the men's bodies, but the two brothers were never found. This is still a place that people feel superstitious about and while many Icelanders would like to pave the road and cut the cross-country journey by half, another group think it not a good idea.

If you want to experience the interior but not take too much time and be 'safe', Kjölur is a good place to start. People will tell you that you've got to have a 4x4, but this is the one exception for the interior – all the rivers have bridges and there's enough traffic to keep the road in good shape. Of course, most rental companies expressly forbid taking your tiny Toyota across the disaster-prone interior, and most have stickers on the dashboard saying 'Don't even think about driving the Kjölur route', and yet people still do.

From south to north, the Kjölur road (Route 35) continues unpaved from Gullfoss and continues northwards to the beautiful mountain of Bláfell (1,204m) or 'blue mountain'. From a distance it really does look blue, and once upon a time, these rocks were home to a famous and friendly troll named Bergthór. A less-friendly troll woman also lived in the mountain, and it was her spell over Kjölur that made travellers lose their minds or lose their way. This continued for years until one brave man, Ólafur, shouted out her name (Hallgerður!), after which the valley was saved – though he disappeared into the hidden world to marry the troll, who turned out to be a lovely elfin woman.

After passing Bláfell, the glacier of Langjökull steps into the horizon as it slopes down into the glacial lagoon of Hvítárvatn. This milky lake is 84m deep, which is very deep for a glacier lagoon. The next turn-off (Route F347) leads to the unique glacier and hot-spring area of Kerlingarfjöll, which is still one of Iceland's more secret splendours. As the road rises up to the pass between the two glaciers – to the east is Mt Kjalfell (1,000m) and just ahead of that is Beinahóll or 'bone hill' (where the unlucky party was found in 1781). The land then flattens out into the vast lava field of Kjalhraun, home to Hveravellir. This is the main stop between north and

## PERFECT PEACE

In 1898, the Danish explorer Daniel Bruun (1856–1931) travelled with the Icelandic statesman Páll Briem on an expedition across the interior. They rode horses, slept in tents and marked the path with cairns. Route 35 follows this same path, and you can still see some of these original cairns, now buried under the rocks of more recent travellers. In the opening pages of his published account of the trip, Daniel offers sound travel advice and a passionate recommendation:

*for the Tourist [sic] who will not be satisfied by making one of the traditional, I am almost tempted to say, too commonplace tours, which all strangers are induced to – for the Tourist, who is a real outdoor man, and does not mind spending a few days in uninhabited regions, I would recommend a ride through the deserted inner Highlands from North to South, or vice versa. Take the route over Kjölur!*

Daniel Bruun's descriptions of each area are just as vivid and accurate as if he had written them today. Reflecting on the tranquillity of Hveravellir:

*there is no sound of rolling carriages nor the baying of dogs in the distance, and no smoke rises from human dwellings. There is perfect peace. Only now and then the hoarse warning and weird cry of a raven is heard across the plain or in the valleys. Today, as it did a thousand years ago, the everlasting ice glitters on the beautiful mountains, seen on the horizon.*

*Both quotes taken from* Iceland – Routes over the Highlands *Sprengisandur and Kjalvegur, Nordisk Forlag, 1907.*

south and the most popular halting place on the Kjölur route, because you can have a quick dip in the hot pool there.

The road then approaches the strange, milky-green lagoon of Blöndulón. This manmade lake is the result of damming the Blanda River for the Blanda power station. There's a lookout point at the top of the hill that allows one to see out over the lake. Because of the fact that it's manmade and recent (about a decade old), no two maps show the same shape and size for Blöndulón. The Kjölur route joins the ring road at Skagafjörður, just south of Blönduós (see page 318) and Varmahlíð (see page 321).

**WHERE TO STAY AND EAT** There's a mountain hut at Hvitárnes (sleeps 30) but it's said to be haunted. Both Hveravellir and Kerlingarfjöll have ample bunk space and small shops that sell scant food supplies.

The remotest farm in the whole of Iceland is on the Kjölur road at **Áfangi** (*32 beds;* m *869 0334;* e *afangi@emax.is;* ⌚ *Jun–Aug;* **$$**). Not only does it make a convenient stop, but it's also the real deal – a genuine Icelandic sheep farm in the middle of nowhere that has the added advantage of being run by the nicest family. Beds are dormitory-style but bedding is available, and there are hot showers and a nice hot tub too. Their roadside café and shop serves very Icelandic fare – waffles with jam and cream, coffee and *kleinur*, and *hangikjöt* (smoked lamb) (⌚ *09.00 until last client*).

## THE HVÍTÁRNES–HVERAVELLIR TRAIL

Hiking the old-time Hvítárnes to Hveravellir trail is a spectacular three-day journey below the glaciers of Langjökull and the smaller Hrútfell (1,470m). This is truly well off the beaten path, with lots of raw terrain, so plan well (about five hours of hiking per day). There are cosy mountain huts to stay in at each stop (*www.fi.is*).

**Day 1** Hvítárnes hut to Thverbrekknamúli (15km)
**Day 2** Thverbrekknamúli to Thjófadalir (13km)
**Day 3** Thjófadalir to Hveravellir (11km)

## HVERAVELLIR

'The field of hot springs' is a lonesome and windswept frontier right in the middle of Kjölur. At first glance the lava flats seem bare and unexciting, but off in the distance shines the great round bluish shield of Hofsjökull. Tiny wisps of steam seep out of the cracked earth to reveal that this is one of Iceland's most terrific hotspots. A wooden walkway takes you through the geothermal area: the main attractions are Bláhver (a serene, milky-blue hot pool that almost glows) and Öskurhólshver (the 'shrieking spring'), a silica-encrusted fumarole with a constant jet of whistling steam pouring from its spout. Beyond the springs lies the hideaway of Eyvindur of the mountains, an outlaw who came and lived at Hveravellir with his wife back in the 18th century. The tumbledown circle of rocks is believed to be his old home and a local spring is named after him (Eyvindahver). Eyvindarrét is thought to be his old sheep pen – a natural volcanic feature where the steam exploding from beneath the lava seemed to have frozen the rock in mid burst. Surely, no sheep could escape from inside that crater. You can still see the old shepherd's hut with thick rock walls and turf roof.

Despite the remoteness, the campsite and station at Hveravellir are becoming busy places in the summer and well into the autumn. For anyone riding or driving across Kjölur, this is the perfect overnight stop. There's a big hut that sleeps a lot of people with a gritty camp kitchen and a small shop (☎ *452 4200*; e *hveravellir@hveravellir.is; www.hveravellir.is*). The hot outdoor bathing pool was built in 1938 and looks natural now that it's covered in silica precipitate. Two pipes direct separate springs into the pool, one ice-old and the other scalding hot. With no control over the flow, a sudden gush of one or the other has everyone leaping out with yelps and screams. Most visitors hike around the hot springs and then set up their tents, whilst others only hike to **Strýtur** (847m), which is unfortunately a little underwhelming given the other nearby trails. To really enjoy this exquisite hinterland though, head towards Langjökull. You need a 4x4 to get there as the road dips through a few rivers (unless you're hiking or riding, in which case you'll get a little wet). On the other side lies the hidden valley of **Thjófadalir** beneath the shadow of the glacier. This is a truly enchanted landscape to walk through.

## KERLINGARFJÖLL

The 'woman's mountains' is a group of pointed peaks, marbled with the white of tiny glaciers and shields of ice that drop into valleys of highly active hot springs.

It's odd that such a beautiful place is named after a troll, whose remnants stand as a rocky pillar at the base of the range. Similar to the colours and shapes of Landmannalaugar, what sets this place apart are its massive scale and fewer crowds. For all the talk of 'fire and ice', no other place in Iceland lets you experience both in such an active way. Kerlingarfjöll is used as a private ski lodge because of the permanent snow patches and the steep slopes, but it's the mountains, ice, and steam that make this such a remarkable hiking destination. The road to Kerlingarfjöll (Route F347) crosses a few streams, so you must have a 4x4 to get there. The **base camp** is at Ásgarður where you'll find lots of sleeping-bag accommodation with facilities, as well as a wonderful natural outdoor hot pot next to a rushing glacial stream (there is also a small but sporadically open petrol station at Kerlingarfjöll). The season is short and the demand great, so book ahead (m *894 2132;* e *info@kerlingarfjoll.is; www.kerlingarfjoll.is;* **$$**). Hikers have plenty of interesting paths to choose from, all of which lead to great views across the whole interior. The most difficult climb is to the top of **Mt Snækollur** (1,477m) for which you will need crampons. It is also possible to hike or ride to the Thjórsa Valley on the other side of Hofsjökull, the unofficial trail between Kjölur and Sprengisandur.

## SPRENGISANDUR

The longest route across the interior is the most desolate place in the whole country. Here the land appears lifeless – barren, black lava flats interspersed with shifting sands, giant boulders dropped by ancient glaciers, and distant black mountains that offer no way out. For the most part, Sprengisandur is true Arctic desert, where all the water is trapped in nearby glaciers and the summer is too short for the melted ice to do anything of consequence.

Some attribute the name 'Sprengisandur' to the Icelandic word 'jump', since the route offered no food or water for horses, and riders would have to *sprengja* across the landscape to make it to the other side. However, the verb *sprengja* also means 'blast' and there are days when 'blasting sands' makes a rather fitting description. Sprengisandur is the epicentre of Iceland's terrific sandstorms in which cars, people, horses, and anything else get sandblasted with crushed pumice.

The official Sprengisandur road is Route F26 that goes from Mt Hekla all the way to Goðafoss; around 200km long. Travelling this route is not for the faint-hearted, as you must ford dozens and dozens of streams and rivers. The road varies in quality and getting stuck in sand is quite common. Regardless of physical dangers, it also takes a special mental stamina to travel in these parts. When you're hiking or riding across such nothingness for so long, it's hard to keep your mind from falling into a post-apocalyptic stupor. The Icelanders add to the psychodrama with lots and lots of ghost stories about the unsettled natures in this region. Superstitions surrounding Sprengisandur make the Kjölur route seem like a fairy-tale. Fear of the supernatural is exactly why nobody travelled this way for centuries, even though the route had been set up much earlier. The first car ever to cross Sprengisandur did so in 1933, and had to be ferried across plenty of water.

**WHERE TO STAY** Anyone who's travelling across Sprengisandur should make a stop at **Hrauneyjar** (*99 rooms;* ☎ *487 7782;* e *hrauney@hrauneyjar.is; www.hrauneyjar.is;* **$$$**). As a base of operations for all things highlands, the **highland centre** features a filling restaurant, petrol station, and lots of useful tourist amenities (like good maps and fishing licences for the lakes), along with a hotel and guesthouse. These make a perfect stopping-off point for this part of the country, with lots of helpful staff who know the region and who are keen to share it. Some rooms are nicer than others, but for the most part it is a comfortable, ranch-style travel hotel with inexpensive spaces for travellers in sleeping-bag spaces (bathrooms are shared) – they are open year-round. There are mountain huts and campsites at both Nýidalur (sleeps 120) and Laugafell (sleeps 35). Both get very busy with hikers in the high season (the only season), so you must book ahead (*www.fi.is*).

**WHAT TO SEE** After the road becomes unpaved (from the south), it follows the shores of Thórisvatn. Travelling south of the lake (on Route F228) takes you into **Veiðivötn** or the 'fishing lakes'. If Iceland has a lake country, this is it (green growth, crystal-clear water, and about 60 pools, all of them kettle lakes from the glacier that was here only 500 years ago). The midpoint is at **Nýidalur**, right at the base of Tungnafellsjökull (1,520m), where hikers walk through the 'pass of hope' or Vonarskarð. If you're looking for the most treacherous, bone-rattling jeep route in all Iceland, Route F910 turns off at Nýidalur right next to Tungnafellsjökull and heads over the north side of Vatnajökull to Askja. On the way, you pass the very wet region of **Gæsavatnaleið** at the back of the glacier. The road also circumnavigates **Mt Trölladyngja** (1,468m) or 'the troll's volcano'. This is Iceland's largest shield volcano and a perfect sloping cone. It is possible to ascend the peak, though the only approach is from the north side and it is a long and difficult walk across the lava field. **Ódáðahraun** is the largest lava field in Iceland, and the largest desert in Europe (over 6,000km$^2$). The name means 'crime lava' and stems from the number of outlaws who were banished to this forsaken place. Because the landscape is so difficult (no water, bad trails, high winds and sharp lava rocks), it's become a right of passage for Icelandic hikers who want to prove their mettle. The trek from Askja to Mývatn is not a good first-time walk in Iceland, but it's something to consider for when you return, or you can drive it (Route F88). Most travellers will have to ignore Route F910 because it's too rough. Instead, stay on Route F26 to Goðafoss or else divert to Laugafell (Route F752) towards Akureyri. **Mt Laugafell** (700m) or 'bath mountain' is a high plateau and geothermal area renowned for its hot springs. Legend relays the tale of Thórunn, a woman who avoided the black plague by running away from the coast and into the highlands. She had a pool cut out of the rock, and today, 600 years later, you can still swim there.

## MT ASKJA (1,510M)

Mt Askja is an impressive volcano that rises straight out of the Ódáðahraun lava field. Its name comes from the Icelandic word for caldera, the most prominent feature of Askja. The volcano of Askja originated some 10,000 years ago, but the caldera was only formed in the mighty eruption of 1875. After spitting out a huge amount of ash and gas, the magma chamber from whence it came could no longer support the volcano above, so that the middle of the mountain slowly began to collapse. The subsequent depression filled with water and formed the lake you see today. **Lake Öskjuvatn** is now the deepest lake in Iceland (220m) and is considered one of the greatest calderas in the world. Both scientists and tourists admire the volcano for its perfect shape and mammoth size, exaggerated by the flatness of the surrounding lava field. The lake is a brilliant blue colour and has been the subject of much study – in 1907, a pair of German geologists disappeared in the lake while studying its chemistry, most likely drowned. A monument to them now stands near the other crater lake of **Víti**. 'Hell' was also formed in the eruption of 1875, but differs from the larger lake in that it is hot. The milky-blue water averages a temperature of 25°C, which is a little cool for swimmers in Iceland, though many people try. If you do swim, be very careful getting in and out of the steep sides and don't touch the bottom because it's very hot!

Askja is still active – the lake is sinking deeper and the last full-blown eruption was only in 1961. In places around Víti it's possible to see compacted snow that was captured underneath the new lava flow – a 135-year-old snowdrift covered in stone. The newest lava field is the shiny, reddish-black rubble to the northwest. In preparation for the first manned flight to the moon, NASA pinpointed the lavascapes around Askja as the most lunar-like on planet earth. Both Neil Armstrong and Buzz Aldrin travelled to Iceland in the mid 1960s to undergo training for the moon landing.

The hike around the top rim of Askja is long (about eight hours) and complicated, not least because of the unco-operative weather. If there is any wind at all, do not make the hike, as the slope down into the lake is very steep and the ridge on which you are walking quite narrow. For now, the only place to stay is the mountain hut at Drekagil (sleeps 60).

**GETTING THERE AND AWAY** Askja is such an iconic tourist spot in Iceland that it's always possible to get transport in summer. Tour buses run regularly from Mývatn (see page 366) (3 hours), or one can simply drive from the ring road on Route F88. It's about a 30-minute hike from the car park up to the caldera.

## MT HERÐUBREIÐ (1,682m)

Icelanders look upon Herðubreið as the 'queen of all mountains' and consider it no small coincidence that it lines up perfectly with Dettifoss (see page 388), the 'king of waterfalls'. This is a wildly stunning mountain, standing tall against the silent desert with broad shoulders (hence its name). Like a queen in chess, Herðubreið seems to have chased all the pieces away, but when there's ice and snow on top the view is truly regal.

Herðubreið is what is known as a *tuya*, a volcano that erupts beneath a glacier and forms a lava pool that is confined by the ice. Thus the volcano grows vertically and becomes the table-shaped mountain that you see today, right next to the Jökulsá á Fjöllum (see page 383). The first successful attempt at reaching the cinder-cone summit of Mt Herðubreið came only in 1908, after which every climber has been dying to try. There's about a six-week period in which you might have the right weather window to try to reach the top. Realise, however, that this is a very steep mountain and that most of it is very loose rock; the trail begins from the west side of the mountain.

On the banks of the Lindaá is **Herðubreiðarlindir**, considered by some to be an actual oasis. The hot springs mixing with glacial rivers support a lively little ecosystem in the midst of the desert, and in summer this is a delightful place to stay. There are pink-footed geese and lots of flowers and not so many people. A campsite offers full facilities and there's also a comfortable mountain hut (sleeps 30).

**GETTING THERE AND AWAY** The quickest way from the ring road is along Route F88, but it is also possible to connect through east Iceland from the bridge on Route 910.

## KVERKFJÖLL

Route F902 heads south (but up, up, up) until it reaches the back of the Vatnajökull glacier. Arriving at the Kverkfjöll mountain pass feels a bit like taking the back door into Iceland's steamy kitchen. The gargantuan black landscapes are taken over by the blue-and-white ice, and the hot springs have melted out incredible ice caves. As gorgeous and nifty as this is, one should never step into the caves – to do so is to risk your life. The mountains of Kverkfjöll also form several calderas (like Askja), but whilst some are beneath the ice, others are not. A popular hike crosses the glacier tongue of Kverkjökull, but is best done by those who have the right experience and the right equipment. There is a warm river (which is safe for bathing). Kverkfjöll is also the source of the mighty Jökulsá á Fjöllum glacier river that shapes the whole northeast of Iceland. The hut at Kverkfjöll is called Sigurðarskáli (sleeps 82) and has full facilities, along with a campsite. It's a 3km hike from the hut up to the edge of the ice and the cave Íshellir.

# Appendix I

## LANGUAGE

Icelanders will approach you speaking English because they are accustomed to foreigners making little to no effort to learn their language. As a traveller, any attempt to communicate in someone's native tongue (no matter how disastrous) communicates much more about the respect and admiration you feel towards that person's country and the people themselves. In Iceland, speaking Icelandic is good manners and a great goodwill gesture.

Icelandic is a rich and complex language, with a fascinating grammar and odd sounds that are completely unknown in modern English. Deciphering the signs and sounds you see and hear can only enrich your experience, so make your best effort and enlist the help of the locals. A properly pronounced *Góðan daginn [Góthan dá-yin]* is the best way to set yourself apart from the general tourist melée and ingratiate your hosts. Understand that more than most languages, learning Icelandic is an exercise in stages, from basic, to confident, to 'fluent for a foreigner', to the 'real Icelandic'. That final stage involves declining Icelandic nouns to match corresponding grammatical structure and knowing all the nuances of Icelandic (which this book doesn't even attempt to tackle). That can take a lifetime and is precisely what sets natives apart from everyone else. Don't be discouraged by how overwhelming it all looks – just roll up your sleeves and enjoy the ride. Good luck!

**THE ICELANDIC ALPHABET** The Icelandic alphabet has 32 letters. The 'extras' are mostly vowels (Á, É, Í, Ó, Ú, Ý, Æ and Ö) and the two consonants, Ð and Þ. The letters C, Q, W and Z only exist in foreign words. Note that the alphabetical order is followed in the way listed.

| Letter | Sounds like | | |
|---|---|---|---|
| Aa | *ah* as in *awesome* | Mm | *m* as in *mummy* |
| Áá | *ow* as in *cow* | Nn | *n* as in *needle* |
| Bb | *b* as in *boat* | Oo | short 'o' as in *John* |
| Dd | *d* as in dog | Óó | long 'o' as in *oh!* |
| Ðð | *th* as in *this* | Pp | *p* as in *pineapple* |
| Ee | short 'e' as in *fed* | Rr | rolled 'r' as in *Puerto Rico* |
| Éé | *yeh* as in *yes* | Ss | *s* as in *salt* |
| Ff | *f* as in *frank* | Tt | *t* as in *telepathy* |
| Gg | *g* as in *good* | Uu | short 'i' but with round lips |
| Hh | *h* as in *hair* | Úú | long 'u' as in *you* |
| Ii | short 'i' as in *hit* | Vv | *v* as in *vespers* |
| Íí | long 'i' as in *feet* | Xx | *x* as in *relax* |
| Jj | *y* as in *yokel* | Yy | short 'i' as in *thick* |
| Kk | *k* as in *kite* | Ýý | long 'i' as in *feet* |
| Ll | *l* as in *luscious* | Þþ | *th* as in *think* |

| | | |
|---|---|---|
| Ææ | *ai* as in *eye* | pursed lips |
| Öö | *uh* as in *curl* but with | |

**ICELANDIC SOUNDS** Sadly, Icelandic is less phonetic than English. Here are a few tips for getting started:

- Double consonants are emphasised – pronounce both letters in the diphthong
- The double *ll* is pronounced 'tl' with the tongue behind the front teeth, the same as in the Welsh *ll*
- If double *nn* follows an accented vowel and ends a word, it sounds like 'tn'. For example, *einn* (one) sounds like *eit(n)*
- *hv* is a common diphthong and sounds like 'kv'; *hvað* (what) sounds like *kvath*
- Sometimes, F becomes P: Keflavík sounds like *kepla-veek*, September sounds like *seftember*, and Hafnarfjörður sounds like *hapnarfjörður*
- The vowel diphthong 'AU' sounds like 'oy', as in swimming pool, *sundlaug* (*sind-loyg*)

## VOCABULARY

### Verbs

| | | |
|---|---|---|
| I *am* | ég *er* | *[yeg air]* |
| You *are* | þú *ert* | *[thoo airt]* |
| He/she/it *is* | hann/hunn/það *er* | *[han/hoon/thath air]* |
| We *are* | við *erum* | *[vith airoom]* |
| You (plural) *are* | þið *eruð* | *[vith airooth]* |
| They *are* | þeir (m)/þær (f)/þau (n) *eru* | *[their/thayr/thoy airoo]* |

### Getting by

| | | |
|---|---|---|
| Hello | *Sæll* (to a man); *Sæl* (to a woman) | *[saitl, sile (as in 'sigh')]* |
| Good day | *Góðan daginn/Góðan dag* | *[gothan dayinn, gothan dag]* |
| Good evening | *Gott kvöld* | *[gott kvuld]* |
| Good night | *Góða nótt* | *[gotha note]* |
| Goodbye | *Bless* | *[bless]* |
| See you later | *Við sjáumst* | *[vith syaw-umst]* |
| My name is … | *Ég heiti …* | *[yeg hatey]* |
| What is your name? | *Hvað heitir þú?* | *[kvath hate-ir thoo]* |
| Where are you from? | *Hvaðan ert þú?* | *[kvathan airt thoo]* |
| I am from … | *Ég er frá …* | *[yeg air fraw]* |
| America | *Ameríka* | *[amaireeka]* |
| Britain | *Bretland* | *[brettland]* |
| England, Scotland, Wales | *England, Skotland, Wales* | *[Ehngland, Skotland, Wales]* |
| Canada | *Kanada* | *[kanada]* |
| How are you? | *Hvað segirðu?* | *[kvath sey-ir thoo]* |
| I'm fine | *allt gott* | *[atlt gott]* |
| Pleased to meet you | *Gaman að kynnast þér* | *[gaman ath kinnast thyair]* |
| Thank you | *Takk Fyrir* | *[takk feer-ear]* |
| Thank you very much | *Takk Kærlega* | *[takk kire-lega]* |
| Same to you | *Sömuleiðis* | *[sumoolay-this]* |

| | | |
|---|---|---|
| That was nothing | *Það var ekkert* | *[thath var aikkairt]* |
| Cheers! | *Skál!* | *[scowl]* |
| excuse me | *Afsakíð* | *[afsakeeth]* |
| pardon me | *Fyrirgefðu* | |
| Yes | *já* | *[yow (as in owl)]* |
| No | *nei* | *[neigh]* |
| I don't understand | *Ég skil ekki* | *[yeg skill eyk-kee]* |
| Could you please speak more slowly? | *Gætir þú talað svolítið hægar?* | *[guy-teer thu talath svoleeteeth hie-yar]* |
| Do you understand? | *Skillur þú?* | *[skitler thoo?]* |
| Do you speak English /Icelandic/Danish? | *Talar þú ensku/íslensku/dansku?* | *[talar thu enskoo, eeslensku, dansku]* |
| I do not speak Icelandic | *Ég tala ekki íslensku* | *[yeg tala eyk-kee eeslenskoo]* |

## Questions

| | | |
|---|---|---|
| How? | *Hvernig?* | *[kver-nig]* |
| Who? | *Hver?* | *[kvair]* |
| What? | *Hvað?* | *[kvath]* |
| Where? | *Hvar?* | *[kvar]* |
| Where from? | *Hvaðan?* | *[kvathan]* |
| Which? | *Hvort?* | *[kvort]* |
| When? | *Hvenær?* | *[hvenayr]* |
| How much? | *Hvað kostar?* | *[kvath costar?]* |

## Colours

| | | |
|---|---|---|
| red | *rauðar* | *[roycher]* |
| orange | *appelsínugulur* | *[apple-seenaguller]* |
| yellow | *gulur* | *[guller]* |
| green | *grænn* | *[grite]* |
| blue | *blár* | *[blawr,* rhymes with *flower]* |
| purple | *fjólublár* | *[fjolablawr]* |
| brown | *brúnn* | *[brute]* |
| black | *svartur* | *[svarter]* |
| white | *hvítur* | *[kveeter]* |
| grey | *grár* | *[grawr]* |
| pink | *bleikur* | *[bleyker]* |
| colourful | *litskrúðugur* | *[litskroothuger]* |
| rainbow | *regnbogi* | *[raiñbogey]* |

## Numbers

| | | |
|---|---|---|
| 0 | *null* | *[nutl]* |
| 1 | *einn* | *[eyt, sounds like ate]* |
| 2 | *tveir* | *[tvayr]* |
| 3 | *þrír* | *[threer]* |
| 4 | *fjórir* | *[fjo-rir]* |
| 5 | *fimm* | *[fimm]* |
| 6 | *sex* | *[seks]* |
| 7 | *sjö* | *[syuh]* |
| 8 | *átta* | *[out-ta]* |
| 9 | *níu* | *[nee-ya]* |

| 10 | *tíu* | *[tee-ya]* |
|---|---|---|
| 11 | *ellefu* | *[etlevu]* |
| 12 | *tólf* | *[tolf]* |
| 13 | *þrettán* | *[thret-town]* |
| 14 | *fjórtán* | *[thret-town]* |
| 15 | *fimmtán* | *[fimm-town]* |
| 16 | *sextán* | *[seks-town]* |
| 17 | *sautján* | *[soy-tyown]* |
| 18 | *átján* | *[ow-tyown]* |
| 19 | *nítján* | *[nee-tyawn]* |
| 20 | *tuttugu* | *[toot-tu-yoo]* |
| 21 | *tuttugu og einn* | *[toot-tu-yoo og eyt]* |
| 30 | *þrjátíu* | *[thryow-teeya]* |
| 40 | *fjörutíu* | *[fyuhr-ateeya]* |
| 50 | *fimmtíu* | *[fimm-teeya]* |
| 60 | *sextíu* | *[seks-teeya]* |
| 70 | *sjötíu* | *[syuh-teeya]* |
| 80 | *áttatíu* | *[owt-tateeya]* |
| 90 | *níutíu* | *[neeya-teeya]* |
| 100 | *hundrað* (n) | *[hundrath]* |
| 1,000 | *þúsund* (n) | *[thu-soond]* |
| 1,000,000 | *milljón* (f) | *[mitl-yon]* |
| 1,675,458 | *ein milljón sex hundrað sjötíu og fimm þúsund, fjögur hundrað fimmtíu og átta* *[eyt mitlyon seks hundrath syuh-teeya og fimm thu-soond fyuhyur hundrath fimm-teeya og owt-ta]* | |

## Time

| What time is it? | *Hvað er klukkan?* | *[kvath air klook-kan]* |
|---|---|---|
| today | *í dag* | *[ee dah]* |
| tonight | *í kvöld* | *[ee kvuld]* |
| tomorrow | *á morgun* | *[ow morgan]* |
| the day after tomorrow | *hinn daginn* | *[hin dayinn]* |
| yesterday | *í gær* | *[ee guyr]* |
| morning | *morgunn* | *[morgan]* |
| evening | *kvöld* | *[kvuld]* |

## Days of the week

| Sunday | *Sunnudagur* | *[soonadagur]* |
|---|---|---|
| Monday | *Mánudagur* | *[mownadagur]* |
| Tuesday | *Þriðjudagur* | *[threethyoodagur]* |
| Wednesday | *Miðvikudagur* | *[mithvikudagur]* |
| Thursday | *Fimmtudagur* | *[fimmtadagur]* |
| Friday | *Föstudagur* | *[fustadagur]* |
| Saturday | *Laugardagur* | *[loygardagur]* |

## Months of the year

| January | *Janúar* | *[yan-oo-ar]* |
|---|---|---|
| February | *Febrúar* | *[feb-roo-ar]* |
| March | *Mars* | *[mars]* |
| April | *Apríl* | *[apreel]* |

## EMERGENCY

| | | |
|---|---|---|
| Help! | *Hjálp!* | *[hyowlp]* |
| I need help | *Ég þarf hjálp* | *[yeg tharf hyowlp]* |
| I'm lost | *Ég er villtur (m)/villt (f)* | *[yeg air vitl-tur/vitlt]* |
| Go away! | *Faruð!* | *[farooth]* |
| Police | *lögreglan* | *[luh-greglan]* |
| Fire | *slökkvistöð* | *[sluhk-kvistuhth]* |
| Ambulance | *sjúkrabifreið* | *[syookrabifrayth]* |
| Doctor | *læknir* | *[like-near]* |
| Hospital | *sjúkrahús* | *[syookrahoos]* |
| Thief | *þjófur* | *[thyofur]* |

| | | |
|---|---|---|
| May | *Maí* | *[ma-ee]* |
| June | *Júní* | *[yoo-nee]* |
| July | *Júlí* | *[yoo-lee]* |
| August | *Ágúst* | *[ow-goost]* |
| September | *September* | *[seftembair]* |
| October | *Október* | *[aktobair]* |
| November | *Nóvember* | *[novembair]* |
| December | *Desember* | *[daysembair]* |

## Getting around

| | | |
|---|---|---|
| A one way ticket to… | *einn miða til…* | *[eyt mitha til]* |
| I want to go to… | *Ég ætla að fara til…* | *[yeg aytla ath fara til]* |
| How much is it? | *Hvað kostur þetta?* | *[kvath costar thet-ta]* |
| one way | *aðra leið* | *[athra layth]* |
| return | *báðar leiðir* | *[bowthar laythir]* |
| plane | *flugvel* | *[floog-vel]* |
| airport | *flugvöllur* | *[floog-vuh-tlur]* |
| ferry | *ferja* | *[ferya]* |
| port | *höfn* | *[hupn]* |
| car | *bíll* | *[beetl]* |
| taxi | *leigubíll* | *[lay-goo-beetl]* |
| coach | *rúta* | *[roo-ta]* |
| motorcycle | *motorhjól* | *[motorkyol]* |
| bicycle | *reiðhjól* | *[raythkyol]* |
| arrival/departure | *koma/brottför* | *[koma/brottfuhr]* |
| here | *hér* | *[hyer]* |
| there | *þar* | *[thar]* |
| Have a nice trip! | *Góða ferð!* | *[gotha ferth]* |

## Accommodation

| | | |
|---|---|---|
| room | *herbergi* | *[herbergi]* |
| hotel | *hótel* | *[hotel]* |
| guesthouse | *gistiheimili* | *[gistihaymily]* |
| youth hostel | *farfuglaheimli* | *[farfuglahaymli]* |
| campsite | *tjaldsvæði* | *[tyaldsvai-thi]* |
| Where is the nearest accommodation? | *Hvar er næsti gisting?* | *[kvar er nice-tee gisting]* |

| | | |
|---|---|---|
| Do you have any free rooms? | *Eigið þið nokkur herbergi laus?* | *[eygith thith nok-kur herbergi loys]* |
| …one person | *…eins manna* | *[eyns manna]* |
| …two people | *…tveggja manna* | *[tveg-gya manna]* |
| …with two beds | *…með tvö rúm* | *[meth tvu room]* |
| …sleeping-bag space | *svefnpokapláss* | *[svefn-poka-plahs]* |
| …made-up bed | *uppbúin rúm* | *[upboo-in room]* |
| with private bath | *með baði* | *[meth bathi]* |
| sink/wash basin | *handlaug* | *[hand-loyg]* |
| Where is the toilet? | *Hvar er salernið?* | *[kvar air salernith]* |
| Is breakfast included? | *Er morgunverður innifalinn?* | *[air morgunverthur innifallit?]* |

## Shopping

| | | |
|---|---|---|
| Where is the shop? | *Hvar er sjoppa?* | |
| How much does it cost? | *Hvað kostur?* | |
| I need to buy… | *Ég þarf að kaupa…* | *[yeg tharf ath koypa]* |
| a map | *kort* | *[kort]* |
| hiking boots | *gönguskó* | *[gungoosko]* |
| coat | *frakki* | *[frak-ki]* |
| a woolly hat | *húfa* | *[hoofa]* |
| gloves | *hanski* | *[hanski]* |
| postcard | *postkórt* | *[postkort]* |
| stamps | *frímerki* | *[freemerki]* |

## Dining

| | | |
|---|---|---|
| Breakfast | *morgunverður* | *[morgunverthur]* |
| Lunch | *hádegisverður* | *[howdegisverthur]* |
| Dinner | *kvöldverður* | *[kvuldverthur]* |
| I am a vegetarian | *Ég er grænmetisæta* | *[yeg air grine-metisaita]* |
| I am allergic to… | *Ég hef ofnæmi fyrir…* | *[eg hef ofnaimi feerir]* |

## Food

| | | |
|---|---|---|
| bread | *brauð* | *[broyth]* |
| butter | *smjör* | *[smyur]* |
| cheese | *ostur* | *[ostur]* |
| ice cream | *ís* | *[ees]* |
| fish | *fisku* | *[fiskoo]* |
| salmon | *lax* | *[lahks]* |
| Arctic char | *bleikja* | *[blay-kya]* |
| lamb | *lamb* | *[lamb (pronounce the 'b')]* |
| chicken | *kjúklingur* | *[kyooklingur]* |
| hot dog | *pylsur* | *[pilsur]* |
| vegetables | *grænméttir* | *[grine-myettir]* |
| fruit | *ávöxter* | *[owvuhkster]* |
| apple | *epli* | *[ehp-li]* |
| banana | *banana* | *[banana]* |
| grape | *vínber* | *[veen-bair]* |
| orange | *appelsína* | *[apple-seena]* |
| blueberry | *bláber* | *[blau-bair]* |

| | | |
|---|---|---|
| potatoes | *kartafla* | *[kartafla]* |
| onion | *laukur* | *[loykur]* |
| carrot | *gulrót* | *[gull-rote]* |
| mushrooms | *sveppur* | *[svep-puhr]* |
| water | *vatn* | *[vatn]* |
| juice | *safi* | *[safi]* |
| milk | *mjólk* | *[myulk]* |
| coffee | *kaffi* | *[kahf-fi]* |
| tea | *te* | *[tay]* |
| wine | *vín* | *[veen]* |
| beer | *bjór* | *[byor]* |

## Directions

| | | |
|---|---|---|
| Where is it? | *Hver er þetta?* | *[kvair air theta]* |
| Left | *vinstri* | *[vinstri]* |
| Right | *hægri* | *[haie-ri]* |
| North | *norður* | *[northur]* |
| South | *suður* | *[soothur]* |
| East | *austur* | *[oystur]* |
| West | *vestur* | *[vestur]* |

## On signs

| | | |
|---|---|---|
| open | *opið* | *[opith]* |
| closed | *lokað* | *[lokath]* |
| from _ to _ | *frá _ til _* | *[frow til]* |
| all year | *allt árið* | *[atlt owrith]* |
| every day | *alla daga* | *[atla daga]* |
| opening hours | *opnunartimi* | *[opnunartimi]* |
| information | *uplýssingar* | *[uplees-singar]* |

## Good words for Iceland

| | | |
|---|---|---|
| swimming pool | *sundlaug* | *[sindloyg]* |
| hot pot (tub) | *heittur pottur* | *[heyt-tur potter]* |
| I'm cold | *mér er kalt* | *[myer air kalt]* |
| breathtaking | *hrífandi* | *[kreefandi]* |
| rocky | *klettótur* | *[klet-totur]* |
| man/woman | *maður/kona* | *[mathur/kona]* |
| this/that | *þetta/það* | *[theta/thath]* |
| expensive/cheap | *dýr/ódýr* | *[deer/odeer]* |
| beautiful/ugly | *fallegur/ljótur* | *[fatlegur/lyotur]* |
| old/new | *gamall/ný* | *[gamatl/nee]* |
| good/bad | *góður/vondur* | *[gothur/vondur]* |
| big/small | *stór/lítill* | *[stor/leetil]* |
| early/late | *snemma/seitt* | *[snemma/seyt]* |
| hot/cold | *heitur/kaldur* | *[heytur/kaldur]* |
| difficult/easy | *erfiður/léttur* | *[airfithur/lyettur]* |

**INTERPRETING ICELANDIC PLACE NAMES** Icelandic toponyms are almost always very basic compound words that date back to the Viking era. Most often the names reflect apt descriptions of the physical characteristics of a place, or announce an event that took place there. Some of these words are repeats, but with this small handful you can interpret half the map of Iceland.

| | | |
|---|---|---|
| *dalur* | valley | *[dalur]* |
| *fjall, fell* | mountain | *[fyatl, felt]* |
| *hlíð* | cliff | *[kleeth]* |
| *heiði* | heath, moor | *[haythi]* |
| *brekka* | slope | *[brekka]* |
| *staðir* | stead, place | *[stathir]* |
| *land* | land or country | *[land]* |
| *strönd* | coast | *[strund]* |
| *nes* | point | *[ness]* |
| *eyjar* | island | *[ey-yar]* |
| *bakki* | riverbank | *[bak-ki]* |
| *vatn* | water | *[vatn]* |
| *foss* | waterfall | *[foss]* |
| *fjörður* | fjord | *[fyurthur]* |
| *höfn* | harbour | *[hupn]* |
| *lón* | lagoon, pool | *[loan]* |
| *vík* | cove | *[veek]* |
| *höfði* | cape | *[huv-thee]* |
| *hraun* | lava | *[hroyn]* |
| *sandur* | sand | *[sandur]* |
| *ís* | ice | *[ees]* |
| *jökull* | glacier | *[yuh-kutl]* |
| *rauð-* | red | *[royth]* |
| *græn-* | green | *[grine]* |
| *hvíta-* | white | *[kveeta]* |
| *svart-* | black | *[svart]* |
| *eld* | fire | *[eld]* |
| *svín* | pig | *[sveen]* |

## In town

| | | |
|---|---|---|
| *gata* | street | *[gata]* |
| *torg* | square | *[torg]* |
| *stígur* | path | *[steegur]* |
| *hof* | temple, farm | *[hof]* |
| *borg* | town, fort | *[borg]* |

### PLACE NAME ESSENTIALS

Icelanders are amazingly tolerant towards those of us who mutilate the names of their towns and mountains and valleys. For foreign tongues, the place names of Iceland can be daunting. Listen to how others say them and sound them out when looking at a map. These are the three most mispronounced roots in Icelandic:

- *fjörður* (fjord) sounds like *fyurther*
- *vík* (as in Reykjavík) sounds like *veek*
- *jökull* (glacier) sounds like *yuh-kutl*

# Appendix 2

## FURTHER INFORMATION

**FURTHER READING** Icelanders read a lot (winter is long) and your journey is made better by reading up on all things Icelandic. Books are much more expensive in Iceland (at least double the price of those in the UK), however there are a few English-language titles that you can only buy in Iceland so bibliophiles might want to budget extra.

### History and culture

Byock, Jesse *Viking Age Iceland* Penguin, 2001. The first 300 years of Iceland's history and a very interesting read with a focus on society and relationships.

Karlsson, Gunnar *Iceland's 1,100 Years: The History of a Marginal Society* C Hurst & Co, 2001. Another academic tome, this time with a more Marxist critique.

Karlsson, Gunnar *The History of Iceland* University of Minnesota, 2000. The be-all, end-all academic 'introduction' to 1,100 years of Icelandic history.

Krakauer, Jon and Roberts, David *Iceland Land of the Sagas* Villard, 1998. A picture book with heavy emphasis on sombre photography and the sagas.

Magnusson, Magnus *Iceland Saga* NPI Media Group, 2005. Relates the story of Iceland in his great TV-presenter style.

Magnusson, Magnus *The Vikings* Tempus, 2004. A classic for Old Norse scholars and history buffs. A truly fascinating read and one of the very best books on the subject.

Rosenblad, Esbjörn and Sigurðardóttir-Rosenblad, Rakel *Iceland from Past to Present* Norstedts, Stockholm, 1993. Written by the Swedish ambassador to Iceland and his Icelandic wife. Sadly, the book is out of print, but it is a real treasure chest of culture, history, and politics.

Sale, Richard *The Xenophobe's Guide to the Icelanders* Oval Books, 2000. A humorous pamphlet on all the silly things Icelanders do.

Simpson, Jacqueline and Magnusson, Magnus *Icelandic Folktales & Legends* Tempus, 2004. Some of the wonderful tales that make Iceland so enchanting.

**Sagas** You should definitely try reading a saga or two before heading to Iceland because you're bound to visit some of these same places. The best place to start is Egils saga, which is such an iconic tale. For fear that I might get hate mail from professors of Old Norse studies, I can quickly add that Njáls saga is equally classic and can also be a good starting point. Where you travel to should determine what you read (Egils for west Iceland, Njáls for south Iceland, Grettis saga for the West Fjords, and so forth). The deluxe edition *Sagas of the Icelanders* (Penguin, 2001) is a very useful, 750-page compilation of many of the more popular sagas, but this is not good in-flight reading. Individual paperback copies of some of the sagas are also available, such as the Erbyggja saga (Penguin, 1989) and the Laxdæla saga (University of Toronto Press, 2001). If you really want to go all out, read the *Heimskringla* by Snorri Sturluson (see page 20).

**Literature** I highly recommend starting with *Independent People* (Panther, 2001) by Halldór Laxness. It is the epic tale of an Icelander, his farm, and his family and is the definitive work of Icelandic literature in translation today. It also is a great introduction to the style and personality of Iceland's Nobel laureate. In the last few years, many of his other books have been brought out again in English: *Under the Glacier* (Vintage, 2005) is the comical novel regarding Icelandic superstition and the glacier of Snæfellsnes (see page 263). *Iceland's Bell* (Vintage, 2003) is a historical snapshot of Iceland leading up to the independence movement, and *Paradise Reclaimed* (Vintage, 2002) explores the struggle between farm and city life in Iceland's belated industrial revolution. One of my favourite Laxness books is *World Light* (Vintage, 2002), but like much of his work, it is bleak – the story of a struggling orphan longing to be a poet. The same goes for the touching but tragic *Fish Can Sing* (Harvill Press, 2001), which is both heart rending and powerful. Laxness dealt with his own time in his book *The Atom Station* (Harvill Press, 2004), in which he brilliantly lays out his beliefs on contemporary Iceland, its politics, and its history. Every bookshop and major tourist office in Iceland sells English-language versions of Laxness, but once again, you can buy it at home for much less.

Another author to read is Gunnar Gunnarsson (see page 398), who only has a few works in translation, including *The Black Cliffs*, *Ships in the Sky* and *The Good Shepherd* (if you can find it). For something a bit more contemporary, read *101 Reykjavík* (Faber & Faber, 2002), the hit novel written by Halgrímur Helgason (see page 39).

**Others to consider** Search and find and read *Letters from Iceland* by W H Auden & Louis MacNeice (Faber, 1965). It is the poetry-heavy and slightly tongue-in-cheek travelogue of the two English poets as they travel around Iceland in the mid 1930s (see page 87). There's a whole library of old travel books on Iceland, but most of them fall under the antique and collectors' categories. In Iceland, you can buy a whole series (in English) regarding Iceland's natural history, its birdlife, fish, and mammals (and its horses), but outside that tight monopoly, visitors must cope with *Iceland (Classic Geology)* by Thór Thordason and Arman Hoskuldsson (Terra Publishing, 2002).

## Language

Jónsdóttir, Hildur *Teach Yourself Icelandic* McGraw Hill, 2004. A little more intense language learning (also with audio CDs).

Moser, Brian D *Lærum Íslensku: Let's Learn Icelandic* Publish America, 2005. A textbook and grammar for the serious student.

Neijmann, Daisy *Colloquial Icelandic* Routledge, 2001. Probably the best thing to take along for a casual trip and the best place to begin; the book also comes with audio CDs.

I would recommend purchasing any English–Icelandic dictionaries in Iceland, since they are far more comprehensive and of much higher quality. Outside Iceland, the only easily available dictionary is the *Hippocrene Concise Icelandic–English/English–Icelandic Dictionary* (Hippocrene, 1989) by Arnold Taylor. A concise but meaningful 'pocket' version is the bright-yellow *Ensk–íslensk/íslensk–ensk Orðabok* (Orðabókaútgáfan, 2005), which sells in Iceland for about US$50, and the classic English–Icelandic dictionary sells for about US$200! (don't think Icelanders don't value their language).

**ICELAND ON THE INTERNET** As one of the most wired countries on earth, Iceland is very well represented on the internet. Thought most Icelandic websites will feature an English page (click on the British or American flag), the breadth of information relayed in English is rarely equivalent to the Icelandic text. Though hundreds of sites are listed throughout the book, the following English-language sites are recommended:

## Official resources

| | |
|---|---|
| **www.althingi.is** | Icelandic parliament |
| **www.fisheries.is** | Ministry of Fisheries |
| **www.hi.is** | University of Iceland |
| **www.iceland.is** | Ministry of Foreign Affairs |
| **www.icelandnaturally.is** | Icelandic products and tourism |
| **www.lmi.is** | Iceland's Land Survey |
| **www.statice.is** | Iceland's official statistics |
| **www.thjodskra.is** | Iceland's National Registry |
| **www.us.is** | Iceland Traffic Council; information on driving |

## Travel information

| | |
|---|---|
| **www.fi.is** | Iceland's hiking club |
| **www.fjallamennska.is** | Mountaineering and hiking |
| **www.goiceland.org** | North American and English-language tourism information |
| **www.travelnet.is** | Trip-planning website |
| **www.vedur.is** | Weather in Iceland |
| **www.visit.is** | Online travellers' resource |
| **www.visiticeland.org** | Iceland Tourist Board |
| **www.visitorsguide.is** | Visitors' online guide to Iceland |
| **www.whatson.is** | General travel information on Iceland |

## Natural history and environment

| | |
|---|---|
| **www.floraislands.is** | Flora of Iceland |
| **www.fuglavernd.is** | Icelandic Society for the Protection of Birds |
| **www.hi.is/%7Eyannk/indexeng.html** | Icelandic birding pages |
| **www.icelandicgeographic.is** | Icelandic Geographic |
| **www.ust.is** | Icelandic National Parks (Umhverfisstofnun) |

## Regional travel sites

| | |
|---|---|
| **www.east.is** | The east |
| **www.northiceland.is** | The north in its entirety |
| **www.reykjanes.is** | The Reykjanes Peninsula |
| **www.south.is** | The south |
| **www.visitreykjavik.is** | Reykjavík |
| **www.westfjords.is** | The West Fjords |
| **www.westiceland.is** | The west |

## News

| | |
|---|---|
| **www.grapevine.is** | Reykjavík's alternative newspaper |
| **www.icelandreview.is** | *Iceland Review*, culture, arts, and news magazine |
| **www.mbl.is** | *Morgunblaðið*, Iceland's main newspaper |

| | |
|---|---|
| **www.news.bbc.co.uk/2/hi/europe/country_profiles/1025227.stm** | BBC Iceland profile |

## Iceland blogs

A few favourites…

| | |
|---|---|
| **Icelandeyes.blogspot.com** | Iceland Eyes; Iceland |
| **Icelandreport.blogspot.com** | The Iceland Report; an American in Reykjavík |
| **www.icelandweatherreport.com** | The Iceland Weather Report; a globalised Icelander on Iceland |

## Get involved

| | |
|---|---|
| **www.icelandairwaves.com** | Iceland's biggest music festival |
| **www.marathon.is** | Reykjavík marathon |
| **www.savingiceland.org** | International environmental activist network |
| **www.wf.blog.is** | Veraldarvinir; a project to clean up all the coastlines of Iceland |
| **www2.btcv.org.uk** | Repair trails in Iceland's largest national parks |

# Index

Page numbers in **bold** refer to major entries; those in *italics* indicate maps